This Is PR

The Realities
of Public Relations

Wadsworth Series in Mass Communication
Rebecca Hayden, Senior Editor

General

The New Communications by Frederick Williams

Mediamerica: Form, Content, and Consequence of Mass Communication, 3d, by Edward Jay Whetmore

The Interplay of Influence: Mass Media & Their Publics in News, Advertising, Politics by Kathleen Hall Jamieson and Karlyn Kohrs Campbell

Mass Communication and Everyday Life: A Perspective on Theory and Effects by Dennis K. Davis and Stanley J. Baran

Mass Media Research: An Introduction by Roger D. Wimmer and Joseph R. Dominick

The Internship Experience by Lynne Schafer Gross

Journalism

Media Writing: News for the Mass Media by Doug Newsom and James A. Wollert

Excellence in College Journalism by Wayne Overbeck and Thomas M. Pasqua

When Words Collide: A Journalist's Guide to Grammar & Style by Lauren Kessler and Duncan McDonald

News Editing in the '80s: Text and Exercises by William L. Rivers

Reporting Public Affairs: Problems and Solutions by Ronald P. Lovell

Newswriting for the Electronic Media: Principles, Examples, Applications by Daniel E. Garvey and William L. Rivers

Free-Lancer and Staff Writer: Newspaper Features and Magazine Articles, 3d, by William L. Rivers and Shelley Smolkin

Magazine Editing in the '80s: Text and Exercises by William L. Rivers

This is PR: The Realities of Public Relations, 3d, by Doug Newsom and Alan Scott

Writing in Public Relations Practice: Form and Style by Doug Newsom and Tom Siegfried

Creative Strategy in Advertising, 2d, by A. Jerome Jewler

Telecommunications

Stay Tuned: A Concise History of American Broadcasting by Christopher H. Sterling and John M. Kittross

Writing for Television and Radio, 4th, by Robert L. Hilliard

Communicating Effectively on Television by Evan Blythin and Larry A. Samovar

World Broadcasting Systems: A Comparative Analysis by Sydney W. Head

Broadcast/Cable Programming: Strategies and Practices, 2d, by Susan Tyler Eastman, Sydney W. Head, and Lewis Klein

Advertising in the Broadcast and Cable Media, 2d, by Elizabeth J. Heighton and Don R. Cunningham

Strategies in Broadcast and Cable Promotion by Susan Tyler Eastman and Robert A. Klein

Modern Radio Station Practices, 2d, by Joseph S. Johnson and Kenneth K. Jones

The Magic Medium: An Introduction to Radio in America by Edward Jay Whetmore

Audio in Media by Stanley R. Alten

Television Production Handbook, 4th, by Herbert Zettl

Sight-Sound-Motion: Applied Media Aesthetics by Herbert Zettl

Electronic Cinematography: Achieving Photographic Control over the Video Image by Harry Mathias and Richard Patterson

THIRD EDITION

This Is PR

The Realities of Public Relations

DOUG NEWSOM
Texas Christian University

ALAN SCOTT
University of Texas at Austin

To JoAnn —
who is practicing (well!)
all I taught her.

Alan

NEW PRINTING

Wadsworth Publishing Company
Belmont, California
A Division of Wadsworth, Inc.

Senior Editor: Rebecca Hayden
Production Editor: Leland Moss
Managing Designer: Paula Shuhert
Designer: Adriane Bosworth
Copy Editor: Elaine Linden
Technical Illustrator: Larry Jansen
Cover Designer: Diane Hillier
Cover Illustrator: Tim Mitona
Print Buyer: Barbara Britton

Part Opening Photo Credits

1: *Stock Boston*/Jeff Albertson
2: *Archive*/Mark Godfrey
3: *Stock Boston*/Peter Vandermark
4: *Magnum*/Raymond Deparden
5: *Magnum Photo*/Alex Webb
6: *Stock Boston*/Fredrik D. Brodin

Printed in the United States of America

4 5 6 7 8 9 10—89 88 87

ISBN 0-534-04287-2

Library of Congress Cataloging in Publication Data

Newsom, Doug.
   This is PR.

   (Wadsworth series in mass communication)
   Includes bibliographies and index.
   1. Public relations. I. Scott, Alan. II. Title.
III. Series.
HM263.N49   1985   659.2   84-15322
ISBN 0-534-04287-2

CONTENTS IN BRIEF

DETAILED CONTENTS

FEATURED MATERIAL

PREFACE

"Tell it like it is," challenged a friend in PR practice. So in 1976, *This Is PR* was first published. Since then, the need for a basic, professional book that serves practitioners as a useful reference and colleges as a contemporary text has increased.

THIS IS PR, THIRD EDITION

Now that the Information Age is here, public relations is on the front line. Since that first edition, PR practice has changed significantly. Real evidence of change is the increasing demand for theory and research techniques. Reviewers of the first edition (1976) were wary, but demanded more of both by the second edition (1981). Research is growing in significance as PR practitioners increasingly find it necessary to measure results. An emphasis on theory is a natural outgrowth of the research emphasis.

Part 1 of *This Is PR* is devoted to discussing what PR is and isn't, how it began and what it is today. Part 2 includes research methods, both informal and formal. Part 3 is a careful look at publics and target audiences, because so much of PR planning depends on understanding audiences and responding to public opinion.

Communication is the topic of Part 4, including concepts and theories, channels and working with media people and other communication professionals. In Part 5 the case study approach is outlined from two points of view, the historical and the current. The PR campaign is included in this section, as are some professional examples. An entire chapter (13) is devoted to learning from the experiences of others. Cases have been grouped into three types: issues management and crisis PR, behavior change, and the PR/marketing mix.

In the final portion of the book (Part 6), two chapters look at the legal and moral environment for public relations practice. Standards for professional performance, the PRSA code, are in the appendix. The index has new entries, representing items that students called to our attention, as well as some omissions found by colleagues.

Deciding what to keep from the second edition was less of a problem than getting a handle on the real changes. For example, trying to find two people to agree on computer terms to include in the glossary proved impossible. We gave up on that and included only the language most commonly used.

IMAGES

PR looks formidable if the book is a tome, and both students and professionals are frustrated by unused (but paid for) chapters. *This Is PR* contains the essentials of PR information, prepared for a single course. (There is a PR writing book, but it is a separate text.)

PR people should be able to see themselves in various PR roles. Since a majority of PR students today are women, that is not possible if the language is sexist—if examples always use the masculine pronoun. And it is also difficult if all of the role models are male. *This Is PR* always has been a nonsexist text, in language and example.

PR research, as it is published in journals, is included to keep the text abreast, often ahead, of the field. Professionals and students frequently fail to see PR as a field for serious scholarship and this text represents an effort to improve that oversight. There is a real need for PR *scholars*.

CONTRIBUTORS AND CRITICS

Colleagues in the field as well as students from all over the nation have had an important part in changes in this third edition. Colleagues have been encouraged to send suggestions and students asked to write critiques. The response was important because, to borrow from computer terminology, we wanted the book to be "user friendly"—easy to use, easy to learn from, easy to teach from.

We are indebted to editor Rebecca Hayden, who has guided us through three editions and has been both an inspiration and a mentor.

Special thanks go to the reviewers who examined our changes for this third edition. Some have been with us since the first edition, and others joined us for the second. Enlisted especially to review this third edition are: Frank Wylie, APR, and former PRSA national president, who began making notes and sending them when he changed from the corporate world to academia as director of Public Affairs for California State University at Los Angeles; Linda Scanlan, APR, of Norfolk State University and PRSA Educator's Section officer and AEJMC PR Division officer as well as national PRSSA liaison; Bill Baxter, APR, of Marquette University and

1984–85 chair of PRSA Educator's Section; William R. Berry of the State University of New York–Geneseo; Michael Hesse, APR, of the University of Alabama; and Frank Walsh, J.D., APR, of the University of Texas at Austin, who was especially helpful in reading the law chapter. We also appreciate the detailed notes on the law chapter in the second edition provided by Wayne Overbeck, J.D., California State University, Fullerton.

Finally, we are extremely grateful to Jim Haynes, APR, assistant dean of the College of Communication, University of Texas at Austin, who prepared the Instructor's Supplement for this edition.

To our colleagues and our students, who have made us better teachers and PR practitioners

This Is PR

**The Realities
of Public Relations**

The Role of PR

The purpose of this unit is to start you thinking in PR terms. In it you will discover the origins of PR activities, the scope and nature of public relations work and the people who use and benefit from public relations.

CHAPTER 1

PR—What Is It?

PR Fundamentals

Maintain the integrity and credibility of yourself and your client.

Practice or adopt policies that are in the public as well as private interest.

Don't do or say or write anything you wouldn't want to see on the front page of the New York Times.

Kerryn King, Senior Consultant, Hill and Knowlton, New York

In my opinion, the best prevention and the most effective form of communication is behavior itself!

Stephen A. Greyser, Professor of Business Administration, Harvard Business School

Television viewers of the evening series soap *Dallas* were given a jaundiced view of public relations when the CBS show introduced "a slithery character" called Leslie Stewart, a PR woman who promised to help J. R. Ewing improve his image. J. R., recovering from a gunshot wound, was trying to regain control of the family oil business. The PR character showed him a new logo for Ewing Oil at their first meeting and promised to make him someone everyone would want to work for, "the richest, most desirable man in town."[1]

PR practitioners protested. CBS's management described Stewart as "almost a female J. R., and not intended to be a caricature of the ethical PR person." The weekly national newsletter *pr reporter* said the PR character's conduct would deserve censure under the ethics code of the Public Relations Society of America because she promised specific results in areas over which she had no control.[2]

The complaints of PR practitioners were based on their concern that erroneous ideas about what public relations is and can do would be reinforced. CBS knows better. One of the best examples of a genuine application of public relations techniques occurred at CBS.

On Sunday afternoon June 2, 1957, CBS's *Face the Nation* had as its guest Nikita Khrushchev, then First Secretary of the U.S.S.R.'s Communist Party. A real coup? Not in the Red-hunting days of the 1950s—especially when Khrushchev chose this occasion to say, "I can prophesy that your grandchildren in America will live under socialism."

---

[1] "PR Industry Gives 'Dallas' Some Flak," *Wall Street Journal*, February 13, 1981, p. 17.

[2] "Practitioners May Want to Shoot J. R. Again as 'Dallas' Introduces a Mythical 'PR Gaff'—But It Shows Perception of Field as Powerful," *pr reporter*, Vol. 24, No. 6, February 9, 1981, p. 2.

Monday morning newspaper headlines enlightened those who missed the telecast, and by Monday afternoon it was clear that CBS had rocked the ship of state. Secretary of State John Foster Dulles was outraged, and President Eisenhower was also reported to be upset. Broadcast stations and networks generally have been more sensitive than individual newspapers to public clamor, especially from the government. Thus on Tuesday morning CBS executives began a marathon meeting that went well into Wednesday.

CBS News saw the program as a plus; corporate executives did not, fearing restrictive legislation in Congress or loss of licenses for the network's five affiliated stations. According to Sig Mickelson, then president of CBS News, it took the arrival of an outside public relations counsel to resolve the dilemma:

> He encouraged the adoption of an affirmative position rather than a negative one. He urged CBS to take the offensive; show pride in *Face the Nation* rather than embarrassment; brag to the country about having made a major contribution to better world understanding rather than apologize for having given the Russian leader an opportunity to speak directly to the American people.
>
> Even more significantly the CBS response—reflected in full-page ads in the New York and Washington newspapers on the next morning—became the springboard for a campaign on behalf of broadcasters' freedom of the press that was to last for several months. The campaign demanded First Amendment protection for broadcasting.[3]

The *counseling* of public relations not only restored CBS's faith in itself and aroused public opinion to speak in its support but also, for the first time, raised the critical issue of constitutional freedom for broadcast news, which was already guaranteed for printed news. This was no false front, no image making. The threat was real, and it was serious.

In many minds, of course, PR has long been associated with image making and the false front. Public relations practitioners have been looked upon as "flacks," "hucksters," P. T. Barnum-style con artists interested only in taking your money and getting you inside the tent.

Such an impression of public relations practice might have been the key to the downfall of the only U.S. president to resign from office.

After reviewing the 1,120 pages of *R. N., The Memoirs of Richard Nixon, Time* magazine described "a few admissions about what he thought was just a public relations problem."[4]

Nixon's ignorance of PR is apparent in his diagnosis of his own legal and political situation after the break-in at Democratic National Committee headquarters in the Watergate office complex. When the break-in was shown to involve officials of his 1972 reelection committee and former White House aides, he tried to shield the event from public scrutiny. The cover-up did not restore public confidence, though, and Nixon thought it had been just a PR ploy that had failed. He

---

[3] Sig Mickelson, "The First Amendment and Broadcast Journalism," *The First Amendment and the News Media: Final Report*, p. 55, Annual Chief Justice Earl Warren Conference on Advocacy in the United States, June 8–9, 1973, Cambridge, Mass., sponsored by the Roscoe Pound–American Trial Lawyers Foundation.

[4] "Nixon's Memoirs: 'I Was Selfish,'" *Time*, May 8, 1978, p. 26.

said that after the cover-up he sensed "a cloud of suspicion still hung over the White House. Yet I felt sure that it was just a public relations problem that only needed a public relations solution."[5] Nixon was equating "cover-up" with public relations. Before the Watergate episode was over, other players in the drama also equated PR with "stonewalling it," that is, not talking to the news media, and with "PR scenarios," where role playing to predict possible public effects was used until the most attractive set piece could be found in which to place the staged action. It was never pointed out that PR involves encountering a problem openly and honestly and solving it.

Yet, as media scholars David Clark and William Blankenburg point out, "Ideally, public relations is not just a matter of saying good things, but of doing good as well. Though much of PR is just a slather of frosting on stale cake, the best is a disclosure of an active social conscience."[6] It is our intention in this book to educate for PR by showing how practitioners can be identified with social responsibility, and in Chapter 3 we will consider this in some detail.

PR AND RELATED ACTIVITIES

Public relations may include all of the following activities, but it is never just any one of them: press agentry, promotion, public affairs, publicity and advertising. PR activities also coexist with marketing and merchandising, terms that are not synonymous. Since many people confuse public relations with one or more of these activities, let us distinguish among them.

Public Relations

PR is responsibility and responsiveness in policy and information to the best interests of the institution and its publics (see 1.1). The public relations practitioner is the intermediary between the interest represented and all of the involved publics. Public relations involves research into all audiences—receiving information from them, advising management of attitudes and responses, helping set policy that will demonstrate a responsible attention to these attitudes and responses and constantly evaluating the effectiveness of all PR programs. This inclusive role embraces all activities having to do with ascertaining and influencing the opinion of a group of people (see 1.2).

The complexity of PR's role prompted the Public Relations Society of America to attempt a description, not a definition, of public relations (see 1.3).

---

[5]Richard M. Nixon, *R. N., The Memoirs of Richard Nixon* (New York: Grosset & Dunlap, 1978), p. 156.
[6]David G. Clark and William B. Blankenburg, *You & Media* (San Francisco: Canfield Press, 1973), p. 175.

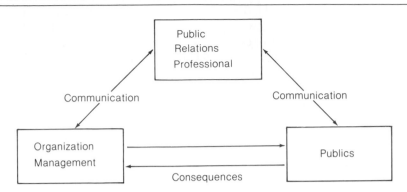

What PR problems you should address depends on your definition of public relations and on the PR activities of your organization. The diagram above defines PR in terms of relationships. PR activities differ among corporate, government, association education, and non-profit public relations.

The diagram shows that an organization–publics relationship exists when one has a consequence for the other. For example, if an organization's acts impact on a group, that group comprises a public for that organization. Likewise, if a group can affect an organization, then it is a public for that organization. When consequences occur—when one does something that affects the other—the organization and the publics must communicate with one another. Management delegates this function to the public relations professional, who communicates with management to be able to explain management decisions to the public and to explain public opinion to management. The public relations professional also communicates with the public in order to explain public opinion to management and management decisions to the public.

Drawing reproduced courtesy of James E. Grunig from a July 1979 newsletter to the Public Relations Division of the Association for Education in Journalism and Mass Communication.

Press Agentry

Because PR had its origins in press agentry, many people think that is all there is to public relations. Press agentry involves planning activities or staging events that will *attract attention* to a person, institution, idea or product. Sometimes these are just stunts, but pure hokum is seldom palatable these days. There is nothing wrong with simply attracting crowds and giving people something to see or talk about, provided there is no deception involved. Today's press agents are polished pros who steer clear of fraud and puffery, unless it is strictly in fun and is recognized as such.

Although a press agent's principal aim is to attract attention, rather than to educate or achieve understanding, some press agents manage to do both. An example of good press agentry was a series of free outdoor concerts with a program of light classical music offered by the Dallas Symphony Orchestra one summer to stimulate interest in its season ticket sales drive. The events attracted a warm response from music lovers, and probably helped people see the symphony as a "fun-giving" rather than as a formal institution. "Press agentry" can be one element in an overall public relations effort.

1.2 THE PRINCIPLES OF PR

1. Public relations deals with reality, not false fronts. Conscientiously planned programs with the public interest in the forefront are the basis of sound public relations policy. (Translation: PR deals with facts, not fiction.)

2. Public relations is a service-oriented profession, with public interest, not personal reward, as the primary consideration in its practice. (PR is a public, not personal, service.)

3. Since the public relations practitioner must go to the public to seek support for programs and policies, public interest is the criterion by which a professional selects not only who will be represented to the public but also the programs and policies that will be offered to the public for support. (PR practitioners must have the guts to say no to a client or to refuse a deceptive program.)

4. Because the public relations practitioner reaches many publics through mass media, which are the public channels for communication, the integrity of these channels must be preserved. (PR practitioners should never lie to the news media, either outright or by implication.)

5. Because PR practitioners are in the middle between an organization and its publics, they must be effective communicators in the true sense of the word, conveying information back and forth until understanding is reached. (The PR practitioner probably was the original ombudsman.)

6. To expedite the two-way communication necessary for practicing public relations and to be responsible communicators, public relations practitioners depend heavily on scientific public opinion research. (PR cannot afford to be a guessing game.)

7. To understand what the publics are saying and to reach them effectively, the public relations practitioner employs the social sciences—psychology, sociology, social psychology, public opinion, communications study and semantics. (Intuition is not enough.)

8. A lot of people are doing PR's research. The PR person appropriates the work of other, related disciplines. PR practice draws from learning theory and other psychology theories, from sociology, political science, economics and history. (See Chapters 4–8 especially.)

9. Public relations practitioners are obligated to explain problems to the public before these problems become crises. (PR should alert and advise so people won't be surprised.)

10. A public relations professional should be measured by only one criterion: ethical performance. (A public relations professional is only as good as the reputation he or she has earned and maintained.)

Promotion

There is a hazy line between the old press agentry and today's promotion. Although promotion incorporates special events that could be called press agentry, it goes beyond that into *opinion making*, for promotion attempts to garner support and endorsement for a person, product, institution or idea. Promotional campaigns depend for their effectiveness on the most efficient use of various PR tools; and *more* is not always better. (See Chapter 7 on external publics and public opinion.) Examples of promotion are the various fund-raising drives conducted by churches, charities, health groups and conservation interests. Among the successful promoters in the country are the American Red Cross, the American Cancer Society and United Fund organizations. Promotion, fund raising and all that goes with such drum beating are a variety of PR activities, incorporated into an overall public relations program. What makes promotion activities worthwhile is the merit of the cause. The legitimacy of the cause is also important from a purely pragmatic viewpoint: It won't receive media coverage if it isn't legitimate.

1.3 OFFICIAL STATEMENT ON PUBLIC RELATIONS

This statement was formally adopted by the PRSA on
November 6, 1982.

Public relations helps our complex, pluralistic society to reach decisions and function more effectively by contributing to mutual understanding among groups and institutions. It serves to bring private and public policies into harmony.

Public relations serves a wide variety of institutions in society such as businesses, trade unions, government agencies, voluntary associations, foundations, hospitals and educational and religious institutions. To achieve their goals, these institutions must develop effective relationships with many different audiences or publics such as employees, members, customers, local communities, shareholders and other institutions and with society at large.

The managements of institutions need to understand the attitudes and values of their publics in order to achieve institutional goals. The goals themselves are shaped by the external environment. The public relations practitioner acts as a counselor to management, and as a mediator, helping to translate private aims into reasonable, publicly acceptable policy and action.

As a management function, public relations encompasses the following:

- Anticipating, analyzing and interpreting public opinion, attitudes and issues which might impact, for good or ill, the operations and plans of the organization.
- Counseling management at all levels in the organization with regard to policy decisions, courses of action and communication, taking into account their public ramifications and the organization's social or citizenship responsibilities.

- Researching, conducting and evaluating, on a continuing basis, programs of action and communication to achieve informed public understanding necessary to the success of an organization's aims. These may include marketing, financial, fund raising, employee, community or government relations and other programs.
- Planning and implementing the organization's efforts to influence or change public policy.
- Setting objectives, planning, budgeting, recruiting and training staff, developing facilities—in short, *managing* the resources needed to perform all of the above.
- Examples of the knowledge that may be required in the professional practice of public relations include communication arts, psychology, social psychology, sociology, political science, economics and the principles of management and ethics. Technical knowledge and skills are required for opinion research, public issues analysis, media relations, direct mail, institutional advertising, publications, film/video productions, special events, speeches and presentations.

In helping to define and implement policy, the public relations practitioner utilizes a variety of professional communication skills and plays an integrative role both within the organization and between the organization and the external environment.

Reprinted with permission of the Public Relations Society of America.

Public Affairs

Many public relations people are using the term *public affairs* to describe their work. This is misleading, however, because public affairs is a highly specialized kind of public relations that means *community relations* and *governmental relations*, or dealing with officials within the community and working with legislative groups and with various pressure groups such as consumers. It is a highly significant part of a public relations program, but it is not the whole program. Eighteen months before the Dallas/Fort Worth Airport was to open, two PR

1.4 LEGAL BONDAGE

An Act of Congress dated October 22, 1913 often is interpreted to preclude the use of public relations talent by government. The prohibitive words were attached to the last paragraph of an Interstate Commerce Commission statute: "Appropriated funds may not be used to pay a publicity expert unless specifically appropriated for that purpose." The amendment to the bill was introduced by Representative Frederick H. Gillett and thus is referred to in public relations literature as the Gillett Amendment. Most public relations activity of that period was publicity, and the intent of the amendment was to identify and control publicity. Legislators were concerned that the government would become involved in propaganda directed to U.S. citizens.

Most responsible PR practitioners would like to see this amendment repealed, since government is carrying out PR functions but masking them. As a result, taxpayers cannot get any information about money spent for PR. One suggestion is to have the Public Relations Society of America's chapter in Washington, D.C., working with the National Association of Government Communicators, help the General Accounting Office get from each department and agency annual expenditures for activities considered public relations. In 1972 Robert O. Beatty, assistant secretary for public affairs, Department of Health, Education and Welfare, suggested that the ancient rider be repealed or the Freedom of Information Act amended "to recognize and legitimatize public affairs as a valid function of government, define its functions and responsibilities clearly across the broad scope of communications, and to give it the necessary support to do the job it's supposed to do—namely, let the people know what goes on in their government with their tax dollars."*

Specific action to identify clearly the role of public relations practitioners in government, to designate the function in each federal agency, was taken by the Public Relations Division of the Association for Education in Journalism, in cooperation with the Public Relations Society of America (PRSA), in August 1975. Both the educators and practitioners supported a bill (HR 7268) that would establish the public information function at the top level of every federal agency. As written, the bill emphasizes the advisory capacity of the public information experts, designating them as the people's voice in government and empowering them to make the basic advisory decisions under the Freedom of Information Act. In the undeserved bad publicity PR got during the Nixon debacle, PRSA did not push for the legislative change. The bill has not been reintroduced. Public relations people in government have given themselves some identity through their National Association of Government Communicators.

*Some information from Robert O. Beatty, "Advocates for the Public," *Public Relations Quarterly* (Summer 1972), p. 13; update from David Brown, historian, the U.S. Printer, 1983.

firms were hired—one to handle public affairs, the other to handle media relations. There were good reasons for having two firms. Public affairs was complex, not only because the airport was paid for by cities in two different counties, but also because the airport was located astride two counties and within the municipal boundaries of four suburban cities. The media relations were complex as well, since they involved arranging the special events, advertising and publicity connected with the opening; producing informational materials about the airport; and conducting media relations that were international in scope.

In the military, *public affairs* is the term commonly used to designate a broader responsibility than *public information*, which is merely publicity—handing out information. Because of a rather shortsighted law that precludes government use of people identified as public relations personnel (see 1.4), military public affairs officers often have broad public relations functions, that is, responsibility for all facets of both internal and external public relations.

Publicity

Because publicity is usually involved in helping to call attention to the special events or the activities surrounding a promotion, there is confusion over this term. Essentially, publicity means *placing information in a news medium*, either a mass medium such as television or newspapers or a specialized medium such as corporate magazines or industry newsletters. Publicists are writers. Use of the term *public relations* by institutions to describe publicity jobs is unfortunate. Publicists perform a vital function—disseminating information—but they generally do not help set policy. (Only PR counselors, usually at the executive level, are in a position to effect substantive management changes.)

A college student's first awareness of public relations activity is often through some personal experience with publicity. A note comes from home, "Congratulations on making the dean's list. Love, Aunt Susie." A clipping is attached. How did that get into the hometown newspaper? Mother? No. The university's news bureau sent a story with that student's name and others from the same town.

Publicity isn't always good news. For campus PR people, the political strife of the sixties and early seventies was an ulcer-provoking period. At Drake University in Des Moines, Iowa, radicals planted a bomb that exploded in the science building. The university's public relations office gave information to the local and campus news media immediately. The next day, the office sent out a four-page mailing piece that included a letter from the president telling what had happened, describing the extent of the damages, estimating when repairs would be made and emphasizing that the incident was not caused by university students. The mailing piece also carried reproductions of the newspaper stories and photographs. It was sent to alumni, parents, students, faculty, staff and others on the university's mailing list. Such prompt action helped clarify a situation that could have resulted in actions even more detrimental to the university such as the removal of students by concerned parents or the withdrawal of funds and support by alumni and donors.

Advertising

Advertising is concerned with *buying time or space* for ads and helping to *design and write copy* for ads. Advertising is usually separate from PR and should complement the total PR program. If a public relations person has no expertise in advertising, an agency should be hired to work under his or her supervision. Advertising is needed for special events and successful promotion. Although it is a major part of marketing, it is a distinct activity with its own needs for research and testing. Advertising as paid-for time or space is a tool of PR, often used to complement publicity, promotions and press agentry (for example, the appearance in supermarkets of the Jolly Green Giant).

Marketing

As in advertising, research and testing play a vital role in marketing, but the kind of testing advertising uses may be only a part of market research. Marketing specialists want to know if there is a *need or desire* for a product or service and, if so, *among which audiences* and in *what form* is it most likely to be received. Marketing is directed toward consumers, although it must interact with other publics such as the sales force, dealers, retailers and the advertising department. Market research is invaluable to the PR practitioner because it provides information about consumers—and relationships with consumers are an important PR consideration.

All marketing activities have public relations implications and occasionally a direct impact. For example, a marketing campaign launched to promote a new type of double-edged razor blade turned into a public relations problem when samples of the product (enclosed in an envelope with promotional literature) were inserted into newspapers, provoking complaints about, for instance, a dog cutting its mouth and children getting to the blades before their parents. Most often, however, marketing is an asset to public relations.

Merchandising

Merchandising, often confused with marketing, is concerned with the *packaging* of a product, an idea or perhaps even a president.[7] Its research asks what subtle emotions play a part in acceptance of the product, what shape of package is easiest to handle, what color is likely to attract more attention, what kind of display will make people react. The answers are important information for salespeople and dealers and should supplement the marketing and advertising research in a campaign. Merchandising experts are strong in the area of graphics, color, tactile responses and emotional reactions to physical imagery. Their work is vital, often part of the public relations milieu. However, it is not in itself public relations.

THE PERSONAL QUALIFICATIONS OF A PR PERSON

Edward L. Bernays, pioneer PR practitioner, author and educator, observed that many people use words without knowing their exact meaning, particularly words that designate new professions. If nothing else, we hope that in this initial discussion we have been able to clear away some misconceptions about what PR is. Now let us consider what kind of person might achieve success as a PR practitioner.

Charles W. Pine, a PR agency president in Phoenix, Arizona, lists the personal qualifications a public relations person should have as follows. That person should:

- Be able to express him- or herself fluently but also know when to listen
- Be observant, quick to learn and have a good memory

---

[7] See Joe McGinniss, *The Selling of the President, 1968* (New York: Trident Press, 1968).

- Possess the gift of human understanding
- Have courage and integrity and be able to think in bold concepts
- Be sufficiently self-disciplined to execute the smallest detail
- Have intellectual maturity, sound judgment and sufficient leadership qualities
- Be a prolific producer of new ideas
- Be able to think and act efficiently in emergencies, able to make decisions quickly
- Be able to write rapidly and well
- Be able to interpret miscellaneous information, marshall thoughts in an orderly sequence, recognize facts and know where to find them
- Have a sound knowledge of the workings of business
- Be versed in psychology, philosophy and economics and know something about politics and current events
- Be able to organize him- or herself and other people
- Be able to formulate priorities and not resent interruptions that require revising the priorities list
- Not agree automatically with authorities
- Be able to be diplomatic
- Recognize that a PR person is a teacher, not a crusader.

Does this seem superhuman? No doubt it is, though Pine's characterization is a goal worth pursuing. However, there are other specific qualities we feel will help you become a professional public relations person.

1. You should read copiously and consistently. Keeping up with newsmaking events and with the media themselves (all of them) is fundamental if you are to think in public relations terms.

2. You must learn to skillfully use two fundamental elements of PR: publicity and advertising. Underlying publicity and advertising is semantics, or what words mean, an entire discipline in itself. The words you choose are critical. You have to be sure your message gets across *and* produces the desired result.

3. You need to know something about the *target audience* for whom the message is intended. For example, a man wanting to surprise his wife with Mother's Day flowers enlisted his six-year-old daughter in the secret so she could help intercept the florist's delivery. When the child asked what to do with mommy's surprise, he responded, "Put it in the icebox." But on Mother's Day, when he looked in the refrigerator, the flowers were not there. The little girl had put them in what she understood was an "icebox"—the freezer.

4. For your ideas to succeed with the public, you must learn to *understand people*. You must be familiar with the relevant discoveries of sociologists and psychologists. Applying these ideas is involved and complex. Realizing this complexity makes a practitioner or PR professor smile weakly when a student claims an interest in PR because "I like people."

5. You must learn how to research target audiences to find out what people know or think they know, what they want, what they do or say they will do and

how their attitudes and hopes affect and are affected by the social, economic and political climate.

6. You must learn to deal with both mass and specialized media. You must try to find out everything you can about the media you work with, how they function and why. Part of this is learning to be of service to the media, an aspect of the publicity function.

7. Since the simple but significant function of public relations, getting the message to the public, has for so long been considered a manipulative process, we must emphasize a pivotal aspect of public relations—*integrity*. You must learn to distinguish quickly the good from the bad. This is accomplished only through a keen awareness honed by reading, observing and listening.

The PR practitioner today needs to be researcher, counselor, strategic planner, educator, communicator and cheerleader, according to former PRSA president Pat Jackson, publisher of *pr reporter*.[8]

Bernays lists these personal characteristics needed by the PR practitioner: (1) character and integrity; (2) a sense of judgment and logic; (3) ability to think creatively and imaginatively; (4) truthfulness and discretion; (5) objectivity; (6) a deep interest in the solution of problems; (7) a broad cultural background; (8) intellectual curiosity; (9) effective powers of analysis and synthesis; (10) intuition; (11) training in the social sciences and the mechanics of public relations.[9]

Of these, most relate to effectiveness as a problem sensor and problem solver—a critical role for the PR person.

Problem solving often requires teamwork and a tolerance for different views. As a public relations person, you must gather different views and help hammer them into a solution. At the same time, you must reflect confidence and hope that a solution exists. Perhaps this is why in a crisis, such as that with Khrushchev and CBS News, people tend to look to a public relations person. Confidence and hope come only from viewing problems with complete honesty and learning to live with some that seem, for the moment at least, insoluble, while diligently pursuing solutions. This leaves no room for the view of public relations as a cover-up for problems or difficulties.

THE EDUCATION
OF A PR PERSON

Formal preparation for public relations careers received a great deal of attention from both educators and practitioners during the early 1980s, primarily because public relations and advertising majors outnumbered others in journalism/mass communication courses at most U.S. colleges and universities. The first nationally accepted standard for public relations education was devel-

---

[8] Pat Jackson, "The Practice of Public Relations, 1982," *pr reporter*, Vol. 25, No. 1, January 4, 1982, p. 3.
[9] *pr reporter*, Vol. 25, No. 50, December 20, 1982, p. 126.

oped in 1975.[10] In 1981 this report was updated.[11] Because colleges and universities outside of the United States also were beginning to offer public relations courses, still another model was developed to include all schools.[12, 13]

Specifics vary in career preparation, but there is universal agreement that public relations practice demands expertise in the following:

1. *Planning*: Ranges from counseling top management in other than PR problems to dealing with the details of the PR department's own organization and functioning. It incorporates the development of policy, procedure, action and the communication of these to other departments.

2. *Administration*: Goes beyond administering the PR department itself to interpreting top management to the entire organization, participating in association activities, coordinating all outside agencies and activities, accumulating information about the organization and preparing and allocating the corporate PR budget.

3. *Advising*: Implies doing the research into opinion, attitudes and expectations necessary to provide authoritative counsel, as well as educational and informational materials, to stockholders, lobbyists and others.

4. *Analyzing*: Examining future trends and their consequences and preventing conflict and misunderstandings through promoting mutual respect and social responsibility.

5. *Industry Relations*: Helping to attract and retain good employees and working with personnel to improve employer-employee relations. It involves initiating communication systems with employees and suppliers, helping to improve labor relations by participating in meetings and conferences with labor representatives and working closely with labor negotiators in labor contracts and discussions.

6. *Economic Relations*: Maintaining relations with competitors, dealers and distributors. It encompasses advertising and promotion, which often requires working closely with marketing and merchandising and harmonizing the public and private interest.

7. *Social Relations*: Being concerned with both human relations, including preservation of personal dignity and employee protection (security), and social welfare, incorporating recreational, medical and civic activities.

8. *Political Activities*: Being involved with the community's administrative, educational and religious groups, as well as with legislative bodies and interna-

---

[10] Carroll Bateman and Scott Cutlip, "A Design for Public Relations Education," *Report of the Commission on Public Relations Education*, published by the Foundation for Public Relations Research and Education, 845 Third Ave., New York, NY 10022.

[11] Kenneth Owler Smith, "Report of the 1981 Commission on Public Relations Education," *Public Relations Review*, 8, no. 2 (Summer 1982), pp. 61–70.

[12] IPRA Education and Research Committee with the IPRA International Commission on Public Relations Education, "A Model for Public Relations Education for Professional Practice," Gold Paper no. 4, January 1982, published by International Public Relations Association, 49 Wellington St., London, England WC2E 6BN.

[13] Robert Kendall, James L. Terhume and Michael B. Hesse, eds., *Where to Study Public Relations—A Student's Guide to Academic Programs in the U.S. and Canada, 1982*, PRSA/PRSSA; 845 Third Ave., New York, NY 10022 and IABC, 870 Market St., Suite 940, San Francisco, CA 94102.

tional contacts. It implies an interest in the international affairs of the world community.

9. *Communication*: Knowing how to communicate through both mass and specialized media by advertising and publicity and setting up a system for a two-way flow of full information.

10. *Educational Activities*: Encompasses working with employees, the general public, schools, consumer groups and company representatives such as salespeople and dealers and arranging appearances and writing speeches for corporate executives. Also included are in-house educational activities such as employee training programs.

THE JOB OF THE PR PRACTITIONER

Applying the skills PR demands in the job market is somewhat different for the entry-level person than for the experienced practitioner. Frank Wylie, former PRSA president and now both practitioner and educator (at the University of California, Los Angeles), explained that mature public relations people divide their time in the following way: 10 percent on techniques, 40 percent on administration and 50 percent on analysis and judgment. The average entry-level PR employee generally finds him- or herself spending 50 percent of job time on techniques, 5 percent on judgment and 45 percent on running like hell![14]

Wylie saw PR being done by fewer people as a result of economic necessity. Consequently, he predicted that more PR practitioners will be generalists rather than specialists. He warned, however, that this does not mean a new PR practitioner can know less about more aspects of PR but rather must know more about more.[15]

Wylie noted that "every beginner is a 'go-fer,' and it's important that you not only go for something, but that you bring back something usable."[16] The retrieval emphasis implies reportorial skills, including knowledge of research techniques. Other skills stressed by Wylie are thinking (first and foremost), writing of all types, speaking, being persuasive, understanding and appreciating media, knowing graphics and photography, respecting deadlines and developing an ability to deal with and solve multiple PR problems at one time.[17]

The way these skills are applied depends on whether the PR person is a *staff member*, an *agency employee*, an *independent PR practitioner* or *PR counselor*. A staff member's job description is usually determined by specific corporate or institutional needs. The PR professional working for an agency will find that the

---

[14] Frank Wylie, "The New Professionals," a speech to the First National Student Conference, Public Relations Student Society of America, Dayton, Ohio, October 24, 1976, published by Chrysler Corporation, p. 5.

[15] Ibid., pp. 5–6.

[16] Ibid., p. 6.

[17] Ibid., pp. 6–11.

Reprinted by permission. © 1983 NEA, Inc.

structure of the agency itself determines the duties, but generally speaking the president of an agency also handles accounts, as do the salespeople, who may be account executives too. An agency may employ a bookkeeper, secretary, publicity writer, advertising or graphics specialist and an artist, although the writer may prepare both publicity and advertising copy and the artist be responsible for both illustrations and layout. Large agencies have copy editors, media specialists, several artists and a complete production facility. Most agencies, even the largest ones, have contracts with printers, typesetters and photographers.

The independent public relations practitioner is usually hired to accomplish a task, ordinarily predetermined, but not always. Payment may be on a flat-fee basis, fee plus expenses or a base fee plus hourly charges and expenses. The less experienced the independent practitioner, the more often it will be necessary to work for an employer on a flat fee.

A PR counselor is called in at an advisory level and works for a consultant's fee, which he or she sets, with hours and expenses added. The counselor studies and researches a situation, interviews, outlines recommendations and offers these in formal presentation format. The program is then implemented by other PR workers.

SPECIALIZED AREAS OF PR

The breadth of PR services gives a wide career choice. Many practitioners are experienced in more than one area.

Nonprofit Organizations

The growing number of nonprofit organizations offers a practitioner several advantages and opportunities, although the compensation is often lower than that in other areas. Because of their structure (small production staff answerable to a volunteer board of directors), the PR person generally has a great deal of freedom in designing a program. An attractive program that does not need a large bankroll probably will be accepted. This kind of PR usually requires a considerable amount of promotional activity and sometimes fund raising and seeking foundation grants. However, a particular plus is the reception given publicity materials by news media representatives; they usually make every effort to use information from nonprofit institutions as long as the preparation is professional. Even advertising gets a break with special rates (sometimes called "church rates"). The only drawback besides red ink is a dependency on volunteer support in many areas. Responsibility for training volunteers usually falls on the PR people. Their interest in and enthusiasm for the organization can be stimulated and kept alive by a viable program. Especially expanding areas are health care organizations such as hospitals, museums and associations of all types. Many nonprofit PR people get involved in fund raising, which is both a campaign and a promotion.

Educational Institutions

Although educational institutions are generally also nonprofit organizations, they may be either public or private. The private institutions generally conform to the nonprofit organizational pattern. Although they have significant dealings with government, their work is not at all like that of public institutions, which, being a part of government, are more open to the scrutiny of taxpayers and the whims of politicians. The type of PR practiced in state educational institutions usually requires the kind of person who also would enjoy dealing with the government. PR people in all educational institutions are likely to be involved with development, which is fund raising. Generally the functions of PR and development are divided but must work closely together.

Government

There are three areas to this category. All have the same focus, but the internal workings vary.

Federal, State and Local—Inside Government As an Employee   Although the federal government is prohibited from labeling PR activities as such, the U.S. government, as well as state and local governments, uses PR talent under a variety of titles—public information is one, public affairs is another, departmental assistant still another.

Public Affairs—Outside Government, in an Institution Working with Government   The term *public affairs* is also used by institutions to designate staff who deal with government. Most institutions, profit and nonprofit, have specialists to handle their relations with the various departments of government on all levels—federal, state and local—with which they have contact. Public affairs means dealing with problems that come under the jurisdiction of public officials who are elected or appointed.

Politics—Working for Candidates or Elected Officials   Political PR involves working with candidates for office and often continuing to work with them after their election to handle problems, strategies and activities like speech writing or publicity. Many PR practitioners will not support a cause or person they cannot endorse; others see PR services as being the same as legal advice and will offer their services to anyone who will pay for them.

For all three areas—government, public affairs and politics—a strong background in government and history is useful. Political PR, as all others, can be high-pressured, especially since the Freedom of Information Act has opened most previously closed doors to governmental secrets. Also, recent restrictions on campaigning and campaign financing mean PR people must be even more judicious in collecting, reporting and spending money. State and federal laws must be adhered to.

Lobbying—Working for Special Interests Outside Government   Many lobbyists are not public relations specialists (many are former government officials). But many public relations practitioners are getting into lobbying activities through their jobs with corporations or utilities. Some PR practitioners become professional lobbyists, generally representing a particular industry such as oil and gas or special interests, such as senior citizens or health care. Lobbyists work closely with the staffs of federal and/or state representatives and senators who depend on them to explain the intricacies and implications of proposed legislation. Lobbyists draw on information and influence to persuade to a point of view.

Industry

Public relations for industry also requires a good feel for political PR because so much of industry is regulated by government. You must develop a high tolerance for bureaucratic procrastination if you work for a company handling government contracts. One PR staffer for a defense contractor has said the average time required to get an "original" release—meaning one with all new material—cleared for dissemination to the news media is twenty-three days. Once the release clears, though, the practitioner is free to use the same information in other releases. Much of the emphasis in industrial public relations is on internal PR, a significant sector being labor relations. That is why a strong background in the social sciences and business helps.

PR practitioners in the utilities industry must work with both government and consumers. They must also know financial PR because most utilities are publicly held. Industry's PR practitioners may be involved in product promotion, which means they need to understand and appreciate marketing and advertising activities.

General Business

Sometimes called "retail PR," business PR is nevertheless somewhat broader than the first term implies, and involves working with government regulatory bodies, employees, the community, competitors and, generally, the full complement of publics both within the company and without. Consumers represent an increasingly significant segment of the external publics because they talk to politicians and can arouse public opinion against business. Product promotion—of either a service or goods—is also often an aspect of general business.

International PR for Institutions and Agencies

As multinational companies become more common, this area of public relations expands. International PR is not limited to businesses, however, since many organizations and associations are international in scope. Many PR agencies have offices abroad to represent both their own domestic clients and foreign clients. International PR requires special sensitivity to public opinion because practitioners deal with people whose language, experience and frame of reference differ from their own. Areas of particular concern are language and knowledge of its nuances, not just vocabulary; customs affecting attitudes toward media, products and services; and symbols stemming from customs and laws, because incompatibilities between one country's laws and another's may make harmonious relationships impossible. The International Public Relations Association (IPRA) was formed in 1955 after meetings with PR executives in the United States, Britain, France, Norway and the Netherlands. Currently, members represent sixty countries.

Financial PR

Sometimes referred to as *corporate PR*, financial PR includes such activities as preparing material for security analysts to use, developing an annual report acceptable to the auditors and readable by the stockholders and knowing when and to whom to issue a news release that could affect corporate stock values. It is a rather hazardous occupation because the consequences of a wrong move can be so detrimental. However, it is exciting, remunerative and challenging.

Sports

Before sports became such big business, the term *public relations* was sometimes used, but the job was actually a combination of press agentry and publicity. Today, however, business enterprises in professional sports are of such size and scope that the PR title is legitimate. The pro teams have intricate relations with investors, their own players, competing teams and players, stadium owners, transportation and housing facilities (at home and on the road), community supporters, media (in terms of both publicity and contractual obligations as in live coverage) and other important publics. Most pro sports organizations employ both full-time staff PR people and also contract for special PR activities. Sports are increasingly important to colleges and universities with sports information officers primarily handling relations with media and fans.

Leisure-Time PR

The leisure-time market, which has been expanding since World War II, includes all recreation and recreation-related industries. It covers real estate promotion, public park development, resorts and hotels, travel agencies, airlines and other mass transportation systems, sports, hobbies and crafts and some educational and cultural activities. The only real hazard in the leisure-time market is its close tie to a somewhat erratic economy. Public relations generalists can function here quite comfortably if they are creative and inventive in the promotional area.

PR ISSUES: MANAGERS/FUTURISTS

By the mid-1970s as many as one in five Fortune 500 companies had a "futurist" on the payroll, owing to the acceleration of crises. Their role is to serve management as an early warning system.[18] The 1970s was an era of uncertainty. Most Americans worried about economic problems, shortages of natural resources, especially energy, and a lack of confidence in American institutions. These concerns have continued in the 1980s, giving impetus to planning based on predictions of internal company development and external social, political and economic conditions. Detecting emerging issues and watching social and economic trends has become an important PR function, casting PR people more in their role as social scientists. Information and intelligent analysis can help restore confidence in our economy and government. The challenge to PR practitioners is to provide leadership in developing creative, pragmatic communications programs, giving the public full information that is candid, factual and understandable. Further, PR workers must draw more extensively on their innovative skills to maintain good relations with their audiences. Audiences are the public of public relations. PR involves maintaining good relations with a number of diverse publics (see Chapters 6 and 7).

POINTS TO REMEMBER

- Most people wrongly assume that public relations means image making in the sense of creating a false front or cover-up.
- Good public relations involves encountering a problem openly and honestly and then solving it; the best PR is disclosure of an active social conscience.

---

[18]Liz Roman Gallese, "More Companies Use 'Futurists' to Discern What Is Lying Ahead," *Wall Street Journal*, March 31, 1975, pp. 1, 10. See Chapter 3, pages 64–65, for a discussion of the role of futurists.

- Public relations may include all of the following activities, but it is never just any one of them: press agentry, promotion, public affairs, publicity and advertising. Such PR activities also coexist with marketing and merchandising.
- PR is responsibility and responsiveness in policy and information to the best interests of the institution and its publics.
- Public relations is a social science.
- Good PR practice involves anticipating, interpreting and analyzing public opinion; counseling management; researching and evaluating on a continuing basis; planning; and implementing and managing resources to carry out goals that are socially responsible.
- PR practitioners have to master diverse skills, be creative in solving problems and well-adjusted enough to withstand the considerable stresses of the job of working between the institution and its various (and numerous) publics.
- The formal education of a PR practitioner in U.S. colleges and universities has been developed by the cooperative efforts of professionals in PR education and PR practice.
- PR skills may be applied as a staff member, agency employee, independent PR practitioner or PR counselor in a variety of institutional settings.
- PR practitioners increasingly are futurists, whose planning is based on detecting social and economic trends. They are skillful communicators personally and in every medium, innovative adapters to the world community and persons with a high sensitivity to social responsibility.

THINGS TO DO

1. Write your own definition of PR, put it aside, and compare it later with the definition you will write at the end of Chapter 15. Has your definition changed? For now, find five different definitions of public relations. Compare them, noting how the source of the definition may have affected the description.

2. Look in the classified columns of your local newspaper for a job described as a public relations position. From the contents of the ad and from a call to the advertiser, determine if it is truly a job that calls for a public relations practitioner. Why do you think it is or is not a job for a PR person? What aspect of PR would it require?

3. Read your daily newspaper for a situation you would describe as a potential public relations problem. Why do you think it is? What are the characteristics of situations you would define as "public relations problems"?

SELECTED READINGS

F. E. Bair, *International Marketing Handbook* (Detroit: Gala, 1981). Profiles 138 nations.

Robert T. Bronzan, *Public Relations, Promotions, Fund-Raising for Athletic Programs* (New York: John Wiley, 1976). For the growing field of sports PR.

J. A. Califano, *Governing America: An Insider's Report from the White House and the*

Cabinet (New York: Simon and Schuster, 1981). Government issues, positions and adversaries.

Phillip Currah, *Setting Up a European Public Relations Operation* (London: Business Books, 1975). Offers some insight into the international field.

L. M. Helm and others, *Informing the People* (New York: Langman, 1981). A guide to government relations and the activities of various departments.

Sidney Kobre, *Successful Public Relations for Colleges/Universities* (New York: Hastings House, 1974). Good special-interest book.

Harold P. Kurtz, *Public Relations's Fund Raising for Hospitals: A Practical Handbook* (Springfield, Ill.: C. C. Thomas, 1980). A useful reference.

T. L. McPhail, *Electronic Colonialism: The Future of International Broadcasting and Communication* (Beverly Hills, Calif.: Sage, 1981). Describes the use of electronic media and the international politics involved.

L. A. Maddalena, *A Communications Manual for Nonprofit Organizations* (New York: AMACON, 1981). A helpful guide.

Patrick Monaghan, *Public Relations Careers in Business and the Community* (New York: Fairchild, 1972). Reasonably up-to-date guidebook.

Robert Oaks, *Communication by Objective* (South Plainfield, N.J.: Groupwork, 1977). A guide for nonprofit PR.

Public Relations Society of America, *Careers in Public Relations* (New York: Public Relations Society of America, 1983). A single copy is free.

Public Relations Society of America, *Public Relations Guides for Nonprofit Organizations* (New York: Public Relations Society of America, 1977). An excellent series of six booklets.

W. Emerson Reck, *Changing World of College Relations* (Washington, D.C.: Council for Advancement and Support of Education, 1976). A guidebook from the organization for people in educational PR.

Arthur R. Roalman, *Investor Relations Handbook* (New York: AMACON, 1974). A special association publication.

Frances Schmidt and Harold M. Weiner, *Public Relations in Health and Welfare* (New York: Columbia University Press, 1966). Needs updating, but gives some ideas of possible fields.

G. J. Voros and P. H. Alvarce, eds., *What Happens in Public Relations* (New York: AMACON, 1981). A description of various PR activities.

D. E. Zand, *Information, Organization and Power* (New York: McGraw-Hill, 1981). A description of the transformation of the United States from an industrial to an information society.

CHAPTER 2

PR—Where Did It Come From?

The public relations field, in all its variety, inventiveness, flamboyance and solemn pretentiousness, can perhaps best be approached, at the outset, by an examination of a representative sampling of its hardiest practitioners.

Irwin Ross, The Image Merchants

Today's public relations worker has inherited a legacy of criticism.

From The Mass Media and Modern Society *by Theodore Peterson, Jay W. Jensen, and William L. Rivers*

As far as we know, the words *public relations* were first used together in an address by lawyer Dorman Eaton to the Yale graduating class of 1882.[1] Eaton, however, was using *public relations* in the sense of "the general good." The term was not used formally, that is, more in the current context, by business until 1897, when it appeared in the Association of American Railroads' *Yearbook of Railway Literature*.[2] The real success of the term can be credited to Edward L. Bernays, whom Irwin Ross calls "the first and doubtless the leading ideologue of public relations."[3] Bernays was the first to call himself, in 1921, a "public relations counsel." Two years later he wrote the first book on the subject, *Crystallizing Public Opinion*,[4] and taught the first college course on PR at New York University (see 2.1). Thus it was around the turn of the twentieth century that PR came into being as a term, as a profession and as an academic discipline.

But it took more than a name and a book and a college course to launch what we now know as public relations. During the important decades near the turn of the century, a number of precedents were set that have affected modern PR ever since. For example, in 1888 the Mutual Life Insurance Company hired an outside consultant, Charles J. Smith, to write press releases and articles to boost the image of their company.[5] In 1889 the Westinghouse Corporation established what was

---

[1] According to a report by Professor Eric Goldman of Princeton University, referred to by Edward L. Bernays in the International Public Relations Association (IPRA) *Review*, September 1977, p. 4 of reprint. However, according to Sanat Lahiri of Calcutta, president, IPRA, in *pr reporter*, December 17, 1979, the phrase "public relations" was used much earlier by Thomas Jefferson.

[2] Ibid.

[3] Irwin Ross, *The Image Merchants* (Garden City, N.Y.: Doubleday, 1959), p. 51.

[4] Edward L. Bernays, *Public Relations* (Norman: University of Oklahoma Press, 1952), p. 84.

[5] Scott M. Cutlip and Allen H. Center, *Effective Public Relations*, 5th ed. (Englewood Cliffs, N.J.: Prentice-Hall, 1978), p. 73.

2.1 EDWARD L. BERNAYS (BORN 1891)

Like his uncle, Sigmund Freud, Edward L. Bernays has devoted his career to the study of the human mind. His specialty is mass psychology—how the opinions of many people can be influenced effectively and honorably. When he arrived on the scene, public opinion was considered philosophy. Sociology was just getting its start and Walter Lippmann had begun to define what Bernays calls "the American tribal consciousness." His psychology is exemplified in the advice he gave the Procter and Gamble Company when it presented him with a problem: a boycott of its products by black people. Bernays advised Procter and Gamble to eliminate its racist advertising campaign, to hire blacks in white collar jobs and to invite black people to open-house gatherings at the plant.

The Bernays style is often subtle. He helped the Beech-Nut Packing Company sell bacon, not by promoting bacon itself, but by promoting what all America could respond to, a nutritious breakfast. In 1918 Bernays even changed the course of history: He urged Thomas Masaryk, the founder of modern Czechoslovakia, to delay the announcement of that country's independence by a day in order to get better press coverage.

Bernays is adamant in his belief that his profession is more than mere press agentry. He is not, however, above staging events. In 1924 he helped President Coolidge overcome his aloof image by staging a White House breakfast, to which were invited Al Jolson and several other movie stars. In 1929 he publicized the fiftieth anniversary of the electric light bulb by having Thomas Edison reenact the discovery in the presence of President Hoover. Among Bernays's many clients have been Enrico Caruso, Henry Miller, the Diaghilev Russian Ballet, the United Fruit Company, General Motors, the American Tobacco Company and the American Nurses' Association. He also worked for the Creel Committee during World War I. He turned down an appeal for PR assistance from Hitler through an intermediary in 1933, just before Hitler came to power. However, Bernays says a correspondent for the Hearst newspapers told him that when he interviewed Joseph Goebbels, Hitler's minister of propaganda, some years later, he saw Bernays's 1923 book, *Propaganda*, on the Nazi's desk.

In 1922 he married Doris E. Fleischman, another PR pioneer. Their marriage and their business partnership lasted for more than fifty years.*

*Based on Irwin Ross, *The Image Merchants* (Garden City, N.Y.: Doubleday, 1959), pp. 51–64, and a story by Clayton Haswell of the Associated Press, which appeared in the Milwaukee Journal, November 14, 1983, pt. 1, p. 12.

essentially the first in-house publicity department under the directorship of E. H. Heinrichs, an ex-newspaper reporter.[6] In 1900 in Boston, Massachusetts, the nation's first publicity agency, the Publicity Bureau, was formed.[7] Within only a few years there were many such agencies competing for the job of presenting American industry in a favorable light to the American people. The first professional association of public relations people was the Bank Marketing Association, formed in 1915.[8]

These are only a few examples of the flurry of PR activities accompanying its "official" beginnings at the turn of the century. It is easy to see why public relations, like jazz, has been called an American product of the twentieth century. But just as the elements of jazz are evident in Bach, and the roots of jazz go back to the

---

[6] Forrest McDonald, *Insull* (Chicago: University of Chicago Press, 1962), pp. 44–45.

[7] Scott M. Cutlip, "The Nation's First Public Relations Firm," *Journalism Quarterly*, 43 (Summer 1966), pp. 269–280.

[8] Cutlip and Center, *Effective Public Relations*, p. 91.

2.2 PR: A CAPSULE HISTORY

In the United States the evolution of PR has gone through four distinct stages:

1. **Communicating/initiating**—a time primarily of publicists, press agents, promoters and propagandists
2. **Reacting/responding**—a period of writers hired to be spokespeople for special interests
3. **Planning/preventing**—a maturing of PR as it began to be incorporated into the management function
4. **Professionalism**—an effort by PR to control its development, use and practice.

These stages of evolution are marked by particular periods in U.S. history, which fall into the following divisions:

1600–1799	The Beginnings—American Revolution
1800–1859	Evolution of PR
1860–1899	Civil War and Postwar Growth
1900–1919	Opinion Molding—A Concern
1920–1939	A Turning Point for PR
1940–1949	PR and the War Effort
1950–1965	PR and Policy Making
1966–1970	The Consumer Movement's Impact
1971–1980	PR and Its Struggle for Status

breeze in the trees, so evidence of effective "public relations" can be seen throughout human history, from the dawn of society.

This chapter examines where public relations came from; how the functions, uses and tactics of PR have influenced American history and vice versa (see 2.2); how PR took form in the early years of this century and how it has developed since then into the vital profession it is today.

THE BEGINNINGS OF PR

It has often been said that twentieth-century public relations grew out of nineteenth-century press agentry. In some ways this is true: Many early PR practitioners got their start as press agents. Though few were as flamboyant as the great showman, P. T. Barnum (see 2.3), a great many were publicity writers whose main target had always been the press; and many of the functions and tactics of PR during its infancy were essentially those performed, served and used by press agentry. But the two are not the same thing. Saying PR grew out of press agentry is like saying jazz grew out of ragtime: partly true, but not the whole truth.

Press Agentry?

Press agentry really began about 1830 with the birth of the penny press. When newspaper prices dropped to a penny each, circulation and readership boomed, but so did the price of newspaper advertising. To reach the huge new audience, therefore, without paying even the price of a single copy, promoters and publicity people developed a talent for "making news." The object was simply to break into print, often at the expense of truth or dignity. Press

2.3 PHINEAS TAYLOR BARNUM (1810–1891)

The most famous and successful of the nineteenth-century press agents was P. T. Barnum, who created, promoted, and exploited the careers of many celebrities, including the midget General Tom Thumb, singer Jenny Lind, and Chang and Eng, the original Siamese twins. Early in his career, in 1835, Barnum exhibited a black slave named Joice Heth, claiming that she had nursed George Washington a hundred years before. Newspapers fell for the story because of its historical value. Then, when public interest in Joice Heth began to die down, Barnum kept the story alive by writing letters to the editor under assumed names, creating a controversy about her authenticity. He didn't care what the papers said, as long as he got space. When Heth died, an autopsy revealed her age to be about eighty. With the fraud exposed, Barnum claimed that he also had been duped.* True? Why not? After all, "There's a sucker born every minute."

The great circus showman was himself often the center of public attention, for which he gave credit to his own press agent, Richard F. "Tody" Hamilton.** However, it was another circus that first formally used the term *press agent*. In 1868 the roster of John Robinson's Circus carried the name W. W. Duran with the title Press Agent.[†]

*Edward L. Bernays, *Public Relations* (Norman: University of Oklahoma Press, 1952), pp. 38–39.

**Dexter W. Fellows and Andrew A. Freeman, *This Way to the Big Show* (New York: Viking Press, 1936), p. 193.

†Will Irwin, "The Press Agent: His Rise and Decline," *Colliers*, December 2, 1911, pp. 24–25. (William Henry Irwin)

agents exploited freaks to publicize circuses, invented legends to promote politicians, told outrageous lies and generally provided plenty of popular entertainment if not much real news.

The main ingredient of press agentry—imagination—is still a necessary talent for effective PR. Perhaps the essential difference between the two can be found in Ivy Lee's "Declaration of Principles" (1906), in which he defined the important ideals of public relations, his new profession: "Our plan is, frankly and openly . . . to supply the press and public of the United States prompt and accurate information concerning subjects which it is of value and interest to the public to know about."[9] Press agentry was usually prompt—so prompt that it didn't bother much with frankness, openness, accuracy or value.

PR has grown considerably since Ivy Lee and the end of the press agentry era. PR now contains many diverse elements that never had much connection with press agentry, including marketing, opinion research, merchandising and public affairs. However, almost all these elements actually predate both modern PR and its predecessor, press agentry. So we'll have to look farther back than P. T. Barnum to find the roots of public relations.

The Functions of PR Throughout History

Broadly defined, public relations is as old as civilization itself, because underlying all public relations activity is the effort *to persuade*. For society to exist, there has to be at least some agreement among people. This agreement is usually achieved by interpersonal and group communication, which in turn

---

[9]Sherman Morse, "An Awakening on Wall Street," *American Magazine*, 62 (September 1906), p. 460.

2.4 MARCUS TULLIUS CICERO (106–43 B.C.)

PUBLIC AFFAIRS IN A TIME OF TRANSITION

Cicero was a brilliant politician who had trouble with his image in the stormy political climate of the late Roman Republic. He held many public offices, including senator and consul, but he was exiled in 58 B.C. and his country houses were plundered and burned by order of the state. He staged a political comeback, but when he made the mistake of opposing Julius Caesar he was again forced into retirement. After Caesar was murdered in 44 B.C., Cicero returned for the last time to public life, waging a campaign to reconcile the political parties who were grappling for power and especially to restore the Republic in which he believed so fervently. But the last great hope of the Roman Republic vanished when Cicero was again declared an outlaw and put to death by Julius's nephew Octavius, who in time became Augustus Caesar, the first Roman emperor.

Cicero's persuasive tools were oratory and rhetoric. He boasted that no one had ever written more speeches in so many different styles. His speeches and writings were full of original ideas and wit, his points were clear and interesting and his language was elegant and moving but always in good taste and his words rang with rhythm.*

*Oskar Seyffert, A Dictionary of Classical Antiquities (London: William Glaisher, 1891), p. 133.

usually involves not just passing on information but also a strong element of persuasion.

Persuasion is still the driving force of public relations, and many of the tactics that modern PR people use to persuade have been used by the leaders of society for thousands of years.

Monuments and other art forms of the ancient world reflect early efforts at persuasion. Pyramids, statues, temples, tombs, paintings and early forms of writing announce the divinity of rulers, whose power, then, derives from the religious dedication of the public. Ancient art and literature also proclaim the heroic deeds of leaders and rulers, who are thus considered gods or godlike. And speeches by the powerful or power-seeking use institutionalized rhetoric (artificial or inflated language) as a principal device for persuasion, as anyone who has lived through a national election in the United States will recognize.

A look at some early techniques used in persuasion and the tools employed will put today's PR activities in perspective. For example, let us look at the early years of the Roman Empire, to see how that culture's leaders performed some of what we now call the functions of public relations. The Romans, of course, did not invent these PR functions. Indeed, by the time of the Caesars, PR (though not known as such) was already a practiced and sophisticated art.

Cameo: Functions of PR for the Caesars Although the early Roman Empire was no democracy, the rulers were aware of the importance of public opinion. *Opinion research* was carried on constantly throughout the empire by means of the most sophisticated courier and postal system of the ancient world, not to mention an equally sophisticated network of spies.

Opinion making was also a practiced art, especially among the persuasive orators of the Roman Senate. Cicero was one of the most polished (see 2.4). The senators were concerned not only with persuading one another; they also had to sell their policies to the ruling family and to the Roman citizens. In 59 B.C. when he was consul, Julius Caesar was able to accomplish this latter by establishing what has been called the first newspaper, the *Acta Diurna*.[10] The *Acta Diurna* was written in Latin, the language of the general populace, and it served chiefly to inform all Romans who could read how lucky they were to have such fine leadership. His commentaries too were less for the sake of history than for recording his own exploits. *Publicity* was a tool used also by the emperors who followed Julius Caesar. They continued his practice by publishing throughout the empire news of the imperial family, state and city affairs and the latest laws. The Roman leaders were also concerned with *opinion response*. Though it wasn't in their plan or in their power to make everybody happy, they did what they could to keep the people pacified and content by giving them what they wanted most: "bread and circuses."

Statues, monuments and arches, which can still be seen today, served as *promotion* for the imperial and military leaders. And all the Roman emperors from Augustus on used the ultimate promotion campaign: They made themselves gods and required the people to worship them. Augustus also had Virgil's *Aeneid* published for *propaganda* purposes. The epic poem glorified the origin of the Roman people and, by implication, the house of Caesar. Before that, Virgil had written *Georgics*, a master plan of practical goals for Italy's rehabilitation after the civil wars, which directed Rome toward a Golden Age. Finally, the Roman leaders used *press agentry*, the staged public event. Nero, for example, reputedly had half the city burned to the ground. Nero blamed the Christians for the fire and used it as an excuse to persecute the new religion.

PR Uses Throughout History

Most of the uses modern society has found for public relations are not new, and modern PR practitioners have learned a lot by studying the experts of the past. In 1095 Pope Urban II used PR *to promote a war* upon his Muslim neighbors to the east. He sent word through his information network—the cardinals, archbishops, bishops and parish priests—that to fight in this holy war was to serve God and to earn forgiveness of sins; it also gave Christians a once-in-a-lifetime chance to visit the holy shrines. The response was overwhelming, even if the Crusades were not an unqualified success.

In 1215 Stephan Langton, Archbishop of Canterbury, used PR tactics *to lobby for a political cause*. He mobilized an influential group of barons to stand up for their rights against King John and forced the king to agree to the terms of the Magna Carta. That document has been used as a political banner ever since by people fed up with oppression and control. In the fifteenth century Machiavelli put his PR talents to use *to support a political party* in power. His *The Prince* and *Discourses* are essentially treatises on how people can be governed firmly and effectively. Machiavelli's political psychology seems quite modern. His PR work for Cesar Borgia relied heavily on opinion control and propaganda, which might suggest that "issues management" is not a new technique.

---

[10] *Encyclopaedia Britannica*, 15th ed., s.v. "History of Publishing."

Saint Paul wrote his *Epistles* to encourage membership growth and boost morale among the early Christian churches, which were spread about the Roman Empire. His PR campaign was a great success, and his slogans and words of encouragement are still quoted.

Dante Alighieri's *Divine Comedy* was written in Italian rather than Latin to reach a wider audience. In the book Dante, a political activist, eloquently put forth his moral, political and intellectual views.

William Shakespeare's *history plays* contained poetry and ideas for the intellectuals and jokes and violence for the rest of the audience. But they also appealed to those in power because they glorified and reinterpreted the War of the Roses to justify the Tudor regime.

John Milton spent much of his career writing pamphlets for the Puritans. He also wrote for the Cromwell government. His greatest work, *Paradise Lost*, is considered the most beautiful and influential statement of the religious views of his time.

PR was used *to promote religion* in 1351. John Wycliffe called for a reform of the Catholic Church and particularly for an English translation of the Bible to give the word of God more directly to more people. Wycliffe took his campaign to the people themselves, addressing them on the streets and in public places. Although it was forbidden, he and his followers distributed books, tracts and broadsides.

During the early colonization of America, PR was used *to sell a product*, in this case real estate. The Virginia Company in 1620 issued a broadside in England offering fifty acres of free land to anyone who brought a new settler to America before 1625.[11] In 1643 PR was used in the colonies *to raise money*: Harvard College solicited funds by issuing a public relations brochure entitled *New England's First Fruits*.[12] Another college first used the publicity release in the New World— *to publicize an event*. King's College (now Columbia University) sent an announcement of the 1758 commencement to various newspapers, where the item was printed as news.[13] (See 2.5 for examples of PR best-sellers and what they accomplished.)

PR Tactics
Throughout History

Many of the functions and uses of public relations, then, have existed throughout the history of our culture. The same cannot be said, however, for many of the *tactics* of twentieth-century PR, since so many depend on inventions that weren't around before the nineteenth century. For example, much of modern PR relies on electronic communication—telegraph, telephone, even satellites— and the electronic mass media—movies, radio and television. PR has also been radically affected by the more recent rise of the computer.

---

[11] Theodore H. White, *Caesar at the Rubicon* (New York: Atheneum, 1968), p. 9.

[12] Marcus Lee Hansen, *The Atlantic Migration, 1607–1860* (New York: Harper & Row, 1961), p. 30. Also see E. I. McCormac, *White Servitude in Maryland, 1634–1820* (Baltimore, 1904), pp. 11–14.

[13] Cutlip and Center, *Effective Public Relations*, 4th ed., p. 49.

DEMONSTRATOR FOR A POPULAR CAUSE

PR practitioners have always known the value of capturing the public's attention. Public "happenings" have often been used to draw a crowd, to win support or to prove a point. The more sensational the staged event the better, although, as in the case of Lady Godiva, the costumes didn't need to be elaborate.

Lady Godiva sympathized with the overtaxed citizens of Coventry, and she took their cause to her husband, the earl. Trying to discuss it with him proved fruitless, so to convince him of her sincerity she agreed to ride a horse naked through the marketplace. She won her case, and the earl removed all tolls from the town (except for people on horseback).

In fact, however, the whole event had been staged from start to finish. The citizens had agreed beforehand not to take advantage of Lady Godiva's generous display of public spirit. The only person who cheated has lived on in history with a name as famous as that of Lady Godiva herself. He was the original Peeping Tom.

Of course, not all tactics of modern PR are recent. Far from it. Even Lady Godiva used a PR tactic to persuade (see 2.6). And PR still uses *rhetoric*, which has been around as long as human speech; *symbols*, which have been around as long as the human imagination; and *slogans*, which have existed as long as people have been conscious of themselves as groups.

Before the Industrial Revolution, the most significant period in the development of PR tactics was a hundred-year period starting about 1450. During that time the Renaissance was at its height, the Reformation began and the European discovery of the New World occurred. These events gave people a new view of themselves, of one another and of their environment. This period also marked the beginning of the age of mass media, for it was around 1450 that Johann Gutenberg invented printing from movable type—and the press was born. Few other inventions have had such a profound effect on human culture; the spin-offs of this discovery have been used by PR practitioners ever since in books, advertising posters, handbills, publicity releases, party organs, newspapers and so on. Of course, these media existed before Gutenberg and his press, but never before could they be used so efficiently to reach so many people at once for the purpose of persuasion.

Cameo: PR Tactics in the American Revolution   Though public relations as such did not exist in 1776, many if not most of PR's functions, uses and tactics were well developed by that time. The patriots who promoted the American Revolution overlooked no opportunity to use PR in their efforts to persuade—that is, to boost the war effort and to rally support for their new political plans. (See 2.7 for a capsule portrait of one of the best of the patriotic publicists.)

The press was the young emerging nation's most powerful weapon. By the time of the American Revolution, there were thirty-seven newspapers in the colonies, and they had become a focal point for political appeals.[14] Many of these pa-

---

[14]William L. Rivers, *The Opinionmakers* (Boston: Beacon Press, 1965), p. 3.

PUBLICIST FOR THE PATRIOTS

In spite of his Harvard education, Samuel Adams was a failure in every business venture he tried until he discovered where his true talents lay: public relations. His specialty was what Bernays later labeled "crystallizing public opinion." Adams was one of the first to cry out against "taxation without representation" and against the presence of British military forces in the colonies. He publicized the Boston Massacre, planned the Boston Tea Party, signed the Declaration of Independence and ended his political career as governor of Massachu-

setts. "He was a nonstop talker and writer of sizzling revolutionary polemics. He was a dusty man with a quavery voice constantly heard on street corners. . . . He was indignant, impassioned, incensed and outraged, and never shut up about it. He was the first American to get up in a public assembly and declare for absolute independence. As an agitator he makes Vladimir Ilich [Lenin] and Trotsky look like pikers."*

*Richard Bissell, *New Light on 1776 and All That* (Boston: Little, Brown, 1975), p. 32.

pers were owned and run by patriotic writers and editors like Benjamin Franklin of the *Pennsylvania Gazette*,[15] and Isaiah Thomas, publisher of the *Massachusetts Spy*, who often found it necessary to relocate his operations. The printing press was used for other means of propaganda too, such as books of political philosophy by Jean Jacques Rousseau and inflammatory pamphlets by Thomas Paine—the works of both men were distributed widely to promote the spirit of rebellion. General Washington is said to have read Paine's *Common Sense* to his troops on Christmas night in 1776, before they crossed the Delaware to trounce the British in the Battle of Trenton.[16]

American patriots made the most of heroes (George Washington, Ethan Allen), legends (Yankee Doodle and the Spirit of '76), slogans ("Give me liberty, or give me death!"), symbols (the Liberty Tree) and rhetoric (the speeches of John Adams and the writings of Thomas Jefferson, including the *Declaration of Independence*). They founded public-spirited organizations (the Sons of Liberty and the Committee of Correspondence). They grabbed every opportunity to interpret events in a light most favorable to their cause: A brawl on March 5, 1770, in which five unruly Bostonians were shot was billed by the revolutionary press as the "Boston Massacre" and denounced as an atrocity to inflame passions against the British.

When there was no event to exploit, the patriots didn't hesitate to create one. On December 16, 1773, a group of them put on war paint and feathers, boarded a British ship and tossed its cargo of tea leaves overboard. The "Boston Tea Party," whose main function was to attract attention, has been called an early example of American press agentry.[17] Historian Richard Bissell states, "Of all the crazy hoo-

---

[15] Frank Luther Mott, *American Journalism* (New York: Macmillan, 1950), pp. 26–28.

[16] Ibid., p. 33.

[17] Vernon L. Parrington, *Main Currents in American Thought* (New York: Harcourt Brace Jovanovich, 1938), pp. 233–247.

ligan stunts pulled off by the colonies against England, the Boston Tea Party was the wildest."[18]

Any PR technique the patriots could put to work for the cause, they employed: rallies, parades, exhibitions and celebrations, poetry, songs, cartoons, fireworks, effigies and even crude lantern slides.

PR and the Growth of the United States

Right from the beginning public relations functions, uses and tactics have played an enormous role in American politics.

The Early Years   The men who drafted the Constitution had to wage an intense PR campaign to sell the document to their colleagues and to the American people. Their propaganda took the form of eighty-five letters written to the newspapers. These letters, by Alexander Hamilton, James Madison and John Jay, became known as *The Federalist Papers*, and they did much to form the political opinions of the young nation. In time the Federalists established their own party newspaper, the *Gazette of the United States*. Hamilton's bitter political enemy, Thomas Jefferson, responded by hiring Phillip Freneau, the "Poet of the Revolution," to establish the Anti-Federalist party newspaper, the *National Gazette*.

In spite of the fractious rivalry between these early parties, the Bill of Rights, a propaganda piece supported by that spectacular campaigner Patrick Henry, had guaranteed freedom of the press. Without the adoption of the Bill of Rights and this guarantee of freedom of the press, public relations would never have become what it is today.

As the nation grew, political sophistication got a boost from the PR innovations of Amos Kendall, the first man to function, although without the title, as a presidential press secretary. In Andrew Jackson's struggle with Nicholas Biddle and the Bank of the United States, both sides bombarded the press with propaganda. That the administration prevailed was largely due to the talented Kendall, who, like many other members of Jackson's "Kitchen Cabinet," was an ex-newspaper reporter. Kendall's official position was Fourth Auditor of the Treasury,[19] but in fact he wrote speeches and pamphlets, prepared strategy, conducted polls, counseled the president on his public image, coordinated the efforts of the executive branch with other aspects of the government and with the public and constantly publicized Jackson in a favorable light.

Influencing the Vote   PR techniques were also important in the heyday of the political machine. By the late 1850s Tammany Hall of New York was using interviews to gather information. This marks the beginning of poll taking by special interest groups for both strategy planning and publicity.[20]

---

[18]Richard Bissell, *New Light on 1776 and All That* (Boston: Little, Brown, 1975), p. 26.

[19]Mott, *American Journalism*, pp. 179–180.

[20]Jerome Mushkat, *Tammany: The Evolution of a Political Machine* (Syracuse, N.Y.: Syracuse University Press, 1971), pp. 373–374. "Public opinions" are noted, not "polls" specifically in this reference. Also see Gustavas Myers, *The History of Tammany Hall* (New York: Gustavas Myers, 1901).

2.8 HARRIET ELIZABETH BEECHER STOWE (1811–1896)

MINORITY ADVOCATE

Harriet Beecher Stowe began her career in the field of education, helping her sister, Catharine Beecher, establish a pioneer college for women. But she is best known as a political agitator and writer. Stowe used the partisan press to publicize her cause, the abolition of slavery. Her influential writings appeared in the *Atlantic Monthly*, the *New York Independent* and the *Christian Union*; and her best-known work, *Uncle Tom's Cabin, or Life among the Lowly,* was first published in serial form in the *National Era*, the Washington antislavery journal. When the novel was published in book form in 1852, it was a best-seller above the Mason-Dixon Line (300,000 copies the first year) and was read all over the world in twenty-three languages. The author traveled to Europe in 1853 to establish relations with influential women sympathetic to her views. Even after the Civil War and the emancipation of the slaves, Stowe remained a talented promoter, occasionally giving public readings of her works.

Although public relations has always been used in political campaigns in an effort to persuade, the 1888 Harrison–Cleveland presidential race showed a growing sophistication in its use. First, far greater use was made of the press—newspapers, pamphlets, fliers and the first official campaign press bureau—during that election year. Also Harrison met the public directly by inviting them to his front porch, where he spent most of the campaign, and shaking hands. The political campaign grew even more sophisticated during the 1896 race between Bryan and McKinley.[21] Both parties established campaign headquarters and flooded the nation with propaganda. Campaign trains and public opinion polls were also extensively used.[22]

Politicians were not the only ones to sell their ideas through PR. Agitators of many persuasions discovered that publicity could help change the nation's thinking. Relying mainly on appeals to public sentiment, groups like the antivivisectionists, the American Peace Party and the Women's Christian Temperance Union met with varying success. Leaders of the women's suffrage movement publicized their cause at the 1876 Centennial celebration in Philadelphia. On July 4 Elizabeth Cady Stanton, Susan B. Anthony and Matilda Joslyn Gage staged a demonstration to dramatize that their rights as citizens had not yet been won.[23]

The most absorbing and compelling protest movement of the nineteenth century was the abolitionist or antislavery movement, which had many organizations allied to the cause. These organizations found that their cause was helped not only by news releases and press agentry stunts but also by getting public figures and newspaper editors to endorse their efforts and their ideas. The editorial alliance of a mass medium extended the reach of their message and gave it prestige and credibility. (See 2.8 for a capsule portrait of one important figure in the movement.)

---

[21] Stanley L. Jones, *The Presidential Election of 1896* (Madison: University of Wisconsin Press, 1964), pp. 276–296.

[22] Ibid., p. 295.

[23] Deborah J. Warner, "The Women's Pavilion," in *1876: A Centennial Exhibition*, ed. Robert C. Post (Washington, D.C.: Smithsonian Institution, 1976).

2.9 WILLIAM FREDERICK CODY (1846–1917)

**MERCHANDISING
THE GREAT AMERICAN SOCIETY**

Beginning at age sixteen, Buffalo Bill devoted his life to the opening of the West—as a Pony Express rider, a buffalo hunter, an army scout, an Indian fighter and a politician. When he was thirty-seven, the West returned the favor and gave Buffalo Bill a handsome living—as a press agent, showman and self-promoted living legend. His Wild West Show toured Europe and gave the crowned heads a glamorous picture of the American frontier, with rodeo stunts, wild animals, Indians and stars like Chief Sitting Bull and sharpshooter Annie Oakley. But the real attraction was Buffalo Bill himself, America's first superstar. He was also the hero of countless dime novels, which told the story of his life as one daring, dangerous episode of heroism after another.

Movement West   PR was also an important factor in America's westward expansion. From the beginning the western frontier was sold like real estate, and to do this the forerunners of modern PR made the most of legends and heroes. John Filson, for example, promoted land deals by making a legend of Daniel Boone, an unschooled, wandering hunter and trapper.[24] And a hero was made of George Armstrong Custer—partly to justify the U.S. position toward the American Indian, partly to promote the settling of the west and partly to sell newspapers and dime novels. Perhaps the most effective publicist of westward expansion was *New York Tribune* publisher Horace Greeley, whose editorial "Go West, Young Man, and Grow Up with the Country" changed the lives of many people and the demographics of the entire nation.

But if the West was sold by PR, it was also exploited by some of the same PR techniques. Press agent Matthew St. Clair Clarke brought Davy Crockett, the frontier hero, to the public's attention and used Crockett's glory to win political support away from Andrew Jackson. The adventures of western personalities like Buffalo Bill (see 2.9), Wyatt Earp, Calamity Jane and Wild Bill Hickock were publicized out of all proportion, to the benefit of their promoters in the eastern press. Even outlaws became adept at using the press for glory—and to mislead the authorities (see 2.10).

Entertainment, Education and the Military   The role of PR in the growth of America's entertainment industry was substantial. In fact, PR's immediate predecessor, press agentry, grew up with the entertainment business in the nineteenth century, a flamboyant era of road shows and circuses. Barnum was only one of many circus showmen who employed press agentry. Another was Hackalian Bailey, who brought the first elephant to the United States in 1815 and was the first to use display advertising to tell about it.[25]

---

[24] Cutlip and Center, *Effective Public Relations*, 4th ed., p. 49. Also see John Walton, *John Filson of Kentucke* (Lexington: University of Kentucky Press, 1956).

[25] Robert Parkinson, "The Circus and the Press," *Bandwagon*, 7 (1963), pp. 3–9, published by Ohio Historical Society.

2.10 JESSE JAMES (1847–1882)

GLORIFYING CRIME IN THE WILD WEST

Train robber Jesse James was also a publicist. To be sure no one else got credit for his gang's holdup of the St. Louis & Texas express train January 31, 1884 at Gads Hill, Missouri, one gang member handed the conductor an envelope containing a press release. The release was signed by Ira A. Merrill and it read:

THE MOST DARING TRAIN ROBBERY ON RECORD! The southbound train of the Iron Mountain Railroad was stopped here this evening by five [there were ten] heavily armed men and robbed of _____ dollars. The robbers arrived at the station a few minutes before the arrival of the train and arrested the agent and put him under guard and then threw the train on the switch. The robbers were all large men, all being slightly under six feet. After robbing the train they started in a southerly direction. They were all mounted on handsome horses.
P.S. There is a hell of an excitement in this part of the country.

Newspapers ran the release the next day, but it contained one significant error. The robbers rode west, not south.*

*Irving Wallace, David Wallechinsky and Amy Wallace, "Significa, June 20, 1982," *Parade.*

Publicity stunts were even used to attract attention to books and their authors. For example, in 1809 the *New York Evening Post* ran a story about the mysterious disappearance of one Diedrich Knickerbocker from his residence in the Columbian Hotel. In follow-up stories, readers learned that Knickerbocker had left a manuscript, which the hotel's owner offered to sell to cover the cost of the unpaid bill. Later, the publishing house Inskeep and Bradford announced in the same newspaper that they were publishing the manuscript, entitled *Knickerbocker's History of New York*. The whole story was a hoax, a publicity campaign by the book's real author, Washington Irving.[26]

In the field of education, the value of PR was recognized, as we have seen, even before the Revolution. After the Revolution, the trend continued. In 1899, for example, Yale University converted the office of the secretary into a PR and alumni office, showing that even the most established institutions were ready to accept the budding profession and use it to help them create favorable public opinion.[27] In 1900 Harvard University hired the Publicity Bureau, the nation's first PR firm, formed in Boston in 1900, but refused to pay the Bureau's fees after about 1902. Nevertheless, the Bureau continued to service the client for the prestige it involved.

Of course, the growing nation found military uses for PR—even the bloodiest of war efforts depends as much on persuasion as on might. It was a military effort that gave birth to a PR practice that has been used effectively ever since, the fund drive. During the American Civil War, Jay Cooke, a banker, floated a state loan. His success led the Treasury Department to put Cooke in charge of selling war bonds to the public. Not only did the bonds finance the army, but the mass sales effort also roused public opinion in support of the Union cause.[28] Also, the "yellow

---

[26]Bernays, *Public Relations*, pp. 36–39.

[27]Cutlip and Center, *Effective Public Relations*, 4th ed., p. 83.

[28]Parrington, *Main Currents*, pp. 31–43, especially p. 40.

journalism" of Joseph Pulitzer and William Randolph Hearst "sold" the Spanish-American War to the American people in the last decade of the nineteenth century. The newspapers were successful, although one story has it that the war was created to sell newspapers. Either way, the episode was largely an exercise in the power of public relations.

Development of Industry   The development of industry, however, brought about the most significant changes in the history of PR. The Industrial Revolution brought technological advances that changed and modernized the tactics and techniques of PR. It was steam power, for example, as well as inventions like the linotype, that made newspapers a truly democratic, nationwide mass medium.

Big business was not at first overly concerned with public relations, except insofar as the early industrialists used advertising to sell their wares and services to a growing market. The prevailing attitude was summed up by William Henry Vanderbilt, head of New York Central Railroad: "The public be damned." [29] During the years between the Civil War and the turn of the century, industrial profit and power controlled and reshaped American life; it was answerable to no one and immune to pressure from the government, labor or public opinion.

An example of the corporate attitude at this time was the behavior of tycoon Andrew Carnegie during the Homestead strike. When labor problems in his steel plant erupted in violence, Carnegie retired to his lodge in Scotland, thirty-five miles from the nearest railroad or telegraph. Carnegie wanted to be known as a cultured philanthropist, and he let the London press know that he remained aloof from the labor struggle only to protect his company from his own generosity. But professionally, he had not amassed a fortune of $400 million by worrying about the working or living conditions of his underpaid employees, and he was content to have his right-hand man, Henry Clay Frick, crush their strike and their union with the help of the state militia. [30]

In time industry had to reckon with the monster it had created, a labor force unwilling to be exploited by the likes of Carnegie, Morgan and Rockefeller (see 2.11), DuPont, Gould and Astor. As we shall see, the labor disputes of the twentieth century came to be fought more and more with public relations, less and less with violence.

In the meantime, a few of the large corporations recognized that in the long run they would have to woo the public's favor. In 1858 a producer of dairy products, the Borden Company, set a PR precedent by issuing a financial report to its stockholders. [31] In 1883 an even more important precedent was set by Theodore N. Vail, general manager of the American Bell Telephone Company. Vail directed a letter to the managers of local exchanges, urging them to look into the services they were offering and the prices they were charging. [32] His letter is significant because it shows concern for the consumer and an interest in improving

---

[29] Roger Butterfield, *American Past* (New York: Simon and Schuster, 1947), p. 476.

[30] Richard Bissell, *The Monongahela* (New York: Rinehart, 1952), pp. 184–191.

[31] John Brooks, "From Dance Cards to the Ivy League Look," *The New Yorker*, May 18, 1957, p. 74.

[32] Ibid.

2.11 JOHN PIERPONT MORGAN, SR. (1837–1913) AND JOHN DAVISON ROCKEFELLER, SR. (1839–1937)

PR—WHO NEEDS IT?

"I don't owe the public anything," said J. P. Morgan. Of course, this was not to say he never received anything from the public. When he died in 1913 he left an estate of $70 million, and that had to have come from somewhere. Where? Well, for one thing, he was accused of gold profiteering during the Civil War and of financing the sale of obsolete equipment in the Union Army. He did do the U.S. government a favor by bailing it out of near bankruptcy in the panic of 1907, but he came out ahead in the deal. Morgan was not a man of the people. He was a railroad reorganizer, a lay leader in the Episcopal Church and a collector of expensive art and rare books. He despised publicity; what he did was none of the public's business. In the end Morgan did give most of his art treasures to the Metropolitan Museum for the public to see. But he didn't do it until he was through looking at them.

J. D. Rockefeller, however, wanted the public to like him. Of course, he was no pushover in the world of finance, and he didn't get his vast fortune by being a nice guy. But he did want the public to like him as a person. Whether out of vanity, conscience, honest generosity, or because he was tired of what journalist Ida Tarbell was saying about him, Rockefeller gave away thousands of dimes to children and over half a billion dollars to charities. And his feelings were hurt when he was accused of doing it for the sake of PR. The Rockefeller business organizations were, nevertheless, among the first to recognize the value of public relations, to hire PR consultants and to establish PR departments within the company.

relations between Ma Bell and the public. In 1888, as we have seen, the Mutual Life Insurance Company hired an outside consultant to handle its publicity, and the following year Westinghouse established an in-house PR department. Individuals also began using PR people.

PR's incubation period ended with the nineteenth century. America was now a powerful, industrialized nation with sophisticated mass media and a well-informed public. The time was right for a new profession, one that would synthesize and coordinate the talents—publicity, promotion, propaganda and press agentry—that had developed with the nation's growth.

PUBLIC RELATIONS IN THE TWENTIETH CENTURY

The age of unchecked industrial growth was over. The new century began with a cry of protest from the "muckrakers," investigative journalists who exposed the scandals involved with power capitalism and government corruption.

The Turn of the Century

The first of the muckrakers was perhaps Joseph Pulitzer, whose editorials supported labor in the Homestead strike of 1892 and who, as early as 1883, had waged a campaign whose slogan, "The public be informed," parodied the attitude of William Vanderbilt.[33] But the great age of muckraking journalism began with the twentieth century.[34] Lincoln Steffens, staff writer for *McClure's* magazine, wrote articles and books exposing the corruption of municipal politics. Frank Norris, who covered the Spanish-American War for *McClure's*, took on the railroads and the wheat traders in his novels *The Octopus* (1901) and *The Pit* (1903). Ida Tarbell's *History of the Standard Oil Company* (1904), which began as a series for *McClure's* in 1902 and consisted mainly of interviews with former Rockefeller employees, exposed the company's business corruption and its unfair competition with the smaller companies. Her book and Upton Sinclair's *The Jungle* (1906), which described unsavory conditions in the meat-packing industry, resulted in social legislation that is still law.

Big business was also under fire from the government. President Theodore Roosevelt decided it was the federal government's job to uphold the public's interest in the fight among management, labor and the consumer. Using the Sherman Antitrust Act of 1890, he challenged big business, including U.S. Steel, the Standard Oil Company and the Pennsylvania Railroad, to respond to the public's disfavor.

Industry *had* to respond. It was no longer enough simply to ignore the public and the press. Nor did simply threatening to withhold advertising from uncomplimentary media work. No longer could the railroads butter up the press by giving free passes to reporters. No longer would the public buy whitewashed statements like that of coal industrialist George F. Baer, who in 1902 told labor to put their trust in "the Christian men whom God in His infinite wisdom has given control of the property interests of the country."[35] When the coal industry came under fire again in 1906, the coal owners had learned their lesson, and instead of relying on puffery and rhetoric, they turned for their defense to the talents of a young ex-newspaper reporter named Ivy Lee (see 2.12).

It is no coincidence that most of the first public relations specialists came from the newspaper profession. Newspaper advertising had long been the only way that many companies communicated with their markets. The newspapers were also the medium in which many companies were being attacked. And newspaper coverage had been the main goal of nineteenth-century press agents; it was the legacy of press agentry that inspired the first publicity agencies of the twentieth century.

The first publicity firm, formed in Boston in 1900, was called The Publicity Bureau.[36] The idea of publicity caught on quickly, and soon there were several such firms made up of ex-newspaper people, including the firm of William Wolf Smith in Washington, D.C., which specialized in what we would now call public affairs—publicity aimed at influencing legislators.[37] From a historical standpoint,

---

[33] W. A. Swanberg, *Pulitzer* (New York: Scribner's, 1967), pp. 73–122.

[34] Cornelius C. Regier, *The Era of Muckrakers* (Chapel Hill: University of North Carolina Press, 1932).

[35] Ross, *Image Merchants*, pp. 29–30.

[36] Cutlip and Center, *Effective Public Relations*, 4th ed., p. 72. Also see Scott M. Cutlip, "The Nation's First Public Relations Firm," *Journalism Quarterly*, 43 (Summer 1966), pp. 269–280.

[37] William Kittle, "The Making of Public Opinion," *Arena*, 41 (1909), pp. 433–450.

2.12 IVY LEDBETTER LEE (1877–1934)

"THE FATHER OF PUBLIC RELATIONS"

After graduating from Princeton, Ivy Lee became a reporter in New York City. He gave that up, first to become a political publicist, and then in 1904, to form with George F. Parker, the nation's third publicity bureau. By 1906 he was the most inspiring success in the young field of PR. Lee represented George F. Baer and his associates (who were allied with the J. P. Morgan financial empire) in a public controversy over an anthracite coal strike. Lee tried a radical approach: Frankly announcing himself as a publicity consultant, he invited the press to ask questions, handed out news releases and presented his client as cooperative and communicative.* Lee's "Declaration of Principles" issued at that time to city editors all over the country won respect for public relations (and it didn't hurt the Baer bunch either). The same year Lee represented the Pennsylvania Railroad when an accident occurred along the main line. Instead of hushing the incident up, Lee invited the press to come, at company expense, to the scene of the accident, where he made every effort to supply reporters with facts and to facilitate photographers. As a result, the Pennsylvania Railroad and the railroad industry got their first favorable press coverage in years.**

Lee's remarkable, straightforward style came from his frank admiration of industry and capitalism, and he made it his goal to get big business to communicate its side of the story to the public. By the time he was thirty, Lee had sired a profession, chiefly by introducing and promoting its first code of ethics.

Lee's career continued to be successful, if not so influenced by high ideals. He began working for the Rockefeller family in 1913, when he presented the "facts" of a coal strike in Colorado called the "Ludlow Massacre." Lee later admitted that the "facts" he handed out about the bloody affair were the facts as management saw them, and that he had not checked them for accuracy.[†] Lee's many clients also included the American Russian Chamber of Commerce and the German Dye Trust, from whom he earned $25,000 a year and a sticky PR problem of his own—how to defend his working for the Nazi organization.

Lee once wrote, "The relationship of a company to the people . . . involves far more than *saying*—it involves *doing*."[‡] Nevertheless, it is perhaps an example of Ivy Lee's public relations talent that he is now remembered not so much for what he *did* at the height of his career as for what he *said* when he was still in his twenties.

*Frank Luther Mott, *American Journalism* (New York: Macmillan, 1950), pp. 179–180.

**Irwin Ross, *The Image Merchants* (Garden City, N.Y.: Doubleday, 1959), p. 31.

[†] Ibid.

[‡] Ibid., p. 32.

however, the most important publicity bureau during this period was that of George F. Parker and Ivy Lee. That company lasted only four years, but it launched the career of Ivy Lee, whose contribution to modern PR is enormous.

The public relations profession grew rapidly, and before long publicity had become a standard and necessary tool for many businesses, individuals and organizations. Big businesses especially, such as communications, railroads and the automobile industry, found that publicity agencies and in-house publicity bureaus helped their relations with both the public and the government. In 1904 two major universities—the University of Pennsylvania and the University of Wisconsin—set up publicity bureaus.[38] Publicity also proved valuable for public service organizations. The Young Men's Christian Association (YMCA) employed a full-time

---

[38] Cutlip and Center, *Effective Public Relations*, 4th ed., p. 83.

publicist to call attention to its fund drive in 1905;[39] the National Tuberculosis Association started a publicity program in 1908;[40] and the American Red Cross followed suit the same year. The Marine Corps established a publicity bureau in 1907 in Chicago.[41] In 1909 the Trinity Episcopal Church in New York City hired Pendleton Dudley as a public relations counsel to help combat criticism of its ownership of slum tenements.[42] Three years later the Seventh Day Adventist Church established a formal publicity bureau to answer complaints about its opposition to Sunday laws.[43]

Many tactics and techniques were developed during the early period of PR. One PR pioneer with many new ideas was Samuel Insull, who handled publicity for the Chicago Edison Company.[44] Insull had a demonstration electric cottage constructed in 1902 to show how convenient the new technology was. In 1903 he communicated with the company's customers by means of bill stuffers and a house organ that was distributed to the community. In 1909 the innovative Insull found a new medium of publicity: He was the first to make movies for public relations purposes.[45] (This was appropriate since Thomas Edison himself was one of the first movie tycoons.)

The growing scope of public relations was also demonstrated by the Ford Motor Company. Ford established a house organ, *Ford Times*, in 1908, which is still printed today.[46] In 1912 the company introduced the use of public opinion surveys for market research.[47] And in 1914 Ford established the first corporate film department.[48]

A rapid rise in nationwide advertising also occurred during this period, and it is not surprising that the first national public relations organization, the Bank Marketing Association, founded in 1915, was part of the Associated Advertising Clubs of the World.[49]

Making the World Safe for Democracy

By the time the United States entered World War I in 1917, the war had been going on for several years, and PR had proved an effective weapon for Europeans. The British in particular aimed a "hands across the sea" propaganda

---

[39] Scott M. Cutlip, *Fund Raising in the United States: Its Role in America's Philanthropy* (New Brunswick, N.J.: Rutgers University Press, 1965).

[40] Ibid.

[41] Ibid.

[42] Ibid. (Letter from Pendleton Dudley to Major Earl F. Storer.)

[43] Howard Weeks, The Development of Public Relations as an Organized Activity in a Protestant Denomination, unpublished master's thesis, American University, 1963.

[44] McDonald, *Insull*, p. 3.

[45] David L. Lewis, "Pioneering the Film Business," *Public Relations Journal*, June 6, 1971, pp. 14–18.

[46] Cutlip and Center, *Effective Public Relations*, 4th ed., p. 82.

[47] Ibid.

[48] Lewis, "Pioneering the Film Business," pp. 14–18.

[49] Cutlip and Center, *Effective Public Relations*, 4th ed., p. 91.

campaign at the American government and people, urging them to join the fight. They publicized the Allies' side of the *Lusitania* incident, for example, characterizing the Germans as vicious "Huns." When President Wilson finally gave up his policy of peacemaking and neutrality, the U.S. entered the war with money, military might and a highly sophisticated public relations effort.

In selling the "war to make the world safe for democracy," the U.S. government solicited cooperation from many sources. AT&T was convinced that the government needed control of the phone company for the war effort.[50] The press was persuaded to exercise self-censorship and to contribute free advertising space for the war effort.[51] Academics served too. College professors acted as a force of "Four Minute Men," which meant they were prepared to speak for that length of time on propaganda topics relating to the war. The world, not just the classroom, was their forum. The government also solicited cooperation directly from the public: Herbert Hoover's Food Administration persuaded the American people to conserve food during this time of emergency. The greatest example of the government's salesmanship, however, was the Liberty Loan Drive, which financed the war.

The genius behind America's wartime public relations effort was George Creel, a former newspaper reporter whom President Wilson appointed as chairman of the newly formed Committee on Public Information. It was thanks to the Creel Committee that the Liberty Loan Drive was so successful and that U.S. wartime propaganda was so effective both at home and abroad. (Creel's propaganda was not as heavy-handed as that of the British government. He deserves credit for toning down the assaults on the German character and emphasizing loyalty more than fear.) The committee also created a legacy for the PR profession. Many members of the committee who learned their craft in wartime went on to practice it in peacetime. Among them were Edward L. Bernays, who coined the term "public relations counsel," and Carl Byoir.[52] As assistant chairman of the Creel Committee, Byoir publicized the draft and was in charge of distributing the *Red White and Blue Textbooks* that described the goals of the war. He went on from there to become one of America's most successful public relations practitioners.

The Roaring Twenties

The 1920s were characterized by prosperity, power and pleasure, and in spite of a national mood of isolationism, America's economic boom was heard around the world. Much of the boom was the sound of advertising, which grew tremendously during this decade. In 1920, for example, the Illinois Central Railroad began what was to become the oldest continuous national advertising campaign in America.[53] Advertisers discovered many new media. In addition to

---

[50] L. L. Golden, *Only By Public Consent: American Corporations Search for Favorable Opinion* (New York: Hawthorn Books, 1968), pp. 37–39.

[51] George Creel, *How We Advertised America: The First Telling of the Amazing Story of the Committees on Public Information That Carried the Gospel of Americanism to Every Corner of the Globe* (New York: Harper & Row, 1920), especially pp. 18–19.

[52] *Who Was Who In America*, vol. 3 (Chicago: Marquis–Who's Who, Inc., 1960), p. 129.

[53] Cutlip and Center, *Effective Public Relations*, 4th ed., p. 90.

the tried and true newspaper ads, billboards, streetcar signs and direct mailing, advertisers in the twenties explored radio, film, flashy trademarks, and even sky-writing. And advertising itself was adopted by health and public service organizations, by churches, and by political parties and candidates. By 1929 advertising was a billion dollar industry. Many sociologists attacked the wasteful ethics of the profession, but none disputed its power or its sophisticated psychology.

Public relations in general grew both in scope and in stature during the 1920s. There were now books and courses on the subject, and social scientists were beginning to take notice. Among them was Walter Lippmann, a former adviser of President Wilson, who expressed concern over the implications of public opinion molding. In *Public Opinion* (1922) he said that the public no longer formed its own opinions, particularly about government policy; their opinions, like their knowledge, were fed to them by the media in the form of slogans and stereotypes.[54] He pointed out, however, that opinion molding is a two-way street. Society contains "innumerable large and small corporations and institutions, voluntary and semi-voluntary associations, national, provincial, urban and neighborhood groupings, which often as not make the decisions that the political body registers."[55]

Social scientists' interest in public opinion was shared by industry. Many companies, including AT&T, had learned from their involvement with World War I that social responsibility is good for public relations and hence good for business.[56] Thus the field of opinion research grew as companies developed tactics for finding out what their stockholders, their markets, and the general community wanted. AT&T's cooperation with the government during the war had earned the confidence of both the government and the people. When Arthur Page joined the company in 1927 as vice president and in-house public relations expert, he stressed several points of view that have affected modern PR ever since: that business begins with the public's permission and survives because of its approval; that businesses should have public relations departments with real influence in top management; and that companies should find out what the public wants and make public commitments that will work as "hostages to performance." Page insisted that PR is built by performance, not by publicity.[57] (See 2.13.)

The New Deal

The mood of the 1930s was drastically different from that of the 1920s. Following the stock market crash of 1929, the U.S. economy plunged into a depression from which it took ten years to recover. Public relations during this time faced many challenges as industry was forced to defend itself against public distrust, a discontented labor force and strict regulation by the Roosevelt govern-

---

[54] Bernays, *Public Relations*, p. 84.

[55] Walter Lippmann in *The Essential Lippmann*, ed. Clinton Rossiter and James Lare (New York: Vintage Books, 1963), p. 96.

[56] Golden, *Only by Public Consent*, pp. 37–39.

[57] Cutlip and Center, *Effective Public Relations*, 4th ed., p. 91. Also see George Griswold, Jr., "How AT&T Public Relations Policies Developed," *Public Relations Quarterly*, 12 (Fall, 1967).

2.13 PR AT AT&T—A LONG HISTORY

In 1938 Arthur Wilson Page, first vice president for public relations of the American Telephone and Telegraphy Company, told an international management congress that "the task which business has, and which it has always had, is of fitting itself to the patterns of public desires." A familiar saying of the PR pioneer was that in a democratic society no business could exist without public permission nor long succeed without public approval. Page also helped to popularize opinion survey techniques. In doing so Page was following through on the philosophy of a predecessor who was very conscious of public opinion: Theodore Vail, AT&T president in the early 1900s, had sent a series of questions about service to Bell telephone exchange managers to inquire about how well Bell was serving its customers. He understood the power of public opinion, noting it was based on information and belief. When public opinion was wrong, it was because of wrong information, and Vail said it was "not only the right, but the obligation of all individuals . . . who come before the public, to see the public have full and correct information."*

*E. M. Block, "Arthur Page and the Uses of Knowledge," Inaugural Lecture, Arthur Page Lecture and Awards Program, College of Communication, University of Texas at Austin, April 22, 1982. Used with permission.

2.14 CHARLES A. LINDBERGH (1902–1974)

PR FOR A NEW INDUSTRY

Young Charles Lindbergh, a military and airmail pilot, was only twenty-five years old when he decided to go for it. On May 21–22, 1927, he was the first to fly a plane nonstop from New York to Paris solo. For this stunt he won $25,000, was decorated by the British and French governments and at home was given a promotion, a ticker tape parade and the Congressional Medal of Honor. Press coverage for this historic event was handled by Harry A. Bruno and Richard Blyth. Lindbergh made the most of his publicity to promote commercial flight and air transport. He made a well-publicized air tour covering every state and sixteen Latin American countries.

ment. The greatest challenge to PR, however, was selling good cheer to a confused and frightened populace. The challenge was felt by government, and the president responded by trying to convince the country that the only thing to fear was fear itself and that the return of prosperity was just around the corner. The challenge was also felt by industry, and in 1938 the National Association of Manufacturers and the U.S. Chamber of Commerce conducted a comprehensive campaign based on the slogan "What helps business helps you."[58] It helped too for government and industry to recognize heroes like Lindbergh (see 2.14).

PR continued to develop during the 1930s as a social force. The National Association of Accredited Publicity Directors was founded in 1936, and the American Council on Public Relations was founded in 1939.[59] (These two groups merged in

---

[58] Golden, *Only by Public Consent*, p. 386.

[59] Cutlip and Center, *Effective Public Relations*, 4th ed, pp. 674, 675.

1948 to form PRSA.) The Gallup Poll was instituted during the 1930s, giving a boost to the sophistication and credibility of opinion research.[60]

Many of the trends in the development of public relations during that time are reflected in the history of General Motors. When Paul Garrett joined GM in 1931 as its one-man PR department, the general public distrusted big business. The GM board of directors wanted Garrett to help the billion dollar corporation look small to win public favor, but Garrett did not believe in this approach. Good PR, he felt, had to work from the inside out. Corporate policies in the public interest had to be the beginning of public acceptance.[61] It was up to management to earn the goodwill of the public by acting, not by selling a false image. Garrett insisted it was in the company's best interest to "place the broad interest of the customer first in every decision of the operation of the business."[62]

In spite of Garrett's views, General Motors' problems were far from over. PR worked against GM in 1937 when the Congress of Industrial Organization (CIO) got involved in a labor dispute that ended in a forty-four-day strike.[63] At a time when public sentiment was strongly antiunion, the CIO nevertheless won a major victory for labor by getting public opinion on its side, forcing the nation's third largest corporation to recognize the union. The corporation lost the battle with labor, but under Garrett's leadership it continued to wage the war of good public relations. In 1938 Garrett said, "The challenge that faces us is to shake off our lethargy and through public relations make the American plan of industry stick."[64]

In 1939 *Fortune* magazine carried an article on Paul Garrett, describing his activities "carry[ing] out a long-range program of finding out what people like and doing more of it."[65] This was the first time an important magazine had reported on a corporation's public relations, and the description itself showed how the function had evolved into one directly concerned with corporate policy.

World War II

With the 1940s, the mood of the nation changed again. The country was at war, and, as in World War I, the most conspicuous pubic relations efforts either served the war directly or were the obvious by-products of a wartime economy. The PR talents of the two Roosevelts are widely known (see 2.15). Also, PR firms seized the opportunity. The prestigious PR firm of Hill and Knowlton, for example, firmly established itself by representing war industry groups such as the Aviation Corporation of America, the American Shipbuilding Council and the Aeronautical Chamber of Commerce.[66]

---

[60] Philip Meyer, *Precision Journalism* (Bloomington: Indiana University Press, 1973), pp. 144–145; also see George H. Gallup and Saul Forbes Rae, *The Pulse of Democracy* (New York: Simon and Schuster, 1940), pp. 41–56.

[61] Bernays, *Public Relations*, p. 112.

[62] Ross, *Image Merchants*, p. 25.

[63] Golden, *Only by Public Consent*, p. 386.

[64] Ross, *Image Merchants*, p. 27.

[65] Bernays, *Public Relations*, p. 112.

[66] Ross, *Image Merchants*, p. 102.

2.15 PR STANDS FOR THE PRESIDENTS ROOSEVELT

There was a swagger in Teddy Roosevelt's public image, and he worked hard at getting himself known as a Rough Rider, a trustbuster, a big stick and a Bull Moose. He loved having his picture taken, especially in his hunting clothes, grinning at the camera over a dead animal. As president, TR was a genius at exploiting the media. He made the front page at every opportunity, and he used powerful public persuasion to take on really big game: the Northern Securities Company.

Franklin Delano Roosevelt used every possible public relations trick to sell the radical reforms of his New Deal to the American people.* Advised by PR expert Louis McHenry Howe, FDR projected an image of self-confidence and happiness—just what the American public wanted to believe in. He talked to them on the radio. He smiled for the cameras. He was mentioned in popular songs. He even allowed himself to be one of the main characters in a Rodgers and Hart musical comedy (played by George M. Cohan, America's favorite Yankee Doodle Dandy). Of course, FDR's public image didn't go over with everybody, and there are still some households in which *Roosevelt* is a dirty word. But in general, the American people liked FDR and responded by putting him in the White House four times.

*L. L. L. Golden, *Only by Public Consent: American Corporations Search for Favorable Opinion* (New York: Hawthorn Books, 1968), pp. 37–39.

Communications scholar Charles Steinberg believes that it was World War II that caused public relations to develop into a "full-fledged profession."[67] In 1947 Boston University established the first full school of public relations, later "public communications."[68] By 1949 100 colleges and universities across the nation were offering courses in PR.

Much of the credit for the growth of PR during the 1940s should go to former newscaster Elmer Davis, director of the Office of War Information. Davis's program was even larger than Creel's had been, and it was tremendously successful in winning support for America at home and abroad. The office helped sell war bonds and win cooperation from the public, from industry and from labor.

The use of films for public relations expanded during this period. In 1943 Frank Capra made a documentary film for the U.S. Signal Corps to inspire patriotism and build morale.[69] It was not just the government that used film for PR, however—Hollywood also made countless movies glorifying American fighting forces. This persuasive power of film was not lost on industry. In 1948, for example, filmmaker Robert Flaherty made a documentary for Standard Oil called "Louisiana Story."[70]

Individual companies adapted to the war in different ways, often with the help of PR. Because of wartime shortages, for example, the American Tobacco Company had to change the color of the Lucky Strike package from green to white. Thanks to PR, the change caused the company only a moment's regret. They launched a new campaign promoting a new slogan: "Lucky Strike Green Has

---

[67] Charles S. Steinberg, *The Creation of Consent* (New York: Hastings House, 1975), p. 27.

[68] Bernays, *Public Relations*, p. 145.

[69] Richard Meran Barsam, *The Nonfiction Film* (New York: E. P. Dutton, 1973), p. 129.

[70] Ibid., pp. 151–156.

Gone To War." Lucky smokers everywhere were proud of their new white package because it meant their brand was doing its part for America.

For Standard Oil of New Jersey, the war caused a public relations crisis. At hearings of Truman's Senate Committee on National Defense, Assistant Attorney General Thurman Arnold charged Standard Oil with "acting against American intent."[71] The charge involved a deal that Standard Oil had made with a German company many years before. The oil company's marketing director, Robert T. Haslan, mounted a public opinion campaign, sending letters to customers and stockholders and hiring Earl Newsom as outside PR counsel. In the long run, Standard Oil beat the charges and came out of it with public support.[72]

In 1945 the same public relations fervor that had sold the war effort continued to help with the postwar industrial recovery. In that year Henry Ford II, the young new president of Ford Motor Company, hired Earl Newsom as a PR consultant. Newsom helped Ford with a letter to the United Automotive Workers (UAW) during a strike at General Motors, urging labor to be reasonable and fair. He also helped Ford with his speech to the Society of Automotive Engineers in January 1946 and with an important antilabor address to the Commonwealth Club in San Francisco the following month. With Newsom's help, young Ford became a public figure, a respected and publicized spokesperson for responsible business management.[73]

Earl Newsom was a public relations counsel in a very pure sense: He did not send out news releases or hold press conferences. He simply advised. But his advice was valued and effective. His career also demonstrated the power of PR counsels to affect the policies and behavior of their clients.

The Fabulous Fifties and the Military-Industrial Complex

During the 1950s, America again experienced a booming economy, this one based more on consumer goods. The population was growing faster than ever, and more and more people were getting good educations and entering the white collar work force. Technology progressed on all fronts: Besides putting a television in every living room and satellites in the sky, science further developed atomic energy and introduced the computer. Industry, in spite of "labor pains," continued to grow, both at home and abroad. Yet the mood of the nation reflected fear—of communists, Russians, the bomb, McCarthyism, technology, juvenile delinquency and mass conformity, to name a few. In 1955 Sloan Wilson examined society and described the American white collar worker in a best-selling novel called *The Man in the Gray Flannel Suit*. The hero, Tom Rath, was an in-house PR person for a large broadcasting corporation.

Public relations grew with the economy. That Wilson's typical businessperson was a PR practitioner shows how established the profession had become. In 1953

---

[71] Golden, *Only by Public Consent*, pp. 163–172.

[72] Ross, *Image Merchants*, p. 93.

[73] Ibid., pp. 87–88.

2.16 DORIS E. FLEISCHMAN BERNAYS (1891–1980) and DENNY GRISWOLD (born 1911)

PIONEERING WOMEN

Doris Fleischman Bernays became the PR partner of Edward Bernays in 1919 when the latter left the Committee on Public Information and began a private agency. The two married in 1922. She made headlines by keeping her maiden name, and was the first married American woman to receive a passport in her maiden name. They first called their field "publicity direction." It was a field not open to many women, but by 1931 Fleischman Bernays was writing and talking about public relations as a new career opportunity for women. Her distinguished career was recognized by Women in Communications, Inc., in 1972 with a Headliner Award. She died in 1980.

Denny Griswold and her husband Glenn founded the first journal of public relations in 1944. Since that time she and the *Public Relations News* have reported in detail the activities of the profession. Files of the newsletter provide historians with a valuable chronicle.

the International Chamber of Commerce set up a commission on public relations,[74] and in 1954 the Public Relations Society of America (PRSA) developed its first code of ethics.[75] More and more women entered the field too, and by the end of the 1950s several of the nation's top PR people were women, including Doris E. Fleischman Bernays, early PR pioneer (see 2.16); Denny Griswold, editor and publisher of *Public Relations News* (see 2.16); Jane Stewart, president of Group Attitudes Corporation; and Leone Baxter, president of Whitaker and Baxter in San Francisco.[76] In 1957 President Eisenhower appointed Anne Williams Wheaton associate press secretary, drawing nationwide attention to PR as a potential career for women.[77]

The affluence of the 1950s encouraged businesses to find new uses for their money. And it was the job of public relations to help them reinvest in the society—not only in tax-sheltering foundations but also in health and community interest campaigns, public service drives and educational seminars. Controlling corporate investment in society gained PR greater respect from the general public and also increased PR's influence within corporations.

Television, which conquered America in the 1950s, had an enormous effect on the growth of public relations. It was a powerful medium, and its capacity for persuasion was evident from the start. Social scientists criticized the new medium for the pervasive control it exercised over public opinion, but it was evident that TV's power could also create harmful as well as helpful PR. Joseph McCarthy's credibility was weakened when his manners and his five o'clock shadow were

---

[74] International Chamber of Commerce.

[75] Cutlip and Center, *Effective Public Relations*, 4th ed., p. 673. Also see comments in Golden, *Only by Public Consent*, pp. 347–350, and the Public Relations Society of America, 845 Third Ave., New York, NY 10022.

[76] Richard W. Darrow et al., *Public Relations Handbook* (Chicago: Dartnell Corporation, 1967), pp. 55–56.

[77] *Facts on File*, vol. 17, "National Affairs" (New York: Facts on File, Inc., 1957), p. 116.

presented to the scrutiny of viewers across the nation. The Revlon Company enjoyed glorious PR while it sponsored the nation's most popular TV program, but when the "$64,000 Question" was exposed as a fraud, Revlon suffered acute embarrassment.

The issue of honesty in public relations was examined closely during the 1950s. In the bitter competition between truckers and railroads to win the nation's long-haul freight business, the two groups relied heavily on PR. The Eastern Railroad Presidents' Council hired Carl Byoir and Associates to represent them, and the Pennsylvania Motor Truck Association hired Allied Public Relations Associates. By 1953 both parties had also hired lawyers, and the case was in court. The truckers charged that the railroads (and their PR firm) were violating the Sherman antitrust laws, trying to drive the truckers out of business by characterizing them as (in the words of federal judge Thomas J. Clary) "law-breakers, road-hoggers, completely indifferent to the safety of others on the highway and moochers on the public through failure to pay their way."[78] Byoir and Associates created many "front" organizations with the single purpose of talking and acting against the trucking industry. The agency argued (Byoir himself died before the struggle was resolved) their coalition was not a violation of antitrust laws but merely the exercise of free speech. A ruling from the U.S. Supreme Court in 1961 upheld Byoir's position and established the PR practitioner's right to represent a client's case in public even if the presentation is dishonest. Thus the legal question was resolved, but not the ethical one.[79]

Ethical problems like this led PRSA in 1954 to develop its first code of ethics, a very brief statement. In 1959 PRSA adopted a Declaration of Principles and a more developed code of ethical behavior.[80] To avoid being accused of creating a paper tiger, PRSA established a grievance board in 1962 to push for code enforcement whenever a violation was suspected.[81] Two years later PRSA approved a voluntary accreditation program open to all members of the society; this was the first step in recognizing a level of accomplishment in public relations and the first step toward implementing some standards of behavior among practitioners.[82]

The Times, They Are A-changin'

The 1960s and early 1970s were years of great crisis and change. (Song titles for this and other eras suggest a PR Hit Parade; see 2.17.) Public relations talent was called upon to help cope with the drama and the trauma. Modern PR practitioners needed a broad knowledge of the social sciences, as well as communication and management skills. In addition, there was a new emphasis on nonmarketing problems, more attention given to the worldwide consumer move-

---

[78] Ross, *Image Merchants*, p. 119.

[79] "The Railroad–Truckers Brawl," *Fortune*, June 1953, pp. 137–139, 198–204.

[80] PRSA *Register*. Also see Golden, *Only by Public Consent*, pp. 347–350.

[81] Ibid. (PRSA)

[82] Ibid.

2.17 PR'S GREATEST HITS

"The Star Spangled Banner" heads the list. Francis Scott Key borrowed the tune from an English drinking song, but the words were inspired by rockets, bombs and a waving flag. Despite its twelve-note range, the song has survived as the U.S. national anthem.

"The Battle Hymn of the Republic" was composed by Julia Ward Howe, who wrote new lyrics to "John Brown's Body" and made it a favorite of President Lincoln and a rallying song for the Union in the Civil War.

"Onward Christian Soldiers," the stirring march by Arthur Sullivan, was a favorite, not only among Christian missionaries, but also among temperance leaders.

"Meet Me in St. Louis" promoted the St. Louis World's Fair of 1904, calling attention to its marvelous display of electricity: "Don't tell me the lights are shining any place but there."

"Over There," by the superpatriot of the stage George M. Cohan, was part of the public relations effort to motivate Americans during World War I.

"California, Here I Come" might as well have been written by the California Chamber of Commerce. It beckoned people from all over to come to where "bowers of flowers bloom in the sun."

"Happy Days Are Here Again" was what Americans wanted most to hear during the Depression. It was also FDR's political campaign "song of cheer again."

"Praise the Lord and Pass the Ammunition" boosted morale and rallied support for American fighting forces during World War II. Its message: "We'll all stay free."

"You Get a Lot to Like with a Marlboro," a commercial sung by a satin-voiced vocalist, sold an image of masculinity, complete with a tattoo on the hand. Zsa Zsa Gabor declared that her ambition was to become "The Marlboro Woman."

"We Shall Overcome" was the theme song of the civil rights movement. It had the driving power of a chain-gang chant and the emotional appeal of a Negro spiritual.

"I Am Woman," recorded by Helen Reddy for Capitol, became the rallying song for feminists in the 1970s.

"Flashdance" became the anthem for individual performance dancing—on the dance floor or the street—in the 1980s.

---

ment, a growing emphasis on corporation government relationships, increasing responsibility for PR people within the corporate structure, a more demanding role for PR in multinational companies and cries for help from all sectors in dealing with dissident youth and minorities. Communications satellites, the awesome power of nuclear weaponry and the takeover of data processing for electronic information storage had made the globe smaller, but not its problems.

The nation seemed to divide on one point after another: civil rights, disarmament, the space program, the Vietnam war and the peace movement, conservation, farm labor, women's liberation, nuclear energy, the Watergate affair and on and on. In each of these issues public relations has been important to both sides. For example, PR professionals conducted seminars training people who were in the power structure how to deal directly with activists and how to deal with them less directly through news media and other public channels of communication. But the activists used PR just as much, capturing public attention with demonstrations, organizations and powerful rhetoric. Conservatives charged that the Chicago riots of 1968 smacked of press agentry. Radicals charged that the same could be said of the Gulf of Tonkin incident. Dow Chemical Company faced a PR crisis when antiwar consumers boycotted their household products, including Saran Wrap, because Dow also manufactured the chemical napalm, used with great de-

2.18 RICHARD M. NIXON

PR AND POLITICS IN THE RISE AND FALL AND RISE AND FALL AND RISE AND FALL AND . . .

Throughout his political career, Richard M. Nixon has recognized the values—and the dangers—of public relations. In 1946 he won a seat in the House of Representatives, largely through a campaign of insinuation and suspicion. In 1952 he appeared on nationwide TV to appeal to the public's sentiment and sympathy, reducing the issue of questionable gifts to whether his daughters could keep their family dog. In his 1968 presidential election campaign, he used every device known to modern advertising and promotion in what author Joe McGinniss has called "The Selling of the President." But in his crisis of 1972–74, even the combined talents of Ron Ziegler, Dwight Chapin, Jim Elbourne and H. R. Haldeman (all of whom had come from the J. Walter Thompson advertising firm but none of whom were PR practitioners) were not enough to convince the public that the president had the right to break the law, even in the interests of "national security."

structive effect in the Vietnam war. Industry was outraged by such protest: Contributing to the war effort had always been good for PR in the past. When at last it seemed there was no way to popularize the Vietnam war, the U.S. signed a peace treaty—a decision that was announced during Richard Nixon's reelection campaign in 1972. (See 2.18 for a brief rundown on Nixon's career.)

The urgency of the problems that PR practitioners were handling during this time and the expectations of those hiring PR talent gave the role new dimensions. In 1966 the national accrediting body for PR talent, the PRSA, claimed 1,000 accredited members.[83] By 1980 the number had grown to 3,000. More and more PR practitioners found themselves in the top levels of business management. In 1968 the Public Relations Student Society of America was formed,[84] and as public relations continued to gain status as an academic discipline, the profession became dominated by a generation of people specially trained for the job.

In 1973 the U.S. Supreme Court handed down a decision that greatly affected the role of the PR practitioner. This was the Texas Gulf Sulphur case, which will be discussed further in Chapter 14. Basically, however, the Supreme Court supported the 1968 decision of the U.S. Circuit Court of Appeals in New York requiring immediate disclosure of any information that would affect the market value of stock in publicly held corporations.[85] The significance of this ruling was that now PR had to concentrate more on dealing with public information, less on selecting what information to make public. The Supreme Court also ruled that PR practitioners involved in such cases were "insiders," subject to the same trading restrictions as other members of the corporation whose knowledge of special circumstances prohibited them from buying or selling stock.[86]

---

[83] Ibid.

[84] Ibid. Also see Cutlip and Center, *Effective Public Relations*, 4th ed., p. 674.

[85] *Facts on File*, vol. 29, "U.S. Developments" (New York: Facts on File, Inc., 1969), pp. 266–267; see also vol. 28, p. 625.

[86] Ibid.

The technology of public relations was greatly enhanced by development of computers. PR newswire services responded to the new technology, including the use of satellite transmissions. PR practitioners, who for years had been complaining there was no way to measure their efforts, now found—usually to their pleasure but occasionally to their consternation—that indeed there are ways to measure PR results. Math, statistics and computer science became essential tools of the trade.

The Future of PR

Like any developing profession, public relations continues to change, forever slipping away from a firm definition. The formal definition in the *Encyclopaedia Britannica* calls PR "policies and activities designed to convey information about, and improve the public's attitude toward, an individual, corporation, government agency, or other organization. Major responsibilities of public relations departments or agencies include issuing news releases; arranging press conferences; answering correspondence from the public; planning participation in community affairs; preparing films, pamphlets, employee magazines, reports to stockholders, and form letters; planning advertising programs; planning and publicizing exhibitions and tours; and undertaking research surveys to measure public opinion."[87]

The following statement was adopted by the representatives of the National Public Relations Associations present at the I (First) World Assembly of Public Relations Associations and the I (First) World Forum of Public Relations at Mexico City on August 11, 1978:

> Public Relations practice is the art and social science of analyzing trends, predicting their consequences, counseling organization leaders, and implementing planned programs of action which will serve both the organization's and the public interest.

We noted in Chapter 1 the most recent effort to give identification to public relations. The 1982 PRSA official statement describes, rather than defines, public relations.

The history of PR has not won the profession unqualified respect from every quarter. The *Britannica* notes, "Public relations has been subject to much criticism, both from social scientists, who criticize its techniques, and from the general public, which distrusts it."[88] It is easy to see valid historical reasons for the criticism: the hucksterism of Barnum and press agentry, the self-defensive whitewashing of the muckraking era, the attempts to manipulate the public during Watergate and so on. Thus it is especially important for us to keep an eye on the past, lest we repeat some of the same mistakes.

---

[87] *Encyclopaedia Britannica, Micropaedia*, 15th ed., vol. 8, "Public Relations," p. 285.
[88] Ibid.

- Public relations has been an evolving process, amalgamating various persuasive and communication techniques.

- Throughout history, PR has been used to promote wars, to lobby for political causes, to support political parties, to promote religion, to sell products, to raise money and to publicize events and people.

- Persuasive PR tactics consistent throughout history include rhetoric, symbols and slogans. These developed greater impact with the evolution of mass media.

- The American revolutionaries employed a wide variety of PR tools—newsletters, newspapers, heroes, slogans, symbols, rhetoric, organizations, press agentry, publicity—as well as rallies, parades, exhibitions and celebrations, poetry, songs, cartoons, fireworks, effigies and even crude lantern slides.

- A climate of free interchange, ensured by the First Amendment to the U.S. Constitution, provided the environment for the evolution of public relations to a full-fledged practice.

- The first poll-taking developed to help measure political campaigns, which also employed other PR tools, such as special campaign newspapers, pamphlets, fliers, campaign trains and, by 1896, official campaign headquarters.

- Special interest groups adopted PR strategies—for example, the suffragettes (people in favor of women's right to vote) and the abolitionists (those who were antislavery).

- PR strategies also were used by developers to encourage the population to move west.

- Even criminals, such as Jesse James, used PR to become folk heroes.

- PR was employed to gain audiences for the entertainment industry, including books.

- Educational institutions formalized their public relations activities by opening their own bureaus or using the new agencies.

- The military found a way to finance war by promoting the sale of bonds.

- Industry and retail establishments were slow to adopt PR tactics until muckrakers began to attack monopolies, and PR people became invaluable tools for defense.

- World War I caused the creation of the Creel Committee to win public support for the conflict.

- In the late 1920s, advertising grew to a billion-dollar industry; PR followed.

- During the 1920s, social scientists began to pay attention to efforts to affect public opinion; the best known scholar was Walter Lippman.

- The economic crash of the 1930s stirred concern for social responsibility.

- World War II's PR effort was much more sophisticated, coordinated and integrated.

- PR counseling came into prominence in the postwar period.

- PR's development toward professional status in the 1950s brought concerns for control over the ethics of PR practitioners.

- The fractionalization of the nation in the 1960s and 1970s emphasized the need for PR people who were good social scientists and counselors.

■ Although public relations developed its form and substance in the United States, many elements have been used by other societies, and PR practice around the world is now firmly established.

THINGS TO DO

1. Develop a profile of one or more of the following: Amos Kendall, Samuel Insull, George Creel, John Hill, Doris Fleischman Bernays, Carl Byoir. Interpret the significance of their contributions to the development of public relations activity.

2. Trace the evolution of the public relations function through the development of a public relations department at a major U.S. corporation (such as Westinghouse, Ford, General Motors or AT&T).

3. Examine any major historical event, such as the Civil War, the civil rights movement or the women's movement, and identify the public relations tactics employed.

4. Look at your own school's public relations program from an historical point of view. When was PR first used? What was its function then? How has it evolved since? Comment on its current state in relation to the school's needs and to the media.

SELECTED READINGS

Edward L. Bernays, *Public Relations* (Norman: University of Oklahoma Press, 1977). Remarkable commentary on the development of public relations from one who has been in the forefront.

Arthur Best, *When Consumers Complain* (New York: Columbia University Press, 1981). A discussion of when consumers complain, when they don't (even though they have legitimate complaints) and how consumer problems are handled.

Melvyn Bloom, *Public Relations and Presidential Campaigns* (New York: Thomas Y. Crowell, 1973). A description of the role and effect of PR in presidential races.

David Chagall, *The New Kingmakers* (San Diego: Harcourt, Brace, Jovanovich, 1981). Shows the emerging role of the campaign consultant as an image merchant.

George Creel, *How We Advertised America: The First Telling of the Amazing Story of the Committee on Public Information That Carried the Gospel of Americanism to Every Corner of the Globe* (New York: Harper & Row, 1920). The story of an important milestone in PR by the individual involved.

George H. Gallup and Saul F. Rae, *The Pulse of Democracy: The Public Opinion Poll and How It Works* (New York: Simon and Schuster, 1968). The beginnings of polling are described by one whose name is synonymous with public opinion study.

Kenneth Henry, *Defenders and Shapers of the Corporate Image* (New Haven, Conn.: College and University Press, 1972). A review of the development of corporate PR.

Harold Innis, *Empire and Communications* (Toronto: University of Toronto Press, 1972). A look at PR's contribution to development.

Keith A. Larson, *Public Relations: The Edward L. Bernayses and the American Scene: A Bibliography* (Westwood, Mass.: F. W. Faxon, 1978). An update from 1951; very useful in locating details about the two PR pioneers as well as their comments on PR activities during their lifetime.

Cornelius C. Reigier, *The Era of the Muckrakers* (Chapel Hill: University of North Carolina Press, 1932). A study done when the mud was scarcely dry.

Irwin Ross, *The Image Merchants* (Garden City, N.Y.: Doubleday, 1959). This book traces the first half-century of PR by analyzing the styles of some of its most important practitioners.

John Tebbel, *The Media in America* (New York: New American Library, 1976). An excellent history of the news media, but don't look for "public relations" in the index.

Sloan Wilson, *The Man in the Gray Flannel Suit* (New York: Simon and Schuster, 1955). This novel about a PR professional is entirely fictitious, but it gives one person's view of the state of the art in the 1950s.

CHAPTER 3

PR—All the Things It Is

Managers are like other people. They do not like to be told unpalatable facts. Too often they want only to be confirmed in their fixed opinions. But if the professional in public relations fails to perform his "no" function, others will be found to do it.

L. L. L. Golden, public relations counselor and commentator

Nothing is more indivisible in a company than its reputation and the climate in which it does business. These are the concerns of the company's public relations, which must be unified as the antenna, *the* conscience, *and the* voice *of the whole corporation.*

Philip Lesly, author and PR counselor

One October evening in 1982, a twenty-eight-year-old mother took her two children to a local McDonald's and was distressed by the size of the small toys included with the "Happy Meal" orders of hamburger, french fries and soft drink. She called the head of a local consumers group. The toys, plastic gun-wielding sheriffs and spear-carrying Indians, were withdrawn—ten million of them, largely as the result of events begun by that one phone call. The toys were tested by the U.S. Consumer Product Safety Commission and were found to be dangerous to children under the age of three who would be likely to put the tiny objects in their noses, ears or mouths. As soon as officials at McDonald's learned that the toys had failed the federal test, the toys were recalled. The action of a knowledgeable consumer was attributed to the maturity of the consumer movement. McDonald's quick response illustrated the company's awareness of what *potential* harm could be done to its image. The company, competing with at least two other major hamburger chains, Wendy's and Burger King, could not risk loss of public confidence and goodwill.[1] The corporate awareness and action is significant. Others have not been so sensitive. The messages consumers get from what you say and what you do is important—as General Motors discovered.

Much to the dismay of General Motors, a common production practice suddenly backfired, resulting in a spate of consumer lawsuits. The controversy occurred when GM car purchasers discovered that many 1977 models were hybrids. GM had been routinely installing Chevrolet engines in Oldsmobiles, Buicks and Pontiacs. The Olds engine had been promoted as a rocket engine and the Chevy engine as a gas saver. The whole thing is just a misunderstanding, GM said, and

---

[1] Molly Sinclair, Washington Post News Service, "Recall without injury: McDonald's says you shouldn't get a break today," *Fort Worth Star Telegram*, November 9, 1982, sec. 1B, p. 12.

THE LITTLE WOMAN

"So you're in public relations. Is that where you get me to like something I wouldn't like at all if you didn't do what you do to make me like it?"

made a peace offering to customers that could have cost GM $12 million or more. However, some of the customers were too angry to accept the peace offering. GM continued to juggle motors among makes, but it stopped extolling the virtues of a specific motor and began talking about the "great family of cars." The company declared that it was not doing anything wrong and the whole incident was a "breakdown in communications."[2]

The breakdown, however, was between the reality and the image. The image that car dealers and sellers project is that one car is significantly different from others. The reality is that mass production techniques that are cost efficient result in standardization. Any solution to the problem is difficult because of the PR problem created by the difference between reality and image. A false image was sold to the public, and it became difficult to get them to accept the reality. That point underlies this whole chapter.

A warning about image and reality comes from Frederick D. Watkins, chairman of Insurance Information Institute and president of Ætna Life and Casualty

---

[2]Terry P. Brown, "Bizarre Backfire, Engine Switch Brings 125 Suits against GM, and Practice Continues, but Ads No Longer Eulogize the Olds Rocket Engine; Is There Any Difference?" *Wall Street Journal*, July 27, 1977, p. 1.

Insurance Company. The age of public relations has created confusion between image and substance, he says, and there is a temptation for PR practitioners to settle for the role of image maker. But, he advises, public relations people should do more than serve as mouthpieces: "They can help us develop an outward-looking managerial philosophy that will be translated into actions proving our concern for the public interest."[3] His comments are echoed by PR commentator L. L. L. Golden.

The proper management philosophy can be developed by the PR person by listening and responding effectively, or as Watkins put it, in one of those dog-chasing-its-tail definitions of PR, "by working to interpret the needs of the public to the industry and by helping translate public needs to the industry and reflecting back to the public the actions taken in response to those needs."[4] Listening and responding effectively go together, and when they do, the conscience of management takes on a new perspective. In any institution where policies are inconsistent and management lacks integrity, no public relations effort can be effective. The role of PR is tied to acceptance of the two-way communication definition.

THE ROLE OF PUBLIC RELATIONS

The role of public relations has had three major interpretations: (1) *controlling publics*, directing what people think or do to meet (or serve) the needs and desires of the institution; (2) *responding to publics*, usually in the form of reacting to developments or problems or to the initiatives of others (if only to curb them; see 3.1); and (3) *achieving mutually beneficial relationships among all publics*, including suppliers, producers, consumers and employees.[5] That third role is what Harvard business professor and consumer behavior researcher Stephen A. Greyser calls the *transactional* model, where the consumer is a partner of business. Two other models he describes are the *manipulative* model, with the consumer as victim, and the *service* model, where the consumer is king. The consumer, Greyser says, still sees some distance between the current marketplace and the ideal.[6] These roles for PR are apparent in their evolution, discussed in 2.2: controlling, Greyser's manipulative model, the era of communicating/initiating; responding, Greyser's service model, the era of reacting/responding; mutually beneficial, Greyser's transactional model, the era of planning/preventing. The fourth era, professionalism, emphasizes the peculiarity of public relations practice, one well-defined by Philip Lesly:

---

[3] Frederick D. Watkins, "Top Insurance Men Meet to Discuss Industry's Public Relations," *pr reporter*, 17, no. 5, p. 2. February 4, 1974.

[4] Ibid.

[5] Task Force on Stature and Role of Public Relations, "Report and Recommendations," Public Relations Society of America, November 1980.

[6] Stephen A. Greyser, "Changing Roles for Public Relations," *Public Relations Journal*, 37, no. 1 (January 1981), p. 23.

3.1 THE VALUE OF TWO-WAY COMMUNICATION

When PR people must set priorities, there often is a conflict between the needs of the institution and those of a public; however, two-way communication often helps to resolve these, as a gas utility discovered. In 1977 Oklahoma Natural Gas was confronted with consumer activists demonstrating against the high costs of home heating outside the utility company's downtown Tulsa offices. Chief Executive Officer Charles Ingram went outside and invited them in to talk. Recognizing consumer concerns, he discovered that the federal government would help meet the fuel costs of disadvantaged customers and also that these customers had to be identified and helped in other ways as well.

ONG responded. The company established annual consumer round tables at division offices all over the state and got the practice adopted at the national level of the American Gas Association in which Ingram is active. Then in 1983 ONG began a Share-The-Warmth program, in which more affluent users can donate money to those less well-off. Other utilities have similar plans. Ingram, now chairman of the board of ONEOK, a diversified energy company of which ONG is a subsidiary, says he always learns something from the consumer in exchanges. Two-way communication and the negotiation of priorities is a major value of PR.

> Public relations people have the role of being always in the middle—pivoted between their clients/employers and their publics . . . This role "in the middle" does not apply to any other group that deals with the climate of attitudes. Experts in other fields—journalists, sociologists, psychologists, politicians, etc.—are oriented in the direction of their specialities.[7]

THE VALUES OF PUBLIC RELATIONS

The lack of consistency in PR practices is a result of PR's rapid growth and the lack of control over both practice and practitioners. Public relations *in practice* may still be observed in each of the eras Greyser outlines. The development of professionalism should give some consistency to PR practice and make more obvious the values of public relations. Such values include the following:

1. Public relations is a representative and spokesperson for the desires and interests of various publics to society's institutions, some of which might be unresponsive. While interpreting and speaking for publics, it also speaks to them for the institutions.
2. Public relations helps establish smoother relationships between institutions and society by providing a means to achieve mutual adjustments to benefit society.
3. Public relations offers ways to work out differences so coercion or arbitrary action does not become necessary.

---

[7]Philip Lesly, *Managing the Human Climate*, 54 (January–February 1979), p. 2.

4. Public relations provides information for the communication system to help keep people informed about various aspects of their lives.

5. Public relations personnel can and frequently do help to stimulate an institution's social conscience.

6. Public relations functions in all aspects of life naturally, since the principles are basically human ones of seeking acceptance, cooperation or affection from others. Public relations practice just formalizes that activity.[8]

7. Public relations also can help management formulate better objectives and reach them.

Doing these things is part of the social responsibility of all institutions—public or private, profit making or nonprofit.

SOCIAL RESPONSIBILITY AND COMMUNICATION

Management must be responsible and responsive or else combat a hostile environment. But the pattern of action has often been just the opposite, according to social scientist Hazel Henderson, who graphed what she saw as a normal pattern of business response to social issues. The response pattern she outlined is as follows: (1) Ignore the problem. (2) If publicity calls widespread attention to the problem, admit its existence but present business as a victim of circumstances it cannot alter. (3) When the public takes the problem to lawmakers, lobby, testify in legislative hearings and advertise to get opinion leaders to believe that the proposed solutions mean government interference in private economy. (4) After new regulations are final, announce that business can live with the new law.[9]

Such behavior not only justifies public pressure for government intervention—just what business does not want—but it also undermines a company's credibility. First, the behavior is reactive, said the late William A. Durbin, former chairman of the Hill and Knowlton public relations firm. Second, it is defensive, suggesting there is a conflict between public welfare and industry. Furthermore, business's posture in explaining how it is a victim of circumstances shows a preference for quantification and puts business in a position of talking about "nonproductive dollars" when the public is talking about something like "clean air." Third, the pattern of response concentrates on means and ignores the end—an end that business might actually support, like clean air.[10]

Not just business is challenged, but *all* large institutions these days: governments, of course; schools and colleges; professional sports; churches; health groups; fund-raising groups; even the news media. With such crises in public confidence, the role of the PR practitioner becomes a critical one.

---

[8] From Task Force on Stature and Role of Public Relations, "Report and Recommendations," p. 9.

[9] Hazel Henderson is quoted by William A. Durbin, "Managing Issues Is Public Relations Responsibility," in "tips and tactics," biweekly supplement of *pr reporter*, 16, no. 9 (May 15, 1978), pp. 1, 2.

[10] Durbin, "Managing Issues," pp. 1, 2.

Probably the biggest obstacles to "ideal" public relations, as media scholars David Clark and William Blankenburg observe, are economics and human nature: "The plain fact is that managers are hired to make money for owners, and that a conscience can cost money. In the long run, it is money well spent, but many stockholders and managers fix their vision on the short run. Then, too, an abrupt change in corporate policy amounts to a public confession of past misbehavior— or so it seems to many executives. The natural temptation is to play up the good, and to let it go at that."[11]

As a result, a whole "new math" is entering the corporate structure as those executives who do try to be responsive and responsible attempt to explain social costs to their stockholders. The *Wall Street Journal* called it "the Arithmetic of Quality": "The social critics of business are making headway. Increasingly, corporations are being held to account not just for their profitability but also for what they do about an endless agenda of social problems. For business executives, it's a whole new ball game. Now they're struggling to come up with a new way to keep score."[12]

There are a number of examples of the problems. How can a profit-and-loss statement be made to reflect on the credit ledger the good a company does when its personnel advise minority businesspeople struggling to succeed in a ghetto? How can the installation of pollution-control devices at a factory be accounted a positive accomplishment rather than a drag on productivity? How can the expense of hiring school dropouts and putting them through company-financed training programs be made to appear on the credit rather than debit side of the ledger? Furthermore, asks the *WSJ* writer, how can the "bad" a company does (by polluting, discriminatory hiring and the like) be measured and reflected as a negative factor in the company's performance? All this has had two important implications for public relations: it has meant that PR has had to be (1) *a problem finder and problem solver or preventer* and (2) *an interpreter—a communications link—* for these are really what people who hire PR practitioners need.

Let us consider these two requirements.

PR AS PROBLEM FINDER AND PROBLEM SOLVER OR PREVENTER

As early as 1965, public relations practitioner and author Philip Lesly outlined what he felt were the major problems for business in the second half of this century.[13] These problems—which may also apply to large nonprofit

---

[11] David G. Clark and William B. Blankenburg, *You & Media* (San Francisco: Canfield Press, 1973), p. 175.

[12] Frederick Andrews, "Puzzled Businessmen Ponder New Methods of Measuring Success," *Wall Street Journal*, September 9, 1971, p. 1. Reprinted with permission of the *Wall Street Journal*, © Dow Jones & Company, Inc., 1971.

[13] Philip Lesly, "Effective Management and the Human Factor," *Journal of Marketing*, 29 (April 1965), pp. 1–4. Reprinted by permission of the American Marketing Association.

institutions—are, Lesly said, "the most intangible, immeasurable, and unpredictable of all elements affecting a business":

1. The main problem in production is no longer that of increasing the efficiency of factories and plants, but of dealing with the attitudes of the people whose jobs are to be changed or eliminated because of the introduction of more efficient methods.

2. The principal problem of growth through innovation is not that of organizing and administering development programs, but of dealing with the reactions of the intended customers and dealers to the product.

3. The personnel problem is not that of projecting a firm's manpower needs and standards but of persuading the best people to work for the company—and then to stay and do their best work.

4. The financing problem is not that of financial planning for the company's funding but of dealing with the attitudes of investors.

5. The problem in advertising is not that of minutely analyzing the media, the timing and the costs but of discovering how to reach the minds and hearts of the audience.

6. The problem of business acceptance is no longer that of demonstrating that an institution is operating in the public interest but of getting people to understand that its cornucopia works better when it has a minimum of restraints.

Each problem Lesly isolated suggests a need for awareness of what is going on in the public mind, a sensitivity to issues that are developing in the collective consciousness of those with whom management must interact. To probe the public consciousness, PR people have turned to pollsters and futurists.

Public opinion surveys can help PR people anticipate difficulties and also suggest the climate for a response. The significance of studying public opinion is stressed in the following four chapters. Underscoring the need for public relations practice to move into preventive PR are some disturbing predictions.

Predictions

PR practitioners in the United States and Canada responding to a survey in 1983 by a professional newsletter said marketplace matters had edged out government and the economy in a prioritized list of concerns. The year before they said economic pressures, technological forces and social change were beginning to cause structural changes and new forms of competition in several industries such as the financial community, where banks, savings and loans, investment houses and insurance companies competed with each other. That trend forced marketplace concerns to the top the following year. The respondents also said that government activities were the second biggest public issue: What should be the role of the private sector and what should be the role of government? The third concern was the economy—first the year before. Still there was the issue of *public confidence* in institutions.

A new category of concerns in the 1982 survey had been employee relations, including union problems, unemployment (and layoffs) and training and professional development programs to improve employee and managerial competence.

For the utilities, energy, consumerism and environmental concerns were also significant.[14]

Most of these were forecast earlier by futures researcher William Friedman, vice president of Ketchum Public Relations. The seven trends he listed as prevailing in the eighties were (1) increased public cynicism about all institutions; (2) lawsuits by individuals or groups; (3) growing economic strains as energy costs rise; (4) growing fragmentation of society; (5) increased willingness to let the federal government handle social programs (in spite of the shift to conservatism); (6) decreasing U.S. dependence on the rest of the world; and (7) continued inflation. He also said that until the end of the decade, PR practitioners will have to deal with (1) rising conflict between the haves and the have-nots; (2) more restricted life-styles; (3) more respect for the dollar; (4) greater competition in all phases of American life; (5) higher value of what is useful and practical over the ostentatious; (6) rising patriotism, which will be apparent in the marketplace; and (7) more importance for PR to win public support.[15]

Predictors

Who and what is a futurist? Dr. Jay S. Mendell, editorial chairman of *Business Tomorrow*, a newsletter-format magazine, says there is no particular spot on the organization chart for the futurist. Futurism, he says, "is a guerrilla activity." Creating a collective consciousness of the emerging environment is more important than devising strategies. The strategies will emerge from the collective consciousness. Not only may the futurist be found under many different titles in the organization, but he or she also may come from any of a number of educational backgrounds; all would involve a great deal of self-directed learning. In addition, the futurist will have to be a superior conceptual thinker.[16]

These futurists are called issues managers in some companies, although a more appropriate title might be issues identifiers, predictors and managers. The kind of planning they engage in is called a pre-crisis approach by Archie Boe, president of Sears, Roebuck & Co., who set up one of the first early warning departments when he headed Sears's Allstate Insurance Unit. Atlantic Richfield Company established an issues identification system because it felt its planning was too numbers oriented. Breck Arrington, head of Arco's twenty-eight-member governmental issues team, was quoted by the *Wall Street Journal* as having said, "Single-line numbers forecasting, typically done by economic planners, didn't predict the Arab oil embargo or the environmental revolution. We needed a wider, more qualitative approach to supplement the other work."[17] Efforts to broaden the traditional planning base include computer software services, which are being devel-

[14]"Eighteenth Annual Survey of the Profession, Part I," *pr reporter*, 25, no. 39 October 4, 1982, p. 1, and "Nineteenth Annual Survey of the Profession, Part II," *pr reporter*, 26, no. 41 October 24, 1983, p. 1.

[15]"tips and tactics," a supplement of *pr reporter*, 20, no. 15, August 30, 1982. Used by permission.

[16]Jay S. Mendell, "The Practitioner As a Futurist," *Public Relations Journal*, 36, no. 12 (December 1980), p. 15.

[17]Earl C. Gottschalk, Jr., "Firms Hiring New Type of Manager To Study Issues, Emerging Troubles," *Wall Street Journal*, June 10, 1982, p. 27.

oped to accumulate files on legislative leaders, prominent spokespeople, legislation and speeches, as well as information on voting records and other public documents. Computerizing PR information storage would make cross-listing easier and help PR departments track issues and retrieve information for reports.

Issues and Images

One of the PR issues identified has been the role of the employee. In looking at the automobile industry, the National Academy of Engineering produced a study funded by the National Science Foundation which noted:

> In the case of productivity, product quality and the role of the work force, we are talking about something close to a cultural revolution, about fundamental changes in the way the business is managed and the ways people at all levels participate in the enterprise.[18]

Public relations practitioners have known for a long time that employees are the front line for public relations because they *are* the institutional image. Employees have a strong sense of what an institution really is, what its problems are and what its consumers think. Furthermore, employees, collectively and individually, represent the institution to its publics. In their neighborhoods and within their groups, they are the authority on the institution.

More than any other executive except the chief executive, the PR person must know what is going on inside the organization and how all its activities and functions interrelate. He or she is also expected to bring awareness and objectivity to the job and be able to inject unvarnished, usable facts into the decision-making process.

The PR person must also know what is happening outside the organization. This person gains such knowledge because he or she is in a position to feel the actual pressures generated by various groups seeking support. The role of the practitioner here is sensitive and complex.

The PR practitioner must also sometimes play devil's advocate by bringing up all the points against a proposed action and stating which decisions will have an adverse effect on which groups and why. Sometimes actions will be taken that will offend a major group, and management should be warned in advance and offered some way of successfully explaining to the group why the action had to be taken.

The role the public relations consultant is playing in relation to current social crises is something no one foresaw ten or twenty years ago. No longer primarily a communicator, the PR practitioner is now a sort of moderator who tries to prevent the crisis from getting out of hand. Some of the tools used, such as personal contact and the media—mass and specialized—are the same. However, the measure of performance is not how effectively the client's message gets across but whether a flare-up that can stop a client's business can be avoided. One of the major obligations is to help clients conduct their business in a way that is responsive to the

---

[18] "NSF Study Finds 'Cultural Revolution' Inside Management Necessary to Compete Today," *pr reporter*, 25, no. 34, August 30, 1982, p. 1.

new demands made by concerned scientists, environmentalists, consumerists, minority leaders, underprivileged segments of the community and employees.

The most valuable public relations activity is that planned to prevent problems or at least solve them while they are small.

PR AS INTERPRETER AND COMMUNICATIONS LINK

Perhaps, as suggested by Daniel H. Gray, a management consultant noted for his work on the social role of business, social accounting doesn't exist.[19] Indeed, perhaps the system needed concerns communications more than accounting.

Communications audits have become common for institutions trying to track problem areas. Audits can be either internal or external or both. (See 3.2 for a typical external audit procedure.) PR practitioner Philip Lesly observes that the institution must function in a human climate, and thoughtful managers recognize they don't have the expertise to deal with this element unaided. As human patterns become more complicated, they demand greater expertise and experience. Consequently, says Lesly, "Communications sense and skills, which have been vital and have always been scarce, are becoming more vital and scarcer still."[20]

This is where the PR practitioner comes in, of course. Lesly adds, "Public relations is a bridge to change. It is a means to adjust to new attitudes that have been caused by change. It is a means of stimulating attitudes in order to create change. It helps an organization see the whole of our society together, rather than from one intensified viewpoint. It provides judgment, creativity and skills in accommodating groups to each other, based on wide and diverse experience."[21]

David Finn, cofounder of the PR firm of Ruder & Finn, Inc., says:

> Twenty years ago public relations had its eye on the social sciences, with the full expectation that new discoveries would soon be made which would elevate the art of mass communications into a respectable and responsible profession. Ten years ago some of us thought computer technology was going to do the trick and the phrase "opinion management" emerged as a possible successor to the long-abandoned "engineering of consent." As things turned out, it is not the technique of public relations which has changed so much as the subject matter with which we are concerned.[22]

Emphasizing the communications link role of PR, Finn focused on four developments: (1) The resolutions of conflicts may require the modification of many opinions, including those held by the public relations consultant and the client.

---

[19] Andrews, "Puzzled Businessmen Ponder New Methods," p. 1.

[20] Philip Lesly, "Challenges of the Communications Explosion," *The Freeman*, October 1973, pp. 607–608.

[21] Ibid.

[22] David Finn, "Modifying Opinions in the New Human Climate," Ruder & Finn Papers no. 1, reprinted from *Public Relations Quarterly*, 17 (Fall, 1972), pp. 12–15, 26.

3.2 A TYPICAL AUDIT PROCEDURE

This audit pattern was developed for use by Hay
Communications. The organization calls it
a "Communications Portfolio Assessment."

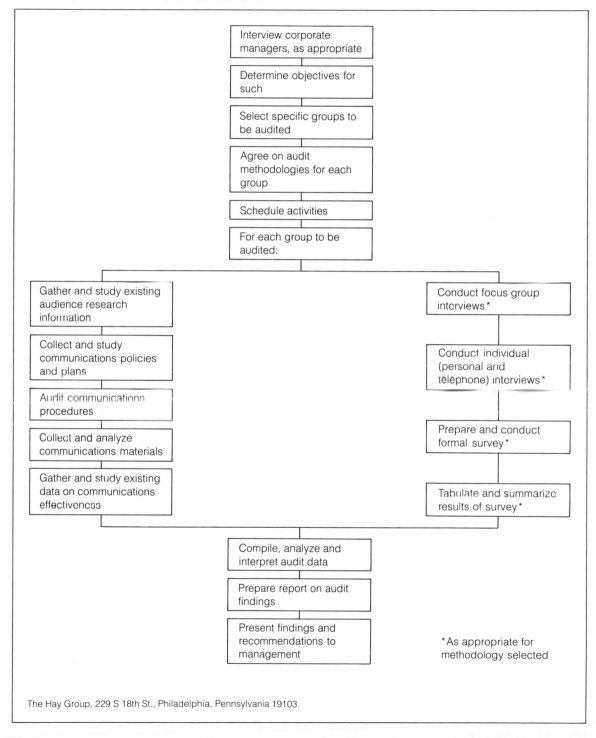

Interview corporate managers, as appropriate

Determine objectives for such

Select specific groups to be audited

Agree on audit methodologies for each group

Schedule activities

For each group to be audited:

Gather and study existing audience research information

Collect and study communications policies and plans

Audit communications procedures

Collect and analyze communications materials

Gather and study existing data on communications effectiveness

Conduct focus group interviews*

Conduct individual (personal and telephone) interviews*

Prepare and conduct formal survey*

Tabulate and summarize results of survey*

Compile, analyze and interpret audit data

Prepare report on audit findings

Present findings and recommendations to management

*As appropriate for methodology selected

The Hay Group, 229 S 18th St., Philadelphia, Pennsylvania 19103.

(2) Patterns of communications in the future may revolve increasingly around smaller groups. (3) The random benefits of public relations activities not directly related to corporate interests will increase. (4) New methods of research are being developed that are especially relevant to times in which opinions are likely to change rapidly.[23]

Public relations, one writer notes, does not "create the corporate image or reputation," rather, "it interprets and advocates the policies, statements, and activities which qualify the corporation for its reputation."[24] The point is PR cannot fabricate a corporate image.

PERCEPTIONS OF PUBLIC RELATIONS

The first challenge facing PR people often is getting management to accept the expertise it is already paying for. The first public to be sold, then, is management. However, although public relations people are on the staffs of almost all major corporations, there is considerable evidence that corporate executive officers go to them for advice only on communications problems. Of course, many PR people perhaps lack the broad base of skills in the social sciences needed for a more expanded role.[25] But part of the difficulty also is that public relations work is not easily evaluated.

For public relations to be an effective instrument in any situation, management must have a clear concept of its role—such as in counseling, research and planning—beyond communication, and the practitioner must be prepared to assume that role. In an article for *Harvard Business Review*, Robert S. Mason, PR consultant and head of his own agency, cautions management not to hire a new public relations director until the job can be specifically delineated. If only a communications technician is desired by management, then there is no reason to hire a highly skilled public relations person qualified to participate in policy decisions. But, Mason warns, since almost every policy decision has some public relations implications, management would be better off with the more expensive, better-equipped public relations practitioner, rather than just the communications technician. Mason also notes that most PR directors have an independent orientation that adds a significant dimension to the decision-making process. When the role is clearly defined, evaluation of PR performance is easier. Mason adds, "Meaningful evaluation of PR's performance can only occur in an environment whe e PR itself is managed consciously as a rational function."[26]

---

[23] Ibid.

[24] John Cook, "Consolidating the Communications Function," *Public Relations Journal*, 29, no. 8 (August 1973), pp. 6–8, 27–28.

[25] John Hill, "The World of Tomorrow," *Public Relations Journal*, 32, no. 10 (October 1976), p. 13.

[26] Robert S. Mason, "What's a PR Director for Anyway?" *Public Relations*, A Harvard Business Review Reprint Series, no. 21490, pp. 95–101, Boston, Mass.; article reprinted from *Harvard Business Review*, no. 74510 (September–October 1974).

One of PR's problems with evaluation, according to a professional newsletter, is the lack of a benchmark against which to measure.[27] At least eight contributions of PR to the "bottom line" are identifiable and measurable: (1) *Publicity and promotion* help to pave the way for new ideas and products. (2) *Internal motivation* can increase team efforts and build morale. (3) *Eliminating surprises* through interpretation of publics to the institution and vice versa may eliminate disruptive surprises. (4) *New opportunities* are identified by PR's outreach to all publics where new markets, new products, new methods and new ideas may be discovered. (5) *Protection of present position* can be handled by PR only when an institution is under siege, because what has to be nurtured is the public's perception of the institution's true values. (6) *Overcoming executive isolation* is PR's job so management really knows what is going on. (7) *Change agentry* is the vital skill PR can offer, since institutions must change to remain viable, yet all of their publics will have to be persuaded to overcome a natural resistance to change. (8) *The double bottom line* is the phrase coined by the Philip Morris Company (manufacturer of tobacco and other products) to explain the effect of social responsibility on the economic health of all institutions.

The role of public relations has been in flux—it has changed from being responsible for "making the cash register ring" to handling the "myriad social problems that beset the corporation," says Harold Burson, chairman of Burson-Marsteller.[28] There are three reasons for the change, Burson believes. The first is affluence. Energies once directed toward making a living are now diverted to social change. The second is technology, which has made bigness possible but reduced the impact of the individual. The third is the transnational or multinational character of the large, modern corporation, which knows no boundaries. (For one company's chart of PR corporate duties, see 3.3.)

THE CHANGING REALITIES OF PUBLIC RELATIONS

Public relations students looking at the roles of practitioners in agency, counseling and staff positions may find that each of these is changing.

Firms

In the late 1970s and early 1980s, several large public relations firms were acquired by advertising firms. Among them, J. Walter Thompson acquired Hill & Knowlton for $28 million; Young and Rubicam bought Burson-Marsteller and Marsteller Inc. for about $20 million; and Benton and Bowles acquired Manning, Selvage and Lee for $2 million. The first big merger (1978) was

---

[27] "Eight Ways Public Relations Contributes to the Bottom Line," *pr reporter*, 26, no. 1 January 3, 1983, pp. 1–2. Used by permission.

[28] Harold Burson, "The 'Bottom Line' in Public Relations," *Burson-Marsteller Report*, no. 46 (November 1980), pp. 1–4; adapted from acceptance address made when Burson was named Public Relations Professional of the Year.

3.3 PR'S CORPORATE RESPONSIBILITIES AND RELATIONSHIPS

The PR process is affected by the feedback from and impact of publics, media, trends, research, experiences and government. These shape actions, messages and their presentation.

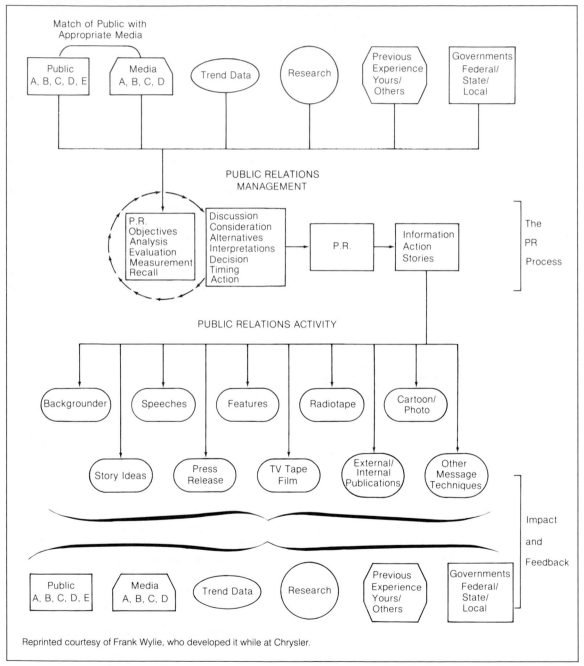

Reprinted courtesy of Frank Wylie, who developed it while at Chrysler.

Carl Byoir & Associates (one of the oldest PR agencies) with Foote, Cone & Belding. This intertwining of functions has already been recognized by many colleges and universities, which combine the academic programs of advertising and PR.

Apparently the trend is continuing. Of the fifteen largest U.S. advertising agencies, seven others, besides the three mentioned, have moved into related fields: public relations, specialized advertising to and for selected groups (doctors, for example), merchandising (including package design), direct marketing and sales promotion. Some agencies have bought successful companies to put under a corporate umbrella. Others have created their own divisions. Some have integrated the units into a superteam to offer clients. Others operate the units separately and independently, but find it advantageous to be able to offer what is called a "full service" agency. Philip Lesly fears the trend places PR strictly in a communications role, subservient to marketing and stripping PR of its counseling role. While some agencies use PR mostly as product/service support, others allow PR its full independence in role and function.

Counselors

Most counselors have been sensitive about their role because of a tendency for people to think of a PR counselor as a strong behind-the-scenes influence peddler and a suspicion that *counselor* is often another term for "unemployed." Public confusion is understandable because counselors are *advisers*. Counselors draw from their own areas of expertise, most of it gained in either agency or corporate work. Their value is their experience, their connections and their skill as researchers, analyzers, communicators and persuaders. Some counselors have developed reputations for helping an institution prepare for and handle crisis communication. Others are known for their ability to help an institution establish and maintain good government relations (at all levels, but primarily federal). Still others are called on for their ability to help with internal problems, generally involving employee relations. Most counselors are senior practitioners, but they often develop staffs that include younger people who have particular strengths.

Staff (Corporate)

Public relations people in institutions (profit and nonprofit) may be in skills jobs in a PR department, may be middle managers of some aspect of the public relations activity or may be considered professional staff. Increased use of computer technology is predicted to decrease the lower-level jobs and expand the middle manager and professional levels while retaining the narrow dimension at the senior level of policy making.[29] Public relations jobs are now considered a route to top management. Handling the different publics of a modern corporation, and their interrelationships, is demanding. Some PR people find the demand beyond their ability to satisfy. Investor relations is one area some, perhaps most, executives would like to put under the PR umbrella but find some PR people not

---

[29]Daniel Goleman, "The Electronic Rorschach," *Psychology Today*, February 1983, p. 43.

trained to handle it. The result of not being able to find people within the field is that management goes outside. For example, one of the highest-paid PR people is a lawyer: Herbert Schmertz of Mobil, who manages the company's public, government and investor relations and earned $300,000 in 1982. Another highly paid exec, Robert Thurston, was named executive vice president of Quaker Oats's grocery products division after fourteen years in company public relations work. (He earned $200,000 in 1982.) While his is a case of movement to the top from PR, another such move is exceptional because the officer is a woman. Mardie MacKimm, public relations officer for Kraft, Inc., was made a senior vice president.[30] Most women in public relations, and their numbers are increasing, are in lower-status positions and earn considerably less than a man in the same position, sometimes only half. In 1982 Matthew M. Miller surveyed the Fortune 300 companies [31] in an update of information from a study of people in corporate PR from the Fortune 500 done in the late 1960s by Dr. Kenneth Henry. He found the following changes had occurred during the seventies. Miller's respondents were older: the median age fifty to Dr. Henry's forty-seven. Almost 50 percent of the younger PR executives were women, up considerably from only 2 percent in the 1960s. However, the top PR spot was still dominated by males; 10 percent of the respondents occupied this slot. Median income for males was $63,800; for females it was $34,900. Most companies still called the function public relations, despite some trends in the sixties and seventies to mask the role and call it institutional relations, public affairs, or consumer relations. The number of employees in the office had increased from nine to eleven, although some companies had as many as thirty-five and some as few as four. PR budgets were at a mean of $1.5 million, but 35 percent were less than $1 million.

Staff (Government)

PR job descriptions in government vary dramatically. Some people who are called public information officers/personnel are really publicists, while those with precisely the same title may have all the responsibilities of a corporate vice president for PR. The reason is that anachronistic law that prevents public relations work in government from being honestly labeled (see Chapter 1, page 11). Many people hired by government, the world's largest employer of public relations talent despite the law, are really communications technicians only. Until the law is changed, there is not and cannot be a civil service job description and test for top public relations at the policy-making level.

Observations

Whatever the PR job, there are some observations that can be made uniformly. First, the salaries in every case are affected by sex, experience, age, job title and duties, as well as by education and the type, size and location of the orga-

---

[30] Sue Shellenbarger, "Work in PR Now a Route To Top Jobs," *Wall Street Journal*, June 24, 1980, p. 31.

[31] Matthew M. Miller, "Corporate Public Relations Update," *Public Relations Journal*, 38, no. 12 (December 1982), p. 22.

nization. Generally speaking, though, the better educated the person, the higher the average salary, regardless of the person's college major, although age and sex are major factors. Second, since anyone can be designated as a public relations practitioner, two of the most controversial areas in public relations at this time are educational preparation for PR (discussed in Chapter 1) and licensing (discussed in Chapter 15). Third, PR jobs are all stressful; in fact, PR practice has been listed as one of the top ten fields for stress. The reasons for stress in public relations practice identified by psychologist Thomas Backer are as follows: (1) *Negative leverage* is the result of the high visibility of mistakes PR professionals make, which multiplies the stress impact. (2) *Multiple bosses* exist within the institution's structure (and there is the stress of a responsibility to all of the different publics as well). (3) *Time pressures* are constant because almost all major tasks are on tight schedules. (4) *Lack of understanding* of the PR role results in such disparaging labeling as "flacks." (5) *Intangible results* still are a problem despite better gauges for measuring PR's effectiveness. (6) *Lack of respect* for public relations work occurs because everyone thinks he or she can do it. (7) *Values conflicts* often occur when the PR practitioner's personal values are not consonant with those of a client or an institution for which the person is working. (8) *Multiple emergencies* are often a part of PR practice because crises tend to perpetrate others.[32]

A fourth observation is that not all PR people have recognized that the information age has created what has been called the global village. Several studies have pointed out that cross-cultural awareness has penetrated the PR function only when the situation is forced by the activities of the institutions like multinational companies, high tech companies, governments and nonprofit organizations with international ties (such as museums). Clearly, public relations practitioners in the field and educators should be taking the initiative in creating such awareness among their publics.

POINTS TO REMEMBER

- The role of public relations has had three major interpretations: controlling publics, responding to publics and achieving mutually beneficial relationships among all publics.

- These roles correspond to the manipulative, service and transactional models of PR.

- PR offers at least seven specific values to society and the institutions it serves, most of them centering on PR's role in working out institutional-social relationships.

- Social responsibility and communication, historically ignored by most institutions, is increasingly recognized as an essential "cost" of doing business.

- PR people have to be problem finders and solvers and, preferably, preventers. Such work involves identifying issues and understanding what images are projected.

---

[32] "Public Relations One of Top 10 Fields for Stress," *pr reporter*, January 24, 1983, p. 1. Used by permission.

- PR people have to be interpreters, functioning as a communications link between an institution and all of its publics.

- PR people must communicate to management a clear concept of their role—as in counseling, research and planning—and demonstrate their ability to assume it.

- The evaluation of PR should be based upon measurable standards and objectives.

- The roles of PR practitioners in agency, counseling and staff positions is changing. One trend is toward increasing agency size and range of services.

- Staff positions are expected to increase at the middle manager and professional levels; PR jobs may now be a route to top management.

- More women are entering the PR field, but at less pay than men at the same level, and access to the top is more restricted.

THINGS TO DO

1. Study the "chain of command" chart from Cleveland State University (see 3.4), as well as the description given to you by your instructor.[33] Then examine the role of public relations at your own college or university. What is the pattern at your school? Is it different from that shown in the chart? In what way? Why?

2. Bearing in mind that to be most effective public relations must have a role in decision making, prepare a case for this management function compared with the role of a communications technician who only carries out the decisions of management.

3. The following minicases each illustrate a particular point, that is, a PR management lesson to be learned. Since public relations should be a preventive rather than merely a cure, offer some additional ways the situations in cases A, C, D and E might have been averted, using *only* the facts provided. Don't alter the existing situation, only the response.[34]

A. *Elephants Remember Ostriches:*   For several years, ABC industries could do no wrong. Major acquisitions were consummated, sales and earnings soared, and large contracts rolled in. Jack Johnson, physicist-turned-president, deserved most of the credit, and he got it. He reveled in the limelight and graciously granted lengthy interviews to all interested press representatives.

Then the economy turned down, and so did ABC. Sales flattened, then sagged, and earnings dropped sharply. Deadwood on the payroll was trimmed, and wholesale cutbacks followed. Johnson managed to hold the company together, and after nearly two years, it started slowly back up the growth curve once again.

But way back at the beginning, the first time he failed to meet his projected sales and earnings, Johnson ducked: No more press interviews. Throughout the hectic two years, he kept a low profile. He met the minimum requirements for release of financial information and other details of material interest to the pru-

---

[33] An instructor's supplement to this text has additional material explaining the chart; this could be reproduced as a handout for student use.

[34] A, B and C are excerpted, by permission of the publisher, from "You Can't Buy Good Public Relations," by David H. Simon, *Management Review*, April 1973. © 1973 by AMACOM, a division of American Management Associations, pp. 25, 26, 29–31, 41. All rights reserved.

3.4 CLEVELAND STATE UNIVERSITY'S ORGANIZATIONAL CHART

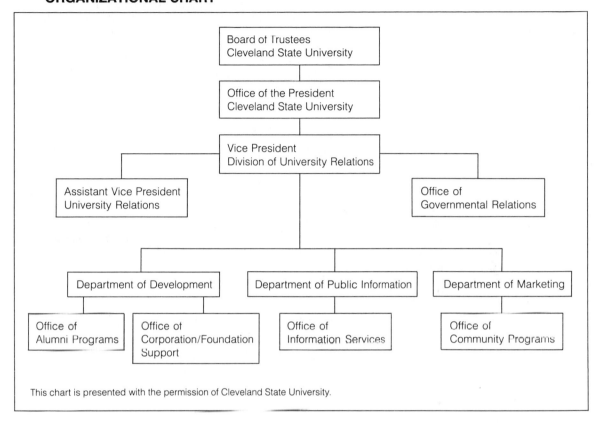

This chart is presented with the permission of Cleveland State University.

dent investor. But he would not amplify the terse news releases, would not explain where the company was headed or how it intended to reverse the downtrend. Nor was any other executive permitted to talk to the press.

When the company finally recovered, so did Smilin' Jack. He was ready to turn the charm back on with his old friends in the press corps. The press conference called to announce the firm's return to profitability, however, played to a virtually empty house. There were more company executives than reporters on hand for the cocktails, canapes, and conversation. The *New York Times* didn't make it, and neither did the *Wall Street Journal*. *Business Week*, which had said it would spare someone if it could, wasn't on hand. Even *Electronics News* wasn't there; perhaps that was the unkindest cut of all. During the halcyon days, *Electronics News* had carried every major story on the firm, frequently on page one and several times with Johnson's picture.

Reporters expect key company executives—particularly the PR spokespersons—to make themselves available in bad times as well as in good. This is especially true when the press corps has been cultivated during good times; if you make yourself available only at *your* convenience, you do so at your own peril. Reporters are human, and they feel used when a PR person who previously took all their calls suddenly can't be reached; they don't easily forget the rebuff.

B. *Yesterday's Rule*:   The small company had grown bigger and was on the threshold of reaching a long-awaited objective: going public. The red herring (preliminary registration statement) mentioned that the firm would soon introduce a version of its equipment for the telecommunications market, signaling an important entry into a new area.

"We're ready," announced the marketing director one day. "Let's break the Model 3000 with big stories and ads in all the telecommunications magazines."

"Can't do it now," the president replied. "We're in registration; we can't do any advertising or PR. We *certainly* can't announce such an important new product because it might be interpreted as an illegal attempt to influence the price of our stock."

"Wrong," said the company's public relations counselor, who produced a copy of SEC Release No. 5180 of August 16, 1971, and personal correspondence he had exchanged with the SEC about that document. He also had notes taken at public and private SEC briefings on the many rule changes and interpretations since the document was issued.

"The SEC specifically permits the dissemination of information that serves a clear marketing function. In this case we're talking about announcing a new product in trade magazines serving the market of interest," noted the PR counselor. "Until a couple of years ago, many people felt that saying nothing during a registration period was the safest course; now, the SEC has made it clear that companies may sometimes err by *not* releasing material information merely because they are in registration."

The company's attorney concurred with the PR man's position, and the product line was introduced successfully without objection from the SEC.

SEC policies and interpretations on dissemination of information, insiders, immediate disclosure, and related matters have changed rapidly in the last few years and continue to be modified. Some lawyers and some PR people specialize in the field; you need to confer with both. (One of the reasons why you need both is discussed in case D.)

C. *Why Didn't You Keep My Big Mouth Shut?*   Before the interview with *U.S. News & World Report*, the PR director carefully briefed Harry Baker, the firm's executive vice president. They covered the nature of the interview, which had been suggested to the magazine by the PR executive. They discussed the types of questions that would likely be asked and the kinds of information that would probably be of most interest to the magazine. They reviewed the areas that were sensitive to the company and that were to be avoided.

The PR director stressed that in most interviews, especially with reporters from "hard news" media, there is no such thing as "off the record": Anything said in an interview is fair game.

When the interview started, the PR director introduced the two and then took a seat in a corner of the room. He stayed throughout the interview but said very little. After the reporter left, the PR director suggested that the two executives should discuss the interview for future reference, but the VP said he was too busy.

Ten days later, the story appeared in print, and the VP was in a rage. His complaints: The remark about a certain competitor being underfinanced and overextended wasn't for publication; the story's emphasis on European marketing plans made it sound as though the firm had committed itself to that course of action, which it hadn't; and the listing of recently departed executives made it sound as though the firm had a lot of management problems, which, the VP maintained, wasn't so.

"You knew how I was coming across," he bellowed at the PR director. "Why didn't you jump in and set the record straight? That's what you're being paid for."

Not so, maintained the PR director. "I knew he wasn't getting the message you wanted to convey. I tried to discuss it with you after the interview, and, failing that, I talked to the reporter about it. But he wrote it the way he heard it from you, not the way he heard it from me, which is his prerogative."

"But you could have kept me out of trouble by pointing out the problems *during* the interview. Afterward was too late."

The trouble with that, the PR director was finally able to explain, is that many reporters are very touchy about PR people who try to take a too-active role in an interview. It is the line executive who is being interviewed, not the PR executive; some of the more sensitive reporters are actually reluctant to conduct an interview in the presence of a PR representative, for fear the PR representative will attempt to modify answers, cut short the line executive's responses, and otherwise interfere with the flow.

It pays for the interviewee to get a thorough briefing *before* the interview, then plan to carry the ball during the session.

It's only fair to point out that while most of the points discussed in this case are agreed upon by most public relations professionals, universal agreement on how interviews should be handled is lacking. Many PR people take issue with the approach expressed, feeling that an active role during an interview *is* an appropriate function for a PR executive. Our own philosophy is described in this case, but if your PR counselor takes a more active role in interviews and if that approach works with the reporters you deal with, stick with it.

D. *An Ounce of Clout*:   The director of a university's news bureau was particularly cautious about the timing of releases and press conferences and tried to balance the offerings to the news media, but one of the newspapers in the city had a competitor in the same time period and consistently and persistently broke release dates on stories from the university. That newspaper would print a story that had also been given to the other paper—which held it for the release date. Although this happened with some frequency, the university's news bureau chief did not take action until a major story was involved.

A nationally known speaker was to appear on campus and biographical material and photos were sent to the newspapers for a Sunday release. The offending newspaper used the story on Friday and thus killed the use of the story by the competitor on Sunday, thereby eliminating a far larger circulation and readership that the paper had. The damage was done and the big story got little play.

The news bureau chief called the staff together and issued this ultimatum: The next time there was a significant story, one the newspapers would want, the news break would go only to the "ethical" paper. This was not a boycott of the offending paper, for routine releases went out as usual, and it was agreed that if a reporter from that paper heard about one of the big stories and called, information would not be withheld. Once the point had been made by the news bureau, the offender was trusted with dated releases. and there was no more trouble.

E. *That's No Solution*:   A director of a small private hospital had just returned from a management training seminar very excited about instituting new communication routines in order to increase rapport and efficiency. He scheduled 7 A.M. meetings on Monday—"briefing sessions," as he called them—"to start the week off right." The sessions did nothing of the sort. Although staff attendance was compulsory, most of the ingenuity for the week was shown in the inventiveness of excuses for missing the meetings.

The director's personal popularity took a dramatic skid, and he was aston-ished to find that he had completely alienated people on the afternoon and late shifts, who had not been invited to the 7 A.M. sessions because they were off duty. What might have been a sound philosophy turned into unsound practice due to thoughtless execution.

SELECTED READINGS

Richard J. Barber, *The American Corporation: Its Power, Its Money, Its Politics* (New York: E. P. Dutton, 1970). Details octopuslike growth of business and examines problems it has created for itself, government and consumers. If you don't read anything else, read the conclusion, "Business, Government, and the Public."

Edward L. Bernays, *Public Relations*, rev. ed. (Norman: University of Oklahoma Press, 1977). The view from PR's pioneer.

Daniel Boorstin, *The Image: A Guide to Pseudo-Events in America* (New York: Harper & Row, 1962). Penetrating and uncomplimentary presentation of the effect of public relations practices on the American public.

R. S. Cole, *The Practical Handbook of Public Relations* (Englewood Cliffs, N.J.: Prentice-Hall, 1981). A handbook to careers in PR.

Scott M. Cutlip and Allen H. Center, *Effective Public Relations*, 5th ed. revised. (Englewood Cliffs, N.J.: Prentice-Hall, 1982). Long a bible of the profession; very comprehensive.

Richard N. Farmer, Barry M. Richman and William G. Ryan, *Incidents in Applying Management Theory* (Belmont, Calif.: Wadsworth, 1966). Because the recommendations of management consultants frequently are sought by business and because they always affect public relations internally and sometimes externally, these are valuable idea generators. See also by the same authors *Incidents for Studying Management and Organization* (Belmont, Calif.: Wadsworth, 1970). Many situations with public relations implications; questions should stimulate thinking along PR lines.

David Finn, *The Corporate Oligarch* (New York: Simon and Schuster, 1969). For those interested in corporate accountability.

L. L. L. Golden, *Only by Public Consent: American Corporations Search for Favorable Opinion* (New York: Hawthorn Books, 1968). Valuable book by one of PR's most valued objective, constructive critics.

James E. Grunig and Todd Hunt, *Managing Public Relations* (New York: Holt, Rinehart and Winston, 1984). Another entry into the growing field of survey PR books; includes some PR writing.

Philip Lesly, *Lesly's Public Relations Handbook*, 3rd ed. (Englewood Cliffs, N.J.: Prentice-Hall, 1983). A collection of articles by specialists; a storehouse of information that should be in the library of a serious practitioner.

H. Frazier Moore, *Public Relations: Principles, Cases, and Problems*, 8th ed. (Homewood, Ill.: Richard D. Irwin, 1981). A valuable book emphasizing specialized areas of PR.

Public Relations Society of America, *Status and Trends of Public Relations Education* (New York: PRSA, 1983). A benchmark.

William L. Rivers, *The Adversaries: Politics and the Press* (Boston: Beacon Press, 1970). The interplay of government and news media is a game the public not only doesn't understand but it also doesn't even have the rules. But the PR practitioner had better.

Raymond Simon, *Public Relations Management: Cases and Simulations*, 3rd ed. (Columbus, Ohio: Grid, 1984). Gives insights into PR problems. See also by the same author *Public Relations Concepts and Practices*, 2nd ed. (Columbus, Ohio: Grid, 1980).

Howard Stephenson, *Handbook of Public Relations*, 2d ed. (New York: McGraw-Hill, 1971). Contributions by authorities in specialized areas; very useful for the practitioner.

G. J. Voros and P. H. Alvarez, *What Happens in Public Relations* (New York: AMACOM, 1981). Discussion of the management aspects of PR.

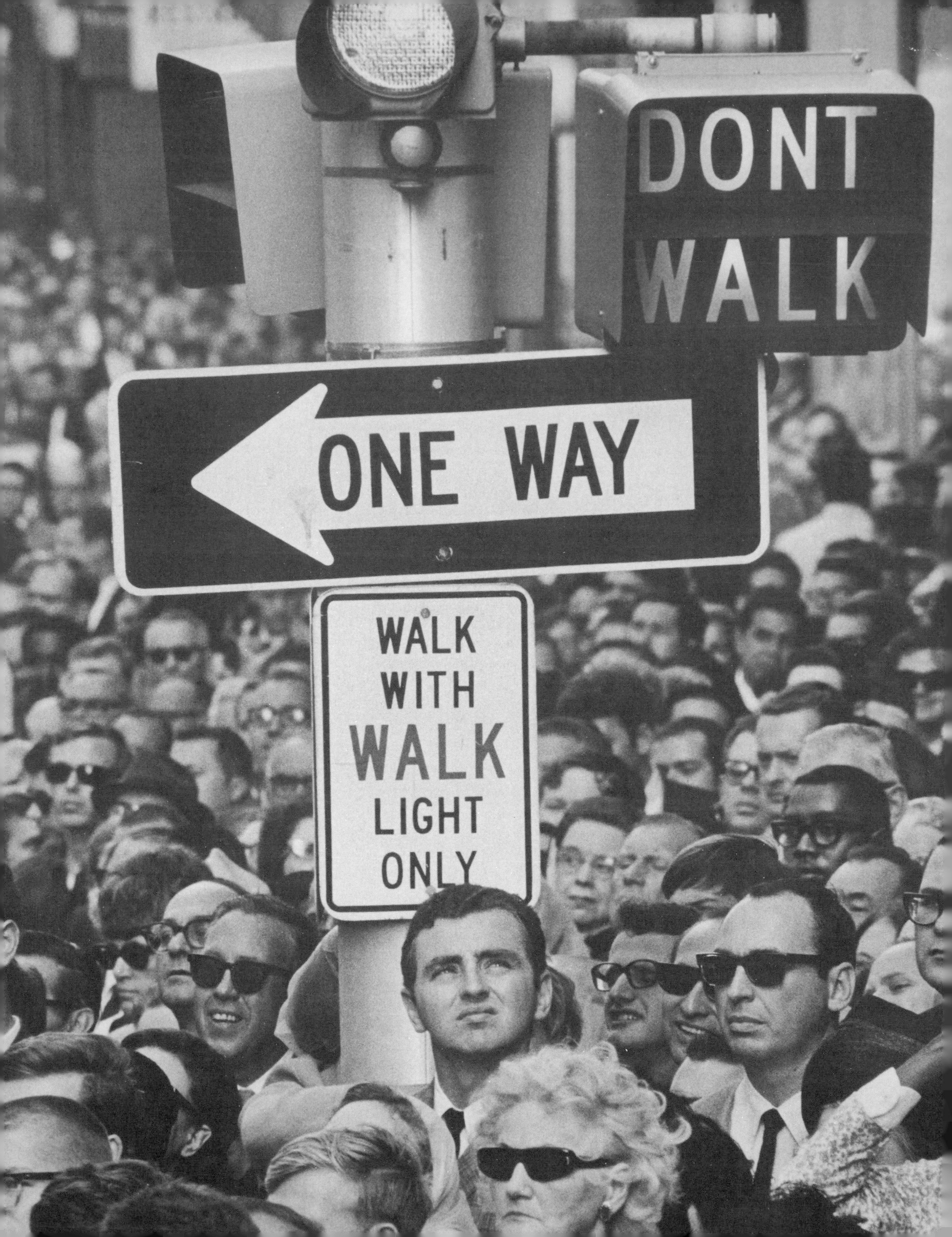
DONT
WALK
ONE WAY
WALK
WITH
WALK
LIGHT
ONLY

PART 2

Research for PR

To the skillful PR practitioner, research is a planning tool, an instrument to monitor and measure and a means for evaluating results. Chapters 4 and 5 are about the use and usefulness of research in public relations.

CHAPTER 4

Research for Backgrounding and Programming

Research is the one important source of ideas for public relations practice.

Edward J. Robinson, management training and development authority

When the crisis occurs the research must be at hand . . . its facts understood . . . the communicators ready to go into action.
*   The modern PR person must know how to research any subject, do it quickly and summarize it well and briefly.*

Frank W. Wylie, Public Affairs, California State University at Los Angeles

"The whole world of information has changed. . . . Just about any question you can ask can be answered out of a data base," says Andrew P. Garvin. He should know because his company, FIND/SVP of New York, is in the business of selling answers.[1] However, a wealth of information is accumulated by institutions in daily operations. Without some thought being given to how that information might be used, though, it is useless. Setting up a system can always be done, but sometimes the opportunity is particular, as the following illustrates:

A senior PR counselor got an urgent call from a colleague, a young woman who is vice president for public relations at a new bank in a metropolitan area. "Please help me think something through," she implored. "Our bank is going to a computer-operated system for all of its reporting. I think this is a wonderful opportunity for me to get a basic customer information sheet to use in handling all of our customer relations and communications." She was right. Information about PR audiences is critical, and research for sound public relations planning can be built into a record-keeping system, provided retrieval is also carefully considered. Information is valueless if it can't be used. For example, a team handling reorganization and five-year planning for a professional organization found that some basic information about membership was crucial to decision making and called the organization's national headquarters for the needed facts. They were told that the information had been gathered, but there was no software program enabling

---

[1]Andrew P. Garvin quoted by Sanford L. Jacobs, "Using Official Data Often Helps Avoid Mistakes, Find Customers," *Wall Street Journal*, January 5, 1981, p. 15.

them to get to the specifics about members they needed. The information was of no use to them.

Record keeping, computer-based or not, ought to be a priority with even the smallest institutions. The PR practitioner needs access to information about people, their ideas and activities and their environment.

A man we know who owns a small PR firm is quick to scorn research as being costly and unreliable. Yet one of his clients is a sports club, and he keeps detailed records of all game statistics, can cite every first in the team's history, holds celebrations for the most obscure anniversaries and is generally rewarded with the publicity he seeks for calling attention to same. He would be aghast if we called something he considers routine matters research, but research it is, and highly significant research because it is done on a continuing basis.

This chapter is about the importance to public relations of keeping records, finding and using existing reports and using research in planning PR programs and evaluating their results. It covers how to get significant information about a subject, how to find out about publics and how to monitor media. It sets out some rules for using research and some guidelines for deciding when to try doing your own and when not to.

THE BASICS: RECORD KEEPING AND FACT FINDING

Research is "the process of obtaining *reliable* knowledge, the kind of knowledge needed to function effectively."[2] The first step in research is keeping adequate records and making good use of them.

A new part-time employee for a hospital's PR department discovered one morning, while sorting out old files, that the hospital would have its fiftieth anniversary *the next day*, and that no plans had been made to celebrate it. Although it was too late to do much, she had a hurried conference with her boss and the hospital's administrator. They, in turn, together with the staff dietitian, were able to convince the chef that a really big birthday cake was in order and that patients should each get a slice with a candle in it. The chef felt better about it all after the local news media had been alerted to the event. The press were given different approaches to the story, and they showed the chef mixing the giant cake (TV), the chef decorating the cake (TV), a patient celebrating the hospital's birthday along with his own (newspaper), and a two-year-old patient devouring her slice with all the enthusiasm and mess typical of that age (newspaper). The celebration and preparation took the better part of a day, with the staff abandoning all else to get the job done. When the part-time PR worker was asked what she planned to do the next day, she replied, "Get those files in order so this will never happen to me again."

---

[2] Edward J. Robinson, "The Fountainhead of Public Relations," a speech at annual meeting, Public Relations Society of America, November 12–14, 1962, Boston University.

Retrieval

Systematic record keeping—collecting facts—may be a drudgery, but it has its reward in that it can supply information when it is critically needed (such as telling us what we did last year), help us plan (such as telling us what we need to put on the calendar), aid us in understanding who our publics are and tell us how they behave in certain situations (such as what events they attended), help us flesh out stories or give us a news peg. Maintaining a file on all major activities and a general how-to file facilitates planning and reduces strain on the nerves—provided you can find what you filed.

Recorded information must be kept in easily retrievable form. It is not valuable unless there is access to it. For example, suppose you have been touting the high food value of your company's canned peaches, and a competitor releases a "market study" showing that actually his frozen peaches have more food value because so much of yours is destroyed in canning. A newspaper food editor calls you for a comment on the challenge. If it takes you too long to get the answer, the competition may win the headlines that day and you may have to settle for a less prominent display for your answer several days later. Professional PR practitioners use two principal storage methods: the computer, in which they can store information that can be called up when needed on visual display terminals; and libraries, where reference materials are filed in a physical form and on VDTs. Some large systems are managed by librarians.

Sources and Resources

The sources and resources a practitioner needs are many and varied. In addition to their own specialized information, PR practitioners use general sources almost daily. Everyone has favorite source books, and each job demands that these be amplified or changed. Because the PR person's greatest importance to a client or to management is as a resource person, the practitioner must either have the information or know where to find it. Research librarians in major libraries will help you select the most fruitful data banks to search in each particular instance. Computer access to data banks is available in some agencies and corporate PR departments.

In your own office library you will want a collection of annual directories and reference books. Two excellent digests of general sources are *Finding Facts*[3] and *Aspen Handbook on the Media*.[4] Also useful is another Aspen publication, *The Mass Media: Aspen Institute Guide to Communication Industry Trends*.[5] Other PR basics are such annuals as *N. W. Ayer & Sons Directory of Newspapers and Peri-*

---

[3]William L. Rivers, *Finding Facts: Interviewing, Observing, Using Reference Sources* (Englewood Cliffs, N.J.: Prentice-Hall, 1975).

[4]William L. Rivers, Wallace Thompson and Michael J. Nyhan, eds., *Aspen Handbook on the Media: Research, Publications, Organizations*, 1977–79 edition (Palo Alto, Calif.: Aspen Institute on Communications and Praeger, 1978).

[5]Christopher H. Sterling and Timothy R. Haight, *The Mass Media: Aspen Institute Guide to Communication Industry Trends* (New York: Praeger, 1978).

odicals; *Editor and Publisher Yearbook*; *Standard Rate and Data Services, Inc.*, *Broadcasting Yearbook*, *Writer's Market*; the *Congressional Directory*, a good world almanac, and a state almanac. Watch the *New York Times Book Review* pages for reviews of new reference books you may want to order. A *new* dictionary is basic, of course.

To these, you should add the technical journals of your own profession—communications. There are also journals of the related social sciences—the *Political Science Quarterly*, for example, and the *Journal of Economic Issues*. There is the National Investment Library of the New York Clearance Systems, Inc., the central business and financial library of written corporate material from the major publicly held corporations. Above all, get on the U.S. Government Printing Office's mailing list; an astonishing amount of information is available at minimal cost from this office. Also, certain libraries are repositories for government publications; find the closest and learn how to use the reference system. Again, government publications provide invaluable information—beyond the obvious such as demographic facts from a census report—and library repositories offer them free. In addition, you will need the technical and trade journals of the fields in which you are practicing public relations—education, business, sports, entertainment, oil, whatever.

Keeping up with all developments is essential. Thoroughness can make the difference between success and failure. Suppose you are handling the political campaign of someone running for city council. A local newspaper reporter calls, saying your candidate's opponent is quoting a federal report on the free lunch program in your city's schools and asking what your candidate thinks about the report. If you do not have the report in hand, it is impossible to fake. But your response in this case should be immediate—even a "Call you back after I check" won't do. You should have read and have copies of all reports on all local issues your candidate is likely to be asked about.

PR Audiences

Besides having on hand, with ready access, all information needed to answer questions about your subject—the industry, the field, the company, individuals within the company, competitors—it is imperative to know all of your audiences thoroughly.

When we talk about public relations audiences, that is, the various publics with whom PR is in contact, the first one that should be thought of is often omitted. That one, the administration of the organization or company for which the public relations effort is being planned, is the most obvious and the most ignored. However, the image that administrators of that institution have of themselves and of the institution must be considered first. Questions must be asked such as Who are we? What are we doing? Why are we doing it? Is this what we should be doing? Is it all we should be doing? How well are we doing what we are doing?

One PR firm's president always first investigates his clients' own self-perceptions. He says it is critical for what he calls "positioning." By "positioning" he means his need to know where the leaders of the institution *see* themselves in relation to the marketplace. This consideration is just as important for educational

4.1 PRODUCTION LINE PROBLEM

Should you always take workers' complaints at face value? Think twice before you do! Maybe communications problems are the real cause of the trouble.

St. Louis public relations consultant Alfred Fleishman, in his [1973] book *Troubled Talk*, tells of a client who was having "all kinds of problems" at one of his plants. In this plant, two identical production lines existed side by side.

Employees on the first line complained about their physical working conditions. It was "too cold in the winter, too hot in the summer." There "wasn't enough light. The machines were too close together." Employees complained about high accident rates and other matters. Absenteeism was high.

But researchers noted that employees on the second production line had few complaints, low absenteeism and a low accident rate. So instead of making the physical changes in the factory called for by the first group, the investigators dug deeper. And here's what they found:

In answer to the question "How does your boss criticize you, in public or in private?" more than 75 percent of the first group said the boss always criticized them in public. This compared with about 10 percent in the second group. Other questions revealed similar differences between the two groups. The answers convinced Mr. Fleishman that neither new lights nor new air conditioning and heating systems would solve the problem.

Instead, the supervisor of the first production line was taken off his job and sent back for more training. The supervisor of the second group replaced him. Months later, a follow-up study showed that the first group's complaints had dropped sharply, along with absenteeism and accidents. Nothing physical had changed; only the boss.

Alfred Fleishman and William D. Meyer, *Troubled Talk* (San Francisco: International Society for General Semantics, 1973); printed in "persuasion," 21, edited by Chester Burger, May 27, 1974, supplement of *pr reporter*, Meridan, New Hampshire. Used by permission.

institutions, health care organizations and other nonprofit groups as for commercial institutions.

While initial research with administrators is always important, it becomes absolutely critical when dealing with a public relations problem. Public relations counselors can cite case after case of being called in and told by management "what the problem is," with the request that the counselor come up with a solution. The wise counselor, however, researches exactly what the problem is because management's perception of the real cause of the difficulty may or may not be correct (see 4.1).

Management's perception of target audiences may not always be accurate either—this is another thing research often points out. Perceptions may be off-base with internal audiences as 4.1 shows, or with external audiences as the following story demonstrates.

The owner of a specialty store with a reputation for expensive, quality merchandise was asked by other local retail merchants to join them in a downtown promotional campaign. The owner was skeptical. "We have the carriage trade," she said, "and a great deal of out-of-town, even international business. Frankly, I can't see that it would be worth our time." Someone who had noticed that the specialty store was highest both in dollar volume and in individual receipts asked the owner where the store's volume of business was centered. Might not the customers responsible for all those receipts be the young professionals, many of whom worked downtown? They were the kind of people who could afford only a

4.2 SCIENTIFIC ANSWERS TO SCIENTIFIC QUESTIONS

Increasingly, . . . scientific questions about communication are being asked of professional communicators.

"How do I know that anyone will look at this ad you are preparing for me?" the advertiser wants to know. He is not satisfied with the artistic answer—"It's beautiful, isn't it?"

The government official says:

"We have only three months to teach these Peace Corps volunteers Swahili. How do I know that this method you are proposing is the best?"

"Well, it is traditional. It is the method we've always used. Don't the lesson plans seem well-organized to you?"

The company president remarks:

"You say this public relations campaign has changed public attitudes toward my company and that I should hire your firm for another year. I'm not quite satisfied. Give me some objective evidence."

"Well," the public relations practitioner says with some hesitation, "I have a lot of newspaper clippings here in a folder."

The politician inquires:

"I am going to be facing a hostile crowd tonight. I want to get away with a whole skin and perhaps influence them a little in my direction. What shall I do?"

"Well," his adviser replies, "in a similar situation, Mark Antony . . ."

The politician is likely to say, "To hell with Mark Antony! Give me something scientific."

The point is simply this: Interest in science and in asking the scientific question is part of the spirit of our times. Professional communicators cannot avoid these questions. They encounter them all the time. They frequently ask them themselves. And they cannot indefinitely avoid giving them a scientific as opposed to an artistic answer.

This is basically what communication research is all about. It is an attempt to give scientific answers to scientific questions about communications.

Wayne A. Danielson, speech to Sigma Delta Chi, University of Texas, Austin, October 26, 1967.

couple of high-priced outfits but were willing to make the investment to get the style and quality the specialty store offered. In addition, the questioner asked, might not many of these people, since they were climbing the career ladder, often buy smaller-priced gifts simply to get the store's label? Intrigued, the owner did some research. To her amazement, she found that, although she did have the carriage trade, which made substantial purchases, the daily volume came from downtown career workers. She participated in the downtown promotion and became as excited as any businessperson with a new market discovery.

Knowing who the target audiences are implies knowing what to say to them and how to say it. You need to know how your messages are likely to affect the various publics you depend on for goodwill. A university administrator once forgot this when, during a talk to prospective students and their parents, he thoughtlessly said, "To maintain high standards of teaching, we try to have as few teaching assistants as possible." His remark, dutifully reported by the university's student newspaper, aroused a predictably hostile reaction from the graduate students serving as teaching assistants, or TAs.

Awareness of publics and their responses really means heightened sensitivity and constant alertness, but there is a lot of guessing involved, unless you have, and regularly update, a statistical profile of these publics (see 4.2, on the need for scientific information). The president did not set out to offend the TAs, of course; it was just a thoughtless remark, but one he might not have made had he been particularly conscious of the composition of his audience.

One way to help us understand and appreciate audiences is through what one research company president calls cross-tabulation of data. He takes the company's own fact-finding operation and extracts from it a general picture of their publics. He combines this with even more generally available research in the field, such as published public opinion studies, to get a broad picture. Then he develops a set of questions to use in talking with small segments of the publics in an interview situation. The quantitative information furnishes the base from which he can go after the specifics or the qualitative information, a technique he laughingly calls "coloring by numbers." There is a broad outline and a number suggesting what color might be used, but until colors—the qualitative research—are applied, the picture is not whole.

One aspect of this technique deserves particular attention: the integration of available research studies with the institution's own fact-finding operation. See 4.3, which shows areas with related subject fields where existing research is available.

FINDING AND USING EXISTING RESEARCH

There is a great deal of research literature around (as 4.4 shows). What is useful in communicating with publics is information from communications research that shows audience profile and credibility ratings. The research is usually already available. You simply need to know where to look for it, know enough about research techniques to interpret the results correctly and then apply them. If, for instance, you are interested in advertising for the youth market, you would be interested in a study by Professor Stephen Unwin, who concluded that "differences in opinion of the advertisements and the products advertised were predictive of response difference between cultures but not between generations and sexes."[6]

Wayne Danielson, former dean of the University of Texas's College of Communication, observes that the communications industry has established committees on research and research organizations.[7] Additionally, many media have research data that are available to the public.

Besides communication research, Danielson also cites *scholarly research* published in professional journals and in the trade press. Much of the scholarly research is available through computer data access terminals in major libraries. Ask a research librarian for help. *Commercial research*—the kind invested in by local media by highly competitive markets—is also available. Companies invest in *internal research* and sometimes publish the results, which can be examined for relationship and significance. The social sciences provide a wealth of information;

---

[6] Stephen J. F. Unwin, "How Culture, Age and Sex Affect Advertising Response," *Journalism Quarterly* (Winter 1973), p. 743.

[7] Wayne A. Danielson, speech to the Society of Professional Journalists, Sigma Delta Chi, University of Texas, Austin, October 26, 1967.

4.3 THE MOLECULE OF PR LITERATURE

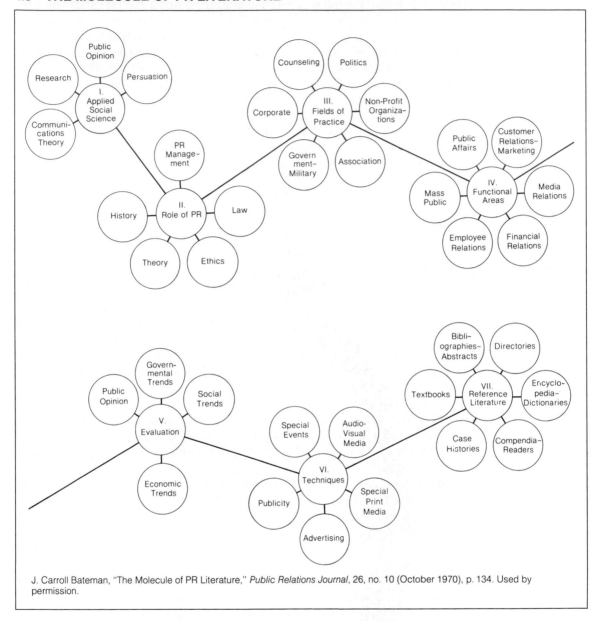

J. Carroll Bateman, "The Molecule of PR Literature," *Public Relations Journal*, 26, no. 10 (October 1970), p. 134. Used by permission.

although such research is often not directly relevant, the PR practitioner can learn how to pull out what can be used most effectively.

A word of warning is needed. It is sometimes difficult to convince others of the usefulness of adapting research. For instance, an argument arose between an artist and PR practitioner charged with coming up with a brochure to explain a new downtown one-way street plan. The practitioner cited graphics studies to support an argument for color choice and placement of copy and artwork, but the

4.4 THE U.S. CENSUS: A FUND OF RESEARCH INFORMATION

For retail operations "demographics are absolutely imperative," says Andrew Konstandt, who specializes in counseling small firms, many referred to him by the Small Business Administration. "You have to know the number of people, the disposable income and the competition in the area," he says. Census information can provide the information. Population data contain the number of residents, the number of families and their incomes by state, county and municipality. Within municipalities, there are breakdowns by neighborhood units, known as "census tracts," so that the high, low and middle-income areas of a town can be determined.

The Census Bureau also does a census of businesses every five years, in years ending in 2 and 7. Jeffrey L. Hall, a Census Bureau Services Officer in New York City, flips through "The 1977 Census of Retail Trade in New Jersey" (one is printed for each state) to demonstrate how the data can be used. Suppose someone is considering a bar in Jersey City, he suggests. He should forget it. The city already has 611 drinking places; they had total sales of $39.1 million in 1977, or average annual sales of only $64,000 a bar. That's well below the New Jersey statewide average for bars of $107,000, the census booklet discloses.

Sanford L. Jacobs, "Using Official Data Often Helps Avoid Mistakes, Find Customers," *Wall Street Journal*, January 5, 1981, p. 15. © Dow Jones & Company, Inc. 1981. All rights reserved. Used by permission.

artist was unwilling to consider them because they conflicted with her own aesthetic concept of the brochure. Finally, the practitioner conceded that the artistic merit of the brochure might be lessened, but he stressed that the important thing was that it be read; he painted a grim picture of potential traffic snarls, buses going the wrong direction down one-way streets and delivery trucks being delayed while drivers tried to figure out new routes. The artist thereupon relented, and some weeks later called the practitioner to ask for a copy of two of the studies. Her explanation: "I need them to convince this client that what I've drawn will do the job for him. You can't imagine what a stupid thing he wants to do."

There is yet another source for research: public opinion surveys. One of these comes from the marketing department of *U.S. News & World Report*. The study is done for the magazine by Marketing Concepts, Inc., and the opinions are gathered from heads of U.S. households, plus a sample of 3,000 executives listed in Poor's Register of Directors and Executives, 2,500 federal government leaders listed in the Congressional Directory and deans and professors who are members of the American Assembly of Collegiate Schools of Business. The report includes summary statements of public opinion on major national issues, such as the energy crisis; a list of attitudes on emerging issues and some ratings of various U.S. institutions. Also, a compendium of information about what is to be comes from the World Future Society. The Society offers a catalogue of books, cassette recordings on different subjects, films, the Society's magazines and even games.[8] For someone searching actively, studies are available, either without charge or at a minimal charge. And the best reason for being familiar with research methodology is to be able to apply, successfully, the many surveys available to a particular company, market or client.

---

[8]World Future Society, 4916 St. Elmo Ave., Washington, DC 20014.

What to Look for in Research Data

Evidence of one corporation's awareness of some generally available statistical information is found in the following piece from the *Wall Street Journal*:

> Gerber Grows Up with a pitch at the adult market. The baby food market, aware of a declining birth rate, starts market tests this week for a line of 12 single-serving entree and side dishes for adults. Also, in a four-city test, it pushes some regular baby foods as adult snacks, desserts, and topping.[9]

Colleges and universities are having to adjust to the same type of declining market information. Owing to a smaller pool of eighteen-year-olds from which to recruit freshmen, many are beginning to emphasize continuing education, the "retreading" of professionals and the "fill in the blanks in your background" types of studies for people already in the job market. Other information like this, which comes under the category of *demographics*, is the projection, based on current trends, that the American household will reflect couples marrying at a later age, having fewer children, getting divorces more often and having in the family working wives who may also be mothers (see 4.4).

To complement the demographics is *psychographics*, an area of study that plans programs to meet the needs of a changing public. Psychographics describes the personality traits of audiences. Its value lies in its ability to show likenesses in audiences of great demographic difference. For example, what do an eighty-year-old engineer and a twenty-five-year-old sociologist have in common? Maybe they both like to grow roses, prefer classical music to country western and so on. In applying this to PR, we may find, for example, that industries may want to know how working mothers would feel about bringing their children to work with them and leaving them in a child-care facility on the premises. And if one is already located at the workplace, what ages of children are likely to be kept there and how much of an educational facility should it be? Such attitudes and opinions are the psychographics of a public.

Using Research to Describe Publics

Public relations practitioners generally divide publics into two broad categories—external and internal (see Chapters 6 and 7). Describing the characteristics of these publics is the function of research.

Both demographics and psychographics are important in describing publics. Public opinion studies often offer both. An example is a Gallup Poll taken during 1978, which was summarized for PR practitioners in a professional newsletter, *pr*

---

[9] "A New Market Search," *Wall Street Journal*, April 4, 1974, p. 1. Reprinted with permission of the *Wall Street Journal*, Dow Jones and Company, Inc., 1974.

reporter.[10] Gallup found America's 25 million teenagers (1) more tolerant than their elders of persons of different backgrounds; (2) highly religious though turned off by organized religion; (3) greatly inclined toward "helping professions" of medicine, education, social work; and (4) in favor of stiffer school workloads, more parental authority. But they are also (5) abusing alcohol in epidemic proportions; (6) committing a high proportion of all crimes; (7) willing to cheat on exams (6 in 10 say they have); (8) violence-prone to the point of attacking teachers and classmates (1 in 5 is fearful of bodily injury during school hours); (9) turning away from politics, as careers or even as voters. The conclusions of the pollsters were that while the 1960s were marked by revolt, the 1970s by disillusionment, the 1980s would be a period of "severe dislocations in society . . . a not very pleasant decade in which to live," and the year 2000 was set as the time when most traditional relationships would be lost. Public relations practitioners in many different fields may find that information useful, though ominous.

Some research institutions, like Opinion Research Corporation, founded in 1938, offer comprehensive reports compiled from various clients' projects. These reports are not inexpensive (each is several hundred dollars) but considerably less expensive than any research project.[11]

Good survey research is costly, and so small companies especially depend a great deal on a careful analysis and application of the results of surveys taken by others and published or made available within the industry. A principal source of such surveys is the research done by professional associations and made available to their members. Social problems and issues with significance to government or to social agencies are studied and published by public polling agencies. A recent national study showed that one in every seven men and one in every ten women is an alcoholic. Many civil, religious and social organizations have conducted studies to see how their community compares.

Applying Research Information

Two questions should be asked before you use survey research. First, is it valid? Second, what does it mean to me or my client? Such information may be only a warning sign—a signal to the alert PR practitioner that a problem is brewing. Then it is important to find out whether the problem already exists within your own scope of responsibility. For instance, a church or denominational office might react to the Gallup religion survey by calling for statistics on attendance. If attendance is sliding, the prudent move would be to design a survey to answer questions directly relative to that church or denomination. Many churches responded to the Gallup survey in just that way.

Just how useful already existing research can be was called to the attention of

---

[10] "Gallup Sees Teenagers as Demonstrators of What's Right and Wrong in Society, Finds Public Wants Electoral Change," *pr reporter*, 21, no. 47 November 27, 1978, p. 2.

[11] Opinion Research Corporation, Center for Management Research, 850 Boydston St., Chestnut Hill, MA 02167.

political strategists by Herschel Schosteck whose firm handles political accounts. Schosteck's example of media research, which he calls "nothing more or less than an expansion and refinement of the issue, image, voter identification and voter preference opinion research, which has become a necessary ingredient of the modern political campaign,"[12] used information about who watched which television newscasts to determine the most effective time buy for calling attention to political candidates. He says media research is better than using television rating services for political time buying because those surveys are tied to the "average" viewer and what he was after was the viewing habits of a key audience of undecided voters—those who were most likely to be susceptible to persuasion. Knowing who views TV newscasts is important because many who are average TV viewers do not watch news. The viewing habits of this group are sometimes "dramatically different" from those of the average viewer. Of using existing media research, Schosteck says, "Particularly in the new age of limited media dollars, this increased effectiveness takes on appreciable importance."[13]

Surveys and polls can be extremely useful as long as they are interpreted correctly. To assist those using poll data, the National Council on Public Polls (NCPP) has issued some poll release standards. NCPP considers it essential that the following be specifically incorporated in published or broadcast reports on polls: (1) who sponsored the poll; (2) dates of interviewing; (3) method of obtaining the interviews: in-person, telephone or mail; (4) wording of the questions; (5) population that was surveyed; (6) size of the sample; (7) size and description of the subsample if results are based on less than the total sample.[14]

A word of caution came also from the American Association for Public Opinion Research (AAPOR). Taking an activist stance, AAPOR president Hope Lunin Klapper said that the organization writes letters to those who do "alleged" polls, pointing out that these—such as one called a "national" poll whose sample was 80 percent Californians—are not polls at all. Dr. Klapper cited advocacy organizations as being the most guilty of abusing poll methodology, primarily by the way the questions are asked.[15]

One of the biggest stumbling blocks to overall acceptance of market research is "who is going to test market the test marketers." The Advertising Research Foundation hoped to provide the answer and find out just how market research firms operate and how valid their findings are. Research firms were asked to allow the foundation to audit research techniques. Findings were made available to foundation member firms, and participating research companies received the "Registered for the ARF Open Audit Plan" seal.[16]

---

[12] Herschel Schosteck, "Media Research and Political Time Buying," *Practical Politics*, 1, no. 2 (December 1978/January 1979), p. 29.

[13] Ibid.

[14] Statement issued in 1978 by the National Council on Public Polls, 1990 M Street, N.W., Washington, D.C. 20036, President Albert H. Cantril; Vice President, Burns W. Roper, Secretary-Treasurer, Frederick P. Currier and trustees: Archibald M. Crossley, Mervin Field, George Gallup, Louis Harris and Richard M. Scammon.

[15] "Gathering Public Opinion Is a Business So Be Wary, Warns AAPOR President; A Survey of New Items to Be Wary of," *pr reporter*, April 3, 1978, p. 1.

[16] *Advertising and Sales Promotion*, February 1972, p. 38.

RESEARCH AND
PLANNING

Although it helps to have research to win arguments or counteract a competitor's claim, the particular value of research is in planning. In planning any program, whether a continuing one or a campaign, the PR person should examine all the available research—that is, all records and materials—to determine the realities. This may mean, for instance, calling on special departments, such as sales or product research, for information. It is important here that you ask for *specific information*. Know what you need before you ask for it; don't waste others' time on a fishing expedition. On the other hand, give them enough information about your situation so that, because they know their area better than you, they may be able to volunteer information you would not have known how to ask for. Be cooperative and considerate, appreciative of others' work and time schedules, but *get what you need*.

Issue Forecasting

Research for planning involves issue forecasting. Of more than 150 forecasting techniques, only nine are commonly used, says Raymond P. Ewing, issues management director of Allstate Insurance.[17]

1. *Trend extrapolation*, one of the most widely used techniques, is based on the assumption that most trends follow the ups and downs of an "S" curve ($\backsim$). However, social and environmental factors have to be considered, and events like wars or strikes can intervene.

2. *Trend impact analysis* is a process by which the impact of events is anticipated. A computer-generated trend is reviewed by experts who try to list future events that could affect the trend and describe how this could occur.

3. *Scanning* involves having a number of people review various general and specialized publications on a regular basis and write abstracts, adding their own personal comments. The abstracts are reviewed by an analysis committee, which reports to a steering committee so the information can be used in planning.

4. *Monitoring* is a technique that picks up where trend analysis and scanning stop. Once an identifiable element of significance is discovered, monitoring tracks its development. Research institutions use surveys and content analysis of mass media to follow identified issues.

5. *The DELPHI technique*, discussed in the following chapter, is used to identify issues by polling experts. Anonymity prevents the experts being influenced by authority figures, interpersonal persuasion or majority opinion. A summary of the predictions is then circulated among a panel for refinement to reach a consensus.

6. *Cross-impact analysis* is an attempt to discover how all of the trends discov-

---

[17] Raymond P. Ewing, "The Uses of Futurist Techniques in Issues Management," *Public Relations Quarterly*, 24, no. 4 (Winter 1979), pp. 15–18.

ered or predicted by other means might occur, influence each other or affect the timing of events.

7. *Computer simulations* are used if a mathematical formula has been developed. All of the information and the formula can be programmed and the computer will use the formula to arrive at the "answer," a conclusion that is a prediction.

8. *Scenario writing* is a "what if" form of research developed to project a number of possibilities, including unpleasant ones, to plan for contingencies. These are sometimes used to sensitize management to issues or even to communicate trends to the public.

9. *Technology assessment* attempts to predict the costs, benefits and negative impact of various technologies to help plan for development and adoption.

Finding Out about Publics

After you have accumulated all the needed facts, begin exploring the publics involved. Reexamine their profiles to see how each might be affected by the situation. This is a critical area, and it is important that *no* public be overlooked. In this manner you will often discover areas where, because publics are divergent, there is a conflict of interest. A college PR administrator frequently encounters this, since a college is an institution with great differences among publics—trustees, administrators, alumni, faculty, staff, parents and students.

Setting Priorities   You have to decide which are the major and minor publics. "It's not exactly deciding who you can afford to offend," one practitioner put it. "It is more deciding which one has to be appealed to most effectively and figuring out how to do that while offending the others the least." To be able to do this at all means you must be aware of what these publics know and what they think they know. Only research will tell you how many real facts a public has, and only research will tell you what a public thinks it knows—the myths it holds, the rumors it has embraced. Some research professes to tell you how a public is *likely* to think, what it might do. This is worth examining, but cautiously.

Research also helps you examine the dynamics of your publics. You want to know how these groups act collectively, if and when they do. This is something more and more institutions are doing with employee surveys. For example, the following appeared in the *Wall Street Journal*:

> Burlington Northern Inc., mails its first employee attitude survey this week, asking 8,000 workers their views on pay, job conditions, and company structure. Metropolitan Life boosts the frequency of surveys to see how workers feel about their jobs, asks retirees how they're faring. Responding to worker gripes discovered in surveys, General Motors recently revised the management system of a Georgia car plant.
>
> Ford Motor increases use of surveys, sees them as "upward communications" from employees. More unions are cooperating with surveys, a Chicago consultant says, because "even the unions can't figure out what's on the worker's mind." Demand for conducting surveys is up 30 percent or more this year at a Booz Allen & Hamilton research unit.
>
> Uncovering corporate flaws "hiding under the rug" is only the beginning. "It takes an exquisite agony" to solve such problems, one survey expert notes.
>
> *Product testing* by employees helps firms head off consumer gripes.

Levi Strauss & Co., the California pants maker, says employees test new styles because "we can't make pants in a vacuum. They have to be tested, and our employees are accessible." Worker testing of kitchen and household items often helps Rubbermaid Inc., clarify instructions given to buyers. Thom McAn asks workers to report on shoe wear and fit regularly for eight weeks.

A North Carolina hosiery maker finds testing by employees a key aid in preparing size charts for prepackaged panty hose. Miami footwear retailer Caressa Inc., finds employee testing helped catch a manufacturing problem in a new line of platform shoes and "saved our retailers a lot of trouble." Most employees keep merchandise they test.

But Bob Evans Farms in Ohio turns to consumer groups to test its pork products because workers "tend to give us the answers we want to hear."[18]

Surveys are one way to get at a public's issues and problems, but some managements are using a direct approach with employees and consumers. Managers, even CEOs, are sitting down with a few employees at a time at different sites to listen to problems. Officers, accompanied by some directors, of ONEOK—a diversified energy company—go to different locations during a month to present employee awards and listen to problems. Hyatt Hotel employees, about fifteen of them at a time, get to meet face to face with President Patrick Foley. He listens to everything from minor complaints to difficulties that suggest problem areas, investigates the problem and then writes a letter of response.

Some companies have adopted a Japanese technique called "quality circles," in which groups of employees meet regularly with managers to review problems. Listening to those who are doing the work and in contact with consumers and suppliers may be good for morale, even if nothing is done. On the other hand, if employees or consumers don't see some tangible evidence of the upward flow of communication, they will lose interest and may use the meetings for personal or political benefit.

The dynamics of a public often will give you a clue to possible interactions and suggest shortcuts for effective communication. For example, charged with selling candy in the local YMCA's fund raising drive, a boy debated whether to hand out a mimeographed sheet furnished by the YMCA that described the candy sale and had his name and phone number, to ask his school principal to include the Y message in the morning announcements read over the public address system or to go to each classroom and make the appeal personally. He decided on the latter, reasoning that the younger children could not and the older ones would not read the printed sheet and that the students seldom paid much attention to PA announcements, but that everyone welcomed an interruption in the classroom and probably not only would pay attention but also would buy some candy to prolong the interruption.

A different set of dynamics would go into a corporation's marketing plan for the introduction of a new product. For example, the soft drink Dr Pepper, made and sold mostly in the South and Southwest, was going to be offered for the first time in New York. Trying to make an impact in that market can be costly, but the company did it economically and effectively. How? By bypassing the general public and instead staging an all-day meeting for new distributors, supplying them

---

[18] *Wall Street Journal*, March 26, 1974, p. 1. Reprinted with permission of the *Wall Street Journal*, © Dow Jones Company, Inc., 1974.

with useful promotional ideas and materials. This logical solution was the result of considering the dynamics of the various publics and the possibilities of a variety of programs. Discovering the dynamics of publics means interpreting their behaviors.

Interpreting the Behavior of Publics James E. Grunig, PR professor at the University of Maryland, says likenesses between and among publics may depend entirely on situations. Any examination of publics, Grunig says, should consider first a grouping by the nature of that public's communication behavior and then a grouping by the similarity of that public's situational perception and behavior—or how people look at certain situations and how they behave in them. For example, an ordinarily outgoing person who talks with ease may be silent and reserved in particular situations. Grunig says we must take into consideration that people *control* their behavior. He urges us to group publics in these two ways to help us predict the attitudes people will assume in certain specific situations; and he offers us a way to discover what is likely to be going on in the situations.

Grunig tells us to look for communications behaviors of different types from information seekers and information processors.[19] An information seeker is someone interested enough in the problem or situation to want to know more about it. An information processor is aware of the communication and may be touched by the message but is not actively seeking such information. For example, the professor in your class announces that Friday is the last day to add and drop classes. If you are interested in adding a class or dropping one, you will try to find out more information, such as how to do that on or before Friday. You are an information seeker. However, if you do not "need" the information, you will process it but not seek for more. So if your roommate says, "My schedule is all messed up; I wonder when the deadline is for changing," you may say, "Well, it's Friday, but that's all I know."

Problem recognition, which the roommate has, is one of the communication situations Grunig explains. He says problem recognition increases the probability that a person will communicate about a situation. Communication is reduced, though, if a person thinks limitations retrict his or her behavior. Grunig calls that *constraint recognition*. These two concepts combine to make four types of perceived situations: problem-facing behavior (high problem recognition, low constraint recognition); constrained behavior (high problem recognition, high constraint recognition); routine behavior (low problem recognition, low constraint recognition); and fatalistic behavior (low problem recognition, high constraint recognition). Now add another variable, *referent criterion*. A referent criterion is a guide or rule by which a person measures a new situation in terms of an old experience. If a person is confronted with a new situation, an old criterion is employed to handle it. If the old criterion doesn't work this time, the person develops a new criterion to guide behavior in the new setting, and the referent criterion applies to that person's communication behavior in this situation too. Grunig has found that when a person is motivated to communicate about a situation, he or she is also

---

[19]James E. Grunig, "An Assessment of Economic Education Programs for Journalism Students," paper presented to the Public Relations Division, Association for Education in Journalism Annual Convention, Houston, Texas, August 5, 1979. Used by permission.

motivated to develop a solution for the situation—an attitude. Therefore, why a person communicates or why one does not in a situation can be explained by these three variables: problem recognition, constraint behavior and referent criterion.

A fourth variable—perceived level of involvement—tells whether the person will be an information seeker or an information processor. A person who is involved in a situation seeks information, but only processes it if not involved. Grunig's theory now produces sixteen types of communication behavior (four combinations of problem recognition and constraint recognition subdivided by presence or absence of a referent criterion and the level of involvement). With this variable added, probabilities can be used to decide whether either information seeking or information processing by a public is likely to be worth the investment of preparing information (brochure, videotape, film) for that group.

An example would be a new admissions policy that would affect students transferring from two-year colleges. Many of these students may not be considering going on to a four-year institution, and others might if they thought they could be admitted. A nonrestrictive policy would need to be communicated to this latter group to show them how to qualify for admission—how to overcome obstacles. They are a very cost-effective group as are the active publics who are interested in what to do and what is going on. However, money is wasted on those students who are not very interested in a college education, who think admission is impossible, and who really want to learn a skill.

Setting Objectives

One of the reasons for the success of the Dr Pepper plan described earlier was that objectives had been clearly defined. You have to decide with each effort, very specifically, what you want to accomplish—that is, what the end result should be. Once you know where you are going, it becomes a lot easier to know when you get there. You can design and implement research to measure a specific goal set as a measure of the success of a program and monitor progress along the way. PR has often hidden behind a cloak of imponderable variables that would preclude any evaluation of its impact. Smart PR managers facing budget cuts, however, have found a way to evaluate their programs to save them; the way is by setting an objective, a goal, that has measurable checkpoints along the way.

Considering Possibilities

Any time you are considering a plan, you should examine all possibilities of what can go wrong, as well as right. Simply discussing these possibilities can often prevent a poor plan from getting beyond the talking point. Few practitioners are willing to share "wild ideas" that were scrapped in the planning stages, but often something occurs that makes those with public relations awareness wonder if the plan had ever been put to this "possibilities test."

Such is the case of the nerve gas story. As the result of a reporter's initiative, a story broke that the government had not intended to get out. As with most coverups that refuse to stay covered, this one got wide dissemination. Front-page headlines told the nation—with heavy play in the local communities involved—that the government was moving by train nerve gas it had decided to destroy. One wonders if anyone ever asked, "What if someone finds out and makes this move public?" Surely if someone had, a more careful program would have been worked out.

In another case a university discovered that it would have to increase room rents. Except for the administration and the school's business office, no one knew of the plan—until housing contracts were sent to students who had indicated they planned to return the following year. The shock and resentment caused many students to cancel contracts and move off campus, and other students' bitter attitudes toward the institution were increased. Again, didn't anyone ask, "What will be the reaction when these contracts are received?"

Examining the possibilities of any plan often reveals that unknown areas exist. You must then decide whether additional research is needed. Is the missing information critical enough to be worth the cost? Usually it is. This is particularly true when a campaign is being developed. Although existing research in each area—the situation, the publics and the media—may have been applied, pretesting is essential. Secondary research—materials and information from other sources—is important, but each situation is unique and may merit its own testing before an entire campaign is launched. Any time you receive in the mail one bar of soap of a brand you have never seen before, the accompanying information will probably reveal you are in a "test market." Sometimes an ad will appear in one split run of a magazine as a test. Or a person may interview you and show you several different ads to get your reaction. All such pretests are worth the expense if they prevent an expensive error, indicate an unanticipated response or suggest a different approach.

Monitoring

It is also important to arrange for feedback after a plan has been set in operation. Careful planning may have preceded a campaign, but that does not ensure success. Monitoring during the campaign can reveal problem areas before they become crises. (Monitoring a PR operation is a specific check on results—measurement, as opposed to general monitoring of the climate of public opinion, which goes on in issue management.)

Monitoring can be as simple as checking a broadcast to be sure advertising is running in the time slots purchased or reading a magazine to be sure an ad really did get in. Or it may be as difficult as finding out whether a consumer even noticed a new package. The result of monitoring is illustrated by a resort area's hurried decision to buy radio time after discovering that a magazine story counted on to increase Labor Day crowds would, in fact, hit the newsstands the day after the holiday instead of two weeks before. Monitoring may also result in a hurried call to a broadcast station to stop commercials for a sale because someone failed to notice the termination date on the commercial and all sale merchandise has been sold.

The importance of keeping up with what is going on was not lost on one politician's campaign manager. He had hired youngsters one Friday morning to set up stake signs. The following Monday he could find no signs in place. He arrived at the office ready to kill a bunch of kids, but instead had to answer a call from city officials who informed him that his signs had been removed because all 500 had been placed in the easement area just behind the curb. That was city property; political signs could not be displayed. How had city officials known? The opponent was "monitoring," of course.

Ketchum Public Relations has developed a tracking model, a computer-based measurement system to formally monitor the use of publicity. The first stage is to program the objectives, strategies and results of a campaign. The model is programmed with demographics of the top 120 markets with a formula that shows how much more or less valuable a quarter page of newspaper space is versus three minutes of radio, or a full page in a national magazine versus five minutes on network TV or local TV. When a campaign's results are fed into the model, the report shows in terms of the programmed goals how well publicity reached the target audience (the number of exposures) and how effective the messages were (the quality of the message).[20]

The Concentric Effect

Using research, then, helps the PR practitioner anticipate problems, evaluate ongoing programs, pretest the effectiveness of certain tools, profile a public and its attitudes, accumulate information about effective use of media and evaluate completed programs and campaigns.

What results is a circle of activity, a concentric effect, as follows:

1. Some research is begun either as routine record keeping or specifically to gather facts for planning purposes.

2. After the PR objective is determined, facts are used to formulate a hypothesis, to test the hypothesis and to make revisions if it does not seem to work.

3. Once the PR objective is developed, additional fact finding may be required to determine what needs to be known about the situations, the publics or the media to be used. Here we consider how to best present the PR objective to a particular public. We must evaluate the image the public holds and determine whether to keep the present identity or modify it. We must also arrive at methods of reaching the audience and decide what type of message will be most effective—publicity, speech, meeting, display or advertising. In addition, we need to consider the best timing for activities and messages.

4. Then, to be sure the plan is working properly, we monitor.

5. Afterward, an evaluation should be conducted to see what went according to plan, what deviated and why. An evaluation can help clarify a public's profile or suggest the greater use of a particular medium, and it may be used as resource information in the development of future plans. Thus a continuing pattern of research needs to be developed for each public relations situation. The greater the continuity of any research project, the greater its potential effectiveness.

---

[20] "Computer Measuring System for Publicity Compares Exposure in Various Media," *pr reporter*, February 21, 1983, p. 2.

The first question in initiating survey research is whether you should commission an outside agency or do it with your own internal staff. The advantage of an internal staff is that it knows your organization and channels of communication and will have its trust and access. An external research agency must often battle hostility and suspicion and can have a rough time if the internal PR staff has not smoothed the way.

The negative side of the internally handled research is often misinterpreted as a plus—the price tag. Well-done survey research takes an enormous amount of time and labor, so it probably is less often handled by internal staff than by external staff. Internally done research can be even more costly. If the staff is thereby tied up and becomes too busy to handle day-to-day PR business, snafus may result and things may not get done. Also, the external team may have the advantage of impartiality. Facts revealed by research may not be exactly what management would like to hear. An internal staff may have a tendency to soften disclosures or even nullify results in an instinctive self-defense effort to protect its own budget or paychecks.

A public relations practitioner should know when to call in outside research and also know enough to be able to recommend several agencies. This gives management a choice and can result in a better decision. The PR practitioner should also help management set the research objective and design the project. This is important because the PR practitioner will have to draw conclusions from the results and perhaps help in planning programs to answer the needs the research reveals. Inaccurate conclusions can nullify an entire research project.

If costs prove prohibitive or if management decides for other reasons that the research should be done internally, the PR director must analyze the human and physical resources. Time and personnel must be made available; talent must be evaluated. The qualifications of the staff to handle the particular research problem must be considered. Mechanical matters such as printing questionnaires and reserving computer time must be taken care of. Above all, project costs must be carefully worked out. Research paid for out of the public relations department's budget may jeopardize other programs. Priorities must be established *before* the project is undertaken.

Planning the Survey

After calculating the resources, the practitioner must focus on the objectives, determining what information is wanted from the research. This, in turn, will indicate the design of the study. A timetable should be worked out allowing for pretesting, collection and interpretation of data.

It should be decided early who will interpret the research results and prepare the report for management and other important publics. For instance, a utility company that was battling a unionization attempt ordered an employee-attitude study. The company made the questionnaire results available to employees as soon as the study was completed, and this policy contributed a great deal to management's success in the contest. In contrast, a private university that had worked for two years to get a faculty and administration evaluation program off the ground made it through the trial run and a first attempt, but had the whole program scratched by the faculty senate, whose members protested because they had not yet been shown the results of the first student evaluation of faculty, which had been held the year before. Although the failure to communicate results may not have been the only reason for the protest, it was a serious error by those trying to implement the program. If the utility company's employees had been interviewed extensively about the company but had been unable to review the results, it is not difficult to imagine that the union, rather than the company, might have been successful. Plan your research to fit into a timetable so you can implement action the research might suggest.

Steps in Research

The steps in an experimental research process (which appear in most standard research books) are basically as follows:

1. State the problem.
2. Select a manageable portion that can be measured.
3. Establish definitions to be used in the measurement.
4. Conduct a search in published literature for studies similar in subject or research approach.
5. Develop a hypothesis.[21]
6. Design the experiments.[22] Included here is defining the universe or broad group you want to study, then choosing a sampling method and a sample.
7. Obtain the data.
8. Analyze the data.
9. Interpret the data to make inferences and generalizations.
10. Communicate the results.

Stating the problem with precision certainly aids in the second step: deciding which part of the problem most needs study or which part lends itself to testing that would cast light into other dark corners. Many inexperienced practitioners design unwieldy research projects.

A realistic researcher usually designs a simple project that keeps the significance of the research in proper perspective. That requires isolating a testable por-

---

[21] For exploratory or descriptive research, which is often done in public relations, you develop, instead of a hypothesis, a simple statement of what you want to find out and do so as specifically as possible.

[22] In designing the experiment, you will want to pretest the instrument since you will be dealing with respondents' interpretations of your questions. You need to discover any misconceptions that might skew results.

tion of the problem and knowing specifically what is being sought. It is important to spell out what you want to know. Don't set a goal like "Find out how to establish effective communications with employees" when what you really want to know is whether they would like to have an employee publication; if that is the question, find out what kind of publication they want, how often it should be published and what subjects should be covered. By establishing definitions, you also set parameters for your research. If you want to find out what people think about the Center for Battered Women, what do you mean by "people"? Social workers? Battered women? The people in the city or county or just the neighborhood in which it is located? The *purpose* of your study is the determining factor. If you want to try to get municipal funding, how can you best *show* with your research that the center deserves funds? Your need, tied to your purpose, is what affects a definition of a research project and a definition of the universe, or set, containing all the elements of the problem.

A literature search simply means seeing if someone has already done the work for you. Has someone conducted research you can appropriate, apply or use as a model? Answering this question usually requires searching through journals of research in the social sciences, communications and business. Buried deep in one or more may be precisely the information that offers a unique insight into your research approach.

As an example of how *not* to go about doing a survey, consider the case of the student who managed a child-care center established in a local shopping center for the benefit of shopping parents. The center was about to go broke after six months when he told a class about the situation. Some of his classmates who were young parents asked, "What made you think parents would want to park their kids anywhere while they shopped? Why did you think they wouldn't take them along? How much is it? Doesn't that add to the cost of the shopping trip?" He responded that a survey had been taken that *proved* the advisability of opening the care center. Actually, he said, the owners had felt intuitively that the center was needed, but the only space available had been on the subterranean mall level. Hence they had conducted the survey primarily to learn whether parents would object to, in effect, "leaving the kids underground" while they shopped. The survey had consisted of ten questions, such as "Do you often bring your children with you when you shop? If not, where do you leave them? Would you use a child-care facility here at the shopping center if one were available? How much would you be willing to pay by the hour for such a service?" Shoppers were asked about leaving the children on the lower level. Women college students, chosen for their good looks because it was assumed shoppers would talk to them more easily, had been hired to administer the questionnaire. They placed themselves at high-traffic points on the mall and stopped only shoppers with children. The survey had been conducted the two Saturdays before Christmas. "No wonder you got a favorable response," one older student replied. "About that time of year I'd be willing to hang my kids from trees!" Asked how the results had been tabulated, the manager said each woman just totaled her pages, wrote down what she considered important responses and turned in the results. In short, the amateur research and the uncritical acceptance of it were at the root of the problem, and the enterprise folded shortly thereafter.

POINTS TO REMEMBER

- Systematic record keeping is the first step in research. Records must be kept in easily retrievable form; the two principal storage methods are computers and libraries.

- Maintain your own resource library with general resource books, communication and public relations resource books and books on the field in which you are practicing public relations.

- Investigation of the PR audience is a primary research task; a statistical profile is useful here.

- Much research already has been done and is readily available in public and specialized libraries. Some sources are the social sciences, government and the media.

- Survey research is the primary research tool to describe publics. Survey research may yield information about the demographics (statistics about people's social and economic status) and psychographics (personality traits) of publics.

- Determining what publics are likely to be concerned about is called issue forecasting, and there are nine principal techniques used: trend extrapolation, trend impact analysis, scanning, monitoring, the DELPHI technique, cross-impact analysis, computer simulations, scenario writing and technology assessment.

- Discovering the dynamics of publics by interpreting their behavior is another research task.

- Research planning involves gathering information, finding out about publics, setting objectives, considering possibilities, monitoring so you can fine-tune a plan and evaluating the results.

- The PR practitioner should be able to determine whether a company should do its own research or commission an outside agency.

- The ten steps in research are state the problem, select a manageable portion to measure, define the measurement, search the literature, develop a hypothesis, design experiments, get the data, analyze it, interpret it and communicate the results.

THINGS TO DO

1. Select a topic, such as the differences between public relations and marketing, and go to your school library's electronic search center. Ask for a search of that topic—or any other related to the public relations field. What data bank was used in the search? What sources were used in the search, such as trade or scholarly journals, magazines or newspapers? What questions did the search leave unanswered for you? How would you go about getting those answers?

2. Evaluate a locally conducted survey—one conducted on campus or one handled by a local advertiser or by the local media. To do the job right, find out the design of the research, who did it, what research was done and who interpreted it. Examine particularly the questionnaire used. Are the questions clear, unbiased? Do the results of the survey reinforce or contradict assumptions you would have made or

opinions you held? Do you think the research is valid? Support either a negative or positive answer.

3. Find five news stories using research data. Determine, in each case, whether the significance of the data is pointed out, whether the conclusions drawn are supported by the data, and whether the data themselves seem logical and possible. Example: A news story about the reading ability of elementary school age children reported that one school's students were "in the 99th percentile of the national average." What does that mean? Is it a valid statement?

4. Take the same five news stories and see if the research study fulfills the seven requirements of the National Council on Public Polls found on page 94.

SELECTED READINGS

Earl Babbie, *The Practice of Social Research*, 3rd ed. (Belmont, Calif.: Wadsworth, 1983). This is *the* book for social science research and you should be familiar with it.

Jacques Barzun and Henry F. Graff, *The Modern Researcher*, 3rd ed. (New York: Harcourt Brace Jovanovich, 1977). Basic book for anyone in the business of collecting facts to write; there is a fascinating chapter on verification, valuable advice on handling ideas in written communication and a discussion of pattern, bias and the reasoning of historical systems.

H. M. Blalock, Jr., *Conceptualization and Measurement in the Social Sciences* (Beverly Hills, Calif.: Sage, 1982). Stresses attention to theoretical assumptions to ensure the correct use of statistical techniques.

Harper W. Boyd, Jr., and Sidney J. Levy, *Promotion: A Behavior View* (Englewood Cliffs, N.J.: Prentice-Hall, 1967). Paperback.

Edward W. Cundiff and Richard R. Still, *Basic Marketing* (Englewood Cliffs, N.J.: Prentice-Hall, 1971).

Lana M. Daniells, comp., *Note on Sources of External Marketing Data* (Boston: Harvard Business Service, 1980). A review of existing research.

Paul E. Green and Donald S. Tull, *Research for Marketing Decisions*, 4th ed. (Englewood Cliffs, N.J.: Prentice-Hall, 1978).

Eugene J. Kelley, *Marketing Planning and Competitive Strategy* (Englewood Cliffs, N.J.: Prentice-Hall, 1972). Paperback.

Philip Kotler, *Marketing Management*, 4th ed. (Englewood Cliffs, N.J.: Prentice-Hall, 1980).

John D. Leckenby and Nugent Wedding, *Advertising Management* (Columbus, Ohio: Grid, 1982).

David J. Luck and O. C. Ferrell, *Marketing Strategy and Plans* (Englewood Cliffs, N.J.: Prentice-Hall, 1979).

Philip Meyer, *Precision Journalism: A Reporter's Introduction to Social Science Methods*, 2nd ed. (Bloomington: Indiana University Press, 1979). Easy-to-read guide to simple game theory, use of statistics for interpreting data and testing hypotheses, analysis of polls and surveys; includes a how-to-do-it for the survey taker and user.

National Association of Broadcasters, *A Broadcast Research Primer* (Washington, D.C.: National Association of Broadcasters, 1971). Excellent reference for those trying to use broadcast lessons effectively as well as those charged with station promotion.

Jeffrey L. Pope, *Practical Marketing Research* (New York: AMACOM, 1981). A good application guide.

R. F. Roth, *International Marketing Communications* (Chicago: Crane Books, 1982). The international aspect of this field is increasing in importance.

William L. Rivers, *Finding Facts: Interviewing, Observing, Using Reference Sources* (Englewood Cliffs, N.J.: Prentice-Hall, 1975). Prevents a lot of wasted effort by telling its readers what type of information is available from a particular source; also evaluates the source. Offers guides to the effective use of language in all forms of writing.

———. *Writing: Craft and Art* (Englewood Cliffs, N.J.: Prentice-Hall, 1975). Tells how to combine facts in a readable way.

Frederick E. Webster, Jr., and Yoram Wind, *Organizational Buying Behavior* (Englewood Cliffs, N.J.: Prentice-Hall, 1972). Paperback.

Frederick E. Webster, Jr., *Social Aspects of Marketing* (Englewood Cliffs, N.J.: Prentice-Hall, 1974). Paperback.

CHAPTER 5

Common Methods of Research

Good research and management's openness to communication, working in tandem, generate a favorable climate for public relations.

Peter Finn, Chairman, Research & Forecasts, Inc., New York

Any superimposing of preconceived ideas which forces patterns upon people's reports loses the richness, the uniqueness, the flavor, or the authenticity of what they are trying to say about themselves. What is needed is information which transmits reliably, in people's own terms, what they are feeling.

Hadley Cantril, social psychologist

Public relations research focuses on finding the answers to these questions: Who is our audience? What is our action/message? What channels of communication reach our audiences? What is the reaction to our efforts? What should we do to keep in touch? With every public relations activity we should consider: How is this activity going to be understood by everyone whom we try to inform or persuade? What are they going to say or do as a result of our efforts? What is their feeling about us (that is, the client—individual or institution) and what we are doing and saying? Research is used for exploration, description, explanation and control.

PR's need for accountability—to prove the value of PR activities—had a great deal to do with the boost PR research got in the eighties.

Research in public relations isn't new, just the focus, says James B. Strenski, chairman of Public Communications, Inc., Chicago.[1] Strenski cites five areas of common PR research that have taken on a somewhat different emphasis in recent years:

1. *Opinion audits* are made in three areas—social, economic and political. Greater attention has been paid to detail, to the nuances of these opinion studies and to their reliability as predictors or as evidence.

2. *Communications audits* are used to determine the attitudes of key publics toward existing communications programs and to form a benchmark for measurement. An initial study, before any PR intervention, shows what is oc-

---

[1] James B. Strenski, "New Concerns for Public Relations Measurement," *Public Relations Journal*, 37 (May 1981), pp. 16–17.

curring. When a PR plan is implemented, measuring it during the activity and afterward against the benchmark, or starting place, makes it possible to talk about effects with some assurance.

3. *Peer perception studies* are often done to find out how a company or institution stacks up alongside its competition against key predetermined criteria. Other similar institutions are asked to name the best or worst of something. For example, a recent study by *U.S. News & World Report*, which used 1,308 four-year college and university presidents to rank the best schools in the country, resulted in a response of slightly more than 50 percent who put Stanford first, Harvard second, Yale third, Princeton fourth and the University of California at Berkeley fifth.[2]

4. *Benchmark communications studies* of publicity clippings and electronic exposure analyzed by message, medium, audience and frequency give a value equivalency comparison. For example, the number of times a release is used may not be as meaningful as the media that used it. Strenski says such studies can relate the quality as well as quantity of the exposure to the cost of the particular PR method.

5. *Environmental monitoring* in the social, political and cultural areas is already a reality, but evaluating message content about *thought trends* has begun to be an accepted practice. Ideas have become an area for observation as well as practices. For example, to determine if students were considering staying in school longer, college freshmen were recently asked if they intended to get a graduate degree.

Strenski says communication measurement is moving from an inexact to an exact science. The change is in response to a need. "Management," Strenski says, "wants to know the return on its public relations investment because increasing sums of money are being spent on communications —with more expenditures in the offing."

We begin our research with the activities discussed in the preceding chapter: looking at records, doing some basic fact finding and examining what is already known through existing research. From there we initiate research to fill in the blanks. One research firm president said public relations is accomplished in four steps: research, analysis, communication and evaluation.

When the word *research* is mentioned, PR people immediately think of two kinds: internal and external. The merit of external and internal research was pointed out by Burson-Marsteller public relations agency in one of its newsletters: "The great value of opinion research and attitude audits is that they keep companies from becoming egocentric: that is, from thinking in terms of what they want to say instead of what their publics want to hear. Listening, of course, shouldn't be limited to the mass audience; it is equally important to listen to all segments of the public, especially employees. . . . Employees should be a corporation's most sympathetic supporters, but often they aren't. The reason is that management tends to ignore what employees want to know."[3]

---

[2] "Stanford on Top," *Parade*, February 5, 1984, p. 6.

[3] "Is Anybody Listening?" *Burson-Marsteller Report*, no. 49 (New York: Burson-Marsteller Public Relations, August 1978).

INTERNAL AND
EXTERNAL RESEARCH

Internal research is conducted within an organization. It may include conferences with employees involved in a particular problem, studies of the organization records, reviews of employee suggestions and surveys of their opinions. Some internal research considers external opinion: ideas of opinion leaders that affect the organization's management; incoming mail; reports from field agents or sales personnel; press clippings and monitoring reports of broadcast media; opinion polls, elections and legislative voting patterns or similar reflections of public opinion that may be shared by internal audiences; and the work of advisory committees or panels of people experienced in a particular field. The danger in much internal research, which is often done informally, is that it is seldom representative and almost always lacks objectivity.

External research, almost always formal, may deal with public opinion[4]—that is, the opinions of large groups of the public, such as a nation, which are usually described demographically—and it always deals with specific target audiences outside the organization that are of particular significance to it. For example, in the airport construction situation mentioned in explaining the role of public affairs (see Chapter 1, pages 10–11) one of the problems was getting the individual municipalities to vote the bond issue providing funds for construction. Dallas was a particular challenge because it already had an airport on its doorstep and voters were not enthusiastic about spending $175 million to drive 45 minutes to a new one. The research company employed (MARC) was hired to find out the bond issue's probabilities for success. MARC broke the city into ten areas to find out which of the ten issues in the bond program were in trouble in each of the areas. Then town meetings were held in these areas to emphasize the problem issues. A campaign, "Dallas at the Crossroads," emerged. These efforts were successful. Now travelers through the Southwest are likely to go through Dallas/Fort Worth Airport, billed as the second largest in the world.

To determine what an external public thinks, since it usually involves a large number of people, we must question a sample of it. Taking a sample is necessary because it is impossible to truly measure an entire population unless it is by its nature extremely small (for instance, all blonde, blue-eyed, left-handed, female nineteen-year-old tennis players who have won their last forty matches). The sample need not be large. Large samples cost too much, and moreover they really do not make much difference once a certain size is reached. With very small sample sizes, predictability increases rather dramatically at first, but once the sample reaches a certain size other elements enter, such as error. So a sample of 1,000 is not likely to be much better than a sample of 500, although a sample of 100 is considerably more reliable than one of 50. That is why, in a country of more than 211 million, quite reliable national estimates are made based on samples of

---

[4]Public opinion can be considered collective thought, that is, the ideas of certain designated groups of people. Definitions of public opinion refer to its being an aggregate or mass of individual views, attitudes or beliefs about a particular topic as expressed by a significant proportion of a community.

only 1,500 to 3,000 people. Researchers do this work with a margin of allowable error. The size of the sample depends upon how much error can be tolerated in the results—how close a call you need to make.[5]

PROBABILITY

Sampling is based on probability. The researcher is gambling on how well a sample represents a population. But the gamble is not wild. Those selected for a sample are chosen *randomly*, and a random sample is usually free of bias or predictability of outcome. The use of a mechanical method eliminates any bias the researcher might have or any peculiar homogeneity in a group or segment of a group selected for study. (*Bias* is the tendency of an estimate to deviate from a true value, for reasons such as nonrandom sampling.) In a random sample each element of a population has an equal or known "chance" of being selected for study. For example, students in a mass communications class were subjects for a survey on media use. To select a random sample from the class, every *other* student seated in the classroom was given a survey to complete. Since seating was selective, not assigned, every student had an equal opportunity to be selected for the sample. This is random selection.

With any large number of chance events, it becomes possible to make predictions based on the relative frequency of the occurrence of the events in the observations. Using such observations as "experience," for instance, it is possible to make some educated guesses. This is the application of rules of probability. Because every other student in the classroom was chosen, half of the students completed the questionnaire; thus, each student had a 50–50 chance of being selected. This is the probability that any given student would be chosen.

Two types of errors can occur in probability sampling: sampling errors and nonsampling errors. *Sampling errors* can occur if a sample is too small for the audience or population being sampled or if the selection is not random enough. (Sampling errors are the chance difference of a statistic from the corresponding population constant for which it is a measure.) *Nonsampling errors* are simply mistakes made by the research team in recording or calculating data or even in gathering data. Nonsampling errors are reduced if there are fewer data to record and calculate—another argument for having a small sample size.

As researcher W. Edward Deming observes, a survey's usefulness and reliability "may actually be enhanced by cutting down on the size of sample and using the money so saved to reduce the nonsampling errors,"[6] such as tracing

---

[5]For an easy-to-follow discussion of the sampling process, see Earl Babbie, *The Practice of Social Research*, pp. 148–158, which includes the standard formula for choosing a sample size

$$S = \sqrt{\frac{P \times Q}{n}}$$

where S = the standard error of deviation from the mean,
P and Q are the population parameters ($P = 1 - Q$ and $Q = 1 - P$) and
n = the number of cases in each sample.
[6]W. Edward Deming, *Sample Design in Business Research* (New York: John Wiley, 1960), p. 61.

wrong and missing information. (*Reliability* is the extent to which a test always yields the same results. *Validity* is how well the evidence explains what is occurring—how meaningful the empirical measures are to the situation or concept. It is the use of intercorrelated items to form scale.) These savings, he points out, might mean more time and money being available for constructing the questionnaire, for hiring fewer but better interviewers, for providing better training and supervision in the field and for making more recalls on people not previously at home.

There are three major types of nonprobability or nonrandom sampling: accidental, purposive and quota. A reporter who stands outside the campus cafeteria and asks people leaving what they think of the food is getting an *accidental* sample; it is accidental because you never know who will come out (suppose you catch all the members of the football team, and they all liked the ground round?). *Purposive* samples are exemplified by the reporter interviewing teachers and students in the food and nutrition department about the quality of food in the college cafeteria. (They will have different ideas about food from those in, say, engineering.) *Quota* samples are shown by the reporter designing a sample that closely resembles the school's population: the proper proportion of freshmen, transfer students, sophomores, juniors, seniors, staff, faculty. The sample would be improved if it were already known what percentage of these different groups ate regularly in the cafeteria. Each group should be proportionately represented.

The concept of stratified sampling is similar to quota sampling. Both recreate the population in microcosm, and both types have population representation. However, the selection process is different. In stratified measurements, selection is random but the overall population has been divided into categories or strata. Selection is a matter of probability; in quota sampling, the interviewer may select.

TYPES OF INFORMATION ABOUT AUDIENCES

Quota sampling recreates a small, representative unit of the audience being studied, based on a knowledge of the demographics of that audience. Some of the research most valuable to persuaders goes beyond telling who an audience is; it tells who the audience thinks it is, or better still, who it wants to be. *Who* makes up an audience—that is, information about age, sex, level of education, geographic location, occupation and such—is called the *demographics*[7] of that audience. But demographics alone isn't sufficient. A group of individuals, even a large one, may fall into one category where all of the demographic data matches—however, they may not all think alike. And a key to how people are likely to respond often lies in their value systems. Getting at these—what goes on inside an audience's head—is important to the field of *psychographic*[8] research.

A demographer is a social scientist who keeps an ongoing record of the size and characteristics of human populations and how they change—their births, deaths, longevity, migrations and such. Demographic statistics are important because of the dollars-and-cents consequences of these changes. Demographics is important to those trying to develop educational systems to meet future needs, to those in utilities who furnish equipment and services to changing populations and to many others.

Psychographics is a specialty of psychologists employed by polling and attitudinal research firms to help them figure out what is going on in the minds of people represented by the demographics.

Advertisers have been interested in psychographics for a long time because the science is part of marketing strategy often referred to as "positioning."[9] For example, many commercial products are chemically the same—it's how they are presented that makes the difference. When the antiperspirant Dry Idea was first brought out, its manufacturer, Gillette, backed the introduction with more advertising and promotion than any other product in its seventy-seven-year history, an $18 million outlay, and all of it dealing with the *appeal* of the product. The company conceded to a *Wall Street Journal* reporter that Dry Idea won't stop perspiration any better than at least five other products on the market, but it was designed to "feel better" to the user. The market for roll-on deodorants was determined to be women, and the specific target group was women twenty to forty-five years old who were to be made to feel good about the product—that "it was a nice thing to use." Women dressing for work in a hurry with no time to wait for the wet deodorant to dry were the psychographic group. As the *Wall Street Journal* said: "It is an industry in which what a so-called 'emotional' product does is apt to be less important than what the public can be convinced it does. And it is a business in which huge sums are spent to track, measure and gratify the consumer's whims and yearnings."[10]

Psychographics can be just as important to internal research. While doing research into what employees want to know from administrators, a New York-based

---

[7]Demography is the science of vital statistics. An important factor is the tolerable margin of error—how wrong can you be 5%, 10%, 20%?

[8]Psychographs are charts outlining the relative strength of fundamental personality traits in an individual.

[9]PR clients, like products, can be "positioned," whether they are individuals or institutions (see Chapter 9). Images are important to positioning, which means finding an emotional appeal that will segment the market.

[10]Neil Ulman, "Seating It Out; Time, Risk, Ingenuity All Go into Launching New Personal Product," *Wall Street Journal*, November 12, 1978, p. 1.

firm discovered how value systems affect employee attitudes and expectations. The following study results come from psychologist Steven Zimney, a vice president of the Yankelovich, Skelly and White polling and attitudinal research firm. The study sample came from among junior executives in the leadership pool of a large American corporation. The research firm found at least five, and possibly six, classes of executives with fundamentally different values, although one group predominated among these employees. Executives who were primarily oriented toward their families made up 34 percent of the total. Career advancement ranked highest with the next largest group. Making money was foremost with a third group, and for a fourth it was being able to balance work with time off the job for pleasure, hobbies, recreation. The fifth group ranked developing personal skills on the job as most important. A possible sixth group put the highest value on getting power.[11]

COMMON METHODS OF GATHERING DATA

When it comes to gathering data, journalists and researchers have a lot in common. Philip Meyer, author of *Precision Journalism*, observed that "the role of the fire-engine researcher may come naturally and readily to journalists. The ground rules are no different from those on which we've always operated: find the facts, tell what they mean, and do it without wasting time."[12] The journalist is trained in getting information from two principal sources: secondary (public records, media files, libraries) and primary (mainly by interviewing people). Sound interviewing techniques are fundamental. The journalist learns to phrase questions neutrally, to avoid "leading" questions or putting words in the mouth of the respondent. A good journalist also learns how to organize questions so they are logically sequential, with the easiest always offered first. The kind of rapport a journalist becomes skilled at developing with interview subjects is an important part of the technique for getting answers from people who are under no obligation to give them. Also, a journalist learns how to pin down an evasive respondent to get at something only suggested or implied.

The journalist also learns to listen and observe. Both are important to the researcher. A few journalists are so skillful they can recall entire conversations, although most rely on recorders, audio and video. These methods, the records journalists use (called archives) and observations are what social scientists classify as unobtrusive measures.[13]

The tools of reporting are also the tools of research. Furthermore, the re-

[11] Noel L. Griese, "Feedback: the Vital Link," *Public Relations Journal*, 33, no. 12 (December 1977), pp. 12–14.

[12] Philip Meyer, *Precision Journalism* (Bloomington: Indiana University Press, 1973), p. 15. Copyright © 1973 by Indiana University Press; reprinted by permission of the publisher.

[13] Eugene J. Webb, Donald T. Campbell, Richard D. Schwartz and Lee Sechrest, *Unobtrusive Measures, Nonreactive Research in the Social Sciences* (Chicago: Rand McNally, 1966), p. 3.

searcher, like the journalist, must try to make sense out of all the information gleaned; must be sensitive to trends, contradictions and conflicts; and must be able to communicate efficiently and effectively what has been discovered through the research—usually under deadline pressure. Only the form the journalist uses is different.

The most familiar forms of data gathering for researchers are cross-section surveys, survey panels, in-depth interviews, focus group interviews, content analyses, questionnaires and the DELPHI process. The situation in which one or the other might be used depends upon which might offer the best solution to the problem. (See 5.1 for an outline of steps in research.)

Cross-section Surveys

There are three generally used types of cross-section surveys: quota samples, probability samples and area samples.

In a *quota sample*, a population is analyzed by its known characteristics, such as age, sex, residence, occupation and income level. A sample selection is made by quota in the same proportion as these characteristics exist in the whole population.

In a *probability sample*, people are chosen at random, ordinarily by using a random number table or by a mechanical formula such as every nth name on a list, a method called "systematic sampling."

In an *area sample*, geographical areas, such as cities or units of cities, are used; an area sample can be designed by using city directories as sources for housing units. Using a *cluster plan* in an area sample may reduce the time and money spent on travel, although it also somewhat reduces the randomness. (In a cluster plan areas are selected, and sample small block clusters are drawn. A random sample may then be drawn from each cluster.)

Survey Panels

Survey panels, such as consumer panels, are often used for research purposes by businesses or institutions. One unusual consumer panel employed by a toy company consists of panelists five years old and under. Once a panel is selected, the members are interviewed several times over a certain period of time. The toy manufacturers get around verbal communication problems by merely watching their consumer panel. Some research firms videotape the sessions so the client can see the results without inhibiting panelists by being there. (Using one-way glass in the viewing area doesn't fool many panelists.) Videotaping aids in analyzing the sessions too, because body language as well as words may be evaluated.

Survey panelists are usually selected on a cross-sectional basis and generally by quota, which is effective for controlled experiments. One disadvantage is that the panel, over a period of time, tends to become less representative. For example, newspaper editors have found that citizens on press councils—small panels of readers from the community—have tended to become less critical as they learned more about the problems of getting out a daily paper.

5.1 STEPS IN RESEARCH

This diagram for research planning comes from the most used reference in the field, *The Practice of Social Research* by Earl Babbie.

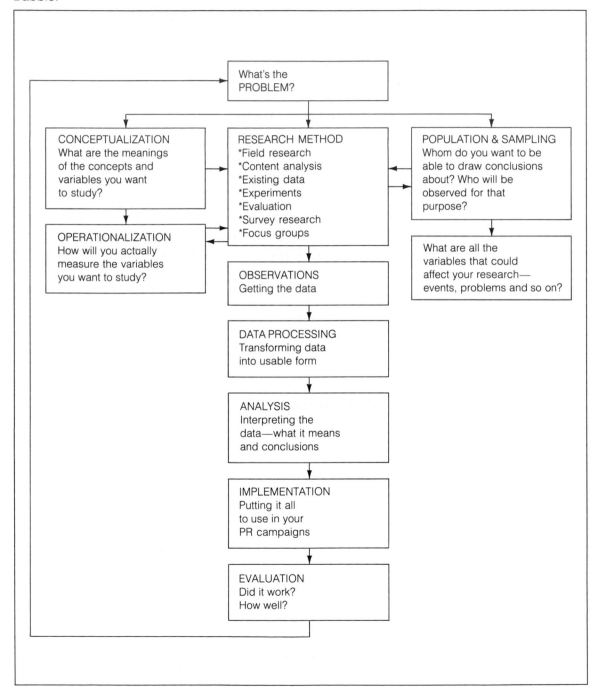

In-depth Interviews

In the in-depth interview, selected respondents are encouraged to talk freely and fully. This technique is used extensively in motivational research—the study of the emotional or subconscious reasons behind decision making. However, motivational research requires highly trained interviewers and skilled analysis.

Open questions are used with in-depth interviewing. These give the interviewer an opportunity to learn more by following up with more probing questions. For example, trying to ferret out employer bias toward hiring representatives of minority groups, some in-depth interviewers asked general questions at first and then zoomed in with such things as "But if you had two applicants absolutely equal in terms of educational background and experience, and one was a woman or a member of a minority race, or both, which would you hire?" The employers' answers could then be questioned directly, based on a particular response.

Some researchers also feel that open questions reduce error in reply since the interviewee can respond in his or her own words, rather than trying to find a category to fit his or her answer. However, errors are often made in evaluating such questions. As a consequence, most researchers—to reduce the interviewer's bias—prefer that the answers be coded in the office rather than in the field by the interviewer.

Focus Group Interviews

A hybrid of the survey panel and in-depth interview is the focus group interview. In this technique, interviewees represent different publics. In a university setting such publics might be faculty, staff, administrators, students, alumni, maybe parents and perhaps regents or trustees. Or the group may represent different types within a single public, such as a panel of alumni representing different majors and different graduating classes.

The key to the session's success is the moderator, who must be a skillful interviewer, adept at keeping the conversation moving and tactful when acting as referee or devil's advocate. Research groups often videotape these sessions too, and often use a live monitor. The monitor enables viewers—the researchers or the client—to slip notes to the moderator during breaks in the session and get additional questions on the agenda. The focus interview is often used as a prelude to development of a questionnaire.

Content Analysis

Transcripts of panel discussions or interactions, in-depth interviews and focus group interviews are often subjected to content analysis. Broadcast media transcripts and newspaper and magazine clippings also undergo content analysis. Content analysis allows for the systematic coding and classification of mass media content that relates to the client. When monitoring information specifically about the client, content analysis tells what is published or broadcast and the context in which it is presented. This provides helpful clues to the kinds of information the various publics are being exposed to (although not necessarily what they consume and believe). As a data-gathering technique, content analysis can also be used to assess what is being said about the goals set by the organization and about its specialized areas of interest, such as proposed legislation. The main difficulty with the technique is setting up a model that will give an unbiased analysis.

The classic definition of content analysis is one by Bernard Berelson who calls it a research technique for the "objective, systematic, and quantitative description of the manifest content of communication."[14] The research procedure developed by H. D. Lasswell is one of the earliest quantitative measures of communication. The procedure follows Berelson's definition. It is *objective* because categories used in the analysis are both precise and normative, with no evaluative terms (good–bad) used; *systematic* because selection is by a formal, unbiased system that does not allow for subjective collection of data; *quantitative* because the results are usually expressed in some numerical way—in percentages, ratios, frequency distributions, correlation coefficients and so on. It is *manifest* because it is a very direct sort of measure; no effort is made to figure out the intent of the person using the words, only the fact that the words were used is measured. Some, more complicated, research designs apply symbol or phrase coding to al-low for the "context" of the words used.

Questionnaires

The most familiar data-gathering device is the questionnaire. A questionnaire is often administered in face-to-face personal interviews, with the interviewer asking the questions and noting the responses on a form. However, it is also administered over the telephone or by direct mail, or it is printed either in a mass medium, like a newspaper, or in a specialized one, like an organization's own newsletter.

The telephone survey is more economical than the personal contact survey, but fewer questions can be considered because the interview may be interfering with the interviewee's activities. Too many questions shorten responses and upset respondents' tempers. Moreover, only homes with listed telephones can be reached, and up to 30 percent of the telephones in any area may have unlisted numbers. Thus a telephone survey sample is not as likely to be representative of the entire market. It loses people at both ends of the economic spectrum—those who cannot afford phones and the more affluent with unlisted numbers. One solution to this problem is to get from the telephone company a list of exchanges and the number of telephones served by each. A computer can then be programmed to draw at random four-digit numbers to be added to the prefix. This method is reliable enough to be used by national research companies.

Often a questionnaire is sent by direct mail. When this is done, the researcher can increase responses by enclosing a self-addressed, postage-paid envelope. These questionnaires can be longer than those used in telephone or personal

---

[14] "Content Analysis in Communication Research," in *Reader in Public Opinion and Communication*, 2d ed., ed. Bernard Berelson and Morris Janowitz (Glencoe, Ill.: Free Press, 1953), p. 263.

interviews, but a long, formidable-looking questionnaire will draw fewer responses. One important element in the rate of return is the respondent's interest in the subject. For general questionnaires sent to a large population, you can expect a 5 to 20 percent return. But when returns are small, it is doubtful that the respondents represent the population well. However, a 30 to 80 percent response to a carefully designed questionnaire is likely if respondents have a vested interest or some special knowledge of the subject. Many members of a professional organization, for example, may answer a long, detailed questionnaire that asks about their professional interests. Women in Communications, Inc., reported a 75 percent return on a salary questionnaire sent to all its members without a return envelope. Texas Instruments Corporation tried a special gimmick. It got almost a 60 percent response to a questionnaire sent shareholders by printing questions on the back of dividend checks.[15]

When people don't have a vested interest, money is the best way to get a response. The *Wall Street Journal* quoted an official of a New York market-research firm, Erdos & Morgan, as saying that sending a dollar bill usually guarantees at least a 50 percent response. If you don't include something, the response percentage falls to below 30. Quarters still work for shorter queries, but Montgomery Ward sends $5 for its ten-page questionnaires. *Newsweek* finds affluent readers respond better if the publication offers to give a charitable contribution in their name than if they are offered a gift.[16]

In a study collating findings from surveys in the social sciences since 1935, Arnold S. Linsky concluded that we may need to change overall research strategy to ensure a high return on mail questionnaires. He found the following devices to be effective (they are listed in order of effectiveness): (1) Send one or more follow-ups, such as postcards or additional letters, as reminders. More intensive follow-ups, such as phone calls or letters sent by special delivery or registered mail, work best, however. (2) Contact the respondent in some way before the questionnaire is sent. Again, the most effective method is by phone. (3) For best response, send mail by some type of special handling, such as special delivery, and use a hand-stamped return envelope rather than a postage permit envelope. (4) Send a reward with the mailing. Promises to send something on receipt of the questionnaire are less effective. (5) Be sure the sponsor of the survey and the name of the person signing the cover letter are both impressive to the audience you are trying to reach. These affect the level of returns.

Linsky's study did not show anonymity of respondents to be a decided asset. Personalizing the questionnaires seems to be somewhat effective but it does confound the anonymity issue so the situation and the issues might be the deciding points to consider here. The length of the questionnaire was only inconsistently related to the level of returns, so again, very interested audiences may tolerate a longer questionnaire (or perhaps a highly rewarded one). What does not seem to work are appeals for the respondent's cooperation based on the significance of the study, the personal help it would be to the researcher or any other altruistic

---

[15] Roger B. May, "Business Bulletin," *Wall Street Journal*, December 30, 1976, p. 1. Used with permission of the *Wall Street Journal* © Dow Jones Company, Inc., 1976.

[16] "Business Bulletin," *Wall Street Journal*, July 31, 1980, p. 1.

motivation. But evidence is mixed, Linsky says, for explaining the place and importance of the respondent for the survey. Again, it may be the audience.[17]

Alan R. Andreasen in "Personalizing Mail Questionnaire Correspondence" (*Public Opinion Quarterly*, summer 1970), says, "Use a cheap method for the first wave, then bear down with a high-return method for the second. This system gives you the advantage of being able to compare first-time respondents with those who had to be nudged and thus estimate the substantive biases, if any, of reluctant respondents."[18]

Increases in postage force researchers to examine content and systems very carefully to stay within budgets. Some research agencies use Western Union Mailgrams or other electronic mail systems, such as Datapost, a unit of TDX Systems, Inc., for both speed and drama. The implied urgency of the communication system commands attention. Computer systems offer an even more direct access and immediate response. As offices become electronically equipped and more individuals have home computers, research designs for electronically administered surveys can be used.

How to Prepare a Questionnaire   The best way to encourage a good response is to write a good questionnaire. The questionnaire should be clear, simple and interesting. You should decide whether the questions are to require specific answers or be open ended, eliciting free response. (These are much more difficult to tabulate and almost demand content analysis.)

You must try to elicit all pertinent information easily and quickly and in a form that can be analyzed. It takes skill to break up a general question into its parts. Questions should be definite and separate, not overlapping, and should invite answers.

Be careful of phrasing. There is usually some resentment of personal queries. In 1970 the Bureau of the Census, for example, reported a great deal of difficulty getting answers to some of its questions, such as one that asked people whether they owned a vacation home. Perhaps an indirect question would have drawn the candid response the direct one didn't. (When you vacation out of town, do you ordinarily stay in a hotel or motel? If not, where? With friends? With family? In own home?) (See 5.2 on pages 122–23 for tips for framing questions.)

Because the source of a questionnaire may bias the answer, it is sometimes important to hire an outside agency. An interviewer conducting a door-to-door survey for an aluminum foil company received a long list of the many ways one woman used aluminum foil in her kitchen, but when the interviewer talked to the woman's next-door neighbor, who was also her daughter, he was told, "Don't bother going over there. My mother lives there and she doesn't cook a thing. She eats every meal with us." Obviously, the mother just had not wanted to disappoint the interviewer.

It is important to group questions in a logical sequence so the arrangement

---

[17] Arnold S. Linsky, "Stimulating Responses to Mailed Questionnaires: A Review," *Public Opinion Quarterly*, 39, no. 1 (Spring 1975), pp. 82–101.

[18] Reprinted from *Precision Journalism* by Philip Meyer, pp. 315–316. Copyright © 1973 by Indiana University Press; reprinted by permission of the publisher.

encourages response. If a respondent is to fill out a questionnaire unaided, the instructions must be clear as to whether responses are to be checked, underlined or crossed out. Many survey results have been skewed because respondents put "x" by what they thought they were deleting. Also, every question must be accounted for, but there should also be an allowance for "Other," "Does not know," "Does not wish to answer" or "Omitted." One way to ensure a good questionnaire is to pretest it by asking a few people to complete it. Pretesting may tell you which questions are ambiguous or cause resentment. For example, an American Heart Association questionnaire had to be reworked four different times when pretests showed the eight- to twelve-year-olds in the study misinterpreted the questions.[19]

The difficulty with some questionnaires that require a specific response is that they do not measure the *intensity* of the response.

Semantic Differential A semantic differential questionnaire does measure intensity.[20] It is designed to measure variations in the connotative meanings of objects and words (see 5.3, 5.4). In this procedure the respondent rates the object being judged (person or concept) within a framework of two adjectival opposites with seven steps between them. In rating a person the adjectival opposites might be active–passive, strong–weak. A political pollster may use the semantic differential in asking respondents to select qualities, positive or negative, they attribute to persons or issues. Its unique application to marketing was advanced by William A. Mindak, who views it as a useful tool in rating images of brands, products and companies.[21] As large a set as nineteen rating scales will reduce to five factors, and a varimax factor analysis[22] can be used for measurement. Weighting is based on value of attribute (colorful–colorless, measured as positive or negative) to factor (appearance).

Summated Ratings Summated ratings are similar to the semantic differential. Here the responses to a series of statements are arranged along the lines of "strongly approve, approve, undecided, disapprove or strongly disapprove." Weights of 1 to 5 are assigned each position, so the high score consistently represents one of the two extremes—for example, 5 to the "strongly approve" and 1 to the "strongly disapprove." After testing, the weights are totaled and individuals are given a single numerical score. Those who score high and those who score low are selected for further study. Then each question on the questionnaire is evaluated by determining whether the high scorers respond to the particular item with a higher score than those who are low scorers. If there is internal consistency in the questions, there should be no correlation of answers between these extreme

---

[19] See example in Doug Newsom and Tom Siegfried, *Writing In Public Relations Practice: Formal Style* (Belmont, Calif.: Wadsworth, 1981), pp. 36–39.

[20] Some researchers disagree, saying semantic differential measures *degree* of response but not intensity. Others claim that "degree" reflects intensity.

[21] William A. Mindak, "Fitting the Semantic Differential to the Marketing Problem," *Journal of Marketing*, 25 (April 1961), pp. 28–33.

[22] Varimax gives a clearer separation of factors. Most students use computer programs in handling reserve data, but for an explanation of the mathematics see Jae-On Kim and Charles W. Mueller, *Factor Analysis Statistical Methods and Practical Issues* (Beverly Hills, Calif.: Sage, 1978).

5.2 TIPS FOR FRAMING QUESTIONS

These tips are the suggestions of John R. Wirtz of Dix & Eaton, corporate communication consultants in Cleveland, Ohio.

FOLLOW THESE TIPS WHEN FRAMING QUESTIONS.

There are . . . some general questions you should always ask yourself when drafting a survey. Some of these questions, and examples of those that may not be obvious to most people, include:

1. Are the words understandable?
2. Do they contain abbreviations or unconventional phrases/jargon?
3. Are the questions technically accurate?
4. Are there appropriate time references?
5. Are they too vague?
6. Are they biased? Bias can occur at least four ways:

■ *Bias from behavioral expectation*

Question: More people have attended pro football games than any other sport. Have you ever seen a pro football game?

1. Yes
2. No

Revision: Have you ever attended a pro football game?

1. Yes
2. No

■ *Bias from leading information*

Question: If the election were being held today, who would you vote for: Jimmy Carter, the incumbent; Ronald Reagan, the Republican challenger; or John Anderson, the independent?

Revision: If the presidential election were being held today, who would you vote for: Jimmy Carter, Ronald Reagan or John Anderson?

■ *Bias due to unequal comparison*

Question: Who do you feel is most responsible for the high oil prices?

1. Service station owners
2. People drilling for oil
3. Executives of the oil companies

Revision: Who do you feel is most responsible for the high oil prices?

1. Service station owners who pump it
2. Refiners who process it
3. Businessmen who operate the oil companies

■ *Bias due to unbalanced categories*

Question: Currently our country spends about $40 billion a year on social services. Do you feel this amount should be:

1. Increased
2. Stay the same
3. Decreased a little
4. Decreased somewhat
5. Decreased a great deal

Revision: Currently our country spends about $40 billion a year on social services. Do you feel this amount should be:

1. Increased significantly
2. Increased a little
3. Stay the same
4. Decreased a little
5. Decreased significantly

7. Are questions offensive? If so, there are at least three ways to overcome offensive questions:

■ *Using a series*

Question: Have you ever had an abortion?

Revision: As you know, there is a great deal of controversy about abortion in this community. Some folks think it's a serious problem, others do not. Do you consider abortion to be a serious, moderate, slight, or no problem at all in your community?

1. Serious
2. Moderate
3. Slight
4. Not at all

During the past few years do you think the number of abortions has increased, stayed the same, or decreased in the community?

1. Increased
2. Stayed about the same
3. Decreased

Please try to recall the time when you were a teenager. Do you recall personally knowing anyone who had an abortion?

1. No
2. Yes

How about yourself? Did you ever consider having an abortion?

1. No
2. Yes

If yes, did you actually have one?

1. No
2. Yes

■ *Using general categories to overcome offensive questions*

Question: How much money did you earn in 1979?
_____ dollars

Revision: Which category below best describes your income during 1979?

1. Less than $7,000
2. $ 7,000 to $ 9,999

3. $10,000 to $14,999
4. $15,000 to $24,999
5. $25,000 or more

■ *Using narrative material to overcome offensive questions*

Question: "Big business is the root of society's problems." Do you:

1. Agree
2. Disagree

Revision: Next, let's talk about your feelings about the relationship between big business and society. Here are various, popular opinions, both negative and positive. With each statement, check whether you are in agreement or disagreement.

"Big business is the foundation of our society's problems "

1. Agree
2. Disagree

"Big business is the root of society's problems."

1. Agree
2. Disagree

(Other statements could follow.)

■ *Do they require too much effort to answer?*

Question: What percent of your time each month is spent on meetings?

Revision: How many hours do you spend a month in meetings? _____

How many hours do you spend on the job each month? _____

From "The Communication Audit—Your Road Map to Success," *Journal of Organizational Communication*, 10, no. 2, (February 1981), p. 16.

5.3 SIMPLE SEMANTIC DIFFERENTIAL QUESTIONNAIRE

This questionnaire was administered to former journalism
students to determine which courses had benefited them most.

INSTRUCTIONS FOR COMPLETING PART I OF QUESTIONNAIRE: Beside
each of 23 courses listed below is a rating scale. Please rate
the value of each course you studied; if you did not take the
course named, just leave that scale blank. If you feel that
the course has been extremely useful to you in your work, place
an X at the extreme left of the scale. If the course has been
useless to your work, place an X at the extreme right. If the
course has had no effect, place an X near the center of the
scale. Varying degrees of usefulness are indicated by the distance your mark is placed from one of the extremes. For example,
the mark on the sample scale below indicates that the course
was slightly useful.

Sample:

FEATURE WRITING   Useful : : :X: : : : :   Useless

                                    Extremely — Moderately — Slightly — Neutral — Slightly — Moderately — Extremely

1.	NEWSWRITING	Useful : : : : : : : :	Useless
2.	RADIO-TV NEWSWRITING	Useful : : : : : : : :	Useless
3.	EDITING	Useful : : : : : : : :	Useless
4.	GRAPHICS OF JOURNALISM	Useful : : : : : : : :	Useless
5.	PUBLIC RELATIONS	Useful : : : : : : : :	Useless
6.	HISTORY OF JOURNALISM	Useful : : : : : : : :	Useless
7.	LAW OF THE PRESS	Useful : : : : : : : :	Useless
8.	THE PRESS AND CON-TEMPORARY AFFAIRS	Useful : : : : : : : :	Useless
9.	NEWSPAPER DIRECTION: EDITORIAL	Useful : : : : : : : :	Useless
10.	EDITORIAL WRITING AND DIRECTION	Useful : : : : : : : :	Useless
11.	ADVANCED FEATURE WRIT-ING	Useful : : : : : : : :	Useless
12.	MAGAZINE EDITING	Useful : : : : : : : :	Useless
13.	PROBLEMS IN PUBLICITY AND PUBLIC RELATIONS (High Noon Agency)	Useful : : : : : : : :	Useless
14.	NEWSPAPER PROMOTION	Useful : : : : : : : :	Useless
15.	RESEARCH PROBLEMS IN JOURNALISM	Useful : : : : : : : :	Useless
16.	SHORT STORY WORKSHOP	Useful : : : : : : : :	Useless
17.	ETHICS OF THE MASS MEDIA	Useful : : : : : : : :	Useless
18.	PUBLIC AFFAIRS REPORT-ING	Useful : : : : : : : :	Useless
19.	COMMUNICATION THEORY	Useful : : : : : : : :	Useless
20.	PUBLIC RELATIONS SPECIALIZED AREA (After 1967)	Useful : : : : : : : :	Useless
21.	STRATEGY OF POLITICS AND PUBLICITY	Useful : : : : : : : :	Useless
22.	EVOLUTION OF THE MASS MEDIA IN AMERICA	Useful : : : : : : : :	Useless
23.	PUBLIC RELATIONS INTERNSHIP	Useful : : : : : : : :	Useless

24. List any other courses, taken in any department, which you
feel have been useful to you:

_____

_____

_____

Roger D. Christensen, "The University of Texas' Public Relations Curriculum—An Evaluation by 1960–1971 Graduates." Master's thesis, University of Texas, Austin, May 1973.

groups. If there is correlation on some questions, they are deleted from the scoring, so that only the items reflecting divergence of opinion with greatest consistency are used as a scale.

Scale Analysis   In its simplest form, scale analysis is concerned with such questions as: Is your grade point average 4.0 (yes or no)? Is it 3.5 (yes or no)? And so on. Such questions often appear on questionnaires about salary and position in relation to years of experience in professional fields.

The DELPHI Process

A Rand Corporation research group developed a method for polling an audience in order to reach a consensus. Management has used this method, called the DELPHI process, to improve relations with employees. The process involves six steps. First, a questionnaire is designed to allow an open-ended response. Second, the sample is chosen on the basis of cost and amount of sampling error acceptable. Third, the questionnaire is sent to respondents as individuals, not handed out by a supervisor or given to the respondents in a general assembly. Fourth, the responses are all organized into one, composite list. Although corrections in spelling and grammar are made as a common courtesy, no value judgments are made, such as discarding an idea because it is too costly or has been tried before. Fifth, each respondent is given this composite list of responses, together with a rating scale such as high to low from 5 to 1 and asked to order the responses. Tabulations of this second series of responses, that is, a ranking of items on the list, can be made on a computer. When a number of issues from the list are rated in the highest category, they have to be grouped according to some relationship of ideas. Once categories of ideas are developed, the items can be rank-ordered within the categories, according to what the responses were. Sixth, the ordered list is sent back to respondents along with their individual responses. Of course, this cannot be done if the responses are anonymous; however, if the respondents' anonymity is important, you can provide an automatic copy they can tear off and keep to compare with the results. Employees, for example, can see if their opinion is representative of the majority. If the results of the polling are to be reported to management for some action, those in the minority may want to present a minority report also. This opportunity to participate in issue description and the setting of priorities has given employees more of a sense of participation, and certainly aids in communication.

DELPHI has been used successfully by Charleston County Public Schools in Charleston, South Carolina, to draw out specific proposals concerning school vandalism and student disruptions. Included in the sample with students and teachers were a variety of community groups. The ideas ranged from improving remedial reading programs to using guard dogs, and owing to a proposal prepared from the report, the schools were granted more than $1 million to implement the ideas agreed upon.[23]

The Complexity of Measurements

Complex questionnaires and tests have been designed to measure changes in attitudes, personality, knowledge and behavior—against a background of such variables as education, income, religion, social status, sex, occupation and race. One writer listed the following kinds of measurement dimensions as examples of their variety:

- *General evaluative dimension*—pleasant–unpleasant, valuable–worthless, important–unimportant, interesting–boring
- *Ethical dimension*—fair–unfair, truthful–untruthful, accurate–inaccurate, biased–unbiased, responsible–irresponsible
- *Stylistic dimension*—exciting–dull, fresh–stale, easy–difficult, neat–messy, colorful–colorless

---

[23]John C. Cone, "DELPHI: Polling for Consensus," *Public Relations Journal*, 34, no. 2 (February 1978), pp. 12–13.

Questionnaire A

LAST SESSION'S NEWSPAPER COVERAGE
OF THE LEGISLATURE IN YOUR HOME DISTRICT

Extr. Modr. Slgt. Neut. Slgt. Modr. Extr.

Attractive		Unattractive
Incomplete		Complete
Fair		Unfair
Weak		Strong
Good		Bad
Backward		Progressive
Careful		Careless
Biased		Unbiased
Active		Passive
Wrong		Right
Relaxed		Tense
Inaccurate		Accurate
Impartial		Partial
Unpleasant		Pleasant
Balanced		Unbalanced
Untruthful		Truthful
Colorful		Colorless
Uninteresting		Interesting
Superior		Inferior

Questionnaire B

LAST SESSION'S TELEVISION COVERAGE
OF THE LEGISLATURE IN YOUR HOME DISTRICT

Extr. Modr. Slgt. Neut. Slgt. Modr. Extr.

Responsible		Irresponsible
Vague		Precise
Alert		Dull
Weak		Powerful
Colorful		Colorless
Disreputable		Reputable
Important		Unimportant
Backward		Progressive
Fresh		Stale
Hazy		Clear
Wholesome		Unwholesome
Inaccurate		Accurate
Good		Bad
Careless		Deliberate
Safe		Dangerous
Unpleasant		Pleasant
Interesting		Uninteresting
Meaningless		Meaningful
Pleasing		Annoying

Above are two fairly complex semantic differential questionnaires (and their scoring sheets) used in measuring how legislators view the news coverage of their work by newspapers and television stations in their home districts.

This material is from a study by John Merwin, "How Texas Legislators View Coverage of Their Work," prepared as a Master's thesis at the University of Texas at Austin. A mail questionnaire was used since the legislature was not in session during the research period. There was a covering letter, personally addressed and personally signed by Mr. Merwin; the letter guaranteed anonymity to the respondents. A postage-paid envelope was enclosed.

In the questionnaire, some of the pairs of adjectives appear in a positive-negative order and some in a negative-positive order. This arrangement is used to forestall a tendency to answer in one *vertical category*—for example, positively if all items are in a positive-negative order.

Note the factor scores appearing below the scoring sheets on the opposite page. Factor scores reduce data to manageable figures that are easily compared. Factor scores are measurements of the factor. Here they show nuances of difference. Certain pairs of adjectives—following each of the factors—were selected to reflect opinions in the topical categories. Without such an arrangement, it would have been difficult to make any conclusive statements. The attributes differ for newspapers and television because of the technological and perceptive differences in the media.

- *Potency dimension*—bold–timid, powerful–weak, loud–soft
- *Evaluative dimension*—accurate–inaccurate, good–bad, responsible–irresponsible, wise–foolish, acceptable–unacceptable

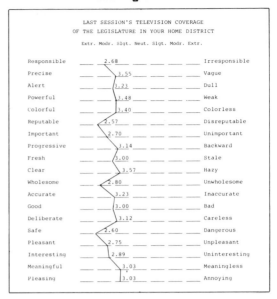

Scoring Sheet A

LAST SESSION'S NEWSPAPER COVERAGE
OF THE LEGISLATURE IN YOUR HOME DISTRICT

Extr. Modr. Slgt. Neut. Slgt. Modr. Extr.

Attractive	3.65	Unattractive
Complete	4.07	Incomplete
Fair	3.50	Unfair
Strong	3.81	Weak
Good	3.72	Bad
Progressive	3.93	Backward
Careful	4.06	Careless
Unbiased	4.40	Biased
Active	3.92	Passive
Right	3.50	Wrong
Relaxed	3.86	Tense
Accurate	3.54	Inaccurate
Impartial	4.36	Partial
Pleasant	4.17	Unpleasant
Balanced	3.86	Unbalanced
Truthful	4.47	Untruthful
Colorful	4.07	Colorless
Interesting	4.42	Uninteresting
Superior	4.24	Inferior

Scoring Sheet B

LAST SESSION'S TELEVISION COVERAGE
OF THE LEGISLATURE IN YOUR HOME DISTRICT

Extr. Modr. Slgt. Neut. Slgt. Modr. Extr.

Responsible	2.68	Irresponsible
Precise	3.55	Vague
Alert	3.23	Dull
Powerful	3.48	Weak
Colorful	3.40	Colorless
Reputable	2.57	Disreputable
Important	2.70	Unimportant
Progressive	3.14	Backward
Fresh	3.00	Stale
Clear	3.57	Hazy
Wholesome	2.80	Unwholesome
Accurate	3.23	Inaccurate
Good	3.00	Bad
Deliberate	3.12	Careless
Safe	2.60	Dangerous
Pleasant	2.75	Unpleasant
Interesting	2.89	Uninteresting
Meaningful	3.03	Meaningless
Pleasing	3.03	Annoying

Newspaper Factor Scores

Ethical (3.841): Fair–Unfair; Good–Bad; Unbiased–Biased; Right–Wrong; Relaxed–Tense; Accurate–Inaccurate; Impartial–Partial

Potency (3.930): Complete–Incomplete; Strong–Weak; Progressive–Backward; Active–Passive

Quality (3.951): Attractive–Unattractive; Careful–Careless; Balanced–Unbalanced; Superior–Inferior

Appearance (4.243): Colorful–Colorless; Interesting–Uninteresting

Style (4.319): Pleasant–Unpleasant; Truthful–Untruthful

Television Factor Scores

Importance (2.707): Importance–Unimportance

Quality (2.775): Responsible–Irresponsible; Reputable–Disreputable; Wholesome–Unwholesome; Safe–Dangerous; Pleasant–Unpleasant; Pleasing–Annoying; Good–Bad

Attractiveness (2.974): Fresh–Stale; Interesting–Uninteresting; Meaningful–Meaningless

Potency (3.311): Alert–Dull; Powerful–Weak; Colorful–Colorless; Progressive–Backward

Accuracy (3.369): Precise–Vague; Clear–Hazy; Accurate–Inaccurate; Deliberate–Careless

- *Excitement dimension*—colorful–colorless, interesting–uninteresting, exciting–unexciting, hot–cold
- *Activity dimension*—active–passive, agitated–calm, bold–timid [24]

[24] Hugh M. Culbertson, "Words vs. Pictures: A Comparison as to Perceived Impact and Connotative Meaning," paper presented at Association for Education in Journalism convention, University of Southern Illinois, Carbondale, August 1972; published in *Journalism Quarterly* (Summer 1974), pp. 226–237.

All attitude tests must be used promptly, since opinion is highly subject to change. However, old data should not be discarded; the information can be used later in developing simulated tests that will give some probable responses. When John F. Kennedy was running for president in 1960, his campaign strategists used cards from the Roper Public Opinion Research Center in Williamstown, Massachusetts (depository for the old cards of the Gallup and Roper polls), to design a program simulating how people around the United States would react to various critical questions and issues, based on how they had reacted in the past. In fact, the simulation came closer in predicting the November election outcome than did the public opinion polls taken in August. The reason, Philip Meyer explains, is that the simulation designed by Ithiel de Sola Pool "was acting out how the voters would react to a [campaign] strategy that had not been fully implemented. After it was implemented and the voters began to react, the polls began to reflect the results and came into closer correlation with both the simulation and the final outcome." [25] (See 5.5 for an effort to measure attitudes.)

Computer Use

Most of the research methods we have discussed can be adapted so the information can be compiled and collated on a computer, shortening the time gap between data gathering and results and eliminating many nonsampling errors. Using the computer also enables researchers to contrast and compare elements, a procedure that would take too many human hours of calculation to be feasible.

In addition, the information may be stored in the computer, which makes a vast amount of data readily available. For example, when a professional organization switches to a computer service to handle its mailing, it can also put other information in the computer besides its members' names and addresses. Thus it can call for printouts on its members by state, by city, by area of specialization, by salary and by institution where highest degrees were obtained. All this information may have been in the organization's files, but it could scarcely be considered readily available. Accumulated information like this can be used to study trends, cycles, seasonal variations and the like. (See 5.6 for an example of a computer-generated profile.)

BROADCAST RESEARCH

Basically the same type of research methodology is applied to TV and radio broadcasting, although some tests are peculiar to the industry. The National Association of Broadcasters publishes "A Broadcast Research Primer" that indicates which methods a novice may use and which should be avoided (see 5.7).

---

[25] Philip Meyer, *Precision Journalism* (Bloomington: Indiana University Press), p. 184. Copyright © 1973 by Indiana University Press; reprinted by permission of the publisher.

5.5 OPINION SURVEY DESIGNED TO MEASURE ATTITUDES

The first portion of this page of the questionnaire is designed to elicit responses to nostalgia questions. The bottom half is attitudinal and value oriented.

GOOD OLD DAYS

THE "GOOD OLD DAYS", WHILE SUBJECT TO SOME DEGREE OF "SELECTIVE MEMORY", ARE FILLED WITH FOND THOUGHTS OF EVENTFUL TIMES IN OUR LIVES WHEN WE WERE GROWING UP AND/OR ENGAGED IN ACTIVITIES THAT WERE VERY IMPORTANT TO US. MANY TIMES, THE AUTOMOBILE PLAYS A SIGNIFICANT PART IN THOSE MEMORIES.

FIRST

PLEASE TAKE A MENTAL TRIP DOWN "MEMORY LANE" THROUGH SOME OF THE PERIODS AND POSSIBLE MILESTONES IN YOUR LIFE THAT WE'VE SELECTED BELOW, AND TELL US THOSE SITUATIONS IN WHICH A PARTICULAR CAR STANDS OUT IN YOUR MIND.

CHECK (✔) THOSE PERIODS/EVENTS WHICH BRING TO MIND A SPECIFIC CAR YOU OWNED OR PARTICULARLY LIKED AT THAT TIME.

1. WHEN YOU WERE "JUST A KID", AND THINKING ABOUT BEING ABLE TO DRIVE ☐
2. WHEN YOU GOT YOUR DRIVER'S LICENSE AND HAD ACCESS TO A CAR AT LEAST PART OF THE TIME ☐
3. WHEN YOU FIRST ACQUIRED A CAR TO CALL YOUR OWN ☐
4. WHEN YOU WENT OUT ON YOUR FIRST DATE IN A CAR ☐
5. WHEN YOU BOUGHT YOUR FIRST NEW CAR ☐
6. WHEN YOU GRADUATED AND WENT TO WORK FULL TIME (if applicable) ☐

7. WHEN YOU WERE ENGAGED TO BE MARRIED ☐
8. WHEN YOU RETURNED HOME FROM MILITARY SERVICE (if applicable) ☐
9. WHEN YOU STARTED "DOING WELL" IN YOUR JOB OR PROFESSION (if applicable) ☐
10. WHEN YOU REACHED THAT POINT WHEN YOUR LIFE STYLE COULD ACCOMMODATE THE KIND OF CAR YOU REALLY WANTED ☐

ANY OTHERS YOU CAN THINK OF? _____ ☐

SECOND

NOW, PLEASE SELECT 4 OF THE MOST SIGNIFICANT PERIODS/EVENTS FROM THE LIST ABOVE IN TERMS OF YOUR MEMORIES OF AUTOMOBILES .... AND TELL US MORE ABOUT THEM.

MOST SIGNIFICANT 4 OR 5 PERIODS/EVENTS (Write in ID Number From the List Above)	OUTSTANDING CAR IN YOUR MIND (Write in Make and Car Line)	DID YOU ... OWN IT	HAVE ACCESS TO USE IT	JUST ADMIRE IT	WAS IT A ... U.S. CAR	IMPORTED CAR
			------(CHECK ONE)-------		-- (CHECK ONE) --	
		☐ 1	☐ 2	☐ 3	☐ 1	☐ 2
		☐	☐	☐	☐	☐
		☐	☐	☐	☐	☐
		☐				

THIRD

THINKING NOW OF THE PRESENT TIME, WHAT CAR (MAKE AND CAR LINE) WOULD BE YOUR "MOST WANTED" CAR, IF PRICE WERE NO OBJECT?

MOST WANTED CURRENT CAR _____ (MAKE) (CAR LINE) DO YOU: OWN IT ☐ 1 ADMIRE IT ☐ 2 IS IT: A U.S. CAR ☐ 1 OR AN IMPORT ☐ 2

RELATIVE TO YOUR INDIVIDUAL TASTES AND PREFERENCES FOR DIFFERENT KINDS OF CARS THROUGHOUT YOUR LIFETIME, PLEASE TELL US YOUR AGREEMENT OR DISAGREEMENT WITH THE FOLLOWING STATEMENTS.

(5 = STRONGLY AGREE ....., 1 = STRONGLY DISAGREE)

. WHILE MY "NEEDS" MAY HAVE CHANGED THROUGHOUT MY LIFE, I STILL HAVE THE SAME "TASTES": I PREFER "PLAIN VANILLA"...OR A "SPORTY FLAIR"...OR A "TOUCH OF LUXURY", ETC.   5 4 3 2 1

. PEOPLE GROWING UP TODAY HAVE DIFFERENT VALUES FROM THOSE OF YESTERDAY....I THINK WE WILL SEE A DIFFERENT PATTERN OF CAR PREFERENCES (by size...type...U.S. vs. Import, etc.) IN THE FUTURE THAN IN THE PAST.   5 4 3 2 1

. YOUNG PEOPLE'S ATTITUDES GO IN CYCLES. THE RADICALS OF THE 60'S HAVE BECOME QUITE CONSERVATIVE IN THE 80'S. THERE'S NO REASON TO THINK THEY WON'T LIKE THE SAME KINDS OF MATERIAL THINGS SUCH AS THE TYPES OF CARS THAT OLDER PEOPLE LIKE TODAY.   5 4 3 2 1

. YOUNG PEOPLE TEND TO FAVOR SMALL ECONOMY OR SPORTY CARS BUT AS THEY GROW OLDER, THEY USUALLY CHANGE TO SOMETHING BIGGER AND MORE COMFORTABLE.   5 4 3 2 1

. MAYBE WE'LL NEVER GET BACK TO THE ULTRA BIG LUXURY CARS OF THE PAST, BUT THERE ALWAYS WILL BE A DEMAND FOR RELATIVELY LARGE, LUXURY CARS AS WELL AS ECONOMY CARS, SPORTY CARS, ETC.   5 4 3 2 1

. IMPORTS HAVE BEEN GOOD FOR ECONOMY ...AND SPORTS-CARS, BUT FOR FAMILY NEEDS, U.S. CARS TRADITIONALLY HAVE BEEN BETTER.   5 4 3 2 1

. WHEN I BOUGHT MY FIRST CARS, IMPORTS FIT MY BUDGET, AND WHEN I PROGRESSED IN MY "ABILITY TO PAY", I JUST NATURALLY STAYED WITH THE IMPORTS.   5 4 3 2 1

. IMPORTED CARS MAY BE REALLY NICE CARS, BUT I HAVE A STRONG BUY-AMERICAN ATTITUDE.   5 4 3 2 1

. MANY YOUNG PEOPLE DRIVING IMPORTS TODAY WILL SWITCH TO U.S. CARS AS THEIR NEEDS AND TASTES CHANGE WITH AGE.   5 4 3 2 1

. I DON'T THINK MOST PEOPLE ARE LOYAL TO EITHER IMPORTS OR U.S. CARS PER SE, BUT THEY BUY ACCORDING TO THEIR PARTICULAR NEEDS AT THE TIME.   5 4 3 2 1

. ONCE A PERSON OWNS EITHER AN IMPORT OR A U.S. CAR AND HAS GOOD LUCK, HE IS LIKELY TO "STAY LOYAL" TO THE SAME KIND OF CAR NEXT TIME.   5 4 3 2 1

. FOR SOME PURPOSES, U.S. CARS OFFER THE BEST CHOICE, WHILE FOR OTHERS, AN IMPORT IS MUCH BETTER, SO MANY FAMILIES OWN ONE OF EACH.   5 4 3 2 1

Reprinted with permission of the Survey Center, Inc.

5.6 COMPUTER-GENERATED PROFILES

Whimsy is not the point of these computer-generated profiles of some corporations. Although these profiles are from financial data, it is not unlikely that a model for a public opinion profile also could be generated. The computer financial profile is a project of the University of Pennsylvania's Wharton School, and is described in the following article.

WITH COMPUTER HELP, MARKETING PROFESSOR FACES UP TO CORPORATIONS' FINANCIAL DATA

When a computer drew the faces on this page, it wasn't just doodling.

Notice General Motors Corp.'s frown. It indicates the auto maker's return on assets. And U.S. Steel Corp.'s eyebrows: They're a clue to the company's cash turnover. International Harvester Co.'s long nose shows the ratio of retained earnings to total assets. International Business Machines Corp.'s big eyes are a sign of strong capitalization and cash flow, as well as impressive turnover of accounts receivable.

GM

In other words, the drawings are supposed to personify complex financial information. Rather than slog through a welter of data in an annual report, say the computer cartoon's developers, it may be possible to look at computer-drawn faces and get the same information.

"It's fun," says Vijay Mahajan, a professor of marketing at the University of Pennsylvania's Wharton School who is involved in the project, "but I think there's also a lot of potential here." He says the faces could indicate which stocks to buy or sell, which companies other firms might want to acquire or signs of trouble for corporate managers.

Financial information from a company's annual report is assigned to 11 facial features. The angle of the eyebrow, for example, represents cash turnover, and the eyebrow's length shows inventory turnover. Features change as

the variables change. Thus the mouth shifts to a frown from a smile as the return on assets declines. And the diameter of the ear widens as the ratio of current assets to current liabilities improves.

U.S. Steel

The looks on the faces here are supposed to correspond to the companies' financial health as described in their most recent annual reports. IBM, says Mr. Mahajan, "looks like the cat who just swallowed the canary." General Motors is "the kid whose toy has just been stolen." International Harvester is angry; U.S. Steel is sad.

Harvester

To draw these faces Mr. Mahajan and two fellow marketing professors—David Huff of the University of Texas and William Black of the University of Arizona—used a technique developed in 1973 by Herman Chernoff, a mathematician at the Massachusetts Institute of Technology. Troubled by the difficulty of presenting lots of information in an easily comprehensible fashion, Mr. Chernoff tried plotting them on a face.

The computer-drawn face, he reasoned, would be more revealing than a list of numbers or a group of charts. People's "library of responses to faces exhausts a huge part of our dictionary of emotions and ideas," Mr. Chernoff wrote in an article explaining his technique. "We perceive the face as a gestalt, and our built-in computer is quick to pick out the relevant information."

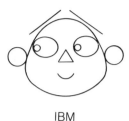

IBM

Mr. Mahajan and his associates concede that their technique needs perfecting. Individual viewers may interpret a face differently depending on whether they focus on the mouth, eyes or another feature. A happy or sad face may result from data that doesn't justify such a look. And an extremely high or low variable may distort a face.

Still, the three marketing professors say their technique—the first use of Chernoff faces for business data—has plenty of practical applications. To demonstrate, they've used the method to compare two companies over a five-year period. At first, the companies' faces were similar: wide-eyed, smiling and generally happy. Then the financial condition of one of them declined, and its face took on a squinting, frowning, sour look. That company eventually filed for bankruptcy.

Bill Abrams, "With Computer Help, Marketing Professor Faces Up To Corporations' Financial Data," *Wall Street Journal*, July 22, 1981, p. 25. Reprinted by permission of the *Wall Street Journal*. © Dow Jones & Company, Inc., 1981. All rights reserved.

The Diary

Used by a network to measure a program's audience, the diary method requires that some member of a household keep a written log of program listening or viewing. Researchers get much the same data by attaching a recorder to the television set or radio to measure the frequency of viewing and channel selection, although the automatic device does not tell when the TV or radio is playing in an empty room.

The Interview

Broadcast researchers also use different types of personal and telephone interviews.

The *personal coincidental* method consists of personal interviews made during a given time period or during a specific program. Respondents are asked what program they are listening to or watching at that moment.

The *personal roster recall* consists of showing respondents a list of programs and stations and asking them to indicate which they watched or listened to within the given time span, usually the day before or the week before.

The *unaided personal recall* seeks the same type of information. Respondents are asked what they listened to on the radio or watched on TV during whatever time span the survey is to measure. It differs from the personal roster recall in that the respondents must remember the names of programs and stations without the help of a list.

The *telephone coincidental*, a survey method that local stations or area research bureaus can use effectively, is basically the same as the personal coincidental method, only it is conducted over the telephone. The *telephone unaided recall*

What You Should Do

In do-it-yourself research, these are important points:

1. The types of surveys you can best handle yourself are those dealing with: (a) the audience of a station or other media—the people as listeners, viewers, or readers; (b) the market in which a station operates—the people as consumers and users of advertising; (c) public opinion—what people think about issues, conditions, governments, their lives.

2. Confine your survey to the precinct, the city, the metropolitan area, or the county. Difficulties arise when a beginning researcher attempts to cover more.

3. Collect information by telephone or face-to-face interviews or observation. Mail surveys can have some value, although it is limited considering the costs involved.

4. Question interviewees directly, but avoid asking for information about others in the family. Use a standardized questionnaire. Self-administered and leave-behind forms are generally not recommended.

5. Primarily, use closed-end or structured-type questions, eliciting explicit replies. Although open-end questions are not discouraged and are sometimes necessary, they are more difficult to handle, during both interviewing and tabulation.

6. Make interviews relatively short—from 1 or 2 minutes up to a maximum of 15 minutes. Professionals can successfully handle interviews up to an hour or more, but such questioning requires wide experience, and the analysis can be ponderous.

7. Gather the information through sampling—a cross-section of relatively few people—rather than a complete enumeration.

8. An adequate sample can be as small as 100; it is seldom more than 1,000.

What You Should Avoid

Aside from the limitations mentioned in the preceding paragraphs, there are some definite areas for the layman researcher to avoid:

1. *Advertising effectiveness* can now be measured in new and intriguing ways, but most require more technical know-how than the average businessperson or beginning researcher has. Many problems arise in attempting to measure not only advertising effect on sales but exposure to advertising—commercials, print, outdoor or others. It may seem perfectly natural to ask, "What led you to buy that?" or "What type of advertising helps you most?" but such simple approaches usually yield misleading results because respondents are likely to give superficial responses and may not understand really what motivated them.

2. *Motivation research* has become a popular term, widely misused. In its true meaning, it is research that describes *why* people act as they do. Conducting it usually requires training in psychology or at least knowledge of techniques developed by behavioral scientists. Certainly you can ask people their reasons for many things, but don't expect to probe the subconscious for basic motives with everyday research tools. Depth interviewing is one of the techniques of motivation and attiude research. A real depth interview that probes intensively behind expressed opinions and reactions demands skills not commonly available.

3. *"Iffy" questions are dangerous*. To ask a respondent what he or she would do if certain changes were made or if other conditions existed seldom produces realistic results. Perhaps you cannot completely avoid questions like, "If the 6 o'clock evening newscast were changed to 7 P.M., would you listen to it more, or less, or about the same?" Such questions can at best give you a general indication, but not a precise estimate.

4. *Use of products by volume* is a tricky thing to measure. Consumers can readily tell you whether they use a product or not, but it is another thing to find out how much they use.

5. *Loaded surveys* mislead. Some advertising researchers have attempted to "document" what they don't actually have by using "research." Going through the motions of a *loaded survey* does not produce facts. In your eagerness to make a good showing, avoid biasing a survey unconsciously.

6. *Trend measurements* are not taboo, but you should realize that for one result to be comparable to a later one, close attention must be paid to the comparability of each survey in a series—comparability as to method, timing and the manner in which it is conducted.

7. *Panels*, requiring that the same people be reinterviewed at intervals or that the members do something between intervals, are best left to specialists.

8. *Store audits* are also for specialists. Although simple in concept, they demand more control than the layman is usually able to exercise.

9. *Consumer tests*—Taste tests, advertising copy tests, package tests, and the like are highly specialized and should be used cautiously, if at all.

10. *Ratings*, the measurements that tell how many people are listening to a given station at a given time, are not recommended as part of broadcast do-it-yourself research. As should be obvious from this guide, there is much more to station research than ratings. The most widespread use of research by radio and television has, indeed, been in ratings, and demand for them continues. But there are many reasons why they should be left to the services that specialize in such surveys or to other experienced researchers. . . .

Although it seems simple, accurate measurement of audience size is highly technical. One needs only to read the hearings of congressional investigations into ratings to become aware of the intricacies and pitfalls. NAB is active in the effort to police the ratings through the Broadcast Rating Council, which audits the operations of the major rating services. . . . To be effective, and useful, ratings also need to be comparable from market to market; so they must be conducted by organizations that operate nationally. Ratings are available from such services as American Research Bureau, Hooper, Mediastat, Nielsen, and Pulse. Only if you must estimate audience size for *internal* use and can't afford a professional firm should you try ratings research. The simplest and least expensive method is usually the telephone coincidental—calling a sample of homes during the time segment you wish to measure.

The evaluation of the impact or effect of media on publics can be tested in a number of ways, but one of the most common is the control group study or experiment where there are two groups selected to be matching samples. One is exposed to the program and the other is not. Through either panel studies or surveys the differences are determined and thus the impact of a program measured. The survey method is used here generally when a program has been activated in one geographical area and not in another. The panel method may use the already selected advisory group. However, the problem with this test is matching the two sample populations. Another program of measurement is the study of similar groups over a long period of time. The measures may involve observable changes over the time span as well as measurable differences in individual and group reactions. The in-depth interview also is a valuable tool and is used to determine reactions to various aspects of a program.

Adapted from *A Broadcast Research Primer* (Washington, D.C.: National Association of Broadcasters, 1973), pp. 10–12.

is essentially the same as the personal unaided recall, as those called must think of the program they were watching or listening to. The *telephone aided recall* is like the personal roster recall.

Broadcasting researchers also use *combinations* of these tests: the combination telephone coincidental and telephone recall, the combined telephone coincidental and personal roster recall or the telephone coincidental combined with the diary.

The Program Analyzer

The program analyzer makes use of panels, although when cable television is more widespread its use may be extended to general audiences. To analyze a program, the viewer or listener presses a button or switch that records his or her reaction to a specific part of the program. There are two buttons—Like and Dislike—and the reactions are recorded on tape and then matched with the program to see which parts of the show elicited which response. Cable systems with such response buttons to give instant ratings have been used, but only on an experimental basis.

THE SEMANTICS OF RESEARCH

The PR practitioner needs to know something about the language of research. For example, the real meanings of *average* or *typical* might be "mean" (sum divided by the number in the sample), "median" (midpoint) or "mode" (number recurring most often). Also, a basic statistics course required at some universities for PR majors will give you a working understanding of *variance* and *standard deviation*, which are derived from mathematical formulas. These concepts will help you to test the validity of data and gauge their usefulness by allowing you to apply what was learned from the sample to the whole population. You also should learn how to test for the significance of sample means and sample proportions, and to be able to use probability equations. The course can also help you become familiar with the useful and common chi-square formula and the Kolmogorov-Smirnov test, as well as the F-test for the significance and confidence limits of a sample variance. Further, you can gain an understanding of the hypothesis-testing procedures and a knowledge of regression and correlation formulas, which are helpful because researchers deal with many variables. Rank-order correlation formulas (Spearman's rho and Kendall's tau) are useful even if you are not applying them to anything more serious than contest judging.

Some of the other tests, particularly for significance, are very important to understand. Why?

Suppose you are handling a political candidate, and the opposition publishes the results of a private poll that shows she had 48 percent of the vote and your candidate had 44 percent, with 8 percent undecided. What is your response? Is she really ahead? How would you figure it out? You definitely need to know! The first question you need to ask is what was the population? What was the response to the sample? How were the statistics compiled? What was the 100 percent base? If the number of "Don't Knows" or "No Answers" (different from *undecided*) is dropped, the percentage will be different. What is the error allowance? If the confidence level is 95 percent, then to be 95 percent sure, you will have an error of 5 percentage points! Here, to be sure, you would need an error allowance of 2 percentage points or less. There is a statistical formula and procedure to use. (Set error at 2 percent and solve for z, $z = 2E \sqrt{2}$. Then use the z table to determine the percentage by which the opposition is ahead.) Only then are you certain.

To consider another example, imagine that you are in charge of media relations for a federal agency and an enterprising and influential journalist, who has compared voter records with grants made by the agency, has accused your agency head of pork barrel politics. Is he correct or is it a coincidence? If you say the latter, can you prove it? Or, suppose you just want to figure out how large a sample you would need for a test. If you know how much error you can tolerate, you can use a simple formula.

A professor who teaches broadcast research enjoys telling the story of a businessman who was explaining the results of a costly media survey. In asking about the sample size, the professor asked the businessman what the error margin was, to which he replied: "Oh, there wasn't any error. This was a very reliable research firm." There is *always* error, and reliable researchers allow for it.

PUBLIC AND PRIVATE POLLS

We are all aware of public polls, such as those taken by Louis Harris and George Gallup, which sample the nation's moods and pass on the information to the public. There are also less widely known pollsters such as Albert Sidlinger and Jay Schmiedeskamp, who measure consumer confidence. "By taking frequent samples of household buying intentions," says the *Wall Street Journal*, "they claim to be able to determine whether the nation's consumers have enough confidence in the economy to commit themselves to such major purchases as new cars, big appliances and houses. The results of such surveys are increasingly important in government economic planning and in corporate decision making."[26] Another private pollster is William R. Hamilton, head of Independent Research Associates, Inc., a political polling and analysis concern that "works directly, and confidentially, for political candidates who want to know as precisely as possible what the electorate thinks so they can devise an effective campaign strategy."[27]

The U.S. president's private pollsters are frequently in the spotlight. Pat Caddell was in the spotlight at an early age. He was twenty-five the year Jimmy

---

[26]Jack H. Morris, "Pollsters Gamely Try to Measure the Moods of Volatile Consumers," *Wall Street Journal*, October 4, 1972, p. 1. Reprinted with permission of the *Wall Street Journal* © Dow Jones & Company, Inc., 1972.

[27]Fred L. Zimmerman, "How Political Pollster Influences Candidates, Stays in Background," *Wall Street Journal*, October 5, 1972. Reprinted with permission of the *Wall Street Journal* © Dow Jones & Company, Inc., 1972.

Carter was inaugurated. Caddell has said his function is not just to do surveys but to figure out what they mean and to contribute advice on certain issues. Caddell is also a pollster for other Democrats, and he got into a verbal battle with a fellow pollster during a heated U.S. senate race in Texas. Caddell's polling technique was criticized publicly by pollster V. Lance Tarrance. The Tarrance polling firm was being used by incumbent John Tower, a Republican, and Caddell's Cambridge Survey Research firm was being used by the Democratic challenger, Bob Krueger. Tarrance claimed he had to respond with criticism when Caddell accused him of unprofessional behavior, because Krueger's camp was using the Caddell poll as a "propaganda" device. The difficulty with private polling, especially in politics, is that even when the pollsters make every effort to be objective about wording a questionnaire or picking a geographical area to sample, there is an ideological bent.

Most political research organizations are identified with one party or the other. Yet, the private pollsters say, politics and partisanship do not prevent them from doing honest research. They use the same measurements as the public pollsters and report objectively to their clients. Indeed, they cannot afford to do inadequate research.

The reliability of polls has from time to time been questioned, as when Harris and Gallup predicted an overwhelming Labour Party victory in the 1970 British elections and the Conservative Party won instead. Nevertheless, both Gallup and Harris claim accuracy of polls in general. Gallup says since 1948 his organization has, on the average, been off the actual balloting in important elections by a little less than 1 percentage point.

The problem with public understanding of any poll, but particularly political polls, was stated succinctly by authors and researchers Charles W. Roll and Albert H. Cantril: "There is nothing immutable about the results of a poll. The way polls are treated by the press and politicians, one might be led to think otherwise. However, what a poll provides is a picture of the public's view at only one point in time and on only the questions that were asked. Yet, inferences of sweeping proportion are frequently drawn from a poll, leading to fundamental misunderstandings of what the state of public opinion really is." [28]

Some polls are just for fun and say so. For example, during the 1960 Kennedy–Nixon presidential campaign, an Iowa radio station asked listeners favoring Nixon to turn on toasters or irons at a specified time and Kennedy backers to do the same at another time. A crew at the local power plant recorded the rise and fall of electrical power. Kennedy, it was reported, "out-kilowatted Nixon, two to one."

A St. Louis dairy found the same margin in a poll of ice cream eaters: Nixon backers were supposed to ask for vanilla (an advantage for Nixon in normally Democratic St. Louis, since vanilla outsells chocolate or any other flavor), and Kennedy supporters were supposed to ask for chocolate; JFK won—140,276 chocolate cones to 69,136 vanillas.

Similarly, in Nashville, Tennessee, a popcorn distributor has conducted a poll during each presidential election since 1948. In 1960 he had boxes or bags

---

[28] Charles W. Roll, Jr., and Albert H. Cantril, *Polls: Their Use and Misuse in Politics* (New York: Basic Books, 1972), p. 117. © by Basic Books, Inc., Publishers, New York.

printed with Democratic donkeys or Republican elephants; in November of that year, the final tabulation showed 53.4 percent of the popcorn electorate for Kennedy.[29]

Politicians are not alone in polling public opinion. Business and nonprofit associations and institutions also measure the climate in which they operate. The accuracy of such surveys is often, as one reporter noted, "a matter of interpretation."[30] This Associated Press reporter noted two reports about small business in the United States—one optimistic and the other showing conditions deteriorating. The latter report was from the National Federation of Independent Business, which had an eight-year track record of surveying the climate for small business in the United States. The report was its own summary of the current survey. The optimistic report was an interpretation by a public relations firm of a survey done for Dun & Bradstreet. The survey researcher told the AP reporter that the total of responses was 444, not "nearly 500" as the PR firm's news release had said. Also, the release had stated that "more than half the respondents felt that inflation would decrease," whereas the survey results actually recorded 33 percent saying it would increase, 32.7 percent saying it would decrease and 23 percent saying it would remain the same. The erroneous "more than half" had come from a breakdown of companies with revenues of more than $1 million. Indeed, 52 percent of these did expect a decrease. Of the 444 respondents, 100 of them were companies of more than $1 million.

Another difficulty with both interpretation and process is reported by anthropologist-market researcher Steve Barnett, who notes that most opinion polls are adequate for superficial questions but that people often behave differently from how they say they will.[31] He cites research his firm did for a group of electric utilities. Their fuel-use projections had been based in part on poll-takers' reports of customer interviews and were falling short of reality. To find out why, Barnett put TV cameras in the room where the thermostat was kept in 150 homes. He discovered that the discrepancy was due to "guerrilla warfare" over the thermostat between the person who paid the bill and everyone else. The constant adjusting was changing the use of heat, and that actual use was far different from reports.

PR RESEARCH AND THE SOCIAL SCIENCES

The difference between public opinion researchers and PR people was stated many years ago by Fred L. Palmer, partner in the PR firm of Earl Newsom and Company: "The public opinion researchers' function," he said, "is to know, measure, analyze, and weigh public opinion. The practitioners' function is

[29] Based on article by Robert W. Wells, "Popcorn for President," *This Week*, August 18, 1968, p. 6.

[30] John Cuniff, "Accuracy of Surveys a Matter of Interpretation," Associated Press story in the *Fort Worth Star-Telegram*, November 20, 1981, p. 5C.

[31] Frederick C. Klein, "Researcher Proves Consumers Using Anthropological Skills," *Wall Street Journal*, July 7, 1983, p. 21.

to help people deal constructively with the force of public opinion."[32] The study of public opinion in motion ties this type of research to both behavioral psychology and economics. Opinion research reflects seasonal or other types of trends in attitudes that raise questions of behavior patterns, and this in turn often means taking a look at the economic picture to determine if the roots of the problem might be there. Anyone who questions this sort of correlation might find some adequate, if unscientific, support in simple observation. Read the front page headlines of the newspaper and check the Dow Jones averages. Any security analyst or stockbroker will tell you there is a correlation between news on the AP and UPI wire and subsequent information on the Dow Jones ticker. Even a first-year economics student learns that the only thing giving the monetary system value is confidence.

The study of public opinion is particularly important to public relations people for another reason. There is a difference between information and opinion. Understanding that difference means taking into consideration the difference between understanding and knowledge. Hadley Cantril, public opinion authority and pollster, delineated the difference when he said public understanding is "knowledge that is function, that has been built up from experience, that has been tested by action."[33] On the other hand, public knowledge is more a matter of intellectual data that do not play a role in concrete perception. Cantril suggested that what public opinion surveys should watch for is when "knowledge" is used for "understanding" and the reasons for its being linked to purpose and brought to bear on the decision-making process. Many public relations projects now involve behavior modification. One of these is the American Heart Association's efforts to get young people to take care of their hearts in a lifelong program. What public relations people are dealing with in any behavior modification problem is perception versus reality. Therefore, what Cantril is saying about perception is particularly important.

The study of opinion, then, is critical. There yet is no continuing system of measurement for the "climate of public opinion." There are specific tests for specific issues, which are valuable in that they measure public opinion on a particular issue at a given time. But there is no continuing study of consumers' state of mind—how much they are willing to sacrifice in craftsmanship, for example, in return for mass-produced, less expensive products. Who knows what the real religious temper of the nation is, what spiritual values are held and by whom and why and when these change? Such attitudes can have a great deal to do with politics, as Italians can relate after their 1974 vote, which finally provided a legal process for divorce in that Catholic country. (Or was that really a question of economics or may be personal freedom?) Who really knows how much freedom people in the United States are willing to relinquish for security? This is a question politicians and businesspeople alike would benefit from knowing. The Opinion Research

---

[32] Fred L. Palmer, "Opinion Research as an Aid to Public Relation's Practice," address at roundtable discussion, International Conference in Public Opinion Research, Eagles Mere, Pa., September 13, 1948.

[33] Hadley Cantril, *Understanding Man's Social Behavior* (Princeton, N.J.: Office of Public Opinion Research, 1947), p. 31.

Corporation makes such probes. *Collectivist Ideology in America* is their most comprehensive study to date. One of the few long-term series of public opinion polls in the United States is the Link Audit, by the Psychological Corporation, which tests attitudes toward eight large U.S. companies. This is the kind of continuing research that has application potential.

There is a value in "pure" research and the searching for and use of new research techniques. There also is a great need for speedier and less expensive ways to measure opinions and reactions so government and business can be responsive; and a technological society that can explore space certainly should be able to meet the challenge.

In recent years the advertising industry has shown an awakened responsiveness to public opinion. As advertising commentator Herbert D. Maneloveg noted in *Saturday Review* back in 1970, the brightest marketing people move to the client's side rather than the agency's and the brighter clients seek help from people more in tune with the times, people oriented to new needs and life-styles. The ad agencies have been forced to meet the mood of consumerism, which demands that ads tell what the public wants to know about a product or service, rather than what the company wants to tell.

THE PR PERSON AS CATALYST

The public relations person has a certain obligation to be a catalyst between the social sciences and industry. Social scientists have the skills, knowledge and time to study social problems, but the meaningfulness of their work depends on implementation.

There are problems in using and applying social science theories and research techniques.

PR educator Michael Hesse, Ph.D., APR, noted that social science research for public relations should carry the following caveat:

> Social science research is imprecise. The hard sciences can easily observe and measure their concepts such as velocity, temperature and mass. Social science public relation concepts are not so easily observed, and thus, social scientists should not make great claims on their data. In public relations, we are associating phenomena at best. Concepts such as awareness and understanding reflect enormous individual differences—yet we try to measure them, and predict on the basis of our imprecise measures all too frequently. Additionally, social scientists apply sophisticated statistical tests (designed for analyzing more measurable phenomena) to unsophisticated data—the result in all too many cases is invalid research. We are probably not measuring what we think we are measuring and it appears we are attempting to use "advanced robotics" to do very simple tasks. Our tools may be too sophisticated for our work and may be misleading us.[34]

---

[34] Michael B. Hesse, Ph.D., APR, The University of Alabama, personal correspondence, 12/9/83. Used by permission.

The advantages of research, however, are many. Opinion research, as pollsters Charles Roll and Albert Cantril point out,[35] can contribute in a number of specific areas: First, it can uncover areas of public ignorance, misunderstanding and indifference. For instance, at a time when the Johnson Administration was reassessing U.S. policy in Southeast Asia, the finding by pollsters that a quarter of the American public did not even know mainland China was ruled by a communist regime could have been of the utmost importance.

Second, because the public often does not understand how specific actions or policies relate to long-term objectives, public opinion research can delineate these areas of confusion and help leaders convey to the public what must be taken into account in formulating policies.

Third, research can reveal the public's realistic expectations of what will follow from some action. Research can help leaders maximize their leadership potential in this regard.

Fourth, the opinion survey can reveal what various publics' perceptions of issues and events are. Perceptions are important because they are the realities with which the public relations practitioner must deal.

The public relations practitioner is in a good position to recognize the usefulness of opinion research and social science research and assist in its application by organizations, particularly business, with the tools, systems and financing to put the concepts to work. A knowledge of the social sciences makes it possible for a PR practitioner to analyze problems in definable, specific terms; set realistic, achievable goals; develop a workable program; gauge the use and usefulness of materials to achieve goals; and evaluate the results. Since this involves judging programs that are often the brainchildren of practitioners, it is only by taking the posture of scientists that PR people can avoid subjective analysis of research and take an objective view.

The public relations person also can help management with the climate of opinion within the institution. Where management is committed and involved, a twenty-question survey can be developed that covers areas important to employee morale, motivation and productivity, according to a study done by the American Press Institute.[36] When institutions are large, samples of employees can be used, just as in sampling external publics; but with small numbers of employees, all should be personally interviewed. Privacy has to be observed and the survey should be done at the place of work, not sent to the home, to eliminate bias from that area. All employees should be given the statistical results, and management should be committed to improving weakness and problems the survey reveals. If no improvements are made, employees may be reluctant to participate again or they may not take the survey seriously.

Communication research can show that PR improves the company's bottom

---

[35] Charles W. Roll, Jr., and Albert H. Cantril, *Polls: Their Use and Misuse in Politics* (New York: Basic Books, 1972), pp. 154–155.

[36] Malcolm F. Mallette, "How Newspapers Communicate Internally," (Reston, Va.: American Press Institute, 1981), p. 31.

5.8 A CORPORATE RESEARCH ACTIVITIES MODEL

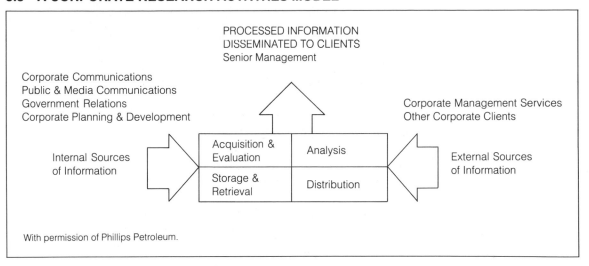

PROCESSED INFORMATION
DISSEMINATED TO CLIENTS
Senior Management

Corporate Communications
Public & Media Communications
Government Relations
Corporate Planning & Development

Corporate Management Services
Other Corporate Clients

Internal Sources
of Information

| Acquisition & Evaluation | Analysis |
| Storage & Retrieval | Distribution |

External Sources
of Information

With permission of Phillips Petroleum.

line by improving relations with its critical audiences, says PR counselor Peter Finn.[37] A second value of research, according to Finn, is to provide hard, reliable information to guide policy decisions, and a third is to verify the role PR must play in effectively answering a company's challengers.

PR practitioners should be involved in opinion studies of both internal and external audiences and provide survey studies and results as a department service (see 5.8). But the idea that public relations practitioners should be skilled in the social sciences isn't new. It was expressed by Edward L. Bernays in his 1955 book *The Engineering of Public Consent,* a title widely considered to mean the "manipulation" of public consent. What he details in his book and has commented on at great length since then, however, is his belief in the efficiency of the standardization of public relations practices, as they are standardized in the engineering profession. Reinforcing the Bernays position is a statement from James F. Tirone, Public Relations Director, Planning, for AT&T in New York. Tirone says, "My inference is that Bernays is suggesting that the PR person should be oriented toward research in the social sciences, be able to do the research work, or, at least, be qualified to understand it in such a way so that the data may be utilized in behalf of the client. I have never found a client, in and out of the large corporation, who expected otherwise even though the requirement might not be stated explicitly."[38]

---

[37] Peter Finn, "Demystifying Public Relations," *Public Relations Journal* (May 1982), p. 12.

[38] James F. Tirone, "Theory, Research and Public Relations," invited paper presented to the Association for Education in Journalism, Seattle, Washington, August, 1978, p. 3.

- Currently, the focus in PR research is on (1) opinion audits, (2) communication audits, (3) peer perception studies, (4) evaluations of the quality of media attention and (5) evaluation of message content about thought trends.

- PR research is either internal or external. Formal research often deals with the opinions of specific target audiences and depends on sampling populations and selecting samples based on probability.

- PR research describes populations in terms of who people are (demographics) and what people think (psychographics).

- The most familiar forms of data gathering for researchers are cross-section surveys, survey panels, in-depth and focus group interviews, content analyses, questionnaires and the DELPHI process.

- Questionnaires are the most familiar data-gathering device, but developing an effective one involves a careful study of how the questionnaire will be administered (mail, telephone and so on) and of who the respondents will be.

- Semantic differential and summated ratings are techniques of questionnaire construction that measure the intensity of responses.

- Broadcast research uses three basic types of research formats: diary, interview and program analyzer.

- Polling, a research technique that can be either public or private, may have problems of accuracy and interpretation.

- The public opinion researcher's function is to know how to measure, analyze and weigh public opinion. The PR practitioner's function is to help people deal constructively with the force of public opinion.

- Most public opinion studies are of specific issues at specific times. Continuing studies of attitudes and states of minds would have useful applications in business and politics.

- Public relations practitioners have an obligation to be a catalyst between the social sciences and industry. They must take the objective position of social scientists to avoid subjective analysis of research.

_____ **THINGS TO DO**

1. Design a readership survey for your college newspaper regarding both editorial and advertising content. Determine how the survey will be taken and prepare the questionnaire.

2. Design a survey to determine where students get most of their information about public affairs: from newspapers, news magazines, radio, television or whatever. Develop the questionnaire to test not only source but also credibility.

3. Choose a new organization on campus or a campus service that doesn't have much visibility (perhaps counseling or career placement). Do the research and plan a strategy to call attention to your "client."

SELECTED READINGS

For Statistics

Allen L. Bernstein, *A Handbook of Statistics Solutions for the Behavioral Sciences* (New York: Holt, Rinehart and Winston, 1964). Standard reference in the field.

Hubert M. Blalock, Jr., *Social Statistics*, 2nd ed. (New York: McGraw-Hill, 1972). Another standard text; readable.

D. J. Champion, *Basic Statistics for Social Research* (Boston: Houghton Mifflin, 1981). A good survey test.

Solomon Diamond, *Information and Error* (New York: Basic Books, 1959). Simplifies some basic steps.

Robert R. Johnson, *Elementary Statistics*, 3rd ed. (North Scituate, Mass.: Duxbury Press, 1980). A simple text with easy-to-find basic formulas.

Donald H. Sanders, A. Franklin Murph and Robert J. Eng, *Statistics: A Fresh Approach*, 2nd ed. (New York: McGraw-Hill, 1980). An excellent book for applications of statistics.

Frederick Williams, *Reasoning with Statistics: Simplified Examples in Communications Research*, 2nd ed. (New York: Holt, Rinehart and Winston, 1979). An excellent guide through the mathematics maze.

Roger D. Wimmer and Joseph R. Dominick, *Mass Media Research* (Belmont, Calif.: Wadsworth, 1983). A superior treatment of statistics; also a good basic research methods text. Special attention is given to research in advertising and public relations.

Especially for Probability

W. J. Youden, *Risk, Choice, and Prediction* (North Scituate, Mass.: Duxbury Press, 1974). More a set of games than a book, but helpful in understanding probability. Now out of print, but still in some libraries. See Wimmer and Dominick.

For Computers

Norman H. Nie, Dale H. Ben and C. Hull Hadlai, *Statistical Package for the Social Sciences*, 2nd ed. (New York: McGraw-Hill, 1978). More help in understanding how to use computers. (See Nie and Hadlai, *SPSS Pocket Guide*, 1981). Also see Wimmer and Dominick, which contains a chapter on use of computers in research.

For Survey Research

Earl R. Babbie, *The Practice of Social Research* (Belmont, Calif.: Wadsworth, 1983). An introductory research methods text, stressing practice as well as method. Also see Babbie's *Survey Research Methods*, also from Wadsworth, 1973.

Charles H. Backstrom and Gerald D. Hursh, *Survey Research*, 2nd ed. (New York: John Wiley, 1981). A basic how-to-do-it approach.

Donald T. Campbell and Julian C. Stanley, *Experimental and Quasi-Experimental Designs for Research* (Chicago: Rand McNally, 1966). A basic text for design of field experiments.

Cales-Magnus Cassel et al. *Foundations of Inference in Survey Sampling* (New York: John Wiley, 1977). Combined with survey sampling techniques is inference theory to give a new approach to the survey.

Cochrane Chase and Kenneth L. Barasch, *Marketing Problem-Solver*, 2d ed. (Radnor, Pa.: Chilton, 1976). Includes marketing strategies and research, as well as pricing, legal constraints, advertising and PR.

Paul Cozby, *Methods in Behavioral Research*, 2nd ed. (Palo Alto, Calif.: Mayfield, 1981). An introductory text in research with good explanation of correlational methods.

Lloyd A. Free and Hadley Cantril, *Political Beliefs of Americans: A Study of Public Opinion* (New York: Touchstone Books, a division of Simon and Schuster, 1968). The study is more interesting than the results; often used by politicians.

Institute for Social Research, *Interviewer's Manual* (Ann Arbor: Institute for Social Research, University of Michigan, 1976). Also offers other helpful guidance.

"Measuring Public Relations Impact," *Public Relations Review*, Vol. X, No. 2 (Summer 1984). A complete issue on research, covering research attitudes, opinion surveys, focus groups, readability studies, readership surveys, research bibliography.

Philip Meyer, *Precision Journalism* (Bloomington: Indiana University Press, 2nd ed. 1979). If polling intrigues you, consult this book. It discusses the effects and effectiveness of polls, including some really critical information for PR people using polls. (Now out of print but available at libraries.)

Delbert C. Miller, *Handbook of Research Design and Social Measurements*, 3d ed. (New York: Longman [David McKay Co.], 1977). A useful guide through the mathematics maze.

Ralph O. Nafziger and David M. White, eds., *Introduction to Mass Communication Research* (Baton Rouge: Louisiana State University Press, 1963). Covers the fundamental areas of communication research and is easy to read.

——— and Marcus M. Wilerson, *Introduction to Journalism Research* (Westport, Conn.: Greenwood, 1968).

Edward J. Robinson, *Public Relations and Survey Research* (New York: Appleton-Century-Crofts, 1969). At this point, the only PR research guide and dated but clear and easy to use.

Leroy Wolins, *Research Mistakes in the Social and Behavioral Sciences* (Ames, Iowa: Iowa State University Press, 1982). Good reading.

PART 3

PR Audiences

Anyone and everyone is a potential target audience for public relations. Also, all public relations activities affect and are affected by the climate of public opinion. Chapters 6 and 7 examine PR publics and public opinion.

CHAPTER 6

PR's Publics and Target Audiences

The sharp drop in the credibility of most U.S. institutions means that the message must be designed with the background of a specific public in mind, so that it will be fully understood. It means also that the real questions in the minds of these publics must be solicited— and answered.

Carl Hauver, former president, Public Relations Society of America

The word *publics* refers to audiences for public relations. But what exactly are these publics? The best way to understand them is to think of the various publics you, as an individual, belong to (see 6.1).

First, you belong to a group of consumers that, no doubt, has been well defined by marketing people. You may, for instance, be in the eighteen- to twenty-one-year-old "college" market; this market receives a great deal of attention because—though you may not believe it—it is responsible for a vast outlay of cash. Second, you have organizational identities. If you belong to a social or civic organization—the Rotary, Lions, PTA, League of Women Voters, a fraternity, political action group, professional society or athletic team or club—you are a member of still another public. If you are in college, you may be a member of a preprofessional organization affiliated with a national group. You may also belong to other publics because of race, religion, ethnic group or national origin. *A public, then, may be defined as any group of people tied together, however loosely, by some common bond of interest or concern.*

In traditional public relations literature, publics are divided into two categories: external and internal. *External publics* are those outside an institution that have some relationship to the institution and can have widespread impact—such as a government regulatory agency.

Internal publics are those to which an institution most closely relates—ones that share the institutional identity, such as management, employees, supporters (investors, for example, or members of an organization) and others who may be defined only in relation to a specific institution. Occasionally in public relations practice, the term *internal publics* is used in reference only to employees, that is, workers. The usage is unfortunate when it distinguishes management or administrators from employees because this results in employees being considered as

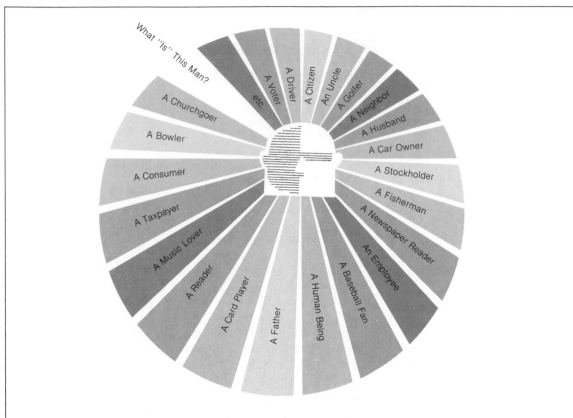

What "Is" This Man?

A Voter etc.
A Driver
A Citizen
An Uncle
A Golfer
A Neighbor
A Husband
A Car Owner
A Stockholder
A Fisherman
A Newspaper Reader
An Employee
A Baseball Fan
A Human Being
A Father
A Card Player
A Reader
A Music Lover
A Taxpayer
A Consumer
A Bowler
A Churchgoer

Reprinted by permission of Macmillan Publishing Co., Inc., from *Communications: The Transfer of Meaning* by Don Fabun. Copyright © 1968 by Kaiser Aluminum and Chemical Corp.

separate from management instead of all being thought of as part of a team. Such thinking has a ghetto effect that creates serious communications problems. In a strong union situation, the separation is real and a team concept is not likely. However, the adversary relationship can be healthy as long as communication between the two is maintained.

To help you think about publics, visualize throwing a rock into a pond. The action moves across the water in concentric circles. The innermost circles are closest to the action, like internal publics. The circles on the periphery are remote, but still tied to the action. When one of the circles touches a lily pad, it has come in contact with an external public, one remote from the action, but touched by it. External publics around a campus, for example, are shopkeepers in the immediate campus area who are not really a part of the university, but who are touched by what occurs there. Internal publics are the student, faculty, administrators, staff. Alumni also would be an internal public because they share the institution's image.

Any particular public, either internal or external, may become the focal point for a public relations effort. When that occurs, the public singled out for attention is called a "target audience."

IDENTIFYING TARGET AUDIENCES

To suggest how a public becomes a *target audience*, consider the example of health care programs. When any national health care programs are proposed, the opinion of the American Medical Association—as a public—is critical, and so pro-health care PR forces must be concerned with AMA members as a target group. However, not everyone favors the concept of "target audience." The dean of communications researchers, Wilbur Schramm, disparages the phrase:

> For nearly thirty years after World War I, the favorite concept of the mass media audience was what advertisers and propagandists often chose to call the "target audience." . . . A propagandist could shoot the magic bullet of communication into a viewer or a listener, who would stand still and wait to be hit! . . . By the late 1950s the bullet theory was, so to speak, shot full of holes. Mass communication was not like a shooting gallery. There was nothing necessarily irresistible about mass communication or mass propaganda. Many influences entered into the effect of the mass media. The audience was not a passive target; rather, it was extraordinarily active.[1]

Certainly no audience is static, and any audience is as unpredictable as human behavior has proven to be. Still, we will use the term *target audience*, consider it valid and emphasize that it is a *particular* public, clearly defined by research—a silhouette, a statistical profile, not a life-size, four-color portrait. The term is used because there must be some definable audience for whom advertising and information is specifically prepared. The "mass audience" is indeed a myth, and the scattershot approach is both foolish and uneconomical.

As a public relations practitioner, you must carefully define each public or target audience pertinent to your particular project and determine other publics that might be affected. The key to this is *research*—finding out who these publics really are and what they think, not what you believe they are or think. An example of what happens when research is ignored is the difficulty an armaments company had in a community the company dominated. Because the company contributed so much to the economy of the community, executives couldn't understand reports that their employees were being shunned socially by other members of the community. Eventually this affected the company's ability to recruit top employees locally, regardless of the pay it offered. Finally, an attitude study of the community by an outside research agency revealed that the community did not know what the company's employees did, that because of the high salaries and government se-

---

[1] Wilbur Schramm, *Men, Messages, and Media: A Look at Human Communication* (New York: Harper & Row, 1973), pp. 243–245.

curity, they looked like a lot of high-priced Ph.D.s pushing paper at the expense of the community's tax dollars. An informational campaign kept within the confines of government security restrictions helped clear up the resentment.

The danger of *assuming* what a major public thinks or knows is quite serious. The alert public relations practitioner must consider not only the position of the majority in each of the publics but also that of the dissenters. Failure to do so may cause future problems, as the Democratic Party leadership discovered in the early 1970s when women and other ethnic minority groups were demanding representation. In 1983 Republican President Ronald Reagan discovered that women saw him as unresponsive to feminist issues. Except when votes are being counted, there is a tendency to underestimate the significance of publics categorized as "minor."

To develop sensitivity to the attitudes of various target audiences, a PR person must develop empathy, doing research to get a profile of a public as an actor studies a role and then projects himself into the character. The PR person must say, "If I were this public, with this background, these situations, this set of concepts, how would I react to the set of circumstances being introduced by the institution I represent?" Developing such empathy for a public, trying to imagine how that public will react, not only helps in planning for a specific situation but also helps in media selection.

Each institution has its own particular primary audiences. A university, for instance, has trustees, administrators, faculty, staff, students, parents, alumni, financial supporters, the intellectual community, business community and residential community. All are important; all represent people of varying ages, backgrounds and views of what the university should be. A business has internal primary audiences (stockholders, employees, dealers, sales representatives) and external primary audiences (customers, government regulatory agencies, suppliers, competitors, the financial community—security analysts and investors in addition to their own stockholders—and the local community). At any time one or more of these primary audiences can become a target audience—the focus for the institution's attention.

DESCRIBING TARGET AUDIENCES

Target audiences can be described in three ways. The first is merely by giving the audience a name, such as stockholders. The second is by looking at the demographics of the audience—who comprises the group in terms of statistical characteristics like age, sex, income, education and so on. The third is by looking at the psychographics—the emotional and behavioral characteristics that define the group. The psychographics often show how one primary public may be like another in interests or actions.

Such descriptions are becoming more and more important with the increasing diversity of audiences. For example, AT&T's public relations organization (supposedly the world's largest) has done some target marketing that seems to contradict conventional wisdom. Vice President for Public Relations Edwin Block says, for example, that supporting the arts is a good business proposition because a higher percentage of the people AT&T wants to reach is interested in the arts. Those who enjoy symphonic music (a psychographic characteristic) have what Block calls "remarkably appealing demographics." He cites some examples: The median age is forty, slightly under the national average; the median income is $21,000, 50 percent above the national average; on educational levels, 70 percent are college graduates and 30 percent hold advanced degrees. Furthermore, the audience size is larger than that of professional sports in almost every major market. He concludes, "If you talk about numbers of people who pay their own good hard money to go to an event, there is a higher percentage of the kind of people we want to reach in the arts."[2]

A more general type of psychographic casting is done by SRI International, which has a system for categorizing publics according to *values, attitudes,* and *lifestyles* called VALS.[3] VALS divides people into groups: the *Inner Directed,* the *Outer Directed* and the *Integrated.* The *Inner Directed* group consists of two subcategories: (1) the *need driven,* about 11 percent of the adult population, are described as "money restricted," those struggling to buy the basics, including *survivors* who are old, poor, depressed and far removed from the cultural mainstream and *sustainers* like female single heads of households, who are relatively young, angry, crafty, struggling on the edge of poverty, willing to do anything to get ahead; and (2) the *self driven* who are predicted to make up 28 percent of the adult population by 1990 and include *I–am–me's* who are young, zippy, exhibitionistic, narcissistic, dramatic, impulsive, fiercely individualistic and inventive; *experimentals,* a mature version of *I–am–me's,* who want direct experience and vigorous involvement and are concerned with inner growth and naturalism; and the *societally conscious* who are attracted to simple living and smallness of scale and tend to support conservation, environmentalism and consumerism. The *Outer Directed* Group, SRI says, make up more than half (59 percent) of the adult population and has three subcategories: (1) *belongers* who are traditional, conservative, conventional, nostalgic, sentimental, puritanical and unexperimental; (2) *emulators* who are trying to burst into the system and make it big and are ambitious, upwardly mobile, status–conscious, macho and competitive, but also distrustful and angry, with little faith that the Establishment will give them a fair shake; and (3) *achievers* who are leaders in business, professions and government and are characterized by efficiency, fame, status, the good life, comfort, and materialistic values. The other group, the *Integrated,* who display the power of the Outers and the sensitivity of the Inners, are described as psychologically fully mature, tolerant, assured, self–actualizing and often having a world perspective. They account for about 2 percent of the population and are heavily represented in corporate and national leadership.

SRI's descriptive categories are similar in attempting to predict behavior from observed or reported behavior to those resulting from a study by NPD, a market

[2] "Audience Targeting Gets Ever More Critical," *pr reporter*, vol. 25, no. 32, August 16, 1982, p. 1.

[3] "Psychographics Combines Values, Attitudes, Lifestyles," *pr reporter*, vol. 25, no. 37, September 20, 1982, p. 1.

research firm that has attempted to categorize people by their eating habits—another expression of values.[4] NPD, going beyond traditional market research polls, employed in addition to questionnaires a research technique borrowed from broadcast research—the diary. Their survey spanned two years. On the basis of the information gathered, NPD groups people as eaters into five categories: (1) meat and potatoes eaters; (2) families with children—the soda pop and sweet cereal buyers; (3) naturalists—the fresh fruit, granola and yogurt crowd; (4) sophisticates—the bagels and wine bunch; (5) dieters—the skim milk and sugar substitute users. However, what they discovered is the groups are consistent in behavior, but in behavior that questions the purity of the categories. Naturalists may eat less sugar than most of the others but they ate chocolate chips more frequently. (The study dealt with frequency, not volume.) There was a logical explanation—the naturalists also liked to cook from scratch—so they probably made the cookies. An NPD competitor, Market Research Corp. of America has completed a ten-year study which it claims to be more comprehensive. The bottom line for the studies is to make products the public likes and will buy. Translating research into action is what gives most decision makers pause.

THE FRAGMENTED PUBLICS

The sheer size of U.S. institutions today has created many problems. Rarely can an irate housewife carry a wilted head of lettuce to a grocery store owner, complain that it was sent in response to her phoned-in order and be recompensed. The consumer today faces an endless chain of command proficient at buck passing, and persons at all levels—consumers and employees—suffer a loss of identity and influence.

From the PR practitioner's standpoint, dealing with this loss of *identity* in an era of increasing sophistication can be a considerable problem. Employees in industry worry about being replaced by robots, and individual achievement is likely to be submerged in group effort. The employee of a large corporation, for example, may wet a finger and try to smear the "signed" signature of a congratulatory letter from management to see if it is handwritten—or if it is akin to the "personalized" computer-written letter we often get in the mail. The efforts to personalize, to identify, to recognize members of a large target audience demand originality and heavy financing. Computer information delivery systems through cable television have further fragmented publics, but do offer some potential for identification of these audiences/users. A study by International Resource Development, "Paperless Consumer Information Services," shows electronic communication efficient but missing the human touch. The most personal communication, a letter, has been depersonalized by electronic mail systems. As a result, letters on personal stationery, IRD says, will be even more important, as will greeting cards.

---

[4]Betsy Morris, "Study to Detect True Eating Habits Finds Junk-Food Fans in the Health Food Ranks," *Wall Street Journal*, February 3, 1984, p. 19.

6.2 EFFECT OF "PAPERLESS" CONSUMER INFORMATION

Category	Negative High	Negative Low	None	Positive Low	Positive High
Catalogs	X				
Directories	X				
Newspapers		X			
Magazines			X		
Business Forms					X
Greeting Cards				X	
High-Quality Stationery					X
Commodity Stationery		X			
Checks		X			
Trade Books			X		
Technical Books	X				
1st Class Mail		X			
2nd Class Mail	X				

Impact

"Depersonalized computer communication will affect many media, adding value to personal ones. Electronic communication will have a high negative impact on catalogs, directories and technical books—most used as references. This information will probably be on data banks. Also, second-class unit messages will be electronically delivered. Very personal media, such as letters on personalized, high-quality stationery, will increase in value due to the human touch."

pr reporter, September 12, 1983, vol. 26, no. 36, p. 2.

Less personal paper communications, such as newspaper classifieds, will probably disappear and be supplanted entirely by electronic ads (see 6.2, which shows the media that will be affected by electronic mail). A suggestion in *pr reporter* is to take advantage of this information by personalizing your medium.

PR people must also contend with a loss of a *sense of community*. High mobility has weakened family ties, almost dissolved neighborhood alliances, reduced civic involvement and changed loyalties so that, as one editor complained, "No one buys this paper just because it's a hometown newspaper anymore." This mobility has weakened loyalty to employers too. Other companies can lure executives with promises of greater success and attract lower-level employees with more money.

In addition, workers suffer from a loss of *creativity*. Because so much progress in our highly technological society depends on teamwork, individuals often think their accomplishments are meaningless. No longer does a cobbler make a pair of shoes, see them worn and pride himself on his reputation as a fine craftsman. People on the assembly line feel little personal involvement with the shoe that comes off and may be highly critical of the production process itself if they perceive it to be producing shoddy merchandise.[5] Some corporations try to combat this discontent by rotating production-line workers from time to time so they are challenged by learning new jobs and begin to understand the production process itself, although the technology of some jobs or union restrictions may not allow this.

[5]W. Lloyd Warner and J. O. Low, "The Factory in the Community," in *Industry and Society*, ed. William F. Whyte (New York: McGraw-Hill, 1946), pp. 21–45.

The environment, then, created by the remoteness of an impersonalized system of business, industry, agriculture, government, education and even religion has isolated many publics, including those they are supposed to serve. Underlying all these factors is the difference between what an institution is and what it says it is.

INTERNAL AUDIENCES AND THE ORGANIZATIONAL IMAGE

"Every organization has an image. The only question is whether it has the image it wants to have—in fact as well as in fantasy," says Harry Levinson, a clinical psychologist. Levinson explains:

> [Psychoanalyst Sigmund] Freud point out that individuals in any cohesive organization identify with the ego ideal [ideal stereotype] of their leader. As an organization expands and matures, this ego tends to become the collective aspirations of its people. Diffuse as this may sound, it is real. Industrial psychologists have long known that people, if they have any choice in the matter, will not work for an organization when they disapprove of its image, its self-image, and its ego ideal.[6]

In other words, employee attitudes often accurately reflect an organization's image of itself. When employees are indifferent to the organization's ideal of itself, as reflected in its imagery, they may stay on the payroll, but will do nothing beyond the minimum demanded.

For employees to react in any way to an organizational ideal, the ideal itself must be defined, communicated and understood. Many institutions have never tried to define an ideal accurately, and the result is often a fragmented reaction to the institution, its policies and products. Sometimes the ideal is too vague or is just rhetoric, as when an oil company says it believes understanding and goodwill must be earned through the application of sound and ethical principles in the conduct of every phase of its business.

The real difficulty, however, is not in stating an ideal but in living up to it. When an organization fails to act consistently with its projected ideal, not only employees but also customers and the community are disillusioned. But while the customers may take their dollars elsewhere, employees express their disillusionment in other ways, particularly if economic circumstances do not permit them to quit. If they stay, they often have feelings of depression, apathy, alienation and outright anger. This is compounded sometimes by a company's image advertising. If a company advertises that people are its most important asset, but employees are having a different experience, they will, of course, see their leaders as hypocrites and react hostilely. Negative feelings can also result when employees cannot act positively toward attaining an ideal. The pride a company has in the steel panels it makes may be shared by all employees except those in the paint department, who

---

[6]Harry Levinson, "How to Undermine an Organization," *Public Relations Journal*, 22, no. 10 (October 1966), pp. 82–84. Used by permission.

know that because the company does not have the money to invest in the process for baking on the enamels, the paints will wear off faster. The resulting cynicism causes high turnover.

Clinical psychologist Levinson compares an organization to a human being:

> If you want to understand a person, you examine him. You may do so systematically, as a physician does, or you may get to know much about him over a long period of time, as a friend does. First, you try to learn who and what he is. Second, you try to learn how he behaves under various circumstances. Third, you want to know what he believes and how he sees the world, how he presents himself to the world and why he does so that way. If there is a wide gap between the image he projects and the person he really is, emotional conflicts are inevitable.[7]

The measures Levinson would use to establish an organization's image are as follows:

- *What it does* as evidenced in its products and services and the way it regards its employees ("economic units to be purchased and directed" or "capable, mature people").
- *What it says* through communication with employees ("exhortation and persuasion" or "mutual definition of common problems") and its customers ("someone to be conned by promising more than can be delivered" or "to be duped by clever packaging").
- *What people believe it to be.*

Although the best way to find out what various publics think is by scientific research, you can also ask a few informal questions: (1) If the institution has an image, does it live up to it? Or does it say one thing and do another? (2) If there is an image, can employees live up to it? Or are there conflicting demands, low pay, or other reasons why they cannot? (3) When there must be an image change, have the employees been helped to make the change through participative management? (4) If there is no recognizable company image, is it desirable to have confusion, limited identification and disparate values?

Internal publics are those most likely to be particularly sensitive to how an institution is presented to an external public because, as a part of that institution, their ego is involved.

A university deciding to do some advertising just before registration discovered just how closely egos were involved when the returning students who had heard the radio commercials created a storm of protest. What the protesters *said* was, "A really excellent institution of higher learning shouldn't have to *advertise*." However, when the protesters were asked in small group sessions if it was unseemly to "call attention to the programs and services the university had to offer, just in case people were unaware of them," they agreed that this was acceptable. What, then, was the problem? The problem turned out to be more than the type of advertising. They considered broadcasting a bit flamboyant, although they admitted it was the best way to reach the target audience of eighteen-year-olds. How-

---

[7] Ibid., p. 84.

ever, the medium had not offended. The *style* of commercials had. The students who were protesting did not *see* the style of the commercials as consistent with the image they had of the university they were attending and from which they hoped to have a degree. They complained about the lack of "dignity" in the appeals. The problem was consistency of imagery.

The university's solution was to involve students more in all its planning for presenting the university to its publics, especially to potential students. It had found that current students need to feel comfortable with an image being portrayed because they share that image. The philosophy behind this solution was that current students are the best recruiters a university has. That is always true of an internal public. Students and faculty of a university, members of an organization, employees of a corporation—all, as internal publics, have the highest credibility among external publics. They are supposed to know how it really is. Often because of poor internal communications, they don't. The wise public relations practitioner focuses on internal publics to keep them involved and informed because they are the voices external publics are most likely to hear and to believe.

Internal publics are considered authorities, whether they really are or not. For example, a plant manufacturing planes for the U.S. government was given some unfortunate publicity when one of the multimillion-dollar aircraft failed to function. Since the plane was new, each time one aircraft malfunctioned, all were grounded until the fault could be detected. The community in which the planes were being made was very sensitive to the publicity. One employee whose job was plant security told of being asked constantly by people at his church, at his lodge, even at the grocery store and when he was working in his yard, "Come on, tell me, what's *really* wrong with those birds." He honestly didn't know. The reasons, like the plane, were very complex. Besides that, he had no engineering experience and was not even involved in the design or construction of the plane, only in the security of the plant. But his judgment was sought and his words taken as authoritative because, after all, others reasoned, since he worked there, he ought to know.

The realization that each person who could be described as an "internal public" is a potentially significant public relations asset could make most public relations directors' jobs ultimately easier. (Tools to use in accomplishing the task are discussed in Chapter 9 on communication channels.) The internal publics can serve effectively as PR's front line. The best way to promote this is for management to make employees feel involved. PR researcher Grunig says (see Chapter 4, page 98) a person involved in a situation seeks information, and a person motivated to communicate about a situation also is motivated to develop a solution for the situation. As an example, a city having difficulty with some old gas meters that are recording higher customer usage than exists needs to give information about the problem to those on the front line—the meter readers. They will be in contact with customers, and if they understand the problem and what the company is doing, they are more likely to communicate. If the company goes a step farther and provides them with some information to give the customer, the typical communication constraint—that it's someone else's job—is removed. If the company generally informs its front-line meter readers, receptionists and so on, the referent criterion is strengthened and the effectiveness of the PR front line improved.

EXTERNAL PUBLICS AND
THE ORGANIZATIONAL IMAGE

External publics are not the exclusive property of any institution. Any external audience may become a target audience, and as such may become the subject of communication. For example, high school students and recent graduates who might become college freshmen are target audiences for university recruiting. Other prospective candidates for college are students in community colleges and working people who might want to return to school or enter for the first time.

Looking at those who might constitute external publics helps a public relations practitioner avoid the fallacy of considering external audiences as a "mass public." *There is no such thing as a "mass audience."* External publics have larger segments of people than internal publics but never should external audiences be thought of as an indescribable "mass."[8]

External publics may be a constituency, like the residents of cities that have a professional sports team. Or an external public may be an adversary, like the antinuclear advocates are to electric utilities. Both must be considered in public relations planning and communication strategies. External publics also have a great deal to do with an institution's image. When external publics have similar perceptions of what the institution is and what it should be to those of the internal publics, the institution's image is likely to be sound. To be sound is to be consistent (see 6.3).

External publics have perceptions of corporate identity, and often these perceptions vary with different external publics. Internal publics are sensitive to and affected by the corporate identity which they share. Corporate identity is the sum of all the factors that define and project what an organization is and where it is going—its business mix, management style, communication policies and practices, nomenclature, competencies, competitive differentiation and visual presentation. Identity is the essence of the corporation, according to corporate PR practitioner Stephen Downey.[9] Downey says American corporations have a great deal of redefining and projection of their images ahead, owing to significant economic, technological and demographic changes in the business environment. He observes:

> Corporate identity (in most companies still the province of public relations) will be expected to define and project—accurately, understandably, efficiently and memorably—the essence of those surviving and emerging companies. Moreover, it must do so within what is becoming truly a world economy and internationally competitive marketplace. Those companies which communicate their identity most compellingly

---

[8] Melvin L. DeFleur and Sandra Ball-Rokeach, *Theories of Mass Communication*, 3d ed. (New York: Longman, 1982), p. 157. "Mass society refers to the relationship that exists between individuals and the social order around them. In mass society . . . individuals are presumed to be in a situation of psychological isolation from others, impersonality is said to prevail in their interaction with others, and they are said to be relatively free from demands of binding social obligations."

[9] Stephen M. Downey, "Corporate Identity's Role in Economic Recovery," *PRSA Newsletter*, 11, nos. 4–5, April/May 1983, p. 1.

6.3 INSTITUTIONAL IMAGE

Problem Profile

1. What an institution's employees think it is. ○
   What employees want it to be. ⃝

2. What an institution's management thinks it is. △
   What management wants it to be. ▽

3. What an institution's external publics think it is. ☐
   What external publics want it to be. ▭

Levinson's Image Theory Illustrated

	Problem Profile	*Positive Profile*
What an institution does.	○	○
What it says.	☐	○
What people believe it to be.	△	○

Difficulties occur when the two profiles overlap and the lines are not harmonious. For example, in problem profile 3, the public wants the institution to be ▭ (buses to all major shopping districts on the hour, six days a week, for 50 cents fare), but it is ☐ (buses to three major shopping districts, 10 A.M. to 6 P.M., five days a week, for 75 cents fare plus area add-on tolls). The result is ⊏⊐ —a poor fit. Levinson's chart says an institution is a mix of what it does and what people believe it to be. If this fits, the image is consonant.

by cutting through customer confusion and gaining the allegiance of key audiences are most likely to prosper in the new order (translate opportunity).

Downey says that organizations must reexamine their identity under the following circumstances:

■ When public perceptions of a company do not reflect reality. Vestiges of past management mistakes, poor earnings, environmental problems, and the like may still be having a negative impact.

■ When external forces such as a new competitor, a breakthrough product, deregulation, or an existing competitor's new identity require identification countermeasures.

■ When competitors are slow to form clearly defined and effectively projected corporate and/or product presentation. In this sense, identity is opportunistic and can become a competitive advantage in itself.

Reexamining a corporate image can offer many insights, as this story of Sperry suggests:

In the business community, Sperry was highly regarded. But its image was blurred. There was a lack of focus, internally as well as externally, about what the company stood for and where it was strong. In short, there was no defined culture that served as a rallying point. Company management recognized that it had to forge a single corporate identity—something unmistakably Sperry.

Their first step involved communications research—an attitude audit—to determine how its various publics perceived Sperry. What they discovered surprised them. One finding, in particular, stood out: Sperry was widely respected for giving thoughtful attention to suggestions, complaints and ideas. One customer summed it up: "You guys listen better."

The listening concept turned up among employees, as well. And listening, as the research revealed, is not a passive act. It connotes interaction, problem solving, sensitivity. All were factors of Sperry's culture, identified by communications efforts. Then Sperry chose to unify its image with the listening theme, letting one element stand for the whole culture.

The general public knows this image through corporate ads that stress listening and offer booklets about it. What the general public did not see were the thousands of hours devoted to internal communications: a companywide schedule of listening seminars, special mailings, bulletin boards, items in employee publications and booklets. Meanwhile, the program attracted a favorable press. Articles on Sperry's listening habits appeared in the *New York Times*, the *Washington Post* and Sylvia Porter's syndicated column. Sperry people began to turn upon TV talk shows as experts on how to listen.

Communications helps Sperry capitalize on its culture.[10]

In contrast, a company that tries to impose a culture on the organization is headed for trouble. The corporate culture is "real and powerful," according to a *Fortune* article. "It's also hard to change, and you won't find much support for doing so inside or outside your company."[11]

TARGET AUDIENCES AND PLANNING

As we indicated, tailoring public relations programs to fit various target audiences depends on your ability to identify the audiences and their characteristics, through both formal and informal research methods, and then translating this information into a sensitive understanding of their needs. To develop a program both real and realistic—not a facade of imagery that disillusions and alienates—it is essential to have respect for and empathy with the target groups.

A target audience is the group most affected by or most influential in accepting an idea, policy, event, decision or product. Once identified, the group must be studied for its other relationships. For instance, are some of the stockholders employees? An incautious communication to corporate stockholders once suggested that their dividends were high because the company had resisted the demands of employees. When an outraged employee-stockholder shared the message with other employees, there was considerable loss of confidence in the company. Are all members of a group men? A professional organization sent newsletters about its annual meeting and listed recreational activities for "the ladies," not noting that some members attending with their husbands did not fit that category. After two years of protests by female members, the wording was changed to "spouses and families." Insensitivity to the composition of target audiences, to their interrelationships and to their ideals and attitudes may waste much time, effort and money on public relations programs that not only miss an audience but offend as well. Tailoring messages to fit a designated audience is rather like the concept clothing manufacturers use. A certain style in a certain size certainly will not fit or please

---

[10] "Corporate Culture and Communication," *Burson-Marsteller Report*, Fall 1981, pp. 1–2. Reprinted by permission.

[11] Bro Uttal, "The Corporate Culture Vultures," *Fortune*, October 17, 1983, pp. 66–72.

all for whom it was designed. But when accepted by most of this particular type of customer, it is considered a success.

The importance of knowing a particular audience is apparent when you consider the variety and disparity of the publics. A PR practitioner must have the acumen of a political scientist and the instincts of a politician to work effectively, for example, with the countless government agencies that directly regulate or indirectly affect an institution. A thorough knowledge of all levels of government and the political system itself is essential, as is keeping open lines of communication with elected representatives and administrators. Better to get a warning from a friend and have time to cope with a problem than to read about it in the newspaper and then have to improvise, as did cereal company executives one morning in 1972 when they learned of publicity from a government source that accused them of producing food items with no nutritional value. For weeks shoppers in grocery stores were seen clutching the "official" list of the few "nutritional" cereals. The cereal companies knew nothing of the release until they read the papers, then had to get information from their own research departments before they could respond with counterarguments. Company publicity, when printed at all, did not make the front page.

The news media are a target audience often overlooked by some PR practitioners. Those who regard the press as "the enemy" generally find this attitude reflected in the news coverage of their organization. A corporation that had always cooperated with the news media and continued to do so when its plant was racked by explosions received front-page coverage of the explosion—but only for one day—and it was generally sympathetic, telling what the company was doing to help the victims and how it was attempting to discover the cause. The PR practitioner should thus keep close contact with both mass and specialized media such as trade, industry and association publications.

An important public that is seldom mentioned is the competition. The competition is an important public to know, communicate with and work with. Institutions that maintain fair and honest dealings with their competitors usually have established this relationship through trade or association organizations. It is harder to insult someone you know personally, perhaps because mutual respect for the industry or profession prevents open hostilities. As an example, in 1974 a paint company received an order from an important customer that it could not meet because of problems resulting from the energy crisis. It called a competitor close to the client who could fill the order, and the two competitors agreed on a commission for the first company. The second company made a sizable sale and the first company kept an important customer. Keeping a channel of communication open benefited both companies, the industry and the customer.

POINTS TO REMEMBER

- Publics are the audiences for public relations. A public may be defined as any group of people tied together by a common bond of interest.
- Publics may be external, outside an institution but with some relationship to it; or internal, sharing the institutional identity.

- A public singled out for attention is a target public; its profile may be revealed by research and understood through empathy.
- Target audiences can be described in three ways: nominatively, demographically and psychographically.
- VALS is a psychographic means of categorizing people according to their values, attitudes and life-styles.
- Today's publics are fragmented by technology and population trends, leading to loss of identity, of a sense of community and of creativity. Fragmentation is exacerbated by differences between what institutions are and what they say they are.
- Employee attitudes often accurately reflect an institution's reality—its public image—for better or worse.
- An organization must act consistently with its projected ideal.
- To achieve credibility, what an institution says it is in its advertising should be closest to how employees see the institution.
- External publics are not a "mass" audience; each public can be identified and described.
- The perceptions of external publics also affect an organization's image. Reexamining an organization's identity includes determining the attitudes of the organization's various publics toward it.
- Target audiences are the priority audiences of PR planning.

THINGS TO DO

1. A plan to construct a coed dormitory housing both men and women on a private college campus has created a furor among trustees, parents, alumni and conservative students. A donor has contributed the entire amount for construction and promises to see the project through to furnishing and landscaping by getting donations from friends. Housing is critical. Operational money is needed from tuitions this additional housing would permit. You are PR adviser to the college's president. What would you suggest?

2. You are publicity director for the athletic department of Majestic State College. The Majestic football team has just been defeated on their home field by the University of Lincoln, 14–6. Immediately after the game, Charlie Snider, Majestic's star quarterback, tells his coach, James "Rip" Tide, he, Snider, threw the game for $1,500 from a gambling syndicate, and he cites several incidents that seem to bear him out. For instance, he tells the coach he deliberately fumbled the ball in the last three minutes of play—one foot from Lincoln's goal line, when Majestic was trailing 6–7—when he should have scored easily. When he dropped the ball, perhaps deliberately, Lincoln recovered and in four plays scored its second touchdown. The coach tells you all this while the players are still in the dressing room. The crowd has left the stadium, but the reporters who covered the game are still in the press box and will be there for at least the next thirty minutes. You have called Majestic State College's president, John Snyder, and he is hurrying back to the stadium to render his okay or disapproval for releasing the story to the press. Perhaps he will say to hold it, but if he says to release it, you should have a complete story to hand out. How would you handle the situation? What specific wording in the release needs to be watched? If the president asks for your own evalua-

tion and a recommendation for whether to release any information, what would you suggest? List all publics to be considered. Since time is critical, prepare a 200-word statement with the awareness that it might be broadcast.

3. Public utility companies in many areas are building nuclear power plants to help meet the need for energy, owing to the shortage of fossil fuels. Concern has been expressed from various sources about the safety of such plants, and employees of the utility company are the ones who must answer—individually and collectively. One company in the process of building a nuclear plant has done a thorough job of winning support from the community in which the plant is located, but it still has other publics with which to contend. List the publics that should be target audiences for information in such a situation. What general knowledge areas—such as economics, engineering and law—are involved in putting together messages to these publics? What information areas can you cite, that is, where must research on new energy sources, the environment and legislation on various governmental levels be done? What are some of the messages the utility company would want to convey in its communications? Be specific in delineating the ways in which avenues of communication—mass media and corporate media—can be used for an informational campaign. In this campaign, what functional management areas would be involved?

4. As a research project, investigate the PR aspects of the Three Mile Island nuclear plant accident in April 1979. With an appreciation for the fact that all hindsight is 20/20, outline events noting where other PR alternatives might have been used.

SELECTED READINGS

Human Relations

Bernard Berelson and Gary A. Steiner, *Human Behavior: An Inventory of Scientific Findings* (New York: Harcourt, Brace and World, 1964). A sourcebook for theories.

B. B. Gardner, *Human Relations in Industry* (Homewood, Ill.: Richard D. Irwin, 1950). A thoughtful work, but dated.

Erving Goffman, *Relations in Public* (New York: Harper & Row, 1972). This sociologist's approach gives a valuable dimension.

Harry Levinson, *Emotional Health in the World of Work* (New York: Harper & Row, 1964). A good insight into the significance of our emotional environment on the job.

Gardner Lindzey and Elliot Aronson, *The Handbook of Social Psychology* (Reading, Mass.: Addison-Wesley, 1968). Should be in every practitioner's library.

Larry A. Samovar, Richard E. Porter and Nem C. Jain, *Understanding Intercultural Communication* (Belmont, Calif.: Wadsworth, 1980). A look at communication behavior from an interpersonal, intercultural point of view.

Andrew D. Szilagyi, Jr., and Marc J. Wallace, *Organizational Behavior and Performance*, 3rd ed. (Glenview, Ill.: Scott, Foresman, 1983). A good survey of the field.

Management

Peter Blau and W. Richard Scott, *Formal Organizations* (San Francisco: Chandler, 1962). A sociologist's view helps us understand internal structures.

Mortimer R. Feinberg, *Effective Psychology for Managers* (Englewood Cliffs, N.J.: Prentice-Hall, 1975). Some useful ideas.

Roy G. Foltz, *Management by Communication* (New York: Chilton, 1973). Interesting assessment of significance of internal communications; a good how-to manual.

Saul William Gellerman, *Management by Motivation* (New York: American Management Association, 1968). Brings evidence from behavior sciences to bear on everyday business problems such as persuading people to upgrade skills or accept necessary changes; stresses problem prevention.

Claude S. George, *The History of Management Thought*, 2nd ed. (Englewood Cliffs, N.J.: Prentice-Hall, 1972). Good reference for various schools of management thought, placed in historical context.

Newsletters and Directories

Bulldog, 6420 Wilshire Blvd., Suite 711, Los Angeles, Calif. 90048. A twice-monthly report on PR in the West, as it describes itself. Offers news of PR and news media in California and the West.

Directory of Business Writers, Association of Business Writers, 1450 S. Havana, Suite 620, Aurora, CO 80012.

Directory of Business and Organization Communicators, Association for International Business Communicators, 870 Market St., Suite 940, San Francisco, CA 94102.

Directory of Public Affairs Officers, Public Affairs Council, 1220 Pate St., NW, Washington, D.C. 20036.

Gale Research Co., Book Tower, Detroit, MI 48226. Publishers of a number of directories, including a directory of directories; and encyclopedias, including ones for associations.

Index of Public Interest Groups, Foundation for Public Affairs, 1220 Sixteenth St., N.W., Washington, D.C. 20036. Lists nationally organized activist, special-interest and pressure groups.

Jack O'Dwyer's PR Newsletter, 271 Madison Ave., New York, NY 10016. Good source for current information. O'Dwyer also publishes annual directories, including ones for PR firms, corporate communications and PR executives.

Poor's Register of Corporations, Directors and Executives, Standard and Poor's Corporation, 345 Hudson St., New York, NY 10014. Annual publication. A single volume updated by quarterly supplements. Lists 45,000 American companies with titles and duties of leading executives and brief biographies of directors, including intercorporate affiliations, alma maters, home addresses. Includes number of employees for each company, list of products and approximate annual sales; geographical index and industry classification.

pr reporter, PR Publishing Co., Inc., 14 Front St., Exeter, NH 03833–0600. Weekly newsletter; also has, as supplements, "tips and tactics," a biweekly "how to" bulletin of PR methods and procedures and "persuasion," a monthly bulletin; indices are provided.

Public Relations News, 127 E. 80th St., New York, NY 10021. The oldest newsletter for the PR profession; produced continuously since 1944.

Pro/Comm, Women In Communications, Inc. POB 9561, Austin, TX 78766. Monthly newsletter.

Professional Guide to PR Services, Public Relations Publishing Co., 888 Seventh Ave., New York, NY 10016. In addition to public relations books, the company publishes a directory of investment newsletters, military publications, college alumni publications, directory of syndicated columnists, news bureaus in the United States and others.

The Ragan Report, Lawrence Ragan and Associates, 407 S. Dearborn St., Chicago, IL 60605. A weekly survey of ideas and methods for communications executives; primarily directed toward corporate PR.

Reader's Guide to Periodicals. A reference source in all libraries; tells what was published by whom in a selected but large list of magazines. An indispensable source for research.

The SEC, The Stock Exchanges and Your Financial Public Relations, published in New York by Hill and Knowlton, Inc., Financial Relations Unit. A very useful guide.

Shopping Center Directory, National Research Bureau, subsidiary of Automated Marketing Systems, Inc., Burlington, IA 52601. Statistics on major U.S. shopping centers, name, location, mailing address, phone, designer, developer, tenant stores, size, parking spaces, cost, manager.

What's Happening, When, National Research Bureau, subsidiary of Automated Marketing Systems, Inc., Burlington, IA 52601. Annual publication; includes a list of special promotion days, weeks, and months, plus the historical dates to tie them into. Includes list of sponsors of events and promotional materials available.

The Working Press of the Nation, National Research Bureau, General Resource Publications, a subsidiary of Automated Marketing Systems, Inc., Burlington, IA 52601. Four volumes of media contacts, roster of addresses, phone numbers and publicity requirements. Includes daily and weekly newspapers, trade and consumer magazines, radio programs, TV shows, all major news syndicates and names of free-lance writers and photographers.

Services

American Institute for Economic Research, Great Barrington, MA 01230. Same as Behavioral Research Council; self-described as "for scientific inquiry into the problems of [people] in society."

American Institute for Political Communication, 402 Prudential Bldg., Washington, D.C. 20005. Produces a monthly newsletter and has a number of books such as *The 1972 Presidential Campaign: The Nixon Administration—Mass Media Relationship and The New Methodology: A Study of Political Strategy and Tactics*.

Behavioral Research Council, Great Barrington, MA 01230. Good resource.

Communication Research, Sage Publications, P.O. Box 776, Beverly Hills, CA 90210. An international quarterly. Scope includes journalism, political science, psychology, economics, sociology, marketing and speech communication. Focus is on explication and testing of models that explain the processes and outcomes of communication.

Direct Mail Marketing Association, 6 East 43rd St., New York, NY 10017. Bibliography.

Exchange Bibliographies, Council of Planning Librarians, P.O. Box 229, Monticello, IL 61856. The Exchange Bibliographies may be purchased from the above address, and a list of bibliographies in print with prices is available on request. Corporate reference librarians may be interested in CPL membership. Bibliographies include all types related to city planning, such as "Energy Crisis in the United States—A Selected Bibliography of Non-Technical Materials" and "Voluntary Associations in Exchange and Conflict," as well as "An Annotated Interdisciplinary Guide of Information in the Social Sciences with Special Emphasis on Urban Studies."

National Investment Library, services of the New York Clearance Systems, Inc., 80 Wall St., New York, NY 10005, is the central business and financial library of written corporate material published by a majority of public corporations in U.S. Users of Library are limited to security analysts, investment banking departments of broker dealers, research libraries, banks and other segments of the financial community, as well as officers of participating corporations. No charge to users.

Publicity Break, Public Relations Aids, Inc., 305 East 45th St., New York, NY 10017. A publication telling where and how to place releases. The company also publishes

Public Relations Quarterly and various media contact lists; also has mailing list service and press release production and distribution service.

Standard Rate and Data Service, Standard Rate and Data Service, 5201 Old Orchard Road, Skokie, IL 60077. Lists all major advertising media; gives names of key personnel.

Television Information Office, 745 Fifth Ave., New York, NY 10022. Research in the medium, available on request.

Journals

Ad Age, 740 Rush St., Chicago, IL 60611. Weekly.

AEJMC *Journalism Quarterly*, Association for Education in Journalism and Mass Communication, College of Journalism, University of South Carolina, Columbia, SC 29208.

Audio Visual Communications, 475 Park Ave., S., New York, NY 10016.

Broadcasting Weekly, 1735 DeSales St., NW, Washington, D.C. 20036.

Business Week, McGraw-Hill Bldg., 1221 Avenue of the Americas, New York, NY 10020.

Columbia Journalism Review, 700 Journalism Bldg., Columbia University, 116th St., and Broadway, New York, NY 10027.

Direct Marketing, 224 Seventh St., Garden City, NY 11530. Monthly.

Editor and Publisher, 575 Lexington Ave., New York, NY 10022. Weekly.

Graphic Arts Monthly, 666 Fifth Ave., New York, NY 10103.

IABC News, 870 Market St., San Francisco, CA 94102. Also publishes a directory.

IPRA Review, International Public Relations Association, Keswick House, 3 Greenway, London, N20 8EE, England. Quarterly.

Journalism Advertising Research, Advertising Research Foundation, 3 East 54th St., New York, NY 10022.

Journal of Broadcasting, Broadcast Education Association, Temple University, Philadelphia, PA 19122. Quarterly.

Journal of Communication, International Communication Association, Annenberg School of Communication, University of Pennsylvania, Philadelphia, PA 19174. Quarterly.

Public Opinion Quarterly, 700 Journalism Bldg., Columbia University, 116th St. and Broadway, New York, NY 10027.

Public Relations Journal, Public Relations Society of America, 845 Third Ave., New York, NY 10022. Monthly.

Public Relations Quarterly, PRQ, subsidiary of Public Relations Aids, Inc., 44 W. Market St., Box 311, Rhinebeck, NY 12572.

Public Relations Review, College of Journalism, University of Maryland, College Park, MD 20742, editorial office. Business office: Communication Research Assn., 7100 Baltimore Blvd., Suite 500, College Park, MD 20740.

Quill, Society for Professional Journalists, 35 East Wacker Dr., Chicago, IL 60601. Monthly.

Television Radio Age, Television Editorial Corp., 666 Fifth Ave., New York, NY 10019. Monday biweekly.

U.S. Department of Commerce, Office of Minority Business Enterprise, *Directory of Minority Media* (Washington, D.C.: U.S. Government Printing Office, 1973). The best listing of minority (black, Oriental and Hispanic) news media—print and broadcasting.

Special Publications

Ayer's Directory of Publications, Ayer Press, 426 Pennsylvania Ave., Fort Washington, PA 19034. A guide to publications printed in the United States and its territories, the Dominion of Canada, Bermuda, the Republic of Panama and the Philippines, with descriptions of the states, provinces, cities and towns in which they are published. A basic book for PR planning. Also publisher of *Hotel-Motel Register* useful in setting up meetings.

Bacon's Publicity Checker, Bacon's Publishing Co., Inc., 14 E. Jackson Blvd., Chicago, IL 60604. List of magazines and newspapers where publicity releases may be placed. Published annually in October with three supplements to update. Gives publications, editors, addresses, phone numbers and specialized markets. Same firm also has clipping service.

Black Press Periodical Directory, Black Press Clipping Bureau, 78 Merchant St., Newark, NJ 07105. First published 1973–74. Lists 288 black newspapers, 196 magazines, 87 newsletters, 280 foreign publications, 68 college publications, 34 specialized publications, 46 media services and supplements, 120 black-oriented radio stations.

Broadcasting Yearbook, Broadcasting, 1735 De Sales St., Washington, D.C. 20036. Lists TV and radio stations and gives information about the station. Names the principal personnel.

Congressional Staff Directory, Congressional Staff Directory, P.O. Box 62, Mt. Vernon, VA 22121. Gives names of staff in House and Senate members' offices.

Cooperative Advertising Plans Directory, National Research Bureau, subsidiary of Automated Marketing Systems, Inc., Burlington, IA 52601. Includes name and address of manufacturer, products included in the co-op plan; cost division or how much manufacturer shares in cost; other aids for dealers, including media-approved co-op advertising.

Editor and Publisher International Yearbook, Editor and Publisher Co., 850 Third Ave., New York, NY 10022. Lists U.S. dailies and weeklies and major foreign papers.

Educators Guide to Free Films, Educators Guide to Free Film Strips, Educators Guide to Free Tapes, and Scripts and Transcriptions, Educators Progress Service, Randolph, WI 53956. Source for teaching aids.

Fund Raising Management Magazine, Hoke Communications, Inc., 224 Seventh St., Garden City, NY 11535.

Newsletter Yearbook Directory, Newsletter Clearing House, Box 311, Rhinebeck, NY 12572. A compilation of worldwide subscription newsletters.

Gale Research Company, Book Tower, Detroit, MI 48226. Publishes a number of useful reference books, among them *Encyclopedia Associations, Directory of Directories, Trade Names Directory, Consumer Sourcebook.*

Gebbie House Magazine Directory, National Research Bureau, subsidiary of Automated Marketing Systems, Inc., Box 1000, Palty, NY 12561. Has information useful in placement of stories in the house magazine field, including company name and address, name of magazine and editor, frequency of issue, circulation, material wanted and special interest subjects cross-indexed.

Hudson's Washington News Media Contacts Directory, 2626 Pennsylvania Ave., NW, Washington, D.C. 20027. A guide to the entire Capitol Press Corps, including news bureaus, wire services, newspaper correspondents, syndicates, broadcast networks, magazines, newsletters, photo service and free-lancers.

If You Want Air Time: A Handbook for Publicity Chairmen, Public Relations Service, National Association of Broadcasters, 1771 N St., NW, Washington, D.C. 20036.

Alvin B. Zeller, 475 Park Ave. S., New York, NY 10016. Catalogs of mailing lists.

CHAPTER 7

Persuasion and the Impact of Opinion

The pressure of public opinion . . . "is like the pressure of the atmosphere—you can't see it, but all the same it is sixteen pounds to the square inch." In a democracy this pressure begs to be explored and understood. But so do the techniques by which the "pressure of public opinion" is examined. Otherwise, in an era of mass communication, public opinion can become not what people think but what politicians and pollsters say they think.

Bill D. Moyers, television commentator and columnist

People's opinions on a public issue depend very much on how that issue is posed to them, and on the circumstances in which they are asked to express themselves.

Charles Frankel, Saturday Review/World *columnist*

During the Arab oil embargo of 1974, a New Jersey coffee shop owner, Barry Warfel, began doing a booming business from motorists waiting in gas station lines. He even had to take on another employee. Then an enterprising eleven-year-old, Billy Halliwell, appeared with a red wagon and began peddling coffee and snacks. Billy used some aggressive business tactics to pull customers away from Warfel's coffee shop, including making disparaging remarks about the quality and prices of the merchandise. Warfel let his temper get the better of him, yelled at the red wagon entrepreneur and chased him away from the coffee shop entrance. The local health inspector happened to be a friend of Warfel's and told him the red wagon competitor couldn't sell food without a license. The result, as *Wall Street Journal* columnist Sanford L. Jacobs summarized it, "An irresistible national news story was created: enterprising youth thwarted by monopoly-minded businessman and government bureaucrat."[1]

Warfel didn't think he did anything wrong. He had worked with youth groups for years, but was unable to convince people after this incident that he didn't hate kids. People avoided his coffee shop, and he got ugly phone calls. The loss of sales caused Warfel to sell his shop and become the manager of a fast-food outlet in another town. Billy got an award from the White House Conference on Small

---

[1] Sanford L. Jacobs, "Attention to Public Opinion Helps Firms Avoid Blunders," *Wall Street Journal*, June 15, 1981, p. 21.

Business. Public relations advisers commenting on the case said Warfel should have given Billy an award, in addition to offering to back his business. Warfel probably would have had a hard time accepting that advice since he saw Billy as being in the wrong and himself in the right. The problem was the public believed Warfel did Billy wrong.

GETTING A HANDLE
ON PUBLIC OPINION

Public relations practitioners function in a climate of public opinion, one that often conditions responses significantly. Climates of public opinion can be as broad as that of the international community on a nation's presumed leadership in an arms race or as narrow as that of security analysts when a company's bonds are rerated, downward.

Public opinion is what most people in a particular public think—in other words, it is a collective opinion of, say, what voters, or teenagers, or senior citizens think, or sometimes what politicians think.

Bernard Hennessy says, "Public opinion is the complex of preferences expressed by a significant number of persons on an issue of general importance."[2] Public opinion has five basic elements according to Hennessy. First, public opinion must be focused on an *issue*, which Hennessy defines as "a contemporary situation with a likelihood of disagreement." Second, the public must consist of "a recognizable group of persons concerned with the issue." A third element in the definition, "complex of preferences," Hennessy says, "means more than mere direction and intensity; it means all the imagined or measured individual opinions held by the relevant public on all the proposals about the issue over which that public has come into existence." The fourth factor, the expression of opinion, is any form of expression—words, printed or spoken, or symbols, such as a clenched fist or stiff-arm salute—even the gasp of a crowd. This does rule out including what could be called latent public opinion. Hennessy would reserve that term for "describing a situation in which a considerable number of individuals hold attitudes or general predispositions that may eventually crystallize into opinions around a given issue." But to measure public opinion, it has to be expressed. The final factor, the number of persons involved, is different in each case and may not be ascertainable, but whatever the number it would produce some effect. The effect, he notes, may be as much a result of the intensity of opinion and the organization of effort as it is the size of the public.[3]

Public opinion is the expression of a belief, based not necessarily on fact but on the *conception* or *evaluation* of an event, person, institution or product. In the

[2] Bernard Hennessy, *Public Opinion*, 4th ed. (Monterey, Calif.: Brooks/Cole, 1981), p. 4. Also, social scientist Ithiel De Sola Pool said an opinion is cognitive, an attitude evaluative: "An opinion is a proposition, while an attitude is a proclivity to be pro or anti something." For his discussion of public opinion, see "Public Opinion," *Handbook of Communication* (Chicago: Rand McNally, 1973), pp. 779–835.

[3] Hennessy, *Public Opinion*, pp. 4–8.

United States it is widely assumed that "public opinion is always right." Perhaps this phenomenon should be expected in a country with a democratic form of government, for certainly elected officials are concerned with the impact of public opinion.

Long before the pollsters were on the scene, nineteenth-century essayist Charles Dudley Warner said, "Public opinion is stronger than the legislature, and nearly as strong as the Ten Commandments."

Obviously, however, public opinion can be misused—as Adolf Hitler's master propagandist, Joseph Goebbels, showed. And, of course, it does not have to be misused to be wrong. It can be distorted through a lack of accurate information— just as in pre-World War II times, many Americans were applauding Mussolini's efforts at "straightening out the Italians" (tourist translation: getting the trains to run on time), while many Italians were beginning to live in fear of the black-shirted troops.

Public opinion also is not stable. It is about as reliable a measurement as body temperature. For accuracy, doctors say, "The patient's temperature was 101 degrees at 7 A.M.," not "The patient's temperature is 101 degrees" (unless the thermometer has just been read), and PR people would be a lot safer in their judgments if they would take the same precautions. Public opinion can be changed by exposure to new information or events to such an extent that if these are not taken into consideration in research, an erroneous reading of the public's opinion results.

"Majority opinion is a curious and elusive thing," columnist Charles Frankel points out. "People's opinions on a public issue depend very much on how the issue is posed to them, and on the circumstances in which they are asked to express themselves. A minority today may well be a majority tomorrow, depending on what transpires between today and tomorrow."[4]

Frankel also notes that the majority opinion on a particular issue "may not in fact express opinion on *that* specific issue. It may express a general party loyalty; it may express the individual's sense that he should go along with a coalition of interest with which he is broadly sympathetic even if he disagrees with the particular policy at issue; it may reflect simply his judgment that he does not know enough to have a reliable opinion on the specific question he has been asked, and his decision, therefore, to accept the opinion of people in authority."[5]

In trying to keep pace with constantly changing public opinion, a few basic precepts must be accepted. Not everyone is going to be on your side at one time. The best you can hope for is a majority consensus. To achieve this, you need to retain the partisans you have, try to win commitments from the undecided or uncommitted and neutralize or win over the opposition.

Winning over the opposition is the most difficult part. Most of us read and listen for reinforcement of our own ideas. We really do not like to hear ideas that conflict, and we make every effort to reject them. There are many ways we accomplish this. We simply tune out and fail to hear or remember what we have been exposed to. We discredit the source, without objectively determining its legit-

---

[4]Charles Frankel, "The Silenced Majority," *Saturday Review*, December 13, 1969, p. 22.
[5]Ibid.

imacy. We mentally distort meanings so what we hear or read conforms to what we believe. No doubt you have seen letters to the editor of a magazine from two different people, each complimenting the publication for an editorial they each saw as taking a stand on a particular issue that was the opposite of what the other saw; the readers simply read into the editorial what they wanted the publication to say.

PERSUASION AND PEOPLE'S CHANGING ATTITUDES

When an opinion is strongly held, you are probably wasting your time trying to win that person over to your view. All you can hope to do is to nullify whatever effects the person may have on the undecided or uncommitted. In particular, you should not waste time on recent converts to the opposition, for new converts to anything react with more emotion than reason and are almost impossible to reach with factual materials, much less a persuasive argument. You should concentrate your efforts, then, on preserving what favorable opinion exists and winning over the undecided to your point of view.

Ways to get people to do what *you* want have three sources basically: *power*, *patronage*, and *persuasion*. Power involves the use of authority. One obvious source of power is the legal system, with laws that demand compliance. Other sources of power may be more subtle, but they are equally binding: Employees may not be legally bound to follow a supervisor's suggestions, for example, but if they don't, they may soon be looking for other jobs. Through group pressure peer groups are also a strong source of power. (If you don't believe that, consider how often you hear, "But I must have one. Everyone else has.") An example of the use of power by public relations practitioners is when, in planning for the United Fund, they use the tactic of asking employers to solicit contributions from their employees. The request is for a good purpose, an honest cause, certainly, but it still involves the use of power.

Patronage as a means of changing people's behavior may be as crude as bribery, but it may also be more subtle, particularly if a favorable opinion is sought or if there is an implied threat of denial. Patronage may involve the payment of money to a celebrity to make advertising endorsements or public appearances on behalf of a campaign, or it may involve a substantial contribution to a civic improvement project campaign from a realtor owning property in the area.[6]

Public relations is most involved with persuasion. Examples of persuasion are, of course, public relations or advertising campaigns, which are generally

---

[6] Somewhat different motivational patterns are given by Daniel Katz and Robert Kahn in *The Social Psychology of Organizations* (New York: John Wiley, 1966), p. 341. Given as "motivational patterns for producing various types of required behaviors" are the following: (1) legal compliance; (2) the use of rewards or instrumental satisfactions—either individual rewards or "system" rewards such as earned memberships or seniority, earned approval of leaders or affiliations with peers that win social approval; (3) internal pattern of self-determination and self-expression; (4) internal values and self-concept.

highly visible because of the publicity. In persuasion, the critical factor in opinion change usually is information or the lack of it and how this information is presented or withheld.[7] Social scientist Herbert I. Schiller contends that information is power, and he is correct.[8] Information resides in controllable sources—among the upper echelons of government, business and education. It is made available to the public, Schiller says, through disseminators who usually are public relations people with the power to control the flow of information. Their access to information and their selective use of it combine the tools of power and persuasion. Schiller rails against such "mind managers," and his arguments sound persuasive. However, they fail to take into account social responsibility on the part of these institutions or their representatives, plus the social responsibility assumed by news and advertising personnel in the media.

Media Orientation

There is no black magic involved in the efforts of PR people to win public opinion. First, public relations means deciding what to tell, whom to tell it to, how and through what media. The choice of medium is critical. It must be a believable source, able to reach those who are to receive the message and with the technological capacity to carry the message. Television, for example, has high credibility and certainly mass penetration. But something complicated like a change in Social Security benefits simply cannot be communicated through this medium. All television can do is alert people to the change and tell them where to find the information; the details demand a print medium. However, safety officials wanting to alert residents about an impending hurricane certainly will take to the airwaves.

In looking at all of the elements to be considered in getting people from just first attending to a message to believing consistently in the desired way, William McGuire developed what he calls the Communication/Persuasion Matrix (see 7.1).

Message Orientation

In determining the suitability of the medium, the message itself should be evaluated. We are not always rational human beings, able to make calculated judgments. We know too much coffee is not good for us, but may drink six cups a day anyway because we like it. Yet we may make cautious decisions about buying a car. Thus to be effective, persuasive appeals must combine both the rational and the irrational.

Think about an effective speaker you have heard recently. No doubt he or she illustrated the facts in the talk with examples—anecdotes that entertained you as well as helped you recall the major points. Compare that with a talk where you took notes furiously to get down the flurry of facts. How much do you remember?

---

[7] The basic principles of persuasion taken from available research studies are conveniently collected and described in a book by Marvin Karlins and Herbert I. Abelson, *Persuasion: How Opinions and Attitudes Are Changed*, 2nd ed. (New York: Springer, 1970).

[8] Herbert I. Schiller, *The Mind Managers* (Boston: Beacon Press, 1973), pp. 134–135.

7.1 THE COMMUNICATION/PERSUASION MODEL AS AN INPUT/OUTPUT MATRIX

At each step in a PR campaign, the campaign designer has to determine how each input variable will affect each output variable. For example, McGuire says, deciding whether to use a male or female source, literal or metaphorical speech will affect the whole chain of twelve output steps.

Input: *Independent (Communication) Variables* / Output: *Dependent Variables (Response steps mediating persuasion)*	Source — *Number, Unanimity, Demographics, Attractiveness, Credibility*	Message — *Type appeal, Type information, Inclusion/omission, Organization, Repetitiveness*	Channel — *Modality, Directness, Context*	Receiver — *Demographics, Ability, Personality, Life-style*	Destination — *Immediacy/delay, Prevention/cessation, Direct/immune*
1. E: Exposure to the communication					
2. A: Attending to it					
3. L: Liking, becoming interested in it					
4. C: Comprehending it (learning what)					
5. S: Skill acquisition (learning how)					
6. Y: Yielding to it; attitude change					
7. M: Memory storage of content and/or agreement					
8. N: Information search and retrieval					
9. D: Deciding on basis of retrieval					
10. B: Behaving in accord with decision					
11. R: Reinforcement of desired acts					
12. P: Postbehavioral consolidating					

William McGuire, "Theoretical Foundations of Campaigns," *Public Communications Campaigns*, ed. Ronald E. Rice and William J. Paisley (Beverly Hills: Sage, 1981), p. 45.

7.2 MOTIVATIONAL THEORIES BEHIND COMMUNICATION/PERSUASION RESEARCH

Initiation of action / Termination of Action State	Need / Provocation / Relationship	Stability		Growth	
		Active	Reactive	Active	Reactive
Cognitive	Internal	1. Consistency	2. Categorization	5. Autonomy	6. Problem-solver
	External	3. Noetic	4. Inductional	7. Stimulation	8. Teleological
Affective	Internal	9. Tension-reduction	10. Ego-defensive	13. Assertion	14. Identification
	External	11. Expressive	12. Repetition	15. Empathy	16. Contagion

Looking at motivational theories, McGuire had determined how they differ on four dimensions of contrast in motivation. From these four, the first two have to do with what starts human action and the third and fourth with what ends the action. The result is sixteen families of dynamic theories shown in the cells of the chart, each focusing on one element or aspect of human motivation in an effort to provide some insight. He relates the dimensions in terms of contrasts: stability versus growth and cognitive versus affective. The latter, he says, deal with forces that initiate human action; the first two terminate action. Some of the communication theories in the matrix conflict. His advice is to apply theory creatively but not to overlook theories that may offer alternative possibilities.

William McGuire, "Theoretical Foundations of Campaigns," *Public Communication Campaigns*, ed. Ronald E. Rice and William J. Paisley (Beverly Hills: Sage, 1981), p. 55.

Unless compelled to take notes and learn them later, you probably don't recall a single significant fact. When it is a matter of choice, as listening to most public relations material is, you probably would not choose the straight facts over the fact-story.

The complexity of the individual in the audience also was addressed by McGuire in a design incorporating the theories about dynamic forces that would propel a person through the Communication/Persuasion Matrix (7.1). The interaction of the motivational theories (7.2) provide clues to what people do or don't do. Some of the theories conflict; McGuire is the first to say that the theories are simply ideas people develop, with some evidence, about behavior.

To be persuasive a message has to present something of value to the audience. It must be compatible with the motives of the public you are trying to persuade. If your audience has to make some adjustment to accept a new or different idea, you must provide that adjustment and the rationale for it. In a free society where communication is open, we are attentive to persuasion that involves the choice of the person being persuaded. If it challenges your listeners' sense of security or self-image, you must provide an ego defense, or the argument will be repelled by their instinct to defend the ego. If you are suggesting acceptance of something that has been rejected before as socially taboo, you must offer a value that can be adopted to replace it or rationalize it. For instance, while it may be difficult to get white Americans to adopt black or Asian-American children, they may adopt *foreign* children of different races—as they did in the 1975 Vietnam "babylift"—because of an emotional appeal to guilt or conscience.

News media often are considered to be agents of change in a free society, but agenda-setting theory studies suggest that all the news media are able to do is to give importance or significance to an issue by giving it space or time and through repetition of coverage. Sometimes the news media are so out of touch with the "average" citizen that the real public opinion on an issue grows not only independently but also totally ignored by the news media. Such was the case in the groundswell of public opinion against 1983 legislation to withhold tax on interest and dividends. When Congress was pressured to repeal the law by an outraged constituency, the news media attributed the repeal to pressure from the banking lobby. Actually, the banking industry had always opposed the legislation. The news media were relying only on news releases from the administration in Washington.[9]

The source of the message also has an effect, so we need to examine the role of news managers and opinion makers.

News Managers and Opinion Makers

A news manager may be someone who creates an event that becomes news because it is made to happen, usually on a carefully detailed and pre-arranged schedule. The event may be Mickey Mouse's visit to a children's hospital or a PLO (Palestine Liberation Army) bomb threat, and may continue over an extended period of time, as the 1979–80 hostage crisis at the American Embassy in Tehran, Iran. A news manager may also be someone who focuses media attention on an event that might otherwise be overlooked. In addition, a news manager may control information as well as events, as many tried to do in the Nixon White House. This is not news, however. As media critic William L. Rivers notes, "Nothing is quite so absurd as thinking of news control by government as a modern phenomenon. . . . Information policy has been at the very center of governing the U.S. from the beginning."[10]

U.S. Presidents as News Managers Presidents of the United States and their spokespeople draw the most accusations for "managing" the news, and there may be some justification for this since that branch can claim "executive privilege." No one expects to find out too much from the judiciary branch because of the American Bar Association's code of ethics, but in the legislative branch, what one party won't tell, the other will. The management of news by U.S. presidents goes back to George Washington, who leaked his Farewell Address to a favored publisher he knew would give it a good display. When Thomas Jefferson was in Washington's cabinet, he put a newspaper reporter on the federal payroll to establish a party newspaper to present Jefferson's point of view; later, when he became president

---

[9]Fritz M. Elmendorf, "Press Ignored Power of Public in Withholding Revolt," *Business-Economic News Report*, 2, no. 8 (September 1983), pp. 1, 5.

[10]William L. Rivers, *The Opinionmakers* (Boston: Beacon Press, 1965), p. 1.

he relied heavily on his "party press" and limited the access of other newspapers to him.

Abraham Lincoln sought out newspaper editors he thought might get his ideas to the people and help win their support for his policies. The significance he placed on public opinion is apparent in his famous statement that "Public sentiment is everything. With public sentiment, nothing can fail; without it, nothing can succeed. Consequently, he who moulds public sentiment goes deeper than he who enacts statutes or pronounces decisions."

Theodore Roosevelt developed the "trial balloon" device: He called favorite reporters to the White House to get their reaction to his ideas before he tried them on the public. Woodrow Wilson developed the first regular formal press conferences, although he later regretted the idea, for he was a reserved man who never won popularity with the press. He also complained that the press was interested in the personal and trivial rather than in principles and policies—a statement to which the press responded that presidents just want them to print what they tell them, not what the public wants to know. Franklin Roosevelt's candor and geniality delighted reporters, but even he later regretted holding press conferences and in a pique once said he would like to award a Nazi Iron Cross to a news reporter whose stories he felt had earned it.

Dwight Eisenhower acknowledged the needs of television and radio news media when he allowed them to record his press conferences, and John Kennedy permitted live TV coverage of his meetings with the press.

Richard Nixon, who blamed TV for his 1960 defeat for the presidency, was determined to master his television technique and did. The live coverage of two of his news conferences following Watergate allowed viewers to see him withstand ruthless questioning by the press. President Nixon's press spokesman was not permitted much candor, however, and was not a professional public relations practitioner; in fact, Ronald Ziegler was experienced only in advertising. The one person with media experience, Herb Klein, was relegated to the relatively innocuous post of working with the newspapers in the "hinterlands," and the single person on Nixon's staff with PR background, William Safire, was made a speech writer.

Jimmy Carter hired Jody Powell as his press secretary when he first took office. However, when President Carter felt his work was not being taken in the proper context by the citizenry, he hired the man who had managed his media campaign during his candidacies for both governor of Georgia and president of the United States, Gerald Rafshoon. Jerry Rafshoon's job was to coordinate policy statements within the executive branch so unity and cohesiveness of position were reflected. In response to descriptions of his role as an "image maker," Rafshoon said he was coordinating, not creating.

President Ronald Reagan's deputy press secretary, Pete Roussel, said he faithfully adhered to what he called the "Press Secretary's Prayer": "Oh, Lord, let me utter words sweet and gentle, for tomorrow, I may have to eat them."[11] Roussel was one of several public-opinion-sensitive specialists Reagan put in place. An-

[11] Dave Montgomery, "A Texan Meets the Press (and Says a Little Prayer)," *Fort Worth Star Telegram*, April 10, 1983, p. 29A.

other, pollster Richard Beal, was charged with looking at public views on questions likely to arise as issues in the future.

In doing this, Reagan was following a trend that started with John F. Kennedy's use of polling, according to Sidney Blumenthal, author of *The Permanent Campaign*.[12] Blumenthal called Reagan "Communicator in Chief," and made this observation: "Ronald Reagan is governing America by a new doctrine—the permanent campaign. He is applying in the White House the most sophisticated team of pollsters, media masters and tacticians ever to work there. They have helped him to transcend entrenched institutions like the Congress and the Washington press corps to appeal directly to the people."[13]

In addition to filling the major public relations posts with experienced professionals, Reagan's appointments people also filled many posts not traditionally considered public relations ones with PR pros. Of the three top advisers to the president, two were lawyers and one, Mike Deaver, a public relations professional.

After press secretary Jim Brady was severely injured in the assassination attempt on Reagan, Larry Speakes became acting press secretary. Speakes sometimes felt he wasn't as fully informed as he might have been, and some newspeople agreed. However, Speakes said, not knowing is the lesser of the two sins of a press secretary. Lying was a "cardinal sin," and unforgivable.

There is protection in not knowing, because you can't lie. However, if you don't know, you are vulnerable to committing a near-equivalent—misleading. Not knowing everything, Speakes said, left him vulnerable in a briefing with the risk of saying something that might embarrass the president. About a fourth of the time he is bound by strict guidelines of what he can say to the news media.[14]

Other Opinion Makers   What is true of news management by government is true of any group in business, science, education or whatever with specialized information: Those in command of information control its dissemination. The public's only defense, then, is in being aware that someone is always trying to influence its opinion. A sophisticated person will ask, "What am I being asked to think? What am I being asked to do? By whom? Why?"

In a democracy these questions often are raised by the opposition—and thus the resulting struggle for public opinion, which confounds both our allies and our enemies. One genuinely bewildered Russian journalist visiting with a group of professional journalists in the United States just after the Pentagon Papers controversy remarked: "I don't see how your government stays in power. This sort of thing would never happen in my country." It was pointed out that the freedom to compete for public opinion is inherent in our conception of democracy. The public relations practitioner becomes involved in such struggles because each side of a controversy employs him or her as a professional adviser or spokesperson. Practitioners usually represent the side corresponding to their own beliefs, although there are ethical practitioners who, like lawyers, will serve any client with loyalty,

---

[12] Sidney Blumenthal, "Brave New World: Marketing the President," *Dallas Morning News*, September 20, 1981, p. G1.

[13] Ibid.

[14] Maureen Santini, "Presidential Spokesman Speaks on Life under Fire," Associated Press column in the *Fort Worth Star Telegram*, February 22, 1983, pp. 1, 2.

whether they personally subscribe to the position or not. What differentiates the professional practitioner from the unprofessional news manager—who unfortunately is often confused with the PR person—is a strict adherence to a code of ethics that endorses a sense of social responsibility. A professional public relations practitioner will never lie to the news media, although in the interests of a client it may sometimes be necessary to say to the press, "I know, but I cannot tell you." The success of those who control certain areas of information in affecting public opinion is only as strong as their credibility. A loss of credibility is something a professional public relations practitioner cannot afford to risk.

PERSUASION APPEALS

People who sway opinions use a variety of appeals—not all of them honest. There are numerous ways to mislead. Here are some of them—they are also known as propaganda devices:

1. *Name Calling*: This can be positive or negative. Someone can be called "wise and conscientious" or "a liar and a cheat" (or it can even be left open to interpretation, such as "He's a character!").

2. *Glittering Generalities*: There are many nebulous words here—for example, "enthusiastic crowds," or "throngs of greeters."

3. *Transfer*: This occurs when a movie star or other celebrity campaigns for a politician or product, and some of the famous person's aura is transferred to the less well-known person or idea.

4. *Testimonial*: This is an actual endorsement, as opposed to a transfer device. It is a common advertising technique in which professional athletes and other celebrities encourage the product's use by saying they use it.

5. *Plain Folks*. A favorite of politicians, this device is to convince the public that despite their high office or aspirations thereto, they are still "one of us."

6. *Bandwagon*: A compelling device to sway the undecided to go with the majority, however slight; this device is considered so powerful that networks avoid telecasting election returns in the East until polls close in the West although there is some research evidence to indicate that such coverage has no impact.

7. *Card Stacking*: Frequently gaining recognition as "one side of the story," this device selects facts representing one point of view, while obscuring other facts. The result is distortion and misrepresentation.

8. *Emotional Stereotypes*: These evoke all kinds of images, and are so designed: "good American," "housewife," "foreigner," and so on.

9. *Illicit Silence*: This device falls into the area of subtle propaganda, such as innuendo, suggestion and insinuation; it means withholding information that would correct a false impression.

10. *Subversive Rhetoric*: An offshoot of card stacking is the device of discrediting a person's motivation in order to discredit the idea, which may be good and useful—for example, discredit the mayor because he wants to build a bridge because he owns property on the other side of the river. In the meantime, the

bridge building may still be a good idea for opening up commerce, traffic, tourism.

Obvious forms of propaganda techniques are easily recognizable, but their application by skillful users often is not. Anyone who communicates may employ propaganda devices—spoken, written, pictorial or whatever. Such devices also may be in the form of synthetic events: The 1960s were filled with "demonstrations"—all of them propaganda devices. And among the most skillful of the news managers were the youths of this era. Reared on the media, they knew how to use them effectively.

Despite these techniques, which are used to mislead, the word *propaganda* should not be thought of as totally negative. Propaganda can be used to change attitudes and behavior in a constructive way. Propagandists differ from educators in that educators teach people how to think, but propagandists try to teach people what to think.[15] Propaganda has been used also to appeal to basic human emotions in order to effect opinion changes in the public interest (see Chapter 8).

Social legislation, income tax, Medicare, civil rights laws and so on—all reflect changes in public opinion that were sensed and acted upon by politicians. Generally, such public opinion is an emotional response to information or events. Social psychologist Hadley Cantril developed some "laws" purportedly governing this emotional response (see 7.3). Although critics say there cannot be anything like a law for something with as many variables as public opinion, Cantril's laws do follow five basic ideas that seem to describe all studies of opinion expression: (1) Events are most likely to affect opinion. (2) Demands for action are a usual response. (3) Self-interest must figure heavily for people to become involved. (4) Leadership is sought, and not always objectively and critically. (5) Reliability is difficult to assess.

Earl Newsom's principles of persuasion build on the concept of personal identification with an idea or problem, and suggest actions to be taken in response to it.

1. *Identification*: People will relate to an idea, opinion or point of view only if they can see some direct effect on their own hopes, fears, desires or aspirations.

2. *Suggestion of Action*: People will endorse ideas only if they are accompanied by a proposed action from the sponsor of the idea or if the recipients themselves propose it—especially a *convenient* action.

3. *Familiarity and Trust*: People are unwilling to accept ideas from sources they don't trust, whether people or institutions. Thus PR must see that an institution deserves and gets such confidence, that it increases the trust of numbers of people and keeps the trust of those it counts as friends.

4. *Clarity*: The meaning of an idea has to be clear, whether it is an event, situation or message.[16]

---

[15] Philip G. Zimbardo, Ebbe B. Ebbesen and Christina Maslach, *Influencing Attitudes and Changing Behavior* (Menlo Park, Calif.: Addison-Wesley, 1977), p. 156.

[16] Taken from Earl Newsom's published speeches: "Elements of a Good Public Relations Program," presented to public relations conference of Standard Oil (New Jersey) and affiliated companies,

7.3 HADLEY CANTRIL'S LAWS OF PUBLIC OPINION

1. Opinion is highly sensitive to important events.

2. Events of unusual magnitude are likely to swing public opinion temporarily from one extreme to another. Opinion does not become stabilized until the implications of events are seen with some perspective.

3. Opinion is generally determined more by events than by words—unless those words are themselves interpreted as an "event."

4. Verbal statements and outlines of courses of action have maximum importance when opinion is unstructured, when people are suggestible and seek some interpretation from a reliable source.

5. By and large, public opinion does not anticipate emergencies—it only reacts to them.

6. Psychologically, opinion is basically determined by self-interest. Events, words, or any other stimuli affect opinion only insofar as their relationship to self-interest is apparent.

7. Opinion does not remain aroused for any long period of time unless people feel their self-interest is acutely involved or unless opinion—aroused by words—is sustained by events.

8. Once self-interest is involved, opinion is not easily changed.

9. When self-interest is involved, public opinion in a democracy is likely to be ahead of official policy.

10. When an opinion is held by a slight majority or when opinion is not solidly structured, an accomplished fact tends to shift opinion in the direction of acceptance.

11. At critical times, people become more sensitive to the adequacy of their leadership—if they have confidence in it, they are willing to assign more than usual responsibility to it; if they lack confidence in it, they are less tolerant than usual.

12. People are less reluctant to have critical decisions made by their leaders if they feel that somehow they, the people, are taking some part in the decision.

13. People have more opinions and are able to form opinions more easily with respect to goals than with respect to methods necessary to reach those goals.

14. Public opinion, like individual opinion, is colored by desire. And when opinion is based chiefly on desire rather than on information, it is likely to show especially sharp shifts with events.

15. The important psychological dimensions of opinion are direction, intensity, breadth, and depth.

Selections from "Some Laws of Public Opinion," in Hadley Cantril, *Gauging Public Opinion* (Princeton, N.J.: Princeton University Press, 1944). Copyright 1944, renewed © 1972 by Princeton University Press, pp. 226–230, without illustration or examples. Reprinted by permission of Princeton University Press.

Successful advertising copywriters certainly would endorse the latter two principles, namely, that the people doing the buying have to trust those doing the selling and those selling have to communicate clearly to have any effect at all.

The element of trust needs to be emphasized in any study of opinion change. All of us are more likely to assume attitudes and accept ideas uncritically from those we love and trust. Observers predicted all kinds of voting patterns for eighteen-year-olds in the United States before they were given the right to vote. What actually happened? Most youths voted like their parents—probably because they loved and trusted them. However, even if they did not love and trust their parents, they did receive information from them over a long period of time. One

December 3, 1946; "A Look at the Record," presented to Annual Public Relations Conference of Standard Oil (New Jersey); "Our Job," presented to Reynolds Metal's executives, March 21, 1957.

communication theory—called the "sleeper effect"—suggests that even a distrusted source is apt to be forgotten after a long period of time, leaving a residue of information accepted as fact.

Identification and suggestion of action are also important. As for identification, most of us feel an association with others—by education, religion, occupation, social or economic status or whatever. What our identification groups say and do suggests courses of action for us. These associations have potential power, for when events demand, opinion can be mobilized along lines of self-interest. Such mobilization, Philip Lesly says, can be activated by highly visible leaders. Lesly says there are at least three separate groups in the "leader" category:

1. *Vocal Activists*, who devote themselves to visibly propounding a cause.

2. *Opinion Leaders* (actually broken down between mass media and individual thought leaders throughout society . . . but for simplicity we'll group them together).

3. *Power Leaders*—legislators, government officials, judges, regulators who have the power to take actions that affect organizations and society.

The focal group increasingly is the Power Leaders. They have the ability to make things actually happen. The vocal activists, media, influential individuals and groups, and the general public provide input to the Power Leaders, but have little power themselves. The input that gets to the Power Leaders is *much greater from the vocal activists and the opinion leaders than from the public and most private organizations*. The Power Leaders are getting much more impact from the few articulate activists and the vocal opinion leaders than from either the public at large or the business community.[17]

Opinion mobilization by a leader results in a pressure group. Even if we are not directly involved in a particular controversy, we are still likely, because of our personal loyalties, to side with the pressure group representing us. For example, during the 1970s strife in Ireland, international problems resulted when Americans of Irish descent became involved in gunrunning.

EFFECTIVENESS OF PERSUASION

In making appeals to various human motives, you must consider two elements: (1) that there is the possibility of so-called *cognitive dissonance* and (2) that truth may be personal.

A theory of cognitive dissonance (see Chapter 8) by sociologist Leon Festinger describes what people do when they act in a way not consistent with their own beliefs—as a result of pressures from power, patronage or persuasion.[18]

---

[17] Philip Lesly, "Guidelines on Public Relations and Public Affairs," in "Managing the Human Climate," no. 24, adapted from *The People Factor: Managing the Human Climate* (Homewood, Ill.: Dow Jones-Irwin, 1974).

[18] Leon Festinger, "The Theory of Cognitive Dissonance," in *The Science of Human Communications*, ed. Wilbur Schramm (New York: Basic Books, 1963), pp. 17–27. See also Festinger's *A Theory of Cognitive Dissonance* (Stanford, Calif.: Stanford University Press, 1982) and Zimbardo et al., *Influencing Attitudes and Changing Behavior*.

When the act sets off internal dissonance, the people try to resolve it by modifying their opinions. This, says Festinger, explains "the frequently observed behavior of people justifying their actions."[19] For instance, when the equal rights amendment was ratified by many states, compelling observance of equal rights for women, many people modified their opinions about woman's position in society.

Subtlety sometimes is the best persuader, says Stanford University psychology professor Philip Zimbardo, who believes that more attitude change can sometimes result from *less* social persuasion. For example, if people think they have a free choice in deciding in ways that are against their values but get just enough of a push to move them, sometimes only an appeal for support, they then have to justify their act. They do this by rationalizing what they think they did freely in conflict with their values.

To see that truth is personal we need only take a look at the religions of the world. All disciples claim their religion represents the truth, yet there are obviously many conflicts in doctrine. Of course, there are certain objective truths that are generally accepted, such as that "football is a contact sport," but there are also many less definitive "personal truths."

Also, there is always the question of manipulation of public opinion. Is it only a matter of communications skills and knowledgeability? Not always. Earl Newsom once pointed out an example of a major failure in a six-month "skilled-persuasion" effort in an Ohio city (see 7.4). It is not true, Newsom said, "that if you have enough money to pay for printing, advertising, and 'propaganda,' you can change people's minds."[20] It is also possible to overcampaign, arousing suspicion and backlash when it is apparent that a lot of money is being spent on the media. (See Chapter 12 for an intensive look at the effects of public communication campaigns.)

Such overcampaigning might be part of the problem with the U.S. government's seven-year (1971–1978), $5 billion war on cancer. A cure for cancer is still in the future and public support for the battle lags. Some government officials feel that a too simplistic approach to the disease was taken originally, stimulating false hope. Others believe that the source of disillusionment and confusion has been the government's placing of bans on various products that cause cancer in animals,[21] but that have not been tested adequately on humans. The basis of the public's cooling on the "war on cancer" may have been the false promise implicit in its initiation. Some legislators talked of having the battle won by the 1976 bicentennial. But "actions speak louder than words"—which was also the real lesson of the UN effort, as Newsom concluded.

Worse than the propaganda itself is the danger of a public either numbed by or made sensitive to the point of resistance to all messages interpreted as propaganda. First, issues like finding a cure for cancer may be ignored or abandoned. Second, simple truths become suspect. For example, columnist Meg Greenfield observes:

---

[19] Festinger, *Science of Human Communications*, p. 19.

[20] See 7.2, source.

[21] Rich Jaroslovsky, "Elusive Quest, Cancer Research Drive, Begun with Fanfare, Hits Disillusionment," *Wall Street Journal*, October 24, 1978, p. 1; and "Elusive Quest, War on Cancer Is Hurt by Animal Test Fight, Moves to Ban Products," *Wall Street Journal*, October 26, 1978, p. 1.

7.4 MAKING CINCINNATI "UNITED NATIONS CONSCIOUS"

During a six-months' campaign, almost 13,000 people were reached directly through the PTA; every school child took home literature on the UN programs; 10,000 in the Catholic PTA were exhorted by the Archbishop to support the UN; club women sent 1,000 letters and 1,350 telegrams to the American delegation; local radio stations averaged more than 150 spots a week. There were newspaper features, club speakers, and car cards. In all, more than 59,000 pieces of literature were distributed.

At the end of the six months, only half as many people considered the United Nations a means of preventing war as thought so at the beginning. There was almost no change in the number of those who thought the UN should take an active part in world affairs.

At the beginning, 76 percent of Cincinnatians were in favor of the United States joining a movement for an international police force; at the close, 73 percent. Fewer people favored UN control of atomic bombs. There was no change in the number of those feeling the U.S. should trade more with other countries. There was no improvement in those knowing what the UN is and how it works. Criticism of the record of the UN actually increased during the campaign.

Why did people respond this way? Perhaps because most of us tend to resist when somebody tries to sell us something that is going to change our views. But I suspect that the people in Cincinnati during that six months got their chief impressions of the United Nations not from the campaign, but from their observations of what was happening at the UN during that particular time. [The UN was ineffective in reconciling a widening gulf between North and South Korea, with the U.S. and U.S.S.R. pulling at opposite ends. The U.S.S.R. refused to let a UN team go into North Korea.]

Corporate managements are fast learning that their public behavior in times of crisis and trial does far more to create public attitudes toward them than most of the "literature" they develop to "educate the public" in between times.

Earl Newsom, "A Philosophy of Corporate Public Relations," An Interview with Earl Newsom, *Public Relations Journal*, 16, no. 2 (February 1960), pp. 13, 25. Reprinted in "Persuasion," a supplement of *pr reporter*, December 17, 1973. Also see Gilbert Bailey's account, "To Make Us Aware," *New York Times Magazine*, March 7, 1948, of the effort sponsored by the American Association for the UN, which was testing this as a pilot model to use throughout the nation. Opinion polling prior to and immediately following (March 7, 1948 weekend) was by the National Opinion Research Center.

Some of us have become self-conscious and afraid to espouse or defend American democratic virtues wholeheartedly and out loud. And we have become equally skittish about saying what is self-evidently true of the—yes—evil of the Soviet system of repression. . . . what a cruel irony it is that our determination to protect ourselves against fraudulent speech and ideas has resulted among other things, in our being afraid either to articulate or acknowledge certain simple, central really all-important—truths.[22]

We need to make a distinction between persuasion that takes place in a face-to-face situation and persuasion that uses the mass media. Differences are apparent in two areas: the means of social influence used and the effects. In mass media the persuasion is limited to information control, but in interpersonal persuasion there can be both information control and reinforcement because of the opportunity in direct contact to punish or reward. The effect of interpersonal persuasion can result in basic cognitive changes in people, but in mass communication efforts that is not attempted. Mass persuasion appeals are efforts to channel attitudes and some existing behavior patterns into a particular direction.[23]

---

[22] Meg Greenfield, "Not Everything Is Propaganda," *Newsweek*, March 21, 1983, p. 84.

[23] Mary John Smith, *Persuasion and Human Action* (Belmont, Calif.: Wadsworth, 1982), pp. 320–322.

POINTS TO REMEMBER

- Public opinion is what most people in a particular public think on a particular issue; it is a collective opinion.

- Latent public opinion is attitudes that have not yet crystallized around an issue and been expressed.

- Public opinion is not necessarily based on fact but on the conception or evaluation of something; it is unstable and often elusive and indirect.

- Persuasion is the means PR practitioners use most often to influence public opinion.

- In persuasion the critical factor in opinion change usually is information or the lack of it and how the information is presented or withheld.

- In effective persuasion, the message must first be attended to, then understood, received and accepted and finally acted upon.

- A persuasive message must present something of value to the audience and be compatible with the motives of the audience.

- News managers and opinion makers may be creators of events that focus attention on people or issues.

- Public relations people, like managers in government, business and other institutions, are opinion makers through their control of the dissemination of information.

- Propaganda, an effort to teach people what to think, is often used to mislead.

- Cantrell's "laws" of public opinion include the following: (1) Events are most likely to affect opinion. (2) Demands for action are a usual response. (3) Self-interest must figure heavily for people to become involved. (4) Leadership is sought, but not always objectively or critically. (5) Reliability is difficult to assess.

- Newsom's principles of persuasion are (1) personal identification with an issue, (2) suggestions of action, (3) familiarity and trust and (4) clarity.

- Persuasive efforts must consider the elements of cognitive dissonance and personal (as opposed to objective) truth.

- Interpersonal persuasion may effect basic cognitive changes in people; mass media persuasion tries to channel attitudes and existing behavior into a particular direction.

THINGS TO DO

1. Since it is most important to know when an attempt is being made to influence your own opinion, try this political opinion exercise. (Please put some thought into your answer.) Much of PR is sensitivity to attitudes and opinions and observation of effects of events, planned or unplanned. Even after an election, politics and policy are often indistinguishable. The elements of politics make it personal, so give your opinion in responding to the following questions:

   a. What current major issues are points for partisan differences in the future? Have the news media suggested these to you? How? Be specific.

b. Is all fair in love, war and politics? That is, are the media obligated to print or broadcast the name calling and other clearly propagandistic devices politicians employ during campaigns? How do off-year battles differ from campaign struggles? Are the devices different? Are media used in different ways?

c. What media are employed currently by politicians to gain your attention? Be specific and tell how each medium is used for what purpose.

d. Do you feel that any news medium is prejudiced in its coverage of the news of political figures? Which is for whom, and how is this favoritism reflected?

e. Local, state and national politics figure heavily in the daily news. Can media avoid being used? Are PR representatives responsible for most of the political-based newsmaking?

2. Locate a newspaper's publication of the most recent national public opinion poll by Louis Harris or George Gallup. Design a questionnaire based on the same questions and use it in selected classes, perhaps within your department, to see how closely responses from the audience you choose (journalism majors or any other group) match those from the national poll. It would be important for you not to use a poll that had just been published because some being asked might recall having read the national poll. On the other hand, if the poll study was published some time ago, events since then could make an important difference in responses.

3. Review John Naisbitt's *Megatrends* (see Selected Readings) and comment on how these are or are not reflected in current public attitudes.

SELECTED READINGS

Persuasion

D. J. Bem, *Beliefs, Attitudes, and Human Affairs* (Monterey, Calif.: Brooks/Cole, 1970). A practical application of theories.

Winston L. Bembeck and William S. Howell, *Persuasion: A Means of Social Influence*, 2d ed. (Englewood Cliffs, N.J.: Prentice-Hall, 1976). An excellent overview.

Marvin Karlins and Herbert I. Abelson, *Persuasion*, 2d ed. (New York: Springer, 1970). Research data correlated with theory.

John W. Keltner, *Elements of Interpersonal Communication* (Belmont, Calif.: Wadsworth, 1973). Excellent source for information about communication; see particularly "Changing Behavior: Persuasion."

William S. Howell, *The Empathic Communicator* (Belmont, Calif.: Wadsworth, 1982). The chapter "Persuading and Being Persuaded," pp. 144–175, is especially pertinent.

Sidney Kraus and Dennis Davis, *The Effects of Mass Communication on Political Behavior* (University Park: Pennsylvania State University Press, 1976). Citations of abstracts and bibliographies for the chapters are particularly helpful to researchers.

Mary John Smith, *Persuasion and Human Action* (Belmont, Calif.: Wadsworth, 1982). A critical look at social influence theories gives strength to some and suggests which ideas are not holding up. See "Nature of Persuasion," pp. 3–26; and Part 2, "Active Participation Theories of Persuasion," especially Chapter 13, "New Theoretical Directions in Persuasion: A Critical Appraisal," pp. 309–340.

Propaganda

Jacques Ellul, *Propaganda: The Formation of Men's Attitudes* (New York: Random House, 1973). A classic.

H. D. Laswell, R. D. Casey and B. L. Smith, eds., *Propaganda and Promotional Activities: An Annotated Bibliography* (Minneapolis: University of Minnesota Press, 1935; reprinted by University of Chicago Press, 1969). An annotated list of books and articles from all over the world on public opinion and the practice of propaganda.

Philip G. Zimbardo, Ebbe B. Ebbesen, Christina Maslach, *Influencing Attitudes and Changing Behavior* 2nd ed. (Menlo Park, Calif.: Addison-Wesley, 1977). Superior treatment and well written. Includes the famous Stanford prisoner experiment.

Public Opinion

Albert H. Cantrell, ed., *Polling on the Issues* (Cabin John, Md.: Seven Locks Press, 1980). Excellent insight into how the way a question is posed affects the response.

Hadley Cantril and Research Associates, *Gauging Public Opinion* (Princeton, N.J.: Princeton University Press, 1944). Although Cantril's laws and other ideas have been challenged, there is much evidence to support them.

———, ed. *Public Opinion 1935–46* (Princeton, N.J.: Princeton University Press, 1978).

———, *Sophisticated Poll Watchers' Guide*, rev. ed. (Princeton, N.J.: Princeton Opinion, 1976).

George Gallup and Craig Norback, *America Wants to Know: The Issues and the Answers for the Eighties* (Madison, New York: A & W Press, 1983).

B. C. Hennessey, *Public Opinion*, 4th ed. (Monterey, Calif.: Brooks/Cole, 1981). Good text on opinion formation and relationships between opinions and public policy. Some examples outdated.

Morris Janowitz and Paul I. Hirsch, *Reader in Public Opinion and Mass Communication*, 3rd ed. (New York: Free Press, 1981). Most of the major theorists are included.

Walter Lippmann, *Public Opinion* (New York: Harcourt, Brace, 1922). Despite its date, still important reading, a "classic"; reissued by Macmillan, 1965. Also see Edward L. Bernays, *Crystallizing Public Opinion* (New York: Boni and Liveright, 1927).

Max McCombs and Donald Shaw, "The Agenda-Setting Function of Mass Media," *Public Opinion Quarterly*, 36 (Summer 1972), pp. 176–187. The concept is set here. Later research has refined it.

John Naisbitt, *Megatrends* (New York: Warner Books, 1982). A popular version of trend analysis.

Richard W. Olshavesky, *Attitude Research Enters the 80s* (Chicago: American Marketing Association, 1980).

William L. Rivers, *The Opinionmakers* (Boston: Beacon Press, 1965). Highly readable, thorough, well-documented study of Washington people in power and those who write about them.

———, *The Other Government* (New York: Universe Books, 1982). Rivers has followed this thesis: An action occurs and is relayed through several layers to the news media, which then interpret the message, not necessarily the action.

PART 4

Communication—
Art and Science

*The backbone of a successful public
relations program is thoughtful, thorough
and appropriate communication, as
Chapters 8 through 11 show.*

CHAPTER 8

Communication Concepts and Theories

Many of our problems in communication arise because we forget to remember that individual experiences are never identical.

Don Fabun, communication specialist and author

The most hazardous undertaking of man—is the transmitting of an idea from one mind to another.

Frank McGee, former NBC commentator

Most theories about communication have been borrowed from the social sciences. It is important to remember that theories are not laws. A theory, according to sociologist George Homans, is something that makes it possible to derive a wide variety of findings under a number of different conditions from "a few higher order propositions."[1] These propositions are constantly undergoing examination, testing and revision. From propositions that survive the testing, principles emerge. Some principles as to how communication works provide a useful framework, both practical and theoretical, for the day-to-day operations of public relations.

HOW WE COMMUNICATE

The theoretical base for much public relations theory about communication comes from Carl I. Hovland's idea that to change attitudes you must change opinions and that going about the process involves communication. With this approach, for communication to be effective, the object of the communication effort must first pay attention to the communication, understand it, accept it and remember it. When the communication has reached the level of acceptance,

[1] George C. Homans, "Contemporary Theory in Sociology," in *Handbook of Modern Sociology*, ed. Robert E. L. Faris (Chicago, Ill.: Rand McNally, 1964), pp. 951–952. Also, Wilbur Schramm's definition of theory is helpful: ". . . a set of related statements, at a high level of abstraction, from which propositions can be generated and tested by scientific methods the results of which help explain human behavior." This definition appears in "The Challenge to Communications Research," in *Introduction to Mass Communication Research*, ed. Ralph O. Nafziger and David M. White (Baton Rouge: Louisiana State University Press, 1972), p. 10.

then the question of credibility comes in. A prominent PR practitioner, the late Earl Newsom, made the following comment about credibility:

> It *does* seem to be true that the attitudes of people are formed by what they see us do and say—not by our insistent attempts to tell all about ourselves and persuade them that we deserve their confidence. It *does* seem to work out in practice that before we can move people to have confidence in us we must appear to them to be solving the problems *they* want to see solved—to be headed where the people are headed.[2]

Another definition states that a theory is "an abstract, symbolic representation of what is conceived to be reality . . . a set of abstract statements or rules designed to 'fit' some portion of the real world."[3] The definition appears with two sets of rules for using "a theory (a set of symbolic statements)." One set is called the *correspondence rules*; it states that some of the symbols, called "conceptual independent variables," must relate with another set, called "conceptual dependent variables," and to what occurs (behavior of an object or person in a situation). The other set of rules is called *functional relationships*; it describes how to manipulate the symbols of the theoretical concepts to derive testable hypotheses.

The second part of the Hovland approach is presented in the question posed by Lasswell: "Who said what to whom with what effect?"[4] "Who" is the source for the communication; when "who" is a PR practitioner, the practitioner is spokesperson for an institution whose credibility depends on the audience's perception of that source's power, competence, trustworthiness, goodwill, idealism and dynamic qualities and the similarity between the source and the self-perception of the audience. (A source can be either a person or a medium of communication, as in an expression like "The *New York Times* said today.") The medium used for the communication conveys information, either factual or emotional, to effect an opinion change on the audience.

The final part of the question is critical for public relations people: ". . . to whom with what effect?" That is, who was the audience, and what effect did the communication have on it? We examine these questions in the following sections. But keep in mind that trying to change attitudes is complex—it means a person relinquishes one way of looking at the world or part of the world for another. What audiences do with a message is the focus in finding the effect.

Reception Test for Media

Although media research departments can show tables of statistics that theoretically profile their audiences, you should still ask some important questions. For example, are the selected "receivers" chosen from a physical or

---

[2] Earl Newsom, *A Look at the Record*, text of an address before the annual Public Relations Conference of Standard Oil (New Jersey), December 16, 1947, published by Earl Newsom & Company. Used by Permission.

[3] Philip G. Zimbardo, Ebbe B. Ebbesen and Christian Maslach, *Influencing Attitudes and Changing Behavior*, 2d ed. (Reading, Mass.: Addison-Wesley, 1977), p. 53.

[4] H. D. Lasswell, "The Structure and Function of Communication in Society," in *Communication of Ideas*, ed. Lyman Bryson (New York: Harper & Row, 1948), pp. 37–51.

intellectual base? To answer this, a university, for instance, may define all those to whom its alumni magazine is mailed as readers, yet a substantial number are probably "nonreceivers" (they throw the publication away without ever lifting the cover) and another segment may be "lookers" (they thumb through the magazine but never read anything except photo captions). The real readers would be those who read at least one article per publication in the time period sampled. The same applies to news releases. To quote Ohio State University PR professor Walter Siefert, "Dissemination [of news releases] does not equal Publication, and Publication does not equal Absorption and Action! Which means, in simpler words: All who receive it won't *publish* it, and all who read or hear it won't understand or *act* on it."[5]

Credibility Test for Media

Another question to ask concerns a medium's credibility: How much do the surveys tell you about reception if they talk in terms of numbers reached? If you send out a news release to the media, not all of them will publish it and many who read or hear it will not pay any real attention to it. For instance, in a presentation designed by the Magazine Publishers Association to show the impact of magazine advertising, it was claimed such ads reached women in the twenty-five to thirty-five age bracket who, it was asserted, do most of the buying. The presentation offered supporting data to show response to and recall of specific advertising messages, but it did not state the *proportion* of readers recalling these messages. Remember that just as some people read editorial content and ignore advertising, some do just the opposite.

Thus in talking about the reception of media, we first must talk in the broad terms of publicity and advertising. Many studies are available on the receptivity of advertising because of its ties to marketing. Publicity is more difficult to measure, because it is almost impossible to evaluate the use, much less the reception, of publicity materials released to the mass media. Publicity is assumed to have a higher degree of credibility because it appears as a nonbiased "news" source that is often referred to as third-party credibility.

Studies bear out these generalities. Ethnic and religious publications have a higher credibility with their readers than do other media with theirs. The industry, trade, association and professional press also ranks high with their selected audiences. Suburban and small-town weekly publications (generally newspapers) are next highest with credibility ratings. Specialized magazines also rate high—again, perhaps because their readers have a concentrated interest in the subject matter. In terms of mass (as opposed to specialized) media, television dominates perhaps because of the "seeing is believing" phenomenon and because TV has the capacity to disengage the critical senses. Daily newspapers have more credibility than their critics often are willing to concede and a higher persuasive impact than even publishers and editors are sometimes willing to admit. Radio stations, owing to their specialized appeal and the emotional impact of the medium, significantly affect their own loyal audiences, but these are comparatively small. At the bottom are

---

[5]Walter Siefert, personal communication. Used by permission.

company publications, which get mixed reviews for credibility, perhaps because they are so diverse in quality.

Interesting enough, in an era when everything else about the government seems suspect, government publications consistently get rather high credibility ratings, particularly the consumer-oriented studies. Although the narrowness of the appeal makes the specialized media and smaller mass media (suburban papers, radio) easier to evaluate, the mass media present a complex study.

Studies among young people show television news rated higher in credibility than newspapers. A college sample gave these newscasts a 3-to-1 lead over newspapers.[6] A high school sample gave TV as a preferred news source because news could be seen happening. Radio and newspapers almost tied for second place with this high school audience, but newspapers were cited as more believable and news magazines rated last.[7]

A term you will hear in relation to the use of media is *agenda setting*. This refers to the idea that the attention the mass media give to certain ideas or issues or themes lends them signficance. There seems to be a symbiotic relationship (mutually beneficial coexistence) between message source and medium, in that mass media may pick up ideas that would seem to represent broad appeals and popularize them. Also, media agenda may suggest to leaders some public concerns that could be exploited. There is no clear-cut "cause and effect" in agenda setting, but the impact of the mass media in calling attention to an idea, regardless of source, is considerable.

HOW TO CHOOSE THE RIGHT MESSAGE

After you have estimated the reception and credibility of the medium, you must plan the correct message for it. If you are using billboards, there is more to determining the message than simply concluding that someone driving at 55 miles per hour cannot possibly read even twenty words of copy—and still be a safe driver. We have to consider the purpose of the message, as well as its form and color and its language.

The Purpose of a Message

The purpose of a message is tied to the objective of the communication. What is it you wish to accomplish? Accomplishment is tied to something tangible like increasing the enrollment of a university, not to something nebulous like improving the image of the institution. PR pioneer Edward L. Bernays is ada-

---

[6]Raymond S. H. Lee, "Credibility of Newspapers and TV News," *Journalism Quarterly*, 55, no. 2 (Summer 1978), pp. 282–287.

[7]Paul A. Atkins and Harry Elwood, "TV News Is First Choice in Survey of High Schools," *Journalism Quarterly*, 55, no. 3 (Autumn 1978), pp. 596–599. Also the Roper poll study for the Television Information Office shows TV has better than a 2-to-1 advantage over newspapers for credibility (The Roper Organization, *Trends in Attitudes Toward Television and Other Media*, New York, 1983).

mant about not even using the word *image* in a public relations context. Bernays says the word suggests that PR deals with shadows and illusions when in reality the practitioner deals with changing attitudes and actions to meet social objectives.[8] The reality of PR's job is reduced to basics—experience not imagery—by Southwestern Bell Telephone area public relations director Jim Pattillo. Pattillo is blunt and very specific: "All the image building goes down the drain for the telephone industry the very first time the customer starts having a hard time with his telephone service or with company representatives."[9] Some problems of institutional credibility cited by PR practitioner Philip Lesly must be attributed directly to peddling images instead of dealing with realities. These include the handling of information about Vietnam as a foreign policy example, and the New York financial crisis of the 1970s as a domestic one.[10]

Once the purpose of the message is clearly defined, then the motivation and inspiration decisions are easier. Psychologist Abraham H. Maslow has devised a hierarchy of human motives.[11] We may think of the purpose of our message as appealing to at least one of these needs in other people.

- *Self-actualization* is the need to develop individuality and make constructive use of one's abilities. This also encompasses creativity and aesthetic appreciation. A subtle aspect of this motive is the need to know and to understand.

- *Esteem* includes the need for achievement and recognition of that achievement by others. It also involves the face-saving compromises we often engage in to rescue our esteem, like settling for a fancier title instead of a salary increase.

- *Love* means more than a need for affection. It encompasses the need for belonging to a group and the longing for a friendly social environment. It is the strength of this motivational need that pulls young people, particularly teenagers, together in a seemingly impenetrable peer group.

- *Safety* means protection against violence, economic hazards and unpredictable reality.

- The most fundamental motivations are the *physiological* needs—hunger, thirst, sex, fatigue and such.

Some principles go along with these needs. One is *homeostasis*. People constantly make an effort to maintain the status quo. Another is the principle of *deprivation*. Related to physiological needs, it never wanes in intensity; if people are deprived of a physiological goal (for instance, food), they will continue to seek it. (One compulsive chocolate eater explained that a childhood allergy had deprived her from eating chocolates when very young!) However, when deprivation in-

---

[8] Edward L. Bernays, "Down with Image, Up with Reality," *Public Relations Quarterly*, 22, no. 1 (Spring 1977), p. 12.

[9] Jim Pattillo in a speech for a public relations workshop in New York City, January 1977; taken from a copy of his address printed by American Telephone and Telegraph (1977), p. 8.

[10] Philip Lesly, "Another View of the Communications Gap," from the newsletter *Managing the Human Climate*, published by the Philip Lesly Company, Chicago, Ill., no. 44, May–June 1977.

[11] See Abraham Maslow, *Motivation and Personality* (New York: Harper & Row, 1954). See also Maslow's *Toward a Psychology of Being* (New York: Van Nostrand-Reinhold, 1962).

volves social goals, it often can be effective only up to a point and then it loses intensity and people may abandon a goal—for instance, resigning themselves to a certain social class or status. The principle of *satiation* weakens physiological drives and can weaken social motives, but it seems to have no effect on emotions—good news for lovers, perhaps. The principle of *goal evaluation* is based on tension—a straining for something—to earn a karate black belt, to be a master at bridge. However, goals that are not socially acceptable are either abandoned or another principle takes over. This occurs also when certain goals prove impossible to achieve. For example, if you can't be an "A" student, perhaps you can be a "solid B" student. One other principle works in these basic motives, the *barrier* principle. A barrier placed between people and the fulfillment of their goals will enhance the appeal of the goal unless the barrier proves too great, in which case they will probably change goals.

Goals are tied closely to what we want to be, and an advertising creative director we know steadfastly maintains that everyone is a snob of one kind or another. When some educators protested, he told them they probably were intellectual snobs. The promoter of a national magazine keyed to intellectuals (*Harper's*) played on that very idea with a mailing piece in a "plain brown envelope" carrying this question in the lower left corner: Should you be punished for being born with a high IQ? The envelope probably was opened by most recipients. What we value is often a key to our personality.

The Texture of a Message

Once you know which needs and values you want to appeal to, you then know the purpose of your message and which persuasive appeal is likely to work.

The texture of the message is chosen for its persuasive effect too. The medium dictates to some extent the range of textures. In television you have the widest range—color design, movement and sound. In print the size, shape and feel of an object—as most people trained in graphics know—may mean the difference as to whether a brochure is picked up (much less read), whether a package is taken off a supermarket shelf, whether an ad catches people's attention. Motivational studies involving form need to be interpreted by both public relations and marketing people in approaching particular problems.

Regarding color, it is important to know, for instance, that most businesspeople will not respond to a questionnaire printed on hot pink, will make little response to one on blue, but will give many answers to a questionnaire printed on green, beige or white. Label colors that look dramatic on clear glass may look unappetizing, even sickening, when the product is inside.

Most of us psychologically favor certain colors; this is likely to manifest itself (perhaps unconsciously) in our choice of colors for clothes, cars and furniture. The public relations person needs to know which colors will appeal to a particular audience and the fidelity of those colors in the medium chosen for communicating with that audience. One despairing art director, after having to change colors for a campaign owing to problems in reproducing them in different media, said with some resignation, "I'm ready to go back to the basics: red, white and blue."

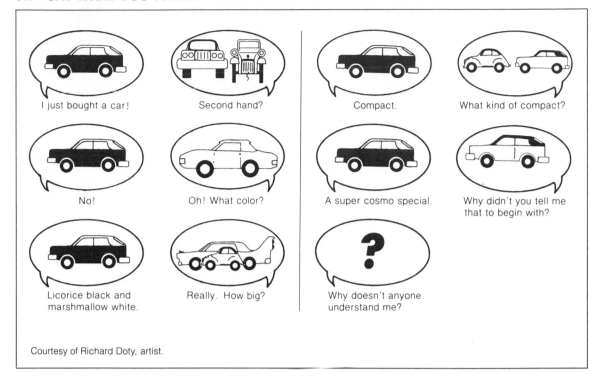

Courtesy of Richard Doty, artist.

The Language of a Message

Problems in communication are often caused by semantics. It is essential that words mean the same thing to the receiver that they do to the communicator. It isn't important that you say something in words *you* like to use or hear; rather, you must know what those words mean to the viewer or listener (see 8.1).

Common words cannot possibly have meanings in themselves—only people can bestow meanings, says communications specialist Don Fabun, adding, "When we act as if we believed that a word symbol is the event that was originally experienced, we ignore all the steps that have made it something else."[12]

Samuel Johnson once made a bet with his companion James Boswell that he could go into the fish market and reduce a Billingsgate stall tender to tears without saying a word she could understand. Here is what took place:

Johnson began by indicating with his nose that her fish had passed the stage in which a man's olfactories could endure their flavor. The Billingsgate woman made a verbal

[12] Don Fabun, *Communications: The Transfer of Meaning* (Encino, Calif.: Kaiser Aluminum and Chemical Corp., distributed by Glencoe Press, 1969), p. 19. Used by permission.

assault, common enough in vulgar parlance, that impugned the classification in natural history of Johnson's mother. The doctor responded with, "You're an article, ma'am." "No more an article than yourself, you bloddy misbegotten villain." "You are a noun, woman." "You . . . you," stammered the woman, choking with rage at a list of articles she could not understand. "You are a pronoun," said Dr. Johnson. The woman shook her fist in speechless rage. "You are a verb . . . an adverb . . . an adjective . . . a conjunction . . . a preposition . . . an interjection!" the doctor continued, applying the harmless epithets at proper intervals. The nine parts of speech completely staggered the old woman and she dumped herself down on the floor, crying with anguish at being thus blackguarded in a set of terms unknown to her and which, not understanding, she could not answer.[13]

As we all know, jargon and obfuscation abound in government, education and elsewhere. Sometimes even attempts to clarify go wrong. In 1972 Pennsylvania's education secretary reportedly exhorted his underlings in a memo to write English instead of bureaucratese; ironically, he wrote the memo in the sort of language he was out to eliminate: "A determination has been made that the communications effectiveness of department personnel suffers from low prioritization of clarity and correspondingly high thresholds of verbosity and circuitous phraseology."[14]

Clarity Obscurity in language has reached ridiculous proportions in American usage. And since PR practitioners are not around to explain what their messages mean, the language they use had better be self-explanatory. You must choose your words with a feeling for the *associations* the receivers will make, based on their individual frames of reference; the *images* the words will conjure up for them, based usually on stereotypes they hold; and simply on identification of the word itself (see 8.1). As an instance of clarity, John F. Kennedy's inaugural address ("Ask not what your country can do for you . . .") was written almost entirely in single syllable words and was comprehensible, as well as elegant and eloquent, to almost all who heard it.

Emotional Impact This element of language has nothing to do with clarity; it depends on emotional association. Emotional impact is, of course, a significant weapon in all propaganda battles. In World War II Axis Sally and Tokyo Rose tried to entice American defections, and two incomparable commanders of the English language, Winston Churchill and Franklin Roosevelt, urged on their countrymen with eloquent propaganda.

Verbal Settings The *context* of messages is also important. As one writer advises:

> There is no easy way of choosing words. They must not be so general in meaning as to include thoughts not intended, nor so narrow as to eliminate thoughts that are intended. Let the meaning select the word.

---

[13] Herbert R. Mayes, "Trade Winds," *Saturday Review*, October 19, 1968, p. 12.
[14] Reported in *El Dorado* (Kansas) *Times*, July 13, 1972.

© 1974 United Feature Syndicate, Inc.

A word is ambiguous when the reader is unable to choose decisively between alternative meanings, either of which would seem to fit the context.

A great deal of unclear writing results from the use of too many broad, general words, those having so many possible meanings that the precise thought is not clear. The more general the words are, the fainter is the picture; the more special they are, the brighter.[15]

Because we know from research that the behavioral attitudes of seeking or avoiding a message exist, it is important to consider the significance of both *repetition* and *consistency* in public relations messages. Repetition increases the opportunity for exposure. Consistency helps increase credibility. Communications scholars who conducted experiments on cognitive discrepancies and communication called the act of seeking "information search" and of avoiding a message "information preference."

To be sure a message gets through to an intended receiver is the first goal; repetition increases chances. To be sure the message is believed is next, and consistency helps. But both of these are based on a time element, and the communications scholars have some other disquieting discoveries. First, they found that when pressed for time people often make decisions based on less information than they would normally require (a fact of significance especially in political PR), and second, writers must decide whether their audience needs information object by object (which is all right if the audience members already have made their decisions) or whether they need an evaluative structure or frame of reference to permit making comparisons between alternatives.[16]

Messages, then, should be in a semantic structure the audience needs, in a context they understand and be said with words that mean the same thing to the hearer as to the user. These messages also must have a consistency to be believable and a repetition to penetrate selectivity.

---

[15] "The Discipline of Language," newsletter, Royal Bank of Canada.

[16] Steven H. Chaffee, Keith R. Stamm, Jose L. Guerrero and Leonard P. Tipton, "Experiments on Cognitive Discrepancies," *Journalism Quarterly Monograph*, December 1969. Illustrations are as follows: (1) Deadline pressures affect the selection of wire copy by wire editors—when under such a constraint their biases affected the selection of material whereas on other occasions, with no time pressures, they were impartial. (2) In an election campaign there are one-sided exposures early and late, which attempt to persuade voters of the opposition to cross over; these should be timed to coincide with the period when they are likely to listen to arguments that run counter to their loyalties—certainly not at the last minute, however, such as an election eve telethon.

RECEIVING AND
ACCEPTING MESSAGES

Evidence suggests that people who have grown up with lots of television (which means most readers of this book) learn to tune out messages they do not wish to receive. Everyone does this to some extent—otherwise we would all be drowning in noise. But the high degree of unconscious selectivity on the part of the electronic generation creates particular challenges to the PR person in reaching them.

Great stock was once put in the two-step flow theory that ideas flowed from opinion makers down to the public at large.[17] The concept is that opinion leaders, attending to mass or specialized media, are early adopters of new ideas. Their adoption influences others, starting with people who are like themselves—those in the same occupations or social/economic class. However, politicians have recently, with enormous success, conducted public opinion studies to see what the people are interested in and concerned with, and then have enunciated these feelings as ideas or policies. Presidential programs reflecting this upward flow are John Kennedy's War on Poverty, Lyndon Johnson's Great Society and Jimmy Carter's New Foundations.

The Sources of a Message

How audiences perceive the source of a message is significant, and one effective source is people. We are in almost constant conversation with people, and the information we get this way has a higher credibility than any other—depending on the attitude we hold toward the speaker. Is it someone we like? That we respect? That seems smart? Someone who seems to be like us or someone who accepts and likes us?

Something interesting happens to the credibility of "people" sources. It fluctuates. The most recent polls show clergy, educators and physicians at the top of the credibility list, winning back their place that was relinquished for a while to celebrity sports or television figures. We tend to seek out not only people but media that reflect our opinions and attitudes. For this reason, many PR veterans advise us to forget about persuading those vehemently against us—rather we should try to neutralize them so they will do minimal harm. Boost those already on our side, and try to sway the undecided.

Everyone seems to be aware that a sender must encode—translate information into something personally meaningful. However, we tend to forget the static of competing messages, credibility disturbances and the interference of selectivity

---

[17] For the evolution of the two-step flow, see Elihu Katz and Paul Lazarsfeld, *Personal Influence: The Part Played by People in The Flow of Mass Communications* (New York: Free Press of Glencoe, 1955), pp. 15–42; Katz, "The Two-Step Flow of Communication: An Up-to-Date Report on a Hypothesis," *Public Opinion Quarterly*, 21 (Spring 1957), pp. 61–78; Paul Lazarsfeld and Herbert Menzell, "Mass Media and Personal Influence," in *Science of Human Communication*, ed. Wilbur Schramm (New York: Basic Books, 1963); Johan Arndt, "A Test of the Two-Step Flow in Diffusion of a New Product," *Journalism Quarterly*, 45 (Autumn 1968), pp. 457–465; Melvin L. DeFleur and Sandra Ball-Rokeach, *Theories of Mass Communication*, 4th ed. (New York: Longman, 1982), pp. 192–194.

8.2 A COMMUNICATION MODEL

Models are useful in understanding communication as a process of sending and receiving
messages. Although communication is infinitely
complex, and no model can indicate all that
goes on during communication, this model
shows how something (Referent) triggers the
source (Encoder) to start a message, and it
suggests some of the intervening or mediating
factors that influence the receiver's (Decoder)
perception of the message.

One well-known communications theorist,
Joseph T. Klapper, gives the following as additional mediating factors: selective exposure,
selective perception, selection retention, interpersonal dissemination, personal influence and
leadership and the nature of the media. For
more details on these factors, see Klapper's
The Effects of Mass Communication (Glencoe,
Ill.: Free Press, 1960).

Other theorists, in formulating a *mass communication model*, have suggested that the
concept of dropping information into the public
awareness is like dropping a pebble into a pool
and then having its concentric rings strike

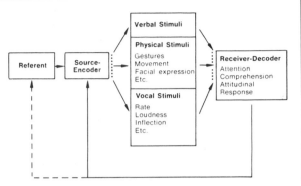

shore and return. See Ray Hiebert, Donald F.
Ungurait, and Thomas W. Bohn, *Mass Media:
An Introduction to Modern Communication*
(New York: McKay, 1974), p. 10.

The above model is from John Keltner's *Interpersonal
Speech-Communication* (Belmont, Calif.: Wadsworth, 1970),
p. 19; it is adapted from Gerald B. Miller's *Speech Communication: A Behavioral Approach* (Indianapolis: Bobbs-Merrill,
1966), p. 73. By permission.

on the part of the receiver. If the receiver does accept the message, it then must be
decoded and some response encoded.

Considering the environment of distortion from our family, social, educational, religious and ethnic experiences, it is a wonder any communication gets
through to us at all. And of course, many messages do not. To grasp some of the
complexity, take a look at communication models (see 8.1 for instance). Sometimes too our intended messages are countermanded by our "body English" or
other symbols.[18] Indeed, symbols are important whether in advertising or art,
whether trademarks or company logos, in conveying the meaning we want to
convey.

In utilizing symbols, however, we often resort to stereotyping, a mental short-
hand that can be useful in processing information. The word *chair* makes you
think of a certain type of chair, as you have *all* chairs filed under that mental image. Often this is adequate for communication and for understanding the situation. However, the context may make you seek a particular symbol. And you may
go, for example, from your basic chair to a desk chair in a classroom setting. But
stereotypes—the pictures in our heads—are personal and may misrepresent reality (as 8.2 shows). Communication, imprecise at best, takes on an even greater risk

---

[18] Albert Mehrabian, *Silent Messages*, 2nd ed. (Belmont, Calif.: Wadsworth, 1981).

when using stereotypes.[19] If one had a target audience that was clearly defined, and had well-grounded knowledge of which stereotypes would be effective and appropriate with this audience, it might be wise to proceed. But there are monumental examples of where stereotyping resulted in failure. For example, look at various situations where the ways women were represented resulted in boycotts, demonstrations and even loss of elections. The stereotyping of females in advertising, television programming, news columns and by public speakers (especially politicians) has lessened in the face of activity by women's groups, but it is still in evidence. The main criticism of the use of stereotypes to represent roles people perform or to represent groups of people is that for many the image becomes the reality. During the civil rights movement in the United States, for example, the concern of blacks over racial stereotyping was that people who had limited contact with blacks accepted the representation as the reality.

Effects of Other Stimuli

Our interpretation of different message stimuli is constantly being measured. Some of the most interesting research now centers on an effort to involve yet another of our senses in the communication process—the olfactory sense. Advertisers have put out ads that, when scratched, smell like lemon, perfume or martinis. However, research by Edward Gillenwater reveals that though such ads increase reader involvement, there is no evidence that readers remember them any more than they do other ads.[20]

The Responses to a Message

Information processing is critical in evaluating the impact, or potential impact, of communication. Carl Hovland established the idea of changing attitudes to change opinions, which has become known as the Yale approach to persuasion.[21] He pointed out that effective communication involved attention, comprehension, acceptance and retention. Using Lasswell's model of who said what to whom with what effect, Hovland named the source, message, audience and audience reaction as the elements of the processing cycle. (Zimbardo reduces these to four components of the Yale model: attention, comprehension, acceptance and retention. Smith adds a fifth action.) The source had to evidence power, competence, trustworthiness, goodwill, idealism, similarity (to audience) and dynamism.[22] The credibility (trust, goodwill, idealism, similarity) of the source and

---

[19] Walter Lippmann, "Stereotypes," *Reader in Public Opinion and Mass Communication*, ed. Morris Janowitz and Paul M. Hirsch (New York: Free Press, 1981), pp. 29–37.

[20] Edward Gillenwater, "The Effect of Olfactory Stimulation on the Retention of Advertising," paper presented to the Advertising Division, Association for Education in Journalism Convention, Carbondale, Ill., August 1972.

[21] Mary John Smith, *Persuasion and Human Action* (Belmont, Calif.: Wadsworth, 1982, p. 214, and Zimbardo et al., *Influencing Attitudes and Changing Behavior*, pp. 56–62.

[22] Ibid. (Zimbardo et al.) pp. 62–64.

the authority (power, competence, dynamism) of the source are the major conceptual factors in the Yale model.

William McGuire saw a flaw in the Yale information-processing theories.[23] Hovland and his associates, McGuire felt, had ignored the relationship between comprehension and acceptance. Instead of the *source*, McGuire focused on the *receiver*. His modifications clarified the relationship between comprehension and acceptance, indicating their separate effects on a persuasive message's impact. Personality traits of message recipients, he said, affected comprehension, acceptance of messages and persuasibility in general. McGuire reduced the steps of the Yale processing to two: reception of message content and yielding to what is comprehended (see 8.3). McGuire says a person has to receive a message effectively and then yield to the point for an attitude or opinion to change.

McGuire, as well as Hovland and associates, assumed that new cognitive information was learned from the content of the messages. That was challenged by Anthony Greenwald, who said it was not message content that was learned, but the interpretative reactions of people and the covert messages they produced in response to the message. However, according to Smith, Greenwald's cognitive response approach tells more about "the *covariation* between self-generated messages and their effects than it does about *why* covert conditions generate cognitive realignments and behavior changes."[24]

Other theories of social and cognitive behavior also help explain message effects. Social psychologist Kurt Lewin observed that people process information and "compute" attitudes to make logical combinations.[25] *Group dynamics* are important in this process because a person tries to adjust his or her opinions and perceptions in response to group norms and pressures toward uniformity. Motivation, said Lewin, is socially based, which means the group has the power to reward for compliance or punish for deviation.

In Chapter 8, we noted Leon Festinger's *theory of cognitive dissonance*—that people strive to reduce discrepancies that may exist within an individual's own cognitive system.[26] Experiences may be consonant (compatible with values), dissonant (conflicting with values) or irrelevant. The greater the ratio of dissonance to consonance, the more the dissonance is felt. Of course, for cognitive conflict to occur, the opposites have to be important to the person. *Cognitive overlap* occurs when there is more than one choice; the choice closest to compatibility creates the less dissonance. J. W. Brehm and A. R. Cohen suggested that the dissonance would be greater if one committed oneself to a course of action while aware that another path was possible, whereas Eliot Aronson said that conceptualizing dissonance was a consequence of violating expectancies or rules, especially regarding one's self-concept (for example, honest persons more bothered by lying than thieves).[27]

---

[23] Smith, *Persuasion and Human Action*, pp. 215–218.

[24] Ibid., p. 236.

[25] Kurt Lewin, "Studies in Group Decision," in Dorwin Cartwright and A. F. Zander (eds.), *Group Dynamics* (Evanston, Ill.: Row Peterson, 1953). Third edition: *Group Dynamics, Research and Theory* (New York: Harper & Row, 1968).

[26] Zimbardo et al., *Influencing Attitudes*, pp. 64–72.

[27] Smith, *Persuasion and Human Action*, pp. 121–123.

8.3 McGUIRE'S TWO-STAGE MEDIATION MODEL

McGuire places emphasis on the receiver rather than
the communicator.

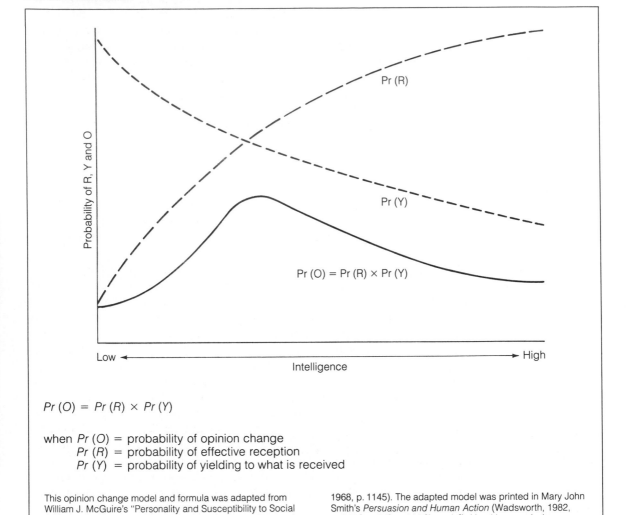

$Pr (O) = Pr (R) \times Pr (Y)$

when $Pr (O)$ = probability of opinion change
$Pr (R)$ = probability of effective reception
$Pr (Y)$ = probability of yielding to what is received

This opinion change model and formula was adapted from William J. McGuire's "Personality and Susceptibility to Social Influence," in *Handbook of Personality Theory and Research* by E. F. Borgatta and W. W. Lambert, et al. (Rand McNally, 1968, p. 1145). The adapted model was printed in Mary John Smith's *Persuasion and Human Action* (Wadsworth, 1982, p. 217 [model], p. 216 [formula]). Used by permission.

The explanation of people's efforts to make sense of others' behavior is called an *attribution theory.*[28] According to Fritz Heider, two potential causes are used to explain behavior: situational (external) and dispositional (internal). The one we choose depends upon some suppositions. If people often do something unusual in different situations that don't have very evident causes, we may attribute an in-

---

[28] Zimbardo et al., *Influencing Attitudes*, pp. 73–80.

ternal or dispositional cause. The problem with these assumptions is a tendency to oversimplify and overestimate people's consistency in behavior and a tendency to see an internal reason when the situation might have had more bearing. But people do take behavior cues from their environment. People also have some reason to explain their behavior. These reasons affect their attitudes. The question is which comes first: Is it reasoned behavior or behavior which is reasoned?

Social learning theory holds there is continuous reciprocal interaction and continuous feedback, between a person's internal cognition and the situation.[29] What we learn through experience, observation, listening or reading and establishing symbolic relationships teaches us to expect different consequences in different situations for the same behavior. Also, according to the theory, reinforcements are different for various people, depending on such factors as value systems. Another element of this theory states that for learning to occur, a person must remember, expecting something to occur again. Extinction is one way to change behavior. Extinction may occur when the anticipated result of an action is withheld (for example, not responding with attention to a child's tantrum as the child expects). Rules or instructions or communications can also be used to change behaviors.[30]

The public relations practitioner has a choice of several theories to apply in planning message strategy to reach a goal. It may be to encourage people to belong (Lewin). It may be to avoid a choice that conflicts with values or—if people are already in a state of cognitive dissonance—to help them reconcile the value conflict through rationalization (Festinger). Self-persuasion, remember, is the most successful. The strategy might also be to provide environmental cues (Helder) that are likely to appeal to a target group (an impressive setting—for example, a black tie event—to mark the opening of a new building). Or it may be an ongoing educational program to develop expectations: Antismoking campaigns aim at making smokers feel uncomfortable when they light up in a public place.

Some researchers feel that a model devised by Martin Fishbein is useful in predicting group attitudes. Because the *Fishbein model* can be used to identify and categorize consumers according to criteria that are significant to the consumers themselves, Jose Guerrero and David Hughes conclude that the model has practical implications for the marketing specialist in particular.[31]

Fishbein himself contends that his model can measure both a person's emotional evaluations about a concept or object and also his or her beliefs about that object, and can show that a person's belief (defined as a perceived probability of the existence of some relationship between an attitude object and a defining criterion) can change independently of an attitude, with the result that two people may differ in belief but have similar attitudes.[32]

For example, two people might be against school busing to achieve integra-

---

[29] Ibid., pp. 80–84.

[30] Ibid., p. 84.

[31] See Jose L. Guerrero and G. David Hughes, "An Empirical Test of the Fishbein Model," *Journalism Quarterly*, 49 (Winter 1971), pp. 684–691.

[32] Martin Fishbein, "Investigation of Relationship Between Belief about an Object and Attitude Toward That Object," *Human Relations*, 16 (1963), pp. 233–239.

tion—that is, they have the same attitude. However, one may favor integration, but through neighborhood school attendance—desiring to integrate schools by integrating neighborhoods. The other may oppose busing because of opposition to forced socialization.[33]

Some researchers say that both opinions and facts represent answers to questions, and so it is impossible to draw a sharp line between them. There may also be a fuzzy line between opinions and attitudes, although opinions can be "verbalized," while attitudes often cannot (they may be unconscious).

The opinions, attitudes and actions of people are all affected by family, friends, informal work groups and formal groups such as clubs and organizations. Group influence and pressure particularly become apparent during controversy, according to this research evidence. (1) When issues are clear, group pressure influences at most only a third of the people, with two-thirds standing firm. (2) If even a small supporting voice comes in, the third shrinks away. (3) Only where there is ambiguity and confusion can you count on a bandwagon effect, which means factors other than the propaganda device itself are determinative.[34]

Getting people to believe something is easier than trying to keep them from accepting something you don't want them to believe. One popular idea is that early exposure to some enemy arguments will inoculate hearers against future belief in the enemy. Other evidence suggests, though, that any message may have an impact on a persuasive enemy attack that might follow. Some evidence also suggests that trying to get a critical response set in the audience can either inhibit or enhance the effect of a message that is to come. If you try to turn people against a message or the messenger, your efforts could have the opposite effect of inoculating them against further negative criticisms. The effect could make them more vulnerable to future enemy persuasive appeals. But reception and acceptance of a later persuasive appeal are determined by both the target of criticism and the nature of the critical act. Therefore, the situation could be manipulated to have some bearing on the outcome.

The purpose of a persuasive communication is often concealed, becoming apparent only after careful examination. The examination of the obvious content compared with its intent is the study of such organized propaganda campaigns as those launched internally by a government or those of one government against another (psychological warfare). Psychological warfare is as old as war itself. Although it has become sophisticated, its goals have remained basically the same: first, to convert subjects from one allegiance to another; second, to divide the opposition into defeatable groups; third, to consolidate existing support (this was

[33]While the illustration used here for simplicity involves individuals, the validity of the Fishbein model as a predictive tool for *individual* attitudes is disputed by Guerrero and Hughes (Jose L. Guerrero and G. David Hughes, "An Empirical Test of the Fishbein Model," *Journalism Quarterly*, 49 [Winter 1971], pp. 684–691), who see its best application to *group* attitudes—certainly a significant observation for PR.

[34]Solomon E. Asch, "Effects of Group Pressure upon the Modification and Distortion of Judgment," in *Groups, Leadership and Men*, ed. H. Guetzkow (Pittsburgh, Pa.: Carnegie Press, 1951), pp. 177–190; R. S. Crutchfield, "Conformity and Character," *American Psychologist*, 10 (1955), pp. 191–198. See also Asch and Crutchfield quoted in Rex Harlow's *Social Science in Public Relations* (New York: Harper & Row, 1957), pp. 64–69.

mentioned earlier as important to all persuasive efforts); and fourth, to counteract or refute another propaganda theme.[35]

Regarding retention of information, researcher Carl I. Hovland finds there is an initial period when people forget verbal material rapidly; this forgetfulness gradually decreases until little further loss is noticeable. (Sometimes, in fact, there is even an increase in what is remembered over a period of time.) He also has found that people retain more meaningful material better than less well understood material, but that overuse of even good material merely for reasons of emphasis can have a boomerang effect. Moreover, the more completely people learn material initially, the longer they will remember it. However, Hovland also found that a higher number of repetitions of a message, up to about three or four times, usually increases the degree of people's attention, but that too frequent repetition without reward is likely to lead to loss of attention, boredom and disregard of the communication[36] (a point that might account for the failure of long-term campaigns).

Communications researcher Steuart Henderson Britt has developed a whole set of learning principles that are particularly applicable to consumer behavior:

1. Unpleasant appeals can be learned as readily as pleasant ones.
2. Appeals made over a period of time are more effective.
3. Unique messages are better remembered.
4. It is easier to recognize an appeal than to recall it.
5. Knowledge of results increases learning of a message.
6. Repetition is more effective when related to belongingness and satisfaction.
7. Messages are easier to learn when they do not interfere with earlier habits.
8. Learning a new pattern of behavior can interfere with remembering something else.[37]

One thing is certain about communication, you never are sure that you have achieved understanding of your message unless you give the recipient a method of response. To measure understanding, rather than just message reception, was the task of two researchers, M. Beth Heffner and Kenneth M. Jackson.[38] They used pictures and verbal descriptions of the pictures to see if the verbal descriptions resulted in the same mental impressions on the readers as the pictures. Results

---

[35] Michael Burgoon, Marshall Cohen, Michael D. Miller and Charles Montgomery, "An Empirical Test of a Model of Resistance to Persuasion," *Human Communication Research*, 5, no. 1 (Fall 1978), pp. 27–39.

[36] Carl I. Hovland, Irving L. Janis and Harold H. Kelley, *Communication and Persuasion: Psychological Studies of Opinion Change* (New Haven, Conn.: Yale University Press, 1953), p. 270.

[37] Steuart Henderson Britt, "Are So Called Successful Advertising Campaigns Really Successful?" *Journal of Advertising Research*, 335 (June 1969), pp. 3–9. Also in Britt's *Consumer Behavior in Theory and Action* (New York: John Wiley, 1970), pp. 46–48.

[38] M. Beth Heffner and Kenneth M. Jackson, "Criterion States for Communication: Two Views of Understanding," paper presented to Theory and Methodology Division, Association for Education in Journalism convention, Carbondale, Ill., August 1972.

8.4 GRUNIG'S THEORY OF MESSAGE RECEPTIVENESS

Conditional Probabilities for Information Processing and Information Seeking

Audience potential is important to cost-effective communication. This diagram of the Grunig theory of message receptiveness in communication behavior attempts to illustrate that importance.

Publics:	Active	Active	Active	Active	Active	Latent	Aware	Aware	Latent/ Aware	Latent/ Aware	Inactive/ Latent	Inactive/ Latent	Latent	Latent	Latent	Inactive	Inactive
Behaviors:	Problem facing	Problem facing	Con-strained	Con-strained	Active rein-forcing Routine	Routine	Problem facing	Problem facing	Con-strained	Con-strained	Routine	Routine	Fatalistic	Fatalistic	Fatalistic	Fatalistic	Fatalistic
Variables:	Problem recog-nition	Problem recog-nition	Con-straint recog-nition	Con-straint recog-nition	Con-straint recog-nition		Problem recog-nition	Problem recog-nition	Con-straint recog-nition	Con-straint recog-nition							
	Referent criterion	Referent criterion	Referent criterion	Referent criterion	Referent criterion	Referent criterion	Referent criterion	Referent criterion	Referent criterion	Referent criterion	Referent criterion	Referent criterion	Referent criterion	Referent criterion	Referent criterion	Referent criterion	Referent criterion
	High involve-ment	High involve-ment	High involve-ment	High involve-ment	High involve-ment	High involve-ment	Low involve-ment	Low involve-ment	Low involve-ment	Low involve-ment	Low involve-ment	Low involve-ment	High involve-ment	High involve-ment	Low involve-ment	Low involve-ment	Low involve-ment
Information seeking:	High	High	High	Mod-erate	High	Low	High	Mod-erate	Low	Low	Low	Low	Mod-erate	Low	Low	Low	Low
Information processing:	High	High	High	High	High	High	High	High	High	High	Low	Low	High	Low	Low	Low	Low
Cost-effectiveness scale, 1–10 (10 best)	5	4	7	6	3	8	10	9	2	1							

showed that understanding seems to occur independently of the messages taken verbally (which is something that can occur without understanding them). Conversely, understanding can occur when messages are altered. They also found that a cognitive frame of reference helped students in determining meaning. If students had the same basis for organizing information, it increased meaning. Some of the verbal descriptions were more reliable than the pictures themselves. Interestingly, one of the things also noted was that symbols can be misunderstood. This has happened occasionally when American advertising has been "exported" without due research into the culture or mores of another country.

The complexities of an international community are heightened by the sophisticated technology of instantaneous satellite communications. This increases the communicators' responsibility to ensure the fidelity of message reception through conscientious research and attention to its findings.

Because information processing is such a critical factor in communication, models that are the most predictive of behavior are important in planning a communication campaign. Grunig's model has some potential (see Chapter 4, p. 98 and the chart in 8.4, developed from his theory). Of the four independent variables he identifies, three explain when a person will communicate: problem recognition, constraint recognition and the presence of a referent criterion. The fourth is the controlling variable, explaining when and how a person will communicate—the level of involvement that results in either information processing (low level) or information seeking (high level of involvement). Beyond that, the recognition of a problem and awareness of some constraints results in four types of perceived situations: problem facing, constrained behavior, routine behavior or fatalistic behavior.[39] The result is an anticipation that in a communication effort, four of those sixteen possibilities will be so low in cost-effectiveness as to be scarcely worth any investment: the low-level (information processing) routine behavior and the fatalistic. Twelve will be fairly high in cost-effectiveness. Of these, the active publics are a *second* target audience because active public needs organizing communication and the active reinforcing needs maintenance communication. The primary publics to win would be the latent, aware and latent/aware publics.

Discussions about how people's behavior can be affected through persuasion troubles many of us, even though most of us have been doing it all our lives. You learned as an infant what kind of behavior got you picked up. As you got older, you learned the right words to use and the best timing to get money from a parent.

Behavioral psychologist B. F. Skinner made the following observation about the positive aspects of affecting what people do:

> I am concerned with the possible relevance of a behavioral analysis to the problems of the world today. We are threatened by the unrestrained growth of the population, the exhaustion of resources, the pollution of the environment, and the specter of a nu-

[39]James E. Grunig, "Communication Behaviors and Attitudes of Environmental Publics: Two Studies," Association for Education in Journalism and Mass Communication Monograph, Number 81, March 1983.

clear holocaust. We have the physical and biological technology needed to solve most of those problems, but we do not seem to be able to put it to use. That is a problem in human behavior, and it is one to which an experimental analysis may offer a solution. Structuralism in the behavioral sciences has always been weak on the side of motivation. It does not explain why knowledge is acquired or put to use; hence it has little to tell us about the conditions under which the human species will make the changes needed for its survival. If there is a solution to that problem, I believe that it will be found in the kind of understanding to which an experimental analysis of human behavior points.[40]

POINTS TO REMEMBER

- To change attitudes, you must change opinions; this process involves communication.

- For communication to be effective, it must result in the desired behavioral objective.

- It is important to determine the credibility of various media for message reception.

- In choosing the right message, we must consider its purpose, texture and language.

- The purpose of a message should appeal to one or more basic human motives, like the need for self-actualization or esteem.

- The texture of a message—color, movement, sound—is chosen for its persuasive appeal.

- Clarity, emotional impact and context are important factors in language choice; repetition and consistency are also significant.

- Information processing has been studied by many theorists: (1) The Yale theorists established the idea of changing attitudes to change opinions and named Lasswell's source, message, audience and audience reaction as the elements. (2) McGuire condensed these elements to two—reception of a message and yielding. (3) Lewin emphasized conformity to group norms. (4) Festinger theorized that people try to reconcile the discrepancy between their experiences and their beliefs. (5) Attribution theory explains behavior in terms of internal and situational causes. (6) Social learning theory holds that reciprocal interaction and continuous feedback occurs between a person's internal cognition and the situation. (7) Fishbein's model can be used to predict group attitudes as consumers.

- Principles of learning, especially those concerning retention of information, are particularly applicable to consumer behavior; for example, information is retained better if it's clear and meaningful and repetition is effective only until boredom sets in.

- Grunig's information-processing model has some indicators of cost-effective communication in selecting target audiences.

---

[40] B. F. Skinner, "Origins of a Behaviorist," *Psychology Today* (September 1983), p. 31. Reprinted by permission.

THINGS TO DO

1. Apply one of the "fog" readability indexes—the Gunning, Flesch, Dale-Chall or Cloze—to a newspaper story, a news magazine story, broadcast wire copy, a page from a government publication, a page from a university handbook or a page from a textbook.[41]

2. Find examples of obscure language in instructions, descriptions or explanations, from any source.

3. Give examples of emotion-laden words in editorials, news stories, ads or commercials.

4. Check the following media one day only for the number of PR source stories: a daily newspaper, a local radio newscast (preferably in early A.M. or noon), a major TV newscast (at noon or evening), a weekly news magazine. (a) How many newspaper stories can be attributed in some way to PR sources? Include columns and features. (b) What percentage of broadcast time is devoted to PR source stories? List the news items by topic and indicate how many other stories were in the newscast.

SELECTED READINGS

Rudolf Arnheim, *Visual Thinking* (Berkeley, Calif.: University of California Press, 1980). Unique approach; Arnheim sees the mechanism by which the senses understand the environment as almost identical with thinking processes. Excellent discussion of imagery.

David K. Berlo, *The Process of Communication: An Introduction to Theory and Practice* (New York: Holt, Rinehart and Winston, 1960). Easy-to-read basic book; highly recommended as a starting point in study of communications theory.

J. Samuel Bois, *Explorations in Awareness* (New York: Harper & Row, 1957); and *The Art of Awareness*, 3rd ed., Dubuque, Iowa: Wm. C. Brown, 1978). Informational, interesting and easy to read.

Stuart Chase, *The Tyranny of Words* (New York: Harcourt Brace Jovanovich, 1959). Valuable insight from a lover of the language.

---

[41] For further information about the readability indexes, see: (1) Robert Gunning, *The Technique of Clear Writing*, rev. ed. (New York: McGraw-Hill, 1968); (2) Rudolf Flesch, *How to Test Readability* (New York: Harper & Row, 1951); *The Art of Plain Talk* (New York: Harper & Row, 1946), p. 197; and "A New Readability Yardstick," *Journal of Applied Psychology*, 32 (June 1948), p. 221; (3) Edgar Dale and Jeanne Chall, "A Formula for Predicting Readability," *Educational Research Bulletin*, Ohio State University, 27 (January–February 1948); (4) Wilson L. Taylor, "Cloze Procedure: A New Tool for Measuring Readability," *Journalism Quarterly*, 30 (Fall 1953), pp. 415–433; and "Recent Developments in the Use of 'Cloze Procedure,'" *Journalism Quarterly*, 33 (Winter 1956), pp. 42–48. Also you might want to read Irving E. Fang, "The Easy Listening Formula," *Journal of Broadcasting*, 11 (Winter 1966–67), pp. 63–68; B. Aubrey Fisher, *Perspectives in Human Communication* (New York: Macmillan, 1978); Rudolph F. Flesch, "Estimating the Comprehension Difficulty of Magazine Articles," *Journal of General Psychology*, 28 (1943), pp. 63–80 and "Measuring the Level of Abstraction," *Journal of Applied Psychology*, 34 (1950), pp. 384–390; Davis Foulger, "A Simplified Flesch Formula," *Journalism Quarterly*, 55, no. 1 (Spring 1978), pp. 167, 202.

Melvin L. DeFleur and Sandra Ball-Rokeach, *Theories of Mass Communication*, 4th ed. (New York: Longman, 1982). Excellent theory from social science perspective.

Edward T. Hall, *The Silent Language* (Westport, Conn.: Greenwood Press, 1980). One of the first books on nonverbal communication.

William V. Haney, *Communication and Organizational Behaviors* (Homewood, Ill.: Richard D. Irwin, 1967). Applies communications theory to everyday life.

Samuel I. Hayakawa, *Language in Thought and Action* (New York: Harcourt Brace Jovanovich, 1964). By the "dean of semantics"; a good introduction to the field.

John W. Keltner, *Elements of Communication* (Belmont, Calif.: Wadsworth, 1973). Primarily about personal communication, which is also important in public relations.

George R. Klare, *The Measurement of Readability* (Ames: Iowa State University Press, 1963). An overview of the literature on readability, with descriptions of the formula.

Alfred Korzybski, *Science and Sanity: An Introduction of Non-Aristotelian Systems and General Semantics*, 4th ed. (Lakeville, Conn.: Institute of General Semantics, 1958). A long-standing primary source on general semantics.

Irving Lee, *The Language of Wisdom and Folly*, 3d ed. (San Francisco: International General Semantics, 1977). Reprint from a master's work.

Irving Lee and Laura Lee, *Handling Barriers in Communication*, 2d ed. (San Francisco: International General Semantics, 1978). Insightful completion of Lee's work by his wife.

Albert Mehrabian, *Silent Messages*, 2d ed. (Belmont, Calif.: Wadsworth, 1980). Brief, readable book about what we say but don't speak.

Edwin Newman, *Strictly Speaking* and *A Civil Tongue* (New York: Warner Books, 1980). For avoiding gobbledygook.

Wilbur Schramm, *Men, Women, Messages, and Media: Understanding Human Communication*, 2d ed. (New York: Harper & Row, 1982). Superb analysis of the communications process and the positive and negative effects of mass communication on society; includes classic case studies such as the "War of the Worlds" broadcast and the Kennedy–Nixon debates.

Rudolph F. Verderber, *The Challenge of Effective Speaking*, 5th ed. (Belmont, Calif.: Wadsworth, 1982). Should be in every speechwriter/maker's library.

———, *Communicate*, 3d ed. (Belmont, Calif.: Wadsworth, 1980). Repeat of an excellent text.

Philip Zimbardo, *The Cognitive Control of Motivation: The Consequences of Choice and Dissonance* (Glenview, Ill.: Scott, Foresman, 1969). Good reference.

Philip Zimbardo, Ebbe B. Ebbeson and Christian Maslach, *Influencing Attitudes and Changing Behaviors: An Introduction to Theory and Applications of Social Control and Personal Power*, 2d ed. (Reading, Mass.: Addison-Wesley, 1977). A must for PR practitioners and researchers.

CHAPTER 9

Communication Channels

It is no use putting whipped cream on the manure pile because the sun comes out in the morning and you have the same old manure pile.

L. L. L. Golden, PR counselor and author

Even the most helpful editor does not look at the problem from the viewpoint of the publicist, and it simply does no good for the publicist to have a perennial chip on his shoulder.

Richard Weiner, PR practitioner and author

Channels of communication are the paths for messages, and media are the conveyances. Channels of communication may be either public or private, the media internal or external. The practitioner is able to choose the appropriate channel by knowing the intended audience or message. Channels of communication for external audiences are usually newspapers and magazines, and television and radio, although they may also be billboards, posters, signs in or on transportation carriers, flyers, point of sale and window displays, bill stuffers, films, sky-writing, trade fair exhibits or public newsletters (those to which anyone may subscribe). Additionally, there are some unique items with limited messages, like campaign buttons and even institutional clothing items such as tee shirts, windbreakers or corporate ties (special colors and usually the logo).

Internal audiences are reached by special magazines and newsletters, closed circuit TV programs or special videotape presentation, speeches and meetings, in-house displays and exhibits and posters, as well as flyers, memos and paycheck stuffers.

For the communicator, the important consideration is which will be the right channel for the audience and the message. The PR practitioner must select the medium that will reach the target audience and be received by it as credible. Television is regarded as the number one source for news, including local elections, and it is the most believable medium. Most people think the news and information shows present a balanced view, although minorities and women have a problem with the way they are portrayed. People who watch TV also read magazines but don't use other media to a great extent. TV viewing by the college educated has declined and not many people in the upper economic bracket watch TV. In fact, television viewing by all audiences is down and radio listening is up (usually a particular station is chosen). Television is used primarily for entertainment by people who use news for decision-making. Most people go to print media for details on a story that interests them which they first heard on the broadcast media (often radio, which is taking on more permanency as a part of a person's day).

TV viewing as a family activity is low. Most people accept commercials on TV but almost half of the audience misses one or more of the commercials in any half-hour show. (Most likely to miss commercials are women with school-age children.) More than half of the homes have cable available, and a fourth have it—primarily for local news and weather.

Younger audiences of the print media, especially newspapers, tend to be "news consumers"—they want only what is useful to them. From newspapers they want consumer information, how-to-do-it pieces, film reviews and TV logs, as well as restaurant reviews and guides. The older print audiences (thirty-five plus) prefer local and national news, spectator sports coverage and articles on hunting, fishing and gardening—a preference that indicates more acceptance of the newspaper's traditional role.[1]

Another medium with a changing role and a changing audience is a publication once regarded almost as a class, not mass, medium and a "throwaway" effort at that—the airlines' in-flight magazines. Now more and more advertisers have realized the advantage of using these publications. The advertisers also found from their research agencies that almost 40 percent of the readers are women, most of them on business trips.[2] They further learned, to their delight, that they were winning with these publications in two ways: Some passengers took the magazines home to keep the article and respond to the ads, and those who left them increased the ad's exposure to several times the expected readership for magazines.

The use of a medium by its audience will give the communicator an idea of how, when and under what circumstances the audience will be exposed to the message and what the life span of the message might be. The medium itself offers clues by providing to some degree its own environment. You learn, for example, to seek certain types of advertising both in specific sections of the newspaper and in certain types of publications. However, advertising agencies have determined that the intrusion of an ad into "foreign territory" can make it stand out and therefore become a success if other elements are right for acceptance of the message—in other words, if the audience is there. Marsteller, Inc., was the first to use the *New York Times Book Review* for a nonbook ad and let the first to use local radio to sell small computers for IBM.

Among the channels of communication experiencing the greatest change in use are the group called audiovisuals: 35mm slides, videotapes, 16mm films, super 8mm motion picture cartridges, 35mm and 16mm sound filmstrips and the 2-inch slide tape. The environment these media create, and their great adaptability and flexibility, are reasons for the eager acceptance of new technology in this field.

---

[1] The Roper Organization, "Evolving Public Attitudes Toward Television and Other Mass Media 1959–80" (New York: Television Information Office, 1981); "Who Watches Commercials," Marketing, *Wall Street Journal*, May 20, 1982; p. 33 and John Consoli, "Under 35 Readers Want 'Tailored' Newspaper," *Editor and Publisher*, April 16, 1977, pp. 9, 11. Report of research by Ernest L. Larkin and Gerald L. Grotta of the University of Oklahoma, H. H. Herbert School of Journalism, and Philip Stout, research manager of the *Oklahoma City Oklahoman and Times*.

[2] Martin J. Shannon, "Business Bulletin," *Wall Street Journal*, August 24, 1978, p. 1.

HOW TO CHOOSE
THE MEDIUM

The PR person choosing among controlled media (those in which you can control the message content and appearance, such as a billboard) and uncontrolled media (those over which you can exert little or no control, such as TV coverage of an event) must weigh the advantages and disadvantages of each before investing time, creativity and money (see 9.1A and B and 9.4). There is an element of uncontrollability in every aspect of communication. There is never any guarantee that the audience to whom the publicity or advertising is directed will pay attention to it or respond to it. Nevertheless, the greater care you take in planning, the greater your chance of success.

There are three questions to consider in selecting the proper medium for your message:

1. *What audience* are you trying to reach, and what does your research tell you about the media received by it and the credibility ratings for each medium?
2. *When* do you need to reach this audience, and by what date does it need to receive a message in order to respond to it?
3. *How much* do you need to spend, and how much can you afford to spend?

After all the questions are answered and evaluated, you then need to ask these four questions:

1. Which medium reaches the broadest segment of your target audience at the lowest cost?
2. Which one has the highest credibility and what is its cost?
3. Which medium can you count on to deliver the message within the necessary time element for the message to be effective? (See 9.2 and Chapter 11.)
4. Should a single medium be used? If not, which media should be used to complement each other, if indeed a media mix is desirable?

One of the most common faults in media selection was voiced by audiovisual specialist Lee Harrison:

> All of us generally choose our communication media by considering the simplest and cheapest form of *production* rather than carefully examining the cost effectiveness of the whole communication process. That's the natural lazy tendency of man. Our duty, perhaps, is to make people aware of how costly our ineffective communications really are, for I believe that change is governed by economics.[3]

To make effective use of the media selected, you must know enough about the mechanics and technology of each medium to prepare the copy properly. Students usually are surprised to discover the amount of writing—and different

---

[3]Lee Harrison, in remarks at the 1973 Visible Thought Perspective Seminar, from *Avcom Report* no. 185, February 1974, published by Audio-Visual Communications. Used by permission.

9.1A PRINCIPAL MEDIA: ADVANTAGES AND DISADVANTAGES

Television

Advantages

1. Combines sight, sound and motion attributes
2. Permits physical demonstration of product
3. Believability due to immediacy of message
4. High impact of message
5. Huge audiences
6. Good product identification
7. Popular medium

Disadvantages

1. Message limited by restricted time segments
2. No possibility for consumer referral to message
3. Availabilities sometimes difficult to arrange
4. High time costs
5. Waste coverage
6. High production costs
7. Poor color transmission

Radio

Advantages

1. Selectivity of geographical markets
2. Good saturation of local markets
3. Ease of changing advertising copy
4. Relatively low cost

Disadvantages

1. Message limited by restricted time segments
2. No possibility for consumer referral to message
3. No visual appeal
4. Waste coverage

Magazines

Advantages

1. Selectivity of audience
2. Reaches more affluent consumers
3. Offers prestige to an advertiser
4. Pass-along readership
5. Good color reproduction

Disadvantages

1. Often duplicate circulation
2. Usually cannot dominate in a local market
3. Long closing dates
4. No immediacy of message
5. Sometimes high production costs

Newspapers

Advantages

1. Selectivity of geographical markets
2. Ease of changing advertising copy
3. Reaches all income groups
4. Ease of scheduling advertisements
5. Relatively low cost
6. Good medium for manufacturer/dealer advertising

Disadvantages

1. High cost for national coverage
2. Shortness of message life
3. Waste circulation
4. Differences of sizes and formats
5. Rate differentials between local and national advertisements
6. Poor color reproduction

Leon Quera, *Advertising Campaigns: Formulation and Tactics* (Columbus, Ohio: Grid, 1973), pp. 71–74. Used by permission.

9.1B SUPPLEMENTAL MEDIA: ADVANTAGES AND DISADVANTAGES

Direct Mail

Advantages

1. Extremely selective
2. Message can be very personalized
3. Little competition with other advertisements
4. Easy to measure effect of advertisements
5. Provides easy means for consumer action

Disadvantages

1. Often has poor image
2. Can be quite expensive
3. Many restrictive postal regulations
4. Problems in maintaining mailing lists

Point-of-Purchase Displays

Advantages

1. Presents message at point of sale
2. Great flexibility for creativity
3. Ability to demonstrate product in use
4. Good color reproduction
5. Repetitive value

Disadvantages

1. Dealer apathy in installation
2. Long production period
3. High unit cost
4. Shipping problems
5. Space problem

Outdoor Posters (on stationary panels)

Advantages

1. Selectivity of geographical markets
2. High repetitive value
3. Large physical size
4. Relatively low cost
5. Good color reproduction

Disadvantages

1. Often has poor image
2. Message must be short
3. Waste circulation
4. National coverage is expensive
5. Few creative specialists

Transit Posters (on moving vehicles)

Advantages

1. Selectivity of geographical markets
2. Captive audience
3. Very low cost
4. Good color reproduction
5. High repetitive value

Disadvantages

1. Limited to a certain class of customers
2. Waste circulation
3. Surroundings are disreputable
4. Few creative specialists

Movie Trailers

Advantages

1. Selectivity of geographical markets
2. Captive audience
3. Large physical size
4. Good medium for manufacturer/dealer advertising

Disadvantages

1. Cannot be employed in all theaters
2. Waste circulation
3. High production costs
4. No possibility for consumer referral to message

Continued

Advertising Specialties

Advantages

1. Unique presentation
2. High repetitive value
3. Has a "gift" quality
4. Relatively long life

Disadvantages

1. Subject to fads
2. Message must be short
3. May have relatively high unit cost
4. Effectiveness difficult to measure

Pamphlets and Booklets

Advantages

1. Offer detailed message at point of sale
2. Supplement a personal sales presentation
3. Offer to potential buyers a good referral means
4. Good color reproduction

Disadvantages

1. Dealers often fail to use
2. May have a relatively high unit cost
3. Few creative specialists
4. Effectiveness difficult to measure

Leon Quera, *Advertising Campaigns: Formulation and Tactics* (Columbus, Ohio: Grid, 1973), pp. 71–74.

styles of writing—demanded of PR practitioners. PR professors are not surprised because in recommending students after graduation they find the most frequently asked question is "Can they write?" The question implies "for all media."

ADVERTISING

The use of traditional media in exceptional or untraditional ways and the more common use of what formerly were considered exotic media are sure to blur the lines between advertising and publicity more than ever in the minds of the public. As we noted earlier, advertising and publicity are often confused, even though there is a significant difference between them: Advertising is *paid-for* broadcast time or print media space; publicity is *news* about a client, product or services that appears in broadcast or print media. Perhaps the confusion over the two occurs in format, as when ads in newspapers or magazines are designed to look like articles. When John Fischer was *Harper's* magazine editor, he turned down a lucrative proposal for paid space because the ad would have appeared in the same format as *Harper's* articles but with nothing to identify the supplier of the copy and nothing to tell readers the space was purchased. Fischer thought the public might be misled, and he was probably right.

Before we discuss advertising as defined, we need to look at two deviations from the definition that nevertheless are advertising: house ads and public service announcements (PSAs). Further, we need to understand what the more com-

9.2 ESTIMATED TIMETABLES (VARIES WITH PROXIMITY TO SUPPLIERS)

Items Needed	Advance Time for You (working days)*	Advance Time for Media (weeks)	Media	Total Time (weeks)
35 mm film			Local or network TV	16–20
Approved storyboard	5–10			
Set bids, casting	10 (more for animation)			
Production planning	10			
Filming	7			
Sound track	3 in canned, otherwise 10–15			
Editing	10			
Master prints	3			
16 mm reductions and prints	1–3	6		
4-color process plates	10–15 for color separations	6–8, if they make color separations; 4–6 if color separation provided	Magazines	8
Finished art	Negotiable	8–10 to print and get up; less if 24 sheets delivered; printer needs time, about 4–6 weeks	Outdoor ads	8–12
Finished art	Negotiable	8 if list bought, 4 if own list	Direct mail	12
Mats (plastic) and repro proofs	5 for shooting and processing	2	Newspapers	3–4
Slides and script or Tape	10–40 depending on subject and length, whether advertising or publicity	6 6–8	Local TV Network or local radio	7 8–12

*Add approval time and correction time—about 6 weeks.

monly accepted "PR advertising"—institutional advertising—is and how it is used. These are all different from publicity. Also discussed in this section are specialty and cooperative advertising, the use of broadcast advertising and the recent phenomenon of professional advertising.

House Ads

An institutional ad for itself is a house ad. House ads are an exception to the definition of advertising always being paid-for time or space. These are ads for the publication in which they appear or ads for another medium held by the same owner. No money is exchanged although there are space allotments or "budgets."

Public Service Announcements

This is another exception to the paid-for time or space definitions. PSAs are sales pieces—not news stories, like publicity, but just announcements. However, the promoters of civic events or nonprofit organizations that might qualify for PSAs often are unaware of exactly what a PSA is.

Generally, the broadcast stations will give public service time for announcements, which are prepared just like commercials, from organizations like the United Fund, the American Heart Association or the local symphony. There is no exchange of money, but the station may send the nonprofit organization an invoice for the amount of air time given, with the number of hours and commercial rate typed on it and the notation "paid in full."

One word of warning if you work for a nonprofit advertiser. Just because your free public service time leaves some money in your advertising budget, don't splurge on sizable ads in print media. Broadcasters can read. If a station is running your spots free on public service time and you buy sizable ads from the print space salesperson, you are likely to get a bill instead of a complimentary credit slip.

PSAs are just now beginning to find their way to the cable systems. For placement, a "public service/cable" service now distributes periodically to 100 of the largest cable systems.[4]

Institutional Advertising

The purpose of advertising and publicity may or may not be different. Advertising usually is trying to sell something—commercial advertising is usually selling a product or a service. Institutional advertising is selling an idea, but it's still selling.

Institutional advertising may have as its objective the conveying of a particular message, such as the ads—three full pages—used by the oil companies during the energy crisis in 1974–1975. Such advertising almost amounts to "position" statements directed to the public. Companies seeking public support for corporate policies and programs have begun to invest more in this type of advertising, called *advocacy* advertising. Another type of institutional ad, which can be considered less of a persuasive message and more a reminder, is the type some companies call *sustaining* or *image* advertising. The image ads may also serve the company seeking to modify its public image—and they can present a redesigned logo or a change in policy or copy (see 9.3). The image ad is also used by companies in a monopolistic position who try to represent themselves as public servants. Utility companies frequently use this type of advertising to win favorable public opinion before requesting rate increases or warding off restrictive legislation. Because of the tone of the ad, and its content, institutional advertising may be mistaken for publicity.

---

[4]Planned Communication Services (PCS), 12 E. 46th St., New York, NY 10017.

9.3 INSTITUTIONAL AD

A national company with an established image has a different approach to its institutional advertising. Gannett, publisher of the national newspaper USA TODAY, takes a statesmanlike approach in its cover ad in *Editor and Publisher*.

THE SPECIAL ROLE OF PUBLISHERS

Newspaper publishers across the nation are something special. Like other good local business executives, they make operations go smoothly. They guide department managers. They direct, they sell and they deliver.

But good publishers are much more than that. They have a special responsibility to a special constituency: readers. They bear a unique constitutional responsibility to exercise the First Amendment rights granted to our free press. They play a special role in guiding the agendas for their communities. Ultimately they help their local citizens determine whether mankind's greatest experiment—self government—can work successfully.

Those very special Americans gather this week at the annual convention of the American Newspaper Publishers Association in New York City to share their concerns, ideas and achievements. Among them will be the men and women who publish the 87 Gannett daily newspapers, represented on the map above. To meet these Gannett publishers, please turn to page XX.

GANNETT
A WORLD OF DIFFERENT VOICES
WHERE FREEDOM SPEAKS

Reprinted courtesy of Gannett.

Specialty Advertising

Without looking, can you name the company whose name is on a pen you use or the calendar by your desk. Advertising specialities are useful items, generally of nominal value, that carry the advertiser's message throughout the year and in a very personal way.

Cooperative Advertising

Cooperative advertising offers almost as many advantages as single advertising. When one advertiser shares a message with another—such as when a cheese-dip manufacturer combines with a potato chips manufacturer to buy advertising space and time—it also shares the production and space-time costs. This gives each some participation in both the production and exposure. Sometimes there must be artistic compromises, but it still is a controlled situation.

Broadcast Advertising

What about preparing advertising copy for the broadcast media? Too many PR practitioners are too willing to turn this job over to an advertising agency because they themselves are so print oriented. However, a practitioner must know about broadcast advertising, both public service announcements and commercials.

The most some PR people attempt is PSAs. Although the broadcast media may get blamed when PSAs are not used, poor preparation is generally the real reason. Because stations vary so much, you should become familiar with the preferences of the individual stations within the market area you're concerned with. Most television stations can use videotape cassettes, 16mm color film (with sound or silent) and color slides (with sound on discs or tape, reel-to-reel or cassette or with script for an announcer to read). It is advisable not to offer videotape or super 8mm film to TV stations unless you know something about their equipment. Most radio stations can use records or scripts, although professional quality cassettes and reel-to-reel tapes are preferred. Cable systems prefer videotape cassettes and, like most broadcast stations, are willing to use more than one length of the same spot concurrently (such as a 10-second, 30-second and 60-second version).

The important points to remember are the following:

1. If you send tapes or discs, send a typed copy of the message with them.
2. Indicate on the copy a cut-off date—when the station should stop using the PSA.
3. Mark the precise timing on the copy.
4. Identify where you can be contacted if there are any questions.
5. Send the material early enough—about four to six weeks ahead of time—to be sure there is ample time for it to be considered and scheduled.
6. Be sure the video and audio are of broadcast quality. Your own recordings or slides are not likely to qualify unless you are professional.

Writing for broadcasting has its own set of rules, and it is less flexible than print. In a printed ad when a message won't fit, you can increase the space or use smaller type. If it won't fit the time slot in broadcasting, and you don't condense it, that message just can't be used.

Sometimes a local station will be generous enough to work with a nonprofit organization to help produce PSAs. If offered, accept with alacrity. A television station, for instance, may provide studio, crew and director, with the PR practitioner handling script, talent, costumes, props, special effects or music and all extra video such as slides, art or film clips. The charge for these PSAs and dubbings for other stations to use is minimal. In a small-market area, you can help get your PSA on the air by catering to the whims and idiosyncrasies of each station, whether it is the number of seconds each prefers or the PSA director's preference for having all PSA scripts typed on 4 × 5 cards so they fit his special file box. However, if your audience is much larger, settle for the format most stations can readily use.

Experienced public relations practitioners usually have good working relationships with the persons in charge of PSA time in their own areas. In preparing national releases they generally produce top-quality materials.

Commercials are more common than PSAs in broadcasting. If you are planning commercials, prepare to invest a lot of time, trouble and money. It is advisable to hire a production company, unless you are working with an agency experienced in producing commercials. For a commercial you must write the copy, plan the audio (announcer and actors, voices, music and sound effects) and, for television, plan the video. You may have to audition acting talent, and will have to hire a producer, director, light crew, engineers and other special personnel needed. You may have to take the entire group on location. You may have to commission special music to be written or electronically put together.

Professional Advertising

Both advertising and PR agencies are now learning to deal with another form of advertising and promotion, that involving lawyers, dentists, doctors and other professionals, who until recently were not "allowed" to engage in the commercial process. An increasing number of these professionals are defying hallowed tradition by getting their names in print and their faces on television. And this break is opening up a new market for public relations practitioners.

In 1975 after the Federal Trade Commission began attacking advertising restrictions on lawyers, doctors and dentists, self-promotion began to appear—particularly in local newspapers and on local television. Several Supreme Court decisions (see Chapter 14) created a new market for the media among the professional groups. And it has become a learning experience for both the professions and those retained to handle the promotion. While some PR practitioners are understandably pleased by the development, others consider the handling of medical clients questionable.

ADVERTISING AS CONTROLLED/ UNCONTROLLED COMMUNICATION

Controlled Advertising

One significant advantage in using paid advertising as opposed to most publicity news to present a message to a public is that the advertiser nearly always has *total control*—over the message itself, over the context in which it will appear (size, shape, color) and, of course, over the medium. In buying the time or space, the advertiser knows approximately *when* an audience will receive the message. In addition, because the media do comprehensive audience studies to sell their own particular advantages, the advertiser has access to research about the audience. This means the advertiser knows *who* will receive the message. Because time or space is purchased, he or she knows *how often* the audience will be exposed to the message. Finally, research on the various media will help indicate to the advertiser the usual *impact* of an ad schedule on a target audience.

Uncontrolled Advertising

Uncontrolled advertising consists of the commercials prepared as PSAs for use on radio and television stations. The message is controlled, but the delivery time is not.

Only nonprofit organizations qualify for public service time, which the stations make available free. But because the time is scarce, the United Fund and local symphony season ticket drives are competing for it just as fiercely as any business is competing for dollars. From the national headquarters of organizations like the Heart Association and Red Cross, stations receive highly professional tapes, usually cut with a celebrity's voice and, for television, top quality videotape or 16mm color film. These are mailed far enough in advance for the station personnel handling PSAs to find good slots in the daily programming for these announcements. In contrast, local sources are likely to put in a frantic call the day before a local blood drive asking for some announcements starting immediately— no tape, probably not even any copy. Or someone drops by with a dozen slides and two pages of copy and does not understand why this cannot be aired. Remember, however, that any PSA is used only if the station has the time to give, and then at a time during the broadcast day when the station can fit a free announcement into the log. Even this slot may be sold and the PSA bumped.

Because most commercial broadcasting stations, radio and television, are generous with their public service time and make every effort to cooperate with those who request it, it is often believed that the stations are compelled by their licensing authority, the Federal Communications Commission, to give a certain percentage of each broadcast day to public service time. This is not the case. A station is not compelled by law. Furthermore in 1984 FCC action erased a guideline for TV that had recommended devoting 10 percent of airtime to nonentertainment programming. The guideline for radio was abolished in 1981. Station policy on PSA time is so diverse that it defies any general description. The effective practitioner will simply learn and meet the demands of the stations.

COMMUNICATING THROUGH ADVERTISING

A person writing advertising copy cannot be satisfied with a list of details from marketing and sales that is supposed to be pushed. The copywriter must first determine the purpose of the ad or commercial, the audience for it and which media will be used.

Copywriters must clearly define an ad's purpose. Is the purpose to *inform*? Is it to introduce a new product, introduce a product to a new market, suggest a new use for a familiar product, give a corporate identity to a conglomerate, familiarize an audience with a new trademark? Is the purpose of the ad to *persuade*? Should the ad or commercial try to get its audience to think or do something? The following ad from a laundry company appeared in an English newspaper. Its purpose is quite clear.

Strong, fat women who wish to lose weight wanted for hard but well-paid work.

Sometimes the purpose of the ad is for "positioning." Advertisers have developed this technique as a way of finding a foothold in the marketplace. It is an idea publicity strategists are now borrowing. Here is the way it works: Have you ever asked yourself why Miller's High Life is for sippers and Schaefer's for guzzlers? Why Nyquil is the "nighttime" cold remedy, while Dristan and Contac work all day? The difference is not in the product but in positioning—an advertising technique to isolate a segment of the market in a highly competitive field by creating a unique image for a product that is fundamentally the same as its competitors. This technique artificially segments the audience.

After determining the audience and the appeal, the copywriter must find which media are planned to carry the ad. Often there must be adjustments, for the copywriter may be thinking in terms of a medium that has not even been considered for the advertising. When the media have been chosen, the copywriter takes the facts learned, tested and validated through research; considers the audience to be reached; and with the *specific* media in mind, develops the copy for the ads.

ADVERTISING COSTS

Television commercials are among the most expensive types of advertising. The cost of producing a 1-minute commercial, including rehearsals, filming, reshooting, dubbing, scoring, animation and printing, is usually five times the cost of producing a minute of televised entertainment. A company may then spend a million dollars or more getting the commercial on the air.

PR practitioners must become familiar with the charges for broadcast time and print media space. They must learn to use local rate cards and to consult *Standard Rate and Data Service, Inc.*'s books for the various media. You can hire a media-buying agency, but even then you can get better results if you know as much about the buying as the agency does and use it only to handle the actual placement of the ads.

You should also learn how to verify the audiences offered by the various media. U.S. magazines and newspapers with paid circulations have their readership claims substantiated by the Audit Bureau of Circulations, an outside agency that authenticates a magazine's or newspaper's circulation claims. This is public information available in various reference books that catalog media. Business publications are also audited and these figures published. However, some readership studies done by the newspapers and magazines are private and may or may not be communicated. Occasionally a publication's editorial department has readership studies done and does not even make the results available to the magazine's own advertising staff! However, audience information usually can be obtained from the advertising and promotion departments of most publications. Or the source may be a research department, often a part of the promotion department. However, since these departments—promotion and advertising—obviously have a vested interest, it is best to get a clear statistical picture on competitors. This usually puts the picture in focus, but not always.

The figures on broadcast audiences are even more difficult to interpret. Radio stations have gone to a "magazine" format—that is, they appeal rather clearly to a particular audience—and the size of this audience is usually available from area ratings. Therefore, you can discover the station's general audience profile and listenership. You can't always tell what time of day this audience listens, however, although ratings for various programs usually are available.

In television, the findings really get obscure. The basic problem is that television is the mass medium, and the mass is rather difficult to measure. There are national ratings for network shows and local ratings for the various television programs, but often the latter are not as reliable as even the stations would like them to be. Time salespeople are usually found boosting either network shows, local personalities or prime time (6 P.M. to 11 P.M. nationally). If a considerable investment is involved, you may want to budget a research study of your own.

It is important to pretest ads and commercials to be sure they have the desired effect *before* the time and space is bought. Also, because of the innumerable legal problems that advertising can involve (particularly in this era of consumer consciousness), it is best to have copy and art for a national or large regional campaign checked by your attorney while it is still in the planning stages.

Some television stations, radio stations and newspapers will produce advertising for clients. But you must remember that you are paying for professional services just as surely as though you were going to an outside agency or studio. The only advantage this sort of in-shop production gives you is quality control for your ad or commercial and assurances of its usability by that newspaper or broadcast station. You are still the one responsible for getting all the information needed for the copy or special art, such as logos or photographs. You must also be available for consultation when *needed*, not when it is convenient for you.

Incidentally, when working with magazines, remember the general mass magazines are gone, except for *Reader's Digest* and perhaps *TV Guide* (the first magazine to sell a billion copies in a single year, it now claims 20 million buyers weekly). Most magazines have a specialized audience, and you must tailor your ads accordingly: What works in *Cosmopolitan* misses by more than a mile in *Playboy* (see 9.4).

DIRECT MAIL— THE HYBRID

A hybrid of both publicity and advertising as well as of controlled media is direct mail. In certain instances, such as newsletters from politicians, direct mail can be considered publicity. On the other hand, direct mail that seeks magazine subscriptions, for example, most certainly is advertising. The message can say anything that does not violate a law and can be any size or shape the postal service will accept. It can be sent any time its sender chooses. Mailing lists are available for almost any audience you wish to reach (if not, there's always "occupant"). However, just because the envelope arrives does not mean the message was received. Direct mail has a high mortality rate, which is the reason so much is invested in designing appeals, personalizing the appeal and repeating it often enough so at least one effort reaches the intended audience.

The seven cardinal rules in direct mail are as follows:

1. Know what the objective is and concentrate on it.

2. Address the piece correctly to the right list. Remember that December through February is a significant job-change period; if you don't have time to research, mailings at this time should go to the title and not the person.

3. Write copy to show what it does for the recipients.

4. Make the layout and format fit the image of the product you want to convey.

5. Make it easy for the prospect to take the action you want taken.

6. Tell the story at least three times and repeat the mailings two or three times.

7. Research all direct mail by testing the offer, package and list. Test to see if offer is attractive to target audiences. Use alternative offers to be sure you have the best incentive. Test the package (presentation). Be sure respondents know what to do with the offer, and that directions are clear. Test the list with a sample mailing to be sure it's accurate. Test even if the mailing is as little as 1,000 pieces. Don't ever drop untested pieces in the mail. On the other hand, be sure that all of your pretests really are important. Testing for a second color isn't!

Three important words with direct mailings are recency, frequency and monetary. The *recency* of direct mailings is significant in getting response; stories of delayed-action response are rare. *Frequency* of mailing increases your chances of response because it serves as a reminder. However, what determines both of these, is *monetary*—what you can afford to spend.

Usually direct-mail investments more than pay their way. The key to this success is the list you select. *Occupant* lists—lists organized by addresses—are easy to find and inexpensive. If the geographical area you are mailing in is limited, you can make up your own list from the crisscross, or city, directory. *Specialized* lists are available according to age, income, educational status and almost any other kind of breakdown you want. Many organizations sell lists of their membership, and you can buy lists from direct-mail list companies. Some base their lists on auto registrations, others on phone directories and others on complex sampling strata.

The modest prices you pay for use of a list entitle you to use it only once, and to protect the list, the mailing house actually sends out the material for you. It is important to remember that 23 percent of a general list, 22 percent of all business lists and 35 percent of the business executive lists go bad in a year. Planning a periodic check on your list is the best safeguard of the integrity of a basic mailing file.

Remember that every letter going out of the office, every piece of correspondence, is an image maker or breaker. Careful attention to spelling indicates that you care about the correspondent. Typographical errors suggest that the message

9.4 TARGET AUDIENCE APPEAL

The four faces of *The Deep*'s magazine ad campaign, aimed at, from left: teenagers, middle Americans, "romantic women" and "lusty men."

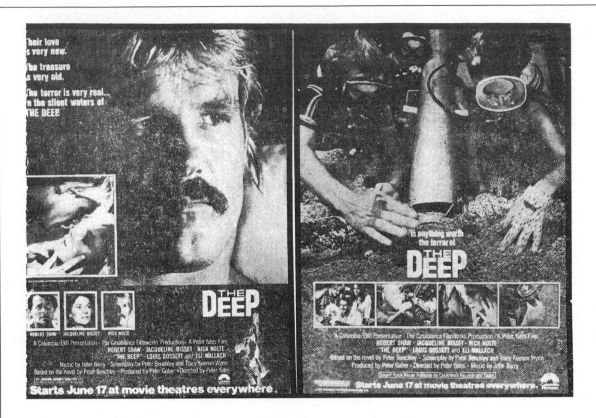

© The Washington Post. Used by permission.

is not important enough to command your attention, and the recipient might wonder why it should deserve any. Accurate spelling and syntax also implies knowledge and authority. Perhaps the most compelling reason for having every piece of copy perfect is that your letterhead is your signature.

PUBLICITY—NEWS AND INFORMATION

What is publicity? Is it a column item in a local newspaper? A cover story in a national magazine? Thirty seconds on the 6 P.M. television news? A bit of chatter by a radio disc jockey? The mention of the company's name once or twice

in a long story about the industry or something related? A single photo in a newspaper or magazine? A 2-inch item in an association publication? An annual report? A house organ? A film? A stamp? It is all of these and more.

Publicity can also be a sales message. Candidates for public office who make frequent speeches and expect to be reported on in the news are selling two things: themselves and their ideas. They hope you will buy them at the ballot box. Other publicity, of course, can be strictly information. Most of a daily newspaper's business pages are either publicity releases or stories based on publicity releases. Here PR people are functioning as reporters, and what they write about their organization or client is hard news they are trying to get into the paper.

Reporters who cover a certain area—for instance, public affairs—are rarely able to talk with the top officials and executives in their field. Consequently, there must be public relations people who are trained to know what the news media want and need and will use, who know their own organization thoroughly, have access to the top echelons and can get the information and prepare it in a form the news media can use. The news media also depend on PR people because there are never enough reporters on a staff to cover absolutely everything going on in a metropolitan area. Much information the news media use comes to them from public relations sources. These are facts they did not have to gather, stories they did not have to write and pictures they did not have to take. But public relations representatives who expect to remain effective must maintain the trust the news media place in them to be accurate, truthful and reliable.

Publications

In-House Publications   Company magazines, sometimes called "house organs," are distributed only to the employees and perhaps to the stockholders of a company; the distribution is usually vertical: Copies go to everyone in the company, from top to bottom. Occasionally in a very large company a publication may go to just one type of employee and thus get horizontal distribution, for example, a publication for supervisors.

Industry Publications   A company may also be a member of an industry group aimed at bettering the entire industry. Such groups often have magazines with rather wide distribution because they are considered to be the voices of the industry. They are received not only by executives of the companies in the industry but also by business editors, financial analysts, economics specialists, government officials—anyone with a particular interest in the industry; the distribution is horizontal—across the industry.

Trade or Association Publications   Also distributed horizontally are trade or association publications—magazines, newsletters or newspapers published at headquarters for a group with particular goals or interests. Among them are labor union publications, religious magazines and newspapers and fraternal as well as professional publications.

Other media are the corporate, industry or association films, which are supervised (though rarely produced) by the public relations staff. The public relations staff also makes use of speeches and meetings and sometimes closed-circuit television.

There are two principal problems in putting out any institutional publication—newsletter, magazine or newspaper (beyond the problem of justifying its existence to some dollars-and-cents-minded person in accounting).

The first is to find out what is going on, principally by setting up "correspondents" in various departments (at all levels) to report monthly to the editor on significant events in their department. Often these are sources for corporate gossip, but not much is printable. The solution to this problem is to seek out the people in each department who have been there longest and ask their supervisors if they can be the correspondents. Then invite all your correspondents to a "news clinic," in which you tell them about the publication needs of an editor and how they can help. Devise a form that will take care of all the basic information you are looking for each month. Be sure the deadline is stated boldly and clearly. You will have to design this yourself because you are the one who has set the editorial policy for the publication and knows what the contents should be. (See 9.5 for a suggestion.) Then figure out a way to reward your correspondents. Listing their names in the publication usually is best because then other people know whom to tell when they have information.

The second problem, which looms large when it is present, is the tendency of management to want to use the publication as a propaganda organ to tell readers what it would like them to believe rather than what the readers would like to know.

When the editor yields to this kind of pressure, the result is an ego treat for management, an unread publication and a truly unjustifiable budget item. Then when enough complaints are heard about the publication, executives conduct a readership survey, discover that the publication is not read and, instead of changing policy, they fire the editor. An editor should not let this drama play itself out.

As editor, you should include what the employees want to know and need to know about the company (see 9.6). Brighten it with entertainment and humor. Reprint articles from professional publications (which will charge little or no fee to nonprofit organizations). When management insists on the inclusion of certain stories, be sure to do a readership survey that tests the readability of various articles. When management loses the poll consistently, it usually backs off and lets editors edit.

Often PR people find they inherit the house publications almost as an afterthought ("By the way, you'll also be doing our publication"); however, there is no need to put it in the category with washing out the coffee pot. Much of what happens depends on attitude and careful planning.

Some corporate publications accept advertising, and this is a way to expand a small budget. Consider what types of ads you could accept and who would sell them (if your staff is small, it may take too much time).

Editing a house publication is an opportunity to be creative. The first thing to consider is the layout. If you have three people on the staff, try to see that one is skilled in art and layout. If your publication is letterpress, the layout is not too time consuming, but if it is offset and goes to the printer camera ready, the layout will take considerably more time. If you can hire someone with a background in art, layout and photography, count your blessings. Photography is another major item. Most house publications are plagued with bad amateur efforts. If you can't afford a professional photographer, even part time, try to find someone in the company who is a semipro and has a darkroom at home, and offer to supply the film and photographic paper and chemicals. Incidentally, the art for some institutional advertising, four-color and well done, is available without charge, even the color separations. Often the source wants only a credit line.

It is wise to make a firm contract each year with a printer spelling out all the special effects (screens, duotones and such) you intend to use per issue, the cost of color separations, cover stock and number of colors to be used on the cover, interior stock (be sure the printer warehouses it for you; it is disconcerting to the reader to find you have changed stocks in mid-year because the printer ran out), number of pages, deadlines and agreements about corrections, delays and delivery. Ingenuity, creativity and determination are qualities of the good house publication editor.

9.5 EMPLOYEE PUBLICATION FORM

```
                        SPECTRUM NEWS




Reporter's Name: _____
Reporter's Department: _____



News Event (please check appropriate category)

_____ Promotion
_____ Award
_____ Sports
_____ Announcement
_____ Other (please explain) _____
           _____


About the event:

        What happened: _____
        _____
        When did it happen: _____
        _____
        Where did it happen: _____
        _____
        Who was there: _____
        _____
                 Names _____
                 Department _____
                 Division _____

        Use this space for additional comments.






Mail to publication office.
```

Prepared for Alcon Laboratories by Betsy Stiteler. Used by
permission.

9.6 THE NEED FOR EFFECTIVE COMPANY COMMUNICATIONS

A few years ago, the executives of a manufacturing company were honoring Joe Zipotas—the name is fictional but the incident is true—for twenty-five years of loyal service. A curious investigator decided to find out just how much Zipotas had learned about the company in his quarter century with it. He discovered that Zipotas did not know the year in which the company was founded; the number of plants it had; more than two of the company's products, which exceeded 200; the name of the president, who had held that office for three years; the location of the company's headquarters; the source of a single raw material going into the company's products; the operation which preceded his or the one which followed it, except in a very general way; and what free enterprise means (he did not even recognize the expression).

On the other hand, Zipotas could give the name and number of his local union; the names of three of five union officers; four direct benefits which, he thought, the union had obtained for him, although it actually had obtained only two of them; and a reasonably accurate definition of collective bargaining.

From William L. Rivers, Theodore Peterson, and Jay W. Jensen, *The Mass Media in Modern Society*, 2d ed. (San Francisco: Rinehart Press, 1971), p. 221.

Employee Handbook Another employee publication that PR departments are responsible for producing is the handbook that should function as both a reference piece and an effective orientation tool for employees. It should provide a definitive statement of what is expected from the employees and what the organization offers them. It should explain thoroughly the promotion structure and company rules and regulations, and indicate how management helps in furthering the education of the employee. A management organizational chart with the names of individuals that employees need to know about or contact in various departments is essential to the handbook. Workers on all levels should be made aware of the way they can get questions answered and problems solved. To this end most corporations are finding it necessary to produce handbooks annually so the information is current.

Newsletters Internal newsletters can be an effective means of communicating frequently with employees. The information in a newsletter should not be a collection of trivia but rather items of interest. Many newsletter items become subjects of fuller treatment in the institution's magazine. One company newsletter editor describes her publication as a "circulating billboard." In other companies it is much more—with short articles, bits of humor, important announcements and notices.

Newsletters are also a publicity vehicle when they are created for and subscribed to by members of the public. The newsletter business is a big one. There are more than 2,500 subscription newsletters listed in the *Newsletter Yearbook Directory*. The total, including association publications, is more like 10,000. Newsletters are obviously intended for a particular target audience; most are on highly specialized subjects, and most enjoy high readership.

Broadcast Publicity

Many institutions find television a better medium than print for some situations and one that should be used together with print for others. An industry that was instituting a new profit-sharing plan, for example, put the executive who could best explain it on a closed-circuit TV show. The show ran each day during all of the lunch periods. PR followed up with handouts so the more complex aspects of the program would be available for reference. The success of closed-circuit TV is attributable partly to employee experience with the medium and partly to the medium itself, which is the next best thing to face-to-face. A Navy public information officer (PIO) put the captain of a carrier on the ship's closed-circuit because, as he put it, "This place is like a city and someone is likely to not even know what the captain looks like if they don't see him on TV."

It requires a sophisticated knowledge of the medium to be able to prepare publicity of broadcast quality. Television can use 16mm color film, either sound or silent, and will accept it for consideration as news. However, it is considered only in situations such as that showing the project plans for a new sixty-story office building, the opening of an airport, the complexity of a space launch. It never supplants spot news—news taken at the time an event occurs—but it is the best way to tell an advance story, and it usually can be done only by publicity. This film is just as subject to editing as a written news release, and it may not be used at all. This is definitely an uncontrolled area, nearly as uncontrolled as the spot coverage of news that results when a television crew is alerted to an event.

The television medium also may use slides, again at the editor's or director's discretion, and the accompanying script (or audio on a cassette) sent with them. Or the director might have a new script written. Occasionally an organization or profession is the subject of a television documentary, and the PR practitioner has usually cooperated with the persons researching, writing and filming it. But that is all that the PR person can do: help and hope for the best. Educational TV often uses PR-produced films if there is no commercialism of the subject matter, and on rare occasions so will commercial TV. Frequently television will use a feature film, generally about three minutes long, offered by a group; generally the film is something entertaining, light and informative. Local stations use these most often on weekends when news is slow and they have time they can fill with nonnetwork shows.

A form of television publicity that cannot be overlooked is the appearance of a representative on a talk show. The daytime and evening talk shows continually present people promoting the latest book, movie, song or maybe just themselves. Most local stations have a format that allows for local bookings. In such events, the only thing a PR person has to worry about is staying off camera and being sure the person on camera is well coached so the results are good.

Regular speeches are also publicity. The very fact of the organization's president speaking to the local Monday club is publicity whether or not the local media cover the speech. Since the PR person usually gets the job of researching and writing the speech, the research must include not only the subject but also the audience. To be well received, the remarks must be particularly tailored for that single group. The speech writer must also remember the personal characteristics of the speaker delivering the speech: it has to sound like the speaker, not the writer!

Some politicians have combined the speech with the interview to produce a tape recording that greets all telephone callers. For the broadcast news media, it offers the speaker delivering a message, sometimes several different ones a day, that is always of broadcast quality, or as close to it as one gets in recording a telephone message that is also a recording. These telephone messages proved so popular during elections that many elected officials adopted them for the government offices they now run. (One official looked slightly hurt at being kidded a bit by a news reporter who said he was glad to be talking to the "real thing." The official replied, "Well, everyone calls Time and the Weather, and no one complains about them being recorded.")

Films

With audiences increasingly oriented toward graphics and the audiovisual, PR practitioners cannot afford to ignore films as a publicity vehicle. One type to consider is the long feature, often called a *sponsored film*, a film without stars put out by an organization or corporation and distributed free except for the cost of return postage. Such films can be produced for as little as $15,000 to $20,000 exclusive of print and distribution expense, although the average cost is nearer $40,000 to $50,000 and some have been known to go above half a million. Large companies may have their own film-producing units, but most use independent film producers in the field. The observations of magazine columnist Stuart Little on such films are informative.

> One sees corporations presenting films on urban development, on consumer protection, on ecological problems, and the only time the sponsoring company allows itself recognition is in a few sunset frames toward the end of the picture when, for example, the wing of the plane tilts skyward and the name of the airline, for an instant, fills the screen like an unexpected rainbow.
> The sponsored film can, of course, serve an explicitly commercial purpose. General Motors and Ford, for example, which are among the largest producers of sponsored films, have libraries of instructional, training and driving safety films that directly relate to commercial goals. The airlines freely distribute travel films that are clearly designed to foster wanderlust.[5]

The customary audiences for sponsored films are specialized, like schools and community organizations, and mass, like television and movie theaters. Hollywood has abandoned making films on short subjects, but exhibitors still need shorts to flesh out their schedules when a 105–minute feature leaves 15 minutes to be filled in the theater's 2–hour schedule. But as PR writer Robert Finehout points out:

> It should be kept in mind that people go to the movies to get away from commercials, station ID's, promos and other back-to-back interruptions. They don't want to be conned by thinly veiled messages or seemingly noncommercial commercials. The

---

[5] Stuart Little, "Sponsored Films Are Better Than Ever," *Saturday Review*, September 12, 1970, pp. 90–92.

mere fact that a sponsor's story is appearing bigger than life means that the message can be subtle—almost subliminal—and still be received.[6]

Another type of film to consider is the 1- to 5-minute film clip, usually 16mm sound. These films generally serve as fillers on feature programs, talk shows or local coverage of sporting events. Their cost is about $5,000,000 exclusive of distribution and any special costs such as expensive talent. Like a news release to print media, the clips must be newsworthy and timely. Also, they must show activity and have only one plug for the sponsor. Film clips have been largely replaced by videotape cassettes, which are cheaper to produce and duplicate.

Other Forms of Publicity

Publicity that is seldom thought of as publicity includes exhibits, multimedia presentations, meetings and closed-circuit television appearances. There are, however, more common forms of publicity. One of the most obvious, and yet one not often considered as publicity, is books. Examples are Frank Tolbert's *Neiman-Marcus* (about the Dallas department store), John F. Kennedy's *Profiles in Courage*, and Richard Nixon's *Six Crises*. A book gives prestige to the subject and can be worth the time invested. Organizations usually save this device for an anniversary or other special occasion. Some books miss being connected to an organization because they are written by a well-known author commissioned to prepare the manuscript. When a political figure, celebrity or executive's name is on the book as author, there is a better than average chance that a ghost writer was employed. Much of the writer's time is devoted to tracking down elusive information, validating information given as fact and searching for illustrations. Nevertheless, a sincere effort, well done, often proves an asset.

If books don't usually come to mind when publicity is mentioned, certainly *stamps* won't. However, any PR person who has shepherded an idea through the maze and actually succeeded in getting a commemorative stamp issued can assure you it is publicity. A postal service panel sifts through 4,000 suggestions a year to get its annual batch of commemoratives. To influence the committee, organizations and individuals proposing stamps often go to considerable lengths. The *Wall Street Journal* reported that Montgomery Ward launched a highly effective campaign in 1972 to get a stamp issued to commemorate the one hundredth anniversary of the mail-order industry:

> The company sent expensive promotion kits to influential members of Congress, including New York's Rep. Thaddeus Dulski, chairman of the House Post Office Committee. Store managers were prodded to write their own legislators. And Walter Trohan, the *Chicago Tribune*'s veteran Washington correspondent, now retired, wrote a column pushing the stamp.
> The proposal, which Montgomery Ward began pushing only last December, was

---

[6] "A Funny Thing Happened at the Cinema Last Night . . . I Saw Your Film," Robert Finehout, *Public Relations Journal*, 30, no. 10 (October 1974), pp. 6–7.

rushed through the advisory panel, and the stamp was issued Sept. 18; the time elapsed was several months less than it usually takes to get a commemorative issued.[7]

One reason companies, institutions and special-interest groups develop symbols and logos is for the visual publicity. Although "obvious," these are not obtrusive, and sometimes they are almost unconsciously accepted. Once such representations are identifiable, all that is necessary to remind a public is to have them see the symbol.

Such a symbol does not have to be a logo. It might even be a picture. PR practitioners had pictures made of children using milk cartons with the tops cut off as modeling clay forms. A national children's educational book for use by both parents and schools printed the photo when it was offered, as an example of the creative application of everyday household items. The photo of the cartons appeared in the book, with the name of the milk company clearly visible. Such pictures, with the product in the background or foreground, are often used. If you ever wondered why hotels always have speaker's rostrums clearly labeled with the hotel's name and insignia, now you know.

PUBLICITY AS CONTROLLED/ UNCONTROLLED COMMUNICATION

Determining where to place publicity demands an objective look at what is likely to happen to it. This means considering whether the medium is an uncontrolled or controlled one. Control means how much control you can exert over the delivery of the message by the medium.

---

[7]Timothy D. Schellhardt, "Why Tom Sawyer and Not Whooda Tom Is on Your Stamps," *Wall Street Journal*, November 30, 1972, pp. 1, 8. © 1972 Dow Jones Company, Inc. All rights reserved.

Controlled Media

There are many specialized media, such as company, industry, trade and association publications, which are under *their* editors' control. If you are the editor, it is a controlled publication, but if you are the PR director for a company submitting publicity to an industry or trade publication, your submissions are subject to editorial discrimination. If you are not the editor, specialized media fall in the category of uncontrolled. Another person makes a decision about whether to use your material.

Uncontrolled Media

News releases may be exceptionally well written, but once they are in the hands of an editor anything can happen and there is not much you can do about it. An editor can use a release as you wrote it; give it to a reporter to rewrite; give the release to a reporter to use merely as a take-off point for a story to be researched and written; or junk the release entirely. Even trade publication editors discard 75 percent of the releases they receive, and radio news people discard 86 percent.

Still, one day on a newspaper copy desk or in the newsroom of a broadcast station will probably demonstrate to you that most PR material that is discarded heartily deserves such an end. The professionally prepared release from sources that have proven trustworthy is treated with respect by the news media, although it may not be used because there is not space or time for it that day.

"Calls for coverage" or queries are PR events called to the attention of the news media for coverage—a presidential press conference, the arrival of Santa to open a store's Christmas buying season, ribbon cuttings and groundbreakings. Whether any of these get any attention is up to the editors, who either assign reporters or not. Of course, even when reporters are assigned, there is no guarantee they will cover the event as the PR person would have wished. But if the event is well planned, the coverage will reflect it.

COMMUNICATING THROUGH PUBLICITY

In contrast to advertising, publicity generally is totally uncontrolled, both in the delivery and in the message. Information about an institution, product or person that appears as news in newspapers or magazines or on the radio or television is used at the discretion of news editors and may be used in any context or not at all.

Information reaches the news media through many routes, with varying impact, but three are basic: news releases, coverage of an event and interviews. To be acceptable, a *news release* must be written in the style used by the particular medium, and it must be in a form that considers the technology of the medium. Awareness of the technological demands of each medium is also important if you expect *coverage of an event*. A speech may be an event, and certainly a news conference is, but the *interview* is obviously something else. It may be formal, arranged by the public relations practitioner, with some expert used by a reporter as a source of information. Or the PR person is "interviewed," though no one is likely to use that term; that is, a reporter contacts the institution that is the source of the kind of news he or she needs, and the PR practitioner acts as an intermediary. This is an informal situation—it may be a phone call or a visit by news media representatives—but it is the most significant source of publicity, for it is generally the one most often used by the media, when events are ignored and releases thrown away.

More and more often direct communication to the media comes from the corporate executive officer (CEO) with the aid of the PR person. The PR person's job is extended, then, to preparing the CEO to be an effective, efficient spokesperson. Some PR agencies, notably Burson-Marsteller, have become specialists in such training. Some aids to decision making in speeches appear in Chapter 11; for audiovisuals used in all publicity, see 9.7A and B.

Most of the bad publicity an organization gets is probably its own fault, owing to poor planning, ineffective communication or bad policies. No publicity at all is probably the fault of the publicist. News people say they throw away *80 percent* of the news releases they get because they are not usable. "Not usable" may mean the stories are incomplete (full of holes) or inaccurate or they just don't fit the news need.

pr reporter carried this item as a warning to its readers:

> One of our volunteer reporters [for the *pr reporter*] scooped up at random an armful of press kits at the recent [1973] National Boat Show in New York's Coliseum, scanned them with the professional eye of a seasoned public relations executive, then sent them along to us with some interesting—if discouraging—observations.
>
> After checking his comments against material in the kits and adding a few findings of our own to the list, we came to the conclusion that some product publicists in the marine field are careless, some are lazy, and some simply don't know how to put together a proper news release. For example:
>
> 1. Three-quarters of the releases were undated.
>
> 2. At least half either lacked any follow-up press contact information (gave only name and address of manufacturer) or the information was incomplete (no telephone number, or PR firm name but no individual to ask for).
>
> 3. Some picture captions were stapled to photographs, while others were so flimsily attached they came apart when handled.
>
> 4. One company's release was single spaced flush left, contained quotes without attribution, and misspelled "Coliseum."
>
> 5. The lead in another company's nine-page release was exactly the same this year as last except that 1973 was substituted for 1972; the president's statement about the new product line also was precisely the same in both years; and the balance of the nine pages closely followed the 1972 pattern—word for word in some short paragraphs.
>
> 6. In one almost unbelievable case, a PR firm handling the publicity for three marine equipment companies (two are competitors, incidentally) not only single spaced all the releases but left practically no margins and then framed the stories with a heavy rule. Included in the kit were several unidentified photographs. Compounding the agony: Every release had a return card attached so the editor could report when and how he planned to use the story.

9.7A A GUIDE TO MAKING AUDIOVISUAL EQUIPMENT DECISIONS

Figures are based on current information and experience of users

Equipment	Reasons for using equipment	Equipment costs (and weight)	Presentation materials costs	Audience size	Image area size	Lead Times Needed		
						Preparing scripts	Producing materials	Equipment rehearsal and first set-up time
Flip Chart	Short lead time; little investment warranted	$63 (15 lbs)	Per word cost: $25–$40 for 1–5 words per page; $75–$90 for charts, cartoons, etc.	10 or under	27" to 34" maximum	From hours to days	Up to 18 pages per day per worker	Minimal, but needed
Chalk Board	Informal in-house communications in board rooms & offices	$13–$134	None	Approx. 16	18" × 24" to 48" × 96"	None	None	None
Veloro Boards, Felt Boards, etc.	Informal but professional presentation to valued audience	$70–$100 (21 to 33 lbs for portables)	$1.50 per letter	Up to 24	48" × 36" to 72" × 48"	From several days to weeks	Usually several days	3 to 4 hours or more
Overhead projector (3M)	Complex materials requiring extensive discussion	$299–$499 (15 to 21 lbs for portables)	$4–$7 made in-house; $25–$85 professional	48 maximum	60" × 60"	Hours to days	Up to several days	Allow a few hours
Slides (1 Projector Presentation) (Kodak)	Important audience & message; professional tone wanted	$300–$875 for random access (10 to 15 lbs)	Type only: $5–$50 Art: $15–$75 +	Usually limited only to room size	6' or more	Plan on 2 or more weeks	Ideally, several weeks from storyboard to finished art	Several hours or longer for script presented live, less with programmed tape

Channel	Features	Cost		Audience size	Viewing distance/size	Production time	Shooting/duplication	Running time
Filmstrip with Sound, Pulse Advance (Singer)	Mechanically somewhat easier than slide & sound	$450 – (20 lbs +)	Same as slides	Same as slides	Same as slides	Same as slides	Same as slides (Note: frame ratio is different from slides)	Same as slides
16mm Sound Movies (Kodak)	Highly important audience; greatest impact; long life; simple, universal display	$735–$1775 (35 to 40 lbs)	$1500–$6000 per minute of finished film	Usually limited only to room size	6' or more	Several weeks	1 to 5 min. of usable footage per day's shooting	One hour or so
Videotape 1. Seen on monitor from prerecorded videocassette (Sony) 2. Seen projected on screen (Sony)	1 & 2: Important audience; credibility; cheaper, quicker production than film; quality not as critical as film	1. $300 (50 lbs) for reel player and monitor 2. $3000 (up to 200 lbs)	1 & 2: Very roughly, half the cost of film and less	1. 1 person per 1" of monitor size; e.g., 25 for 25" monitor 2. 36 or so	1. up to 25' 2. 40" × 30"	1 & 2: days to weeks	1 & 2: 3 to 5 days to duplicate videocassettes	1 & 2: several hours

Other specialty systems that may be of interest are 3M's sound-on slide; multimedia using multiple slide projectors or slides with movies; Super 8mm sound movies; sound tape presentations or sound with auxiliary materials; opaque projectors, which are best for small conference situations

Note: Overtime for professional assistance, studio or lab time can add 50% to 100% to production costs

Reprinted from *Public Relations Journal,* September 1978, with cost updates. Used by permission.

	Feature	User Benefit	Sony Betamax (½")	U-Matic (¾")	Motion Picture (16mm)	Motion Picture (Super 8mm) Cartridge	Sound Film-strip (35mm/16mm)	Slide Tape (2" × 2")
General characteristics	Incorporates all media on timely basis	■ Suitable for all types of programming . . . corporate communications to training	•	•	▮	▮	▮	▮
	Ability to depict motion, color and sound	■ Message has greater communicating effectiveness ■ Can use animation to explain processes ■ Dramatization possible	•	•	•	•	▮	▮
	High impact	■ Message tends to make a strong impression ■ Captures attention and interest faster ■ Increases program effectiveness	•	•	•	•	▮	▮
Ease of operation	Television tube or rear screen display	■ Easily viewable in lighted room	•	•	▮	•	•	On some models
	Cartridge-loading automatic threading	■ No technician or operator required ■ Permits informal scheduling, repeat viewing	•	•	No (Automatic threading available)	•	•	•
	Pause control	■ Allows viewer to concurrently work with other visuals, notes, books and interactive response exercises	•	•	On some models	On some models	•	•
	Fast-forward	■ Permits synchronous accessing of program segments out of sequence	•	•	1	2	On some models	▮
	Rapid-rewind	■ Facilitates repetition and "instant replay" ■ More convenient to handle longer programs	•	•	1	▮	On some models	▮
	Digital index counter	■ Permits indexing programs for reference purposes ■ Makes access more convenient	•	•	1	▮	▮	▮
Extended capability	Random access available	■ *Automatically* accesses any one of many program segments ■ Maximizes benefits of "fast-forward," "rapid-rewind" and "digital index counter"	•	•	1	▮	▮	▮
	Dual audio track	■ Allows choice of different narrative content for different audience requirements		•	▮	3	▮	On some models
	Silent machine operation	■ Usable in quiet areas	•	•	•	Yes (if noise level acceptable)	Yes (if noise level acceptable)	•
	Large screen presentation	■ Increases dramatic impact	Limited	Limited	•	Yes (within limits)	Limited	•

Category	Attribute	Description	C1	C2	C3	C4	C5	C6
	Multiple location viewing	■ One player can feed multiple monitors/screens in other locations	●	●	—	—	—	—
	Portability	■ Allows easy use, either internal or external to the facility. Portability to a function of weight and dimension of the equipment. The quality of parts, frequency and distance to be traveled and the determination of the user. Super 8mm, filmstrip and slice/tape units are more portable than video and 16mm	40 lbs plus receiver	50 lbs plus receiver	35–40 lbs plus screen	15–25 lbs	16 lbs	10–15 lbs
	Field updatability	■ Ease of incorporation changes extends life of program, especially for technical programs	Moderate (with record capability or by recycling)	Moderate (with record capability or by recycling)			No (but low cost replacement possible)	●
Duplication	Recyclable playback materials	■ Significantly reduces expenses for new raw stock	●	●	—	—	—	—
	In-house duplication	■ Can eliminate need for subcontracting ■ Saves money, time ■ Increases control over duplication	●	●	—	—	—	—
	Low duplication cost	■ Savings mount with increase in duplication ■ The more copies, the more savings ■ Figures are for 75 copies of a 20-minute program and are for illustration purposes only	Per copy $14.70 low	$17.97 low	$62.44 high	$43.46 high	$16.48 low	$30.93 medium
Distribution	Duplication time	■ Affects timeliness of message distribution	1 to 3 days	1 to 3 days	2 weeks	2 weeks	2 weeks	1 week
	Capability of easily distributing all other media	■ Allows single distribution format ■ Saves money	●	●	—	—	—	—
	Convenient packaging	■ Easy handling ■ Convenient storage	●	●	●	●	●	—
	Low distribution (mailing) cost	■ Savings mount with increase in distribution ■ The more copies, the more the savings ■ Figures are for a 20-minute program and are for illustration purposes only	Per copy $.90 low	$1.46 medium	$1.81 high	$1.46 medium	$1.01 low	$1.63 high
Storage and maintenance	Storage and space requirements (program materials)	■ Determines space requirements ■ Affects ease of handling	Low	Medium	High	Low	Medium	High
	Extended-play maintenance requirements (equipment)	■ Impacts maintenance expenses ■ Affects utilization reliability	Low	Low	High	Medium	Low	Low

1. Singer graphlex only.
2. Optional on Fairchild models only.
3. Available on customized models only.

The ratings in the chart reflect the suitability of the media for an industrial network application.

Reprinted from *Public Relations Journal*, September 1978. Used by permission.

In all fairness to some 50 companies which had kits stacked in the boat show press room, it should be noted that we looked at only nine. But of those nine, only two came through with flying colors. One was Raytheon Co., whose marine subsidiary makes electronic devices for watercraft. The other was Evinrude Motors—which, as a matter of added interest, included a fascinating story, complete with pictures, of how one of its outboard engines propelled a boat 110 feet through the air for an upcoming James Bond movie.[8]

There are many other horror stories like these, but the point is this: The way to avoid bad publicity and nonpublicity is to—

1. Be sure information offered is appropriate to the medium in content and style, and is *timely*.
2. Check all facts carefully for accuracy, and double-check for any missing information.
3. Should there be any questions, the name of the person to contact and all phone numbers should be given, including the home phone.
4. Photographs should have the name, address and phone number of the supplier stamped or written in felt tip pen on the back in the margin so it won't come through, and captions should be attached with rubber cement—not glue, paper clips or Scotch tape. Most importantly—the captions have to be there.
5. If the story or photo does not appear, *never* call to find out why, and certainly don't ask when your story is submitted when it will appear. It also is highly unprofessional to send out a note with mailed releases asking for clippings. Newspapers do not run clipping bureaus.

Some reasons for the failure of publicity were chronicled by Art Garcia in *The California* magazine:

"There are some good ideas that come across the desk" (statement from Marty Rossman, Financial Editor of the *Los Angeles Times*). "I agree there are, but only when the PR man has done his homework, knows the paper and the kinds of stories it's interested in" (modification and agreement from Garcia).
"PR people call up with an idea that doesn't remotely fit our magazine," complains Ellen Melton, *Forbes* West Coast bureau chief in Beverly Hills. "The stories they propose in a million years couldn't appear in *Forbes*. That really shocks me, and we tell them that, either rudely or kindly, depending on how many other people have done that to us recently. A frequent reaction by them is, tell us the kind of stories you need. Well, the magazine costs a dollar. They should pick it up and look at it." . . .
"The few good PR people in town know exactly what their market is," continues (Tom) Gable (Business Editor of the *San Diego Evening Tribune*). "They study the newspapers, they know the style, they know exactly what I'll take. I've never told them; they know. The bad guys come breezing into the city editor and say, 'Hey, I've got this great thing,' then magically they appear before my desk, calling me by my first name. 'Hi, Tom, read you all the time.' Usually, the thing is just too commercial to use." . . .
One function PR people and their bosses would do well to forget is the press conference, relegated by financial editors to the negative standing of groundbreakings

---

[8] *pr reporter*, February 12, 1973, p. 1.

and ribbon cuttings. "I can't overemphasize how archaic the press conference is," (Jack) Miller emphasizes (Business Editor of the *San Francisco Examiner*). "We just won't go to them." Rarely will anyone from *California Business* go either, mainly because they're infrequently of value. . . .

"The criteria I use is if you can tell it on a piece of paper, then don't have a press conference," says Miller. . . .

Another common complaint is the calls from anxious PR people about whether a story will be used, or worse, whether the editor received a release or story pitch that was sent. "I think it's ridiculous for a PR person to call. If he knows I received it, he knows I'll look at it and will use my judgment and the editorial policy of the newspaper to decide whether it will run," sniffs Gable.[9]

POINTS TO REMEMBER

- Communication channels are the paths for messages, and media are the conveyances.
- The use of a medium by its audience will give the communicator an idea of how, when and under what circumstances the audience will be exposed to the message and what the life span of the message might be.
- Choosing among media where you can control the message content and appearance means weighing the advantages and disadvantages of each before investing time and money.
- The first three questions to consider in selecting the proper medium for your message are what audience are you trying to reach, when and how much can you spend.
- The next four questions involve the target audiences and cost effectiveness in reaching them, credibility, time factors and media mix.
- Advertising with special PR emphasis includes house ads, PSAs, institutional advertising and advocacy advertising.
- Broadcast advertising may be used for both PSAs and commercials. Knowledge of the technical requirements is essential.
- Controlled media are the specialized publications and broadcasts you produce internally, or space and time you buy. PSAs and news releases are uncontrolled media.
- Advertising copy must be written with the purpose and the specific medium in mind.
- Direct mail is a hybrid channel that sometimes is used for publicity and sometimes for advertising.
- Publicity media include in-house, industry and trade or association publications, employee handbooks, company newsletters, broadcast publicity and films.
- Most publicity that is not used is inappropriate for the media, inaccurate or poorly prepared.

---

[9]Art Garcia, *The California* Magazine, February 1975, pp. 39–41. Reprinted courtesy *The California* Magazine as carried aboard Pacific Southwest Airlines. © 1975 East/West Network, Inc.

- Four rules for avoiding errors in publicity are as follows: (1) Be sure information is appropriate for the medium or style and is timely. (2) Be sure story is accurate and complete. (3) Give the name of the contact person and all phone numbers, including home phone. (4) Identify photos and attach captions with rubber cement.

THINGS TO DO

1. Begin a collection of public relations materials. Your list should include: brochures, direct mailing pieces, trade journals, in-house publications. Also, individual publicity releases may be available to you through the student newspaper. In collecting these, don't discard the "bad" examples. These are often good lessons in "how not to."

2. Select five ads you find personally appealing. Analyze them and see why you were attracted. To get variety, choose an institutional ad, a direct sales ad (perhaps one requiring a return), a co-op ad.

3. The academic department you are in has decided to improve relations with alumni of that department. It will publish a bimonthly newsletter. Plan its content and design, and determine how you will get information for it.

4. Prepare the following as a newspaper story or as a broadcast item. A university track team has just won a major track and field event in its conference, but immediately afterward, Sarah Brown, one of the distance runners, was discovered to have been taking amphetamines. The field doctors made the discovery and have the complete information, including the student's statement that she took it on the recommendation of the university's track coach because during practice she had difficulty breathing. You are at the event as the university's sports information officer, but the academic dean, who has jurisdiction in such cases, is not. He has been called and is coming to the stadium. The press is covering the event, of course, but you must give them a story. Write a release to cover the situation.

SELECTED READINGS

Arthur Bellaire, *Controlling Your TV Commercial Costs* (Chicago: Crain Books, 1977). Revision of a 1972 book with chapters on production costs and how to control them, pretesting, low-budget commercial film and videotape distribution.

Philip Ward Burton, *Advertising Copywriting*, 4th ed. (Columbus, Ohio: Grid, 1978). Analysis of what makes good copy; discusses relationship between writer and artist.

Mitchell V. Charnley and Blair Charnley, *Reporting*, 4th ed. (New York: Holt, Rinehart and Winston, 1979). Basic reporting text, telling how news (which is what publicity is) should be written.

Robert S. Cole, *The Practical Handbook of Public Relations* (Englewood Cliffs, N.J.: Prentice-Hall, 1982). A writing and techniques book.

Philip C. Geraci, *Photojournalism: Making Pictures for Publication*, 2d ed. (Dubuque, Iowa: Kendall/Hunt, 1978). A text for beginners that makes taking photos sound easy.

Rolf Gompertz, *Promotion and Publicity Handbook for Broadcasters* (Blue Ridge Summit, Pa.: TAB Books, 1977). Has information on media kits and publicity releases from the author's experience with the NBC press department.

Elizabeth J. Heighton and Don R. Cunningham, 2d ed. *Advertising in the Broadcast Media* (Belmont, Calif.: Wadsworth, 1984). Comprehensive survey of television and radio advertising.

Robert L. Hilliard, *Writing for Television and Radio*, 3d rev. ed. (New York: Hastings House, 1976). Good reference for format and examples.

Otto Heppner and Thomas Russell, *Advertising Procedure*, 8th ed. (Englewood Cliffs, N.J.: Prentice-Hall, 1983). An outstanding text in the field.

Maxwell McCombs and David L. Grey, *Handbook of Reporting Methods* (Boston: Houghton Mifflin, 1976). A procedural approach to writing.

Melvin Mencher, *Basic News Writing* (Dubuque, Iowa: Wm. C. Brown, 1983). Excellent basic text for print media.

Doug Newsom and Tom Siegfried, *Writing in Public Relations Practice: Form and Style* (Belmont, Calif.: Wadsworth, 1981). Comprehensive book of PR writing forms including broadcast media and specialized writing for PR such as annual reports, background and position papers, speeches and slide shows.

Robert T. Reilly, *Public Relations in Action* (Englewood Cliffs, N.J.: Prentice-Hall, 1982). Primarily covers applications of PR.

William L. Rivers, *The Mass Media*, 2d ed. (New York: Harper & Row, 1975). Good information on writing for various media.

Jack Z. Sissors and E. R. Petray, *Advertising Media Planning* (Chicago: Crain Books, 1982). One of the best; a standard text. Includes samples and examples with how-to-do-it information from an advertising professor and an ad agency media director.

Richard Weiner, *Professional's Guide to Publicity*, rev. ed. (New York: Richard Weiner, 1982). A concise handbook.

John S. Wright, Daniel S. Warner, Willis L. Winter, Jr. and Sherilyn Zeigler, *Advertising*, 4th ed. (New York: McGraw-Hill, 1977). The basic introductory text.

Newsletters

Bulldog, 6420 Wilshire Blvd., Suite 711, Los Angeles, CA 90048. News of PR and media people in California and in West; bimonthly.

Jack O'Dwyer's PR Newsletter, 271 Madison Ave., New York, NY 10016. Good weekly source for current information on what is happening in PR field.

pr reporter, PR Publishing Company, Box 600, Exeter, NH 03833. Weekly newsletter, also issues a supplement, "tips & tactics," a weekly how-to bulletin of PR methods and procedures and a monthly "persuasion" bulletin. Indices of each are printed periodically.

Public Relations News, 127 E. 80th St., New York, NY 10021. Oldest weekly newsletter for PR profession; issued continuously since 1945.

Journals

Public Relations Journal, Public Relations Society of America, 845 Third Ave., New York, NY 10022. Monthly.

Public Relations Quarterly, PR Aids, Inc., 44 W. Market St., Box 311, Rhinebeck, NY 12572.

Public Relations Review, College of Journalism, University of Maryland, College Park, MD 20742. Quarterly.

CHAPTER 10

Working with Media People

PR men should realize they really can help us and help their clients just by knowing their market and knowing what are the needs of each financial editor. . . . If they did that, they'd make my life a little easier, and anybody who does that I'm appreciative of.

Tom Gable, business editor, San Diego Evening Tribune

Our foe is not dishonesty; it's laziness.

Bill Marsteller, former chairman and chief executive officer, Marsteller, Inc.

Good working relationships are imperative for smooth functioning anytime, but they are particularly important when personal relationships can facilitate, impede or even destroy the public relations program. The secret of success in placing publicity is in knowing and anticipating the needs of the media. Your PR efforts in handling publicity are usually a two-part operation: (1) providing the information you want to convey to the public and (2) responding to inquiries. Your contacts are valuable as a source for placing stories or story ideas and as a resource for keeping you advised of media changes in personnel or procedure.

Fortunately, some things never change, and among them are the standards by which publicity is measured. Publicity is ranked by editors and TV news directors for news value. They have three criteria:

1. Is it important to this medium's readers? It must be of local significance to be considered.

2. Is it timely? It must be news, not something the beat reporter had three days ago.

3. Is it accurate, truthful and complete?

One PR person, who had heard a newspaper's assistant city editor chew out an unfortunate publicist for having copy with "more holes than a sieve," was asked by the editor if the reaction had been too harsh. "Not at all," he replied. "Sloppy copy just makes it harder for the rest of us." Strict news value is one yardstick. Another is human interest, a story or picture with humor, drama or poignancy. Humorous stories especially have an edge because so much of what editors must print is serious. A publicity piece that is genuinely funny or appealing is usually given good display.

In handling publicity you will be concerned with offering news releases to mass and specialized media, both print and broadcast; interesting them in story and picture ideas they will cover, giving them access to management through interviews and conferences; and preparing materials to tell about the institution, such as newsletters, brochures and pamphlets, television and radio spots, slide presentations and perhaps films. You will be compelled to master the styles of all media and to have a working relationship with professionals in all of these fields.

The PR person must know, for example, the exact copy deadlines for all local media and the approximate deadlines for state and national media. No experienced PR person would call a city editor at 11:30 A.M. and offer lunch—if the editor is working on an evening paper. Why? Because the editor probably began work at six that morning, has already had lunch and is presently fighting a deadline to get the paper out. (Actually, buying the editor lunch or dinner is not the key. If you do take someone to lunch, it should be because you want to, not because you expect a favor or free professional service.) And it might be wise to call a sports, business or whatever section editor to check on the possibility of new deadlines. Such attention to details separates the professional from the inept.

BEFORE CONTACTING THE MEDIA

You are going to be selling an idea in story or pictures to the media, so there is advance work to be done in gathering ideas and information.

Preparing the Story

You should have some basic training as a reporter, for in order to write news you have to know it when you see or hear it. In a large institution, where people may be too busy to be bothered with giving you "news tips," you must be able to search out the news yourself. One way to encourage news cooperation in a large organization is to tell people exactly what you need and how and when to get it to you. Of course, once you have the information, you often are expected to make banner headlines with it.

Sometimes a PR person's news sense becomes dulled by spending too much time reading company materials and too little time on outside news and newscasts—not to mention talking too much to company people instead of to news people. When this happens, he or she is likely to respond with a three-page story to the boss's suggestion for a "great news story," when in fact it deserves only three paragraphs. Although you should listen to the suggestion carefully (never discourage any news source), you should always assess it from a news editor's position, not a company perspective. Is it really worth three pages or is it simply a column item? Or does it deserve any exposure at all? Maybe the idea is good but the medium wrong. Maybe the idea is good for the company newspaper, but it wouldn't be of any interest outside the institution. It is this sense of news value that a publicity person must keep finely honed.

10.1 THE PUBLICIST'S BASIC FILE

A good publicist keeps the following in a "basic file"—a collection of all material useful to a particular organization's intelligence activity:

1. Statistical information
2. Governmental information—regulatory and other
3. Basic reference books for the field of interest and related fields
4. All legislation on problems—pending or proposed
5. Trade association data
6. Trade union literature—each union, how it operates
7. Record of organization—own publications, a file copy of *all*
8. File of ads run
9. File of speeches of officials
10. Clippings of all information about company with publication name and date
11. List of individuals and organizations interested in company, including civic groups appealing for contributions
12. Biography of top executives
13. Pictures of stores, plants, products, other activities
14. Lists of editors and publications
15. People in all media; contact as potential sources of releases or information
16. File on major competition and antagonists and their efforts
17. Timetables of occasions for publicity—indicate news releases

In gathering information for a release, the publicity writer must act just like a reporter would with the same access. You should start with secondary sources, finding out if there is anything written about the subject in the company files—any research or sales reports, any memos. You should then seek out the primary sources, interviewing people to learn everything they know and are willing to share (see 10.1).

Like a reporter, never begin with some predetermined idea about the length of the story. Find out everything you can, since you must have complete information before you condense it—and news people won't later be able to ask you questions you never anticipated (which they will). In doing this you may find that you have accumulated information for not one but several stories. You may find that, with a different emphasis, the story you have researched may be used by the newspaper, the local chamber of commerce magazine, an industry publication and your company's own house organ. If your story focuses on a person, there may be even more opportunities for publication, for (again with a different emphasis) it may be used in professional, religious or other publications of organizations in which that person is active. Research represents your principal investment in time. Make it pay off for you.

Regarding writing style, you should be familiar enough with the medium to which you are submitting copy to be absolutely certain the style of the publicity meets precisely the style of the medium. It is important to know whether a newspaper has an "up" or "down" style—that is, uses capital letters frequently (up) or seldom (down). Find out and accommodate. Beware especially of writing the way people from whom you got your information talk, because they often use unintelligible jargon (business, professional, educational, governmental or whatever). Don't write what someone says, write what is meant. Of course, this is impossible if you don't understand it yourself, so never be afraid to say to a source, "I'm sorry, that is out of my area. You'll have to explain. I don't understand." They probably don't know anything about communications either, so you're even.

Planning Publicity Photos and Illustrations

A publicity story has a better chance of being accepted by a news medium if you can offer an illustration with it. Many newspapers prefer to shoot their own photos, and the wire services almost always do. In such cases, you will need to work in advance of the day the newspaper intends to use the story to preserve its timeliness and still allow the editor to schedule a photographer at a time when you can set up the picture. You should have all the elements of the photo assembled—people, things or both—before the photographer arrives. But how the photographer arranges or uses the subjects is his or her business. Don't interfere.

If you have hired a photographer to take the picture for you, you may have to offer strong guidance, depending on the photographer's background. If he or she has news experience, you can probably trust the person's news judgment. But if he or she is a commercial photographer with no idea of newspaper requirements, it will be your responsibility to make sure of the following:

- Keep the number of subjects down to four or less.
- Be sure you are getting high contrast and sharp detail.
- Avoid the cliché shot of people shaking hands or receiving a plaque.
- Be sure your subjects are close together and that the backgrounds are neutral.

Make the most of the photographer you have hired and get what photos you need—not only for the one particular story but also for use with other versions of the story for different media. Once you have good photographs, you can use them in a number of ways (see 10.2).

In ordering photographic prints, be sure to order some for your own files. Keep your photographic files up to date, so you will not get caught offering an old photo to a news source. The news media often pull photos out of their own libraries to use, but they expect to get something new from someone seeking publicity, even if they initiate the request. Anticipate this with adequate photo files. In addition, do not give competing media the same picture, even if it is only a person's photograph. Round up another.

Be sure that in any arrangement with a photographer *you* own the negatives, particularly for high-cost assignments involving color and aerial photography. Get it in writing in a contract. Otherwise, owing to copyright law, the pictures belong to the photographer and you have only bought specific rights. For convenience

10.2 PUBLICITY PHOTOS

An excellent example of an unusual PR photo is this General Electric Easter idea. It was nationally syndicated by AP, UPI and NEA. There was a series of nationally syndicated photomicrographs issued by GE's Research and Development Center between 1972 and 1974. The series included two Christmas photomicrographs, a crystal chrysanthemum, the Easter symbol shown here and a Halloween shot.

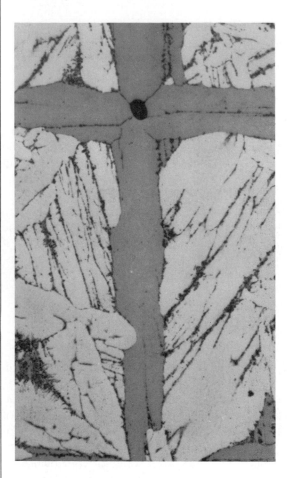

From: Public Information
GENERAL ELECTRIC RESEARCH AND DEVELOPMENT CENTER
Schenectady, New York

Photo No. 32152F1B

FOR RELEASE MONDAY, APRIL 16, 1973

OLD RUGGED CROSS? This Easter symbol is in reality no larger than the head of a pin. It is a tiny speck of zirconium alloy magnified 300 times. The photo was taken by Robert R. Russell as part of studies of alloys at the General Electric Research and Development Center in Schenectady, N.Y.

NOTE TO EDITORS: This photo is available in color.

Photo and news release courtesy of General Electric Research and Development Center, Schenectady, New York.

Another season provided a department store with this opportunity.

CHRISTMAS FACES. The faces of these dolls and stuffed animals may well run through the dreams of toddlers as they await the magical night on which Santa descends their chimney. The toys are from F.A.O. Swartz in New York.

Reprinted with permission of Wide World Photos.

you may ask the photographer to store the negatives for you at his or her studio so additional prints can be made later. However, it is important that you (your institution) own the negatives. If you do not own the negatives, and the photographer moves or sells out or goes out of business, you lose a substantial portion of the investment.

The same is true for other artwork and film. You might invest in elaborate schematics, maps, charts or graphs. Be sure they become yours. When you hire a filmmaker to shoot film for you to use in releases to television (although most TV stations and all networks prefer to shoot their own footage), it is all right to let the company that processes and duplicates the film keep the master, because they have the temperature-controlled environment to preserve it; but be sure you own that master. Although all you may have in mind at the moment is a short segment for a news clip or news feature, you might need that footage later for a corporate film. Be sure everyone knows and understands who the owner is and how much reprintings cost.

News photographers do not have time to develop and print film other than their own or to make extra prints for you; neither do the wire services. Both newspapers and wire services have photo sales departments to take care of reprint requests. Television stations have commercial operations that develop film; be prepared to pay for whatever you ask for. If you ask for videotape to be prepared at a station or illustrations to be handled by a newspaper's art department—whether simply photo retouching or designing the cover for a special section—get your checkbook out. The news media are businesses. They cannot make money on gratuities.

When you hire a photographer or one is assigned by a publication to cover some event, try to think of an original pose to replace unimaginative stock poses. Be sure all the people and the props the photographer will need are ready well before time for the shot. Action shots are best because they help tell a story, but a character study of a person whose face shows deep emotion can do so also.

You should have at least two specific shots in mind (including camera angles) before going to the event. Discuss these with the photographer before the event. Consider publication needs in terms of horizontal and vertical shots, the number of people to be included in the pictures and whether you need color or black and white. You also need to consider the event from the standpoint of the photographer and how close the pictures can be taken. In some cases, the photographer needs to be unobtrusive. For that reason, many PR directors insist that their staffs have firsthand knowledge of photography to understand lens openings and lighting. When you have a picture in mind, look through the lens to be sure it is there. If not, work toward what you want. The more professional the photographer, the less direction is needed. Allow for travel time and rest periods in shooting and be prepared to pay half or all if you must cancel at the last minute.

Planning Gimmicks

Some public relations people plan news-making gimmicks that will attract attention to their clients. For women recruits who failed to meet the Los Angeles Police Department's upper-body strength test, Nann Miller Enterprises got them free workouts at Jack LaLanne Health Spas, her client. At a groundbreaking for the S.P.C.A. (Society for the Prevention of Cruelty to Animals), two trained dogs manipulated the shovel. Stunts of this type are clever and accepted for their general interest. Any stunt that misleads, though, or causes a hazard, such as a human fly who walks up the side of a building and ties up traffic as well as rescue forces from the police and fire departments, is not generally thought of too highly by the news media. One metropolitan paper declined to give attention to one such stunt, burying it inside, although competing media gave it much better play. The editor's comment was he thought the public was getting bored with such things.

ON THE JOB WITH MEDIA PEOPLE

Successful publicity is often closely tied to the relationships one forms in getting and disseminating information. Four groups are especially important to the publicist, newspeople, production people, other PR people and free-lance writers.

WE'RE HAVING OUR ANNUAL KIWANIS CLUB PANCAKE BREAKFAST, AND WE'D LIKE TO GET SOMETHING ON IT IN THE PAPER...

WHAT WOULD IT TAKE FOR YOU GUYS TO SEND A PHOTOGRAPHER OVER TO COVER IT?

YOU'D HAVE TO HOLD THE PANCAKE BREAKFAST AT A NUDIST COLONY.

Reprinted by permission of Jefferson Communications, Inc., Reston, Virginia.

Relations with Newspeople

PR people will go to lengths to meet the requirements of media people and sometimes still not have anything to show for it. Such was the case when *Fortune* contacted K-Mart Corporation Chairman Bernard M. Fauber in Troy, Michigan, about being on the cover.[1] Although the story had been in the works since the middle of July, it was the middle of August, and a Friday at 11 A.M., when K-Mart was told that the picture would have to be in hand that weekend to make the cover. *Fortune* wanted a photo of Fauber on the roof of a K-Mart store. So after the call, Fauber's schedule was cleared, a store in Troy, Michigan, was selected and the PR staff began looking for a "cherry-picker," a truck-mounted elevator, to lift Fauber to the roof. After the publicity director found a cherry-picker operator in the yellow pages, the weather turned bad and the *Fortune* photographer canceled. The shooting was reset for Saturday morning; it rained. Saturday afternoon was clear, but Fauber had to go to a wedding. *Fortune* ruled out Sunday. Monday morning the shot was finally taken and couriers took the film to the Detroit airport to be flown to *Fortune*'s headquarters in New York. Unfortunately for K-Mart, Fauber got crowded off the cover by President Ronald Reagan, although the company's story was in that issue. The magazine has a practice of selecting three possible covers. The decision was made to go with Reagan. Fauber's graceful comment was, "If I had to lose out, I can't think of anyone I'd rather lose out to."

A good PR practitioner knows newspeople's jobs almost as well as they do, and is courteous and considerate with them. The PR professional also knows the importance of getting to know the newspeople, and will be the one to initiate contact. One of the best ways is to hand carry news releases to all the local media. It is time consuming, but by regularly hand delivering releases, the PR person establishes a working relationship with the media that permits extra consideration when the institution he or she represents may be under attack. Take the release to

---

[1] Charles Stevens, "Cherry Picker Got Him to the Roof But Not Onto Fortune's New Cover," *Wall Street Journal*, September 15, 1981, sec. 2, p. 1. Reprinted by permission of the *Wall Street Journal*. © 1981 Dow Jones & Company, Inc. All rights reserved.

the particular editor or reporter who should receive it. Be sure no questions are left unanswered. Visits should not be long. Speak to others, briefly, and leave. Don't engage in extended conversation unless the newsperson invites it (say, by offering you a cup of coffee), and then be sure to take the time. Plan a delivery schedule that allows you such flexibility but still allows you to get the releases to other media with deadlines.

Include among the local media not just the daily metropolitan newspapers but also all the television and radio stations and suburban newspapers. Include the ethnic media too. If it is necessary to translate the release into a different language, call on the faculty of commercial language schools and local college language departments or on one of the relatively new firms of language specialists handling business and industrial translations. (Be sure the translator knows current idiomatic use of the language.)

An illustration of fractured media relations appeared in an account of misplaced publicity recorded by the *Business Wire Newsletter*. According to the newsletter, the San Francisco bureau chief for *Business Week* received in the mail a seven-page feature sent by a local public relations person to the magazine's New York office. New York kicked the story back to the San Francisco bureau, and in checking, the bureau chief found that the "leapfrogging" of his office to New York was not an insult—only ignorance. The PR person did not know that *Business Week* had regional offices, including one in San Francisco. In sending releases to national publications, be sure to check if they have local offices or representatives and deal directly with them.

When special events attract newspeople from outside the local area or members of the specialized media such as travel or outdoor publications, be sure to make personal contact while the opportunity is there. Contacts make smoother one of the more effective PR efforts—alerting news media to stories that might interest them. Usually this is a personal, individual effort, but some organizations have had success by publishing collections of newstips or story ideas for the state and national media.

If you are sending out many releases a week to the local media, you obviously cannot hand deliver all of them, but it is important that you see all local newspeople you are mailing to at least once a month—there are no little or insignificant newspeople.

Most importantly, *be available*. PR people should not only not have unlisted telephone numbers but they should also deliberately list their home phone number (as well as business phone) at the top of each release. A story may be processed after 5 P.M., and if you want it on the 10 P.M. news or in the morning paper, you should be available to answer questions. Often it is not an editor but someone from the copy desk who calls to check the spelling of a name in your story or get some background to flesh out the story. You should stop then and oblige them. The need comes with the request, not later, when it is convenient for you.

In working with news photographers, never tell them how to take their pictures, since they know what their editors expect. However, as the PR practitioner, you know the event, institution and the people, and so you may be able to think of other pictures that might be newsworthy and *suggest*—the word cannot be too strongly emphasized—them to the photographer.

This additional advice comes from Eaton Corporation's *Public Relations Manual*, reprinted here with permission.

> When you think you have a story that rates a picture, call the city editor, the business editor or reporter and present your idea. If the editor thinks it has merit, you will usually find it gets coverage. If you're turned down, there's probably a good reason for it. Try again, but come up with a better idea next time. Unless the picture possibility comes up suddenly, give the paper several days' notice. You'll have a better chance of scoring.
>
> Don't try to get an iron-clad promise from a paper for photo coverage of an event days in advance. An important news break may occur which will prevent the photographer from taking your picture at the last moment. [If you are simultaneously visited by several competing photographers, be sure you do not suggest the same pictures to each.]
>
> Newspapers will accept and publish well-executed pictures by photographers other than their own staff members. There are a number of excellent free-lance press photographers whose services can be acquired at reasonable cost.
>
> Ask other PR people for recommendations and look at their work. Tell the photographer what type of pictures you need, how they will be used and the format. Unless you negotiate the photographer owns the negatives. Also be sure to let the photographer do the "directing" of the subjects.

Relations with Production People

PR people need to work effectively with two types of production people: those in the media and suppliers. In the media, much of the technical work is handled electronically. However, knowing the production staffs and understanding the production processes make it easier for you to avoid problems with the material you supply and to unsnarl the ones that do occur. You need to know what is and is not technically possible in the media, and it helps to be familiar with the terminology.

Knowing the terminology and production processes can be critical when you are dealing with suppliers. Technical suppliers produce the typeset copy for your printed pieces, the printed pieces themselves, color separations for your artwork, slides, videotapes and sound. You have to know what you want and appreciate and be able to pay for quality (or accept less if you don't have the budget). More importantly, your directions will be followed by the producers. If you have scaled a picture wrong, or not fit the copy correctly or, worse, misspelled a word, you will be charged for your mistake when it is corrected. Just like other craftspeople, if the mistake is the suppliers', they will correct it at no charge. Mistakes always cause delays and, if the errors are yours, are costly. A PR project can go over budget quickly owing to technical problems.

Relations with Other PR People

On occasion you may be working with PR people from other agencies. It may be in a cooperative promotion; it may be because you've hired the agency to help with a special event; or it may be you have a long-standing relationship with an advertising agency.

Fiascos have occurred when the practitioner supposedly directing the agency's efforts has suddenly felt threatened by it and has withdrawn his or her support and cooperation. To avoid such traumas, be sure to spell out in the beginning who has final approval of copy, and be sure deadlines and timetables are worked out to preserve your long-established relationships with the media. Then relax and manage. It is your job to supply the major source of information to the agency, to see that work is expedited, that deadlines are kept and that quality is maintained. It should be a rewarding experience from which all will benefit.

Relations with Free-lance Writers

Although it may be time consuming, it is important to cooperate with free-lancers who may be using your PR department as a source of information for a story they hope to sell or a book they are writing. The free-lancer may have a contact you lack; the writer's status as a free agent lends greater credibility to the material.

Of course, free-lancers can waste a lot of time, especially those who are really nonwriters on a fishing expedition. There are a couple of ways to check, without offending them. One is to inquire about what they have written and where it has been published, and then look up the articles in *Readers' Guide to Periodical Literature*. Another way is to ask if they have sent a magazine or newspaper a query on the article idea and received a response; if they say they have, you can call the editor for confirmation. (To make it seem less of a "corroboration" check, you can suggest to the editor that you certainly are willing to cooperate but perhaps could help the writer better if you knew what direction the story was to take and if art might be needed.) Most editors will tell you immediately if the writer is working on assignment or on speculation. You should not dismiss the writer working without assignment, however; on the contrary, you may be able to help an inexperienced writer.

Many magazines use staff for stories or assign writers. Working with a magazine's experienced people usually increases your own appreciation for what you are publicizing and is a pleasurable, albeit time-demanding, experience. One news bureau director and university magazine editor, contacted by a nationally syndicated Sunday supplement about a story on the university, found that three weeks' work with the magazine writers produced not only national coverage but also a handsome reprint she could use as the primary portion of one of her magazines.

Sometimes a writer has malicious intent, but an experienced PR person can take the offensive to advantage. As one practitioner says, "I give them the straight stuff, and I try to keep them busy. Every time I say something, I try to think how it could be distorted, contorted, twisted beyond recognition, and if it still seems to shake out okay, I spit it out. One thing I do know, while they are talking to me they are not talking to the opposition or gathering facts against us." The key here is to anticipate how the truth might be used against you.

If a story seems unfair or distorted, employers will blame the PR person, but the PR person cannot pass it on to the media without aggravating the situation.

Most professional public relations people have never registered a complaint with any news media in their entire careers. The standing rule to the media is call only if they have made a substantial error. If the story is libelous, let your institution's lawyer make the call.

The Media Interview

Public relations people are usually in the position of having to prepare top management for an interview situation. It may be one-on-one in the office of the executive or a press conference on familiar or unfamiliar ground with many reporters. On occasion there may be a series of interviews on what is termed a "media tour," where the spokesperson is taken to different media that have accepted "bookings" (that is, made arrangements) for the executive to talk with editors, specialized reporters or representatives of special-interest publications. The tour may also include visits with news departments of broadcast stations and perhaps an appearance on talk shows. On the latter, the executive may appear alone, as part of a panel or as the guest of an on-air personality. In any event, it is important to remember that the success of all interviews depends less on the interviewee's personality (although certainly important) than it does on the preparation for the interview situation.

Some problems occur when the executive being interviewed has not done the necessary homework and is not fully prepared for questions. The interviewee must not only always be ready with a brief, concise, clear and honest response, he or she should also be aware of the interviewer's style and personal background. One exasperated PR executive said it was a problem to get his company's spokesperson to remember even an interviewer's name, much less background and style. As a consequence, this PR person insists on a role-playing exercise for the executive before any scheduled appearance. The executive is not pleased with the PR person's aggressive interviewing, but does say it is more fun to prepare in this manner instead of "reading all that dry stuff." Even if an executive is willing to prepare, however, it helps to have a run-through, with someone playing the devil's advocate and asking potentially embarrassing questions. It is also important to have the executive listen carefully to the questions asked—a skill that can be learned in rehearsal.

In planning for an appearance, the executive and the PR director should develop some quotable material—hopefully something carefully researched to appear fresh and newsworthy. Remember, the reporter is looking for a story, and it is wise to be able to offer one. Also, if the reporter gets into a sensitive area, it is a mistake to mislead or skirt the truth, since most good reporters can spot such devices quickly and they move in for the kill. Rarely should one try to go "off the record" (although this is possible in certain circumstances with print media). It is usually better to say something, rather than "No comment." It is also a good idea to be certain the reporter has access to the executive in case he or she needs to clarify something (see 10.3).

The best way to ensure an accurate representation in the news media is to give a good performance. Does that mean a mistake-free performance? No, but it means correcting any mistakes immediately, says former ABC affiliate broad-

10.3   CONDUCTING PRESS INTERVIEWS

The element of control that is present with written communications is far less in the interview situation. As a consequence, the danger of looking bad in print is far greater when news is provided through this method. Certain ground rules, however, can make the interview more manageable and at the same time less of a burden on the person being interviewed. Following is a set of guidelines for public relations people to follow in conducting press interviews:

1. Select the place for the interview, one preferably on the home ground of the person being interviewed.

2. Be sure to allow sufficient time for the interviewer to complete an assignment.

3. Know the topic of discussion and have supporting material at hand.

4. School the person interviewed beforehand as to what questions to expect. Be prepared to handle touchy questions.

5. Know your reporter's habits, etc., and give the person being interviewed a verbal sketch. At the same time, be sure the reporter is completely aware of the person being interviewed—background, hobbies, and so on. These things can help establish rapport in preliminary conversation.

6. Set ground rules for the interview and make sure both parties understand them.

7. Avoid off-the-record remarks. If it's off the record, keep it that way. Exceptions might occur if the reporter is known and trusted.

8. Help the reporter to wind up the story in one day.

9. Make sure the reporter gets the story sought. In agreeing to do the interview, you have said in essence that you will give the reporter the story.

10. Stay in the background and do not try to answer questions. If the question is one that requires an answer contrary to company policy and the person being interviewed starts to answer, remind him or her it is not policy to disclose that information. Or, if the interviewee wants to hedge on a question that is perfectly all right to answer, say it is OK to answer.

11. Offer to answer further questions later.

12. Do *not* ask the reporter when the story will run or how big it will be.

Rules for Executives Being Interviewed

1. Know the topic you are to discuss.

2. Anticipate touchy questions.

3. Be completely honest.

4. Answer questions directly. If you cannot answer the question, say you cannot.

5. If you don't know an answer, say so and offer to get one. Follow up on this offer.

6. Keep the meeting as cordial as possible even in the face of bantering and pushing.

7. Avoid off-the-record remarks unless you know and trust the reporter. Explain that the information is not for public disclosure and politely decline an answer.

8. Be sure to answer questions that are public record or not against company policy.

9. Use the personality that helped get you into a management position and look professional.

10. Offer help later if the reporter needs it.

All of this section on press interviews is adapted from the *Public Relations Manual*, Eaton Corporation. Reprinted by permission.

caster Dan Ammerman, who now trains executives to appear on television. (For Ammerman's basics, see 10.4.) Ammerman points out both the importance of television as a medium and the significance of getting your message straight by relating the story of Gerald Ford's slip during his television debate with Jimmy Carter in the presidential campaign of 1976.

Ammerman claims Ford lost the presidency of the United States for violating

10.4 TV INTERVIEW GUIDELINES

TV BASICS

1. Listen—remember.
2. No technical jargon.
3. Smile when answering a reporter's questions.
4. Speak in 30-second quotes. Long answers are seldom used.
5. A simple "yes" or "no" may keep you from being quoted.
6. Lose your temper in front of a reporter and you are assured a spot on the six o'clock news.
7. Same goes for weeping.
8. Never tell a lie. A reporter never forgets.
9. Preface remarks are taboo.
10. You are your company when appearing on radio or TV. No personal opinions.
11. Don't offer ammunition.
12. No third-party discussions.
13. Read a newspaper prior to any interview or hearing.
14. You know more about your subject than they do.
15. Don't use "no comment"; it makes you sound guilty.
16. Don't go "off the record" when talking to a reporter. Earl Butz did and lost his job.
17. In any interview *you* should be interested in *information and education*.
18. The interviewer is interested in *pacing and entertainment*.
19. A good interview mixes all four ingredients.
20. Always have a positive message from your company or industry to deliver.
21. Know why you were asked to be there. The days of being invited on television just to "chew the fat" are over.
22. Dress conservatively for television. No bright colors. No short sleeves.
23. Do your homework! Be prepared! Even in your specialty a brush-up is needed.
24. Question your position. Play the "devil's advocate" and force yourself to justify your position.
25. Go beyond the interviewer for understanding. Make the average tenth-grade student understand your position.
26. While in a television or radio studio consider every microphone and camera to be "on." Don't do or say anything you wouldn't do or say in church.
27. Never leave the set until you have been assured the program is over.
28. Boil down everything you want to say before you say it.

Dan Ammerman, Ammerman Enterprises, Inc., 8323 Southwest Freeway, #920, Houston, TX 77014. Reprinted with permission.

one of the most important rules for being interviewed on TV: Correct your mistake *immediately*. During the debate Ford declared that Eastern Europe was not under Soviet domination, and despite being given three chances to correct his mistake, Ford did not. Ammerman says Ford could have said, "I'm sorry, I didn't phrase that correctly, what I meant to say was" and then say what he meant. Had he done so, according to Ammerman, the slip would not have made headlines the next day. Furthermore, Ammerman quotes Ford's campaign strategists as determining that they had to convert 174,000 voters each day from the day their candidate was nominated to the day of the election. This would have assured Ford a slim victory. For two weeks following the crucial debate, however, no voters were converted. A Gallup poll taken after the election led George Gallup to state that "to the best of my ability to judge" President Ford lost to Jimmy Carter on that one misstatement in their debate. If the strategists had been able to acquire those

10.5 ON CAMERA INSTRUCTIONS (IN FRONT OF THE MAGIC LENS)

The following advice for interviews on camera (tape or live) will help, especially if you practice.

- Appearance is crucial. Create confidence by wearing fairly conservative clothes with muted colors—medium to dark suits or dresses. Don't wear bold stripes or checks. Avoid white shirts or blouses; off-white is better. And think twice about vests. These can make you seem aloof.

- Don't wear flashy jewelry or tie pins which can distract and often reflect bright lights.

- Take a last-minute look in the mirror. Straighten your hair and tie. Button your coat and pull it down in back when you sit down.

- Be on time for the interview. If you're rushing, your harried look will show.

- Don't sit on your hands. Slight head and hand movements can help emphasize key points. But watch out for exaggerated mannerisms or fidgety gestures. Cameras often zero in on hands, capturing you nervously drumming the table or fiddling with a pen.

- Never smoke on camera.

- Be yourself, natural and sincere. You'll come across that way to viewers. Don't forget to smile, too. Of course, if questions turn more serious, reflect the mood.

- Ignore the cameras, maintain good eye contact with the interviewer. Remember, even when the interviewer is asking a question, you still may be on camera. So watch your actions and expressions.

- Speak clearly and distinctly in a normal conversational tone.

- Strive to maintain control of the interview. Your main goal is to convey your key points. Do so with crisp and quotable answers.

- Be your own worst critic. If possible, try to review the actual tape. You'll learn a lot through self-assessment.

Larry E. Schnieders, "O Press, Where Is thy Sting?" *Communications Update*, Southwestern Bell, (Summer 1972), p. 23. Used by permission.

174,000 voters per day for the fourteen days between the debate and the election, Ford would have beaten Carter.[2]

William Jurma analyzed videotapes of the Jimmy Carter–Ronald Reagan debates in the 1980 presidential campaign and concluded that Carter's body language lost him the advantage. He failed to display characteristics of leadership and "lost" the visual debate to his camera-savvy opponent, an actor. (Jurma's study shows that people who only heard the audio of the debates on radio thought Carter "won.") (See 10.5 for hints for TV appearances.)

If you are working with the print media, it is wise to use graphics to illustrate your significant points. Offer figures and statistics that are easily understood or interpretable. Also, furnish all the sources of information and background material on the person being interviewed and the situation represented. If some statements or quotes are appropriate, give these too. If the topic is one often addressed, have copies of previously printed quotes, with a reference to when each appeared. Finally, as with a good speech, the objective of the discussion should be kept clearly in focus, particularly if the interview has been initiated by the PR di-

---

[2] Dan Ammerman, speech to the Texas Public Relations Association, Fort Worth, Texas, February 25, 1978.

rector. The number of ideas offered should be limited so adequate concentration can be given. Remember too that it helps to use analogies to illustrate the more difficult or abstract points.

The role of the PR person in the interview is that of preparer, facilitator and clarifier. The public relations person who tries to inject him- or herself into the process during the actual interview is asking for a hostile reaction. The role of clarifier includes interpreting facts and technical language, giving some background information, reminding the interviewee of questions that might have been overlooked and perhaps extending the interview if necessary. Phillips Petroleum printed "golden rules" for handling newspeople on 3 × 2 plastic cards and gave them to executives who took the company's media training class. The flip side of the card lists the company's public relations contacts with home and office numbers. Among the seven rules is the admonition to *"be brief and to the point.* Be pleasant even when the reporter is hostile. Answer the question, then shut up. Dead air isn't your problem. Correct misstatements." Another rule states, *"Never answer hypothetical questions.* These get you into trouble with speculation." And still another good piece of advice: *"Never use expert talk.* Sharks are sharks, not marine life."[3]

To these rules, Jim Blackmore and Alex Burton add, "Never say 'never' such as 'that never happened here before,'" and they advise tape recording the interview yourself. They also advise correcting an inaccuracy or misrepresentation immediately.

Contracts

Potential trouble with some media arrangements, such as exclusive cover stories or special TV appearances, can be avoided through contracts. Contracts have enormous value as preventives. The PR person will also be arranging contracts with suppliers of services. You should consider having a contract with an outside agency or studio, with a printer, with models, with any artists or photographers, even if they are your best friends or relatives. If your close friend, the photographer, has a contract, you can say, "The boss wants one of those color prints for his office," and your friend can say, "Well, it's not in the contract. How much do you think we ought to charge him for it?" A contract gives you the chance to suggest a fair price or say, "Forget it!" Bad feelings resulting from unexpected charges are avoided if things are spelled out—in friendly but specific language. (See also the section on contracts in Chapter 14.)

Deadlines

Making deadlines is essential to a smooth operation. Allow enough flexibility in planning for mistakes—yours and others. Once you have promised copy to the artist or typesetter or ads to the media, you *must* make that deadline. This is an unforgiving business, and you must function within the framework of time segments or you don't function. Remember the significance of both contrac-

---

[3] *pr reporter*, September 20, 1982, p. 3. Used by permission.

tual agreements and deadlines. The former may be invalid if the latter are not observed. Be sure that you get the ad or commercial to the proper person at the agreed time in a form usable to the medium.

PUBLICIZING SPECIAL EVENTS

A special event may be any newsmaking situation—from a corporate open house or a freeway ribbon cutting to the preview of an exhibition of rare paintings. Each event requires different handling to publicize it, but there are a few basic rules.

The Mechanics of Promoting

First, a timetable must be established because so many events must dovetail. The timetable includes the dates for the first announcement, which must be coordinated with any special invitations and advertising. Second, mailing lists must be prepared for both special activities and the news media. You must start early and set firm policies regarding the handing out of news media credentials. (You should not invite your PR colleagues to any media day functions, unless they had an active part in the planning.) Third, the promotion campaign itself must be planned in detail, with a theme selected that will carry through all advertising, publicity, letterheads, invitations and posters.

The so-called media kit should be one of the most carefully thought-out pieces of the entire promotion. Media kits are sent to people who may not attend the special event but may write something about it. Because they must serve a variety of media—specialized and mass, print and broadcasting—parts of the kits will differ. Publications will get 8 × 10 glossy photographs with cutlines glued on. Broadcast media will get cassettes or small tape reels with important information spoken by the central figures involved in the news event, so these may be used by the broadcast media as "activities." With this will be two brief stories written in broadcast style and format with a suggested release date. Television media kits will also contain a list of specific activities with visual appeal for television camera-people to photograph, as well as 16mm film or slides. The word *press* should never be used in a media kit. Press relates only to the *print* media; a PR person who thinks only in print terms is in the dark ages.

Media Kit Contents

Media kits have to be tailored for each occasion, and if mailed, they should also have a cover letter briefly explaining the event. The contents are as follows:

1. *Basic facts sheet* detailing newsmaking event and explaining significance in strictly factual terms. Include important dates, times, participants and rela-

tionships (for example, company to holding company). Be sure name, address and phone numbers where you can be reached for additional information are on sheet.

2. *Historical facts sheet* giving background of event, individual or organization involved. Use simple date-event format.

3. *Program of event or schedule of activities*, including detailed time data. Give script, when possible, for broadcast media.

4. *Straight news story*, never more than a page and a half of double-spaced typescript for print media and one or two short paragraphs for broadcast media. Give both print and broadcast versions to broadcast newspeople. The print news media need only print version.

5. *Complete list of all participants*, explaining their connection with the event.

6. *Biographical background of principals*, updated with current information about them given priority, unless something in background is particularly related to the event.

7. *Visual material*, consisting of 8 × 10 (or 5 × 7 if head shots of a person) black and white glossy prints for newspapers and magazines and 35mm color slides (transparencies) for television and publications using color. Be sure all are good quality, have significance (tell a story or show an important participant) and have *attached* identification. (If media kits are being mailed, you may want to send slick proofs but certainly not to broadcast media.)

8. A *longer general news story*, tying in background information. May be as long as three double-spaced pages for print media, full page for broadcast media (about 60 seconds of copy).

9. Two or three *feature* stories of varying lengths for print media. There will be no broadcast versions, but the features should be included in broadcast news kits for background.

10. A *page of special isolated facts* that are interesting and that will stand alone. These often are picked up for incorporation into copy written by the newspeople or used as fillers.

11. Any *brochures* available about the event or organization or person, prepared either for the event or earlier (if the latter, be *sure to update* in pen).

Don't forget electronic networks that can help. Put your material on a PR wire service. Have releases and photos (still and slides) ready for the newswire people and actualities (voice quotes) on cassettes for the radio networks (many state and regional ones extra) as well as film clips and videotapes for television.

Setting Up a Newsroom

The next most important planning should go into the media facilities during the event. Find out from the local media what they will need, and then plan for the out-of-town reporters.

Setting up and maintaining a newsroom or media facility for a convention, meeting or any special event requires planning and constant attention. The facility is for those responsible for getting the news and getting it out, so it must operate efficiently. When a newsroom is too small, badly located or understaffed, it can result in poor coverage. The following elements are essential for a smooth-running operation. (See also 10.6 for additional suggestions.)

1. All information must be easily available to media representatives. This means accessibility of news information, background material and releases, illustrations and people to be interviewed.

2. Select for the newsroom staff an experienced crew cognizant of the need to be helpful and friendly. The number of staffers depends on the size of the event and the expected news coverage indicated by past occasions. The importance of having one well-qualified person in charge cannot be over-emphasized. This should be someone able to handle emergencies, opportunities and delicate press or personality relations. Leaving the goodwill of an organization up to an inexperienced person can be damaging.

3. The newsroom must be separated from the traffic of the convention or meeting.

4. There should be separate interview rooms for print and broadcast reporters. It is advisable to have an interview "set" for television coverage, another area for radio interviewing and a third spot where newspaper and magazine reporters can talk with people. There should be plenty of wall plugs and extension cords for lights and other electronic equipment, such as a mult box.

5. Mini-cams and the TV vans have made coverage easier for their reporters. But some television equipment is still bulky, so large doors must be near for this equipment to be brought into the newsroom area. Get information in advance about electrical outlets and other essentials that the TV crews will require. At large news conferences, risers are usually necessary for each camera to have a clear shot.

6. A newsroom should have the following supplies: (a) telephones for local and long distance calls plus metro lines so surrounding cities can be dialed freely, voice transmission equipment for broadcast newspeople and, of course, telephone directories; (b) typewriters, electric and manual (power has been known to fail); (c) copy machines; (d) remote keyboards for electronic equipment; (e) Telex transmitters (electronic message senders) for wire stories; (f) bulletin boards and thumb tacks or blackboards with chalk and erasers; (g) individual desks or tables with comfortable chairs and good lighting; (h) coat hangers and space to hang coats; (i) wastebaskets; (j) paper, envelopes, pencils, correcting tape/fluid, erasers; (k) drinking water.

7. Providing food in the newsroom is practically a must. Food is worth the cost because reporters expect it, and it keeps them from wandering away from the meeting. How elaborate the food table is depends on the budget and generosity of the organization operating the newsroom. The basic requirements are coffee with donuts or rolls in the morning, sandwiches for lunch, and coffee and soft drinks throughout the day. Parties, however, should be held elsewhere. The distinction between working newspeople and partying newspeople is important. Never call a news conference unless it is a working situation; never have a party for newspeople and expect them to work. However, it is customary at large conventions to have a cocktail hour for the reporters at the end of the working day and to provide free tickets for evening meals. If lunchtime includes a regular session of the program, a media table should be set up in the eating area.

10.6 SETTING UP A NEWSROOM: ADDITIONAL POINTERS

Steve Lee, vice president of GSD&M makes the following useful observations about setting up a newsroom:

1. Out-of-town press too often have to remember, or search for in a crunch, telephone numbers and addresses of their local affiliate, nearby photo labs, quick eating places or fast food places that deliver, office supply shops, cleaners, etc. I simply create a list including all the things I would need if I were visiting from outside the city and add a good local media list, with station or publication affiliations. Add this list to a city map and it then becomes a part of the event's press material I provide explaining how the newsroom is set up and what is available.

2. I also use a sign-up sheet system in the newsroom for two reasons—so members of the press can see who's attending, and as an emergency "find 'em" system when the publisher calls to find their people (you would think they would tell their home office where they are staying, but they often do not).

3. A major problem at large conventions and conferences where manufacturers exhibit and supply media kits is the total disorganization these kits fall into on the second day of the show. To solve this problem I mount magazine racks to hold the kits apart and keep them in an orderly fashion. This looks better, is more professional and an exhibitor's public relations person can quickly see if they need to restock the newsroom. I put my "slot" prominent so daily releases and other information will be quickly seen and picked up.

4. More and more print journalists are using lap-portable computers that communicate back to the home office (this memo was written on a portable and uploaded to my micro for editing and printing). This recent trend requires us to think about plug-in telephone connections and newsroom telephones so these writers can communicate back to the office.
   This is not technically difficult as most single-line telephone connections are suitable. The telephone company should be asked to install the telephones with RJ11W or RJ11C type jacks (if you want to get technical). Many portable computers work simply off the telephone receiver, so no special instructions are needed.
   Some restrictions do apply—these computer devices cannot be connected to party lines or pay telephones and the telephone company must be alerted that an FCC registered device is to be used.
   Sharp newsroom organizers have added to their normal stash of misc. items like b&w and color film, an extra camera with flash attachment, extra spiral notebooks and other "newshound" items, the computer-necessitated items like batteries, common computer cables and jewelers' tools.
   One computer show I recently attended set up a computer bulletin board service (BBS) so press people could call in, by computer, from their hotel room and obtain highlights of the day's agenda, information on speakers and key exhibitors activities. This BBS stayed busy with both attending press and news people from out of the area who kept up with the show by this method. One publication downloaded every day's press info and constructed their conference overview from this information.
   This new trend in press tools is *not* slow in its growth. I'm seeing a multitude of desk-portable and lap-portable units appear at out-of-town events. It's fast, it's accurate and it's convenient. In fact, on press information we distribute for Docutel/Olivetti's office products, I'm finding more and more news media who will quickly accept computer-uploaded releases we send at the cost of a two-minute LD telephone call.

Private correspondence, October 6, 1983. Used by permission.

To protect the equipment a newsroom must be secure—for use only by authorized media representatives. It cannot be a social lounge for curiosity seekers, people looking for a cup of coffee (or other nourishment) and registrants to the meeting, who always seem to prefer the newsroom but get in the way. Visitors and unaccredited persons—regardless of who they may be—should be handled firmly and not admitted to the news area, where they are resented by the working newspeople.

To assure a good news operation, put yourself in the place of the reporter or editor. Evaluate what you would need to cover the meeting properly—then plan from that point. If your event didn't get the proper coverage, it's probably because the PR staff didn't really put the time, money and staff into a sincere effort.

Other Special Event Considerations

The day before the event, call local media as a reminder; you can check on their technical needs again at this time too. If you have something like the governor in a wheelchair (see 10.7) to dramatize the needs of the handicapped, or the Goodyear blimp as a symbol of publicity (see 10.8), you don't want to miss getting coverage.

Plan also for the tie-ins to the special event. Motels and businesses around town are usually willing to display special messages on their marquees, especially if the event is an annual attraction or has some civic interests (10.7 is an example of the advantage of others being tied into an event). If you have a boat show, football bowl game or state fair, having the Goodyear blimp attracts attention to the event, as well as to the blimp's sponsor.

Exhibits and displays can be developed and placed with institutions such as banks, utilities, schools and libraries. The Chamber of Commerce usually has a list of conventions and meetings that will be simultaneously going on, and a special offer might be made to the sponsors to show your exhibit or display, if attracting crowds is one purpose of the special event. For example, the Texas Parks and Recreation Department has a wildlife exhibit with real animals that can be booked for an event. Southwestern Bell Telephone has many historical exhibits that can be used by others. A word of caution about all these extras: Each tie-in has more details than a spiderweb has strands. (Plans that go awry also get reported; see 10.9.)

Promotions and Publicity Spin-offs

Often promotions generate publicity without much stimulation. One such situation was the publicity surrounding Marsteller, Inc.'s advertising campaign for Dannon yogurt. The Dannon commercials were filmed in Russia and featured a number of elderly citizens (such as an eighty-nine-year-old farmer and his mother), still hale and hearty, who were yogurt eaters. The commercials were filmed in Soviet Georgia where even some Russians are not allowed to go, so that itself created some interest. Then the commercials began to win awards, which inspired more attention. The photo of the eighty-nine-year-old farmer was chosen for the cover of a book, *The Best Things on TV Commercials*, by Jonathan

10.7 CAPTURING THE IDEA

WHEELCHAIR ANTICS. Governor David Pryor and other political and community leaders in Little Rock, Arkansas, were outfitted with wheelchairs for part of "Barriers Awareness Day." The officials went through the day on wheels to demonstrate the difficulties faced by Arkansans confined to wheelchairs.

Reprinted with permission of Wide World Photos.

Price, and the story of the filming of the commercials appeared as "Diary of a Commercial: Soviet Georgians Eat Yogurt" in Judy Fireman's *TV Book: The Ultimate Television Book*.

In the promotion of film talent, publicity is the name of the game. *Parade* writer Marguerite Michaels explains the formula like this: "The new system is based on four parts—the agent, the manager, the publicist and the would-be star. They generate their own law of supply and demand: the publicist creates the demand, the manager and agent supply the star."[4] The promoter of Farrah Fawcett-

---

[4]Marguerite Michaels, "How Hollywood Harvests the New Crop of Stars," *Parade*, July 23, 1978, pp. 4–5.

Dallas News staff photo by Rick Young

The Goodyear blimp — the ultimate in company trademarks.

Blimp gives PR big lift

By TOM BAYER

year.

name just about everybody — many today learn it as chil- wed at the intriguing Goodyear which happens to be maki

A station wagon and sedan provide additional transportation for the crew. Moran, who said the crew spends about 50 to 60 per cent of its time away me. explained the principle on p operates and example

FOR NIGHT FLYING and presenta- tion of the "Super Skytacular" display, as Goodyear calls it, the crew replaces the seats in th with elec- tronic

which will lift heavy loads straight up and then move them away.

"OUR GOAL NASA

Reprinted with permission of *Dallas Morning News.*

Majors, Jay Bernstein, took as a client Suzanne Somers, who was in ABC-TV's situation comedy, "Three's Company." The publicist on the job was Stu Ehrlich who said Suzanne "had a real Hollywood story. She was pregnant at 16, married at 17, divorced at 18. Carried the baby on her back to college classes. Waited tables, did modeling, lots of struggle. Published two volumes of poetry. Wonderful home- maker, wonderful mother." When an unfavorable story about the actress passing some bad checks threatened the image, Ehrlich turned it around by calling the news media who didn't break the story and offering them an "exclusive" giving the other side: The actress was broke and hungry at the time, the rent had been due and her son was ill. As her agent, Edgar Small, said, "It doesn't matter if the hype is vulgar or dumb. . . . It only matters if it works." P. T. Barnum would not quarrel with that, but most PR people would.

10.9 BAD PUBLICITY

DALLAS FORT WORTH BUSINESS
October 17, 1977

Perspective by John Powers, Editor

I realize there are people—even in public information positions—who do not like the press. That is not as hard to understand as you may think. They have to deal with the media daily, and it is more often than not unpleasant. Few newsmen are likeable. Even other newsmen don't like them.

But few public information people go to the trouble to belittle reporters in public or make their job more difficult when, in fact, it is their job to make things easy.

Take for example (name) college (place). A recent speaker there was Motorola Board Chairman Robert W. Galvin, who stated during a news conference, no less, that the press is important to the business community in getting its story told; that the press isn't to blame if businessmen don't give a good interview.

That press conference, under the direction of someone who will remain nameless to protect the guilty, was set up in the school's cafeteria—not the faculty club or some other private area. The cafeteria. With trays clanking in the background and students meandering around. One radio reporter gave up after being unable to get a decent tape. I heard one tape take by our reporter. The background noise was incredible.

Then, after the press conference, the officials trooped off to one end of the cafeteria. The press was not invited, but was told to go through the line with the students. The press was set up at one long table near a door. A door that was neatly closed at the end of the table to seal off the press as Mr. Galvin spoke to a luncheon group.

I am glad to report every member of the press got up, walked out and didn't go back.

Reprinted with permission of John Powers.

DEALING WITH THE MEDIA DURING EMERGENCIES

All of the California businesses, especially those in geologic fault areas, should be prepared for disaster. The news media are.[5] The *Wall Street Journal* says CBS may have the most elaborate battle plan for covering a major California earthquake. However, both the Associated Press and United Press International also have plans that include specific assignments. The WSJ said it didn't have an elaborate plan, but its Los Angeles bureau did buy a battery-powered radio and television set recently and plan to buy short-wave equipment.

PR people must deal with all sorts of unplanned things including disasters, explosions, fires, late flights, temperamental people. You must anticipate all the things that could happen and develop plans for handling them. No airline expects an airliner to crash, for example, but it must plan for such an event. Airlines have procedures for releasing information to the news media and handling relatives. They even have an arrangement to cancel advertising after a fatal crash. And such plans are not locked up somewhere for when disaster occurs. Likewise, everyone in PR should be trained in disaster procedure so that things go as smoothly as possible when the unexpected happens.

For some guidelines regarding crisis PR, see 10.10, which has been adapted

[5] Scot J. Paltrow, "News Crews, Expecting the Worst, Prepare to Cover a Major Earthquake in California," *Wall Street Journal*, Friday, June 24, 1983, sec. 2, p. 1.

Your operation must contain two specific areas that will serve as a central clearing point for reporters and company PR personnel in a serious emergency. These areas should be equipped with several telephones and some place for the people to sit and write. In the case of _____, one location should be _____ and the other _____.

If the emergency is centered in the area of one of the headquarters, the alternate location should be used. Additionally, company employees should be informed of this fact and thus able to direct reporters to the area from which news will be forthcoming.

At least two secretaries should be made available to the reporter handling public relations if the emergency takes place during working hours, since there will be times when this individual will, by necessity, be away from news headquarters.

If no news headquarters needs to be established, all calls from news media should be directed to one or two designated lines. While the PR person is out assessing the situation, names and phone numbers of callers are taken.

Handling PR in the Emergency

1. Need for the establishment of the news headquarters will be determined by the PR person. News headquarters will keep all visitors to the site under control and out of the way of any emergency work being done. Also, having a news service indicates the company's desire to be cooperative. The size of the emergency will determine whether there is a need for a headquarters.

2. The person handling public relations will maintain contact with reporters, make sure they stay in approved locations while on plant property, and provide as quickly as possible all information determined to be in the company's best interests.

3. The person handling public relations will check with _____ on the text of announcements and help formulate answers to questions.

4. The person handling public relations will be responsible for guiding reporters into the disaster area if company management will permit such a visit.

5. The fundamental responsibility for which facts are to be given to the press and ultimately to the public must remain with top management. It is the responsibility of the person handling public relations to operate with the approval of top management.

6. Maintain close contact with members of media. More often than not they will be able to tell you things you don't already know. This is a great way to stem the flow of false information.

7. Keep a log of all facts given out, with times they were released. This avoids duplication and conflicting reports should new developments change facts.

8. Do not release the names of the victims until you know for a fact that the families involved have been notified. Tell the reporters that the name of the victim will be made available as soon as the next of kin has been told of the mishap.

9. When it is necessary to admit a fact already known to the press, be sure confirmation is limited only to definite information that will not change. If fire fighters carry a victim from the plant in a body bag and the reporter sees it, say only that one body has been recovered. DO NOT SAY that you "don't know how many are dead." Never speculate as to the cause of accidents, amount of damage, responsibility, possible down-time, delays in shipments, layoffs, and so on.

In other words, say no more than to confirm what is already known, and yet give the reporters the impression the company will give all the assistance it possibly can. As facts that won't be harmful become known, clear them and give to news media people.

Questions to Look for in Emergencies

What reporters can get from other sources if forced to

1. Number of deaths.
2. Number of injuries.
3. Damage. (Fire chief will give estimate in dollars—give yours in *general* terms of what was destroyed as soon as known.)
4. What burned, collapsed, etc.
5. Time.
6. Location within plant (paint locker, press room, etc.).
7. Names of dead and injured, following notification of relatives.
8. Their addresses, ages and how long with company, as well as occupation.

9. How many people employed, what manufactured.

Facts desired but not necessarily desirable to give

1. Speculate on nothing.
2. Any delivery delays, etc. (Accentuate positive as soon as course if sure.)
3. How caused. (Let city officials release this— chances are story will die before report is completed.)
4. Specific damage estimates as well as what destroyed. (This information would be extremely valuable to competitors.)

Dealing with the Media During Emergencies

In meeting the press at the scene of emergencies, several things should be remembered. Basic is the fact that the public is represented by the press, and this medium has a recognized right to information that may vitally concern the community, employees, their friends and families, and the victims. It is also common knowledge that the best way to prevent the spread of false rumors and misinformation is through issuance of factual information. At the same time, the company must guard its own interests and insist on relaying factual information only in an orderly, controlled manner.

Remember:

1. Speed in reply to a query is all-important. All reporters have deadlines to meet.
2. Keep cool. If reporters get snappy, chances are it's because they are under considerably more pressure at the moment than you. Try to cooperate to the extent possible.
3. If you don't know the answer, attempt to get it for the reporters.
4. Eliminate obstacles wherever possible. Most reporters will agree that the more obstacles they find in their way, the harder they will work to ferret out the real story—from any source possible. They will almost always use something they have uncovered, and you have no control over what they might uncover.
5. Never ask to see a reporter's story. Time is usually a factor. If you feel the reporter may be misinformed, check back with him or her on the point to make sure.
6. There's seldom a reason why you should not be quoted by name. As a member of the management and one charged with the public relations, you are speaking for the company.
7. Never argue with a reporter about the value of a story.
8. Any information that goes to one source in the emergency is fair game to all. Don't play favorites. They listen to and read each other's copy anyway.
9. Never flatly refuse information. Always give a good reason why it isn't available. (Want to be sure facts are, indeed, factual. Getting information together, etc.)
10. Always know to whom you are talking. Get the reporter's name and phone number in case you need to contact him or her later.
11. Never give an answer that you feel might not stand up. It can embarrass you later.
12. Never falsify, color, or slant your answers. A reporter is trained to see a curve ball coming a mile away, and he's fielded them before. If he thinks you are pitching one at him, he'll remember it a long time and tell his colleagues and other members of the news media over coffee. This will also set him off quicker than getting no information at all.
13. Be especially alert about photographs. You have no control of photos taken off of company property, but you have every right to control photos taken within the plant. Consider the possibility of pool photos and movies where it is impractical to have several photographers on the scene at once. Remember, photos can be as harmful as words.
14. Be sure no time lag comes into play from the time you get information that can be put out and the time it is actually given to news media people.
15. Have safety, labor, employee records available for your reference if possible.
16. Be quick to point up long safety records and any acts of heroism by employees.
17. If damage must be estimated for press immediately, confine statement to general description of what was destroyed.
18. Always accentuate the positive and . . . if your public relations is good, so are your chances for an even break.

From *Public Relations Manual*, Eaton Corporation. Reprinted by permission.

from crisis-handling outlines developed by the Eaton Corporation, a diversified company that made a reputation producing auto parts.

There are many types of crisis PR. One occurs when there is an accident involving property damage, loss of life or injuries. Planning for this type of crisis should always be part of public relations. Although events never occur precisely as expected, of course, some ground rules for handling them should be developed, explained and put in the hands of those who will need to implement them. In an emergency situation it is necessary to facilitate the media coverage the event will attract. *Facilitate* is the proper word, not control. Openness and honesty are not only the best policy, they are the only policy.

Crises and the Bottom Line

Crises always are public relations problems and often the consequences are financial. The impact of crisis on the bottom line is suggested by the following cases:

1. *Three Mile Island*: Major technical difficulties, but no significant releases of radiation or deaths or traceable health damage. Result: Lack of emergency plans and ability to work with media. Metropolitan Edison plant is still closed.

2. *Love Canal*: No proof of health problems and no death. Hooker Corporation donates $1 million to clean up site. Sold twenty-seven years prior to incident. Company gets bad TV coverage. Responds. Public reaction hostile.

3. *Firestone 500*: Deaths and injuries due to faulty tires. Recall urged by National Highway Safety Administration. Not done. Company reputed to be in serious difficulty.

4. *Rely Tampons*: Supposedly related to cause of toxic shock syndrome. Voluntary and prompt recall. Company seen as caring; confidence holds.

5. *Hyatt Hotel* in Kansas City: Skywalk collapses. One injured woman (paralyzed neck down) wins highest damage award ever awarded.

6. *Nestlé*: Infant deaths in third world due to marketing of formula. Company disputed claims, got involved with argument in bottle versus breast; conflict put company opposite World Council of Churches. Boycott of Nestlé products and negative press. PR problem due to failure to anticipate sensitive issue and letting it get out of hand.[6]

It is essential to set up emergency, temporary, usually on-site media headquarters where briefings may be given, bulletins posted and news transmitted.

If an emergency is long term and serious, as in natural disasters, rumor headquarters also must be set up and staffed. In the absence of fact, there will be fab-

---

[6]"Comparison of Recent Cases Suggests PR Philosophy, Willingness to Face up to Bad Situations Is Worth Real Dollars on the Bottom Line," *pr reporter*, November 17, 1980; Dean Rotbart, "State of Alarm, Tampon Industry Is in Throes of Change After Toxic Shock," *Wall Street Journal*, February 26, 1982, pp. 1, 19; Thomas Petzinger, Jr., and Heywood Klein, "Haunted Hotel, Building Snags Dogged the Kansas City Hyatt that Collapsed—1981," *Wall Street Journal*, October 8, 1982, pp. 1, 22; "Burson-Marsteller Report," Spring 1981, p. 3.

Reprinted with permission of Roland Michaud.

rication. The following advice on handling rumor comes from communications specialist Walter St. John.[7] First, try to avoid situations that contribute to a climate in which rumor grows.

Factors Encouraging Rumors

1. Authentic and official information and news is lacking.
2. Authentic information is incomplete.
3. Situations are loaded with anxiety and fear.
4. Doubts exist because of the existence of erroneous information.
5. People's ego needs are not being met (satisfaction from possessing the "inside dope").

[7]Walter D. St. John, *A Guide to Effective Communication*. Copies available from author, Department of Education, Keene State College, Keene, NH 03431.

6. Prolonged delays occur on decision making on important matters.

7. Personnel feel they can't control conditions or their fate.

8. Serious organizational problems exist.

9. Organizational conflict and personal antagonisms are excessive.

Combating Rumors

1. Analyze the scope and seriousness of the nature and impact of the rumor before planning and engaging in any active correction (sometimes it is best to merely ignore the rumor).

2. Analyze the specific causes, motives, sources and disseminators of the rumors.

3. Confer with persons affected by or being damaged by rumors—level with them and assure them of your concern and of attempts to combat the rumors effectively.

4. Proceed to immediately (and massively if it appears advisable) supply complete and authentic information regarding the matter.

5. Feed the grapevine yourself with counterrumors placed by trusted colleagues and confidants.

6. Call the key status and informal leaders, opinion molders, and other influential people together to discuss and clarify the situation and solicit their support and assistance.

7. Avoid referring to the rumor in disseminating the truth. (You don't want to reinforce the rumor itself.)

8. Conduct meetings with the staff at the grass-roots level to dispel the rumors if you deem this approach to be necessary.

Once rumors begin to travel, they spread with considerable speed, and it is extremely difficult to stop them. The best way to combat rumors is to restrict the need for them in the first place by keeping people promptly and accurately informed and by maintaining good two-way communication.

TECHNOLOGY AND PR

A deskman on a New York paper called a friend one day during a strike. "Guess what I have?" he said. No newspaper in the city had been published for several days.

"Nothing to do?" the friend replied.

"Right," the deskman said, "but the New York PR people don't know it. I have three telegrams, five special delivery letters and four just arrived by messenger—all news releases."

The failure to get publicity is often the result of ignorance. It's a PR person's job to keep up.

One area in which a PR person must keep up is in the new technology of mass communications. Recent developments particularly significant to public relations are (1) the use of computers for storing, sending, receiving and producing information, (2) the growth of satellite transmission and cable video, and (3) the growth of specialized PR services, including the monitoring of broadcasts to catch publicity (a parallel to the print media clipping services) and computerized graphics. (To appreciate the potential of new technology, see 10.11.)

Typesetting and Printing Processes

Public relations practitioners began to feel the impact of new technology in the newsrooms early in 1973, and it has increased continuously since then. All news releases that came in used to be simply "processed" with all other newspaper copy, including stories generated by the staff. Often a good publicity release would be checked over by a reporter and go to the copy desk for editing. It had a reasonably good chance for survival.

However, with newspapers converted to photo-offset printing and using visual display terminals (VDTs) to put stories directly into their computer, publicity releases *must* be retyped. The chances of its being used decrease considerably and the chances of its being used "as is" are almost nonexistent. Before electronic handling of copy, it was easier for copy to be "edited" and thrown in with newspaper-originated material to be edited and set in type. The electronic process means that fewer pieces of publicity are going to survive. To escape discard, both staff and agency public relations practitioners are originating electronically acceptable copy.

PR Wire Services

Specialized wire services carry public relations news directly into the nation's newsrooms, both broadcast and newspapers. This capability is especially important for the new technology of newspapers, since the newswires provide tape that can be fed directly into the computers for typesetting. First begun in 1954, the publicity wire concept began to catch on as a result of the technological advances of the media. Its use was further stimulated by the simultaneous disclosure decision of the Texas Gulf Sulphur case (see Chapter 14, p. 413).

There are now more than a dozen privately owned teletype services offering simultaneous transmission of news releases and providing a rather efficient national network. Although they charge for their services, they are run much like news bureaus, and the editors in the bureaus may reject copy as they try to exercise some judgment about what is moved on their wires. Most operate only Monday through Friday, although special arrangements can be made for evening or weekend transmission. An exception is PR Newswire. It is staffed seven days a week, 24 hours a day. Most of the PR wire services charge clients an annual fee and then charge for each release, the price depending on the distribution ordered. A surcharge is usually added for larger than average releases (more than 400 words). In addition to publicity, clients may send advisories or invitations, such as for news conferences. PR Newswire now has a Boston office for its New England

TRY THIS APPROACH FOR BREAKING NEWS

Daniel Johnson

Pratt & Whitney had a very big story to tell last December. It expected to win a contract from Delta Airlines for production of the most fuel-efficient jet aircraft engine ever developed. If the deal came through (and it was by no means certain until the day it was announced) Pratt & Whitney would ring up the largest commercial engine sale in aviation history—$600 million.

This story was a natural for audiences all over the country affected by such news—air travelers, of course, but much more particularly the communities, subcontractors, and competitors involved with Delta, Pratt & Whitney and Boeing (which was building for Delta the fleet of 757s that would receive the engines). We were dealing with a technological breakthrough designed to save significant amounts of energy and enhance United States leadership in the aviation industries.

Our suggested approach for breaking the story was the first satellite video release. Pratt & Whitney agreed and we began phase I: determining what would be needed.
Our shopping list:

- A fully equipped TV news crew to cover the news conference, which probably would be held at Delta headquarters in Atlanta but could be held in Hartford, Pratt & Whitney's home base;
- A satellite and time reserved for the transmission;
- A prepared-in-advance videotape showing and explaining the new engine and the new Boeing aircraft it would power;
- Arrangements to quickly edit the videotaped news conference to present the highlights in a five-minute segment;
- Arrangements for a local station, in Atlanta or Hartford, to handle the first stage of the transmission to the satellite;
- Advance notice to TV news directors at stations in some 35 major markets detailing what they could expect and exactly when they would be able to receive the feed from the satellite. (We decided on three feeds, spaced 15 minutes apart, to give the stations some flexibility in receiving the feed and to give our people a maximum amount of time to alert the news directors.)

Everything Fell into Place

Assembling the crew was no problem. DWJ has crews going on "shoots" all over the country and abroad for a variety of clients. We do territory. Its Los Angeles wire office has a broad coverage of Southern California, serving about thirty distribution points in the Los Angeles area as well as newspapers from San Diego to Seattle to Phoenix. Besides these newspapers, the PR Newswire's "basic news line" includes the broadcast networks and eight newswires—AP, UPI, Dow Jones, Reuters, Manufacts Newswire, USIA, French News Agency and Jiji of Japan. PR Newswire acquired PR Wire Service, Inc., which covered fifteen states from Maine to Florida to Minnesota and other market areas.

A rival operation is the Business Wire, based in San Francisco and the only other PR wire with national coverage. Chet Herald, Jr., Business Wire vice president, says Business Wire serves more than 200 daily newspapers in thirty-three states from New England to Hawaii and from Alaska to Florida. In addition to the San Francisco base, Business Wire also has offices in Los Angeles, Seattle, Boston and New York. The press relations wire counts more than 2,000 customers. Its news circuits reach a total of more than 400 daily newspapers, newswire services, financial disclosure points such as stock exchanges, broadcast systems, trade publications and bureaus of overseas publications and news services.

our own editing and other production and supply the results.

Similarly, production of the videotape B Roll, showing the Pratt & Whitney engine and the new Boeing 757, edited to 90 seconds, was done in our own studios. We also edited the news conference tape.

Hartford was picked for the news conference and we got WFSB-TV to handle the transmission to the satellite ground station in northern New Jersey, where it was combined with the pretaped B Roll.

We selected Western Union's Westar III satellite as the facility best suited to our needs, and reserved time early in the week of December 15 for what we expected would be transmission from Atlanta on December 18 at 4 P.M. Before the eventual transmission from Hartford shortly after 5 P.M. on the 18th, the reservation had to be changed twice, once to Friday when it appeared the conference would be delayed.

We were able to complete editing within an hour of the close of the news conference and get the transmission from WFSB-TV to Western Union and via Westar III to TV stations around the country by 5:30 P.M., one hour after editing began.

Our reports show we reached an adult audience of 9 million (Nielsen figures) on the 21 stations carrying the Delta-P&W story in such cities as New York, Washington, Los Angeles, Seattle, Miami, Atlanta and Chicago. This compares quite favorably with the estimated total viewers of ABC's "World News Tonight" each evening.

We define the satellite video release as breaking news recorded on videotape and released via satellite and local satellite-receive dishes to local TV news operations in widely separated markets.

The key phrase is "breaking news." Pre-break announcements or news reported well after the fact are not candidates for this approach.

The satellite video release solves the problem of getting your story covered—and, usually, with sufficient time devoted to your news event. The story is covered because your crew covers it. It arrives in the local TV newsroom in a form and length you select. Of course, local stations may cut your story, but certainly not down to network length.

The concept is less than a year old, but it has enormous potential for solving difficult communication problems.

Daniel Johnson, "Try This Approach for Breaking News," *Public Relations Journal*, 37, no. 9, pp. 28–29 (September 1981). Reprinted by permission. Mr. Johnson is a managing partner of DWJ Associates, Inc., New York, and former executive producer of WNEW-TV (New York) "10 O'Clock News."

Analyst Wire is Business Wire's private-line newswire network reaching about sixty firms and institutions in the investment banking, securities trading and stock-watch fields. Analyst Wire is a supplement to news-circuit coverage for financial disclosure news releases.

Business Wire also supplies news to information access and data retrieval services to aid public relations research.

Third largest is the Intermedia Group, Inc., based in Southfield, Michigan. In Detroit the company operates under the name of Press Relations Newswire; in Atlanta, Southeastern Press Relations Newswire; in Cleveland, Ohio Media Newswire; and in Washington, D.C., Press Relations Wire.

Chicago is served by PR News Service, which also goes to other cities through affiliated wires. Dallas/Ft. Worth is served by Southwest Newswire, Inc., which covers other major Texas cities and Oklahoma City and Tulsa in Oklahoma.

The largest service, PR Newswire in New York, originated in 1954. In this system a bureau receives releases from clients by messenger, TWX and Telex (commercial wire service direct transmission), telegram, mail and phone. After editing and processing, it offers a basic 300-word-a-minute transmission to a national news line, with many transmissions directly to newspaper computers at 1,200 wpm.

PR Newswire Executive Editor Roland Eckman says the company offers a choice of local, regional or national "News-Lines" that may be ordered as required. It can also provide international distribution to any country in the world. PR Newswire's most popular News-Line is the "Basic News-Line," which serves more than 150 news points in fifty cities, including sixty points in New York City alone—all wire services, newspapers, radio/TV stations and special publications—and newspapers in cities in the East, Southeast, Midwest and Southwest. Its regional lines include the western United States (101 media in fifty-one cities in eight states), Florida, New York (State), New Jersey and New England. PR Newswire serves more than 400 media on all of its lines.

Eckman says an important adjunct to these News-Lines for corporate financial releases is the Investors Research Wire, which transmits the release, in full, to many of the nations's largest brokerage houses, stock exchanges and other financial institutions.

More recently, Eckman says, PR Newswire began transmitting all releases to a number of data bases, including NEXIS, where they can be easily retrieved—again in full—by editors or financial analysts studying a company or an industry.

PR Newswire was among the first wire services in the world to use electronic editing terminals in 1970 and now is fully computerized for faster processing of copy in its offices and for transmission. All copy is formatted to ANPA (American Newspaper Publishers Association) standards and is compatible with newspaper computers around the country.

One particular advantage of the public relations wire services to practitioners is the national coverage now available for the clients of a practitioner working from a single base. Before the wire operation, many practitioners tried to make arrangements with agencies in other cities to help handle out-of-town releases. It was a Rube Goldberg operation at best. Also, it depended greatly on *who* the practitioner knew in other cities. Now it is a strictly business arrangement, easily arranged and with predictable results.

Another advantage to the practitioner is the editorial acceptance of the PR wires. Because copy is carefully checked by PR newswire bureau chiefs before it is moved (even though the practitioners supplying the material are "clients" of the newswire), there is a double check on details, timeliness and other elements that often make PR copy unacceptable. To preserve their own reputations, the PR news bureaus won't move inferior or inaccurate copy. They have built a reputation for reliability with the media they service.

Perhaps best of all, the PR wires are already in the newsroom. Many metropolitan dailies have a PR wire ticking away right beside the Associated Press, United Press International and Reuters. The copy is pulled from that source and considered for use on its merits. Often mailed releases are never even opened by reporters—if they reach them at all. Also, mail service may be delayed by lack of weekend delivery or holiday closing. For all these reasons, a newswire service is a good investment when national coverage is desired, timing is significant and the budget allows.

Use of international circuits has been low, according to Ben Soderquist,

Southwest Newswire president, but investor wires have grown greatly, as has the use of news retrieval. Southwest accesses news articles and analyzes forecasts and stock trading patterns for its clients.

In other expanded services, satellite transmission of newsclip material has been available since 1982 through Newslink (210 East 36th St., New York, NY 10016). Newslink can reach any market where satellite transmission can be received by broadcast stations.

Other Electronic Applications

When a PR person gets a story of regional or national interest in a local paper, there is a good chance that the story will get regular newswire service attention. Once it was necessary for the story to be filed by a newswire editor with the wire service. Today, however, the Associated Press wire service has something called an "electronic carbon." This is a computer-to-computer hookup that allows newspapers to send copies of their stories instantly into local AP bureau computers. The increased flow of stories from member papers to the bureaus increases the use by other papers of PR-generated stories of regional or national significance.

Another AP computer advance is better control of laser photos so that photo-editors will get an opportunity to crop, enlarge, reduce, brighten, darken or otherwise improve the quality of the overseas send.

Newspapers' electronic information delivery systems (EIS) are copy cannibals—immediately relaying facts, breaking news, sports scores, retest stock reports and such. EIS has enlarged the news hole. Cable is another cannibal, using programming 24 hours a day. Much of cable's programming gives PR practitioners special opportunities to reach some TV audiences without the commercial costs. For example, sponsored films can be used on cable, health information from the American Heart Association or the Cancer Society can be shown, and museums can preview new exhibitions.

PR agencies are also finding that computers make preparing graphics much easier. Computer programs are available that permit instant call-up of common illustrations like bar charts and pie charts. The computer system, coordinated by General Electric, has programs stored in it for each type of chart or graph.[8] The artist works on a visual display terminal (VDT) with a lighted display board. The programs contain different designs and type sizes so that the artist, to create a pie chart, for example, must simply type the percentage of the pie to be dissected and the computer does the work. The pie can even be tilted for a three-dimensional effect. The system also allows slides to be produced for meetings and publications.

More exotic uses of computer graphics are described by Dr. James Blinn.

Computer graphics is an efficient way to simulate space photography because it lends itself easily to the function. The pictures can range from simple line drawings to com-

---

[8]See Hirotaka Takenchi and Allan H. Schmidt, "New Promise of Computer Graphics," *Harvard Business Review*, 58, no. 1 (January/February 1980), pp. 122–131.

plex three-dimensional color ones. To make simple drawings, a human being draws on a digitized tablet. The tablet has a special surface, and as the artist moves an electronic pen across the tablet, the computer determines the position of the pen and by using simple arithmetic reproduces the number of the position on a black and white screen.

Three-dimensional pictures can be elicited by a computer basically by assigning a different number for the horizontal, vertical and depth positions. With an elaborate program and data one can project a fairly realistic representation of a picture. However, the computer's calculations are so mathematically precise that the resulting image often appears too perfect, too smooth, unlike real objects, so it becomes necessary to apply various techniques to generate some irregularities. The computer can be given information that will allow it to project highlights, texture, dents, holes and colors. There are many ways of achieving these effects, but they all require the computer to do some arithmetic.[9]

Another electronic advancement that is helping PR people keep up with publicity in the broadcast media is videotape recorder systems, which allow programs to be captured for a "clipping file" that can be used for television promotions. And a new audiovisual tool is the multi-image slide show Jerome McGarry calls the glamour audiovisual of this decade.[10] (The multi-image slide show uses from two to 22 or more projectors covering walls and ceilings, with images changing so quickly that it seems like a film.) Finally, PR in-house use of technology includes access to a variety of data banks, use of word processors to store and manipulate large amounts of data, and communication by teleconferences and electronic mail systems.

POINTS TO REMEMBER

- Personal and professional relationships are critical to working successfully with the news media.
- Before contacting the media, you must do advance work in gathering ideas and information; this includes preparing the story and planning publicity photos and illustrations.
- A PR person has to have the news sense and judgment of news media people and the appropriate professional skills.
- Keeping a complete, updated file is essential in working with news media, as is anticipating news media needs and treatments.
- Four groups of media people are especially important to the publicist: newspeople, production people, other PR people and free-lance writers. Professional standards must be maintained in all these relationships.
- PR people need to prepare management and other corporate spokespeople for

[9]James Blinn, "Photography," Interface, Communications-on-Line: Tapping New Technologies, vol. 3 (Fullerton, Calif.: California State University Department of Communications, 1982).

[10]Jerome McGarry, "Visual Communications: A Look Ahead," *Interface*, vol. 3, 1982. California State University, Fullerton, Department of Communications, p. 27.

their contacts with news media and the public. There are several sources for guidelines for preparing for press and TV interviews.

- Contracts help avoid potential trouble with media arrangements and make deadlines easier to enforce.

- Media kit contents may vary, but basically include the following: facts sheets, program of events, news story, list of participants with photo and bios, visual materials, special facts and special stories.

- Some of the elements necessary in setting up an efficient working space for newspeople are as follows: accessible information, friendly and efficient staff, sufficient space for equipment, full communication supplies and food.

- Crisis PR demands advance planning, constant alertness to details and control of communication.

- Recent developments in the technology of mass communications include the use of computers for information storage and retrieval, the growth of satellite transmission and cable video, and the growth of specialized PR services, including PR wire services and computerized graphics.

THINGS TO DO

Evaluate two media kits, including one prepared for the broadcast media. Some questions to ask are the following:

1. Can the news media use the materials "as is"?
2. Are resource materials offered, such as background or history of corporation, biographies of chief executives, photographs of these with captions attended and some "stock" shots of the event, of the company and so on that reveal action but have no time element?
3. Is the material attractively packaged and easily arranged for use?
4. Does the material reflect careful, thoughtful preparation?

SELECTED READINGS AND SERVICES

Readings

John Budd, *Corporate Video in Focus* (Englewood Cliffs, N.J.: Prentice-Hall, 1983). A "how-to book" for using video effectively.

Lincoln Diamant, ed., *The Broadcast Communications Dictionary*, 2d ed. (New York: Hastings House, 1978). More than 4,000 terms to help those unfamiliar with broadcast media.

Albert Feldman, ed., *Inside News Broadcasting* (Washington Depot, Conn.: Public Relations Plus, 1973). Seminar transcript with input from ABC, CBS, NBC, UPI and United Press Independent Television News.

Clarence Jones, *How to Speak TV: A Self-Defense Manual When You're In the News* (Marathon, Fla.: Video Consultants, Inc., 1983). A good guide with easy to locate references.

Otto Kleppner and Thomas Russell, *Otto Kleppner's Advertising Procedure*, 8th ed. (Englewood Cliffs, N.J.: Prentice-Hall, 1983). Update of valuable book.

Lee Loevinger, "The Politics of Advertising" (New York: Television Information Office, 1973). Address on counteradvertising before International Radio and Television Society.

Burns W. Roper, "Trends in Attitudes Towards Television and Other Media—A Twenty-Four Year Review" (New York: Television Information Office, 1983). A review and comparison of responses to their polls over the years.

Christopher M. Sterling and Timothy R. Haight, *The Mass Media Aspen Institute Guide to Communication Industry Trends* (New York: Praeger, 1978). Analysis of source reliability and validity; 300 tables of data on media industries; references listed for each subject.

Laurence Urdang, ed., *Dictionary of Advertising Terms* (Chicago: Crain Books, 1979). Helpful for those with little ad experience.

Roberta Webb, ed., *The Washington Post Deskbook on Style* (New York: McGraw-Hill, 1978). Deals with issues such as newspaper standards and fairness and problems of usage such as sexism; also serves as a guide for grammar, spelling and punctuation.

Lubomyr R. Wynar and Anna T. Wynar, *Encyclopedic Directory of Ethnic Newspapers and Periodicals in the U.S.*, 2d ed. (Littleton, Colo, P.O. Box 263, 1976). Gives newspapers and periodicals published by sixty-one U.S. ethnic groups; describes content.

"When I see or read something in the media that I don't like . . ." (Brookfield, Wis.: Rexnard Resource Center with the First Amendment Congress, 1982). An excellent booklet with comments of outstanding people in the field and some inserts suggesting how to talk back.

Services

The following descriptions are based on information provided by the services.

- *Anagraphics, Inc.*, 104 West 29th St., New York, NY 10001. Complete in-house design and production facilities for audiovisual presentations and commercial art preparation. Slides, multiimage, videotape, posters, brochures, charts, annual reports.

- *Associated Release Service*, 2 North Riverside Plaza, Chicago, IL 60606. Traces which newspapers, television and radio stations are current users of publicity features, then mails in proper format for clients. Feedback is provided with slips and reply cards, plus typed analyses.

- *Audio Features, Inc.*, 20 East 53rd St., New York, NY 10022. Develops and produces voiced radio news and feature reports for clients and distributes them daily by satellite to approximately 2,000 radio stations nationwide via the broadcast facilities of the Associated Press and United Press International radio networks.

- *Bacon's*, 332 South Michigan Ave., Chicago, IL 60604. A complete package for all public relations and media information needs. Press clippings, publicity, research, ads, competitive reports, media placement analyses. Publicity distribution: 100,000 daily updated media contacts; printing, photo assembly and mailing facilities; on-line access to Bacon's Media Bank. Media directories: magazines, newspapers, domestic and international, and new companion service, *Media Alerts*.

- *Burrelle's Press Clipping Service*, Box 7, Livingston, NJ 07039. Press clipping, television monitoring, information search services, media directories and competitive advertising reports.

- *Business Wire*, 235 Montgomery St., San Francisco, CA 94104. A national press relations wire service reaching more than 400 media across the country via a private-line data communication network. It also transmits news releases to the securities research industry and to certain news retrieval data bases.

- *By/Media, Inc.*, 380 Madison Ave., New York, NY 10017. Offers a full range of electronic media services for the public relations profession. Satellite services include regularly scheduled satellite feeds to more than 400 television stations. By/Media produces and uses existing newsclips, industrials, "infomercials" and other programming suitable for distribution. In addition to cable services, By/Media also produces teleconferences, syndicated broadcast programming, multimedia productions and videodiscs.

- *Connecticut Cartoonists Associates, Inc.*, 14 White Pine Dr., Brookfield Center, CT 06805. An organization of nationally and internationally known artists and illustrators providing professional cartoons, slides, illustrations and other artistic support services to business and industry.

- *Dialog Information Services, Inc.*, 3460 Hillview Ave., Palo Alto, CA 94304. The world's largest information retrieval service currently offering more than 180 data bases in such subject areas as advertising, business (information on companies and products), science and technology.

- *Docuvid*, 220 East 23rd St., 10th floor, New York, NY 10010. The nation's largest independent television news organization with full-service news bureau and satellite organization in Washington, D.C. and New York City. Docuvid's production division produces and distributes video news releases, as well as industrials, commercials, public service spots, training tapes, documentaries and corporate image productions.

- *Dow Jones & Co., Inc. (The Wall Street Journal)*, 420 Lexington Ave., Suite 2540, New York, NY 10017. Dow Jones & Co., Inc., a publishing and communications company, publishes national publications and information services, general-interest community newspapers and books. Dow Jones has equity or other interests in international business and financial wire services; in several English-language publications based in Asia and Europe; in newsprint production; and in telecommunications equipment manufacturing and rental.

- *The Editor & Publisher Co., Inc.*, 575 Lexington Ave., New York, NY 10022. Weekly news magazine of the newspaper industry.

- *Gateway Productions, Inc. (Subsidiary of The Gannett Company, Inc.)*, 304 East 45th St., New York, NY 10017. Producers of films, videotapes, slide presentations and video teleconferences for the corporate community. Also offered are post-production services in both videotape and film.

- *HDO Productions, Inc.*, 237 Melvin Dr., Northbrook, IL 60062. Renters of colorful tent pavilions and free-span structures for all sorts of events. Serving the nation from fully staffed offices/warehouses in New York, Washington, D.C., Chicago and Los Angeles.

- *Heritage Classics, Inc.*, One East Gate Plaza, Morgantown, WV 26565. Designers and manufacturers of high-quality, customized awards, gifts, office decor and desk accessories. Made of top-quality materials—gold on fine pewter, bronze, enamels. Mounted on hand-made wood components in solid rosewood, walnut and oak.

■ *Hi-Net Communications, Inc.*, 3796 Lamar Ave., Memphis, TN 38195. Full-service meeting planning and video teleconferencing to include 300 permanently installed earth stations at Holiday Inn hotels. Satellite transponders uplink facilities and on-site technicians and coordinators.

■ *The Jones Colad Group*, 701 Seneca St., Buffalo, NY 14210. Designers and manufacturers of custom presentation and promotional products. Binders, indexes, folders, boxes and point-of-purchase displays are available in vinyl, film-laminated paperboard, poly- and turned-edge construction.

■ *Karol Media, Inc.*, 625 From Road, Paramus, NY 07652. A sponsored film distributor.

■ *Larimi Communications*, 151 East 50th St., New York, NY 10022. Practical media guides for the public relations professional now include television contacts, radio contacts, television news, cable contact yearbook, trade media news, contacts newsletter, cable hotline. Company also sponsors the National Media Conference.

■ *The Leadership Network*, 254 Fifth Ave., New York, NY 10001. A group of seven of America's premier magazines on public affairs, the arts, the sciences, communication and business, combined as a group to offer the advertiser a market of more than 560,000 affluent and influential subscribers.

■ *Luce Press Clippings, Inc.*, 420 Lexington Ave., New York, NY 10017. Public relations evaluation through clippings. Television monitoring across the nation.

■ *Mead Data Central*, 200 Park Ave., New York, NY 10166. MEXIS is a computer-assisted information retrieval service that provides instant access to the full texts of stories from leading newspapers, magazines, wire services, newsletters and other information sources.

■ *Meadia Distribution Services*, 307 West 36th St., New York, NY 10018. An organization serving public relations executives and publicists in the production and distribution of press and financial information, speeches, reports, newsletters and other materials to media, security analysts, selected target audiences and other special publics.

■ *Modern Talking Picture Service*, 5000 Park Street N., St. Petersburg, FL 22709. World's largest distributor of general- and special-interest public relations films, videocassettes and collateral materials available on free loan to educational and community groups, theaters and television stations. Modern Satellite Network division broadcasts daily to more than eight million cable television homes. Sales offices in New York, Chicago, Washington, D.C. and San Francisco.

■ *Newslink, Inc.*, 210 East 36th St., New York, NY 10016. Provides satellite distribution service for video publicity material, as well as comprehensive consultant services for special corporate communication projects involving television news.

■ *News/Sports Radio Network*, 9431 West Beloit Road, Milwaukee, WI 53227. With offices in Chicago, Los Angeles, Philadelphia and Milwaukee, company covers news, feature and public relations events for nation's largest public relations firms, corporations and associations and provides broadcast-ready stories to radio stations on both nationwide and selected market basis.

■ *North American Precis Syndicate, Inc.*, 201 East 42nd St., New York, NY 10017. Distributes news releases for most *Fortune* 500 companies to suburban dailies and weeklies, television news and talk shows, radio and through an affiliate to minority media. Public relations executives receive clippings, broadcast usage cards, computer printouts with audience and circulation data and usage maps.

- *PR Aids, Inc.*, 330 West 34th St., New York, NY 10001. A complete press release distribution service providing targeted mailing lists of media contacts to any editorial categories and types of media specified by the customer. Once the list is generated, PR Aids can produce, assemble and mail all printed material and photographs—usually within 24 hours.

- *PR Data Systems, Inc.*, 33 Danbury Road, Wilton, CT 06897. A computerized "closed loop" media management system. Provides more efficient media planning, release distribution, clipping feedback and media usage analysis. Option available for remote access to bring total function in-house.

- *PR Newswire*, 150 East 58th St., New York, NY 10155. The firm now reaches the nation's news media by satellite and sends news releases into a growing number of data bases.

- *Rathe Productions*, 555 West 23rd St., New York, NY 10011. Designs and fabricates environments, permanent and temporary exhibits, museums and promotional events.

- *SCW, Inc.*, 20433 Nordoff St., Chatsworth, CA 91311. Publishes newspaper editorial supplements, currently eighteen a year. Newspapers build special advertising sections using the supplement content for editorial fill-in copy. If sections are not sold, the different editors use the supplement content for daily and weekly fill-in needs.

- *Sheridan-Elson Communications, Inc.*, 355 Lexington Ave., New York, NY 10017. The firm specializes in the production and distribution of video news releases, films for television, documentaries, radio news releases and audiovisual presentations. Fully equipped for audio, film and 3/4-inch video editing, as well as programming and pulsing A/V presentations.

- *Trans Global Films, Inc.*, 645 Madison Ave., New York, NY 10022. Sponsored inflight entertainment. Seventeen airlines in network; films reach 4.5 million viewers monthly, all over the world.

- *Videostar Connections, Inc.*, 3390 Peachtree Road, Atlanta, GA 30326. A satellite communication company that provides complete communication services for satellite teleconferencing to first-class hotel meeting rooms throughout the United States and also to university sites through an agreement with the National University Teleconference Network (NUTN). Company takes total responsibility for transmission of domestic or international events.

- *VISCOM International*, International Bldg., Rockefeller Center, 630 Fifth Ave., 22nd floor, New York, NY 10111. International videoconferencing, special production and news crews situated throughout the world, international satellite distribution, film-tape library dating back to 1896, slide-map service of people, places and things in the news, sponsored films, program production and distribution, international standards conversion.

- *Evergreen Satellite Network*, 1733 Broadway, 2d floor, New York, NY 10019. Distributes newsclips, infomercials and other public relations materials to 500 television shows by satellite.

CHAPTER **11**

Details of PR Work

Modern education has frequently been criticized for turning out people who know a great deal more than they understand . . . it is only from concrete experience that one can really build up a capacity to discriminate, to be selective, that is, to be aware of differences.

Hadley Cantril

The success of most things Depends upon knowing how long it Will take to succeed.

Montesquieu, Pensées Diverses

Good public relations consists of (1) planning and (2) attention to detail. We will shortly discuss the importance of planning. Here we describe the details, the nuts and bolts, that make a good PR program possible.

NEWS RELEASE TIMING

These schedules have to be worked out to fit the media served in each case (see 11.1 and 11.2). Deadline, be it noted, means just that: the last minute for notification, not the preferable minute. You should let editors know your plans in advance, when possible, so they can put your story on their schedules.

SETTING UP FOR EVENTS

There are nine steps or stages in planning for meetings or special events such as dedications, open houses and plant tours:

1. Start planning early. Depending on the size of your event, a year in advance is not too soon.
2. Make a blueprint and timetable. Plan every detail no matter how minor, and assign responsibility for each. Have alternates selected as "backups." These can be one or two extras, people without specific assignments but involved in planning so they could step in if necessary. (See checklists 11.3 and 11.4 for special events and meetings.) Once you have all details listed, "walk through" the event mentally as a participant. You will find what you overlooked.

11.1 NEWS STORY DEADLINES FOR VARIOUS MEDIA*

Media	Type of News Story	Deadline*
Newspapers		
A.M. daily, local	General news	4 P.M. day before publication
	Breaking news	8 P.M. day before publication
	Breaking major stories	11 P.M. absolute last
	Features	Several weeks before anticipated publication
P.M. daily, local	General news	8 A.M.–4 P.M. day before publication
	Breaking story	7–9 A.M. day of publication
	New material or important development	10:30–11 A.M. day of publication
	Critical	2–2:30 P.M. (will make only last edition, and then only maybe)
	Features	Several weeks before anticipated publication
Sunday local	General news	First section and front pages close Saturday, usually by noon or early afternoon
	Section news and features	Usually 5 P.M. Wednesday deadline for preprinting on Friday
Weekly	All material	Four days prior to publication's own deadline, generally day before issue
News Wire Services	All material	Any time, but more amenable 9–4 weekdays; short-staffed weekends
PR Wire Services	All material	Some services available on week after business hours by arrangement
Television		
Network	Straight news	Call in to desk or feed to affiliate if local available 4–6 hours prior to airtime
	Breaking story	1 hour prior to airtime
	News on videotape	Send day in advance
Local	Straight news	2 hours prior to airtime
	Breaking news	1 hour prior to airtime
	News on videotape	4 hours prior to airtime
Radio		
Network	General news	Send release day in advance
	Breaking story	Call newsroom
Local	General news	Give release day before
	Breaking news	Need 45 minutes before newscast
Magazines		
Weekly	News	No later than Saturday noon for following Tuesday
	Features	Several weeks before expected use
Monthly	All material	On 10th of month preceding month of publication
	Photos (especially color)	First of month preceding month of publication

*Deadlines are general guidelines. Specific media may differ.

11.2 EXAMPLES OF NEWS RELEASES

Here are two examples of a story prepared for newspaper and broadcast news. The four daily newspapers in the area *each* got different stories. The broadcast version went to the radio and television stations, with TV also receiving a color slide of the choirboys in uniform.

```
TEXAS BOYS CHOIR
5617 Locke, Fort Worth, Texas 76104
Doug Newsom, AC 817-738-5420

                              FOR IMMEDIATE RELEASE

      MEMBERS OF THE TEXAS BOYS CHOIR OF FORT WORTH WILL BE
PERFORMING IN AN AMERICAN PREMIERE OF THE GIAN CARLO MENOTTI
(GEE·AN KAHR·LOH MEN·AH·TEE) SCIENCE FICTION-STYLED OPERA,
"HELP, HELP, THE GLOBOLINKS!" (GLAHB·OH·LINKS)

      "GLOBOLINKS" (GLAHB·OH·LINKS) IS BEING GIVEN BY THE
SANTA FE OPERA IN NEW MEXICO.  PERFORMANCE DATES FOR THE
AMERICAN PREMIERE ARE AUGUST FIRST, SIXTH, NINTH AND
FIFTEENTH.


                              - 30 -
```

```
TEXAS BOYS CHOIR
5617 Locke, Fort Worth, Texas 76104
Doug Newsom, AC 817-738-5420

                              FOR IMMEDIATE RELEASE

      Members of the Texas Boys Choir of Fort Worth are perform-
ing in the American premiere of Gian Carlo Menotti's "Help,
Help, The Globolinks" August 1, 6, 9 and 15 by the Santa Fe
Opera in New Mexico.

      "Globolinks" is Menotti's newest one-act, four-scene
opera "for children and those who love children," according
to the composer's own description.

      The Globolinks are space-age spooks whose mere touch
substitutes electronic noise for the sound of one's own voice
and eventually turns the one touched into one of them.  No-
thing frightens them away except musical tones.

      The operative science fiction story begins with a stranded
school bus full of children saved by their driver, Tony, who
scares away the Globolinks by sounding the horn.  A child armed
with her violin goes to defend her classmates.  There's con-
flict between a music-hating principal, who almost becomes a
Globolink, and a music teacher, Madame Euterpova.  The latter
character was hailed by reviewers seeing the world premiere as
"one of Menotti's most inspired creations."

      Choirboys performing in the opera are from the Choir's 43
members in New Mexico during the summer to appear in 13 per-
formances of the Santa Fe Opera and to work with the faculty
of the Summer Choral Institute being held by the Texas Boys
Choir with Highlands University in Las Vegas, New Mexico.


                              - 30 -
```

3. Form as many committees as you deem feasible. By involving management and employees in this event, you not only spread the workload but get the employees enthusiastic and knowledgeable.

4. Use company professionals wherever possible: artists, design personnel, copywriters, exhibit specialists and the like.

5. Provide special attractions to ensure attendance and to make the event memorable. Examples: prominent personalities, parades, concerts, dances, films, exhibits of historical materials, citations or awards, prizes and drawings, product demonstrations, tours of plants in operation. (See 11.5 and 11.6 for ideas.)

6. Have giveaways and souvenirs (they need not be expensive) for everyone. There should be different souvenirs for various target audiences. Personalize all items and tie them to the event. (Advertising specialty companies have brochures filled with suggestions.)

7. To ensure smooth flow of traffic, arrange for parking or, if the plant is a dis-

11.3 CHECKLIST FOR FACILITIES

Organization is essential in making sure significant details are not overlooked. One of the easiest ways is to make out a checklist far enough in advance—so that you can add those "middle of the night" thoughts to it in plenty of time to plan for and implement them.

1 Week Before	Day Before	Day of Event	Following Week
Complete media kits, including speeches, bios and photos, with event timing indicated for broadcast news.	Have kits available for news media on request.	Meet with news media representatives, distribute kits.	Follow up letters to news media represented.
Advance release out.			
Find out what special facilities news media will need and make arrangements for. Order all supplies and equipment for newsroom or media use area. Check for lighting, sound levels, electric outlets and so on.	Set up media area. Check out all equipment and special facilities. Check all visual displays and logos.	Recheck news media area to be sure all supplies and equipment ready for use.	
Draft final guest-acceptance list.			
Prepare guest information kits including program, brochures and the like.		Distribute guest information kits with badges.	
Prepare media, guest and host badges.	Set up physical facility and procedure for badge distribution.	Check badges and be sure badge issuance recorded.	
Make arrangements definite. Be specific and agree on contingency plans. Plan cleaning of site and arrange for any special decorations. Remember logos, displays and so on.	Check eating area and order. Be sure time of service, place and clean-up are clear. Check site, grounds, all facilities.	Check food preparation, delivery, service.	
Complete speeches and get adequate number of copies for kits, requests and files.	Have kits available for news media who cannot cover.		
Assign hosts for VIPs.	Check with VIP host to confirm schedules.	Be sure all VIPs' needs met.	
Arrange for any citations or presentation materials.	Check to be sure special presentation materials are on hand.	Be sure persons making presentation have materials.	
Detail any necessary safety precautions. Outline plan for emergency situation. Anticipate and be sure to communicate all emergency planning to all who might be involved.			Mail thank-yous.
Arrange for message board for media and guests. Have local airline schedules, taxi numbers, hotel and restaurant lists, with times and phone numbers available.			
Make final transportation and hotel arrangements for guests. If remote, plan transportation and hotel accommodations for news media also.			

11.4 MEETING OR SPEECHES CHECKLIST

This is perhaps the most common arrangement asked of PR people and one often carelessly handled. The following detailed list may be adapted for particular situations.

1. Set up a day in advance when possible; if not, at least two hours before program. Check *podium*; test podium light and microphone.

2. Find out what activity will be going on in the *room next to your speaker*; you don't want the speaker to have to yell to make him- or herself heard. When planning for a large group, it is important to see whether the hotel or restaurant also expects another large group and, if so, what that group is. If your group consists of retired schoolteachers, they may not enjoy being housed in a moderate-sized hotel with a group of boisterous rodeo riders.

3. Check out *sound system*, amplifiers, speakers. Find cut-off for piped-in music.

4. Find access to *lighting* controls.

5. Check access to *electrical outlets*. Have spare heavy-duty extension cords ready for broadcast media.

6. If visuals are used, check out *projector* and check for extra equipment such as spare reels. Test the proper distance for projection. Be sure a table for the projector is set up and at the proper distance.

7. Have proper number of *chairs and tables* and have them placed correctly. It may be desirable to have tables covered with cloths.

Arrange tables so they are as close to the speaker as possible without crowding. However, a smaller room with some crowding is preferable to the yawning caverns of a big hall if attendance is light.

8. Make arrangements for *water and glasses*; also, for coffee or other refreshments. Be sure there is a firm understanding about the *service*: when delivered, replenished and removed and what quantity.

9. Locate a *telephone*. If one is in the room, be sure to arrange for an immediate answer if a ring should interrupt the speaker.

10. Make out *name tags* and have spare blank tags at hand. Remember that women guests may not have pockets for the pocket insert tags. Use pressure-sensitive tags or pin-ons.

11. Set up a table for *guest registration* and name tags.

12. Have a *list of guests* invited, marked for those confirmed as having accepted and those who have sent regrets.

13. Have *place cards* or attendants helping guests to seats.

14. Prepare a *program* of activities for speaker, and guests too, if possible.

15. Have *writing materials*, including cards, available in case speaker wants to make last-minute notes.

16. Have *information kits* to give to guests.

17. Have an easy-to-read *clock* or stopwatch for timing.

---

tance from the population center, provide bus transportation from points of departure. Train guides to conduct tours for visitors, and have knowledgeable employees at strategic points to provide information and answer questions. Use signs and printed maps to direct visitors.

8. Publicize the events well in advance through all possible channels. Use all of the controlled media to keep employees and other publics informed. Use the mass media for the general public—if necessary, use advertising.

9. When it is over say thank you to everyone who helped and participated. A successful dedication or open house requires the services of many, and hard work by quite a few, and their efforts should be gratefully acknowledged.

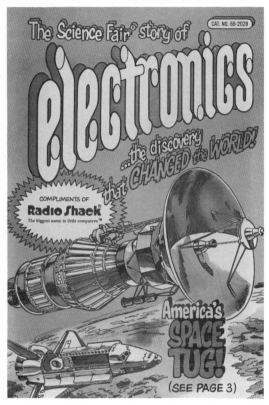

Reprinted with permission of Radio Shack, Tandy Corp.,
Ft. Worth, TX

HANDLING VISUAL PROJECTION DEVICES

Here are comments on various visual presentation methods, including easel pads, overhead projectors and slides.

Easel Pads

The chart pad easel is the best tool to help executives generate ideas and reach conclusions in the shortest time possible. It can stimulate group interest, help organize discussion, help explain or clarify and help summarize and review.

11.6 CHARTING BEGINNINGS

Sponsored traveling museum exhibit generates publicity and
goodwill.

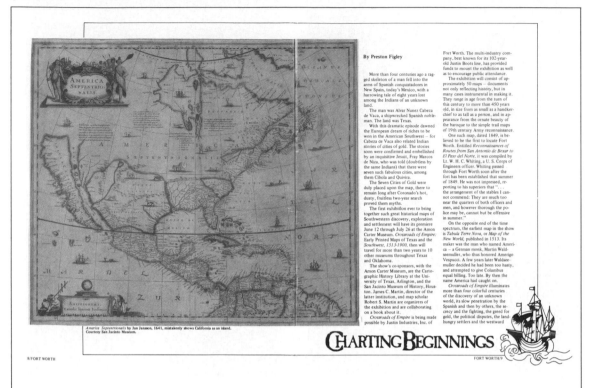

By Preston Figley

More than four centuries ago a ragged skeleton of a man fell into the arms of Spanish conquistadores in New Spain, today's Mexico, with a harrowing tale of eight years lost among the Indians of an unknown land.

The man was Alvar Nunez Cabeza de Vaca, a shipwrecked Spanish nobleman. The land was Texas.

With this dramatic episode dawned the European dream of riches to be won in the American Southwest – for Cabeza de Vaca also related Indian stories of cities of gold. The stories soon were confirmed and embellished by an inquisitive Jesuit, Fray Marcos de Niza, who was told (doubtless by the same Indians) that there were seven such fabulous cities, among them Cibola and Quivira.

The Seven Cities of Gold were duly placed upon the map, there to remain long after Coronado's hot, dusty, fruitless two-year search proved them myths.

The first exhibition ever to bring together such great historical maps of Southwestern discovery, exploration and settlement will have its premiere June 12 through July 26 at the Amon Carter Museum. *Crossroads of Empire: Early Printed Maps of Texas and the Southwest, 1513-1900,* then will travel for more than two years to 10 other museums throughout Texas and Oklahoma.

The show's co-sponsors, with the Amon Carter Museum, are the Cartographic History Library at the University of Texas, Arlington, and the San Jacinto Museum of History, Houston. James C. Martin, director of the latter institution, and map scholar Robert S. Martin are organizers of the exhibition and are collaborating on a book about it.

Crossroads of Empire is being made possible by Justin Industries, Inc. of Fort Worth. The multi-industry company, best known for its 102-year-old Justin Boots line, has provided funds to mount the exhibition as well as to encourage public attendance.

The exhibition will consist of approximately 50 maps – documents not only reflecting history, but in many cases instrumental in making it. They range in age from the turn of this century to more than 450 years old, in size from as small as a handkerchief to as tall as a person, and in appearance from the ornate beauty of the baroque to the simple trail maps of 19th century Army reconnaissance.

One such map, dated 1849, is believed to be the first to locate Fort Worth. Entitled *Reconnaissance of Routes from San Antonio de Bexar to El Paso del Norte,* it was compiled by Lt. W. H. C. Whiting, a U. S. Corps of Engineers officer. Whiting passed through Fort Worth soon after the fort has been established that summer of 1849. He was not impressed, reporting to his superiors that ". . . the arrangement of the stables I cannot commend: They are much too near the quarters of both officers and men, and however thorough the police may be, cannot but be offensive in summer."

On the opposite end of the time spectrum, the earliest map in the show is *Tabula Terre Nova,* or *Map of the New World,* published in 1513. Its maker was the man who named America – a German monk, Martin Waldseemuller, who thus honored Amerigo Vespucci. A few years later Waldseemuller decided he had been too hasty, and attempted to give Columbus equal billing. Too late. By then the name America had caught on.

Crossroads of Empire illuminates more than four colorful centuries of the discovery of an unknown world, its slow penetration by the Spanish and then by others, the secrecy and the fighting, the greed for gold, the political disputes, the landhungry settlers and the westward

CHARTING BEGINNINGS

America Septentrionalis by Jan Jansson, 1641, mistakenly shows California as an island.
Courtesy San Jacinto Museum.

8/FORT WORTH

FORT WORTH/9

Overhead Projectors

Overhead projectors are simple and speedy to set up and use; but it is also easy to clutter your presentation with too much material. Here are some tips on how to get the most from this visual aid:

■ *Don't*—turn the projector on and leave it on. Use the light only when you want to bring attention to the screen. Even a lighted screen with no image on it is distracting. Observe how, when you switch on the light, attention goes to the screen, then when you switch it off, it goes back to you.

■ *Do*—for best effect, locate the transparency on the projector stage before turning the light on. Don't turn on the light, then fumble around trying to position the transparency.

■ *Do*—use a grease pencil to circle, underline or otherwise emphasize key words, figures or portions of the transparency as you are discussing them.

- *Don't*—make rapid, distracting gestures on the stage. Be deliberate in pointing out information. A grease pencil is a handy pointer, showing up well on the screen.

- *Do*—if your hand tends to shake when holding the pointing device, touch it to the transparency to steady it. A small movement can be very obvious when magnified many times on a lighted screen.

- *Do*—in general keep your information toward the top of the sheet. That brings it to the top of the screen for optimum visibility.

- *Do*—use the technique of revelation or development. Best where the bulk of the materials to be communicated is cut-and-dry facts and figures. This is accomplished by covering all but the first point to be discussed by placing a plain sheet of paper over the transparency, then moving it down so as to uncover only what you want to show and discuss at the moment. This brings absolute focus of attention. Many presentations lose their effectiveness when people jump ahead.

- *Do*—in using transparency overlays to develop an idea one step at a time, be sure everyone understands before going on to the next step. Keep each overlay simple.

- *Do*—in making transparencies remember that simplicity is important. A transparency that is too cluttered will be distracting to your audience and you may lose the point you want to make.

- *Do*—obtain a simple guide to screen and image size relationship to ensure easy visibility from the rear of the room. There are several templates available for just this purpose.

- *Do*—remember that using color for the sake of color is a wrong concept and can distract your audience's attention.

- *Do*—remember, however, that in some cases, use of color can add dramatic impact. Some simple techniques exist for this. They include felt pens for marking the film surface, adding color to lines on the transparency with color grease pencils or color transparent film and tapes or putting a sheet of colored foil over the transparency to give a color background. Color lift films also are available.

- *Do*—mix with color. Colored film is currently popular for overhead projectors. Visuals can be made in full color or in black and white with color adhesive film to add color, or color transparencies can be made directly from full-color magazine illustrations with color lift film.

- *Do*—use an executive memo pad, a "lightboard," which can be projected on a screen via the overhead projector. Lightboard is a pressure-sensitive sandwich of film on a cardboard frame that shows a white-on-gray image. Speakers can "talk with their pencils," incorporating ideas from the floor directly into the transparency. When the subject changes, so does the transparency—by simply lifting the top film to erase the image.

- *Do*—try the chalkboard technique for detailing up-to-the-minute information or showing growth. The overhead projector can be used as a versatile replacement for a chalkboard, with a grease pencil replacing chalk. Partial transparencies can be completed right in front of meeting participants.

- *Do*—experiment with an animated box. Sales executives faced with the task of explaining complicated products to a field force can make effective use of animated boxes. Boxes are frames, transparent in the center, with miniature cutouts of the working parts of equipment. A series of strings on the outside of the boxes can be manipulated to cause the visual to actually move on the screen. Boxes can be easily produced in the graphics department.

- *Do*—show design changes by using a basic visual that can be made, and new style and details emphasized, by use of colored felt marking pens. Evolution of style change can be traced by making transparencies of preparatory product sketches.

Slides

Not everything can be made into a good slide. Poor color choice, intricate diagrams, cluttered charts and wrong size type or lettering can leave your audience red-eyed and discouraged. It is necessary to have good color contrast, clear details that are kept at a minimum and the proper size type or letters in the slide.

A good rule of thumb, which almost always works and is helpful in evaluating whether a given piece of material can be translated into a slide, is the following:

1. Measure the widest part of material being considered for a slide.
2. Provide a reasonably wide border and measure the border on both sides.
3. Add items 1 and 2 together.
4. Multiply the total by 6 (giving you a final total in inches or feet as the case may be, from your eyes or from a person with eye vision of 20–40. This is important.

If you or your substitute—with the 20–40 vision—can read the material easily and see all the pertinent details easily, then the material could be a good slide. If it can't be easily read, it must be modified until it does pass the test.

Artwork prepared for 3¼ × 4 inch slide projection should be prepared in a 3 (high) to 4 (wide) proportion, because the image should be masked down in photography and slide binding to 2¼ × 3 inches, which is a 3 to 4 proportion. Artwork for 35mm double frame slides (2 × 2s) should be prepared in the proportion of 2 (high) to 3 (wide); and art for 35mm filmstrip should be prepared, like that for 3¼ × 4 inch slides, in a proportion of 3 (high) to 4 (wide). The use of these proportions is very important. If they are not used, effective space on the slide is lost.

In using slides observe these important points:

1. Use 2 × 2 inch color slides—they are more effective; easier to make; and cheaper, considering darkroom time. Color film is also convenient for black-and-white copy slides.
2. Use a dark-colored background—it is better than black or white.
3. Limit each slide to fifteen or twenty words. The maximum for the presentation is twenty-five to thirty pieces of data. Include no more than you will discuss.

4. Leave space—at least the height of a capital letter—between lines.

5. Include titles to supplement, not duplicate, slide data.

6. Use several simple slides rather than one complicated one, especially if you must discuss something at length.

7. Use duplicates if you need to refer to the same slide at several different times in your talk. It is impractical for the projectionist to reshow a slide.

8. Plan your slides for a good visual pace in your presentation. Don't leave a slide on the screen after discussing its subject.

9. Thumb-spot all slides in the lower left corner when the slides read correctly on hand viewing.

10. Add sequence numbers.[1]

Dos and Don'ts of Visuals

Some general dos and don'ts of visuals include these. The function of a visual is to illustrate a point, to clarify and to fix a fact or image in the minds of the audience. It should correlate with the spoken narrative, whether it be a recorded sound track or a live presentation. It has been proven that people retain more when it is presented to them in a combination of sight and sound than they do when only one of these two senses is employed.

A good visual must have simplicity. It must be capable of being instantly absorbed by the mind. The things that influence simplicity are color choice, design elements, type and lettering and how photos are used, to name a few. The following are a few common pitfalls to avoid if you want to retain simplicity in visuals.

Backgrounds Never use black type on a dark background. This is so elementary one would expect that it is never done. Yet people who should know better, such as qualified commercial artists, make this mistake every day. They usually use black type on a blue background that never seems to photograph as light as they thought it would. Blue isn't a good color for background use where black type is involved. If the blue is light enough to contrast strongly with the type, it invariably washes out and results in a weak visual. Similarly, white letters should never be used against a pastel background.

Overloading A visual with too much detail is another common mistake. Don't use too many design elements, too many shapes—circles, triangles, rectangles, square blocks—in planning a visual. A design may be made so "arty" that the message is lost in a maze of shapes, curlicues and clashing colors. Better to be simple than sorry. Don't use too many type faces in a single visual. Don't overload a visual with too many words. It is better to break up a statement or thought into two or three slides, and let the audience take it in short bites. Similarly, bear in mind that

---

[1] William J. Connelly, "The Why, What and When of Audio Visuals," Association of National Advertisers, in "Staging Techniques," published as a reprint from *Successful Meetings* (formerly *Sales Meeting Magazine*), May 15, 1968 issue.

script type is about 50 percent harder to read than simple, uncluttered Roman letters.

Color Don't make the mistake of having too much white space in a visual either. Remember, white means clear film, 100 percent light transmission and an overpowering glare from a white screen. If you must show a white form, photograph only the essential areas, and cover the rest with color-aid paper or a colored bourgess, with cutouts to allow the important areas to stand out on screen. Your visual will be much more effective.

Conflicting Messages Visuals should correlate with the audio portion of your presentation. They should not fight each other for supremacy. The word or words on screen should be the exact words that are to be spoken. Don't say one thing visually and something else orally. The mind simply cannot accept two conflicting statements simultaneously.

Putting the Show Together The sequence of events in developing a slide show production is as follows: (1) Set your objectives. (2) Work out a budget. (3) Prepare the conceptual plan—an artistic development of the idea. (4) Write the script. (5) Test concept and script on an audience. (6) Shoot the visuals. (7) Produce the visuals. (8) Edit visuals and script. (9) Complete for presentation (record script and synchronize, add music and so on). The show should capture the mood of the message as well as provide content.

Adding Sound If you are a production expert, you can add sound effects and musical themes from suppliers such as audio archives (Films for the Humanities, Box 2053, Princeton, NJ 08530). They can provide anything from a convoy of diesel trucks to an orchestra tuning up. However, many large metropolitan areas also have professional sound studios and sound suppliers. Hire a professional if you aren't one. (See 11.7 for estimated production timetables.)

HANDLING SOUND SYSTEMS

A sound system can make or break a presentation. Here are general rules to follow:

1. *Sound Reinforcement*: Never accept the word of a hotel that adequate sound reinforcement will be provided. Few hotels own acceptable equipment. The electronic rostrums, microphones and portable loudspeakers they provide vary widely in age, quality and condition. Frequently the parts are not physically or electronically compatible with one another.

   Do not check the sound item off your list until a dry run—held in the meeting room—has established that every component in the system is functioning properly. Make certain that any assistant who must operate the equip-

ESTIMATED TIMETABLES (VARIES WITH PROXIMITY TO SUPPLIERS)

Items Needed	Advance Time for You (working days)*	Advance Time for Media (weeks)	Media	Total Time (weeks)
35 mm film			Local or network TV	16–20
Approved storyboard	5–10			
Set bids, casting	10 (more for animation)			
Production planning	10			
Filming	7			
Sound track	3 in canned, otherwise 10–15			
Editing	10			
Master prints	3			
16mm reductions and prints	1–3	6		
4-color process plates	10–15 for color separations	6–8, if they make color separations; 4–6 if color separation provided	Magazines	8
Finished art	Negotiable	8–10 to print and get up; less if 24 sheets delivered; printer needs time, about 4–6 weeks	Outdoor ads	8–12
Finished art	Negotiable	8 if list bought, 4 if own list	Direct mail	12
Mats (plastic) and repro proofs	5 for shooting and processing	2	Newspapers	3–4
Slides and script or Tape	10–40 depending on subject and length, whether advertising or publicity	6 6–8	Local TV Network or local radio	7 8–12

*Add approval time and correction time—about 6 weeks.

ment knows exactly how it works—that he or she knows the location of all switches and controls, knows the proper volume and tone control settings and knows how to operate auxiliary equipment such as phonograph turntables, tape recorders or additional microphones. It is always exasperating to both audience and speaker to have to break the bond of communication between them in order to give mechanical instructions to an equipment operator.

Check out the loudspeaker systems. Adjust volume level to a point slightly higher than you would normally set it—recognizing that the room, when filled with people, will be much more sound-absorptive than when it is empty.

2. *Rented or Company Equipment*: If you cannot rely on the hotel sound equipment, you can rent it from a nearby audio rental facility. Or you can bring it in and have your own firm set it up (subject to local union regulations and convention requirements). The last is probably the most reliable—and the most economical too if your annual investment in sales meetings exceeds $3,000.

3. *Simple Equipment*: When selecting equipment you will use, remember the auto mechanic's maxim: You will never have trouble with the accessories they *don't* include. There is a bewildering variety of microphones, loudspeaker systems, amplifiers and accessory equipment available for highly specialized uses and for startling effects. But keep your equipment basic and simple.

4. *Choosing Components*: The technical information you will need to make a wise choice as to components is not great, and most manufacturers furnish helpful literature in terms that even the novice can readily understand.

   It's a good idea, nevertheless, to choose components to suit your individual needs. Microphones, for instance, are available in a great many varieties and prices, but no other element is so vital to the sound system. However good the other components, they cannot compensate for a poor microphone. Be sure it is suited to the use for which it is intended. Price is no index to suitability.

Numerous evils commonly associated with poor sound reinforcement are actually unsuccessful attempts to offset microphone deficiencies. Amplifier hum or background noise may be caused by a microphone with a low output, inadequately compensated for by turning up amplifier gain (volume). Ear-splitting treble emphasis often occurs because an amplifier's treble control was turned up to overcome a loss of articulation at the microphone. When amplifier gain is held so low that the audience must strain to hear, the microphone is often to blame. In this case, if the gain were turned up, ear-splitting feedback would result because of the microphone's inability to discriminate against unwanted sound.

There are six common sound system troubles. If you check them out in advance, you can avoid them. If they occur during your talk, you know what to do about them.

1. *Feedback*: The most prevalent sound system disorder is the harsh, shrill squeal called "feedback." It happens when the microphone picks up sound from the loudspeakers, reamplifies it and rebroadcasts it. Feedback is most often due to incorrect microphone selection and placement. Before the meeting or performance make a dry run of the sound system as follows:

   ■ Turn up the amplifier gain so that with a normal speaking voice and distance from the microphone (12 inches away) there is adequate sound coverage in all parts of the room.

   ■ If the system operates satisfactorily, try it next with a much louder voice.

   ■ Since gain usually must be turned up higher when an audience is in the room, try raising the gain a little and speak again in a normal voice.

   ■ If there is no feedback or ringing sound, the system should perform adequately during the actual meeting.

If there is feedback during any of these steps, try the following remedies:

- Check microphone to see if it is the unidirectional type. This type picks up sound mainly from one direction (the speaker) and minimizes chances of picking up and amplifying sound from the audience.
- If feedback exists even with the unidirectional microphone, try moving it a few feet to either side or away from the front of the stage or platform. Also try turning the microphone from side to side on its stand.
- If microphone position is critical, avoid moving it during actual meeting.
- If feedback persists and loudspeakers are placed approximately at the sides of the microphone, it would be well to try a bidirectional-type microphone.
- Move loudspeakers, if possible, to minimize feedback.
- In general, the audience will absorb sound and discourage some types of feedback.
- Control your speaking voice. If you suddenly raise your voice without backing away from the microphone or speak so softly that the gain must be increased or stand too far from the microphone, feedback will be produced.

2. *Long Cable Runs*: When the microphone is connected to the amplifier by long runs of cable—that is, more than 25 feet—some frequency response is often lost and volume is reduced. The problem is one of using a microphone of correct impedance (ratio of force per unit area to volume displacement of surface). For normal cable runs, high-impedance microphones are used, since they cost less and since most amplifiers have only high-impedance microphone inputs.

For long cable runs it may be necessary to use a low-impedance microphone connected to a low-impedance input amplifier. A high-impedance input amplifier can be used if a matching transformer is hooked into the line at the amplifier.

Another solution is the multiple-impedance microphone with a switch that changes it from high to low.

3. *More Than One Microphone*: When more than one microphone is used to pick up action or voices from several locations, a mixer is needed. All microphones are plugged into this mixer, which in turn is plugged into the amplifier. The mixer balances sounds coming in from microphones and shuts off those that aren't in use.

The most complicated problem of placing multiple microphones occurs when a dramatic skit is being presented and participants must move about. Microphones must be placed to pick up voices anywhere on stage. If the action can be centered around a desk or similar prop, the problem is simplified. One bidirectional or omnidirectional microphone on a table stand can then serve three or four persons.

Where overall movement and speaking are necessary, several unidirectional microphones can be set up at strategic points over the stage and controlled with the mixer. Here also a dry run is helpful.

4. *Booming or Hollow Sound*: When you hear these sounds, move away from the microphone. You are standing too close and low tones are being accented. If the booming persists, your microphone may have a poor frequency

response that "peaks" and overemphasizes either bass or high sounds or both. Another cause, easy to correct, is faulty adjustment of bass and treble controls on the amplifier.

5. *Hiss and Hum*: This can happen when the microphone or cable is too close to an electric wire or electrical device. Move the microphone, cable or electrical device. If that isn't possible, use a low-impedance microphone and matching transformer. Also check to see that the microphone-cable shield is grounded.

6. *No Sound*: Check to see that the cable is connected to microphone, amplifier and speaker. Make sure amplifier is on. If microphone has an on-off switch, see that it is on. Check that the microphone impedance matches the input impedance of the amplifier. Check plug connections at microphone and amplifier. If the amplifier has more than one channel, see that the proper channel is on. Check amplifier fuses. Check electrical system fuses.

If you master these troubles, you will have overcome 90 percent of the sound system problems that might arise. If the trouble persists even after you have taken all these recommended steps, the next step is to call your sound technician.

HANDLING CELEBRITIES

The presence of celebrities almost guarantees publicity, so luring them and making them glad they came is important. Arrangements for a celebrity's appearance may be made through an organization with which the celebrity is involved, perhaps as the national chairperson of a charity. Or if the celebrity is a columnist or television star, contact may be made through the syndicate or network, using a local publication or network affiliate station as a starting point.

Ultimately, though, there probably will be dealings with the celebrity's agent. It is important to remember that this person is a *business* agent. The agent's primary consideration is what is good for the celebrity, so you must discover a selling point to attract the star. Forget money. Few local groups can afford a celebrity. Anyway, money is just not a big enough attraction for the inconvenience. The appeal must be a highly personal one, or there must be a good business reason for the appearance. For example, a prominent film and television star has a child afflicted with a terminal illness, and because of this intense personal involvement has given countless hours of time and talent to the national organization and will make appearances for the local chapters. A well-known newspaper columnist was once persuaded to visit a city in which the papers did not carry her column, in the hope of making some contact and expanding her syndication.

Once you have the celebrity in hand, you should request updated biographical information from his or her agent or public relations personnel and 8 × 10 glossies of at least two different poses. The biographical data will give you a start in preparing the advance publicity. It is helpful if you can also get a telephone interview to fill in details, since vita sheets are sometimes incomplete. Further, personal information and a personal contact give you some insight into the celebrity's likes and dislikes and some indication of what type of promotion would be best. A publicity schedule for a celebrity does not come out of a cookie cutter. It is important to determine what that person likes to do and does best because this is where he or she will perform best for you.

Some standard things to consider for a celebrity's visit are (1) individual interviews for newspapers, both metropolitan and suburban, and magazines; (2) media conferences or luncheons; (3) personal appearances on radio and television talk shows; (4) VIP treatment at civic functions and organizational meetings; (5) appearances at shopping centers and major department stores that tie in with the sponsor, if dignified and suitable; (6) visits to hospitals, particularly children's hospitals, if appropriate; (7) occasionally, riding in a motorcade to and from events; (8) audio- and videotaped promotion sessions; (9) a note to clubs and youth groups encouraging them to meet the celebrity's plane with welcoming banners.

Be sure all newsmaking events on the schedule are covered by your own staff reporter and photographer. In fact, the easiest rule to follow is just don't go anywhere without your photographers. Some of the best picture possibilities can be missed if you depend on the news media photographers working only on assignment. Also, the celebrity may want pictures, and these are easier to get from your staff than from the media. Someone in the office should keep a log of television appearances and clippings to present to the celebrity or the accompanying PR person or agent.

Media information kits should be prepared and distributed in advance of the celebrity's appearance, but keep extra ones with you at all times. If reporters assigned to the story have not seen the kit, they may ask you a number of questions that could have been avoided.

Make the most of the celebrity's time, but remember that he or she is a human being with public exposure limitations. Put one person in charge of the celebrity's schedule so that it will become immediately clear when the schedule is too taxing or the arrangements unrealistic. A tired, frazzled, hungry celebrity might become snappish with the press or critical of the promotion itself. Remember to allow the celebrity time for a rest and change of clothes before a television appearance—two hours minimum. At least two hours, and preferably three, should be allowed before the celebrity has to make the major appearance of the trip—probably a speaking engagement. The celebrity may have to attend to personal matters. If the celebrity enjoys the appearance, this enjoyment will be reflected.

The interviewing situation can get tricky. Most publications prefer exclusive interviews, but if you have an excessive demand, a conference is the better solution—or luncheon, if that seems suitable. The latter is good for magazine writers, but it takes too much time from the working day of newspaper or broadcast reporters. It is okay to arrange interviews back to back, allowing the same amount of time for each one; however, remember the celebrity, and allow for leg-stretching coffee breaks of a few minutes or so. Most celebrities prefer "block" scheduling (appointments back to back) to get the interviews out of the way. The trick is to accommodate the media, yet conserve the celebrity's energy.

In figuring out the celebrity's schedule, you will probably be working with the agent or a person charged with scheduling. Be sure your communications with this person are clear, concise and definite. Your dependence is mutual, so it is important that you establish rapport. Get off to a good start in your first contact by giving the following information: (1) travel arrangements and who will be meeting the celebrity (and if an airport arrival interview is planned); (2) where the celebrity will be staying; (3) what provision has been made for transportation; (4) what financial arrangements have been made (get this ironed out early!); (5) what the schedule of appearances is; (6) what other group appearances have been scheduled and what special events the celebrity will be participating in. Make multiple copies of the schedule so your staff and the celebrity's have contact information. Include phone numbers at various locations.

Give the celebrity as much background as possible, not only on the groups and people, but also on the city. Personalize: Tie the information into the celebrity's own background, career or special interests. It will help prepare the celebrity for the questions that will have to be fielded and also make a stranger feel comfortable and welcome rather than exploited.

Arrangements too should not only reflect star status but also be personalized. One television actor found that the PR director at an affiliate station had keyed everything, even the fruit in his room, to the TV series in which he portrayed a teacher (the fruit was, of course, apples). For another celebrity, who was an art lover, pictures in the suite were replaced with valuable paintings on loan from the local art museum.

The red-carpet treatment begins at the airport, where most major airlines maintain luxurious VIP rooms for interviews. It may be the best place to have an initial press conference and have the celebrity greeted by a city official. Make arrangements through the airline's local public relations department. Most airlines will also expedite baggage handling. The hotel's PR department is also eager to cooperate in seeing that the star's room is specially prepared with flowers or fruit. You should check the celebrity in before arrival and have the room key in order to make this a smoother operation.

For transportation, a chauffeured limousine is almost a must for important celebrities, or if this is impossible, try to get a new car on loan, say a demonstration model from a promotion-conscious dealer. (You can't promise any free plugs for the dealership, but the car certainly is noticed and sometimes appears in photographs.) Get a driver who understands time schedules and knows the city. Be sure the celebrity knows how to contact the limousine service or driver in case of emergency or change in plans.

Assign someone who is understanding and sympathetic to be with the star throughout the schedule. This person should be able to handle special requests like hairdressers at 6 A.M. or filet mignon at midnight. Be sure it is someone with patience, tact and diplomacy who also understands the significance of keeping on schedule. After an appearance is over, this person can probably suggest the best way to say thank you.

Take care of all departure details such as check-out, bills, airline flight confirmation, baggage check-in. Attention to the celebrity cannot be relaxed just because the itinerary is closed. Remember the farewell remarks of a celebrity are usually recorded and remembered too. One thought to keep in mind is that celebrities talk to other celebrities. A public relations director who was having difficulty getting a celebrity happened to mention it to another celebrity who had once been their guest for the same event. To the PR person's surprise, the celebrity said, "Well, I'll just call and tell her she needs to be here. It's a good promotion vehicle, and you people know how to do things right."

PRODUCING BROCHURES AND PUBLICATIONS

"Publishing" is a highly technical part of public relations activity. It is full of traps for the unwary—and unfortunately, mistakes are very tangible.

Brochure Production

The first decision in making a brochure is to determine its purpose and then its *audience*. This will suggest not only the number to be printed but also the method of distribution. Distribution is critical to planning.

Brochures come in all shapes and sizes, but the size and shape is almost predetermined if it will have to be mailed. If it is going in the *mail*, the decision must be made whether it will be enclosed in an envelope at additional expense or will be a self-mailer, that is, a folded piece with a tab or staple closing with part of the surface reserved for mailing instructions. In either case, it is important to first check with the Postal Service, particularly if your piece will require an especially designed and irregular envelope, since there are regulations regarding envelope size. There are also regulations about sealing and addressing self-mailers. Certainly this would be a bulk mailing and there are regulations regarding that too. Finding out all this in advance is important because it governs brochure design, including the choice of paper stock (see 11.8).

After determining the physical properties of the brochure, and its envelope if there is to be one, use a folded piece of paper as a mock-up. It helps in visualizing. Be sure the size is exactly that of the finished piece. (See 11.9 for examples of different types of brochures.)

Next decide what is to be said and how. Figure out what can be said with illustrations. Brochures usually succeed or fail on their graphics, so it is important to begin working early with an artist. The artist responsible for the design must know the concept and the purpose, as well as the distribution method and how it affects the design. There also must be some decision about color (ordinarily a financial, rather than aesthetic, decision) and about the method of reproduction, whether offset or letterpress (today most printing is by offset). Ask for rough layouts, and let the artist offer a choice of several different ideas.

Once the design has been approved, you must decide on the exact paper stock, finish, weight and color; the precise color of ink; the kind and size of type for each portion of the layout. Paper suppliers, printers and typesetters usually have samples, which many artists also keep on hand. Choose the printer carefully because an attractive layout that is clumsily executed is unusable. The number of brochures printed affects their cost—the more printed, the less the cost for each.

The artist can go ahead with production after all details are settled, copy has been written and supplied and either illustrations have been supplied or artwork approved. Copy fitting and layout usually fall to the artist, but many public relations people have found it expedient to master these techniques. The decision of whether to do it or have it done depends on a PR person's own skills.

After the type has been set and proofread, the finished art readied and everything pasted up, it is time to begin work with the printer. Be sure to arrange with the printer to check proof before the entire printing is run. Mistakes can happen.

11.8 POSTAL REGULATIONS

Note the attention called to the weight and size of the mailing piece. Such a notice prevents the whole mailing being delayed or not returned at all.

Instructions on the layout can be misunderstood or wrong. It is your last chance. Take it.

When a large printing is complete, and the folding done, it may be worthwhile to have the stuffing and mailing handled by a mail service. Such firms offer different services, but nearly all will work with a mailing list and charge for labeling or use your labels. Since most operations are computerized, it is best to provide a mailing service with a printout of the addresses on mailing labels.

After the mailing, be sure to keep enough brochures on hand to meet requests. Keep at least five as copies. You may need them for reference.[2]

---

[2] For production details, such as copy fitting and scaling photographs to fit the designated space, see Doug Newsom and Tom Siegfried, *Writing in Public Relations Practice: Form & Style* (Belmont, Calif.: Wadsworth, 1981).

Both of these very different pieces could be called a "brochure." The Eastern Airlines piece is four folds, printed front and back and four color. The tornado piece is found in rooms of several hotels. Designed by Scriptographic, it is printed in brown on a gray, lightweight paper stock.

EASTERN'S BUSINESSWOMAN
Travel And The Times For Women-On-The-Go
Vol. IX, No. 1, 1983

Three Lifetimes In One Is Postmaster's Goal.

"I spent my first 'life' in the educational community," says Mary Layton, speaking of her hopes for at least three major and very different careers in her lifetime. "I loved teaching and it was very fulfilling."

But she embarked on a second and entirely new career several years ago when she became involved in communications as Public Relations Director for the Port Authority of New York. "I'm not afraid of risk-taking," she explains, "of leaving the security of the known for a new opportunity. It's exciting to go into new areas and try something altogether different."

Ms. Layton's current position as Assistant Postmaster General for Public Relations is a challenge she has been enjoying since she accepted the Washington, DC post in May of 1982. "I really like government public relations," she says enthusiastically. "You have to be very exact in this area, and you're on the spot much of the time. It's quite lively and you're always putting out fires. No two days are ever the same — which is exactly the way I like it!"

As one of 18 Assistant Postmasters General, three of whom are women, Ms. Layton's job includes responsibility for communications, both internally and to the public. "This involves anything to do with the media, as well as the supervision of six publications."

She supervises a staff of more than 50 people, and an art department and audio-visual shop where brochures, posters, films, slides and videotapes are produced.

She's also a member of the Postal Executive Committee, which meets once a month to discuss "top level issues and policies such as the move to cluster boxes, EEO and Affirmative Action matters, reports on safety issues and various real estate properties."

Travel within the five Federal postal regions is another part of her job, as she flies throughout the U.S. for conferences, public speaking engagements and Career Awareness programs for postal workers. A large portion of her personal time is also spent traveling. "One of my favorite pastimes is travel," she offers energetically. "I enjoy getting away and changing my thought processes at the same time I change the scenery." Her explorations have included visits to Europe, Canada, Mexico and the Caribbean, as well as more exotic spots such as Casablanca and Marrakech, Morocco, and an extensive visit to the Ivory Coast. "And I'm hoping to go back to Africa on a photographic safari to Kenya next winter. If I had my way, I'd take at least a couple of really exciting vacations each year!"

Since accepting her new position in Washington, Ms. Layton says her "after hours" activities have suffered somewhat. "My life has pretty much concentrated on my work," she smiles a bit ruefully. "There has been much to learn and it takes a lot of time and energy."

After living the past 15 years in Manhattan, she says she was "almost traumatized at the thought of leaving New York! Making the move was a big transition in my life, but it's gone much smoother than I expected. And Washington is a nice change from the hustle-bustle of the West Village!"

Her retired parents have also lived in Washington for the past several years, which kept her on the Eastern Air-Shuttle while she was living in New York. "My dad was a social worker for years and finally Director of Affirmative Action for the entire Federal Reserve System. We lived in Tennessee, Ohio and Michigan for most of my growing up years, and I later lived in New Jersey before moving to New York." So getting adjusted to new environments has long been a part of Ms. Layton's life.

"I haven't gotten involved in any organizations in Washington, yet," she continues. "But I was an officer of the New York chapter of the Coalition of 100 Black Women, which went national last fall. I plan to remain active in this group, which includes professional women from all walks of life."

Other outside interests include museum-hopping, music and ice skating, a sport learned with her two sisters as girls in Michigan. And on the more adventurous side, "soaring in a glider plane is one of my favorite things!" she says with enthusiasm. "I also hope to try to parachute someday."

As for her third career venture, she says she doesn't know just what that will be yet. "But I know it will be altogether different! Life itself is very exciting — and it ought to be experienced to the fullest!"

Tornadoes, THE WESTIN HOTEL Williams Center and You

You probably have several questions regarding our atmosphere's most violent weather phenomena; the tornado.

In this leaflet, the management of the Williams Plaza Hotel has endeavored to present some basic answers on the dangers of tornadoes and what we can all do to prevent injuries.

THE WESTIN HOTEL
Williams Center

WHAT IS A TORNADO?

Tornadoes are local storms of short duration formed of winds rotating at speeds up to 300 miles per hour, usually in a counter clockwise motion in the northern hemisphere. These storms are visible as a vortex, a whirlpool structure of winds rotating about a hollow cavity in which centrifugal forces produce a partial vacuum. As condensation occurs around the vortex, a pale cloud usually appears — the familiar and frightening tornado funnel.

Funnels usually appear as extensions of the dark, heavy cumulonimbus clouds of thunderstorms and stretch downward toward the ground. Some never reach the surface; others touch and rise again.

WHAT IS A TORNADO WATCH?

TORNADO WATCHES ARE NOT THE SAME AS TORNADO WARNINGS. UNTIL A TORNADO WARNING IS ISSUED, PERSONS IN WATCH AREAS SHOULD NOT INTERRUPT THEIR NORMAL ROUTINES EXCEPT TO WATCH FOR THREATENING WEATHER.

Our hotel security office monitors the weather conditions on a 24 hour basis and when a Tornado Watch has been ordered by the Weather Bureau our own watch will be initiated. Be alert but stay calm. There is no reason to interrupt your normal activities. The likelihood of an actual tornado in this area is still very small even during a tornado watch.

WHAT IS A TORNADO WARNING?

If a tornado is sighted or detected on radar, a WARNING bulletin is issued. Such watch and warning statements are issued at least once each hour, and more frequently as the severity of the storm increases.

TORNADO WARNINGS are issued when a tornado has actually been sighted in the area or indicated by radar. Warnings indicate the location of the tornado at the time of detection, the area through which it is expected to move, and the time period during which the tornado will move through the area warned.

WHEN A TORNADO WARNING IS ISSUED, PERSONS IN THE PATH OF THE STORM SHOULD TAKE IMMEDIATE SAFETY PRECAUTIONS.

TORNADO WARNING SIGNAL

OUR GUESTS WILL BE ALERTED TO A TORNADO WARNING BY MEANS OF OUR EMERGENCY BROADCAST SYSTEM. SPEAKERS ARE LOCATED IN EVERY GUEST ROOM AND PUBLIC AREA OF THE HOTEL AND ALLOW US TO COMMUNICATE EMERGENCY MESSAGES IMMEDIATELY. ALTHOUGH THE LIKELIHOOD OF EVACUATION EVER BECOMING NECESSARY IS EXTREMELY REMOTE, EVACUATION WOULD BE VIA THE STAIRWELLS AT THE END OF EACH GUEST HALL TO THE LOWEST LEVEL AND THEN TO THE HOTEL'S BALLROOMS.

Producing a House Publication

When producing a house publication, all other decisions depend on the first: who the audience is. Since a house publication is going to employees or members only, it will have quite a different design from a publication with a broader distribution. What type of publication, then, is most likely to be accepted and read—a newsletter, a tabloid newspaper format, a magazine? This decision is usually helped by the budget allotted, which sometimes makes such a question academic.

The next decision is frequency of publication. Frequency usually depends on the public relations department, and monthly issues are about all most PR departments can cope with. Some have quarterly publications.

Method of distribution is another consideration. If it is all internal, with distribution either in pick-up boxes or by supervisory personnel or in-house mail service, there is no concern for mailing regulations and labeling. However, many companies have found it advantageous to send the publication into the home. In this case, it is important to keep up with mailing address changes, which the personnel department would have in the employee records, and it is critical to consult with the mailroom so this can be worked into a reasonable schedule with consideration for their other duties.

Once these elements are decided, content deserves the most careful attention. Enlightened management knows that what the employees want to know about the company is more important than what the company wants to tell the employees. Built into the publication should be ways to convey information and allowances for some two-way communication—perhaps through letters to the editor or a response column that answers questions of general concern. The tone of the publication—which includes writing style, layout, artwork, type choice and general design—greatly affects the attitude the employees will have toward it.

To help determine content, and even type and frequency of publication, PR staffs have used a questionnaire to find out what employees might like in the way of employee publication. The difficulty here is that some employees have no idea what might be possible. Choosing among unknowns is a bit of a problem. What seems to work better is to get a sample of house publications put out by others, not necessarily in the same type of company, and select a representative panel to meet on company time and discuss the type of employee publication that might be effective and can be produced within budget time and talent restrictions.

It is a good idea to retain the panel even after the publication appears, since panel judgments provide a check on whether the publication is being read, what part of it is best liked and what is missing.

Develop a dummy or mock-up, suggesting design and general type of content. Estimate how much copy and artwork will be in each publication and approximately how many pages each will be; then determine how the publication will be printed. Larger organizations may have in-house printing plants; however, when an outside printer is being chosen, it is important to get bids from several. The printer will need to see the dummy, know about how many issues will be needed and how often the publication will appear. Together with the printer you will have to decide about paper stock for the cover and inside pages and also headline and body type. The printer will have a price list for artwork and special effects that will help in estimating the costs of each issue. In selecting the printer, you will have to choose between offset and letterpress. If offset is chosen, as it is likely to be for both cost and flexibility, then the printer will have to know whether the publication will be coming to the shop camera-ready or whether setting type and preparing the art (as in getting color separations) will be the responsibility of the printer or the house organ's staff.

Staff is one of the major concerns in starting a house publication. Who will write and edit? Where is help available and talent that can be put to work? Writers, photographers and artists are all important to the success of a house publication, and some reasonable assessment of potential must be made before a publication can be launched. Again, budget is a factor in deciding how much talent can be bought. In the case of an employee publication, however, ego, esprit de corps and gentle persuasion often work in lieu of remuneration.

Whatever is used, a system for gathering information and preparing it for publication on schedule must be developed. Deadlines must be set for all art and photos, as well as specifications for the way material is to be submitted. Some successful operations use reporting sheets, which are handled by a person in each department. These are turned over to the editor and help in gathering news. The longer articles are generally an editorial/administrative decision, and are worked out on an assignment basis. Some editors plan a whole year's content; others plan an issue at a time, working only two or three months in advance on major stories.

Some publications are prepared by institutions to be a reader service, offered at no charge. These bonus publications, from institutions like insurance companies, are designed to make the customers feel good about the institution. The publications are subtle ads suggesting that the company cares about a customer. Often the publications do not call attention to their sponsorship. An example is a fitness magazine sent out by a hospital group.[3]

PRODUCING AN ANNUAL REPORT

Responsibility for the annual report should be shared between two key people, according to Ruder and Finn.[4] One of these should be a communications specialist responsible for deciding the *character* of the report, and the other a high-level management representative responsible for the *content*. The design and the language of the report are the responsibility of the communications specialist, who should not have to yield to the style preferences of others whose expertise lies in different areas.

To give these two the authority they need, it is suggested that all key manage-

---

[3] David Mills, "Publications at No Charge Are Subtle Ads," *Wall Street Journal*, August 5, 1983, p. 19.

[4] William Ruder and David Finn, *How to Make Your Annual Report Pay for Itself*, second booklet in *Management Methods*, a series on public relations by members of Ruder and Finn, Inc.

ment personnel not only know who has the responsibility for the report but also be involved in contributing to the point of view the report will reflect. Through meetings, it is hoped, there can be a consensus on theme and approach. The communications expert should prepare the first draft, working with content supplied by the other key person. The document should be circulated for comment and contributions. It should be weighed for its impact on all audiences, but specifically for its effect on the target audiences. While the report is being planned, the communications expert is responsible for suggesting to other members of management how the published report might be used with various publics, because this could have some bearing on presentation.

Annual reports that used to be almost a synonym for complex and obscure prose are now down-to-earth and occasionally even entertaining. The *Wall Street Journal* quotes Wisconsin Securities Co., of Delaware as describing one of its ventures as "a flop," and the annual report contains enough additional candor for the *Journal* writer to comment, "Now that's telling it like it is."[5] New Hampshire's Wheelabrator-Frye, Inc., has aimed its annual report toward youngsters. The educational effort—to tell fourth through sixth graders about the free enterprise system—was a twenty-page cartoon report telling what this manufacturer of environment and energy systems did with its money that year. Not only did the company get publicity from the circulation of the report among youngsters (whose parents and teachers also were exposed), but the report generated a lot of publicity as the example suggests. Several companies have bought enough pages in magazines like *Time* to present the entire annual report to an audience of millions.

"Millions" may represent a kind of overkill, but to make the most of the published report, it does need to be in the hands of all interested publics. Again, the communications expert is the one who should suggest to other departments the most effective use of this published piece.

Most annual report planning begins three to six months before the close of the fiscal year. The wise public relations person builds some padding into any schedule, and the annual report is the most likely to need it since its publication has such significance.

Shareholders also get quarterly reports, and some companies package these attractively in a newsletter form (see 11.10). Others use a brochure format, or create packages that resemble thick statement stuffers (or see 11.11 for more imaginative packaging).

PRODUCING INSTITUTIONAL VIDEOTAPES AND FILMS

Print media are generally thought of immediately as channels to various specialized publics, but film is popular too. Companies and nonprofit institutions—including the U.S. government—are making considerable use not

---

[5]N. R. Kleinfield, "An Annual Report Is No Comic Novel, but It Can Be Fun," *Wall Street Journal*, April 15, 1977, pp. 1, 29.

Pizza Time Theatre, Inc. 1981 Annual Report

Franchise Operations

Franchise Centers Currently Committed Under Territorial Franchise Agreements

Cummulative Totals by Year

1978	1979	1980	1981	1982	1983	1984	1985	1986
0	1	11	44	123	173	218	248	254

The Company has franchised on both a territorial and an individual unit basis, generally only in areas where there is no existing or planned concentration of Company centers. At the close of 1981, the Company had entered into Territorial Development Franchise Agreements with 26 persons and organizations.

The Company's standard franchise agreement grants the franchise owner the right to use the Company's trade names, trademarks, and service marks, and the right to develop and operate a center in accordance with the Company's system. The Company assists franchise owners with center development, operations and marketing programs.

Thirty-three franchise centers opened in 1981 including the first international units located in Surfer's Paradise, Queensland, Australia, and in Burlington, Ontario, Canada. Currently there are franchise commitments to open more than 200 additional centers over the next five years.

To facilitate communications between franchise owners and the Company, a franchise advisory council with regional representation was formed last year. The six-member council elected annually by the franchise owners meets once a quarter.

Response to the report—Pizza Time's first—"has been definitely favorable," said communications manager Suzie Crocker. "The only people who didn't like it were our auditors."

The company, which has only 4,000 shareholders, already has distributed 15,000 copies of the report, which cost $5 each to produce. "Brokers and analysts all over the country are going crazy. They are requesting them by the boxes and boxes. I think it may become a collector's item," she said.

In the first six weeks after the report was issued, Pizza Time stock rose 35 percent in a down market—from $23 to $31 per share. Crocker said part of the rise must have been stimulated by the report. "Of course, our [growth and earnings] figures were excellent," she added.

In deciding how it would produce its first report, "We looked at hundreds and hundreds of annual reports and saw that we didn't fit into anybody's category. We even looked at Walt Disney, but we didn't fit into that category because they're really a conglomerate.

"We aren't an IBM or a paper company or a widget company. We are a creative, innovative, family entertainment company, and we wanted our annual report to show that," Crocker said.

The original layout had all the graphs, artwork and color in the front of the book and the financial statements in back. But Pizza Time's board of directors said "it isn't fun enough. We need something the kids will pick up." (About 30 percent of Pizza Time's shareholders are children.) The board chairman came up with the idea of putting cartoons in the back.

The cartoons were designed not only to liven up otherwise dull financial pages, but to teach young people what the statements mean.

Crocker cites several reasons why it was easy for her company to produce an unusual annual report.

"Since we're a small company, there were fewer people to shoot it down. And in most companies, the financial department has a tight clamp on the annual report. All they care about is figures. We did it in our marketing department, which has a different approach."

Finally, "We are traded over the counter, which gives us more latitude than if we were traded on the New York Stock Exchange."

Fort Worth Star-Telegram, May 23, 1982. Reprinted with permission.

11.11 IT'S A COMPUTER? NO, AN ANNUAL REPORT

Stockholders of Tandy received annual reports that resembled Radio Shack's popular computer, with a screen that was die-cut so the name came through from the second page (which revealed the boards of the computer).

 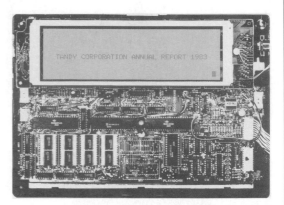

only of the videotape cassette but also of the 16mm film. Since the early 1970s, the trend has been to make these films in 35mm, then reduce them to 16mm. Technology has lowered the cost of this type of treatment, and the larger film gives higher quality and increases the potential use, including possible distribution to movie houses. The life of a film is usually about seven years, with potential audiences in the millions, and the technique of using clips from the film or taking clips from the outtakes for corporate advertising spreads out the costs. Furthermore, the unit cost per public impression must be considered.

When considering whether to produce a film, the first decision must not be how much will it cost, but who is going to produce it—an in-house unit, an outside commercial studio or both? Most corporations have in-house film production units, but their size and capacity varies—even large units occasionally farm out a large undertaking, at least in part. There are a number of commercial studios, but only a few are known for award-winning films. Some commercial studios are just film producers; others are producers and distributors.

More than half the institutions with film titles in circulation use part in-house and part commercial studio for production. An in-house film unit generally handles such things as record shooting, in-plant filming and the shepherding of the script and budget approvals through the corporate structure. The commercial studio is used for the filming that requires extensive staging or remote location or that demands talent. Sometimes the film is all shot by the in-house unit but processed and edited externally.

Distribution must also be considered. Ordinarily, it is better to pay a distribution company to take care of the enormous amount of paperwork, the shipping and the film care. However, some companies large enough for in-house film units can handle distribution easily and at a lower cost. Bypassing the commercial distributor also means bypassing the contracts, and they may be important.

A film should have an objective—a specific, stated purpose. It cannot be expected to "tell the whole story." The more objectives, the weaker the film. The sponsor must determine why a film is needed and have one made to accomplish that purpose. Another decision that needs to be made is what impression or attitude the film should communicate.

Often this is suggested by the audience. Obvious audiences for business films are customers or prospective customers; industry groups or other business groups in related fields; management; stockholders and the professional investment public; employees; the general public through direct distribution to clubs, church groups, social agencies, professional associations; government on all levels—federal, state, local; educational institutions; television, either through purchased time or public service time; theaters; international distribution through any of these channels.

Multiple use of the film has a great deal to do with the planning. Is it going to be made with an eye toward the mass public? Then what should be considered is a contract with a producer/distributor who can deliver the movie theaters for the 35mm production, as well as offer the film in 16mm for private audiences. Should it also be available in 8mm? What about finished copies being distributed in video-cassette form? All of this affects the design of the film. Usage also affects time—how long the finished version will be. Television too puts certain time strictures on the film.

A whole different approach is used for the publicity-slanted film as opposed to a more personal corporate statement. To be acceptable for public use, the corporate message must be so subtle as to be almost unnoticed, with the only blatant tie in the credit line: "sponsored by." Of course, if the film is mostly for corporate use, it can be much more inwardly focused.

Whether the film is produced commercially or internally, however, a great deal of research is involved. Often this falls on the sponsoring PR department, which will be working with a writer and a producer. The first step is to get enough information so the writer can come up with a story outline or suggested script. The next step is a rough storyboard. At this point, it is important to consider getting approval clearances; audience reaction may also be desirable. It may be important, too, to invest in a finished storyboard, since it is difficult for inexperienced people to visualize from a rough.

Once the script is approved and some consideration is given to the footage needed, the producer must know what is available in stills, slides and footage. None of it may be used, but it might suggest ideas or approaches. If film on hand is used, clearances for use of stock footage and for the people appearing in it must be granted.

Another question that must always be decided is whether to use *professional talent* in a film. If a producer is good at getting unstilted performances from nonprofessionals, then this solution is probably preferable to hiring talent. Casting takes time and adds to costs. However, casting is preferable to a distractingly and obviously amateur "performance."

Sound is also a major consideration. It is often the primary reason why corporations with film units go outside for the production of their footage. Technical knowledge is important, too, to make sure either that all music used is in the public domain or that permission has been granted. An expensive film can increase in price overnight if it has to be shelved to avoid a lawsuit or if one is filed.

Editing is another expert's job. Costs vary according to the complexity of the film and the skill of the editor. After the initial editing effort, the producer usually holds a screening of the work print, which shows picture scenes arranged and spliced in approximate relationship. Some sequences may be missing, and it is a very rough product. PR people should be familiar enough with work prints to know what to expect, but it can be a rather unsettling experience for the untrained eye. Much reassurance may be necessary if top management sits in on this approval session. It is important, though, to get as much input as possible, because if changes are to be made, this is the time. Later changes probably will cost more money than they would be worth.

The sound probably will involve narration, which requires a talent fee. Narration and the other sounds in films can be finalized only after the approval of the work print. The next stage is the answer print, sometimes called the "first release print" because it combines picture, sound and optical into one print for the first time. Revisions now come with high price tags.

The master print of the film is never used and should be stored in climate-controlled conditions while its prints travel according to the approved distribution method.

Promotion of the film is an additional consideration. Usually it is handled by the distributor, but often the film's sponsor must also do the touting, and the sponsor may find—with some dismay—that this has not been considered in budgeting.

The biggest user of institutional films is the U.S. government. About 2,300 films are made each year by the various federal agencies and departments. The purposes vary—training, public information and promotion. Users of government films include schools, civic groups, theaters and television stations, as well as some individuals and other agencies. The costs of this taxpayer-supported movie making far outshadow those of any commercial film corporation. While a commercial movie studio in Hollywood may spend between $90 and $100 million a year on movie and TV productions, the government spends more than $500 million on movies, TV shows, filmstrips and similar productions.

Commercially made films are well received by schools and civic groups. About 30,000 requests come each year from such groups and 1,200 from commercial, public and cable TV stations. TV stations also use videotapes.

Videotapes are also a costly project. A video news release can cost from $7,000 or $8,000 to $40,000 or $50,000. The variables are much the same as for film: length, shooting schedules, travel, editing, placement and so on. First, before you get into the area of news, you need to be sure you have a market. Talk to some news stations' personnel to see whether you have the right angle. Your topic has to have either broad or local appeal. Then be sure you have both the professional help to accomplish it and the time to get it filmed, edited and distributed. Because the size of tape varies, ½ inch (Betamax) or ¾ inch (u-matra), you must know what stations use. Or you may decide to hire a media servicer. (See list of services in Chapter 10.)

Cable systems are using more videotape of nonnews from various sources. Some of the segments could almost be called "shows." These are information, not entertainment, but the advertiser-made or sponsored shows have high interest. A 30-minute show can cost as little as $30,000. In many cases the show is a setting for commercial messages and by using particular products certainly suggests if it doesn't actually sell.

Instead of producing your own film, you may only want to see that your product is used prominently. This is expressive, and it is a highly competitive business. However, since you are paying, you can make demands. Mercedes-Benz, for instance, likes to see its cars used in films, but never wants the villain at the wheel. When you see a product close enough to recognize it in a film, the company undoubtedly paid for it to be there. It is a subtle form of promotion/advertising.

The following checklist is given by Howard Bach of National Television News (Woodland Hills, CA) for critiquing films and videotapes.

Before looking at the film, be sure you know its subject, purpose, and the nature of the audience it purports to reach. Only then can you judge whether it meets its goals, or is suitable.

As you look at the film, rate it on each of these ten points:

1. *Attention Span*: Is the film "gripping," or "interesting," or just plain able to hold the audience's attention throughout? This is critical: If the film is boring, *nothing else really matters*!

2. *Subject*: Does the film adequately cover the subject in a clear way, and fulfill its expressed purpose? Is the film too long? Or (seldom) not long enough?

3. *Audience Suitability*: Does it clearly address the audience it's aimed at . . . or the group you plan to show it to?

4. *Visuals*: Are the pictures in focus? Properly exposed? Are the colors true? If there are graphics, do they help to clarify and explain, or are they just there for effect?

5. *Timeliness*: Are the visuals up to date? (Nothing turns off an audience faster than an old-fashioned haircut or clothing style, or any printed matter on screen that shows the age of the film.)

6. *Talent*: Are the participants or actors real, and natural? Do you believe them? Can you hear and clearly understand what they're saying?

7. *Sound*: Are the sound effects and/or music appropriate to the action? Is there proper balance among words, sound effects and music, so that the message gets across in the most effective way?

8. *Editing*: Does the story flow naturally? Is the editing pace good, so the story neither drags, nor moves too fast? Are you jolted by unusual angles, jumps in action, scenes that are too short or too long, or by bad sound?

9. *Script Content*: Someone once said (or wrote) that the best script for a film is one with the fewest possible words. A well-done informational film should rely heavily on visuals to tell the story. Words should fill in, adding information that cannot be seen. Most films have too many words. And words should be simple. Long words or cumbersome phrases are distracting.

10. *Believability*: Is the film "professional," in the sense that it moves along smoothly, in a logical fashion, and you're not distracted by the mechanics of the medium? In summary, did you find the film or tape honest and believable?[6]

---

[6]"Formal Guidelines for Reviewing Information Films or Videotapes," *pr reporter*, February 23, 1982, p. 4. Reprinted by permission.

CHARGING FOR PR SERVICES

Most of the costs of a PR person or firm are for personal time. Thus systematic ways must be developed to keep track of the time spent and charge for it. There are three basic methods for determining client charges:

1. The *fixed fee*, seldom used now because it is a bit risky; it sets a specific fee in advance for all work *and* expenses.

2. The *fee for services plus out-of-pocket expenses*, which is the most popular form of billing. Out-of-pocket costs are such items as travel for a client, hotel rooms and meals, taxis, gratuities, telegrams, long-distance phone calls and entertainment.

3. The *retainer*, which covers counseling, supervision, profit and overhead. Overhead costs include all of the indirect expenses of doing business: utilities, secretarial and clerical costs, office supplies, amortization of equipment. Additional charges are made for services at hourly rates that reflect payroll costs plus out-of-pocket expenses. Many firms charge a retainer that covers counseling, supervision and profit, with an additional charge covering payroll and overhead expenses. All out-of-pocket costs are extra and are billed as such.

The cost of staff time spent on a project is staff salaries, usually prorated to the nearest hour of time spent. The cost of executive time and supervision depends on the size of the agency: Large agencies have executive oversight; small ones include the executive in the staff part of the time.

In running a PR business there are chargeable and nonchargeable expenses. Expenses that can be charged to a client are the following:

1. Meetings with clients to prepare material for the account

2. Interviews, surveys and placement of materials

3. Supervision of mailing and distribution of releases, photograph assignments and other visual material prepared for the client

4. Travel time, including going to and from client's office, as well as time spent in off-hours (evenings and weekends) with client personnel on client matters

Nonchargeable expenses are as follows:

1. Keeping up contacts with media representatives

2. Meetings with office and staff and other group conferences related to PR business in general

3. New business solicitation and preparation of materials for potential clients

4. Professional activities such as seminars, meetings and time spent on professional/firm matters

5. Time spent away from home in hotels at one's own leisure, as well as purely social activities with client, whether or not these occur in the evening or on weekends.

11.12 EXAMPLE OF EXECUTIVE DIARY SHEET

EMPLOYE NAME _____

EMPLOYE NUMBER _____ WEEK ENDING _____

Instructions

| 1) Category columns: 1--Average hours 2--Collateral 3--Research 4--Corporate staff 5--PR | C a t e g o r y | MONDAY | C a t e g o r y | TUESDAY |

2) Time sheets must be turned in weekly.

3) All collateral time must show job number.

Co.	Div.	Client Name	Job Number	Hrs.	Job Number	Hrs.
	32	New Business-Promotion and Publicity				
	33	Administrative				
	34	Company Meetings (nonclient)				
	35	Conventions, etc. (nonclient)				
	90	General				
	91	Absence (7-hour day)				
	92	Vacation (7-hour day)				

Total hours

Reproduced courtesy of Burson-Marsteller.

This type of cost accounting makes it necessary for employees and executives to keep an accurate record of time spent. Time segments are broken out in small sections, such as 5 minutes, 15 minutes and so on. Ordinarily, to simplify matters, clerical, secretarial and mailroom salaries are billed out as "overhead." This means that only the executives have to keep detailed records of time spent. To facilitate this, most executives keep diary sheets (see 11.12) and weekly expense reports. To make the executive billing fair, some of the larger corporations have standards like this one reported in PRSA:

> We set a ceiling on our staff time charged at the same rate as some of our people whose salaries are significantly lower. This is explained to the client so that he understands that our cost accounting system does not tempt us to put so-called lower-priced people to work on jobs. It costs him the same for me when I'm doing operational work as it does for a lot of others who are not principals. Our overhead rate usually ranges between 90 percent and 110 percent. All operational time is accounted for on an hourly basis. Nonoperational work comes out of the fee, but that time is also accounted for on an hourly basis.

Making small accounts earn their keep is sometimes a problem. One of the difficulties you are likely to encounter is that these smaller companies have little experience using public relations services and often make unreasonable demands and expect extraordinary results. It helps if you concentrate your efforts where you are most likely to get demonstrable results: trade publications, weeklies, locally produced Sunday supplements and other regional media. See if the client has a feature appropriate for a local television "magazine" program. You will probably have to do a better selling job to the print and television media on such features because of their limited scope and appeal. Be sure all your efforts are related to the client. Tell every success story to the client, even if it is just a column item. Help the client develop programs that will generate publicity—foot traffic, maybe. You may want to help the client start an internal communications program, a simple one like a newsletter. Help the client use advertising economically. These clients are going to need the effectiveness of a paid-for message. Watch the client's costs carefully. Small budgets can't absorb things like printing overruns or expensive mass mailings. Probably most important, be sure you have a contract that spells out obligations and also provides for prompt payment, such as ten days after billing. If it is a new client you don't know much about, it is not a bad idea to require some prepayment.

BUDGETING A PR OPERATION

In a PR office, salaries and fringe benefits amount to approximately 80 percent of the total expenses, leaving 20 percent for profit, new business and company (rather than client) costs, which means 20 percent of the costs cannot be billed out. Since some of the latter are a matter of discretion, it occasionally works best to have a set budget for them so there are no misunderstandings about travel and entertainment allowances, membership dues, long-distance phone calls and other nonbillable expenses. The other company expenses are usually predictable, since they involve rent, insurance and utilities. Such things as office supplies and postage are variables that just have to be estimated.

The amount that can be invested in seeking new business must also be calculated rather roughly. A firm must decide at what rate it desires and needs to grow. PR practitioner Alfred G. Paulson, author of articles on fiscal planning, suggests that a 20 percent anticipated or planned growth is not realistic and might prove taxing for a company already handling a large volume of business.[7] The cost of attracting new business and finding the staff to handle it are real considerations. If too rapid an expansion takes place, the problem of limited facilities might also

---

[7] Alfred G. Paulson, "Cost Accounting in the Public Relations Firm," *Public Relations Quarterly*, 16, no. 3 (1972), pp. 14–15. Also see "Budgeting in the Public Relations Agency" and "Accounting Reports in Public Relations," *Public Relations Quarterly*, 9, no. 4 (1972). These also are in a brochure, "Budgeting and Accounting for Public Relations Firms," with Paulson's article on fee billing and one by Farley Manning on "How to Charge a Client." Copies available on request: A. G. Paulson, 103 Park Ave., New York, NY 10017.

enter the picture. However, Paulson warns that the percentage of anticipated growth should not be as low as 10 percent, since this would be too low to stimulate the action and enthusiasm needed to develop new business contacts and clients. A growth pattern of roughly 15 percent, he says, allows a realistic profit return expectancy of 25 percent before bonuses, profit sharing and taxes.

Would it ever occur to you to put in your PR budget the cost of responding to news media requests should your institution suddenly become the focus of news? Perhaps you should. Consider what happened to Washington Public Power Supply when its failure to pay on bonds became news.

> "WPPSS is averaging 1,500–2,200 news clips a month just from the Pacific Northwest. Our twice-a-month executive board meetings are regularly covered by 5–7 TV stations, usually at least one national, and some 30 reporters including the *NYTimes* & the *Wall Street Journal. Time* magazine has reported on the Supply System in 3 of its 4 last issues. Three members of my staff regularly handle some 150–200 media inquiries per week (and sometimes 150/day) from all over the U.S. And in a usual week we will have at least 1 or 2 national media visit our sites for 1–3 days. It goes on, but suffice it to say that, to my knowledge, there is no other single company that has this kind of consistent news coverage other than perhaps G.P.U. & Three Mile Island."
>
> Washington Public Power Supply System's (WPPSS) effort to "recover costs" by charging media for document requests elicited some disagreements (see *prr* 6/13). Responding to *prr*'s article, info svcs dir Gary Petersen explains:
>
> "To give you a feel for the volume of requests we have been getting, in 1982 we charged 10¢ a page and received $12,740 for all the records provided. 127,400 pages of text had to be located, copied, packaged & mailed.
>
> "It was only when the total WPPSS staff was reduced by more than 25%, and when the document requests began involving extensive staff & legal research that our records management group suggested a fee to recover costs. If a request was for a specific document (which required no research), we made only the 10¢ a page charge. . . ."[8]

POINTS TO REMEMBER

- Know the production schedules of the news media and provide the appropriately prepared message for each audience.

- Planning events requires at least nine steps or stages to ensure success: (1) Start early. (2) Make a timetable. (3) Form committees. (4) Use professionals. (5) Offer extra attractions to get people there. (6) Have giveaways and souvenirs. (7) Make traffic flows easy. (8) Publicize event well in advance. (9) Thank people who helped.

- Check facilities and equipment thoroughly. Don't trust anything to either chance or promises.

- Easel pads, overhead projectors and slides are several visual presentation methods that require technical familiarity.

---

[8] "Being in the News Proves Costly," *pr reporter*, July 18, 1983, p. 3. Reprinted by permission. (Some companies handling high-volume products like automobiles get similar attention routinely.)

- Rules to follow in handling sound equipment include the areas of sound reinforcement, rented or company equipment, complexity of equipment and choosing components.

- Arrangements for celebrity appearances must be well planned; handling celebrities requires tact and patience.

- Steps in brochure production are determining its purpose, audience and physical properties; deciding what is to be said and how; choosing materials and procedures to carry out the design; and carrying production through printing.

- House publications must be professional-looking pieces because they have many different uses, and they must be appropriate in content for their audiences.

- Annual reports should be the shared responsibility of a communications specialist, who decides the character of the report, and the management representative, who is responsible for the content.

- Producing institutional films and videotapes is a costly, time-consuming venture, although they can be put to many uses. Decisions to be made include who will produce and distribute it, what its objective is and who its audiences are.

- Three basic methods for determining client charges are the fixed fee, the fee for services plus out-of-pocket expenses and the retainer.

- Budgeting the PR operation includes planning for people costs and operations costs.

THINGS TO DO

1. A film personality who is a graduate of your university is returning to the campus for a dedication of a new fine arts complex. What arrangements must be made for the visit?

2. Outline the contents of a media kit for this occasion.

3. There will be visiting newspeople covering the dedication. What do you need to do to arrange for facilities to accommodate them?

4. Assume that you have been asked to produce a brochure for an organization of which you are a member. What steps do you take? Plan a timetable.

SELECTED READINGS

Don Bates, Anne L. New, Alice Norton, Harold N. Weiner, Dorothy Ducas, Frances Schmidt and Frances A. Koestler, *Managing Your Public Relations: Guidelines for Nonprofit Organizations* (New York: Public Relations Society of America, 1977), set of six. Superb collection of ideas, suggestions, recommendations.

Doug Newsom and Tom Siegfried, *Writing in Public Relations Practice: Form and Style* (Belmont, Calif.: Wadsworth, 1981). Includes writing for print media; broadcast media; advertising copy; speeches and scripts; annual reports; magazines and employee publications; newsletters and brochures; backgrounders and position papers, memos and letters, reports and proposals, as well as chapters on research and presentation strategy.

W. E. Scott and L. L. Cummings, *Readings in Organizational Behavior and Human Performance*, rev. ed. (Homewood, Ill.: Richard D. Irwin, 1973). Some useful theories and studies to help the PR practitioner win internal battles.

Gary Wagner, ed., *Publicity Forum* (New York: Richard Weiner, 1977). A collection of some of the more amusing and exotic stories of promotions.

Note: Stylebooks for both print and broadcast media—Associated Press and United Press International—are available. Also, helpful paperbacks are often issued by trade associations and by product manufacturers. Collect these for references. Suppliers, too, can furnish valuable reference aids from type styles to catalogues of prerecorded music to use for sports and slide shows.) An essential book is *Without Bias: A Guidebook for Nondiscriminatory Communication for the International Association of Business Communicators*, 2d ed. Judy E. Pickens, ed., IABC. (New York: John Wiley, 1982).

PART 5

PR in Action

Taken by itself, each component of PR may look easy. But it is the blending of all components into a successful program that makes PR effective. Chapter 12 describes how to launch the PR campaign and Chapter 13 presents case studies of successful PR.

CHAPTER 12

The PR Campaign and the Case Study Approach

Thank God, communication isn't a disease, because we know so little about it.

Bill Marsteller, former chairman and chief executive officer, Marsteller, Inc.

Public Relations is a tough, constant-pressure business. If you don't enjoy working under pressure, stay away from PR.

Frank W. Wylie, director of public affairs, California State University, Los Angeles

Good public relations doesn't just happen. It is a carefully planned, well-calculated effort that brings measurable results. Analyzing campaigns and cases can guide the novice, stimulate the imagination of the expert and offer a resource to both.

PLANNING THE CAMPAIGN

The first task in planning is to clarify the objectives and goals of the PR program that your research suggests is needed. Define the objectives—what you want to accomplish—as precisely as possible and in terms of long-range achievements. Your short-range achievements are your goals. The best way to clarify them is to write them down. (Remember to write for yourself, not posterity; spare prose will keep you from straying into murky bypaths.) If you have a clear statement of objectives and goals, you will be able to evaluate the success of your campaign because you can measure how close you came to achieving them or by how much you surpassed what you expected.

Once you have defined the objectives and goals suggested by the initial fact finding, look at them and ask some probing questions. Are they compatible with the current PR program? Where are they headed, ultimately? Would any of these objectives or goals conflict with your institution's policy? Is there possible conflict with a major public? With any particular public? How significant is the conflict? Could it destroy a program?

A clear delineation of publics is something you should be sure of before planning your strategy. The demographics and psychographics will give you a key to the tactics you can employ to make your strategy succeed. Part of your strategy is deciding the most effective way to reach each public. What does each public need to know? What is the best way to say it? What would be the most likely way to get that public's attention? This is where creativity makes the difference—the creative use of words or symbols, an original approach to the medium.

Choosing the
Theme and Media

The success or failure of a PR campaign depends very strongly on your creativity—in deciding on the theme, in choosing the media and in using the media.

Deciding on the theme may come about in a number of ways—from several persons brainstorming together, from one person's idea, from the adaptation of someone else's successful idea. What is important is to entertain *all* ideas without passing judgment. Criticism kills creativity and may snuff out an idea at birth. Stimulate people to share ideas—no matter how wild—by encouragement and enthusiasm. A good theme won't save a poorly executed campaign, but well-oiled campaign machinery won't save a bad idea either. Remember you can also pretest. Pretesting works for ideas as well as for completed materials.

Your choice of media depends on the publics you want to reach, among other things. A preliminary decision as to which media are right should be apparent once objectives are determined; however, the *creative* choice of media is something different. What is a unique way to reach a special public? What media have not been used before but could be? Someone, after all, was the first to use bumper stickers and skywriting, and silk-screened T-shirts.

The creative use of the media is also important. A media schedule that lists which media will be used when can be the key to a campaign's success—and also to its failure. Cereal companies that began advertising in the comics might have been laughed at by those advertising in women's pages, but the comic-page advertisers knew who their real consumers were and how to reach them. The PR person has to be careful about the complementary use of advertising and publicity. Advertising is a definite, scheduled event that appears along with whatever planned activities it is designed to promote. Publicity is an indefinite event that cannot be guaranteed to appear but will likely happen if the planned activities are news-making enough. The careful exploration of possible publicity makes planning a comprehensive program much easier. Planning adds the unknown (publicity) to the known (advertising).

In the case of both advertising and publicity, what you are presenting is a message—information. People either seek information or just process it. If involved enough in the subject to seek it, they are not likely to turn to mass media, says PR researcher James E. Grunig.[1] Grunig found that only people with extra time to spend are exposed to mass media. The more active people are, the less time they spend with mass media. To reach the involved, you need to use specialized publications because that is where people actively seeking information on a subject

---

[1] Reported in *pr reporter*, May 29, 1978, p. 1.

go. However, if you are aiming at a low involvement and perhaps just want exposure to an issue, then a mass medium is appropriate, especially one like television, which forces audiences to process information. Remember, though, that the public you most want to reach might not be there, and the effort (if publicity) or expense (if advertising) may be wasted.

Setting Goals and Timetables

Visions of grandeur are kept within the realm of the feasible when you set your goals. You have set your objectives and know where you are going. Now you decide how to get there, one step at a time. Have information on hand before you determine the extra research needed, the publics and the media. Above all, don't overplan. You can spend a lot of time creating in management the impression of great thought and forethought, but often, unfortunately, not much but charts gets done.

Goal achievement estimates, like timetables, need be no more elaborate than a marked calendar, but it is imperative that the deadlines be realistic. This means be realistic about what can be achieved within the time periods designed for your goals. Allow for foul-up time, and try to finish work ahead of schedule rather than have to explain why you are behind. Contingency planning means deciding in advance who will pick up the ball if someone drops it and what effect the substitution will have. Downtime from mistakes is reduced considerably if you have a realistic timetable. Don't crowd yourself or your staff. Consider how to integrate the project into the overall schedule of PR activities so it will not conflict with regular duties such as writing the annual report or preparing for a stockholders' meeting. If necessary, allow for calling in extra clerical help when there is an overload. It is not necessary to allow for the ten minutes it takes a messenger to deliver copy to the typesetter, but it is necessary to allow the ten days for color separations to be made. Allow some leeway or one missed deadline will jeopardize the entire effort. Also retain enough elasticity in the schedule so you can take advantage of opportunities and make changes.

You will undoubtedly have the experience of having some critical element in a project barely make it—programs delivered from the printers with the ink barely dry, artwork delivered only an hour before it is needed for production. But if a PR director allows this to happen too often, his or her staff will find the work environment harrowing and unpleasant, and the PR practitioner will risk his or her mental and physical health as well as job and reputation.

Contingency Planning

One cheerful PR person says his smile is the result of always anticipating the worst things happening, then enjoying it when they don't. Unhappy possibilities always have to be kept in the back of your mind. What if a billboard company confuses dates and your ads don't go up on time? Can you use newspaper advertising and radio or TV commercials to take up the slack? What if your publicity is pushed off the news by a disaster or other breaking story? What if your TV time is preempted? Flexibility and contingency plans are needed.

A PR director will get help in contingency planning from his or her staff. The staff will not only make creative suggestions and come up with good alternative proposals, but they will support the project, particularly when it is likely to consume a lot of their time. The director should evaluate accurately and honestly what each individual can best contribute to the project (and think about individual talents rather than just the jobs done before). After the project is accepted by management, the director must write down everyone's duties and responsibilities so there will be no misunderstanding of who does what when.

Selling the Program to Management

After you have set your goals, you must plan the strategy you will use to achieve them. One of your first tasks in mapping your strategy is selling your plan to management. You do this with a carefully reasoned and well-designed presentation, based at least in part on what has received approval in the past. As an example, Jim Fitchette sent a copy of a Phillips Petroleum employee videotape to the CEO for approval because the CEO appeared in it. Although the CEO looked great in the tape, his immediate reaction was "Why are we doing this?" Fitchette noted, "We in PR get so wrapped up in how neatly we produce things that we keep asking management to pat us on the head for how clever we are. We forget anything going to management should spell out the 'why' for the project before anything else. Reminded of the 'why,' management tends to leave the 'how' pretty much to us. . . . A lesson I keep learning."[2] Management approved, after Fitchette explained.

The greatest danger in presenting a plan is not anticipating questions and challenges. Listen to opposing points of view, but maintain control and do not allow "a good plan to get nibbled to death," as one PR director put it, before you have a chance to test its effectiveness. A PR director who has to work in a hostile climate makes a practice of duplicating her presentations and circulating them to management instead of calling a conference because she says people will approve ideas on paper that they would never approve in an open meeting. If necessary, show your plan to several important people first so you know the likely reception it will get before you actually present it formally. The whole process is not unlike caucusing in politics before calling for a committee vote. Also, much verbal battle can be eliminated by careful listening in the planning stages (see 12.1).

IMPLEMENTING THE CAMPAIGN

Implementing the project requires (1) adherence to the timetable and (2) keeping people informed. If the publicity writer says it is impossible to get the information needed for a story to go in the media kit on time, determine

---

[2] Personal correspondence, Jim Fitchette, former public affairs manager (now retired), Creative Services, Phillips Petroleum Company, January 27, 1982.

12.1 THE DEVELOPMENT OF A BROCHURE ON THE CLIENT'S NEW LINE OF SWINGS

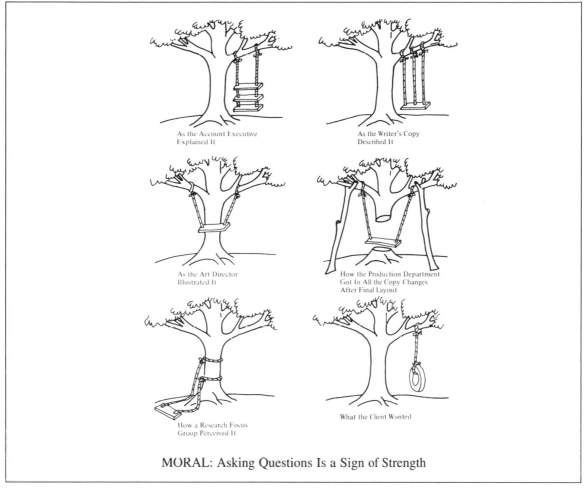

As the Account Executive Explained It

As the Writer's Copy Described It

As the Art Director Illustrated It

How the Production Department Got In All the Copy Changes After Final Layout

How a Research Focus Group Perceived It

What the Client Wanted

MORAL: Asking Questions Is a Sign of Strength

Source unknown

how long the delay may be, set an absolute deadline and be sure it is one you can live with. Most importantly, keep people informed of changes as well as of first plans. Most foul-ups occur because one person does not know the problems besetting another person whose work is related.

There are many ways to solve internal communications problems. The head of one small PR firm, noting that his staffers headed for the coffeepot between 9:30 and 10:00 A.M., scheduled a coffee-break conference time with free doughnuts. In persuading his staff members to sit for a while and discuss their successes and problems, he helped integrate staff work. Staffers, hearing the problems of others, discovered how their own timetables were going to be affected. The chief executive of a larger PR operation, after observing the most horrendous arguments among his staff over who was to blame for a delay, insisted that written communications be sent to everyone. Although he admits that sometimes there are still snafus, he says it is only because someone did not read a communique.

A multibranch operation has an alternative to written communication in a weekly loudspeaker telephone conference (telecon). Every week the advertising and PR staff of a Dallas company, for example, sit around a conference table with a phone loudspeaker operation hooked up to their counterparts in branch offices in other parts of the country. Each person summarizes what he or she is doing and outlines travel plans. As a result of the conference, plans are frequently changed. It may be brought out that someone from Dallas and someone from Chicago are both heading for, say, a plant in Montreal. The PR corporate director, then, can tell the Chicago person to take care of both assignments, thereby reducing costs in travel expenses and staff.

Still, even in the most carefully planned and well-managed effort, complications and confusion will occur. The important thing is to resolve each problem and get the job done successfully. Placing the blame wastes time and energy and can damage working relationships. Good working relationships are imperative for smooth functioning any time, but particularly where personal relationships can either facilitate, impede or even destroy the public relations program.

Whatever the PR projects, all internal publics should be kept informed. This is easy to overlook, especially when there is dynamic leadership. For instance, the director of a concert group that suddenly was given the opportunity to tour Europe was about to relay the story to the news media when it was suggested that the concert group's board of directors should be asked first to grant permission for the tour. Although approval seemed certain, and asking for it made it necessary to call each one of the twenty-three directors, the effort was worthwhile, for those in authority feel their authority has been undermined when they learn of important actions first from the newspapers.

Pleasing everyone is impossible, but the PR practitioner who works according to policy—real policy, not the "unwritten policy"—is usually safe. Unwritten policies may seem as compelling as written ones, but persistence and diplomacy can often change them, although this may be difficult if they represent the principal interests of the major stockholders. Written policy, however, is much less flexible and should be followed carefully until changes are adopted. Policies can be changed by the bold, but you must first devise a strong justification for the change and then determine how to sell it to the publics involved by anticipating how they will perceive it. For example, although Congress once rejected the Alaskan pipeline because the public perceived it as a threat to the environment, it changed its mind when the public perceived the lack of a pipeline as contributing to an energy shortage.

EVALUATING THE CAMPAIGN

Every PR campaign deserves a really soul-baring, honest autopsy. What worked and what didn't and why? What was accidentally a success? What could have been done better?

To make these postmortems successful, it is important to keep all analysis on a professional level; no witch-hunts should be permitted. If something did not work, there is usually more than one reason for its failure and more than one person involved in it. The important thing is to use constructive criticism to suggest, "If we had attempted to do this, would it have worked better than what we did try?" Egos, especially creative egos, are fragile things, yet no one minds looking in the mirror unless someone in the background is pointing an accusing finger.

The most effective evaluations are continuing programs—for instance, annual surveys of what audiences like or dislike, surveys of employee attitudes and measurements of consumer attitudes. Evaluations may also be done by reading letters and taking phone calls from happy and unhappy publics and by talking with various publics to ascertain their attitudes. To say after a campaign, "It's all over, we can forget it," instead of instituting an ongoing evaluation program, means, as one astute advertising executive put it, that you will be "constantly reinventing the wheel."

Although we have been mainly talking about specific campaigns, which may run a year or so, it is important for an organization to have an overall public relations plan projected over five to ten years. This should be a written plan complete with rationale, policy support and illustrations of tools to be used—and it should receive top management endorsement.

SUMMARY OUTLINE OF A CAMPAIGN

The cycle of a PR campaign goes something like this. First, you seek facts to help identify the problem, and then you establish your long-range objectives in terms of specific short-term goals. Second, you design whatever additional research is needed to determine the causes of the problem. Identify all possible solutions. Look at the consequences of the solutions for generating new problems. Third, you determine the publics involved and indicate the target audiences. Evaluate what research tells you about the attitudes and information these publics have and which media reach them most effectively. Plan research to pretest media and messages with these publics. What you need to look for in each of the campaigns is the "self-interest" appeal to each target audience, the key to all effective communication. Search out the other communication strategies in message structure and media delivery that have proved successful (or unsuccessful) in both informing and influencing the target audience. Look beyond the strategies for their base in some theoretical concept so you can apply that to other campaigns.

Fourth, develop a strategy that will achieve your long-term objectives and allow you to reach short-term goals. Decide which tactics will fit the strategy best. Then plan your program by integrating all of these elements into a flexible, feasible timetable and secure management and staff support. Fifth, select the media that will ensure successful and on-time implementation of the program. Finally, evaluate the results or effectiveness of the program through formal posttesting research and through less formal methods of responses from staff and publics.

Used by permission of King Features Syndicate.

Our concept of the PR case problem is much the same as that of a campaign: Both involve a program to achieve a specific objective; and in this sense, both demand the same sort of planning. PR practitioners and educators use case studies in two ways: (1) They may pose a PR problem and outline a possible solution according to specific guidelines (the existing case). (2) They may dissect a PR event as a learning experience to determine what worked and what didn't and why (the historical case). The historical case is generally referred to simply as a case. The existing situation in need of a PR solution is generally called a problem. Many PR texts and courses in fact use the title "PR Cases and Problems."

The device of posing a PR problem for solution is used in many public relations cases-and-problems classes; it is also used each year in a competition for the members of PRSSA (Public Relations Student Society of America), the student organization of PRSA. Usually the cases for class and competition are real, existing PR problems in need of a creative solution.

The case study approach in problem solving parallels the development of a campaign. Bernays called the development of solutions for problems "the engineering of consent." His approach is an eight-point program.

1. Define goals or objectives.
2. Research publics to find whether goals are realistic and attainable, and how.
3. Modify goals if research finds them unrealistic.
4. Determine strategy to reach goals.
5. Plan actions, themes and appeals to publics.
6. Plan organization to meet goals.
7. Time and plan tactics to meet goals.
8. Set up budget.[3]

After an extensive study of public communication campaigns like energy conservation or registering to vote, communication scholars concluded that suc-

---

[3] Edward L. Bernays, "The Engineering of Consent," *Industry*, 43, no. 12 (December 1978), pp. 12, 13, 36.

cessful campaigns are never guaranteed, but they can be implemented on the basis of five principles: (1) assessment of the needs, goals, and capabilities of target audiences; (2) systematic campaign planning and production; (3) continuous evaluation; (4) complementary roles of mass media and interpersonal communication; and (5) selection of appropriate media for target audiences.[4]

Grunig's studies suggest four elements necessary for success with changing behavior, three affecting communication. For success: (1) education, (2) enforcement (legal measures to force behavior change), (3) engineering (constructing preventives or barriers) and (4) peer support. (See discussion of seat belt use in Chapter 13.) The communication requirements are (1) problem awareness, (2) problem acceptance (belief that it *is* a real problem) and (3) construct behavior (a feeling that the individual can solve the problem by acting). (See Chapter 8 for Grunig's theoretical precepts.)

DISSECTING THE PR EFFORT— CASE STUDY OUTLINE

An analysis of a historical case should have three parts. The first section should include a summary of the case, that is, an explanation of the nature of the problems and their background. The discussion of the evolution of the problem with its probable causes should include the objective or goal that was to be reached in the solution. In looking at the steps taken to solve the problem, pay attention to the research into the problem itself, such as how the publics were selected and what was learned about them. Study the techniques and tools used to reach these publics and compare them with other possible techniques and tools. Study too the role of the public relations person in the solution, especially in considering the interaction of PR with other departments. The solution should offer some evidence that it was a workable way to handle the problem. Evidence may be available from the continuation of the program, from letters of endorsement, from evaluation research or from other data, such as responses to the program.

The second part of the analysis should be a detailed description of the institution involved in the problem—what it does, what it is. Samples of all materials used in the program should be included: news releases to all media, special coverage, scripts, posters, advertising, letters, special publications. Also, copies of progress reports should be examined and included in the analysis. Such reports are generally available if the PR problem was handled by a PR firm because the firm must report to management periodically. Internally handled problems are sometimes less well documented because there is some informal reporting.

The third part of the analysis ought to be a consideration and evaluation of what worked particularly well and what could have been improved. There should be thoughtful recommendations about how such a program might be handled better if a similar situation arises again for the same institution.

Dissection of a PR event is not only useful for students trying to develop ap-

---

[4]Ronald E. Rice and William J. Paisley, eds. *Public Communication Campaigns*, (Beverly Hills, Calif.: Sage, 1981), p. 7.

Existing Case	*Historical Case*
Research	
To help identify the problem and establish objectives.	To describe the nature of the problem and its background—the evolution and probable causes. To define the goals involved in the solution. To consider other possible solutions and their consequences.
Publics	
To designate publics and recognize which are target audiences. Learn what they know and believe and how to reach them with available media.	To determine how priority publics were selected and how each was involved in the solution.
Action	
To plan ways of reaching publics in an effective, efficient manner within a flexible, feasible timetable. Develop persuasive strategy. Get management and staff support.	To examine the tools and techniques used in terms of their effectiveness with the various publics. Look for evidence of management and publics' endorsement through continuation of the program or through other results giving evidence of a solution.
	To include samples of action taken—PR tools and techniques.
Evaluation	
To evaluate results or effectiveness of the program as revealed by posttesting research or less formal methods as responses from publics and staffs.	To recommend better ways to approach similar problems should these occur in the same organization. To analyze lessons to be learned from the solution implemented.

proaches to PR problems, but the same careful, detailed study and documentation is also useful for practitioners after a campaign; such a dissection is part of the postevaluation talked about in Chapter 4.

Elements in both the existing and historical case are basically the same (see 12.2).

COLLECTING IDEAS

PR practitioners are idea pack rats and keep a collection of good PR examples "just in case." Cataloging your own collection of case studies means finding an appropriate typology. Some PR librarians classify cases by the type of problem solved, such as an industrial plant closing. Others use the physical evidence from the case, such as brochures and posters. However, problems can arise if you try to save the tortilla that a meeting announcement arrived on or attempt to file half of a child's wooden block sent to announce a move of "half a block away." The indexing you might prefer probably depends on what you are looking for. Ideally, some sort of cross-filing or double-entry system works best.

Following are some examples from files labeled "Consumer Relations," "Legislative Action" and "Image Marketing." Image marketing includes promotions, media events, fund raising, investor relations and entertaining.

Consumer Relations

The natural gas industry became involved in a complex consumer confidence situation in 1983 when it was common knowledge that there was a supply glut and yet prices were up substantially. The price hike had a history. During the energy crises of the 1970s, there was a big push for exploration—at any cost—to create energy independence from foreign sources. Gas from deep wells and other difficult retrieval situations such as tight sands increased the cost at the wellhead. Producers were reluctant to lose money and so passed along the cost. Part of the controversy was the pending deregulation of natural gas and political action, encouraged by consumerism, to control increased prices for utilities. For a utility, it was a bad time for unfavorable publicity to develop over the cutoff of gas supplies to the poor, most of whom included a number of elderly people and children. No gas utility wanted to see stories of an elderly person freezing to death because the gas had been cut off after failure to pay bills. With cutbacks in federal funding that had been available to help in some of these cases, the gas utilities turned to their other customers. One utility, Oklahoma Natural Gas, began a "Share the Warmth" campaign. On the customers' bills was a place to make a contribution to the bill of some person who could not afford to pay. Skeptics said no fool would pay more than was owed. But the appeal was made in a climate of the "new federalism," with its emphasis on the private sector assuming some of the government's burden to reduce the national debt. The response to ONG's request was overwhelming , and many other gas as well as electric utilities followed suit with the same results.

Customers holding a Gulf Oil credit card may be recipients of a brochure telling them how to complain about a product or poor service. Copies of "The Art of Complaining" have been sent to millions of people. Some of the instructions say not to write to the president or the chairperson—although they are interested in hearing from customers—but instead to direct letters to customer relations.

However, the owner of a Ford Granada that had spent more time in the shop than on the road wrote and complained to Ford's president. As a result, the local dealer called, the district director sent a certified letter and the car was repaired quickly.

Companies don't always create their own problems. Others can help. A Houston PR firm was omitted from the telephone book's yellow pages. For their creative correction, see 12.3. But for firms that do create their own problems, the light touch in responding to a customer's complaint may help (see 12.4).

From a missing identification, look at what an institution does about changing its identification: the corporate signature, or logo. Allied Chemical took out a full page ad in the *Wall Street Journal* describing the change of its logo and telling why. That was straightforward and simple. But an announcement can be more complicated. A modification by the Boy Scouts of America was handled by a PR firm that volunteered its services. Normally the PR firm—Murtha, DeSola, Finsilver, Fiore—expects to spend three to six months developing a new corporate

1   ADVERTISING, ERRATA

Nobody's Perfect—

Not Even Ma Bell.

Maybe we're just paranoid, but Ma's neglecting us. She left us off page 11 of the Yellow Pages book (A-L). Really. Look for yourself. Since we're Houston's largest independent full-service advertising and public relations agency, a lot of important people—like yourself—need to look us up. Sometimes just to spell our name correctly. So, if you feel like letting your fingers do the walking, here's your chance to walk all over us. Save this page and stick it to Ma, preferably around page 11. It's the next best thing to being there in the first place.

> **GOODWIN DANNENBAUM LITTMAN & WINGFIELD INC.**
> 7676 Woodway **977-7676**

Reprinted with permission of Goodwin Dannenbaum Littman & Wingfield, Inc., Houston, Texas 77215.

identity program, and an additional three to six months implementing it with new materials.

When AT&T and Southwestern Bell were separated in 1984, the globe symbol, without the bell in the center, was kept. Since the AT&T symbol is used internationally, the sign must be universally accepted. A "good" symbol in one country can be obscene or a bad omen in another.

Communication problems are usually central to PR cases. The following examples point up some solutions to particular PR problems.

The first example: Believing that even an adult audience may need to have a

12.4 THE USE OF HUMOR IN RESPONDING TO COMPLAINTS

This is a reply to a letter complaining about a strange piece of string or rope in a can of cat food, sent over the pawprint signature of the offended finicky feline.

A NOTE FROM MORRIS
582 TUNA STREET · TERMINAL ISLAND, CA. 90731

February 5, 1974

Mini Kitty Newsom

Ft. Worth, Texas

Hi Mini Kitty!

    I'm sure glad that you took the time to write to me. Good grief!! I wouldn't want that stuff in my dinner either. It looks to me like it's somebody's fishing line. Brother - humans can really be human at times, can't they.

    I sent your letter directly to the 9-Lives Quality Assurance Department, with strict instructions that they look into this occurrence -- and that they do something about it! They told me that this sort of thing doesn't happen but once in a long, long, long while, but I asked them to make sure anyway that it doesn't happen again. After all, what will my feline friends think of my gourmet taste in cat food if they get fishing line in their dinners!

    I sure hope that your mistress (master?) will accept the enclosed coupon good for three free cans of 9-Lives. She (he?) can redeem this coupon at a local grocery store, and I sure hope that the din dins you receive will be up to 9-Lives' high quality standards and to your palate's complete satisfaction!

    Again, Mini, thanks so much for letting me know about this goof - I know that it won't happen again. My humans here at 9-Lives pride themselves on the high quality of their pet foods, and I'm sure that they will look into this problem. Keep up your finicky act, okay?!

Sincerely,

MORRIS

P.S. If your mistress happens to still have the can code on hand (that's the letters and numbers on the lid or bottom of the can), the folks here at 9-Lives would love to receive it. That'll help them investigate your weird experience. Thanks --

PRINTED IN U.S.A.

5M-1072-A 4232

Reprinted by permission of Star-Kist Foods, Inc.

message simplified, Texas Electric Service Company's newsletter makes that effort. The cost of service is put in terms of tomatoes (see 12.5).

Another example: Foreseeing a need to create an understanding of energy companies and their problems, Phillips Petroleum formally embarked on a public relations education program (PREP) in 1981. Before that Phillips had sent people to speak on campuses, but PREP was aimed at public relations students—"the

Energy Messenger

A newsletter to keep community leaders informed of developments at Texas Electric Service Company

April 1977

KILOWATTS AND LIGHTNING BUGS
Electric rates aren't as simple as they seem.

The difference between the right word and almost the right word, Mark Twain wrote, "is the difference between lightning and a lightning bug."

In the electricity business, it's often hard to find just the right word to explain something to the public. A lot of utility jargon comes into play unavoidably. Some words sound very similar to the public but mean entirely different things to an electrical engineer.

Take the terms "kilowatt" and "kilowatt-hour," for example. They sound similar. Yet the difference between them, though not quite as great as the difference between lightning and lightning bugs, is very important.

In fact, understanding these two terms can take you a long way toward understanding the complicated nature of electric utility rates. It helps to answer, for example, one of the most frequently asked questions about electric rates: Why do big industries get lower rates than homeowners?

The answer, of course, is big industries do not get lower rates than homeowners. It's true that if you average all the kilowatt-hours a big industry uses and divide that into his bill, he comes out with a lower cents-per-kilowatt-hour cost. But his electric bill, in dollars, will be much greater than the homeowner's, because he uses more electricity.

And the rate is not really lower. The homeowner could request the industrial rate, if he wanted to. But he

wouldn't, because the industrial rate would make his bill higher, not lower.

The reason for all this has to do with the difference between kilowatts and kilowatt-hours. So let's examine just what these terms mean. A kilowatt-hour, as you probably know, measures the amount of electric energy used. But a kilowatt is different. It measures the amount of electric power required at a point in time. In other words, it measures the rate at which electric energy is being used.

To illustrate this, consider an ordinary household steam iron. It requires about 1 kilowatt of power to operate (called a 1-kilowatt "demand"). If you use the iron for one hour, you've used up 1 kilowatt-hour of electric energy. If you use it for 10 hours, you've used 10 kilowatt-hours. Simple.

So what does all this mean for your electric bill? Well, your electric bill is determined by the cost of making electricity. And the most important part of the cost of electricity is the cost of the property that must be in place to serve you at the time of your maximum need.

For example, you might need 5 kilowatts of power during the hottest part of the summer when your air conditioner is running at full load. The equipment needed to supply that amount has to be there all year long, even though you need it all for only a brief time in the summer.

And the cost of that property is

pretty high. Five kilowatts of power plant capacity costs more than a thousand dollars these days. You'll also need transmission lines, and that'll cost about $250 more. Distribution facilities (wires and poles and transformers and things like that) will cost another $600 or so to serve a 5-kilowatt demand.

That should give you some idea of how expensive it is to provide electricity — and we haven't even talked about the cost of fuel to burn in the power plants yet.

(Continued on next page)

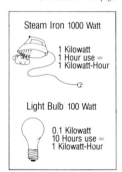

Steam Iron 1000 Watt

1 Kilowatt
1 Hour use =
1 Kilowatt-Hour

Light Bulb 100 Watt

0.1 Kilowatt
10 Hours use =
1 Kilowatt-Hour

Using a steam iron for an hour uses up as much electric energy as a 100-watt light bulb does in 10 hours. That means the steam iron requires 10 times as much power at any given time, and it's that amount — measured in kilowatts — that's the most important factor in determining the cost of electricity.

thought leaders and journalists of tomorrow," as Phillips described them.[5] Phillips' PR director, Bill Adams, told a national PR newsletter reporter that "seeds planted now will affect relationships for at least 50 years."[6] Letters to department heads go

[5] Public Relations Education Program (PREP) Draft Document from Phillips, Bartlesville, OK, 1981.

[6] "Phillips 66 Gives New Twist to Building Relationships with Students," *pr reporter*, May 23, 1983, p. 1.

KILOWATTS AND LIGHTNING BUGS (Continued)

Of course, you don't have to pay the cost of this property all at once. But there are certain costs that must be paid each year — costs like property taxes, depreciation to cover the cost of property wearing out, and interest on the money borrowed to build the property in the first place. And don't forget that some of that money came from the sale of stock, so dividends must be paid as well, just like interest.

When you add it all up, you find that there is a certain cost each year to pay for the equipment you need on those hot summer afternoons. Electric rates are designed so that over the course of a year, the customer will pay those costs.

Ordinarily you think of electricity prices in terms of cents per kilowatt-hour. That's the easiest way to measure electricity use and charge for it. But remember, the main part of the cost is due to those 5 kilowatts you needed in the summer. So the cost of that 5 kilowatts is spread over all the kilowatt-hours you use during the year.

This explains why a large industrial customer generally pays a lower cost per kilowatt-hour than a residential customer. The cost of serving an industrial customer (per kilowatt) is not much different from the cost of serving a residential customer. But the industrial customer generally uses many more kilowatt-hours than

the residential customer for the same maximum number of kilowatts. This means the industrial customer has more kilowatt-hours to spread his costs over. The result is a lower average cost per kilowatt-hour, even though the industrial customer has a much larger total bill.

For example, a residential customer might pay 3 cents per kilowatt-hour, and have a total bill of $15. An industrial customer might pay 1.5 cents per kilowatt-hour, but have a total bill of $15,000! In other words, there's a big difference between cents per kilowatt-hour and dollars — about the difference between lightning and lightning bugs.

TOMATOES ARE EASIER TO UNDERSTAND

To put cost-of-service principles into more familiar terms, let's forget about the electric utility business for a moment. Let's talk about tomatoes.

Acme Tomato Company sells and delivers tomatoes. The company charges 10 cents for each tomato. It also charges a 50 cent fee for deliveries to cover the expenses of the delivery truck and driver.

Acme has two customers. On one side of town is Harriet, a homemaker. She buys two tomatoes each day for husband Harvey's sandwiches. On the other side of town is Craig's Catsup Company. Craig buys 50 tomatoes each day to make catsup.

Acme delivers Harriet two tomatoes and charges her 70 cents. That's two tomatoes at 10 cents each plus the 50 cent delivery fee. That figures out to be 35 cents a tomato.

$$\frac{(2 \times 10¢) + 50¢}{2} = 35¢ \text{ per tomato}$$

Acme delivers Craig's Catsup Company 50 tomatoes each day and charges him $5.50. That's 50 tomatoes at 10 cents each plus the 50 cent delivery fee. That figures out to be 11 cents a tomato.

$$\frac{(50 \times 10¢) + 50¢}{50} = 11¢ \text{ per tomato}$$

That's quite a difference in the price of tomatoes — 35 cents compared to 11 cents. Just looking at the average price per tomato it would seem that poor Harriet is being overcharged.

That's clearly not the case. The cost

of delivering tomatoes remains the same and must be paid, whether it's two tomatoes or 50 being delivered. If it's 50, the delivery cost is spread out thinly over the price of the tomatoes. If it's only two being delivered, it must still be lumped on.

But no one is overcharged, and no one subsidizes anyone else. Everyone pays for the cost of service.

It is the same way in the electric utility business as it is with Acme Tomato Company. A major part of the cost is "delivering" electricity to your house.

And that's why large industrial customers pay a lower average cost per kilowatt-hour. They simply have more kilowatt-hours to spread the delivery cost over. It's just easier to understand it if you're buying tomatoes.

ID5M477

to colleges not previously visited, but personal letters go to those visited or where interest has been expressed and to those not yet contacted. The college sets the date and examines the scope of the presentations. Confirmation letters request the number of handouts needed. These are sent in advance of the Phillips representative's arrival. Presentations vary and there is no set lecture; the representative determines what is appropriate for each class. Afterward, Phillips' PR department conducts evaluations and sends notes to the host school as follow-ups. Each of the seven PR professional staff persons made at least one visit in 1981 and the PREP plan included twenty campuses. By the end of the 1982–1983 school year, the representatives had made presentations at ninety-four colleges and universities in thirty-seven states. The next step is the development of cases to send to the schools for class use. Other companies such as Standard Oil have also prepared cases for college classroom use in the form of class presentations, which are free to the colleges on request. The costs of presentations are often offset by calls on media representatives or other constituencies in the area.

Dealings with consumers should be considerate, creative and candid. Responses, rather than reactions, are more effective. Institutions can defuse hostility and modify negative positions by creating respect for another point of view, making sure everyone knows all sides of an issue, and having the facts translated from scientific, technical or legal data into something consumers and news media can understand. Also, thinking ahead helps in educating audiences. If an institution you are representing is ever the victim of a false or misleading story in the news, it is important to get a correction promptly. It isn't just institutional ego that is involved. The data banks mentioned in Part 2 on research are continuing sources of information to reporters and scholars. If a piece of false information is stored and a correction is not added, it is likely that the error will continue to be disseminated.

Error is one thing, but media bias is another. Trying to discover the effect of bias in television, Chevron did its own research. The company developed three scripts and tested responses to a positive, negative and neutral presentation. Their conclusion was that real or apparent bias of some television personnel doesn't matter much. Most people recognize it. But the oil industry's efforts to downplay or explain large profits are useless. ("Where oil profits are concerned, the rule of reason has been suspended.") The conclusion was to focus communication efforts on how profits are being reinvested in projects to expand U.S. domestic energy supplies. This would not automatically win "widespread admiration," but might eventually win respect for oil companies' technological expertise and for their efforts at reducing foreign influence[7] (see 12.6).

Legislative Action

When consumers began reacting to high medical costs with increasing criticism, one result was a significant increase in malpractice suits. Doctors who had only modest malpractice insurance policies began looking at million-dollar coverage. Arguments that the cost of expensive malpractice coverage had to be passed on to patients through increased charges only inflamed the issue. Legislation was sought to put a cap on the amounts for which doctors could be sued.

Many states were involved in the problem (perhaps most notably California), but the Texas Medical Association put together one of the most comprehensive and effective presentations of the problem. The presentation went to news media, lobbyists, legislators and significant opinion leaders. The clarity of the presentation and the uncluttered, easy-to-use references marked its effectiveness. The

---

[7]"The Influence of Reporter Bias on TV Viewer Opinion," A Chevron Communications Research Project (San Francisco, Calif.: Public Affairs Communications Division, Chevron, U.S.A., Inc., 1981).

twelve-page booklet had a pocket in the back cover for a bound copy of the proposed legislation, and in a smaller binding, in front of the proposed legislation, the documentation. Both pocket pieces could be used independently of the principal document, but they were tied to it graphically by duplicate covers. Contents of the principal document included: "Anatomy of the Crisis," "Exploding Medical Malpractice Claims," "High Cost and Scarcity of Medical Malpractice Insurance," "Skyrocketing Patient Costs," "The Crippling Effects on Health Care," "Problems with Texas Law," "What Texans Are Asking For" (the results of a TMA survey by an independent research organization, Belden Associates, whose information was then compared with a national Louis Harris survey), "What Other States Are Doing" and "Findings and Recommendations of the Study Commission" (a TMA group that spent eighteen months reviewing the problem). Each of the three documents presented was easy to read. Major points appeared in red outside a blue margin separating text material. The blue margin repeated the color of the covers. The presentation facilitated use of the information by lobbyists and opinion leaders as well as doctors.

Many legislators will turn for information to government employees. The influence of government employees is more noticeable on the federal level. In preparing a persuasive effort in Washington, win the support of related government agencies early. It is a long, tedious process: Arguments are not impressive unless they are well documented and civil servants are often young Ph.D.s not impressed by the so-called complexity of a problem. In a bureaucracy it is even more difficult to determine where the decision power lies. Strong-arm tactics directed toward the top may insult a lower-level employee who is actually responsible for making a "recommendation" and doing all of the backup work that is only "approved" at the upper level. Also, many legislators' staff members turn to lower level staff for opinions they then relay to their bosses.

A collaborative effort of government and media investigators, especially in regulated industries or services, is something to anticipate. An investigative documentary, "Home Health Hustle," aired May 1981 on *NBC News Magazine with David Brinkley*. The show was a collaborative effort of the network investigative reporters and members of the U.S. Permanent Subcommittee on Investigations. The result was a series of hearings on home health care abuse and some recommendations for new laws. Some social scientists looked at this media/policymaker collaboration for its impact on business.[8] They found that among the general public, more viewers of the show thought home health care was a problem and government help the solution than did nonviewers. Special-interest groups had little change in opinion, probably owing to a high level of knowledge. While government policy makers did not change their own priorities for the issue, their perception of the issue's importance and the public's concern increased, as did their belief that policy action was necessary.

Because PR practitioners who aren't lobbyists often get involved in helping

---

[8] Otto Lerbinger, ed., "How Media Investigations Influence Public Agendas," in "purview," a supplement to *pr reporter*, April 25, 1983, p. 1; in Fay Lomax Cook et al., "Media and Agenda Setting: Effects on the Public Interest Group Leaders, Policy Makers, and Policy," *Public Opinion Quarterly*, 47 (Spring 1983), pp. 16–35.

TV Reporter Bias:
Does it exist?
Does it matter?

Are TV newsmen biased against business?

Some businessmen — particularly oilmen — would respond with a resounding "yes."

For affirmation they would cite the decision of the National News Council which found that Brian Ross and NBC Nightly News distorted a report about Shell Oil Company titled "Fly Now, Freeze Later."

Or Mobil Oil's newspaper ad, accusing WNBC reporter Liz Trotta of committing a "hatchet job" in a TV series about gasoline prices.

Or Illinois Power's "60 Minutes/Our Reply," the celebrated videotape disclosing what Harry Reasoner and his CBS producers preferred to leave on the cutting room floor.

And more recently, Kaiser Aluminum's hard-hitting response to criticism of its aluminum wiring by Geraldo Rivera of ABC's "20/20."

Whether such incidents are proof of bias — or merely of sloppy reporting — is arguable. Some of each may very well be involved. In any event, when reporter errors are so blatant and obvious, the affronted parties can demand response time, or go public, á la Kaiser and Mobil, to redress their grievances.

But what about the more subtle forms of bias — not your out-and-out factually incorrect reporting, but the raised eyebrow, sly smirk, or disparaging "happy talk" that may prejudice viewers, even though the facts may be reported with reasonable accuracy?

Take, for instance, Mike Jensen's coverage, for CBS Evening News, of 1980 first quarter oil profits, in which he frowns into the camera and righteously intones "...experts

Reprinted with permission of Chevron, U.S.A., Inc.

lobbyists, Ronald N. Levy offers the following suggestions for helping your lobbyist win.

1. Get started early and use material from an executive's speech because it already has been researched and cleared for release.

2. Use arguments people can relate to, ones that affect them.

3. Show how winning on your issue will impact on the major concerns of the day.

4. Don't put all arguments into one release (except for the trade publications). No one wants to know everything, at least immediately, and you need additional material to keep sending.

5. Present only your case, not the opposition's. (That might depend on the situation, though; see communication theories, Chapter 8.)

Methodology

We at Chevron felt it worthwhile to explore this possibility in a dispassionate, analytical fashion, to confirm whether or not subtle reporter bias *is* really worth worrying about.

To probe this question we produced three hypothetical versions[1] of the same news report, about second half 1980 profits of Standard Oil Company of California, parent of Chevron U.S.A. One version was scripted and presented in a neutral style; a second was clearly biased against the company; a third was patently favorable. The three versions were shown to three separate samples of viewers, to assess the differing effects of the differing reporter styles on viewer opinions.

The basic assumption to be tested was that obvious reporter bias — as manifested by tone of voice, expression, or emphasis — has a direct and significant bearing on the opinions formed by a viewer about the topic reported.

"Profits" was knowingly selected as the topic for the test, even though it was anticipated (correctly) that viewers would already have strong opinions on this controversial subject.

It could be argued that a "neutral," less controversial topic would have surfaced a more accurate measure of the impact of reporter style on viewer opinion. In that case, opinion changes should have been due entirely to the reporter's influence, rather than to more complex interaction between the reporter's and the viewer's pre-existing biases.

In the "real world," however, it's extremely doubtful that *any* viewer approaches the day's news without *some* preconceptions; there simply aren't any truly "neutral" issues of any consequence. So on that basis, we concluded that a "gut" issue like profits would be an appropriate topic for this study.

We also considered how viewer familiarity with the reporter might be expected to influence the results. It seems safe to say that a well known and highly credible reporter (e.g., Walter Cronkite) would have the most personal influence, while a relative unknown would have the least. So we chose as reporter a professional newsman not well known in the communities where the study was conducted.

The three versions of the newscast were shown to separate groups of about 200 viewers each by means of closed circuit TV systems in San Diego, Calif., and Albany, N.Y. Prior to viewing a tape, each subject was asked a series of questions probing his/her attitude toward the oil industry's and Chevron's profits. Most of the questions were then repeated after the tape viewing, to assess what effect the reporting style had on the viewer's perception of the content of the newscast, and whether it altered his/her prior opinions.

1/Texts are included in appendix.

3   4

Continued

6. Don't engage in pejorative name calling. If you have to, refer to the other side as "less informed" or "well intentioned."

7. Keep in touch with the lobbyist to get feedback on which arguments seem to be working best.

8. Don't cover just the news media. Also send information to important constituencies so they will have information to reinforce their support.

9. Keep in mind the key objective is winning, not the number of clippings, interviews, editorials and photo layouts. Winning is the bottom line.[9]

---

[9] Adapted from Ronald N. Levy, "How to Help Your Lobbyists Win," *Public Relations Journal* (August 1982), p. 31. Used by permission.

Conclusions

A basic conclusion that may be drawn from this study is an affirmation of the obvious — that high oil company profits are strongly resented by many of the public. Attempts by oil companies to rationalize their profits through factual explanations have been and will be met with stony indifference and disbelief.

Considering the prevailing opinion about oil profits, reporter bias on this broad subject can have at best (or worst) only a nominal impact on the public's attitude. On the other hand, on narrower details about which the viewers have little or no specific knowledge (e.g., profit-per-dollar-of-sales, level of reinvestment), reporter bias does have a more noticeable influence over viewer perception.

Overall, however, reporter bias is not a very important influence in the formation of generally negative public opinion toward oil companies. Nor would a reporter with a *pro*-industry bias have much influence. Even if Dan Rather smiled as he announced increased oil profits, it's unlikely that viewers would be pleased with the message.

The study supports this practical counsel for oil people (and for other business people concerned with public aversion to profits in general):

(1) Don't spend much time agonizing over the real or apparent bias of some TV news personnel. It just doesn't matter that much;

(2) Downplay what have been largely fruitless efforts to convince the public that oil industry profits are not excessive. Where oil profits are concerned, the rule of reason has been suspended;

(3) Focus communications efforts on how profits are being reinvested in projects to expand U.S. domestic energy supplies.

The latter approach may not immediately generate widespread admiration of oil companies or their profits. But it may at least earn respect for the companies' technological expertise, and eventual recognition that reinvestment of profits by the companies provides the most practical and direct means of reducing undue foreign influence over our energy supplies.

This study was conceived as part of Chevron's periodic research into the impact of television news reporting on public understanding of oil industry activities and issues. It is hoped that the findings will make a useful contribution to the almost non-existent body of knowledge on this subject.

The booklet is being distributed as a public service to schools of journalism and public relations, interested broadcast and print news personnel and, of course, to business people.

11   12

Image Marketing

An image is the impression of a person, company or institution held by one or more publics. An image is not a picture, that is, a detailed, accurate representation; it is, rather, a few details softened with the fuzziness of perception. Because all of the following really depend on the marketing of an image to a public, some otherwise unlike elements appear under this heading: personality promotions, media events and fund raising; investor relations; and entertaining.

Personality Promotions, Media Events and Fund Raising   A national business publication described an interviewee as looking like a "wrung-out politician." He was an author on a book promotion tour. A newspaper columnist told how another interviewee asked him what day it was. The man did not know what city he was in either. He was a film star riding the circuit to promote a new movie. The agenda is rigorous: one-night stands in major market cities talking with entertainment columnists, appearing on TV talk shows, opening new buildings and

Appendix III
Scripts

This research project was conceived by Guy M. Carruthers, Manager, Communications, Public Affairs, Chevron U.S.A. Inc., assisted by Nancy J. Arvay, Coordinator of Electronic News Media Relations for Chevron. The methodology and questionnaire were developed in consultation with Dr. Gary Frieden and Dr. Ann Silny of ASI Market Research, Inc., of Los Angeles. ASI also conducted the interviews and collected and analyzed the data.

For further information or additional copies, write Chevron TV Research, Box 7753, San Francisco, CA 94120.

Version 1 (Neutral)

Reporter appears at news desk. Demeanor is neutral. (No smiles, frowns, voice changes or other prejudicial mannerisms.) Graphic shows Chevron Hallmark and arrow pointing up with 40% alongside.

Reporter:

In financial news today, Standard Oil Company of California, also known as Chevron, reported a 40% gain in its profits for the second quarter of this year.

Earnings per share were 3.13 dollars for the second quarter, compared to 2.24 dollars a year ago.

For the six months, Standard earned 1.16 billion dollars, a gain of 60% over the first half of 1979. These profits, the company said, were equivalent to 4½ cents on a dollar of sales, or about 3½ cents a gallon.

The company also reported it re-invested 815 million dollars in new projects around the world, up 41% from the same quarter last year. All together, Standard says, it will reinvest 3.4 billion dollars this year.

Version 2 (Negative)

Reporter appears at news desk. Through voice inflection, facial expression and choice of words, makes it plain that he thinks Socal profits are outrageous and viewer should think so, too.

Reporter:

Another of the oil giants announced huge profits today — Standard Oil Company of California, which also calls itself Chevron around here.

Standard Oil said it made a whopping 535 *million* dollars in only three months — April to June — 40% more than it did during the same three months a year ago!

In just the first six months of this year, Standard made 1.16 *billion* dollars — *60%* more than last year!

The company claims its profits amounted to 4½ cents on the dollar, and about 3½ cents a gallon. From the size of their profits they must have sold us quite a few gallons.

Standard also said its profits were down from the first quarter of this year, when it made a mere 627 million, and had to reinvest 815 million more in the second quarter to stay in business. Don't you feel sorry for them?

Version 3 (Favorable)

Reporter appears at news desk. Demeanor is neutral or upbeat. Report of increase in capital expenditures is voiced over B-roll of large scale field operations.

Reporter:

In business news tonight, Standard Oil of California, also known as Chevron, announced another healthy earnings gain — 40% more in the second quarter of 1980, and 60% more for the year as a whole.

The six months dollar total was 1.16 billion, compared with 726 million last year.

Big numbers, to be sure — but surprisingly, the company said it only earned 4½ cents on each dollar of sales, and only about 3½ cents a gallon.

Standard said it's plowing back these profits at record rates to increase U.S. energy supplies. By the end of the year it will have re-invested a record 3.4 billion dollars — 800 million dollars more than last year — in new energy development ventures. That's good news for Chevron investors.

For summaries of earlier Chevron Communications projects, write to:

Chevron U.S.A. Inc., Public Affairs
P.O. Box 7753, San Francisco, CA 94120

Chevron Communications Project #1:
Does It Pay to Communicate? — Is it smart to keep a low profile when the news gets bad? Or wiser to speak out on controversial issues, even if you take some "heat"? A 1979 study.

Chevron Communications Project #2:
Should You Debate a Politician? — The average businessman is usually mismatched in a debate against a seasoned political campaigner. Should you debate him anyway? A 1980 study.

---

being the guest celebrity for special events in places like shopping malls. The name of the game is *exposure*. Winning national exposure is a bone-wearying job. It means a lot of calls, a lot of small efforts to create some momentum toward a major recognition.

The difference a public relations effort makes is apparent in two cases reported by the *Wall Street Journal*. One case is an orthopedic surgeon who uses a miniature TV camera inserted in bone joints while he operates. He is not the only one using the technique, but he has been the subject of a number of magazine articles and has appeared on many radio and television talk shows. Why? Because he pays a PR firm $1,500 a month to publicize his practice.[10] The other involves a U.S. cabinet member, a once reclusive businessman. Raymond Donovan as U.S. Secretary of Labor was having difficulty gaining union acceptance and the press

---

[10]Jennifer Bingham Hull, "If the Doc's on TV, Maybe It's Because He Takes the PR Rx," *Wall Street Journal*, August 23, 1983, pp. 1, 16.

was having a field day with an investigation by a federal prosecutor looking into charges that Donovan once was involved in payoffs to unions as an officer in a construction company. Donovan got some PR help. He began to make speeches, hold news conferences and make trips to meet with media and business groups. In the process he generated some positive media coverage. Soon there was a change from calls for his resignation to positive comments about his actions. According to *WSJ*, "The critics say Mr. Donovan hasn't improved as much as his press clippings would indicate. But in Washington it often is difficult to separate image from substance."[11]

Politicians use the personal appearance as a media event to help create exposure. Candidates develop a message (called The Speech by media who travel with them). Their message is presented as often as a dozen times in one day to different audiences. The most skillful emphasize some particular portion of it for a particular audience. The result of this single-message presentation is that the news media stop reporting on the speech and begin to report instead on the audience reaction to The Speech or on trivia of the campaign. One gubernatorial candidate, capitalizing on the scarcity of things to report once his campaign was underway, had media kits constantly updated with "The Campaign to Date," his own version of the emphasis in different towns or to particular audiences. A political columnist who was a member of the opposing political party admiringly called the update "useful to us and damn smart politics." What is being sold in tours by personalities is the image of the individual.

Among the more ingenious ideas for image promotion are the ads and public service announcements produced by the Scouts, using such talent as former U.S. president Gerald Ford (see 12.7). Other stars used have included Hank Aaron, Arthur Godfrey, David Hartman, Henry Fonda, James Lovell, Mark Spitz, James Stewart, Howard K. Smith, Rich Little, Willis Reed, and Paul Winfield. The PSAs had the former Scouts, in uniform, reciting a few words of the Scout oath. Getting public service time means you shouldn't buy the advertising space; most groups, therefore, look for space donors. The United Way found one in Sears, which donated a whole back page of its newspaper section, with only the Sears logo appearing (see 12.8).

Corporate Advertising—Image and Advocacy The image advertising companies do is tied to the economy and the company's position in the industry. When money is tight, the image ads go. The risk is if the ads stay out for too long, one estimate is two years before the company begins to suffer, but decline then is said to be quick. Image advertising is just one form of corporate advertising other than commercial. Another is advocacy. Advocacy ads are a form of lobbying. The appeal usually is an indirect one, but is aimed at broadening a base of public support and a political strategy.

Fundraising The promotion of a person, book or film is not unlike what fund raisers must do. What they are selling is the image of an institution. They are also

---

[11] Robert S. Greenberger, "How Donovan Rises from Politician Grave with Help of Hype," *Wall Street Journal*, June 16, 1983, pp. 1, 20.

When you help start a Scout troop, there's no guarantee one of the Scouts will grow up to be President.

But you never know.

For all the facts on how your organization can support a Scout troop, call Boy Scouts of America. The Trinity Methodist Church of Grand Rapids, Michigan did, and look what they've got to show for it.

SCOUTING/USA

Prepared as a Public Service by Foote, Cone & Belding, Inc.

Reprinted with permission of Boy Scouts of America, National Headquarters, Dallas/Fort Worth Airport, Texas 75261.

asking for a direct response. Fund raising is highly competitive and so specialized that it has its own magazine: *Fund-Raising Management*. Marketing techniques, advertising, image making and promotion are all fund-raising techniques. For public relations people fund raising means learning how to write proposals that will "sell," making contacts for resources, arranging and handling meetings that will be productive and presenting the institution and its publics in a persuasive format. The strategy of an appeal is outlined by William R. Conrad, chairman of the board of the Institute for Voluntary Organizations (see 12.9), and the communication process it reflects is significant for PR people.

Fund raisers in campaigns have charted the course of asking techniques. First, planning initiates the presentation of an image that wins identification with a cause; then tactics are used to get emotional support for the cause before targets are asked. If the target says no, there is an analysis of why, and then there is further communication and cultivation before the target is asked again.

Investor Relations   A stockbroker stopped one evening on the way home from her office to bring some material about investments to friends who were also her customers. One of the friends, a public relations practitioner, looked over the materials and handed them back with the comment, "I write this sort of thing. I just

36 A   *The Dallas Morning News*   Thursday, September 16, 1976

HELP THEM

...It Won't Cost You A Dime

Here's Why

Less Than 8¢ Is Required For Fund Raising and Year-Round United Way Administration ...

That Means 92¢ Of Every Dollar You Contribute Goes To Direct Help

Where the money goes

1976 Budget

A. HEALTH SERVICES	17.6%
B. YOUTH SERVICES	20.4%
C. FAMILY SERVICES	14.4%
D. CHILD CARE	14.5%
E. STATE AND NATIONAL AGENCIES	13.4%
F. CENTRAL SERVICES	5.6%
G. AGENCY CONTINGENCIES AND EMERGENCIES	0.7%
H. SHRINKAGE (DEATHS REMOVALS, ETC.)	5.5%
I. CAMPAIGN EXPENSE	4.1%
J. ADMINISTRATION EXPENSE	3.8%

"Rip-off!" An ugly phrase common in an age of inflation and skepticism. Too often it refers to so-called "worthy causes" in which costs of raising money and administration are far too high.

Most people like to help people. Most will back it up with a portion of their hard-earned paychecks. But people understandably get indignant when they learn that sloppy operations take the heart right out of their contributions. Money you work hard for comes hard, and you want it to work hard . . . in United Way, it does

United Way
Thanks to you it works.
For all of us.

Sears
SEARS, ROEBUCK AND CO.

Reprinted with permission of Sears, Roebuck and Company.

12.9 THE GIVING PROCESS

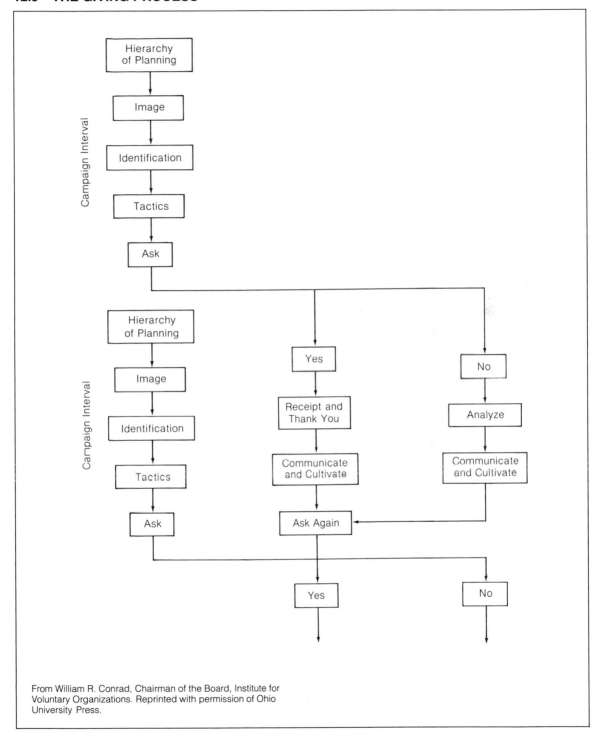

From William R. Conrad, Chairman of the Board, Institute for
Voluntary Organizations. Reprinted with permission of Ohio
University Press.

want to see the recent financial data." The stockbroker was surprised to learn her friend considered the materials "publicity" sent to an "investor public."

The stockbroker had never thought of herself as an investor public—the target for intensive public relations efforts by publicly held companies. As noted by publicly held Tracor's PR director, Judith Asel Newby, "Investor relations is no longer a function concerned only with producing annual and quarterly reports and assisting the financial office in meeting reporting requirements. Investor relations is, and must be, a total public relations type program of its own, designed to meet one overriding objective: to establish, or increase, a company's credibility and recognition in the financial community."[12] The product, Newby said, is the company, and there are more than 5,000 other publicly held companies with the same objective, competing for the same public's attention.

Newby outlines what is necessary for a successful investor relations program:

1. Total commitment and honest participation by the company's key executives
2. Critical, internal evaluation of the management and performance of the company
3. Complete awareness of the nature of the company's business and competition within the industry, including economic factors of the industry, industry trends and attitudes affecting business and industry
4. Specific identification of the diverse publics within the financial community
5. Knowledge of how the company is perceived and rated by each of these financial publics

Entertaining   Part of the PR image is partying. To downplay this, many practitioners have gone to the opposite extreme of pretending that entertaining is never a part of PR practice—when it is. PR people must plan and produce countless business/social functions such as receptions, cocktail parties, lunches, dinners and other similar events. The proper word is *produce*, not *host*, because usually the PR person is not the host. Much business gets done at these informal gatherings, and to facilitate that purpose, the PR person in charge needs to be sure that those on the host team know who is coming, what their background is and why they are being invited.

There should also be a briefing before the party for another look at who is coming and what their interests are, who is responsible for that person's being introduced and meeting others and, certainly, for a review of the correct pronunciation of names and a clarification of titles and connections or relationships among guests. Also at the briefing, those responsible for the party need to find out basic functional information such as where name tags are (if any are used); what the time frame for activities is (should there be entertainment or a speaker or an announcement); and what the physical arrangements are, including where the light dimmers are (in case of slide shows), where the switch is to cut out the PA system or—in the case of a party in a private home—where the telephones are and perhaps even where the mop is kept. The point of entertaining is for people

---

[12] Speech to the Texas Public Relations Association members, Summer 1977, Corpus Christi, Texas.

to have an enjoyable experience. They should feel comfortable and welcome. Social graces and just plain good manners are always a functional part of good public relations.

POINTS TO REMEMBER

- Campaigns and cases are the blueprints of PR—those to be drawn and those already drawn to be studied.
- In planning a campaign the steps are as follows: (1) Clarify the short- and long-term objectives. (2) Delineate your publics. (3) Figure out what you want to happen with each public and the strategy for accomplishing your objectives. (4) Determine the message content for each public. (5) Discover how to deliver that message and through which media. (6) Pretest media and messages for direction to govern decisions. (7) Determine activities, set goals and establish timetables, as well as use of personnel and other resources. (8) Plan for contingencies. (9) Get management approval.
- In implementing the plan, adhere to the timetable and keep people informed.
- Evaluate the results to determine what worked, what didn't and why.
- In outlining a campaign, use Bernays's eight-point approach to problem-solving: (1) Define goals or objectives. (2) Research publics. (3) Modify goals if research shows them unrealistic. (4) Determine strategy. (5) Plan actions, themes and appeals to publics. (6) Plan organization. (7) Time and plan tactics. (8) Set up budget.
- Successful campaigns are based on the following principles: (1) assessment of needs, goals, capabilities of target audiences; (2) systematic campaign planning and production; (3) continuous evaluation for fine tuning; (4) complementary roles for mass and personal media; and (5) selection of appropriate media for target audiences.
- Both types of PR cases, the existing problem and the historical case, are sources and resources for PR practitioners and educators.
- Dissecting the PR case, either a current problem or a historical one, involves research, publics, action and evaluation.
- Major areas for cases are consumer relations, legislative action and image marketing, which includes personality promotions, media events and fund raising; investor relations; and entertaining.

THINGS TO DO

1. This is a case of a PR plan that was not sold to management. The management of a chemical plant employing 30,000 people and dominating a small city's economic life asked its PR director to determine the best way to handle vacations—whether to shut down the plant for two weeks or let the employees individually choose their vacations throughout the conventional three-month summer period. The PR director conducted a survey among employees and residents and found most fa-

vored the individual vacation plan. The results were communicated throughout the media, and the local newspaper editorially complimented the plant on its civic-mindedness and concern for employees. But a month before the three-month vacation period was to start, the company management told its employees that the plant would close for two weeks in July so everyone could take a vacation. The decision was made by the vice president in charge of production, who had sold management on the shutdown so maintenance crews could make repairs and install new equipment. The notice went to the employees before the PR director even knew of the change in plans. She protested, but the plant still closed. There was serious damage to employee morale and community relations. Where was the problem? How could this have been prevented?

2. You have been assigned the job of planning a model fund-raising campaign that can be used either as is or adapted by each individual community. What must be considered in planning for this flexibility? What physical format would you suggest for the model? What media would you recommend being used? What tools would you offer for using these media? What is a reasonable time schedule for development of the model and for implementation by other cities? What will be necessary for the adoption of the model by different communities?

3. You are planning a nationwide campaign for a manufacturer of work clothes made in the South. Is there any particular advantage in planning a regional campaign before launching the national campaign? How would you schedule the campaign activities so they would reinforce each other?

SELECTED READINGS

Jeffery M. Berry, *Lobbying for the People: The Political Behavior of Public Interest Groups* (Princeton, N.J.: Princeton University Press, 1977). A good look at activist politics.

Harper W. Boyd, Jr., and William F. Massy, *Marketing Management* (New York: Harcourt Brace Jovanovich, 1972). An excellent reference source.

Fraser/Associates, *The PAC Handbook—Political Action for Business* (Washington, D.C.: Fraser/Associates, 1981). An agency's review of PAC use and usefulness.

George L. Herpel and Richard A. Collins, *Specialty Advertising in Marketing* (Homewood, Ill.: Dow Jones–Irwin, 1972). One of the best discussions of this widely used but little talked about part of public relations. How useful are those pens with the company name, key chains with the logo or balloons with a slogan? Are they a waste or a tool?

Maurice I. Mandell, *Advertising*, 3d ed. (Englewood Cliffs, N.J.: Prentice-Hall, 1981). Approaches advertising in its relationship to the marketing function; has blueprints for a marketing plan, media plan and behavioral research study (a simple questionnaire, but useful as an example).

——— and L. Rosenberg, *Marketing*, 3d ed. (Englewood Cliffs, N.J.: Prentice-Hall, 1981). A good companion to *Advertising*.

Leon Quera, *Advertising Campaigns: Formulation and Tactics* (Columbus, Ohio: Grid, 1977). Good general book on a complex subject, with outstanding treatment of themes and appeals.

Ronald E. Rice and William J. Paisley, *Public Communication Campaigns* (Beverly Hills, Calif.: Sage, 1981). Discusses some well-known campaigns like the antismoking campaign and evaluates elements needed to make such campaigns effective.

Joseph S. Nagel Schmidt, ed., *The Public Affairs Handbook* (New York: AMACOM, 1982). A useful tool for many references to different aspects of working with government.

Nathaniel Sperber and Otto Lerbinger, *Manager's Public Relations Handbook* (Reading, Mass.: Addison-Wesley Publishing Co., Inc., 1982). A blend of directions and theory from a managerial approach.

Ralph Turner and Lewis M. Killian, *Collective Behavior*, 2d ed. (Englewood Cliffs, N.J.: Prentice-Hall, 1972). One of the best comprehensive treatments of the subject; stresses importance of communication.

Frederick E. Webster, Jr., *Marketing Communication: Modern Promotional Strategy* (New York: Ronald Press, 1971). A formula (mathematical) approach about effects on audience of coordinating advertising, personal selling and other promotional elements.

13

PR in Action—
How They Did It

All experience is an arch to build upon.

Henry Brooks Adams, historian and writer

. . . To be possessed of a vigorous mind is not enough; the prime requisite is rightly to apply it.

René Descartes, philosopher

Three types of cases dominated the early 1980s: issues and crisis management, behavior modification and combined marketing-public relations efforts. The reasons these emerged are clear. They are products of the times. The increasing impact of focused public opinion makes issues and crises command great attention. Demands for proven results, measurements of success, have sent behavioral scientists to work to see if public relations tools work. The merging of advertising agencies and public relations firms has created a dynamic milieu for marketing, sales promotion and public relations. Take a case in each of the three areas, put it in an international arena and you have a representation of PR cases and concerns of the period. PR, like the economy, is no longer "domestic," and many cases have impact, even settings, far beyond one country's borders.

A PR practitioner said one of the most useless activities he could imagine for a professional organization was the preservation of public relations cases, since no two situations were ever exactly alike. This is true, but nevertheless, it is helpful to see how others approached a PR problem and solved it. Their solution might not have been the only solution, but it was one solution. Most of the texts for PR cases-and-problems classes offer historical cases as learning experiences. Unfortunately, most of these are usually ones that had successful solutions. But PR mistakes are also useful; they are just less often shared except by a few rare, professionally se-cure practitioners. Analyzing cases in PR is just as valuable as studying battle strate-gies, or in a less violent vein, bridge or backgammon games. The storehouse of experience and ideas in all professionals results from an accumulation of case studies.

In this chapter are complete cases for you to study as well as some incidents and innovations from which you can learn.

ISSUES MANAGEMENT
AND CRISIS PR

Issues management and crisis public relations have much in common. As a monitoring of the socioeconomic climate and its impact on public opinion, issues management is a public relations tool designed to head off confrontations and crises. Some inevitable crises such as disasters are also easier to manage if issues have been dealt with so the climate of public opinion is favorable enough to be sympathetic toward company management.

Issues

Philip Lesly cautions that an emphasis on issues leads to a siege mentality. He prefers calling the procedure monitoring and management of issues and *opportunities*. Lesly also cautions against long-term, fixed planning; the term *issues monitoring* suggests the need to be flexible and responsive to developing situations and trends.

Lesly has developed a comprehensive checklist for issues and opportunities (see 13.1). Following a similar pattern is the issue-tracking plan used by Phillips Petroleum, called PRISM (Public Relations Issues State Monitoring) (see 13.2 for Phillips's 1982 plan).

Issues monitoring is not limited to the corporate world. Industries, nonprofits and professional groups are also watching their radars. The *Wall Street Journal* has reported on the sensitive monitoring by FACT—the Frozen Food Action Communication Team—who sent a letter of reprimand to New York's Mayor Edward Koch after Koch said on a radio talk show that he preferred fresh food to frozen.[1] FACT began in 1974 with financing from frozen-food processors. The monitoring and communication group's purpose is to keep track of negative comments, collect evidence supporting claims to the superiority of frozen foods and distribute frozen-food recipes. (Public Relations Society of America has a similar, volunteer monitoring system called "PR for PR" to informally censure abusers of the title either in slurs or in job descriptions.)

The handling of issues and crises is not a linear action from sensing the issue or opportunity to a favorable solution. Instead, as consultant John Bitter suggests, it is more like a cycle. The five-step process of sensing the problem, defining the problem, deriving solutions, implementing them and evaluating outcomes (similar to the PR case study approach in Chapter 12) can recur as each portion of a solution is worked through. The feedback causes adjustments in the plans, which in turn causes the next step of a solution to return to phase one each time.[2]

---

[1] David L. Blum, *The Wall Street Journal*, June 11, 1981, p. 29.

[2] John Bitter, "A Basic Training Document: Following a Problem Solving Cycle Steadies the Course in a Crisis," tips and tactics, *pr reporter*, January 24, 1983, pp. 1–2.

13.1 A CHECKLIST FOR ISSUES AND OPPORTUNITIES

MANAGING THE HUMAN CLIMATE

**Guidelines on Public
Relations and Public Affairs**

by Philip Lesly

I. Structure
   1. Public Issues and Opportunities Task Force
      - Corporate planning
      - Operations
      - Finance
      - Marketing
      - Production
      - Law
      - Government relations
      - Public relations
      - Human resources
      - Outside Counsel

II. Preparation for Each Issue or Opportunity
   1. Research what is known about the issue or opportunity
      1.1 Analyze causes
         - Technical factors
         - Supplier fault
         - Company's procedures
         - External problems (blockages, weather, etc.)
         - Snag in employee communication
         - Snag in communication with customers
         - Snag in communication with stockholders
         - Snag in communication with government agencies
         - Snag in communication with legislators
         - Snag in relations with external organizations (environmentalists, minorities, etc.)
      1.2 Study facts, reports, experts within company

   1.3 Review outside sources
      - Government
      - Other industry
      - Associations
      - Libraries
      - Suppliers
      - Publications
   1.4 Analyze the present climate
      - In government
      - Competitors
      - Other industry
      - Critics' groups
      - In media
      - In journals
   1.5 Conduct opinion surveys
      - Among groups affected by issue
      - Activists
      - Employees
      - Stockholders
   1.6 Determine what others are doing on this issue (avoid duplication, coordinate, counteract)
   2. Establish company's position on the issue
      2.1 Write policy as guide for all in company
      2.2 Distribute on need-to-know basis

III. Publics to Be Dealt with
   1. Employees
      1.1 All
      1.2 Select groups
         - Executives
         - Operating staff
         - Subsidiaries' staff
         - Local plant and office level
   2. Government
      2.1 Federal elected officials
      2.2 Federal appointed officials
      2.3 State elected officials
      2.4 State appointed officials
      2.5 Local elected officials
      2.6 Local appointed officials
   3. Financial community

Crises

Trying to stay on top of a crisis creates both internal and external communication problems, as Seattle First National Bank discovered. In 1982, when Penn Square Bank of Oklahoma City failed and was closed, its depositors paid off by the Federal Deposit Insurance Corp. (FDIC), other banks tied to it through major investments also were involved in the national coverage of the bad

4. Stockholders
5. Customers and prospective customers
6. Unions
7. Suppliers
8. Plant and office communities
9. Academia
10. Other opinion leaders—churches, civic groups
11. News media
   11.1 Press
   11.2 TV and radio
12. Other media
   12.1 Books and reference works
   12.2 Business publications
   12.3 Trade publications
   12.4 Alternative press

IV. Activities
   1. Prepare authoritative document on the issue or opportunity that can be the key source for all concerned with it
      ■ Distribute to affected government officials and personnel, colleges, journals, public media, other industry members, associations
   2. Designate company representatives on this issue or opportunity and establish lines of authority for communicating on it
   3. Prepare executives for questioning by media, testifying to committees, conducting meetings
   4. Prepare testimony before Congress, government agencies, etc.
   5. Prepare fact cards on the issue and company sources (with home phone numbers) for distribution to media
   6. Set up emergency plan
      ■ Line of authority
      ■ Facilities for the media on the site
   7. Statements ready as responses to charges or questions
   8. Press conference

9. Press releases
10. Fact sheets and photos for the media
11. Videotape
   ■ Record events
   ■ Provide proof of developments and deter media distortion
   ■ Prepare news footage for TV
12. Literature
13. Employee bulletins or letters
14. Employee publications
15. Advertising
16. Scripts for radio broadcast
17. Customer information—letters and literature
18. Letters to stockholders
19. Bulletin boards
20. Community meetings
21. Speeches
   ■ Key executives
   ■ Others at local levels

V. Set Timetable (with built-in flexibility)

VI. Establish Budget

VII. Review and Evaluation
1. Conduct survey as a measure against analysis of problem or opportunity at the start
2. Analyze cost of manpower utilization in terms of alleviation of the problem or progress in fulfilling opportunity

Philip Lesly, "Checklist on Issues and Opportunities," *Managing the Human Climate*, No. 68, May–June, 1981.

news. As the eighteenth largest bank in the United States, Seattle-First National was the first to announce and detail its involvement with Penn Square and the impact that bank's failure would have on its own fiscal health. Seattle-First also told what it intended to do (including 400 staff layoffs and two senior management resignations). For three weeks the bank handled calls from national, local and trade media, some 300 to 400; the bank felt that the resulting coverage was balanced and fair.

PUBLIC RELATIONS ISSUES STATE MONITORING (PRISM)—REVISED, 1984

I. Background and Rationale for Program
  A. Growth of state and local autonomy on issues of national significance, especially impacting on energy industry. 1984 issues should include:
    1. Continued regulatory problems, including natural gas deregulation
    2. Toxic waste disposal, other chemical-related issues
    3. Mergers, acquisitions
    4. Land use, OCS issues
    5. Taxation (local, state levels especially)
    6. Cost-reduction, manpower utilization and costs
    7. Miscellaneous local, regional and national political issues
  B. Creation of national and regional constituency-contact programs; liaison with Government Relations and GAC program
  C. Ongoing and future media-contact programs
    1. Company-oriented
    2. Industry-oriented (API, NGSA, CMA, etc.)
    3. Government Advisory Committee goals
  D. Need to know what might affect all segments of Phillips operations, in order to professionally counsel management
  E. Need for better system of collecting, evaluating and disseminating information
    1. Coordinate with Public Affairs research staff
      a. Keep management informed of emerging issues
      b. Coordinate information with various company segments
      c. Input for speeches, papers, publications
    2. Attempt to formalize efforts at collecting data, targeting key areas for public relations efforts
      a. Get input from wide array of industry, media and constituency contacts, plus other groups and staffs when possible
      b. Ferret out relevant data from all groups to prepare executives for media contact, etc.
      c. "Beat" system of gathering information focuses on sections of company, not necessarily region or state
      d. PRISM concept allows PR staffers to become familiar with specific geographical areas, issues, opportunities

II. Methods and Implementation
  A. Public Relations Issues State Monitoring system (PRISM), as originally conceived, is based on dividing the country among PR staff members, with each responsible for covering several states. The exceptions are Dan Harrison, who is International and Financial monitor; Bill Adams, who oversees all PRISM activity and gathers regular reports, coordinates information and monitors activity in Washington and New York (including liaison with Gross & Associates, some industry associations and the GAC); Jere Smith will, along with specific states, continue as liaison with Natural Gas Supply Association and coordinate natural gas issues in 1984.
  B. Methods of information gathering
    1. Regular *phone contact with petroleum councils* in assigned states in order to:
      a. Learn about local, state issues
      b. Secure possible speaking engagements for PPCo executives
      c. Monitor advocacy group and/or other "anti-oil" activity for possible counteraction
      d. Monitor state constituency activity
    2. Contact with *Company and industry public affairs peers* headquartered in assigned states
      a. Includes regular interaction with Coal Company; Europe-Africa; Norway; Energy and minerals activity in Denver, etc.
      b. Also involves contact with other energy company and related-industry public relations professionals, local PRSA chapters, etc.
    3. *Media contacts*, energy forums in assigned states, including press associations; assignments in natural gas information program for 1984
    4. Routinely contact *marketing district managers* to:
      a. Learn of state and local problems facing marketing personnel
        (1) Offer public relations counsel
        (2) Offer local speaking opportunities
      b. Consider sending informative materials managers might not be seeing on regular basis (checking first with

Bartlesville marketing department contact)

5. Contact with *state legislative person-nel* concerned with energy issues (liaison with Government Affairs on this segment of PRISM program)
   a. State energy officials
   b. Energy aides to congressmen and senators in district offices, and possibly in Washington

6. *Monitor regional, state and local energy symposiums* and miscellaneous meetings involving utilities, educators, others; consider attendance, participation by company

7. *Miscellaneous contacts* not specifically outlined above

C. State assignments (for routine monitoring as outlined above)

Flesher: California, Oregon, Washington, Alaska, Idaho, Montana, Utah, Wyoming, Arizona

Milburn: Oklahoma, Kansas, Nebraska, Iowa, Wisconsin, Illinois, Missouri, Indiana, Michigan, Ohio, N. Dak., S. Dak., Minnesota

Smith: Texas, Arkansas, Louisiana, Mississippi, Alabama, Georgia, Florida, New Mexico, Colorado

Stoffle: Kentucky, Tennessee, West Virginia, Virginia, Maryland, Delaware, New Jersey, Connecticut, Rhode Island, Massachusetts, Vermont, New Hampshire, Maine, Pennsylvania, New York, N. Carolina, S. Carolina

D. Reporting methods

1. Reports of contacts and general state monitoring activity to be reported on quarterly basis to Bill Adams
   a. Reports will be consolidated by Adams and presented in concise form to Tom Boyd
   b. Recommendations by staff as to possible new PR programs for specific states—resulting from PRISM monitoring—will be discussed with Adams

2. Relevant information gleaned from PRISM is to be shared with other Public Affairs staffs, as well as with contacts in other Phillips groups and subsidiaries

III. PRISM Interfaces with Public Relations "Beat" Concept

A. PR staffers are assigned major corporate areas of concentration

1. Contact to be made on regular basis
2. When possible, PR staffers should try to attend marketing, chemicals, exploration and production, other departmental staff meetings of importance, offer counsel

B. PR staff interaction on "beat" system is crucial to success of PRISM program
   1. "Beat" staffer must share information concerning state not in that staffer's PRISM assignment; potential PR program assignment then discussed with Adams
   2. "Beat" information, along with PRISM data, shared at PR meetings

C. "Beat" assignments:

Adams: Government Relations; Phillips Foundation

Flesher: Staff Groups (Engineering and Services, etc.); Community Relations/U.S. Swimming and Diving (KT)

Harrison: Financial; Pipelines/Petroleum Products (although in touch with all departments as part of Information job including Europe-Africa; Norway; Dallas and Denver)

Milburn: Minerals (and Coal Company); R&D; Chemicals

Smith: Exploration and Production; G&GL

Stoffle: Marketing; Advertising/Video Services

Note. PRISM is first and foremost a *monitoring* concept; it does *not* mean assignments will be meted out only on a PRISM basis. For example, a project involving media calls with an executive in a certain state or states within one person's PRISM "territory" might be handled by another staffer under certain conditions. PRISM assignments also should not be taken to mean travel to *only* those states.

The basic PRISM concept is that the staffer responsible for a specific geographical area can be called upon by *any* Public Relations co-worker for input or suggestions involving a potential or existing project. In most instances, the staffer concerned with a particular state or states will actually handle the project, especially if he or she originates the trip to begin with.

Phillips Petroleum working paper for *Public Relations Issues State Monitoring*, Revised, 1984. Reprinted by permission.

The experience did result in some observations by Arthur Merrick, the bank's vice manager for corporate communications. The media are insatiable in their demands, he feels, especially if they can't get the news elsewhere because of stonewalling, but reporting developments as they occur can result in day-to-day headlines instead of getting it all out and over with at once. Also, reporting as events occur demands quick employee communication to avoid having employees get their news first from the news media. Seattle-First has a telephone newsline, which Merrick said set records for use in two weeks.

Merrick also cautions against overexposure of top management in a crisis because of other pressures and demands on their time. Management needs to be alerted to the opportunities in meeting the media so they won't simply brush them aside as people seeking more dirt but will see it as an opportunity. The competition among news media personnel for new leads and a good story can result in trick questions being asked, unnamed sources being used and even threats being made. But when you are cooperating, Merrick says, you can demand fairness and decency from reporters and set the ground rules in advance.[3]

An agency discovered that most of what Merrick says is true when it, not a client, became involved in a crisis. In 1980 Hill and Knowlton, Inc. (public relations) merged with J. Walter Thompson (advertising), and a JWT Group was formed to establish identity and investment credentials. Working with the chairman of this group was a Hill and Knowlton senior vice president, Donald C. Deaton. As Deaton told a National Investor Relations Institute meeting in Chicago, he was working one Friday in early February of 1982 on the corporate annual report and waiting for the fourth-quarter figures when he got a call to the chairman's office for a late meeting. He learned that outside counsel had turned up financial irregularities in their Television Program Syndication Unit that would have an impact on their profit, not just for the previous year, 1981, but also for the preceding three years. The group of outside investigators was to present their findings and loss estimates to the board of director's audit committee on the following Monday morning.

The only good thing, Deaton noted, was that Monday was a national holiday so the markets were closed. That gave the JWT Group three days to prepare. The syndication unit was responsible for only about 2 percent of revenue, but the effect was to deduct $30.5 million from earnings over a four-year period and to have the additional cost of more than $10 million during 1982 in closing down the operation.[4] Deaton says his support came from JWT Group Don Johnston's commitment to strong communications and a staff to help implement this. The coverage meant up to 200 phone calls a day, extensive use of memos and messengers, plus many meetings. As Deaton reported, "[W]e adhered strictly to the strategy determined the day we discussed the problem. We identified our audiences and communicated to each one clearly, consistently, and honestly. We did not waste

---

[3]"Complete Openness with Media Poses as Many Problems as It Solves Seattle-First National Bank Finds When Caught in Penn Square Failure," *pr reporter*, August 9, 1982, p. 1.

[4]Donald C. Deaton, "Corporate Fraud and Crisis Public Relations," *Public Relations Journal*, 36, no. 6 (June 1983), pp. 18–21.

time with speculation or name calling; we simply told the story as we knew it, updating and amplifying as events unfolded."[5]

The story was in the news for quite a while, and part of it had to do with a suit filed by Marie Luisi who had been JWT's senior vice president for media spot buying and syndication and who was dismissed. Luisi claimed that the company had known since 1978 that there were problems.

The disagreement was over "time banking," in which programs are bartered to stations in exchange for commercial airtime. The time is "banked" for future clients and appears on the books as an "asset." The syndication unit's assets looked good on paper, but didn't hold up well in the review by outside counsel.

Deaton felt that the coverage of the issue in both the trade and popular media, primarily press, had not damaged the company because of the openness of communication. Financially, the close of 1982 left the JWT Group, according to Deaton, essentially where it was before the crisis arose.

Talking Back in Crises   Companies used to take their lumps in the news media when negative publicity occurred, especially if they had tried to be open and cooperative and it had backfired.

Hostility levels between business and the news media go up and down, usually with the PR person trying to ride the tide without drowning. Corporate executive officers (CEOs) often admit they rely on their PR person to handle all contact with the news media because their rage wouldn't permit civility. Of course, when PR people get along well with news media representatives—as they must—their internal loyalty sometimes becomes suspect. Nevertheless, the advice PR people gave for years to irate CEOs who wanted to talk back, or worse, to the news media was "let me handle them." And they handled them with kid gloves.[6]

However, the public relations stance is different now and more companies are talking back. For example, Dow Chemical became involved in the summer of 1983 in combating such "jokes" as "How do you spell dioxin? Some people spell it D-O-W"—these were the words of David Stringham, deputy director of the waste-management division in the Chicago regional office of the Environmental Protection Agency.[7]

Dow was named in a class action suit by Vietnam veterans over the product Agent Orange, a defoliant that the suit claims was contaminated with dioxin. Also, in 1981 an EPA report blaming Dow for contaminating Michigan rivers with dioxin came into the hands of the chemical company, which sent lobbyists to defend its position. Although in 1964 Dow had called attention to other producers to the

---

[5] Ibid., p. 21.

[6] Public Affairs/PR people often differ from CEOs on issues, and some research indicates the major factor is age, since people tend to become more conservative as they grow older and the longer a person is in corporate public affairs, the more likely he or she is to reflect the interests of the CEO. These two factors are discussed, along with other research on the topic, by Fred J. Evans, "Business: Attacked from Without and Undermined from Within?" *IPRA* (*International Public Relations Review*), November 1983, pp. 27–32.

[7] Paul Blustein, "Poisoned Image, Dow Chemical Fights Effect of Public Outcry over Dioxin Pollution," *Wall Street Journal*, June 28, 1983, pp. 1, 20.

potential trouble the presence of dioxin in herbicides could cause, almost twenty years later Dow fought the EPA at every turn on the issue because the company contended that most of the product research was Dow's, not EPA's, and that they should be the ones to evaluate it. Also, Dow noted that if one product was disallowed by the government, others may follow. Then in March 1983 when the EPA came under attack for staff irregularities, the company was accused of influencing the wording of an internal EPA report that involved Dow.

Hooker Chemical, now a part of Occidental Petroleum, took its problems with Love Canal to the public with a public television program responding to media coverage of the Love Canal problem, and distributed numerous printed materials, among them Hooker *Factline* covering such topics as "How would you like to be sued for hundreds of millions of dollars for something you didn't do?" The controversy stemmed from accusations that Hooker had not exercised caution in burying potentially dangerous chemicals in a landfill that was bought by the Niagara Falls School Board in 1953. Subsequent development of the property, which Hooker had contested, caused penetration of the cannisters in which the chemicals had been buried and resulted in seepage.[8]

Liabilities aside, the point is that crises can come from looking forward to potential problems or backward, and companies have been responding to allegations of wrongdoing. What often makes a great deal of difference is the style of the response, as these next two illustrations reveal.

One of the first companies to speak out boldly and loudly was Mobil Corp., when during the 1970s Mobil engaged the news media in a verbal fight. To Mobil, taking the offensive seemed critical to corporate survival during what they knew was going to be a serious oil shortage. The company decided it didn't have to take anything and everything the news media decided to print or broadcast about who was responsible for what, and it structured an aggressive PR program, one that has since been imitated by others.

Director of the public affairs campaign was Mobil vice president Herbert Schmertz. Mobil began buying advertising space in key metropolitan newspapers for editorial columns, usually carrying a cartoon of editorial comment also. When media reports were wrong (in Mobil's point of view), editorial space was purchased to name the offenders, present Mobil's position and offer facts without getting into vituperative repartee. Additionally, Mobil's chairman of the board and chief executive officer met with editorial boards of major print media—newspapers and magazines—to respond to questions and debate issues that were impacting on the industry and on their company.

Getting into the ring with the news media requires the PR counselor to be a heavyweight in the realm of ideas and to know how to handle the company's position politically, economically and socially. Further, crafting aggressive programs that take the offensive requires thorough knowledge of the industry as well as of all factors that affect the climate of public opinion. In some cases, as in Mobil's, it also means defending yourself within the profession. Some PR people were

---

[8]Eric Zuesse, "Love Canal, the Truth Seeps Out," *Reason*, February 1981. Published by the Reason Foundation, Box 40105, Santa Barbara, Calif. 93103.

highly critical of Mobil's aggressive posture and accused it of defensiveness instead of social responsibility.

Writing about Mobil in the *Public Relations Journal*, communication consultant Richard M. Detwiler commented that the result of the "high-decibel advocacy seems to be more low-yield persuasion." Detwiler quotes Herbert D. Maneloveg, communication authority, as having said the public has quietly rebelled against such methods of communication. Detwiler also quotes the negative comments of two business publications. The *Wall Street Journal* referred to "surprisingly widespread public hatred of the company [Mobil]" and *Forbes* noted, "Mobil's monkeyshines would be funny if not so serious."[9]

The repercussions of Mobil's stance were felt in the defeat of Mobil's unfriendly takeover bid of Marathon, a smaller oil company, in 1982. Richard E. Cheney has discussed the positive role for public relations in such takeover battles, for the company being taken over. As public relations counsel for Marathon, he notes that the company was popular with its employees and the local townspeople (Findlay, Ohio). In bad situations, Cheney says, a client has such poor public relations that when he asks company managers what their employees think about the takeover, they say they would ask them but the employees are out on strike. Marathon's situation was a good public relations base from which to build, and the *Wall Street Journal* noted that the public relations campaign Marathon launched strongly influenced the judicial decision when the takeover battle wound up in court. A Mobil lawyer was quoted as saying that policy arguments helped convince the appeals court that heard the case that a combination of Mobil and Marathon would somehow be "morally wrong." What had occurred was that Marathon called on all its forces, employees and townspeople, to condemn Mobil's "perceived 'to-hell-with them all'" attitude, an action *WSJ* called a highly effective guerrilla campaign.[10]

Mobil's PR campaign in the 1970s and other corporate "talking-back" actions have often been spurred by unfavorable investigative reporting from programs like CBS's *60 Minutes* with Mike Wallace—reporting that often amounts to trial by television. Some trade shows won't even let TV film crews in if the shows are private.

Two communication scholars looked at three issues involved in such conflicts: (1) the media criticism of organizations, (2) the new (since 1970) response technique by criticized firms and (3) the related issues of responsibility and performance, especially of media. The result of the study by David E. Clavier and Frank E. Kalupa showed the original source of the information, the news media, suffered loss of credibility when they attacked firms.[11] While cautioning that studies of long-term effects of media credibility need to be made, the researchers' work does give some support to the attacked entering the fray.

[9] Richard M. Detwiler, "The Myths of Persuasion," *Public Relations Journal* (April 1982), pp. 52–54.

[10] Richard E. Cheney, "PR to the Rescue in Takeover Battles," *Public Relations Quarterly*, 28, no. 1 (Spring 1983), pp. 23–26.

[11] David E. Clavier and Frank B. Kalupa, "Corporate Rebuttals to 'Trial by Television,'" *Public Relations Review*, 9, no. 1 (Spring 1983), pp. 24–36.

Supporting those findings against the media are some studies by the Media Institute, a three-volume series centering on television coverage of the oil crisis.[12] The researchers concluded that TV coverage is what provokes companies like Mobil to do battle. The end result is that regardless of the impact on the media or the company, the real loser is the public. So much for social responsibility.

A Crisis Case—Tylenol   In March 1983 the Public Relations Society of America's Honors and Awards Committee took unprecedented action and gave a Silver Anvil Award to Johnson & Johnson with Burson-Marsteller for their handling of the crisis that resulted when poisoned Tylenol capsules resulted in seven deaths within a forty-mile radius of Chicago and a reported 250 more illnesses or deaths, later found to be unrelated to Tylenol.[13]

The public already had given Johnson & Johnson, known for its manufacture of health and infant products, its own reward—confidence.[14] Tylenol had been reintroduced to the marketplace after being immediately removed during the crisis, and the product had been repackaged to deter tampering.[15] A *Wall Street Journal* headline summarized, "Speedy Recovery, Tylenol Regains Most of No. 1 Market Share, Amazing Doomsayers."[16]

Credit for the recovery as well as the crisis intervention techniques belongs also to J&J subsidiary McNeil Consumer Products, which aggressively reintroduced Tylenol, giving away $50 million worth of coupons offering free bottles of the repackaged pain reliever.[17]

Consumer confidence was built on the public's perception that the company was not at fault, a perception that some copycat crimes helped to reinforce. Also, the company already had a strong consumer base of goodwill from which to draw for its long-term involvement in consumer affairs.[18]

Johnson & Johnson had an ethics code that dated back to 1942 and then board chairman James Burke said the code "is one of our greatest strengths."[19] The credo is a simple one: The welfare and protection of the consumer must come first. The author of the code was Robert Wood Johnson, chairman of the board from 1938 to 1963, who disseminated it to consumers, employees, community and stockholders.

---

[12]Leonard J. Theberge, ed., *TV Coverage of the Oil Crises: How Well Was the Public Served?* 3 vols. (Washington, D.C.: The Media Institute, 1973–74, 1978–79.)

[13]Kathy M. Hyett, news release, Public Relations Society of America, March 27, 1983.

[14]Harland W. Warner, "Solid Consumer Relations Can Defuse Crises," *Public Relations Journal* (December 1982), p. 8.

[15]"Tylenol Accelerates Bid to Recoup Market," United Press International story in the *Dallas Morning News*, November 17, 1982, p. 15A.

[16]Mitchell Leon, "Tylenol Fights Back," *Public Relations Journal* (March 1983), pp. 10–13.

[17]Lawrence G. Foster, "Handling the Tylenol Story: Good p.r.," *ASNE Bulletin*, no. 658 (March 1983), pp. 23–24.

[18]"B-M's Tylenol Videoconference Makes News History," *Burson-Marsteller Viewpoint*, January 1983, pp. 1–2.

[19]Michael Waldholz and Dennis Kneale, "Growing Headache, Tylenol's Maker Tries to Regain Good Image in Wake of Tragedy," *Wall Street Journal*, October 8, 1982, p. 1.

Johnson wrote:

> The evidence on this point is clear. Institutions, both public and private, exist because the people want them to, believe in them, or at least are willing to tolerate them. The day has passed when business was a private matter—if it ever really was. In a business society, every act of business has social consequences and may arouse public interest. Every time business hires, builds, sells, or buys, it is acting for the . . . people as well as for itself, and it must be prepared to accept full responsibility.[20]

The story is best told by Lawrence G. Foster, an employee of Johnson & Johnson since 1957 and, at the time of the crisis, vice president public relations:

> The public relations decisions related to the Tylenol crisis and the product's strong comeback came in two phases.
>
> Phase one was the crisis phase, which began on the morning of September 30 with the grim news of the cyanide poisonings. Since the extent of the contamination was not immediately known, there was grave concern for the safety of the estimated 100 million Americans who were using Tylenol. The first critical public relations decision, taken immediately and with total support from company management, was to cooperate fully with the news media. The press was key to warning the public of the danger.
>
> Later it was realized that no meeting had been called to make that critical decision. The poisonings called for immediate action to protect the consumer, and there wasn't the slightest hesitation about being completely open with the news media. For the same reasons the decision was made to recall two batches of the product, and later to withdraw it nationally. During the crisis phase of the Tylenol tragedy, virtually every public relations decision was based on sound, socially responsible business principles, which is when public relations is most effective.
>
> Almost immediately, planning began for phase two, the comeback, and this involved a more detailed and extensive public relations effort that closely followed important marketing decisions and reached out to many audiences [see 13.3]. The comeback began officially with a 30-city video press conference via satellite, an innovative approach suggested by Burson-Marsteller, which has had the Tylenol product publicity account since 1978.
>
> The video conference and all other key decisions were discussed and debated by a seven-member strategy committee formed by Chairman and CEO James E. Burke to deal with the Tylenol crisis. The committee included a public relations executive and met twice daily for six weeks. The decisions it made dealt with every aspect of the problem—from packaging to advertising to appearances on network television. Many required follow-up by the public relations staff at corporate and at McNeil Consumer Products Company.
>
> The Tylenol tragedy proved once again that public relations is a business of basics, and that the best public relations decisions are closely linked to sound business practices, prompt positive action and a responsible corporate philosophy which is in the public's interest.[21]

---

[20] "Evidence That True Social Responsibility Pays Off," *pr reporter*, February 14, 1983, p. 1.

[21] Lawrence G. Foster, "The Role of Public Relations in the Tylenol Crisis," *Public Relations Journal* (March 1983), p. 13. Reprinted with permission.

Reprinted with permission from *Viewpoint*, Marsteller, Burson-Marsteller, January, 1983, pp. 1, 2.

CHANGING BEHAVIOR

Public relations' claim to being a social science is often in jeopardy when an assumption is made that the PR person is a master of manipulative techniques. The United Nations case cited earlier (see Chapter 7) is proof that campaigns that are merely informational don't necessarily change attitudes, but how about more extensive efforts?

Can Laws Change People's Behavior?

In an effort to keep people from killing themselves, auto safety promoters have publicized the benefits of using safety belts. Automakers who didn't voluntarily put seat belts in their cars were finally compelled to by legislation. Not only do cars now have seat belts, but they are also equipped with devices to encourage use. One automaker decided to enforce use by preventing the engine from starting until belts were fastened. That didn't last long. Just as unpopular were the buzzers, lights and other signals that called attention to the use of belts. Ford car windows all carry the slogan "Buckle up." How effective is this effort at behavior modification? Not very, according to research by Leon S. Robertson, senior behavioral scientist for the Insurance Institute for Highway Safety, Washington, D.C. Robertson summarized the situation this way:

> Belt use in automobiles was observed in 19 cities in five countries. In jurisdictions with belt use laws, belt use ranged from a high of 83 percent in Sydney, Australia, to a low of less than 1 percent at expressway exits in Japan. Prior to the belt law in Ontario and Quebec, Canada, and in the United States without a belt law, belt use ranged from a high of 33 percent in Los Angeles to a low of 4 percent in Windsor, Ontario. Persons less than 20 years of age were using belts less often than adults and many people were wearing belts too loosely to be effective in crashes. The 10 to 20 percent reductions in deaths in countries with belt laws are not as high as would be expected from the known effects of belts apparently because of the lower usage by those disproportionately involved in severe crashes and because belts are worn improperly.[22]

Other reports by Robertson and others detail the failure of public information campaigns costing millions of dollars in the countries with free information systems (the only places to legitimately test public persuasion campaigns of public relations origin).[23] Evidence from their studies shows a minor *temporary* behavior change, which drops off after the campaign is over. Legal enforcement seems to have some effect. The effectiveness of a legal mandate with punishment as a consequence is borne out by studies of compliance with the 55 mile-per-hour speed limit in the United States.[24] However, studies in two U.S. cities (St. Louis and Denver) suggest that compliance with the law is not as persuasive as a *continuing* public information campaign.[25]

You have to wonder what the long-term effects would be of continual persuasive messages to buckle up, brush your teeth regularly, exercise, eat less salt and so on. Robertson says that compliance by law or administrative directive seldom exceeds 80 percent, so that perhaps we need to look at some alternative strategies. Acknowledging that "with present technology, behavior change strategies may be the only ones available for some health problems," Robertson says building in some preventives might be better. For the automobile industry, he suggests automatically inflatable air cushions. He asks these questions:

---

[22]Leon S. Robertson, "Automobile Seat Belt Use in Selected Countries, States and Provinces With and Without Laws Requiring Belt Use," *Accident Analysis and Prevention*, vol. 10 (Elmsford, N.Y., and Oxford, England: Pergamon Press, 1978), p. 9. Copyright 1978, Pergamon Press, Ltd. Reprinted with permission.

[23]*Ibid.*

[24]"Newspaper Stories Enforce the 55 mph Speed Limit," United Press International, August 1981 (report of research by Carol Kohfeld, assistant professor of political science, University of Missouri-St. Louis, and Tom Likens, professor of research, University of Denver).

[25]"Promoting Belt Use: Lessons from the Past," Insurance Institute for Highway Safety, *Highway Loss Reduction Status Report*, 16, no. 9 (June 24, 1981), pp. 1–7.

Does it make sense to continue to concentrate on changing every individual's behavior whether by advertising, education, or law enforcement? Or does it make more sense to force decision makers to provide automatic protection where the technology is available to do so? If faced with the choices today, would we purify water at the source or would we launch an ad campaign to attempt to persuade everyone to boil his or her drinking water? Would we require pasteurization of milk before it was sold or would we pass a law that each family had to boil their milk before it was consumed? The choices we face today with respect to motor vehicles are no different.[26]

Can Persuasive Campaigns Mobilize Public Opinion?

While the questions Robertson poses seem to have commonsense answers, the real question in a free society is who is going to make decisions. In the 1960s, when authority was being questioned at all levels, pure food advocates questioned the decision of the Food and Drug Administration (FDA) to add preservatives to foods. The purpose of the FDA's initiative was to protect people from consuming tainted or spoiled foods. Whether the government decides what's best for everyone or whether those who are governed should participate in the decision-making process is at the root of most social issues.

How fundamental this question can be is reflected in the campaign strategy for "selling" the nuclear freeze, worked out by science writer and environmental public relations specialist Peter M. Sandman. Sandman is media and outreach coordinator for the New Jersey Campaign for a Nuclear Weapons Freeze and teaches communication at Rutgers University. His campaign instructions follow:

NOTES ON "SELLING" THE FREEZE

Most of the recommendations listed below are based on communication theory, poll data, or both. Some are just my political instincts. *All* are meant to supplement your own political instincts, not to replace them. If what I am suggesting feels wrong, do what feels right instead.

1. Aim at involvement, not knowledge. Well-informed futility and paralyzed concern are of little value to the freeze movement, short-term or long. Besides, people who become actively involved will find and absorb huge quantities of relevant information. Becoming well-informed, on the other hand, is no guarantee of involvement.

2. Don't bury people in information. Newcomers, especially, have a limited appetite for technical detail; that will come *after* they're involved. Respond to the questions people are asking, of course, but try not to feed their fear that they must become arms experts before taking a stand. Especially avoid prolonged "our experts versus their experts" battles: their experts have more Pentagon titles and classified numbers; the basic issues require far less expertise than people imagine; newcomers respond to technical debate with glazed eyes and paralyzed wills. (But information *is* crucial after involvement; see #18.)

3. For any given presentation or document and for the campaign as a whole, identify 3–5 points that you will keep stressing. For each point, focus on a handful of convincing

---

[26]Leon S. Robertson, "The Great Seat Belt Campaign Flop," *Journal of Communication*, 26, no. 4 (Autumn 1976), p. 45.

arguments, statistics, and quotations—including ones from military and other "unexpected" sources. Hold in reserve prepared responses to the most likely hostile questions on each point, again relying heavily on "their" sources. Fight *hard* to stick to these basics. Move beyond them only if the audience as a whole (not just one questioner or a debate opponent) seems to want you to. The winners of political contests are usually the people who define the terms of the contest. Your goal is to sell the freeze, not to answer its opponents (but see #11). Fight on your own turf.

4. Accept the legitimacy of feelings. People get involved in arms-control issues, not because they are "interested," but because they *care*. This is true even of freeze opponents—they too are feeling people, worried about the survival of what they love. The feelings of potential supporters point the route to more active support; try to sense what feelings are on top (fear? anger? love?) and respond in a way that legitimates them. (But don't necessarily pander to them—see #19.) The feelings of hostile questioners also deserve respect; accepting and responding to the feeling is often more important than answering the question itself.

5. Remember that our audience is not ourselves. Whatever your politics, whatever your moral and religious values, whatever your reasons for working on the freeze, they are *yours*. Other people will become involved for their own reasons, not for your reasons—and your goal is to facilitate the involvement, not to debate the reasons. Bear in mind especially that the audience is not yet involved for *any* reasons; presuming more interest or commitment than is there risks nipping its growth in the bud. Newcomers need nurturing; they grow into seasoned activists in their own time and on their own path. This growth process is determined by a complex amalgam of their histories, feelings, actions, values, and knowledge, probably in that order. We can affect it but not control it.

6. Focus on top prospects. Activating supporters is easier than persuading neutrals, and persuading neutrals is easier than converting opponents. Especially early in the campaign, when you need help and contributions more than votes, concentrate your efforts where you expect to find supporters. As summer moves into fall shift more emphasis into mass persuasion of uncommitted voters. Never waste time on opponents unless there is a neutral audience to win over. But note that your top prospects may not be who you think they are—see #7.

7. Don't write off any group. The freeze movement so far has proved to be wide but shallow—supported by a large majority of virtually every demographic group, but supported with fervor by many fewer. . . .

8. Be patriotic. The vast majority of the U.S. public sees the United States and the Soviet Union as opponents, and is skeptical about the arms-control opinions of those who seem unsure which side they are on. Showing respect for key U.S. institutions and symbols (the flag, the presidency, elections) is essential. Showing disapproval of Soviet repression is extraordinarily helpful as well; so is a healthy (and visible) skepticism about Soviet good will ("verifiability" wins more votes than "trust"). This reality neither requires nor excuses Red-baiting, or denying such home-grown injustices as racism and sexism. It does, perhaps, suggest a muting of ideology in the interests of the widest possible freeze coalition. . . .

9. Go easy on the rhetoric of ideology. Make the connections you want to make, but try to pick connections you think will be meaningful to your audience, not necessarily to yourself. . . .

10. Reinforce audience values. People change more, and act more, when you support their values than when you challenge them. The golden rule of persuasion is thus to look for *existing* audience values to which you can hook your message, values that already incline your audience toward your message. If there are existing values that incline your audience the other way, the less you mention them the better—you want to remind people why they want to agree with you, not why they want to disagree. . . .

11. Respond to key counterarguments. Although it generally pays to fight on our own turf (see #3), four issues are or will soon be so widely debated as to require an explicit response.

(a) "The freeze would tie the hands of the experts at the Strategic Arms Reduction Talks" (which will show predictably optimistic signs by summer's end). Respond with respect for START—argue that it is not enough, not that it is a fraud. In fact, claim credit for it; the president's arms-control policy changed in response to the freeze movement, and can change more if we maintain the effort. . . .

(b) "The Soviet Union is ahead in the arms race, as shown by the following incomprehensible chart." According to poll data, the parity issue is *at the core* of freeze support and opposition; believing that the Soviet Union is not ahead is virtually a prerequisite for supporting the freeze. (Most Americans would feel safest—mistakenly— if the U.S. were ahead, but they will settle for a standoff.) Parity here does not mean quantitative equality; it means essential fairness. So skip the incomprehensible charts for most audiences and rely instead on quotations from military experts to the effect that they would not trade places with their Soviet counterparts. And explain that both sides have enough weapons to obliterate the other no matter who strikes first; this secure deterrent is the only parity that means anything. . . . Make your point without slinging arrows. . . .

(c) "We can't trust the Russians, as the record on chemical/bacteriological weapons, or Poland or Afghanistan or whatever proves." The most effective answer here is not that we can trust the Russians—though it is helpful to point out that honoring a freeze treaty would be in the Soviet Union's interests. Nor is it wise to put great stress on the parallel record of international untrustworthiness of the United States—though you may want to note that trust has never figured greatly in diplomacy. The key response is that we do not *need* to trust the Russians, nor they us. Carry a satellite photo of a Moscow license plate with you, and argue that the freeze is verifiable.

(d) "The United States needs a strong military." The response that the U.S. does not need a strong military, that U.S. military strength threatens the world's peoples, lacks appeal to most audiences, even profreeze audiences. The response that the U.S. already has a strong military goes over better, especially when tied to nuclear parity. But the most effective answer by far is to argue that weapons too powerful to use confer no strength, that the arms race diminishes national security, that a Pentagon grown overdependent on nuclear arms is ill-prepared to fight. Stop short of asserting that the freeze makes the world safe for war.

As the campaign continues, other issues may grow important enough to require an answer—nuclear proliferation is a likely addition to the list, and subversion may become an issue if opponents decide to fight dirty. If you are quite sure your audience is already concerned about an issue (*any* issue), respond to it before you're asked. But don't spend too much time "answering" the opposition; we want to keep the opposition answering us instead.

12. Help people give themselves permission to support the freeze. No one wants a nuclear war, and almost everyone intuitively senses a freeze would help prevent one. But the cost of being wrong is frighteningly high. People worry that the freeze might be a communist plot, or a cowardly cop-out, or a con—or just a terrible mistake. They thus need to hear that experts and authorities also support the freeze; this gives them permission to support it too. (The bandwagon of support from other nonexperts is also important—see #14.) The ideal list of endorsers depends on your audience, of course. Military experts are essential; state and national political leaders confer establishment respectability, especially when the list is bipartisan; religious, moral, and cultural dignitaries help; national heroes can be invoked. Be sure to include *local* persons of stature. Though the freeze movement rose mainly from the grassroots, prestige endorsements are probably crucial to further growth—and it is wise to secure them early while the mood of consensus remains strong.

13. Make working for the freeze personally attractive to people. All of us are concerned about many more issues than we actually commit our time and money to. And that all-important first commitment, the evidence shows, comes because we are given a chance to do something personally fulfilling. Why do people start working for freeze groups?—to meet interesting people; to get out of the house; to feel more a part of the community; to improve old skills and develop new skills; to feel needed; to enjoy a social evening, a rock concert, a stimulating conversation. None of these is enough reason to *stay* involved; once involved people learn about the issue and build a better rationale for their involvement. . . .

14. Help make people feel powerful. Paralysis, fatalism, apathy, and "psychic numbing" are inevitable responses to feeling powerless; acting, caring, and learning make no sense if they will do no good. . . . To unfreeze nonsupporters, stress efficacy and empowerment in three senses: (a) the effectiveness of the individual—that the things we are asking people to do are *useful* and *important*, not makework; (b) the effectiveness of the movement—that they are about to join an irresistible bandwagon, a mass up-welling of grassroots fervor, democracy in action (but guided by experts—see #12); and (c) the effectiveness of the freeze itself—that a nonbinding referendum can genuinely influence national policy and lead to a treaty that works. Supporters as well as newcomers need to hear these things; the single greatest reason why people abandon political movements is that they began to feel futile.

15. Stress the urgency of the freeze movement. People contribute their time and money where they feel their time and money will make a difference. This means they must feel effective (see #14); it *also* means they must feel needed. . . . This stress on urgency is especially important for committed audiences; newcomers need to hear more about confidence (see #19).

16. Make working for the freeze feel like a "controllable" commitment. People normally join new causes tentatively, a step at a time. The first steps must be easy, like wearing a button or signing a petition. And they must be reinforced (see #18) before people are asked to do more. Aim at a graduated series of increasingly serious commitments, alternating with information about the issue and about the effectiveness of past commitments. Avoid "the four outs": (a) Burn-out results from asking for too much too fast. When last week's newcomer is this week's committee chair, s/he may well become next week's ex-member. (b) Cool-out comes from asking for too little, and giving too little reinforcement. People want to be told explicitly what to do next, and why, and what you think about what they did last. (c) Pull-out is what happens when people feel trapped, afraid that unless they quit now the movement will suck up all their energy. Feeling suffocated does not lead to good political work. (d) Keep-out is the feeling many newcomers get from ongoing political groups—the sense that there are invisible walls to be climbed; social, ideological, or informational entrance requirements to be met. Think of the four outs as the corners of a room; commitment grows best in the room's center.

17. Personalize the movement. Perhaps "movement" is the wrong word to begin with. People join groups; they decide to try working with Mary and George. And peace work is not a penance. It can and should be joyful. At every level, then, try to make the freeze movement human and fun. Include quotations and photographs of "ordinary citizens" in your literature. Encourage people to bring their children to meetings, and provide relevant child-care activities. Serve food. Introduce newcomers. Share good news. Consider fielding a freeze softball team.

18. Use information strategically. Instead of inundating newcomers with technical details (see #2), use information to reinforce that first commitment; this leads people to adopt a what-shall-we-do-next? attitude instead of I-gave-at-the-office. Three kinds of information are especially useful: (a) Ammunition is information about the issue itself. People need it to do a good job, of course—but they need it even more to justify their commitment to themselves and their skeptical friends. Though people become involved for personal reasons (see #13), they need sound arguments to *stay* involved.

(b) Mobilizing information tells people what to do next and how to do it. (This article is an example of mobilizing information.) When passive supporters of political movements are asked why they don't do more, their two biggest answers are "I don't know what" and "I don't know how." Mobilizing information meets these needs. (c) Efficacy information stresses the value of what people have already done (see #14). It tells them that they're not wasting their time, that their work is appreciated, that their neighbors are working too.

19. Go easy on fear, guilt, and depression. These are all inward-turning, negative emotions. They may shock the totally ignorant into recognizing the issue, and they may actually galvanize hardened fanatics into further action—but most audiences respond better to uppers than to downers, better to solutions than to problems, better to progress than to catastrophe, better to confidence than to desperation. We must come to terms with nuclear terror slowly or we risk reverting to psychic numbness and paralyzed inaction. . . . In contrast to fear, guilt, and depression, *anger* provokes action rather than avoidance, because it looks outward instead of inward. But even anger is too negative to stand alone without turning sterile; it is best paired with *love* and *efficacy*: someone to fight against, someone to fight for, and the conviction the fight can be won.

20. Don't neglect the mass media. The most *effective* outreach is of course person-to-person. But we're talking about reaching millions of people, and we can't do it without the megaphone of the mass media. In any case, grassroots organizing and media reinforce each other. Active supporters get much of their ammunition and sense of efficacy from media coverage of "their" movement. Potential supporters are far more likely to become involved if they are hearing about the freeze from the media, not just from their neighborhood activist. And millions of politically inactive people will vote almost exclusively on the basis of what they learned from the media. Early in the campaign, then, use media to reinforce your grassroots organizing, to confer visibility and credibility on the freeze. Later, use media to reach those who have not been touched by organizing. Advertising, pamphlets, and the like give you the most control over what you say and to whom you say it. But unpaid media attention—news, talk shows, letters-to-the-editor—is cheaper and more credible. Whatever your budget you can afford to talk to local reporters—and you cannot afford not to.

21. Trust yourself. If you'd asked them, most experts would have told you a year ago that a mass movement for nuclear arms control wouldn't get to first base right now. These notes may be out of date by the time you read them; or inappropriate for your group, your style, your constituency, your situation; or flat-out wrong. Merge what looks helpful with what you're already doing.[27]

This is a model for any movement to get public opinion mobilized and into action. It can be analyzed to watch pressure groups at work, and it can also be used as a predictor. The model blends communication theory with social movement action.

Can an Information Campaign Help?

Many campaigns have attempted to increase public acceptance of the handicapped. The National Paraplegic Association is one of the most active in monitoring enforcement of laws to make public areas like buildings, streets and

---

[27] Developed by Peter Sandman, Rutgers University Communications professor and outreach coordinator for the New Jersey Campaign for a Nuclear Weapons Freeze, 1981.

schools accessible. Building codes have forced institutions to be open to the handicapped. Equal employment laws aid the handicapped in getting jobs. But many parents of handicapped children are reluctant to expose them to a public world. Some parents are ashamed. Some are defensive. Some are protective. When a state law mandated that handicapped children be educated, the first problem was finding them. This public relations case is an illustration of such an effort. The campaign itself was put together in less than a week before it had to be launched. It was called "Child Find."[28]

Child Find—A Statewide Search   In early 1976 new federal and state laws were on the books requiring local public schools to provide free education for *all* children, regardless of the child's condition. Previously, schools were able to exclude some children whose handicaps did not allow them to "fit" into regular classrooms. To be eligible to receive federal funds, public schools were also required to actively seek and assist handicapped children between the ages of three and twenty-one not already receiving education.

The laws were a recognition of—and a giant step toward eliminating—a shameful national situation. For years, thousands of handicapped children had simply been "hidden." The situation was less acute in larger cities, many of which had done commendable jobs in the field of special education. But in lower-income urban areas and in small towns and rural areas, the problem affected the lives of many people. Some schools simply did not provide the special and expensive facilities and instruction needed by the relatively small number of handicapped youngsters. And many parents and guardians of handicapped children didn't know where to seek help or had been rejected for program after program because their children "didn't fit in."

Texas Education Agency (TEA), long a leader among states in special education, had begun long before the laws were passed in Washington to "gear up" a statewide program designed to meet the special needs of handicapped Texas youngsters. With funds from the U.S. Department of Health, Education and Welfare, which became available in March 1976, TEA began implementation of a three-phase program to do the following:

1. Locate handicapped children not in school
2. Assess the needs of the individual child
3. Provide services appropriate to the needs of each child

Called "Child Find," the project broke new ground for government programs. Traditionally, government programs had been established that provided specific services for individuals who met specific criteria. People who could meet the criteria were eligible for the services; others weren't.

---

[28]The case is courtesy of Jim Haynes. Haynes handled the Child Find project when he was working with a not-for-profit agency in Austin, Texas. Haynes is now assistant dean of the College of Communication, University of Texas at Austin. Since the Child Find project, a national organization using the same name has been formed to locate missing children. Used by permission.

Child Find was different. Under this program, educators were challenged to look first at the needs of the children and their families and design individual programs to meet their specific needs. And perhaps for the first time, the traditionally rigid lines separating one agency from another were crossed; education agency people were given permission to seek out, from whatever source available, the services needed by each handicapped child. In government circles, that was a major change, perhaps even a minor revolution. The emphasis was switched from *services* and *eligibility* for those services to a concentration on *people*.

The Texas program was coordinated by TEA's Division of Special Education in Austin. But the state's twenty Education Service Centers and the more than 1,100 Independent School Districts were responsible for implementing Child Find. The need for a coordinated communication program became apparent, and TEA turned to La Mancha Group, Inc., a not-for-profit corporation working exclusively for nonprofit organizations.

Because of a delay in federal funding, the first phase of the program, the "search" phase, was to begin in mid-March and end June 30. During that brief period, people involved in the Child Find program needed to create a statewide awareness of the program, conduct door-to-door contact campaigns in twenty school districts with a minimum of 5,000 schoolchildren each, set up procedures for evaluating the handicapped children located and compile massive directories of services available to handicapped children—a task never before undertaken.

Even before La Mancha Group became involved, some of the twenty Education Service Centers were plunging into work in an attempt to meet the short time schedules. They needed communication materials "yesterday."

Within a few days, La Mancha Group defined the overall objectives of Child Find, wrote goals for the communication program, analyzed principal audiences and designed a three-part communication strategy for the March–June phase of the statewide program.

Designed for implementation first was a strategy to *achieve impact*—to let the people of the state know Child Find existed. For this purpose, La Mancha Group set up a major State Capitol news conference (all major Texas media have representatives at the State Capitol, along with wire services). At the well-attended news conference, Joe Kelly Butler, chairman of the State Board of Education, announced statewide implementation of the program. The news conference was rehearsed, on camera, a day before the actual event. During the rehearsal, 16mm sound-on film was shot; the film was processed, edited, printed and mailed to fifty-five of the state's television stations along with scripts for news anchorpeople. Press packets, fact sheets and news releases were distributed at the news conference and later statewide. During the news conference, audio tape was recorded. Within an hour, it had been edited to select brief "actualities," a professional announcer had taped an introduction and it was fed via telephone to fifty-five top radio stations throughout the state.

Materials from the Austin news conference were modified for use in regional news conferences. These were included in a Child Find Public Information Handbook, a thirty-two-page booklet distributed, literally "hot off the press," at an Austin Child Find conference of eighty TEA, Education Service Center and Independent School District Child Find coordinators from around the state. At this conference, La Mancha Group presented its recommendations for a coordinated communication plan, using more than 300 slides—less than two weeks after becoming involved in the project.

The Child Find Public Information Handbook, printed on brightly colored paper with cartoon illustrations, presented objectives, details of communication plans and strategies, a "how to" section on media relations, a step-by-step discussion on "How to Have a Press Conference," suggestions for local publicity and copies of the Child Find logo designed by La Mancha Group which could be applied to artwork by Education Service Center and school district staffs. This handbook was later to be reprinted in quantity by La Mancha Group and included in a handbook on Child Find distributed across the country by the National Association of State Directors of Special Education. (For sample parts of the handbook, see 13.4.)

With the initial news conferences and the presentation to Child Find coordinators completed, La Mancha Group moved into the second of the three parts of its communication strategy—a series of activities designed to *build and sustain awareness* of Child Find.

For this part of the communication program, La Mancha Group taped 10-, 20-, 30- and 60-second radio public service announcements, among its other activities. The radio PSAs were recorded in both English and Spanish and were localized by inserting contact phone numbers for each of the state's twenty Education Service Center regions. Duplicated by TEA staff members, they were distributed to every radio station in Texas.

Television public service spots were shot on 16mm film, using volunteer talent, a professional film crew and professional English and Spanish voices. The TV spots were transferred to 2-inch television tape, and copies were made for each TV station in the state with local telephone contact numbers "tagged" into the duplicated copies.

Since newspapers typically do not use public service ads, La Mancha Group tried an unusual approach. Newspaper ads for Child Find were prepared in both English and Spanish and distributed to all newspapers in the state along with a letter suggesting that space for the ads be *sold* to advertisers and that sponsors' names be set in type and inserted into the ads.

While the second part of the communication program was being implemented, La Mancha Group was working toward the third part of the program—*maintaining interest* in Child Find after it ceased to be of news interest.

Among its activities for this segment of the program, La Mancha Group produced artwork for information folders, bumper stickers and statement stuffers. Quantities of these materials would run into the millions, since they included folders to be taken home by schoolchildren. To reduce massive inventory and distribution problems and to allow each school and Education Service Center to localize the materials to fit their particular needs, La Mancha Group produced Velox "slicks" of the artwork, inserted instructions and specifications for printing and distributed copies of the artwork for printing in each locality.

The one item that was printed in Austin for this part of the program was an 18 × 24-inch four-color poster containing a photo of a wistful, hearing-impaired youngster, the statewide toll-free telephone number, the Child Find logo and the

NEWS CONFERENCE ANNOUNCEMENT

Announcement of the news conference should be made by personally delivered news conference announcements, by MailGram (Western Union service), or by telephone. . .one or two days (no more) prior to the news conference.

NEWS CONFERENCE ANNOUNCEMENT

You are invited to attend a news conference at __(time)__ , __(day)__ , __(date)__ for a presentation related to public education which is of interest to the people of _____ counties.

Participating in the news conference will be _____ (names and titles).

The conference will begin promptly at __(time)__ at _____ (exact location, with instructions, if necessary) _____ . We hope you will be able to attend or be represented.

(Signature)

(Typed Name)

NEWS CONFERENCE REMINDER

Each news media representative invited to the news conference should be reminded as early as possible on the day of the conference. Phone calls are the most effective way of handling reminders. If you wish to use a printed or typed reminder, simply change the heading on the NEWS CONFERENCE ANNOUNCEMENT to make it read NEWS CONFERENCE REMINDER.

Child Find Objectives   1

All together, we've set out:

- To identify every handicapped child between the ages of 3 and 21 within the state of Texas.
- To locate and/or provide appropriate services for handicapped children located through CHILD FIND, through coordination with local education agencies and other agencies and organizations.

Child Find Public Information Goals

- Establish and sustain a high level of public awareness that every handicapped child in the state of Texas is assured a free public education.
- Create a public awareness of the fact that only 76% of school age handicapped children are receiving appropriate special services and that, through CHILD FIND, TEA and local education agencies are actively involved in locating and serving every handicapped child in the state.
- Increase the level of the general public's understanding of, and appreciation for, programs for all handicapped children in the state.

- Provide the people of Texas with an appreciation for the progress TEA has made in the field of special education.
- Communicate the important role of the individual independent school district in providing for the special education needs of the citizens within its district, with the support of TEA.
- Use unifying identity so local programs will benefit from public information and public education on a state-wide basis and that from other local programs.
- Stress availability of all community resources to aid handicapped children.

Why Statewide Public Information?   2

The reason for statewide public information is to provide a unity to the program so we can each benefit from what other regions are doing. It's called "message reinforcement," and it works!

Message Reinforcement

People retain information for varying lengths of time depending upon

1. The importance the individual attaches to the information
2. The number of times the person is exposed to the information

We can try to influence the importance people attach to our messages, but we can't really control that.

We can control, to a large degree, the number of times individuals are exposed to our messages. But they will recognize it the second time, the third, and the fourth only if it's very similar in appearance and sound to the original.

So the key to getting people to remember the CHILD FIND message is repetition. Repeat the same message over and over in different ways.

Suggestions for Publicity   24

- [ ] Region ____ ESC Begins Planning for Child Find Project
- [ ] Child Find Program Director Named
- [ ] Child Find Regional Staff Selected
- [ ] Child Find Office Established
- [ ] Child Find Contact Number Begins Operation
- [ ] Child Find Door-to-Door Campaign Announced
- [ ] Field Workers Chosen for Child Find Door-to-Door Interviews
- [ ] Child Find Door-to-Door Program Begins Tomorrow (City and Rural Areas Charted and Mapped)
- [ ] Door-to-Door Interviews Begin
- [ ] Door-to-Door Campaign Half Completed (Results Given)
- [ ] Child Find Director Speaks at Rotary Club
- [ ] Child Find Project Leaders Display Materials at "Working Mothers Convention."
- [ ] _____ Donates Wheelchair to Child Find Project (name of organization making donation is used)
- [ ] Door-to-Door Canvass Ends Today
- [ ] ____ Handicapped Children Found By Child Find (fill in with number found)
- [ ] ____ Handicapped Children Found Through Child Find Hotline (fill in with number of children found)
- [ ] Mayor Places First Child Find Bumper Sticker
- [ ] _____ High School Student Council Announces "Locate to Educate" Contest for Child Find
- [ ] _____ High School Child Find Contest Underway
- [ ] Child Find Contest Finalist Announced
- [ ] __(Name)__ Wins "Locate to Educate" Child Find Contest
- [ ] Child Find Field Workers Slate Awards Presentation
- [ ] __(Name)__ Wins "Child Find Tired Feet" Award
- [ ] Chamber of Commerce Provides Transportation for Child Find Children Now in School
- [ ] Mayor Names __(Date)__ as Child Find Day

copy that was used as a theme for radio, TV, newspaper and all print materials in this phase of the Child Find program:

How do you find
the children who stay at home all day
because their parents don't know that
free education is guaranteed to every child
by our state laws?

**YOU ASK EVERY PERSON IN TEXAS
TO HELP.**

Maybe you know a handicapped child who needs
help. Maybe you can help.

MAKE THE CALL THAT MAKES THE DIFFERENCE.

**CHILD FIND
CALL TOLL FREE**
(Telephone number)

Quantities of the poster, which could be modified with local phone numbers, were distributed throughout the state. A TEA computer run was used to place them where they were needed.

Because local groups needed materials for civic club and PTA presentations, La Mancha Group distributed sets of slides for local speech use, while a 12-minute, 16mm film was in production.

Called "We Are Alive," the Child Find film was a dramatic presentation of the needs of handicapped children and the work of the Texas Education Agency and local school districts in meeting those needs. Because the film was to be used longer than other materials, the content emphasized special education in Texas schools, rather than Child Find, which would cease to exist after three years.

Did Child Find work?

There are, of course, as many answers to that question as there were people involved in the program. In terms of statistics, the answer would have to be an unqualified yes. At the outset of the Child Find program, La Mancha Group and TEA estimated that based upon a pilot program in Alice, Texas, there were more than 10,000 "hidden" handicapped children between the ages of three and twenty-one in the state. Considerably more than 10,000 have been found.

For those who use awards to measure professionalism in public relations, certainly the Child Find communication program could be rated high. The overall program received Texas Public Relations Association's Best of Texas award and a top award, a Gold Medal, in Austin competition. The film, "We Are Alive," received

13.5 A CAMPAIGN THAT WORKED TO AFFECT BEHAVIOR

Perhaps repetition is an answer. Smokey is over 40 years old.

Smokey Bear, one of the best-known symbols in the history of advertising, is celebrating his 40th year as the national symbol of forest fire prevention—and one of the most successful programs of mass appeal. Smokey is credited with reducing forest fires by 50 percent since 1944, with resulting savings in human life, wildlife and timber.

The Smokey Bear program has been effective because it accomplishes the three objectives of any successful information campaign: It creates a cognitive structure (awareness), a motivational structure (desire) and a behavioral structure (action). Awareness is measured by recognizability, and Smokey has certainly become a well-known character since he first appeared on a poster dressed in dungarees and campaign hat, pouring water on a campfire.

Surveys show that 98 out of 100 people know who he is, and that most know what he stands for. It is difficult, for instance, to visit or travel through a forested area without encountering some evidence of Smokey and his message: "Only You Can Prevent Forest Fires."

The Smokey Bear program (actually, the Cooperative Forest Fire Prevention Program) goes beyond the familiar posters. In addition to television spots, the campaign uses personal appearances by Smokey-costumed forest rangers, Tournament of Roses Parade floats and a giant Smokey Bear balloon. Smokey gets so much mail he has his own zip code (20252), and his commercial use is regulated by an Act of Congress.

Motivation would appear to be no problem: Who wouldn't want to prevent forest fires? Well, not quite everyone does—one fire of every four is started deliberately. But, if Smokey is even 75 percent successful in convincing us that we shouldn't burn the woods, that's a lot better than the seat-belt folks have done.

Sixty percent of all forest fires result from human carelessness. (Only 9 percent are started by lightning.) What we have, then, in an average year is about 76,000 careless acts that result in forest fires. No one knows how many near-misses occur, but this record isn't bad when one considers the millions of people who live in and visit forested areas.

Although there is room for improvement, Smokey's record in creating a desired behavior structure is the envy of the advertising world. And because Smokey's keepers know they have a good thing, it's very likely that your children and your grandchildren will be just as familiar as you are with Smokey's admonition— "Only You Can Prevent . . ."

Larry Doolittle, "Only He Can Prevent Forest Fires," *Psychology Today*, May 1984, p. 14.

a number of awards, including a Bronze Award from the International Film and Television Festival of New York.

But success should really be measured in more human terms. In almost every community and city throughout Texas, there are handicapped children who do *not* stay at home all day. They are learning to be responsible participants in our society.

As Haynes says, "Was Child Find successful? Just ask any one of those children!" For another PR campaign that works, see 13.5.

THE PR/MARKETING MIX

Marketing reaches out to external publics, and institutions that are not open communication systems are today more likely to make marketing a number one priority. Examples of typically closed communication systems are museums (often because of security and protection of benefactors), hospitals (usually because of privacy), banks (for privacy and security) and airlines.

Until the 1960s neither museums nor hospitals bothered a great deal with either public relations or marketing. In the seventies museums sought to broaden their constituency, to expand collections and buildings. Hospitals found it necessary to explain increasing costs. They also were caught up in the litigious climate that positioned patients against their physicians in malpractice suits.

Banks and savings and loans have become financial supermarkets, offering a variety of services in a competitive marketplace fraught with the dangers of closings caused by overextended loans. Airlines have found that deregulation has created a highly competitive marketplace, which contributed to the bankruptcy of two major airlines—Braniff and Continental.

Marketing the Arts

If the phrase "marketing the arts" had been used in the 1950s, it would have been declared in poor taste. The arts were something special—something for small, particular audiences who were supposed to know what they wanted and appreciate it when it was given to them. The financial base for artistic institutions was small and was generally met by a few large donors. Inflation, however, changed everything, including artistic endeavors. Inflation made everything cost more, and donors began asking for more business accountability in the arts. The inevitable effect was that the arts began seeking a broader base and using marketing skills to get it.

Perhaps the best-packaged artistic event of the 1970s was the King Tut presentation. "Treasures of Tutankhamun" was an exhibit of Egyptian art that had been buried in the tomb of King Tutankhamun 3,300 years ago. The exhibit was sponsored by a consortium of six museums and was overseen by the Metropolitan Museum of Art in New York. The exhibit was extensively promoted, replicas of the artifacts were even available to museum buyers—if you could get in to see the exhibit. The exhibit opened in Washington, D.C., during the inauguration of President Jimmy Carter and lines often meant a 10-hour wait. New Orleans probably experienced the worst crush, however, with people waiting days to get in.

Building on the Tut-mania, the Dallas Museum of Art promoted its Pompeii exhibit extensively. In its brochures mailed almost a year in advance of the showing to museum members, it used the selling point that members would not have to wait in line to get in (see 13.6). That did it. Nonmembers heard about it and plunked down their $25 membership to get into the exhibit free. Museum membership quadrupled to 15,000.

Big exhibits put museums in the position of staging public relations special events, something new to their business. It is a strain on most museum staffs. Dallas used 671 volunteers, not counting their regular docents (trained volunteers) and shop helpers. (Pompeii-inspired artifacts were available for sale, as well as the museum store's usual quality products, including fine jewelry. The most expensive item sold during the show was a $1,500 14-carat gold necklace.) Volunteers logged almost 14,700 hours.

Marketing the event well in advance included getting the next-door Dallas

DMFA comes to life with exhibit of Pompeii's death

By JANET KUTNER
Art Editor of The News

POMPEII'S DEATH has brought new life to the Dallas Museum of Fine Arts. When the blockbuster exhibit of 300 artifacts, buried when Mount Vesuvius erupted almost 2,000 years ago, closes at 6 p.m. Sunday, it is doubtful DMFA will ever be the same.

The record-breaking crowds — close to 325,000 persons in 11 weeks — that have poured through the museum's Fair Park building since *Pompeii AD 79* opened Jan. 2 have crammed the place to capacity, literally flooding the building's aged plumbing system and proving the facilities are totally inadequate to such popular shows. Implications are DMFA indeed needs the new and larger facilities it has been seeking.

Despite its outdated building and cramped quarters, DMFA has demonstrated it can be a place that attracts wide audiences if people are made to feel comfortable and if they are excited about what they are seeing. Even midweek during Pompeii, adults and children were sprawled on the grass or sculpture outside the building, obviously at home rather than intimidated by their museum experience.

Pompeii's bigger-than-art appeal drew throngs of first-time visitors to the Dallas museum, almost quadrupling its membership to 15,000.

From a commercial point of view, Pompeii proved financially successful for the city. No results are in on an economic impact study being conducted by the Dallas Chamber of Commerce, the City of Dallas and DMFA, but the Chamber's Visitor Development Department reported a able increase in the city's tourism business during according to its director James

what director Harry S. Parker calls "general repair to put the place back in order."

POMPEII COORDINATOR Barbara Van Pelt and her assistant, Love Nance, took the Red Cross emergency training course before the show opened, hoping all the while they would never need it.

"We had no major calamities but we did have to administer first aid to a lot of people who fainted because of the crowds," Ms. Nance said.

Pompeii strained DMFA's small staff and the museum depended heavily on volunteers from the Art Museum League. "A total of 671 volunteers, not counting shop helpers or docents, put in 192 hours a day or a total of 14,652 donated work hours during the course of the show," Pompeii volunteer coordinator Betty Zech tallied.

The museum's Pompeii shop sold more than $400,000 worth of merchandise, manager Wyatt Allen reported. The most expensive item sold was a $1,500 14-carat gold necklace and the most popular were $2 coffee mugs and 19-cent pencils.

The museum's off-hours events — everything from tours booked in the mornings by the Dallas County Community College District to black tie evenings at which shrimp and caviar were served — brought a total of $200,000 to DMFA, which depended on these profits and those from the Pompeii shop to help it break even on the cost of bringing Pompeii to Dallas since it charged no admission during public hours.

AS A RESULT OF a last-minute rush to see the show — some people evidently kept postponing while others waited for warmer weather — DMFA was filled with capacity crowds during the last three weeks.

raised

Reprinted with permission of Fort Worth Star-Telegram, Fort Worth, Texas 76101.

Museum of Natural History to put in a volcano exhibit and touching base with all commercial enterprises for tie-ins. Sanger-Harris, a Dallas-based department store chain, sent buyers to Italy the summer before, and planned a merchandising campaign that included window displays and was so extensive that it ranged from items in stationery to sofas upholstered in Pompeii designs. The city's hotels, Gray Line Tours and Charters, and Chamber of Commerce were delighted. The exhibit averaged 4,300 persons a day for 11 weeks—statistics that would have amazed and appalled people in the days before museums became so heavily involved in such public relations activities.

Museums now have memberships, catalogs for their shops (not just their collections) and newsletters for their patrons. A wall-to-wall and floor-to-ceiling Omni Theater in the Fort Worth Museum of Science and History creates a sense of participation in the shows (some patrons have even gotten motion sickness). The popularity of the theater is maintained by frequent changes in the feature attraction, and a newsletter to patrons calls their attention to the latest one. Inside the newsletter readers can keep up with other major events and attractions, such as a story of the rescue and bringing up of two abandoned bobcats who are supposedly part of the "live" exhibit area but spend most of their time with museum staffers.

For nonprofit institutions that emphasize the selling aspect of marketing without paying enough attention to their publics, there can be hazards. Alan R. Andreasen, a professor of marketing at the University of Illinois in Champaign-Urbana, has warned nonprofits to pay as much attention to their clients as they do to their products.[29] He points out that nonprofits are always in financial difficulties and really suffer when the economy is bad and when the federal government makes substantial budget cuts in social services. Clients will remain loyal if they feel a part of the institution.

Merging the Public and Private Sectors

Marriages of the public and private sectors have largely benefited both. Phillips Petroleum's artists work on a series of Phillips ads for the arts, along with product ads. Public service television spectaculars are sponsored by major corporations. The nonprofit side needs the money and the corporate side needs the image.

An example of a public-private cooperative venture is the 1984 Summer Olympic Games. The city of Los Angeles decided early that hosting the games didn't mean having the taxpayers subsidize the event. So the Southern California Committee for the Olympic Games was formed, and with the approval of the International Olympic Committee, went to private funding. An account of early success, summer of 1983, appeared in the Burson-Marsteller Report.

[M]ore than 60 companies have been designated official sponsors, suppliers or licensees for the Summer Games. Still others are paying millions to ABC-TV to be "category exclusive" advertisers for the more than 190 hours of live coverage of the Games.

Specifically, 28 firms have each paid $4 million to $13 million in cash and products and services for the right to use Olympic symbols and refer to themselves as the "official [film, snack food, product] of the 1984 Summer Olympic Games." These same companies are spending additional sums on a variety of trade and consumer promotions, advertising and package identification.

Some companies are using the Olympics to introduce new products or position old ones differently. Still others are expanding into new markets or increasing distribution channels.

And, not all companies that are part of the "Olympic movement" are involved in the Summer Games. Several have chosen to support the U.S. Olympic Committee, which administers—among other activities—the two Olympic Training Centers in Colorado Springs and Lake Placid.

Dozens more have opted to sponsor the Winter Games in Sarajevo, Yugoslavia, where the fees are approximately 10 percent of those required for similar official status for the Summer Games. Other opportunities include sponsorship of specific teams (swimming, boxing, hockey) and their various Olympic trials.

The money is not a gift; it is a promotional investment.[30]

Commercial Blends of PR and Marketing

The most desirable situation for blending PR and marketing might be when both are in the mind of the same person, the one in charge. In writing about Jordache's strategist, agency head J. Wilfrid Gagen, management consultant

[29] Alan R. Andreasen, "Nonprofits: Check your Attention to Customers," *Harvard Business Review* (May–June, 1982), pp. 105–110.

[30] "Going for Gold: Corporate America and the 1984 Olympics," *Burson-Marsteller Report*, no. 67, Summer 1983, p. 1. Reprinted with permission.

Edward Langley said: "The right half of his brain knows what the left half is up to all of the time. If his marketing programs produce negative reactions—and Jordache has had more than a few—Mr. Gagen turns his head around, together with the negatives, to produce a slice of favorable public relations."[31] Gagen has his own diversified public relations firm in New York, including a marketing operation. He quoted a retailer as having once said, "You never know where the company's advertising, promotion or public relations starts or ends." Gagen works with Joe Nakash, one of the owners of Jordache and the CEO, on all these activities.

Humor has been a big part of the Jordache advertising approach, and also what some have called theatrics. An example of the blend of advertising and PR is a problem that Jordache turned to advantage. The *New York Times* had banned one of Gagen's topless leapfrogging ads because "the couple was smiling." Gagen had the ad reshot with the models not smiling. Then in a speech he recounted the incident and said of the *Times*, "We have come to the inexorable conclusion that the morality of the *New York Times* is that you can do whatever you want, as long as you don't enjoy it." His remarks got considerable coverage. On a serious note, when the jeans were said to be selling for their label only, news releases countered by pointing out that tailoring, fit and fashion, as well as a quality that makes them relatively care free, is what customers were paying for, just as they would pay for quality in good tailoring and fabrics in a suit. Extensive coverage also resulted from hiring detectives to track down rivals counterfeiting Jordache products. The news media were invited to go along for the confrontations. Much of this work is promotional, and some of it press agentry. But it is a cohesive blend of the public image of the product and the presentation of the company to all of its audiences.

A "Product" the Public Made   Muse Air is one commercial firm that grew out of an accurate perception of what the public wanted. Airline executive Lamar Muse (who "retired" from another carrier he started, Southwest Airlines) decided the flying public was ready for an airline for nonsmokers. Muse, now chairman of Muse Air, and his son, Michael, based their decision on solid research. The smoking sections of major airlines were shrinking, and they heard nonsmokers complaining that the air conditioning system couldn't prevent the circulation of smoke. Muse's research team reported that only 1 out of every 6 airline passengers requested the smoking section on flights of less than one hour. Some smokers even preferred the nonsmoking section. Muse thought of other times people didn't smoke during periods of similar length—for example, in church—and decided the idea would work.

Muse Air has found there are passengers for longer nonsmoking trips too. There are also cooperative tie-ins. Thrifty Rent-A-Car has 10 to 15 percent of its fleet designated as nonsmoking cars, "guaranteed not to smell like a dirty ash tray." Also, there are hotels with nonsmoking floors and some hotels that are completely nonsmoking. Travel agents now can book travelers on a smoke-free trip to and in some cities.

---

[31] Edward Langley, "Panache at Jordache," *Public Relations Journal* (August 1982), pp. 14–19.

Muse says his planes are cleaner and stay cleaner. Muse Air also offers aids and incentives to help smokers quit. Heavy smokers get a package with a few sticks of gum and some hard candy with a written promise that if the troubled smoker uses the second half of the round-trip ticket on Muse Air and is still uncomfortable being cigarette-free for three hours, the return flight will be refunded.

In addition to what Muse Air sees as a marketing advantage, there have been some public relations benefits. Both the American Association for Respiratory Therapy and the American Heart Association have made official public presentations of commendation for Muse Air. The American Cancer Society sent TV and film personality Dennis Cole, honorary chairman for the 1982 Smokeout, to participate in the roll-out ceremonies for Muse Air's inauguration of its Los Angeles service.[32]

Keeping an Identity in a Name Change   When a bank that shared the city's name changed its name to the holding company it anchored, the community, the customers and the employees were given special attention to retain loyalty and to establish the new identity with publics most likely to resist the change. The Fort Worth National "adopted" the independent school district's financial magnet school, prepared a twelve-page, four-color booklet with original artwork as a tribute to the city, "Fort Worth: Stetsons to Skyscrapers," and put $1 million in an advertising campaign that was called the biggest promotion in the 109-year history of the bank. The bank used the slogan "pulling together to serve you better" to identify its campaign for a united front with the twenty-one Texas American banks, nine of which were in the metroplex. The local paper even ran a news story on the ad campaign. Employees at Fort Worth National had plenty of advance notice of events leading up to the official name change through their weekly newsletter and the holding company monthly magazine. To mark the day of the change, they had a party for employees and customers. The lobby was converted to a carnival with balloons, clowns, booths, games and a Dixieland band. The Fort Worth festival coincided with celebrations at each of the twenty-one facilities. Employees wore "pulling together" pins, and on their desks were cards: "Don't forget to say 'Texas American Bank.'"

PR director and bank vice president Gail Burris observed that the public relations function in a bank is often under the marketing aegis. Both public relations and advertising report to marketing at her bank. However, she said, she had open lines to top management and a close association with them. Trust and credibility are the major benefits of a job like hers, although such corporate PR positions are frequently lower paying than corresponding jobs in PR firms.[33]

Vice president for public relations for GSD&M Steve Lee says many agencies such as his that are primarily advertising and marketing oriented have to be edu-

---

[32] "Muse Air Breathing Easier as No-Smoking Gamble Pays Off," *The Travel Agent*, March 10, 1983, pp. 16–18.

[33] Gail Burris, presentation PR class, Texas Christian University, May 31, 1983.

13.7 HELPING IDENTITY CRISIS

To ease the impact of its name change, TABS began featuring cities in which its banks were located in its quarterly reports. The city features reinforced the name change and also tied the bank to the community, offsetting a sense of remoteness that some customers might connect to a "chain."

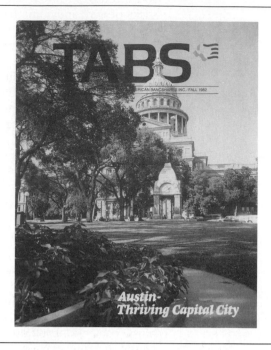

cated to the public relations function beyond publicity and sales promotion. However, Lee says, the proper balance in relationships can result in a very socially responsible and successful operation[34] (see 13.7 and 13.8).

ANNUAL REPORTS—FOR STOCKHOLDERS AND STAKEHOLDERS

What began as a protection for investors has grown into a major, multipurpose public relations tool: the annual report. Even nonprofit institutions have begun using annual reports to offer proof of their responsible use of funds from their publics—their stakeholders. Stakeholders have been identified as those who have an investment (time or money or interest) in an institution and who may have an impact on it, although they are external to the institution. The importance of stakeholders is such that some for-profit companies even issue a report for them.

The American Heart Association, Texas Affiliate publishes an annual report for volunteers, donors, the medical community, legislators and their staffs (see 13.9). The purpose is the same as any other institution's: to tell the accomplishments for

---

[34] Steve Lee, personal conversation, Summer, 1983.

13.8   BIG BUT STILL BACK HOME

When a bank carrying a city's name changes to its corporate name, some estrangement can occur. To avoid this, TAB of Fort Worth published this "tribute to the city." The art work in the book was especially commissioned for the piece.

Fort Worth:
Stetsons
to Skyscrapers

The view from the windswept bluff overlooking the Trinity River convinced U.S. Army Brevet Major Ripley A. Arnold that he had accomplished his mission.

He had indeed found what he had been ordered to seek on the sage-strewn North Texas prairie in 1849 — a site for an army outpost that would protect settlers from the roving bands of Comanche Indians who continued to terrorize them.

He knew the lofty vantage point would thwart any surprise attack and that the abundance of water, fish and wild game would be all those who settled there could possibly ask for.

And as he and a band of 25 privates made camp that night in a grove of cottonwood trees along the river, Arnold declared that he would name the outpost after the man who had seen him to find it, Major General William Jenkins Worth, his commander during the Mexican War and the head of U.S. Army operations in Texas and New Mexico.

But Worth never saw the fort that bore his name. He died of cholera before word of the honor reached him.

And the outpost turned out to be only a temporary facility, because, like Arnold, Fort Worth accomplished its mission as the Indian raids subsided and the Army vacated its log buildings.

But unlike many cities that have prospered as a neighbor to a military installation, yet succumbed to a slow death by abandonment, Fort Worth sensed its destiny.

the past year so the people who have invested in it will feel they have gotten a good return, and to impress the merit of its goals, objectives and activities on those who can have an impact on the institutions (also see 13.10).

Armstrong Annual Report, A Learning Experience [35]

The Objectives   Like many other businesspeople, the management of Armstrong World Industries, Inc., was concerned about two related problems: (1) increasing evidence of the general public's distrust of established insti-

---

[35] This case and the examples are from the manager of corporate information, Armstrong World Industries, Inc., in Lancaster, Pennsylvania. This annual report differed from the regular edition in an important particular: comments on colored paper were bound into this special edition. The comments are intended to help students and others understand more about the purposes and terminology of annual reports—not only Armstrong's but those of other companies as well. Armstrong took this step toward the broad goal of economic education in the belief that a better understanding of America's competitive enterprise system would lead to a greater appreciation of the benefits it offers in comparison with other economic systems.

Reprinted with permission of Armstrong World Industries, Inc., Lancaster, Pennsylvania 17604.

ANNUAL REPORT
Year Ended June 30,

1 9 8 3

American Heart
Association in Texas
Texas Affiliate, Inc.

WE'RE FIGHTING FOR
YOUR LIFE

We are volunteers with a mission.

We are a voluntary health agency. We are supported by public contributions and the donated time of thousands of volunteers. We devote all of our human and financial resources to one mission: the reduction of premature death and disability caused by heart and blood vessel disease.

Heart disease is a significant health problem.

Heart attack, stroke, and related disorders are the most formidable threat to our well-being. Cardiovascular disease is our Number One Killer, claiming almost half of all deaths each year. In 1982, 50,209 men, women, and children died from heart-related causes, 11,014 of them before reaching the age of 65.

Cardiovascular disease is a significant health problem in need of public attention and action. Luckily, something can be done about it. Most heart disease is preventable. And there has been more progess in discovering and treating heart disease in the last decade than in all of prior history.

We support life-saving research.

Your American Heart Association is a major supporter of significant cardiovascular research, second only to the U.S. government. The commitment of federal dollars is not keeping pace with inflation. Deserving scientists with meritorious projects continue to go unfunded. Our support of research is more important than ever. Last year we committed almost $2.4 million to more than 100 researchers in Texas.

We are the premier authority on heart health.

Your American Heart Association is the most credible and authoritative source of cardiovascular health and science information. Taking what we learn in the laboratory, we translate it for use by medical professionals and the public. Our ambitious educational progams reach into the schools and the workplace, teaching people how they can prevent heart disease in themselves and their families.

Through our efforts, Texans are increasingly aware of the crucial role lifestyles play in affecting their risk of these diseases. The role of prevention is especially vital because the initial symptoms are so frequently lethal or permanently disabling.

The public interest in health is at an all-time high. Misinformation abounds. But you can always rely on your American Heart Association for accurate, timely guidance.

We are successful in saving lives.

Your American Heart Association is firmly established. We have a people orientation derived from our grassroots, community-based organization. Our activity is well planned using the most modern, goal-oriented business principles and practices. The result is an active and progressive program which has been successful in saving lives. The death rates for all cardiovascular diseases are falling at a pace double that for all other causes of death. Accelerated progress in reducing the appalling statistics is our goal.

Our task is far from finished, and we need your support.

Continued success for your American Heart Association requires continued effort by thousands of volunteers, with the support of public donations and cooperation from business, education, communication, and governmental sectors . . . indeed, from every walk of life.

Proudly, we can say that support of your American Heart Association in Texas through time and money is a worthy investment which provides an excellent return for self, family, and society.

The problem is real. The results are effective. The results are worthwhile. Your investment pays dividends. Your American Heart Association merits your support.

tutions, especially business institutions, and (2) the relatively few students, even at college level, who have had exposure to sound economic education courses during their schooling.

Armstrong management realized that these problems, nationwide in extent, were too large for any one company to overcome. Nonetheless, they believed they could contribute something constructive toward economic education. If they set an *achievable* goal and reached it, then perhaps other companies would be encouraged to follow suit and the cumulative effect could become significant.

They decided in early 1973 to undertake a program that would develop a better understanding of business operations, motives and accomplishments. The chief target of this effort was to be college and high school students, all of whom would soon be reaching full adulthood, and most of whom appeared ill-informed about the heart of the U.S. competitive enterprise system: business. It was hoped that other publics, including employees of Armstrong and other companies, would also reach a better insight into business operations through this economic education project.

The Method   Already at hand was a good beginning for the program: Armstrong's annual report for 1972, which was then in production. The theme for this report was particularly appropriate. It concerned Armstrong's relationship with the consumer; in copy and illustrations, the report described the company's long-established programs to assure consumer satisfaction with its products and services.

13.10 REPORTING FOR SOCIAL RESPONSIBILITY AND PUBLICITY

Foundations also use annual reports, not only to report to donors and the Internal Revenue Service how the funds were spent, but also to use in soliciting additional funds. People who seek financial support for particular projects also use these reports to see what type of projects are being funded by a foundation.

Over 25 Years of Service

The Foundation for Public Relations Research and Education was established in 1956. Over the years it has been the leader in public relations research and education. Its work has led to many firsts, among them the first documentary on public relations, the first law textbook for the field, the first scholarly journal, and the first guidelines for undergraduate public relations curricula.

The Foundation's annual program of scholarships, project grants, awards, publications, and symposia is funded by tax-deductible contributions from individuals, corporations, and other foundations. Recent contributors are listed in this report.

How You Can Help
See Contributor Categories on inside back cover

☐ Send or pledge an annual personal contribution.
☐ Ask your company or organization to make a corporate contribution.
☐ Make gifts in honor or memory of colleagues or loved ones.
☐ Donate stocks or bonds.
☐ Make a bequest.
☐ Encourage others to support the Foundation's work.

Thank you for your interest and consideration.

Cover photo, and above:
Betsy Ann Plank, Assistant Vice President, Illinois Bell, giving 1982 Foundation Lecture preceding PRSA's 1982 National Conference.

Now the decision was made to take this educational process one step further by explaining in detail how and why a business reports on its activities each year to its stockholders and the general public.

In addition to the regular annual report, the company's Public Relations and Public Affairs organization prepared a "special edition" aimed at students and others who were interested in a better understanding of business (see 13.11). The

CORPORATE INFORMATION ARMSTRONG CORK COMPANY, P.O. BOX 3001, LANCASTER, PA. 17604. TELEPHONE 717/397-0611

FOR RELEASE   ON RECEIPT

ARMSTRONG OFFERS SPECIAL
ANNOTATED ANNUAL REPORT
AS ECONOMIC EDUCATION AID

The current edition of Armstrong Cork Company's annual report is being offered nationally in a special annotated version to students and others who want to know more about how a corporation reports on its activities.

This is the seventh consecutive year the company has produced an annotated version of its annual report as a contribution to economic education. To make up the annotated "special edition," Armstrong has prepared an eight-page supplement to its 1978 annual report. This supplement contains definitions and explanations of some of the basic terms used in annual reports. The supplement answers such questions as: Why is an annual report published? Who reads it and why? What is meant by such financial reporting terms as "replacement cost valuation," "depreciation and amortization," and "unrealized foreign currency translation"? Armstrong has also prepared a companion 20-item quiz consisting of questions whose answers are to be found in either the company's regular annual report or the supplement.

Educators in economics, business, accounting, marketing, and related fields may request classroom quantities of the special edition and quiz at no charge, while the supply lasts. Other interested persons may obtain single copies by writing to Corporate Information, Armstrong Cork Company, P. O. Box 3001, Lancaster, PA 17604.

Armstrong manufactures and markets a comprehensive range of interior furnishings, including floor coverings (resilient flooring and carpets), ceiling systems, and furniture; and a variety of specialty products for the building, automotive, textile and other industries.

12/79

M 2011 11-78J

basic text remained unchanged, but added insert pages were added, printed on gray paper to contrast with the basic report's white stock.

The insert pages were bound into the book to illuminate its various sections. The inserts set forth in layperson's language the "why" of each section. The President's Letter got a terse paragraph, the Theme Section and Operations Review scarcely more. Type covered only one-fourth of some insert pages for the purpose of clarity. The Financial Reports section of the book called for more ingenuity—and more space. Virtually every one of the financial terms used in the book, so familiar to accountants and so poorly understood by many laypersons, was defined and explained. The relationships between money items were made plain, often by drawing analogies the reader could readily understand. The Special Edition inserts raised questions, then answered them: Why publish an annual report, and what does it do? Why must a balance sheet always balance? What is meant by such terms as *stockholders' equity*, *working capital*, *retained earnings*? What are important things to look for in a report's financial section? (New material is added to the Special Edition each year. In addition to new definitions required to explain accounting terms appearing for the first time, special economic education features have included discussions on the role of profits, the distribution of the company's sales dollar and the effect of foreign currency exchange.)

Copies of the 1972 Special Edition went out, with individually typed letters, to more than 250 college and university presidents and to chairpersons of such departments as economics, business, marketing and accounting. Copies also went to heads of secondary school systems in Armstrong's plant town communities across the United States; to educational foundations, local and national business organizations and corporations; and to the Securities and Exchange Commission and other organizations that might have an interest in this explanatory effort. Copies were also distributed widely to Armstrong employees in supervisory positions.

The accompanying letters described the Special Edition and explained its purpose: one company's hopeful contribution to economic education, aimed at a better understanding of the competitive enterprise system. Recipients were invited to request additional copies of the Special Edition if they could use them effectively. Educators were offered classroom quantities at no charge.

As each new Special Edition is issued, the company sends a sample copy to every educator or college administrator who has used a previous year's special edition. Also, it sends copies to the business administration faculties at the many colleges with which it has a close relationship—especially those on whose campuses Armstrong recruits prospective employees—and it attempts to get the Special Edition into the hands of educators, at both high school and college levels, in the areas where Armstrong plants are located. In addition, it sends a copy—along with a news release offering classroom quantities—to several special-interest publications such as the *Journal of Business Education* and the American Assembly of Collegiate Schools of Business *Newsline*, where it is brought to the attention of large numbers of business educators. Finally, through the Joint Council of Economic Education and similar organizations, the Special Edition is made available to many other individuals around the country dedicated to economic education.

An innovation added to Armstrong's Special Edition annual reports beginning in 1975 was a supplemental twenty-question quiz, with answers drawn from both the regular glossy pages and the colored insert pages of the report.

Armstrong had not fully anticipated (but of course is pleased by) the wide range of disciplines of teachers who have asked for classroom quantities—business administration (through graduate level), accounting, financial analysis, government and business, law, economics, communications, public administration, finance, investment, advertising, marketing, portfolio management, industrial management, political science, personal finance, financial management and broader nonbusiness courses.

Perhaps most rewarding to Armstrong is achievement of one of the company's basic aims with its Special Edition: through example, to encourage other companies to undertake similar educational projects. Several have done so. (See Chapter 11 for other educational efforts by annual report writers.)

INCIDENTS, INNOVATIONS, INSPIRATIONS

The "global village" creates new opportunities for PR bloopers as well as for understanding. But unusual public relations tools applied in an innovative way continue to offer inspiration for problem solving.

Incidents

World markets are today the only markets, and public relations practitioners now find that translating materials is a commonplace task. Perhaps in the future PR offices will consider as standard equipment the hand-held computer that translates words and phrases into any one of thirteen languages, with the help of the appropriate tape cassette. Actually, few agencies now (or will) try to handle their own translations, with or without language computer assistance. The problem concerns the nuances of a language. For example, a PR and advertising agency director in Mexico City told with some relish of the agency's U.S.-based affiliate insistence on sending them billboards ready to put up for a client. The Mexico City agency had wanted to handle the art and translations. The client was Parker Pen. When billboard twenty-four-sheets arrived, a secretary in the office opened one package of posters that were duplicates of the billboards, gasped and began laughing. The Spanish translation had not taken into consideration local usage— and it was advertising that its new product would help prevent unwanted pregnancies! The Mexico agency's experience is not unique. Otis Engineering Company displayed a poster at a Moscow trade show saying its oil well completion equipment was effective in improving one's sex life.

Countless such goofs have occurred. The one shown here involves Dr Pepper, the soft drink manufacturer. When the company designed its logo for the Middle East, where its product was to be bottled for the first time, it could have used some expert help. In July 1978 the Dallas-based beverage company took a copy of its new logo for the Middle East production to the *Dallas Morning News*, where

13.12 DR BEBBER—SOMETHING LOST IN TRANSLATION

Reprinted with permission of Dallas Morning News, Dallas, Texas 75222.

Aziz Shihab, chief copy editor of the newspaper and former editor of the *Jerusalem Times* newspaper, noticed a problem. Shihab explained that Arabic has no letter *p* and that Arabs consequently often confuse the letters *p* and *b* when reading English. The Arabic symbol that is used for *p* in translated works is the Arabic letter *b* with three dots, instead of the usual one, under it. The company was thus alerted to the problem, and the *News* shared the story with its readers (see 13.12), showing both the incorrect (left) logo, which spells "Dr Bebber," and the corrected (right) version.

For companies that do have translations done, the cost can be high—$15 to $20 an hour—and the problem of finding type with a foreign language's more unique symbols difficult. When Gerber's faced that difficulty with its labels, it went to King Typographic Service, a Manhattan-based advertising typographer. According to the *Wall Street Journal*, King offers "Happy New Year" in 600 languages "all the way from Abenaqui to Zulu with such exotic stops in between as Ewe, Guipzcoan, Gyengyen, Kanarese, Lur, Ma, Tamul, Tsimihety, Wa, Xhosa and Yahgan."[36]

Words, emblems, gestures—all have cultural connotations. It pays to be aware of meanings, especially taboos. A book by Paul Ekman, Wallace V. Friesen and John Bear tentatively titled *Gestures International* presents a technique they have developed for identifying cultural emblems and their significance to certain groups (see 13.13). U.S. industry and even associations that are international in scope must be alert to such problems now that they are catching up with practices already firmly established in Europe. A resort in the Bahamas, owned and operated by Americans, casually keeps brochures available in other languages.

[36] "Company Sets Type in Almost Any Lingo," *Wall Street Journal*, January 3, 1973, p. 1.

On his first trip to Naples, a well-meaning American tourist thanks his waiter for a good meal well-served by making the "A-Okay" gesture with his thumb and forefinger. The waiter pales and heads for the manager. They seriously discuss calling the police and having the hapless tourist arrested for obscene and offensive public behavior.

What happened?

Most travelers wouldn't think of leaving home without a phrase book of some kind, enough of a guide to help them say and understand "Ja," "Nein," "Grazie" and "Où se trouvent les toilettes?" And yet, while most people are aware that gestures are the most common form of cross-cultural communication, they don't realize that the language of gestures can be just as different, just as regional and just as likely to cause misunderstanding as the spoken word.

Consider our puzzled tourist. The thumb-and-forefinger-in-a-circle gesture, a friendly one in America, has an insulting meaning in France and Belgium: "You're worth zero." In parts of Southern Italy it means "asshole," while in Greece and Turkey it is an insulting or vulgar sexual invitation.

There are, in fact, dozens of gestures that take on totally different meanings as you move from one country or region to another. Is "thumbs up" always a positive gesture? Absolutely not. Does nodding the head up and down always mean "Yes?" No!

To make matters even more confusing, many hand movements have no meaning at all, in any country. If you watch television with the sound turned off, or observe a conversation at a distance, you become aware of almost constant motion, especially with the hands and arms. People wave their arms, they shrug, they waggle their fingers, they point, they scratch their chests, they pick their noses.

These various activities can be divided into three major categories: manipulators, emblems and illustrators.

In a manipulator, one part of the body, usually the hands, rubs, picks, squeezes, cleans or otherwise grooms some other part. These movements have no specific meaning. Manipulators generally increase when people become uncomfortable or occasionally when they are totally relaxed.

An emblem is a physical act that can fully take the place of words. Nodding the head up and down in many cultures is a substitute for saying, "Yes." Raising the shoulders and turning the palms upward clearly means "I don't know," or "I'm not sure."

Illustrators are physical acts that help explain what is being said but have no meaning on their own. Waving the arms, raising or lowering the eyebrows, snapping the fingers and pounding the table may enhance or explain the words that accompany them, but they cannot stand alone. People sometimes use illustrators as a pantomime or charade, especially when they can't think of the right words, or when it's simply easier to illustrate, as in defining "zig-zag" or explaining how to tie a shoe.

Thus the same illustrator might accompany a positive statement one moment and a negative one the next. This is not the case with emblems, which have the same precise meaning on all occasions for all members of a group, class, culture or subculture.

Emblems are used consciously. The user knows what they mean, unless, of course, he uses them inadvertently. When Nelson Rockefeller raised his middle finger to a heckler, he knew exactly what the gesture meant, and he believed that the person he was communicating with knew as well. . . .

In looking for emblems, we found that it isn't productive simply to observe people communicating with each other, because emblems are used only occasionally. And asking people to describe or identify emblems that are important in their culture is even less productive. Even when we explain the concept clearly, most people find it difficult to recognize and analyze their own communication behavior this way.

Instead, we developed a research procedure that has enabled us to identify emblems in cultures as diverse as those of urban Japanese, white, middle-class Americans, the pre-literate South Fore people of Papua, natives of New Guinea, Iranians, Israelis and the inhabitants of London, Madrid, Paris, Frankfurt and Rome. The procedure involves three steps:

- Give a group of people from the same cultural background a series of phrases and ask if they have a gesture or facial expression for each phrase: "What time is it?" "He's a homosexual." "That's good." "Yes." And so on. We find that normally, after 10 to 15 people have provided responses, we have catalogued the great majority of the emblems of their culture.

- Analyze the results. If most of the people cannot supply a "performance" for a verbal message, we discard it.

- Study the remaining performances further to eliminate inventions and illustrators. Many people are so eager to please that they will invent a gesture on the spot. Americans asked for a gesture for "sawing wood" could certainly oblige, even if they had never considered that request before, but the arm motion they would provide would not be an emblem.

To weed out these "false emblems," we show other people from the same culture video-tapes of the performances by the first group. We ask which are inventions, which are pan-tomimes and which are symbolic gestures that they have seen before or used themselves. We also ask the people to give us their own meanings for each performance.

The gestures remaining after this second round of interpretations are likely to be the emblems of that particular culture. Using this procedure, we have found three types of emblems:

First, popular emblems have the same or similar meanings in several cultures. The side-to-side head motion meaning "No" is a good example.

Next, unique emblems have a specific meaning in one culture but none elsewhere. Surpris-ingly, there seem to be no uniquely American emblems, although other countries provide many examples. For instance, the French gesture of putting one's fist around the tip of the nose and twisting it to signify "He's drunk," is not used elsewhere. The German "good luck" emblem, making two fists with the thumbs inside and pounding an imaginary table, is unique to that culture.

Finally, multi-meaning emblems have one meaning in one culture and a totally different meaning in another. The thumb inserted between the index and third fingers is an invitation to have sex in Germany, Holland and Denmark, but in Portugal and Brazil it is a wish for good luck or protection.

The number of emblems in use varies considerably among cultures, from fewer than 60 in the United States to more than 250 in Israel. The difference is understandable, since Israel is composed of recent immigrants from many countries, most of which have their own large emblem vocabularies. In addition, since emblems are helpful in military operations where silence is essential, and all Israelis serve in the armed forces, military service provides both the opportunity and the need to learn new emblems.

The kind of emblems used, as well as the number, varies considerably from culture to culture. Some are especially heavy on insults, for instance, while others have a large number of emblems for hunger or sex.

Finally, as Desmond Morris documented in his book, *Gestures*, there are significant regional variations in modern cultures. The findings we describe in this article apply to people in the major urban areas of each country: London, not England as a whole; Paris, not France. Because of the pervasiveness of travel and television, however, an emblem is often known in the countryside even if it is not used there.

Paul Ekman, Wallace V. Friesen and John Bear, "The International Language of Gestures," *Psychology Today*, May, 1984.

Innovations

Telephoning for the Personal Touch   About twenty years ago many newspapers introduced columns called "action lines," which answered questions about consumer problems, and were somewhat miffed to have them identified as public relations devices. The corporate equivalent to the action-line column in the seventies and eighties has been the toll-free 800 telephone number. American Telephone and Telegraph used it in a campaign, devised by Young & Rubicam, to promote its call-in service, "Let's Talk," which put people in touch with Bell system representatives who were able to converse on a number of subjects. (One youngster called for help on his school paper dealing with fiber optics technology.)[37] And Shell Oil Company followed suit with their call-in "Shell Answer Man" program to respond to questions about fuel conservation. AT&T officials say they are judging the success of their "Let's Talk" operation by the image the campaign projects of the company caring about its customers—whether the customers call or not.[38]

While those two companies were using the telephone call-in system for general information, thousands of other companies found the 800 number a superb marketing tool for customer orders and complaints and also for market research. Campbell Soup researchers used it for responses to their Mailgram questionnaire, and asked viewers to call in with opinions about new commercials.

Media PR   The three commercial networks are increasing their profits by packaging news in videocassettes and videodiscs for academic, corporate and consumer use. The profits are modest when compared with the networks' news budgets, but recently a "CBS Collections" cassette on President John F. Kennedy made *Billboard*'s "Top 40" chart. Materials from the network archives offer many opportunities for both profit and corporate recognition.

A daily newspaper in a metropolitan area with heavy competition found through a survey that circulation was down, not because people wanted more local news, but because news in general was dull and depressing and people didn't have time to read. The PR firm of Regian-McStay broke their promotion for the *Fort Worth Star Telegram* with full-page ads proclaiming "Reach for a Star and Win a Car." The giveaways (seven Thunderbirds and $25,000 in cash and oil changes) followed a trial campaign, "Time Trivia," to see if newspaper readers would respond if offered something of value. They did and the "Reach for a Star" promotion was successful, the first time the newspaper had ever become involved in a promotional campaign of such magnitude.[39]

Employees   "Your Extra Security, Yes" is the title of eight booklets packaged in a case that Phillips Petroleum gives employees for quick reference on benefits. The

---

[37] James A. White, "Ma Bell Starts Spending a Lot to Answer People's Questions," *Wall Street Journal*, November 11, 1982, p. 31.

[38] Ibid.

[39] Greg Regian, presentation to PR class, Texas Christian University, 1983.

booklets, about forty pages each, include a general one on the corporate benefits package and one each on topics like retirement, dental health, disability and so on, each dated on the cover. When benefits in one area change, updated booklets can easily replace the old ones. The inside format poses questions in boldface type set in wide margins with the answers next to them.[40]

Responsiveness to employee communication needs prompted Shell Oil to take an extensive survey of how employees are kept informed. Under examination were Shell's seven publications, but the survey also asked employees to rate fourteen methods of communication. The number one source for information was the supervisor, followed by small group meetings. While senior executives ranked second and third as preferred sources, bulletin boards and the grapevine were given as top current (present or actual) sources. Employees asked for more discussion of public issues, so *Shell News* began publishing an "issue centerfold" presenting the company's viewpoint on specific industry problems. The survey was completed in 1980. Changes were made, and a follow-up survey in 1982 gave the corporate communication system high scores.[41]

"A new corporate name must be properly communicated internally or it will never work externally," says Russell R. Anspach, a principal in Anspach Grossman Portugal, Inc.[42] The New York-based marketing communication and design-consulting firm has handled name changes and corporate identity programs for Sun Company, Texaco, Citibank and Continental Group.

The worst thing that can happen, Anspach says, is for employees to hear about the name change from outside. This can do more than "dampen enthusiasm; it can result in serious resistance." A name change is unsettling to employees and it is important to get their cooperation. A name change is a good time to focus on corporate objectives, and Anspach suggests two principal ways to go about it. One is to announce the name change and come in with the graphics and other details later. That helps to build interest and suspense. The other is to wait until everything is ready and make the presentation of everything at once. That can be very dramatic. In either case, though, the support of senior and middle-level executives should be enlisted first in a personalized effort. Then comes informing all employees of the change and its significance. Open communication during the change is critical, and communication after the change is essential. Anspach suggests providing employees with a name change booklet, periodic news bulletins and specialty items with the new name (pens, paperweights, paper cups, softball team uniforms and the like). A name change generally takes about twelve months from the initial idea to getting senior management's approval to getting the board of directors' okay. This time period also allows for gradual adjustment to the corporate identity transformation. Because everyone shares in the institutional image, changing it is a project in persuasion and winning acceptance.

---

[40]Materials from Phillips Petroleum, 1982.

[41]Materials from Shell Oil Co., 1983.

[42]Russell R. Anspach, "Selling a New Identity Inside," *Public Relations Journal*, 38, no. 7 (July 1982), p. 14.

Inspirations

Good advice on common public relations efforts can make the difference between a mediocre outcome and a success. Two how-to lists are displayed in 13.14 and 13.15. The key to both is being sure the right people come to the event, the ones you want to receive your message and to participate.

POINTS TO REMEMBER

- Three types of cases dominated the early 1980s: issues and crisis management, behavior modification and combined public relations and marketing efforts.
- Issues management is a monitoring of the socioeconomic climate and its impact on public opinion; it is a PR tool designed to head off confrontations and crises and to monitor opportunities as well.
- Handling a company crisis requires socially responsible behavior in communicating with the media and the affected publics.
- More institutions are responding to criticism by talking back, but with mixed results. A conflict aired in the media generally does not serve the public interest.
- The long-term effects of behavior modification through campaigns of information and persuasion are questionable.
- Persuasion and information campaigns have been used with some effect to mobilize public opinion and group effort toward a common goal.
- PR and marketing are inextricably mixed; relatively new clients for such services are museums, hospitals and banks.
- Annual reports have become communication devices for both stockholders and stakeholders.
- Corporate and nonprofit institutions alike issue annual reports to demonstrate accountability.
- Internationalism is making an impact on all PR efforts; this means practitioners must be sensitive to the culture and languages of other countries.
- Some recent innovations in which PR has played a major role are the use of toll-free 800 telephone numbers to secure information; the packaging of news in videocassettes and videodiscs for academic, corporate and other consumer use; and the production of a variety of publications to meet employee information needs.
- The key to successful public relations events like trade shows or awards dinners is being sure the right people come to the event.

THINGS TO DO

1. It is an anniversary year for your university's student newspaper. The editor has asked you to come up with "something special" that will help increase advertising revenues. Develop a promotional campaign.

13.14 TRADE SHOW SUCCESS SECRETS

The following trade show success secrets are from Dallas, Texas, PR counsel Hal Copeland.

- Remember that the amount of exhibitor revenues you reap from your trade show depends on the quality and quantity of people you attract to the show. So don't put the cart before the horse. Registration promotion should get more care and attention than the sale of your show's exhibit space.

- Promote attendance year-round. Begin promoting next year's location and dates at this year's events with banners, invitations, and program notices.

- Help your exhibitors to promote show attendance. Keep them supplied with complimentary admission tickets, decals for their mailings, and camera-ready show logos for their trade advertisements.

- Do not, however, depend upon your exhibitors to bring out the crowds. You have the prime responsibility to promote attendance.

- Recruit, involve, motivate, and recognize as many industry volunteers as possible. You should start recruiting six to twelve months before the show. Also consider involving your allied associations or chapters in the planning and production of your trade show. Give recognition to your volunteers by providing special registration badge ribbons and by publishing their names and committees in your official program. Before you decide upon your educational programs, survey as many industry opinion leaders and volunteers as possible to determine the hot topics in the field. The appeal of your speakers, seminars, and workshops makes a big difference in your total attendance.

- To stretch your promotional advertising consider trading exhibit space for advertising space in the major publications in your field.

- Send the convention schedule and background data to editors of all appropriate business publications at least six months before your convention or trade show.

- Consider adopting a theme. You can build your show's identity with a catchy theme repeated in your promotional materials. The theme should distinguish your show from its competitors' and highlight specific benefits to different segments of the market.

- Stimulate preregistration by offering discounts or tickets for a prize drawing. People who preregister tend not to cancel, and the advance attendance information can help in your planning

- Enlist help in promoting the convention or trade show from the marketing departments of your official airline, travel agency, hotel chain, car rental agency, or other supplier. Under your guidance, they may be willing to distribute preregistration brochures and complimentary tickets, or conduct telephone or direct mail campaigns.

- Involve and honor key members to ensure approval of their employee's participation. When management is sold on the value of a show, employees will follow.

- Conduct specific promotions to special local groups such as federal and state government officials and members of the academic or financial communities whose attendance would benefit the entire convention or show.

- Run an efficient, professionally managed press room to offer services to visiting editors, writers, and photographers. This will enhance your association's media relations, stimulate favorable convention or trade show news coverage, and encourage media support for your next annual event.

- Make sure your guests are treated well. Site selection, weather, and the quality of your program and exhibits definitely influence your attendance, but the treatment your guests receive more directly determines the number that will return next year.

Hal Copeland, "How to Draw a Crowd at Your Next Trade Show," *Association Management*, February 1983, p. 83. Copyright 1983 by the American Society of Association Executives. Reprinted with permission.

13.15 DOS AND DON'TS OF PARTY PLANNING

The dos and don'ts of party planning for an event like observing a fiftieth anniversary of a company or an awards dinner are set forth here by two experts, Kay Partney Lautman, president of the Washington Division of the Oram Group, Inc., and Lynette Teich Caldwell, president of the Oram Group Events.

Before You Even Begin

- *Do* have a reason for a party; a special anniversary, an award to bestow.
- *Do* check your date to make sure you don't have competition that night. Most major cities have a service, or try the local newspaper. (In New York call the NY Cultural Assistance Center at 212/947-6340 and in Washington, D.C., telephone Maggie Wimsatt's Social Calendar at 202/652-7574.)
- *Do* allow a minimum of three months to plan and execute your party.

Leadership Is the Most Important Ingredient for Success

- *Don't* think a good cause will attract an audience. Remember the time-tested saying, "People give to people, not causes."
- *Don't* try to sell the house to individuals. It will take forever to fill the ballroom (or any other room) that way.
- *Do* secure a CEO (Chief Executive Officer) of a major corporation to be your corporate chairman and form a corporate committee to sell corporate tables of ten.
- *Do* ask a leading social arbiter to be cochair or vice chair (not a social climber—there's a big difference).
- *Don't* promise your leadership that they won't have to do any work. If you have paper leadership you might as well start cutting out paper dolls to fill the house.

Invitation Lists

- *Do* invite your $50 and over donors but don't expect them to fill the house, especially if they are direct mail donors.
- *Do* research your honoree and your dinner chairman and co-chairs. Learn which clubs they belong to, the boards on which they sit, who sits on their corporate board, the people with whom they do business, their competition, etc., and add these names to your invitation list.
- *Don't* submit these names to your chairperson as a separate list for obvious reasons. Rather, intersperse these names in your master invitation list in alphabetical order.
- *Do* ask your chair and vice chairs to "first name" your master list to note exactly how they address each. It's not good enough to assume that Robert Rich will be addressed as "Dear Bob." It may be that your chairman and your chairman only still calls him "Curly" or some other nickname unknown to you.
- *Do* ask your honoree for a list of his or her friends and associates, but don't ask for "first naming!" After all, you aren't going to send invitations from your guest of honor are you?
- *Do* befriend the secretaries of your chair, co-chair and vice chairs early in the game. And if you take her to lunch, take her some place just as nice as you would have taken her boss.

The Invitation

- *Don't* automatically send "formal" printed invitations. They do have a role to play in the social world, but in inviting corporations they are no substitute for a letter from one CEO to another.
- *Do* transfer all "first named" flat lists to three inch by five inch cards and note each card with all personalizations. If everyone knows Curly Rich equally well, send the chairman's letter of invitation. But if a vice-chair was the invitee's college roommate, you know what to do.
- *Do* ask those corporate leaders signing invitation letters to allow use of their corporate letterhead (which will get better results than their letter on your organization's stationery).
- *Do* remember, however, that if you use the

corporation's envelope that the "nixies" will be returned to the signer, so research those addresses carefully.

■ *Do* use your "formal" invitations to invite the social crowd at home addresses, but don't send even one without a covering "love" note from a committee member, even if you have to forge the notes or even print them. (Notes written in felt tip pen and printed in blue ink on odd size note paper look very convincing.)

■ *Don't* ask committee members to mail their own invitations. Ideally, they write the "love" notes and address the envelopes, but you put the packages together and mail them if you want to be sure they are mailed on time.

■ *Do* mail the invitations at least six weeks in advance. Eight weeks is preferable.

■ *Don't* wait until the week before the event to begin your follow-up if you don't have a full house. Follow-up by phone is far more effective than another note.

What to Charge

■ *Do* learn what others in your area charge and gauge accordingly. In major cities like New York, per ticket benefit dinners start at $150 and go up.

■ *Don't* have unrealistic expectations. It is the rare organization that can command $500 or more per ticket.

■ *Do* charge more for corporate tables of ten. For example, if individual tickets sell for $150 each (or $1,500 per table) charge $2,000 for corporate tables and be sure to list those corporations prominently in the dinner program.

■ *Don't* forget to include on your response card the potentially profitable tag line, "I/We cannot attend but enclose a tax-deductible contribution of $."

■ *Do* expect everyone to pay including your committee members and then let them beat you over the head for reduced price, never free, tickets.

Hotel/Caterer

■ *Don't* automatically book your town's largest hotel ballroom. Look for a unique setting. The Oram Group managed to organize a sit down dinner for 500 smack in the middle of the country's most visited museum, the National Air and Space Museum, for the Charles A. Lindbergh Memorial Fund. The guests dined with the Spirit of St. Louis spotlighted just above their heads.

■ *Do* realize, however, that catered affairs outside a hotel will be up to one-third more expensive because you have to bring everything in.

■ *Do* bargain with the hotel for better rates and make sure you understand all prices before signing a contract.

■ *Do* ask for a complimentary advance "tasting" of the menu you have selected.

■ *Don't* forget that even though your organization is tax-deductible, in certain cities you will have to pay food and beverage taxes and a set gratuity.

■ *Do* tip your headwaiter that evening in advance and you will then have his undivided attention.

Seating

■ *Do* reconsider whether you really need a dais. No one really enjoys being on view to the world all evening long, especially if they have a "bore" on either side of them.

■ *Don't* forget, if you are having a dais, to organize a "processional" in an adjoining room by putting names on a line up of chairs in the same order as the people will sit on the dais.

Continued

- *Do* (if you are not having a dais) scatter your "VIP" tables throughout the entire room so that even if most of your guests aren't sitting with a "VIP" or a celebrity, they are at least sitting in close proximity.

- *Do* distribute alphabetically printed seating lists to all guests as they arrive. It makes your job easier and people like to know where their friends are sitting. A map approximating table locations also helps.

- *Do* try to have at least one "host" at every table (board member, volunteer, or executive staff) who is familiar with the organization. This also helps in getting feedback later.

Staff

- *Don't* think that you can organize a major special event in your spare time. If you can't devote at least two-thirds of your time for three months, aided by a full-time assistant, hire a professional.

- *Do* be choosy in selecting staff and volunteers to represent you at the benefit.

- *Do* rehearse them carefully, especially if they have no experience. Take them for an on-site walk through prior to the event. The night of the dinner is no time to learn the location of all entrances, exits, stage, kitchen, rest rooms, and coat check room.

- *Don't* assume they know how to dress for the occasion. Make rules: no low-cut dresses or too-heavy makeup for the women or less than proper attire for the men. Budget to rent tuxedos for the men who don't own them.

- *Don't* allow staff to sit at the reception area unless their assignment requires it. Would you sit to receive your own guests?

- *Don't* allow the staff to have drinks at the reception area.

- *Don't* depend on promised volunteers unless you know them personally.

- *Do* have sufficient help—a minimum of four assistants at a dinner for 250, and add about one person for every additional 150 guests. For a dinner of between 500 and 1,000 plan on having 3 greeters and one runner, plus a second runner to remain constantly at your side; two staff members at

the reception and two backstage with the lighting crew, electricians, film people, etc.

The Reception

- *Don't* make enemies by having a VIP reception in one suite while directing the rest of the crowd, who have also paid their $100 plus, to a pay bar. If you must have a special reception that is limited in number, have it at someone's home or club in advance of the general reception.

- *Don't* ever make any guest have to reach into his pocket or her pocketbook at a cash bar after paying $100 plus per ticket.

- *Do* try to obtain underwriting for the wine and liquor. If that can't be arranged, there's nothing wrong with house brands.

The Menu

- *Do* keep it simple. Few hotels can serve complicated dishes to large crowds.

- *Don't* serve chicken if you are charging more than $100 per person.

- *Don't* be cheap with a simple house wine. Figure on two to three bottles per table.

- *Do* have waiters serve the wine and coffee if yours is a buffet-style dinner.

The Program

- *Do* write out a complete script for the entire evening with exact time allocations for each and every segment (i.e., National Anthem— two minutes; Invocation—two minutes; first course—10 minutes, etc.) Then add one half hour and make sure you conclude no later than 10:30 P.M., not including dancing afterwards.

- *Don't* be timid about asking each speaker to keep remarks brief and be specific. Never ask anyone to speak longer than 15 minutes. They will anyhow, but don't encourage it.

- *Don't* schedule your "best act" too early in the program if you want your audience with you at the end.

- *Do* try to get the services of a professional M.C. or someone with extensive speaking, stage or television experience to keep the evening smooth.

Music-Entertainment-Dancing

- *Do* have music, even if it is only for background.
- *Don't* hire Aunt Tillie's best friend's niece who has "such a pretty voice." Hire professionals or do without.
- *Don't* pay for big name entertainers. Try to get talent donated and pay for expenses only. But be sure to find out what those expenses might entail so that you aren't surprised when presented with a hotel bill for a traveling hairdresser, wardrobe mistress, accompanist and three friends.
- *Do* consider dancing, but unless your audience is exceptionally young, don't engage a rock band, not even if the Rolling Stones donate their services.

Gifts and Favors

- *Don't* distribute favors unless they are top quality. Remember, a piece of junk taken home is a lasting memento of your taste and judgment.
- *Don't* pay for favors. Get them donated or do without.
- *Don't* place favors on the tables. Half your guests will never see them.
- *Do* have staff or volunteers hand the favors out as people leave at the end of the evening or by going from table to table.
- *Do* give credit in your printed dinner program to those who donated favors, center pieces or other underwriting, and don't print the credits in six point type. Large type is a cheap way of saying thank you and saying thank you often is a big *"do"* in any type of fund raising.

What Do I Do Now?

(Some sticky situations and how to handle them.)

Sticky Situation #1

It's one week before the dinner and you haven't filled the house. What do you do?

First, get your corporate chair and vice chairs on the telephone selling tables to their friends. Believe us, they don't want this dinner to be a failure either.

If your dinner is to be in a hotel, see if you can change rooms. If the hotel is large, mail announcements of the new room to ticket holders and post staff at the entrance to the original room to redirect guests.

If you can't change rooms, use tables that would have seated ten to seat a group of eight and space the tables further apart. If you're having dancing, enlarge the dance floor and use lots of palm trees. "Bump up" table numbers. No one will notice that tables 4, 8, 12, 16 and so on don't exist as long as you get up to 50.

Sticky Situation #2

The seating lists don't arrive from the printer on time. What do you do?

In anticipation of this potential mishap you have brought six xerox copies of the list with you. You then make six "registration" signs just as they do at conventions. (i.e., A–E, F–J, K–O and so on.) Your staff, posted behind signs, directs guests to the proper tables. On the other hand if your printed programs don't arrive until the dinner is underway, don't throw them away. Instead, have staff members hand them out as guests depart as souvenirs. Remember that those corporate patrons and sponsors want to see their names in print and want to know that everyone else did too.

Sticky Situation #3

You're having a VIP reception, with special tickets, of course, and an angry guest without tickets insists that her party of four should be admitted. You know that she was not invited to the private party. What do you do?

Get her out of earshot of others, apologize for the error and escort the injured party to the VIP reception promising yourself never to have two separate simultaneous receptions.

Sticky Situation #4

The first course has already been cleared when you notice two conspicuous empty tables in the center of the room, both purchased by corporations that didn't show. What do you do?

Move your staff, usually sitting in a side or rear table, to at least partially fill the empty seats, and alert the headwaiter to have the entrees served there. Nothing looks worse to the other guests than empty tables.

Continued

Sticky Situations #5, 6, 7 and 8

Your guest of honor fails to show.

You make up a story that probably won't be found out (i.e., his plane was delayed in a snowstorm).

Your entertainers arrive an hour late.

You decide whether they can be fitted into the program later. If not, scratch them, making no announcement.

The floral centerpieces arrive late.

You have staff and volunteers hand out individual stems (not entire centerpieces) to departing guests. Charming!

Despite signs noting that the centerpieces are being donated to a nursing home, you notice guests making off with them.

You do nothing. That woman carrying a centerpiece under each arm is probably the dinner chairman's wife.

Final Advice

Here's some final advice.

- Work with a reverse timetable and write everything on it. Ten days before the dinner, make a check list by categories and don't rest until everything is crossed off.

- Think through your worst fears and pay attention to your nightmares. Then figure out in advance what you would do if such things happened.

- Buy your new dress, and those desperately needed new shoes, at least a month before the dinner. That last month will fly by and we promise that you won't have time for shopping the last week.

- We know you are busy, but carve out forty-five minutes for yourself about an hour before you have to be at the hotel. If you're too keyed up to nap, try deep breathing, yoga, a bath or whatever works best for you. Dress slowly and arrive one hour early at the reception—relaxed and ready for anything.

- Make up your mind in advance that something probably will go wrong, but that when it does you won't panic because after all, in that crowd, you're probably the only one who will even notice.

Kay Partney Lautman and Lynette Teich Caldwell, "Use Precision Planning to Organize Special Dinners," *Fund Raising Management* (August 1982), pp. 20–23. Used with permission.

2. Collect six annual reports, three from companies offering products and three from companies selling services (utilities, banks and such). Compare the approach to their audiences. Critique the annual reports, listing strengths and weaknesses, and suggest how to make each report a better communication tool.

3. Dissect the Child Find case presented here. Identify and describe the various tools used in the campaign. What else—keeping in mind the short time frame—would you have done to develop this promotion? What could you suggest as a continuing follow-up annual campaign?

4. Analyze the nuclear freeze campaign strategy. Refer to Chapter 5 and determine if the campaign as outlined is likely to be successful or not. Explain your reasoning.

SELECTED READINGS

Allen Center with Frank Walsh, 2d ed., *Public Relations Practices: Case Studies* (Englewood Cliffs, N.J.: Prentice-Hall, 1982). A collection of "how they did its" worth studying.

Hill and Knowlton, *The SEC, the Securities Markets, and Your Financial Contributions, Disclosures, and Filing Requirements for Public Companies*, 5th ed., 1983 (Hill and Knowlton, 633 Third Ave., New York, NY 10017).

Ted Klein and Fred Danzig, *How to Be Heard* (New York: Macmillan, 1974). A how-to book for activists and some case history success stories.

John Marston, *Modern Public Relations* (New York: McGraw-Hill, 1979). Cited earlier for principles information, but cases also compose almost half.

SEC Reporter, *Corporate Directors' Handbook* (Washington, D.C.: Securities and Exchange Commission, 1984). In addition to guidelines for disclosure and restrictions on corporate communication, gives some brief accounts of corporate legal cases.

PART 6

PR's Legal and Ethical Environment

In Chapters 14 and 15 we attempt to show how to handle legal matters relating to PR and to share some experiences with ethical questions.

14

Laws Affecting
PR Practice

*The law is the last result of human
wisdom acting upon human experience for the benefit of the public.*

Samuel Johnson, Miscellanies

A student hired by an advertising agency to distribute circulars was
stuffing them in mailboxes when an official U.S. Postal Service car drove up, and a
man leaned out and said, "Do you know that what you're doing is illegal?"

The student was mystified. "You mean I have to have a license or something?"

"No," the man said, "I mean you can't do it at all. Mailboxes are for officially
delivered mail and nothing else—you can't even put something the occupants
want in them."

The student called the agency and the agency called a lawyer. The lawyer's
opinion: The circulars could be placed in doors or elsewhere, provided they were
secured so that they would not litter the neighborhood, but they could not be put
in mailboxes.

This is only one of the laws that people using advertising and publicity need
to know. PR clients deserve a professional service. The last thing they want is for a
PR person to involve them in some legal entanglement.

THE LIABILITIES OF
PRACTICING PR

PR practitioners themselves are more conscious than ever of their
legal exposure. An Oklahoma City counselor says he now buys malpractice insurance, a business expense he never would have considered as recently as a decade
ago. The policy is his response to the three areas of exposure Morton J. Simon
categorizes as (1) normal legal exposure, like any other person, encompassing
civil and criminal matters, including conspiracy; (2) work-oriented legal exposure (normal PR or publicity activities); (3) extraneous legal exposure, an im-

portant category for PR people because it covers everything from getting sports events tickets for a client to lobbying and not registering as a lobbyist or reporting income and expenses from such activities. This broad category also includes the use of the public relations office by the corporation as a conduit for illegal corporate political contributions and, in the international arena, use of the PR office as a source for bribes or other illicit activities.[1]

LEGAL PROBLEMS

Civil suits involving practitioners may occur either in the course of communications activities—for example, copyright infringements—or in physical activities, such as accidents during plant tours. In addition, the practitioner has statutory and administrative liability related to dealings with government administrative agencies (SEC, FTC, FDA, ICC and others). A publicity release, for example, may violate SEC regulations, cause the company's stock to be closed for trading and result in court action. A carelessly worded ad can result in fines and perhaps court action. The statutory responsibilities are substantial. Sometimes a case is the result of something *not* done as a matter of compliance, rather than something done wrong—failure to disclose information, for example. Or it might not involve a formal public at all. It may be an entirely internal matter, such as a letter to employees suggesting management's position on a unionization effort. The NLRB takes a dim view of persuasive communications that sound coercive.

More so than ordinary citizens, PR practitioners are also exposed to many opportunities for criminal actions such as bribery, price fixing, mail fraud, securities manipulation, even perjury. To yield to these, however, is to risk criminal charges, particularly for conspiracy. It is imperative, therefore, to understand the legal interpretation of the PR person's standing as the agent of the client. As one expert, Morton Simon, explains, "Whatever the PR practitioner does, he usually does by reason of his retainer by his client and in concert with the client. Joint or multiparty action is therefore almost indigenous to the PR function. This is the root of the conspiracy charge."[2] Simon lists five instances in which a PR practitioner can be found liable to a conspiracy charge: he or she (1) participates in the illegal action; (2) counsels, guides and directs the policy behind it; (3) takes a large personal part in it; (4) sets up a propaganda agency to fight enemies of it; and (5) cooperates to further it.

Simon suggests that PR practitioners are usually involved in four specific kinds of cases—the big case, the human interest case, the routine case and the testimony. The *big case*, he says, "may be antitrust action directed at [a company's] entire marketing program, a labor relations hearing involving thousands of employees, suits involving product liability—especially those which deal with basic

---

[1] Morton J. Simon, speech to North Texas Chapter of the Public Relations Society of America, Dallas, Texas, August 29, 1978.

[2] Morton J. Simon, *Public Relations Law* (New York: Appleton-Century-Crofts, 1969), pp. 16–17.

safety or acceptability of a product—minority stockholders' actions charging mismanagement or fraud, and other litigation basic to the continued success of the company."[3]

The *human interest* case may not involve much money but by its nature it has a particular appeal to the news media. Examples, Simon says, are "a minor civil rights charge, a local zoning conflict, a right of privacy suit by a 'glamour name,' air or water pollution charges, suits against a company by a retired employee seeking a large pension, and myriad other kinds of litigation which may concern either an individual or some community interest."

The *routine* types of litigation are the result of simply being in business and include "actions for breach of contract, workmen's compensation claims, tax refund matters." Routine suits rarely involve public relations activities, such as the preparation of documents, publicity releases or media conferences for executives. This type of litigation is not likely to need staff PR involvement or the PR firm's help, if the company is a client.

Of course, the PR person who *owns* a firm or works as a consultant is subject to all of the normal potential litigation of being in business.

Cases calling for a PR person's *testimony* come about either because of his or her participation in the company program that is the cause of the legal action or as a result of being called as an "expert" witness. These may vary from "cases growing out of preparation of the company president's statement before a congressional committee to a $200 supplier claim for tables and chairs used at a company picnic."

Most large institutions, businesses and news media have legal counsel. If your client retains legal help, use it. The client's own counselor is as eager to stay out of trouble as you are. Many practitioners have also built up libraries of cases and regulations relating both to public relations and to their clients. In addition, many PR firms have prepared manuals for their employees to alert them to legal trouble spots. Clients too may have manuals, and the PR person should ask for them and examine them carefully for areas where misunderstandings might create problems.

The public relations person within a corporation needs to establish a liaison with the corporate attorney, advises attorney Morton J. Simon. Simon suggests that the reason some CEOs ask PR to do "Machiavellian" things is because they often don't understand what a PR person is supposed to do, because there are so many "loose" descriptions of the PR job and because PR activities are difficult to define.[4]

David Simon, president of Simon Public Relations in San Francisco, offers another reason.[5] The top PR person now is within inner management councils helping to formulate policy that will affect all of the various publics and must be concerned about how that policy is understood and accepted by those publics. Therefore, the corporate PR person is in a good position to assist corporate coun-

---

[3] Ibid.

[4] Simon, speech to North Texas PRSA chapter, Dallas, 1978.

[5] David H. Simon, "Lawyer and Public Relations Counselor: Teamwork or Turmoil?" *American Bar Journal*, 63 (August 1977), pp. 1113–1116.

sel in planning strategies and suggesting how legal actions are likely to be received by the various publics. The PR person also needs legal counsel's help, especially in reviewing financial materials. The relationship between the two needs to be complementary, not adversary, PR practitioner Simon says.

Attorney Simon agrees and says a good relationship with the corporate attorney is one of the best ways to stay out of trouble. Others he suggests are as follows: (1) Recognize your individual responsibility for your actions—none of this "I only did what the boss said." The law won't look at it that way. (2) Know your business. (3) Ignore the vague lines between advertising and PR because the law often does. (4) Decide how far you are willing to go to run a risk of jail, fine, a cease and desist order or a corrective order. (5) "Know your enemy," that is, which government agency is likely to take out after you. It helps to get on the agency's mailing list and read all speeches its administrators give. Often these may be the first hint of troubles for your company or industry.

Simon suggests there are three general types of legal involvements.[6] The first consists of meeting *government agencies' regulations*—federal, state and local—on everything from antitrust matters to building permits.

The second consists of *government-related activities*, such as libel and slander; right of privacy; contempt of court; ownership of ideas including copyright, trademarks and patents; publicity, political views, registering political activity as lobbying and representing foreign governments; contract disputes; stockholder actions; fair trade problems; use of photos of individuals and groups, preparation of publicity releases and advertising copy, plus games and giveaway promoting and financial collections.

The third type consists of *contracts* with clients and suppliers of goods and services, which deals with such matters as who owns the music for a commercial jingle if the client moves his or her account from the agency that created the commercial or what recourse you have if the photographer you hired messes up the color negatives you gave him to make enlargements.

In any of these three types of cases, a PR person *outside* of the situation is likely to be called by either side as an expert witness. When this occurs, a considerable amount of time must be devoted to research—gathering facts in the case, not relying just on what you are told. (Most PR testimony is for fact finding, in the discovery part of litigation.) Additionally, most PR people alert their own attorney who can advise them of any legal traps or personal jeopardy. Fees are generally paid for expert witnesses. However, excessive fees tend to invalidate the testimony. (The opposition generally tries to get the fee made public, usually as a part of the deposition.)

The danger zones to a PR person are letters and proxy fights, use of photos, product claims, accusations that might be ruled libel or slander, promotions involving games, publicity that might result in charges of misrepresentation, political campaigns. You should keep a checklist covering areas such as contracts, releases, statements of responsibility and rights of privacy.

Most important, don't guess. Get legal assistance. Work closely with media attorneys. The New York Stock Exchange encourages calls and other inquiries.

---

[6]Morton Simon, *Public Relations Law*, pp. 16–17.

Query any government body involved and get a statement of legal precedent or request an informal ruling. Get advice from the Public Relations Society of America.

GOVERNMENT REGULATIONS

There are hundreds of government agencies you may find yourself working with as a practitioner. Although we can't begin to cover them all, we can touch on three that are particularly important: the Postal Service, the Securities and Exchange Commission (SEC) and the Federal Trade Commission (FTC).

The Postal Service

Postal Service regulations prohibit dissemination by mail of obscenity, information about a lottery (two important elements: consideration and chance) and material that would incite riot, murder, arson or assassination. A 1975 law exempts newspapers and broadcast stations from prosecution in publicizing state-operated lotteries. The only restriction is that newspapers may not carry information on another state's lotteries in editions that are mailed.

Certain state laws prohibit the circulation of magazines carrying particular types of advertising, so space buyers have to beware. Furthermore, although there are substantial specifications to inserts in second-class magazines, the total reference to the subject in the *Postal Service Manual* about controlled circulation publications is contained in one sentence: "Enclosures are not permitted."

All mailing pieces face many different regulations regarding size, weight, thickness and where an address may appear. It is best to have the design of a piece checked by the post office.

Reaching audiences by direct mail has been put in serious question by a 1970 decision in a U.S. District Court, which has been upheld by the U.S. Supreme Court.[7] Senders could be compelled to delete an address from their mailing list and prohibited by law from sending or having an agent send future mailings to an addressee.

The case began when a mail-order business challenged a California regulation that states the recipient has a right not to have to receive "a pandering advertisement which offers for sale matter which addressee in his sole discretion believes to be erotically arousing or sexually provocative." If there is a violation, the addressee may report it and the Postmaster General informs the sender, who then has an opportunity to respond. An administrative hearing is held to see if a violation has occurred. The Postmaster General may request the U.S. Attorney General to force compliance through a court order.

---

[7] *Rowan* v. *Post Office Department*, 397 U.S. 728, 1970, Appeal of U.S. District Court for Central District of California, January 22, 1970, decided May 4, 1970.

These three points are significant:

1. The law allows a person absolute discretion to decide whether he or she wishes to receive any further material from a particular sender. (The material need not be erotic.)
2. A vendor does *not* have a constitutional right to send unwanted material into someone's home. A mailer's right to communicate must stop before the mailbox of an unreceptive addressee.
3. The law gives the vendor who sends the material due process. It provides for an administrative hearing if the sender does violate the prohibitory order from the Postal Service, and a judicial hearing is held prior to the issuance of any compliance order by a district court.

As a result, the Postal Service now provides two forms. Form 2150 is directed to a particular sender and is usually requested when a person has received some obscene matter or sex-related materials in the mail. Form 2201 is a request that a person's name be removed from *all mailing lists*. In an effort to counteract legislation that might be directed toward controlling unsolicited mail, the Direct Mail Advertising Association has asked that all persons who wished to be removed from the lists of their members send their name and mailing address to the DMAA (230 Park Ave., New York, New York 10017).

The Securities and Exchange Commission

Public corporations have to be concerned with SEC regulations, and all corporations must be aware of and sensitive to personnel and financial information that might be released (see 14.1). The larger the company, the more likely it is that something will escape that should not have or that the timing will be wrong. This is particularly true when the corporation must be coordinated with one of its clients (especially in the case of companies with government contracts) or with releases being prepared by an outside firm.

For this reason, it is wise to have a pattern for clearing news releases so that no one is confused about what to do and, it is hoped, so no one jumps the gun and turns loose a story that has not been cleared (see 14.2). Some institutions release only the required information, but a case can be made for using releases as early warning signals (see 14.3). Taking the offensive in takeover battles also is a new PR tactic related to this consideration of a consumer financial climate (see Chapter 13 for a discussion of Mobil's attempted takeover of Marathon.)

Timely and adequate disclosure of corporate information affecting investment decisions is a principal purpose of the Federal Securities Acts, as well as the policy of all national stock exchanges, for publicly held companies. Two major court cases, involving Texas Gulf Sulphur and Merrill, Lynch,[8] made it necessary for corporate officials and employees to understand the legal obligations of

---

[8] The involvement of Merrill Lynch was in a 1968 court case of the *Financial Industrial Fund* v. *McDonnell Douglas*, 474 F 2d 514 (1973).

proper corporate disclosure. This is particularly true of the corporation's relationship with financial analysts and the investment community. In the Texas Gulf Sulphur case,[9] a district court ruling, which the U.S. Supreme Court let stand, defined as an insider anyone who has access to information that, if disseminated, might influence the price of a stock. The PR person writing a news release, then, could be considered an insider. A firm must therefore disclose in its news releases that it is acting on behalf of an issuer and is receiving consideration from the issuer for its service. Richard S. Seltzer, former SEC special counsel, writes: "The SEC apparently believes that fraudulent schemes initiated by corporate insiders may be facilitated by the action—or deliberate inaction—of outside professionals: the accountant who 'stretches' generally accepted accounting principles; the lawyer who is willing to 'overlook' material disclosures; and even the public relations practitioner who seeks to portray a convincing, but inaccurate, picture of corporate events."[10]

Another federal court decision also affected financial PR significantly. Pig N' Whistle, a Chicago-based restaurant and motel chain, was headed by Paul Pickle, sentenced at one time to three years in prison for misapplication of federally insured funds. Pig N' Whistle was brought before the SEC in February and March of 1972 to answer charges of having distributed untrue and misleading press releases concerning stock transactions and acquisition of property made in 1969. The firm also was charged with illegal stock registration.[11]

The two releases, one made September 8 and the other December 30, contained untrue or misleading statements about the purchases of the Mary Ann Baking Co., and the Holiday Lodge near Lake Tahoe. Pig N' Whistle stock shot up to $18 per share after the two releases were printed. The releases came from Financial Relations Board, Inc., a public relations company. Pig N' Whistle had been a client of Financial Relations for eight weeks in 1969. The statements released by Financial Relations were handled by only one member of the firm. The president of Financial Relations stated that Pig N' Whistle had not provided the firm with proper SEC registration papers for the stock. The PR firm was told by Pig N' Whistle lawyers that immediate dispersal of the purchase made by Pig N' Whistle was necessary to comply with SEC disclosure requirements.

The SEC investigated the actions of both Pig N' Whistle and Financial Relations and ruled that Financial Relations had not exercised due caution in establishing the truth about the information as furnished by Pig N' Whistle. Financial Relations should have done independent research before allowing any releases to come from their offices. As a result, Financial Relations established within thirty days new procedures for reviewing the credentials of any new clients and also for verifying the facts given to them for publication. This verification of facts is for information that might affect investment decisions by stock purchasers. The SEC also ordered Financial Relations to stop any contact with Pig N' Whistle.

Following the Pig N' Whistle case, the SEC began reviewing possible new disclosure laws designed to protect the stock purchaser. The most important aspect

---

[9] SEC v. *Texas Gulf Sulphur*, 344 F. Supp. 1398 (1972).

[10] Richard S. Seltzer, "The SEC Strikes Again," *Public Relations Journal*, 28, no. 4 (April 1972), p. 22.

[11] SEC v. *Pig N' Whistle Corp.*, 359 F. Supp. 219 (1973).

A. Principles of Public Disclosure

1. The basic rule for corporate officials, when dealing with financial analysts and other members of the investment community, is that no item of previously undisclosed material corporate information should be divulged or discussed unless and until it has been disclosed to the public by a general press release or by an equivalent public statement. Material information as defined most recently by the [SEC] . . . , is information "of such importance that it could be expected to affect the judgment of investors whether to buy, sell, or hold . . . stock. If generally known, such information could be expected to affect materially the market price of the stock." Considering the facts of the cases decided to date, material information in each instance consisted of information about the corporation or its securities, which if disclosed, could be expected to have a reasonably prompt and substantial impact on the market price of the securities involved, i.e., resulting in a market price change perceptible in excess of the usual day to day or week to week fluctuation of the stock in question.

2. The New York Stock Exchange has recommended that corporations observe an "open door" policy in their relations with the investment community. It is appropriate to communicate with stockholders, financial analysts, trust officers, investment counselors, etc., either individually or in groups to answer their questions or to volunteer information, so long as undisclosed material information is not privately divulged. It is important that information should not be given to one individual or group which the corporation would not willingly give to any other individual or group asking the same question. In other words, preferential treatment of any class of community members with regard either to fullness of discussion or to disclosure is to be avoided.

3. If it is expected that any material information, previously undisclosed, is to be revealed at a meeting or interview, a press release should be prepared in advance and publicly released to the financial press and wire services prior to or concurrently with the meeting, unless the press itself is adequately represented at the meeting. If material information is inadvertently disclosed at a meeting a press release must immediately be issued.

4. Further explanatory information within the context of a previous public disclosure may be given to financial analysts and others. Any new material information, however, should be given ony in accordance with the procedures set forth in Paragraph 3.

5. Estimates of future earnings may be dealt with by either of the following methods, depending upon the policy of the individual company:

   a. Those companies which make it a practice not to issue any projections of earnings are frequently asked by financial analysts to comment on estimates made by them with respect to a future period or periods. Some companies do not comment on such estimates; others respond that such a projection is or is not "within the ball park." It may be necessary under certain circumstances to emphasize that the "no comment" implies neither an approval nor disapproval of the estimate. If, however, an independently arrived at estimate is deemed to be unreasonably high or low for the period in question in the light of responsible projections made by management, it may be appropriate to indicate that such estimate is "too high" or "too low" in order to prevent widespread dissemination of a substantially incorrect earnings projection within the investment community.

   b. Companies desiring to issue projected earnings, which are responsibly prepared and appropriately qualified, should do so only by public disclosure. Once such disclosure has been made and the projection remains materially unchanged, the company may discuss with individuals or groups the background and details of such projection. Such projection can also be compared with earnings for prior periods. If a publicly issued earnings projection becomes materially inaccurate, a new correcting public disclosure should be made.

B. Procedures and Practices

1. It is suggested that the following procedures be utilized to implement the Principles of Public Disclosure set forth in Section A:

a. Only certain designated officers or employees be authorized by the corporation to speak before or with members of the investment community;

b. One or more of such designated individuals (referred to hereafter as "the designated official") be given the responsibility for approving, in advance, commitments for speeches or interviews with the press on financial matters;

c. Press releases and texts or outlines of speeches to be reviewed in advance by the designated official to insure, among other things, that they are not misleading, i.e., are accurate, balanced, and do not emphasize facts disclosed out of proportion to their actual importance when considered within the overall context of the corporation's business;

d. Answers to probable questions on sensitive matters be prepared in advance of meetings with the press or members of the investment community.

2. While it is impractical to categorize what constitutes material information, public disclosure should be considered for the following subjects prior to discussion with individuals or groups:

   a. Total sales, sales by product groups, or percentage of total sales by product groups, for any period;

   b. Earnings;

   c. Profit margins;

   d. Plans to borrow funds or to sell additional equity securities;

   e. Proposed changes in dividend policy or rate, stock splits, or stock dividends;

   f. Proposed acquisitions or joint ventures;

   g. Proposed major management changes;

   h. Contemplated major management changes;

   i. Any other important development such as sale by the company of any significant asset, major contracts, pending material litigation, etc.

3. The following subjects are among those which, in the absence of special circumstances, are not ordinarily regarded as constituting material information requiring public disclosure prior to discussion with individuals or groups:

   a. Total project capital or research and development expenditures;

   b. Plans for construction of new plants or expansion of existing plants not falling under Paragraph 2 (g) above;

   c. Existing or planned inventory levels;

   d. General trends of sales or other operating conditions for the industry as a whole;

   e. Estimates of the corporation's effective tax rate and investment tax credit for the current and future years;

   f. Depreciation policy and estimated depreciation rates;

   g. General information concerning the company's business, prospects for various product groups, etc.

4. It may be in a company's interests to prepare a memorandum of each meeting or conversation with financial analysts or other members of the investment community, stating the names of the persons involved, the date of the meeting or conversation, and the items discussed. In addition, a complete record should be kept of all public disclosures.

5. Stricter limitations in addition to the foregoing Suggested Guidelines may apply in the event a public offering is pending or in process.

"Corporate Reporting Requirements," *Public Relations Journal*, 36, no. 4 (April 1980), pp. 25–47.

Note: Although these guidelines are still valid, an important decision was made in September 1976 in the U.S. District Court of Judge Robert J. Ward. Judge Ward ruled that Bausch & Lomb and its chairman, Daniel G. Schuman, had not violated the antifraud provision of the federal securities law during March 1972 when they had granted a series of interviews to four financial analysts who followed the company's stock after there had been some adverse publicity about the company's soft contact lens, Soflens. Schuman had been concerned about the interviews but had been candid within the bounds of proper disclosure. One of the analysts then called him, and in a telephone conversation Schuman attempted to correct the analyst's low first-quarter earnings estimate. Then Schuman called back to change his own rough estimate. The other analysts who had been at the interview were also called and given the same estimate. Then, as further protection, Schuman also gave the *Wall Street Journal* the earnings estimate. Despite his precautions, the SEC had taken the chairman and the company to court. Judge Ward's decision recognizes that a sincere effort was made to supply analysts with raw data that would, in effect, protect investors.

Handling of Product News Releases

1. First draft of copy to primary sources for preliminary approval.
2. Draft of release to Corporate Secretary for his approval.
3. Revised copy to Legal Department for approval.
4. Draft to division General Manager for his approval in certain instances. (Group Public Relations Manager should make judgment in this instance.)
5. Copy of approved news released is then mailed to PR Aids [New York company handling news releases] along with media selection sheets for distribution.
6. Media covered will depend on the nature of the product, its importance to the various markets and industries, and the marketing philosophy behind the development. (Distribution should be as broad as possible without covering media that would obviously not be interested in the development.)
7. Internal distribution of the news release to be determined by the Group Public Relations Manager.

Approval Chain for Agency-Prepared Releases

1. Clear with primary source at division.
2. Send cleared draft to Group Public Relations Manager for purposes of corporate clearance.
3. Following approvals at corporate level, distribution may be made through agency channels.
4. Copies of completed release to all involved in clearances. (News releases that must be approved at the corporate level include features, case histories, new product releases, and any other product-oriented information released to magazines or other news media.)

Handling of Personnel News Releases

1. First draft of copy to individual named in release to check accuracy of facts.
2. Draft of release to source requesting release.
3. Draft of release to division General Manager or individual's immediate superior at corporate level.
4. Draft to Corporate Secretary and Legal Department for legal clearances.
5. Draft to Group Vice President in cases of key promotions at divisional level. In instances of key corporate promotions, the Chairman, President, Executive Vice President, General Counsel, and appropriate Group Vice President must clear release.
6. Media coverage should include plant cities, Cleveland area [Eaton headquarters], individual's home town, association publications, appropriate alumni publications as well as trade magazines covering industries served by division or group with which individual is associated.
7. Internal distribution determined by Group PR Manager, and in cases of key corporate promotions, by Public Relations Director.
8. Copies of news release should be sent to everyone included in chain of approval.

From *Public Relations Manual*, Eaton Corporation. Reprinted by permission.

of this for public relations is that the kind of information to be released has to be more detailed and exact. Statements must be registered and they must include a budget and cash flow projection for the company. Public relations has to provide more information and be more certain now than in the past that the information is true. Further, the underwriters who do the research and write the releases now assume the same liabilities as the company about which the releases are pub-

14.3 DISCRETIONARY DISCLOSURE

The argument is made here for using a preliminary disclosure release as an early warning or advance information system. The release is not a forecast but an announcement. The risk is that management might abuse this technique, using it to manipulate its publics, with a resulting loss in credibility.

Mr. X, chairman of the board of Ajax Company, said today that the company's board of directors intends to increase the annual cash dividend payment on the company's common stock for the coming year to $2 per share from $1.75. The company issues the release three full months before the board actually increases the dividend as described.

Issuing such an anticipatory statement creates a number of potential benefits for the company:

- The issuing company can control the timing of the announcement, an important consideration for companies that have learned through bitter experience that their dividend action, no matter how newsworthy, gets lost in a massive table with dividend action of many other companies. It also allows a company to give an accurate and valuable sig-

nal to investors when the timing may be right to do so.

- A company can show the cause-and-effect relationship linking two corporate events. For example, the above example could be linked with a report of higher earnings for the year, sale of a problem division, or even a change in control of the corporation.

- A corporation can respond to shareholder demands without imprudently putting itself at financial risk too early.

- The impression may grow that a company is well managed; the company thinks ahead, says what it plans to do and then does it.

Robert W. Taft, "Discretionary Disclosure," *Public Relations Journal*, 39, no. 4 (April 1983), pp. 34–35. Used by permission.

---

lished. The information the public relations firm releases—the financial operations, history, future outlook, management and marketing structure of the company for which they are working—now must be considered. The SEC has placed a heavy burden on public relations practitioners by holding them accountable. The agency has also left the public relations firms up in the air about how specific and detailed their information must be. The problem narrows down to a matter of opinion and to the legal interpretation of "reasonable" or "ordinary care."

Curtis L. Anders, former vice president of Carl Byoir and Associates in New York, stresses that, in addition to understanding the impact of the Supreme Court's "insider" decision, it is imperative that PR counsel understand the other element in the court's decision, namely, "timely disclosure." Timely disclosure means getting information that could affect the market value of stocks to all publics simultaneously and promptly. The SEC decides if you got it there soon enough after the fact and if everyone received it equitably. One specialist in investor relations summarized the insider and timely disclosure rulings as, "Tell as few people as possible anything and then tell everyone everything," although it's not quite that simple, of course. Anders suggests the following in regard to timely disclosure:

1. Remember, internal corporate communications channels are not always effective, so include internal notification in the disclosure plans.

2. Since decisions must be made in advance, it is important for the PR person to have continuing access to facts and he or she must work closely with other PR people involved (as in a merger or other type of acquisition situation, for instance). Contingency plans should be made, on the assumption that a leak will indeed occur.

3. Keep the stock exchange notified or consult it if something unexpected occurs or if exchange ruling is not clear.

4. Notify the appropriate official in the stock exchange by telephone either before or simultaneously with the release of the information to the news media.

5. Make the announcement on the broad tape [stock exchange tape] and give the release to Dow Jones, the public relations and business news wires, both national wire services, and any foreign news services that might be especially interested. This is about as close as you can get to telling everyone at once.[12]

The primary responsibility of any confidential adviser is to the company he or she is advising. Curtis Anders offers the following advice, to ensure that a company will comply with the New York Stock Exchange's equal access policy:

1. Make a comprehensive survey of the totality of information regarding the corporation, then establish a clear distinction between what can and should be made freely available to the public and facts that must be withheld and protected by the most stringent security provisions.

2. Designate certain executives to act as official spokesmen and insist that all contacts with the press, security analysts, and others be channeled through them. The corporation must speak with one voice to all.

3. Provide systems that will keep designated spokesmen informed at all times of what can and what must not be disclosed.

4. Avoid all situations that will tend to create the impression that the corporation is willing to give confidential information to anyone, or that it is willing to disclose *any* information to some recipients that it is not equally willing to provide to others or to the public generally at the same time.[13]

Some suggested guidelines (14.1) have been prepared by the American Society of Corporate Secretaries, after conferring with SEC representatives, to assist officers and employees responsible for disseminating corporate information to financial analysts and the investment community. Some companies have developed internal checks (14.2), and some advocate going beyond what is required (14.3).

The annual report and the 10-K are two documents that PR staff or firms must prepare. Annual reports have become promotion tools used by investment brokers and the company itself in presenting the company to all members of the financial public from banks to potential investors to security analysts. An effort to make the annual report an integrated document didn't work too well, and the

---

[12] Curtis L. Anders, "The New Guidelines for Corporate Information," *Public Relations Journal*, 25, no. 1 (January 1969), p. 14.
[13] Ibid.

SEC is using the 10-K—another reporting document—as the best way to integrate management messages with financial reports. (For changes in these documents see 14.4.)

The Federal Trade Commission

If the Securities and Exchange Commission is looking out for the rights of investors, another equally alert agency is looking out for the consumers, the Federal Trade Commission. The FTC's scrupulous surveillance has resulted in false claims charges relating to publicity releases as well as to advertising. As in advertising, both the client making the assertions and the firm disseminating them are legally liable, the only protection being prudent precaution.

Consequently, the publicist should seek some verification for product claims before publicizing them. One suspicious or cautious publicist insists on trying a product before he writes the release. "If it works, and works well, I write a better story. If it doesn't work, I don't write it!" This is fine, if the product or whatever is to be publicized is tangible, but often it is not. Since the writer is legally responsible, some PR writers, especially those in independent firms as opposed to corporate staff, require notarized statements from research and development of product attributes.

Business spokespeople have cited the following particular groups when asking for relief from government agency pressures:

- The ICC, founded in 1887. Although created originally to regulate railroads, it now regulates many aspects of interstate trade.
- The Federal Maritime Commission, created in 1916 as the Federal Maritime Board. It regulates U.S. shipping.
- The Federal Power Commission, created in 1920. It controls interstate aspects of oil, gas and electric power.
- The Federal Communications Commission, organized in 1934. A 1979 communications act would have had a substantial impact on broadcasting, but it failed to pass (see 14.5).
- The SEC, also organized in 1934.
- The CAB, established in 1938.[14]

Additionally, the Federal Department of Agriculture is developing guidelines for consumer advertising initiated by drug companies. The first prescription drug advertising in the fall of 1983 appeared on cable TV shows for physicians, but there is no way to exclude the lay public. Physicians have expressed some concern that the ads will show only the advantages of the product. Nevertheless, the marketing, promotion and advertising of prescription drugs already has the drug companies' PR people heavily involved.

---

[14] From a Burson-Marsteller Report.

14.4 INTEGRATED DISCLOSURE DOCUMENTS: THE ANNUAL REPORT AND THE 10-K CHANGES IN THE 1980 ANNUAL REPORTS

Information in the annual report, proxy or other outside materials can be referenced in the 10-K, provided it meets the requirements of the SEC's regulation SX.

Changes in the 1980 Annual Reports

1. The SEC required two audited balance sheets for the last two fiscal years.
2. The income statement, previously for a two-year period, was increased to a three-year period. There are three columns.
3. The footnotes to the financial statements cover a three-year period.
4. There was the added requirement for five years of selected financial data, including net sales, net earnings, earnings per common share, dividends per common share, total assets, and long-term debt and lease obligations.
5. The biggest change in annual report requirements—which also changes the 10-K—is the need for expanded management discussion and analysis of financial condition and results of operations. This includes a fairly extensive *conversational* discussion of the liquidity and capital resources of the company. It can no longer be a line-by-line analysis of changes in the income statement. The rules say that if there's a 10 percent increase or decrease in a line item, the company must explain it. And, of course, most companies used a good portion of text space to say line so-and-so increased by so many millions of dollars and this was because of new business. However, the SEC said this approach was not satisfactory and called for an expanded narrative explanation.

Changes in the 10-K

1. Part 1 deals with the business of the company, its properties, the legal proceedings, and a discussion of stock ownership. All of this was there before.
2. Part 2 is the financial data for the basic disclosure package. These are financial statements, a five-year summary, and the management discussion. Here the SEC encourages incorporation by record from the annual report to the 10-K.
3. Part 3 is certain proxy disclosures that used to be made in the proxy statement. This was an attempt to cut down on some of the duplication. The SEC allows companies to incorporate proxy material by reference in the 10-K, provided they meet all the rules. The proxy must be filed with the Commission within 120 days of the year-end of the company. If a company does that, it can incorporate information relating to directors, executive officers and management remuneration by reference.
4. Part 4 of the 10-K deals with certain financial statements and schedules and scaled-down exhibits. In the old 10-K, a company reported parent-company financial statements, nonconsolidated subsidiaries, and a host of other information. That has been pushed back into Part 4, and now it can even be filed after the 10-K. The SEC recognizes that no one is really interested in the

The conscientious publicist is less concerned with the action of government agencies than with the consumer's wrath or loss of confidence, but he or she should still be aware that fraud or misrepresentation, as it applies to advertising, is watched over by the FTC, the local Better Business Bureau and state and local law enforcement authorities. And the PR person should certainly be aware that payola and other such illegal promotional activities are grouped by the law in the category of "bribes." (See 14.6 for FTC policies.)

information, so it moved the information toward the back.

The one big change in the 10-K is who signs it. It is now signed by the chief executive officer, the chief financial officer, the chief accounting officer, and *a majority of the board of directors*. This requirement doesn't change the legal liability of the director, but it is an attempt by the SEC to remind directors that they have responsibility for the information going out from management.

The SEC also changed regulation SX to give greater flexibility in the placement of certain financial information that heretofore has been on the face of financial statements. Some items can be combined, and there are certain disclosures—e.g., allowances from accounts—that can be footnoted.

Many of the differences that existed between Generally Accepted Accounting Principles and SX have been eliminated. Many of the disclosures, many of the discussions of short-term debt, rates of interest, supplementary profit-and-loss information, and inventory detail have been eliminated from the requirements.

There was a proposal to have expanded tax disclosure, but the SEC bowed to the dissenters and the proposal was abandoned. However, the SEC is still studying it. The Commission may yet come back with some expansion of the requirements discussing tax disclosures.

Summary

The most significant change in the annual report and the 10-K was in the management discussion. The SEC wants three areas covered: results of operation, liquidity and capital resources. A company must cover three years of financial information in the report and the 10-K, and it must talk about material items, unusual occurrences and infrequent transactions. It must talk about trends and uncertainties, and it must use a somewhat futuristic viewpoint.

The SEC does not want a line-by-line discussion, but if there was a significant change in a line item in any of the financial areas, the SEC wants the company to talk about it. In the area of liquidity, companies need some new approaches. There is no "boilerplate," no prescribed set of words. The SEC leaves it to each company to tell its own story.

The SEC found that mandating disclosure did not work. Everyone conformed to a line-by-line analysis and the management discussions didn't say anything. Now that is being changed. The value of the publications might be suggested by the fact that the annual reports are generally sent, on request, but many companies charge for their 10-Ks.

Vincent Cannella, "Integrated Disclosure: Betwixt and Between," *Public Relations Journal*, 37, no. 8 (August 1981), pp. 8, 9.

LEGAL RESPONSIBILITIES

Many aspects of PR fall into this category. Here we will touch on those that seem particularly important. As an example, in 1978 a Minnesota court ordered Ford Motor Co., to pay $500 for repairs to a buyer's pickup because he had driven it over rough ground as the TV commercial showed and damaged the cargo box. The judge ruled that Ford's advertising became a part of the warranty

14.5 BROADCAST DEREGULATION CONFUSION

When a 1979 communications act failed to pass, the FCC, operating under its authority from a 1934 statute, began making changes for which it then sought approval by the judiciary. The piecemeal changes and their effect are explained here by PR practitioner and educator Frank Walsh, who also is a lawyer. In spring 1983 the American Newspaper Publishers' Association adopted a policy advocating repeal of the equal time and fairness doctrine imposed on broadcasters and cable television. The fairness doctrine requires that equal time be given to persons with views opposing those presented on the air.

While Congress . . . continues to debate deregulation, the FCC went ahead and made some deregulation changes. Then, of course, the judicial branch was asked to determine if the changes were lawful.

The most recent judicial ruling by a Federal appeals court upheld the FCC action that gives radio stations more leeway on the amount of time devoted to commercials and to non-entertainment programming such as news and public affairs shows and public service announcements.

In the same decision, the court asked the FCC to reconsider its action eliminating the requirement that radio stations keep detailed logs of programs. The court questioned the commission's apparent failure to consider the difficulty of overseeing partial deregulation of radio without the logged information.

Leaning even more to the deregulation side, the court also eliminated the requirement that stations ascertain the interests of the community, in order to provide responsive programming.

This kind of piecemeal deregulation by the FCC, and the fact that the courts approve some of the actions and not others, present special problems for the public relations practitioner. Consider the following:

■ The partial deregulation by the FCC applies only to radio. Until this action there were strong parallels between the regulation of radio and television; now the rules differ. Ascertainment, for instance, continues for TV.

■ The primary targets of deregulation—the fairness and equal-time doctrines—have not been changed, although they may be the FCC's next target. Some groups seeking access to broadcast worry that, without those two doctrines, other groups will monopolize the airtime and there will be no legal recourse.

■ The instability in broadcast regulation makes even short-term planning more difficult for the practitioner. Station managers are not sure what to expect or whether different opportunities will be available in the near future. For example, many practitioners are planning for the 1984 primary and general elections. Any change in the equal-time doctrine might significantly change how radio (maybe even TV, depending on the mood of the FCC) would cover candidates.

Regarding deregulation of broadcast, the position taken by Judge J. Skelly Wright, who wrote the appeals court decision, seems to be the best approach: "The current tidal wave of deregulation should be initiated by Congress instead of the commission. It should thus be Congress, and not the unrepresentative bureaucracy and judiciary, that takes the lead in grossly amending the system of government regulation of the broadcast industry."

Frank Walsh, "Broadcast Deregulation Confusion," *Public Relations Journal*, 39, no. 7 (July 1983), p. 33. Used by permission. *Note:* Cable television and radio both are now deregulated. For additional information on current laws regarding all areas of public/mass communication, see *Media Law Reporter*, The Bureau of National Affairs, Inc., 1231 25th St., N.W., Washington, D.C. 20037.

in that it led the purchaser to believe the truck could be operated in the way shown in the commercial. The judge did not say Ford was guilty of false advertising. However, another judge found that the makers of Listerine mouthwash were. Listerine had been advertised as a cold remedy for fifty years, but in 1978 it had to mount a $10.2 million advertising campaign saying the claim was not true. The advertising had to say, specifically, "Listerine will not help prevent colds or sore throats or lessen their severity."

A consent agreement May 11, 1980 between Pat Boone and the Federal Trade Commission was the first example of an FTC policy holding celebrities accountable for the statements they make in advertising. Boone was a spokesman for Acne Statin, a skin preparation manufactured by Karr Prevention Medical Products, Inc. In summary, Boone was accused of making false claims that the product cured acne, was better than other products to do this and that some of his family had used the product with good results. Boone agreed to contribute to any restitution FTC might order but didn't deny or admit the charges.[15] Under the Reagan administration, the Federal Trade Commission became less aggressive, and Boone has even been quoted as saying he would go back on the air to support the product. However, although he had personal knowledge of the product, many celebrities endorse products in name only; their only contact might be in having the product shipped free to their home or office.

Complying with the Freedom of Information Act

Much government-held information is within the reach of the news media and the public in general, much to the consternation of corporate executives who have had to file reams of data to meet the regulations of various government agencies, commissions and bureaus. The public relations corporate staff officer should know what information is filed with these various government offices to anticipate what might cause a problem if released under an FOI request.

Corporate lawyers will advise what is protected under the law, but generally it is restricted to the following: (1) trade secrets (narrowly defined) and (2) information that is confidential, commercial or financial and obtained from outside government. Competitive disadvantage is a legitimate argument to protect confidentiality, but it must be proved; just the possibility of harm to a competitive position is not adequate. Some portions of otherwise protected material still may have to be released if, by eliminating critical portions, the basic confidentiality is protected. Another protection for confidentiality is to show that release of the information will make it difficult for the government to get the same type of information in the future.

Libel Laws

Libel is of two kinds, civil and criminal.

Civil libel is defined as defamation of character by malicious publication tending to blacken the reputation of a living person so as to expose to public hatred,

---

[15] *Facts on File*, September 15, 1978, p. 22.

14.6 FTC'S DECEPTIVE AND UNSUBSTANTIATED CLAIMS POLICY

Advertising claims that came to the attention of the FTC staff are evaluated on the basis of the criteria contained in this protocol.

A. Consumer Interpretations of the Claim

1. List the main interpretations that consumers may place on the claim recommended for challenge, including those that might render the claim true/substantiated as well as those that might render the claim false/unsubstantiated.

2. Indicate which of these interpretations would be alleged to be implications of the claim for purposes of substantiation or litigation. For each interpretation so indicated, state the reasons, if any, for believing that the claim so interpreted would be false/unsubstantiated.

B. Scale of the Deception or Lack of Substantiation

3. What is known about the relative proportions of consumers adhering to each of the interpretations listed above in response to Question 1?

4. What was the approximate advertising budget for the claim during the past year or during any other period of time that would reflect the number of consumers actually exposed to the claim? Is there more direct information on the number of consumers exposed to the claim?

C. Materiality

5. If the consumers do interpret the claim in the ways that would be alleged to be implications, what reasons are there for supposing that these interpretations would influence purchase decisions?

6. During the past year, approximately how many consumers purchased the product* about which the claim was made?

7. Approximately what price did they pay?

8. Estimate, if possible, the proportion of consumers who would have purchased the product only at some price lower than they did pay, if at all, were they informed that the

interpretations identified in response to Question 2 were false.

9. Estimate, if possible, what the advertised product would be worth to the consumers identified by Question 8 if they knew that the product did not have the positive (or unique) attributes suggested by the claim. If the claim can cause consumers to disregard some negative attribute, such as a risk to health and safety, to their possible physical or economic injury, so specify. If so, estimate, if possible, the annual number of such injuries attributable to the claim.

D. Adequacy of Corrective Market Forces

10. If the product to which the claim relates is a low-ticket item, can consumers ordinarily determine prior to purchase whether the claim, as interpreted, is true, or invest a small amount in purchase and then by experience with the product determine whether or not the claim is true? Does the claim relate to a credence quality, that is, a quality of the product that consumers ordinarily cannot evaluate during normal use of the product without acquiring costly information from some source other than their own evaluative faculties?

11. Is the product to which the claim relates one that a consumer would typically purchase frequently? Have product sales increased or decreased substantially since the claim was made?

12. Are there sources of information about the subject matter of the claim in addition to the claim itself? If so, are they likely to be recalled by consumers when they purchase or use the product? Are they likely to be used by consumers who are not aggressive, effective shoppers? If not, why not?

E. Effect on the Flow of Truthful Information

13. Will the standard of truth/substantiation that would be applied to the claim under the recommendation to initiate proceedings make it extremely difficult as a practical matter to make the type of claim? Is this result reasonable?

14. What are the consequences to consumers of an erroneous determination by the Commission that the claim is false/unsubstantiated? What are the consequences to consumers of an erroneous determination by the Commission that the claim is true/substantiated?

F. Deterrence

15. Is there a possibility of getting significant relief with broad product or claim coverage? What relief is possible? Why would it be significant?

16. Do the facts of the matter recommended present an opportunity to elaborate a rule of law that would be applicable to claims or advertisers other than those that would be directly challenged by the recommended action? If so, describe this rule of law as you would wish the advertising community to understand it. If this rule of law would be a significant precedent, explain why.

17. Does the claim violate [an industry] Guide or is it inconsistent with relevant principles embodied in a Guide?

18. Is the fact of a violation so evident to other industry members that, if we do not act, our credibility and deterrence might be adversely affected?

19. Is there any aspect of the advertisement—e g , the nature of the advertiser, the product, the theme, the volume of the advertising, the memorableness of the ad, the blatancy of the violation—which indicates that an enforcement action would have substantial impact on the advertising community?

20. What, if anything, do we know about the role advertising plays (as against other promotional techniques and other sources of information) in the decision to purchase the product?

21. What is the aggregate dollar volume spent on advertising by the advertiser to be joined in the recommended action?

22. What is the aggregate volume of sales of the advertised product and of products of the same type?

G. Law Enforcement Efficiency

23. Has another agency taken action or does another agency have expertise with respect to the claim or its subject matter? Are there reasons why the Commission should defer? What is the position of this other agency? If coordination is planned, what form would it take?

24. How difficult would it be to litigate a case challenging the claim? Would the theory of the proceeding recommended place the Commission in a position of resolving issues that are better left to other modes of resolution, for instance, debate among scientists? If so, explain. Is there a substantial possibility of whole or partial summary judgment?

25. Can the problem seen in the ad be handled by way of a rule? Are the violations widespread? Should they be handled by way of a rule?

H. Additional Considerations

26. What is the ratio of the advertiser's advertising expense to sales revenues? How, if at all, is this ratio relevant to the public interest in proceeding as recommended?

27. Does the claim specially affect a vulnerable group?

28. Does the advertising use deception or unfairness to offend important values or to exploit legitimate concerns of a substantial segment of the population, whether or not there is direct injury to person or pocketbook, e.g., minority hiring or environmental protection?

29. Are there additional considerations not elicited by previous questions that would affect the public interest in proceeding?

*Throughout, "product" refers to the particular brand advertised.

Elizabeth J. Heighton and Don R. Cunningham, *Advertising in the Broadcast and Cable Media*, 2d. Belmont, Calif.: Wadsworth Publishing Co., 1984, pp. 310–11.

contempt or ridicule. It also means injuring the person in his or her trade or profession. Use of "alleged" or other subtle qualifications are no protection.

In libel cases involving public officials and public figures, "actual malice" must be proved. But don't count on it. Definitions of all three designations—libel, malice and public figures—are still a matter of opinion in the courts. Slander is spoken defamation. It does not always apply in broadcasting because multiple copies of a script, even though the copy is eventually spoken, constitute publication and are therefore libelous.

Criminal libel—breach of peace or treason—is inciting to riot or some other form of violence against the government or is the publication of an obscenity or blasphemy. However, criminal libel is rarely considered and one writer, Robert Sack, in *Libel, Slander, and Related Problems*, suggests that it might be unconstitutional.[16]

"Publication" in libel suits is defined as dissemination of more than one copy. It may include office memos, letters, telegrams, certainly broadcasting scripts. All who take part in the procurement, composition and publication of libelous material are responsible, although the original publisher is not responsible for subsequent publications by others. Even those who bring the matter to the attention of anyone connected with possible publication are guilty of a misdemeanor. (See 14.7 for a guide to determining what is libel.)

There are three traditional defenses against charges of libel, plus the constitutional protection as provided by the *New York Times* v. *Sullivan* decision in 1964 regarding public figures.[17] These defenses are as follows:

1. *Truth*: But you had better be sure you have proof and that it is admissable in court.
2. *Privilege*: This is a fair and true report of a public, official or judicial proceedings.
3. *Fair Comment*: This is the loophole that film and book reviewers have. However, it is up to the jury to decide if it is "fair."

A protection, if not a defense, is the *New York Times* v. *Sullivan* decision by the U.S. Supreme Court, which now makes it necessary for a public official to prove malice in a libel suit. The court decides "malice," but basically it involves the intent to harm.[18] The real significance of the *New York Times* v. *Sullivan* case was that the Supreme Court could and would look at libel judgments to be sure that constitutionally guaranteed freedoms were not being denied. The second important point was that it didn't matter that the libelous matter was in an ad. The third point is that the Supreme Court said it was limiting the power of all states to award libel damages for statements about public officials. In that statement, the Brennan opinion, actual malice was defined as knowledge that the statement was false or was reckless disregard of whether it was true or false. The issue is what the writer thinks about the truth or falsity of the statement.

---

[16] New York: The Practising Law Institute, 1980.

[17] *New York Times* v. *Sullivan*, 376 U.S. 254, 11 L. Ed. 2d 686, 84 S. Ct. 710.

[18] State libel laws may be different. For example, in some states consent is a defense.

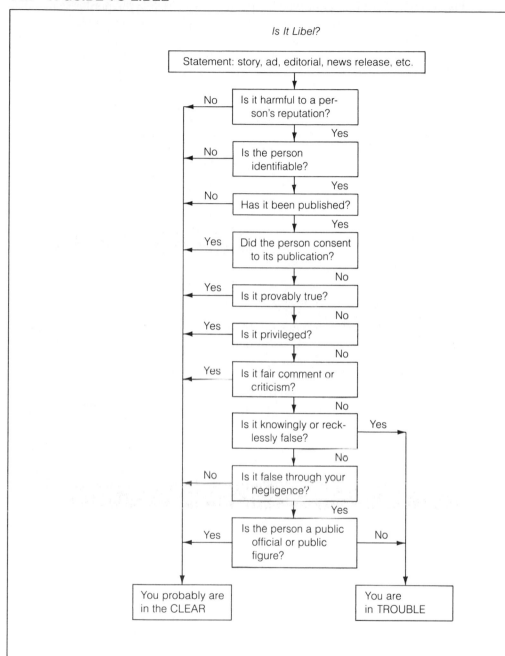

Is It Libel?

Statement: story, ad, editorial, news release, etc.

Is it harmful to a person's reputation? — No / Yes

Is the person identifiable? — No / Yes

Has it been published? — No / Yes

Did the person consent to its publication? — Yes / No

Is it provably true? — Yes / No

Is it privileged? — Yes / No

Is it fair comment or criticism? — Yes / No

Is it knowingly or recklessly false? — Yes / No

Is it false through your negligence? — No / Yes

Is the person a public official or public figure? — Yes / No

You probably are in the CLEAR

You are in TROUBLE

Albert Skaggs, and Cleve Mathews, "'Is This Libelous?
Simple Chart Helps Student Get Answer," *Journalism Educator*
(Autumn 1982), pp. 16–18. Used by permission.

A subsequent case extended this requirement to "public figures" other than just officials—that is, anyone who has put him- or herself in the public arena, such as a United Fund chairperson. However, in a 1974 decision,[19] information conveyed by the press that falsely maligns a person, regardless of public figure status or voluntary involvement, is still subject to jury determination of negligence. What this means to PR people is that carelessness with copy in a news release, such as saying things you can't prove about an individual, can be costly.

Private figures in most states must prove negligence to recover actual damages, and all plaintiffs, private or public figures, must prove reckless disregard for the truth or calculated falsehood to recover punitive damages. Since releases typically go into more than one state, to be safe it would have to be assumed that private-figure plaintiffs would need only to prove negligence to recover actual damages. However, the writer of the release might be in one of a few states that requires a higher standard.

Another limit to libel charges is the *statute of limitations*. In all cases this provides that a person cannot be charged one year after the date of publication. (Some states have varying periods of one to five years.)

Right of Privacy

A picture or letter or name of a living person cannot be used in advertising or publicity without his or her consent. For instance, a cereal company used an artist's representation of a girl, which showed her pregnant. Because she was neither pregnant nor married, she sued.

Although photos may be taken at an event for publicity purposes, the photos may be used later in innocence or ignorance in a brochure about the event. There is some question about whether a brochure is publicity or advertising, and the latter poses a legal problem. The photo might even be used specifically in an ad or accidentally because it is in the files or just available. Furthermore, even in a publicity situation, people may not be aware that their picture is being taken and for any number of reasons may not wish to have their photograph used. Most attorneys for public relations people say to always get a release. In some states, consent is the best defense; newsworthiness is more difficult to defend. For example, employee pictures and names can be used internally, but if distribution is external, "newsworthiness" is lost as a lead defense. Even internal use must be germane to the job—for example, giving information about promotions—or an employee who has not given consent may sue for invasion of privacy. Furthermore, use of an employee's name or image ends with the employment.

Major elements of a consent release are cited by Frank Walsh as *written consent of all parties* (employer, employee and parent of employee if a minor); *consideration* (something of value exchanged, like $1); *scope* of the use *defined* (as photo used in brochure only); *duration* (a set time period, not forever); words

---

[19] *Gertz* v. *Robert Welch Inc.*, 418 U.S. 323, 41 L. Ed. 2d 789, 94 S. Ct. 2997.

binding (which means heirs also have to be considered after death of person giving consent); and *no other consideration* involved such as some sort of inducement or promise.[20]

Contempt

Contempt is what happens if you comment on a case pending before a court in such a way that it can be construed as an attempt to influence a jury or those who might be chosen to serve on a jury. Particularly when a case is in pre-trial stages is it inadvisable to put your argument in advertising or publicity. A company with its case in court can't take it to the public by issuing releases or buying ads explaining its position, or can't even send out a mailing if the judge has ordered no public comment on the trial. The company can be cited for contempt. Even if the news media's coverage of a trial is eroding public confidence and hurting the company, it still can't do it. Even "issue" advertising can cause problems. Aetna insurance's ads about damage suits running up the cost of insurance created a problem in choosing a jury that had not been "exposed." The Sony case (below) was different because the campaign began when the case was on appeal and because there was a lobbying effort with the legislature going on at the same time to change the copyright law. Sony was arguing that the current law permitted their videotapes to be made, sold and used by the public. The Supreme Court upheld their position. However, the fight to change the copyright law in reference to videotapes continues.

"Ownership of Ideas"

Copyright protects a literary work, in form or style, from duplication in any manner.[21] Before quoting from copyrighted works, ask for permission. There are some exceptions, however.

If artistic efforts (writings, art, graphics, photos or other creative work) are done on company time by an employee with company resources, the material belongs to the organization (salary is the compensation). In some cases, an organization will have an agreement to one-time use and permit the artist to earn extra money by selling the work elsewhere. However, the artist's sale of his or her work can be done only when there is an agreement.

When work is purchased from an outside person, a supplier, there can be confusion unless an agreement is drawn up. Most PR people either buy file rights *or* one-time rights. But just be sure there is a written agreement when the work is ordered.

A problem PR people and their media suppliers faced in 1983–1984 was the contention by news media that videotapes of news are a copyright infringe-

---

[20] Frank Walsh, "Elements of a Consent Release," *Public Relations Journal* (November 1983), p. 8.

[21] Write the U.S. Government Printing Office for copies of the copyright law that went into effect January 1, 1978. (Also see Kent R. Middleton, "Copyright and the Journalist: New Powers for the Freelancer," *Journalism Quarterly*, 56, no. 1 (Spring 1979); pp. 38–42.

ment. Some companies regularly supply clips of exposure to clients, and other PR people capture their own. Part of the same issue was the legality of home-videotaping with video taperecorders (VTRs). The issue was resolved in 1984 when the Supreme Court ruled that Sony was not contributing to copyright infringement by making and selling VTRs since VTRs are capable of substantial non-infringement uses.[22]

Trademarks are protected from infringement, previous claim or use without permission. Check with the government registry and ask owners for permission to use.

Publicizing Political Views

Firms cannot be prevented by state laws from publicizing (or advertising) their position on political issues that materially affect their property, business or assets. In 1978 the Supreme Court found unconstitutional a Massachusetts state law that prohibited companies from making contributions to support a point of view on political issues.[23] So on referendum issues, corporations now, like individuals, have the right of free speech in conveying information of public interest whether or not the issue directly affects the company. The Supreme Court has not passed on whether corporations can support candidates. However, since corporate campaign contributions are illegal in most states, corporations have developed political action committees (PACs), which can gather funds and do have some impact.

Registering Political Activity

Public relations practitioners representing foreign governments must be registered with the U.S. government as foreign agents. (When the Justice Department took the PR man for the French-made Concorde SST to court for failing to register, he put a "foreign agent" identification on his Christmas cards.)[24]

Lobbyists on all levels usually have to be registered, although laws vary. For example, New York City requires the registration of anyone who attempts to influence city legislation or is responsible for "articles or editorials designed or intended to influence directly or indirectly any municipal legislation."[25] On the federal level, the following consists of lobbying activities: (1) payment to a legislative agent of $250 or more in a given calendar quarter to lobby; (2) making twelve or more oral lobbying communications per quarter through paid officers, directors or employees with senators or representatives from districts other than those in which the principal place of business is located; (3) making lobbying solicitations (which means asking others to write), if the expense of solicitation on a specific issue costs more than $7,500 in a calendar quarter.

---

[22] *Sony Corporation of America et al.* v. *Universal City Studios*, U.S. Law Week 52 LW 4090, No. 81-1687.

[23] *First National Bank of Boston* v. *Bellotti*, 435 U.S. 765, 55 L. Ed. 2d 707, 98 S. Ct. 1407 reh. den., 57 L. Ed. 2d 1150, 98 S. Ct. 3726 No. 76-1172.

[24] Reported in "Washington Wire," *Wall Street Journal*, January 2, 1976, p. 1.

[25] *Public Relations Society of America National Newsletter*, April 1974, p. 4.

A PR practitioner need not get involved in a lot of contracts, but there are at least four he or she ought to know about: the employee contract, the photo release, the photo agreement and the printing contract.

The Employee Contract

A client has a right to expect loyalty and confidentiality from a practitioner. Some large PR firms have their employees sign a restrictive covenant, and that means everyone, from the account executive to the file clerk. Ted Baron, president of a New York firm, recommends this "because they have access to insider information and documents, some of which your clients' competition or others would love to get hold of."[26] What are the penalties for breaking a covenant? Any sort of punishment management decrees—even firing, if it causes problems for a big client or causes the company to lose clients unnecessarily. A covenant is really a moral commitment as well as a psychological commitment (for, of course, you are less likely to do something if you publicly say you won't). An example of the Baron employee covenant is shown in 14.8.

The Photo Release

One of the most serious legal problems can arise from failure to get a person's permission before using his or her photograph or other likeness in publicity or advertising. The photographer should always have the model sign a photo release form. An example of such a form used by Eaton Corporation is shown in 14.9. A simpler form may also be used. Pads of these photo and model releases are available in most photo or stationery stores. If pictures of minors are used, the permission of parents or guardians must also be gained. The following contract was used by a photographer taking pictures of a group of youngsters.

I _____ parent/guardian of _____
      (Signature)   (Name of minor)

do hereby grant permission for all photographs taken of

_____ during _____
     (Name of minor)   (Time schedule, which

_____ may be used by _____
   included on-site location)   (Name of organization)

for either publicity or advertising for _____
                                             (Name of organization)

---

[26] Ted Baron, "Legal Protection for the PR Agency," *Public Relations Journal* (September 1971): 33.

TED BARON, INC. PUBLIC RELATIONS
104 EAST 40TH STREET • NEW YORK, 10016 • (212) 986-0517

Theodore Baron
President

        I hereby agree that during the course of my employment and thereafter for a period of two years I will not divert or attempt to divert any accounts or business of Ted Baron, Inc. either directly or indirectly for my own account or for the account of any other person or firm. Furthermore, it is hereby acknowledged that all records and other data concerning present or future clients of Ted Baron, Inc. are highly confidential and entitled to protection under the law as trade and business secrets of Ted Baron, Inc.

                                  _____
                                  Employee's Signature

                                  _____
                                  Date

Reproduced courtesy of Ted Baron, Inc.

Note that the permission for use was granted to publicize the organization only. This guaranteed that the pictures would not be used to endorse a product or for any other unspecified purpose.

The Photo Agreement

        This is a contract between a PR practitioner or firm and a free-lance photographer being hired to work on an assignment. A sample of a form is given in 14.10.

PHOTO RELEASE FORM

Name_____ Plant/Division_____

Address_____ Machinery/Equipment_____

_____

     For value received, receipt whereof is hereby confessed
and acknowledged, I DO HEREBY GIVE AND GRANT unto EATON
CORPORATION of Cleveland, Ohio, its successors and assigns,
and those acting under its permission or upon its authority,
full and exclusive permission to copyright, use and publish
for any and all commercial purposes whatsoever any and all
photographs or photographic prints of myself or other reproductions from negatives made of me at their studios or elsewhere in any and all poses, either in conjunction with or
without using my name, and to make changes or alterations
in such photographs, with testimonial copy, with fictitious
name or otherwise, in such manner as to said Eaton Corporation
shall seem proper. I do further certify that I am of full age
and possessed of full legal capacity to execute the foregoing
authorization and release.

_____
(Signature)

WITNESS: DATE:

_____   _____

Photographer's Note:

Identifying Data, such as description of clothing_____

_____

_____

From *Public Relations Manual*, Eaton Corporation. Reprinted
by permission.

PHOTOGRAPHIC AGREEMENT FORM

This form will constitute our agreement with you for the services which you will render as a photographer for Eaton Corporation ("Company"). The specific terms and conditions under which you will render such services are as follows:

1. You will act as an independent contractor and will not be an employee of the Company.

2. Your duties will include photographic assignments for the _____ [corporate divisions] in _____ [countries]. You will perform your photographic assignments under the direct supervision of the Director of Public Relations of the Company or his appointed representative.

3. For each day that you render your photographic services to the Company as set forth above, the Company will pay to you the sum of _____ for your services, plus all reasonable food, lodging, and traveling expenses incurred by you in the performance of your assignment. Upon return from the countries set forth above, you will prepare and submit an expense report and the Company will reimburse you for such expenses. The Company also will pay the cost of all film and shall pay all photograph developing charges incurred by you in the performance of your assignments hereunder.

4. All photographs taken by you in the performance of your assignments hereunder shall be and remain the property of the Company, including prints and negatives. In addition, the Company shall have the right to use all photographs taken by you in the performance of this agreement in any manner whatsoever, without limitations or restriction.

The Printing Contract

In making a printing agreement, remember that no two situations are exactly alike, so the suggestions that follow will not always be appropriate. However, they might be useful in developing your own contract or agreement. Along with the contract, remember you will need to furnish some suggestions of how you want the publication to look. Suggestions for making a printing agreement:

1. *Dummy* a typical issue of the publication, showing the number of columns, widths of columns, page size, number of pages and the estimated ratio of advertising to editorial matter—if you intend to have advertising. Ask the printer for a quote on the price for a fixed number of copies for editions of certain specified pages. Also, ask for the price per hundred for additional copies. You also need to know how much it will cost to add pages or additional color.

2. *Deadlines* for the publication will have to be reasonable for you and for the printer. You might vary deadlines for certain pages in a large publication like a magazine, especially if the pages have color or a great deal of statistical matter (perhaps set in charts or graphs). But be sure the deadline for the final product, as in delivery date and time, is firm.

3. *Corrections* can be costly. Be sure the printer agrees to furnish galley proofs on all copy and advertising. Usually there is an extra charge for making corrections on the page proof.

4. *Makeup* is often the reason for corrections. Be sure you provide the printer with legible dummys, correctly marked and copy checked for accuracy.

5. *Paper* is sometimes a problem. Be sure you and the printer agree on the type and quality of stock you will use, and get some guarantee of continuity of supply (and price if you can).

6. *Art* charges are usually specific. Get a list of art charges from the printer. Go over with the printer the types of art you are likely to use. Keep the information sheet on charges for reference in planning individual issues.

7. *Printing technique* is a basic decision, and usually a primary one since not a lot of printers can handle both letterpress and offset. However involved with printing technique, you also need to consider the quality of the job. If you have color covers, for example, with delicate shades, all the covers will not look the same when printed unless you pay extra for special handling, that is, a cleaning of the press periodically to maintain color consistency. Be sure you are not demanding—after the fact—something you didn't agree to pay for in the contract.

Examples of a printing bid specification and a printing contract are given in 14.11 and 14.12. The contract here is for a quarterly magazine. (The date was left on because prices have risen since, owing to inflation.)

═══════════════════════ **POINTS TO REMEMBER**

- PR people's involvement with law may be categorized as normal legal exposure, work-oriented legal exposure and extraneous legal exposure.

- PR practitioners are more likely to get inivolved in conspiracy charges than the normal citizen, such as for bribery, price fixing, mail fraud, securities manipulation and perjury.

- Four types of events dominate PR involvement in legal matters: the big media case, the human interest case, routine matters and testimony.

- Most general PR activities fall under the purview of three government entities: the Postal Service, the Securities and Exchange Commission and the Federal Trade Commission. Each has its regulations, with which the PR practitioner must be familiar.

- Legal responsibilities in the area of communications, particularly the news media, are open to interpretation of FTC regulations.

14.11   PRINTING BID: EXAMPLE

```
                    PRINTING BID SPECIFICATIONS
                                    Date_____

    Job title _____

    Date job due _____Brown print due_____

    Date of copy or camera-ready layout turnover_____

    Quantity _____

    Size _____

    Type _____Source _____

    Paper stock _____Color _____

    Folds _____

    Color (type, photos) _____

    Other parameters _____

            _____

            _____


    Based on the above information, my quotation for this printing

    job is            _____  per _____

                  _____    _____

                  _____    _____


    Signed bid must be received
    no later than             _____
                              (Signed)
    _____ on _____
    (time)      (date)        _____
                              (Company)

                              _____
                              (Address, city, and state)
```

14.12 PRINTING CONTRACT: EXAMPLE

Printing Contract

		Base prices - 4,000/5,000 copies	4,000	5,000
Name of Printing Company and address	Name of Client Date: June 13, 1984			

Job description
and size

MAGAZINE. Four issues per year.
8½ x 11 page size.

Quantity

Base bid is 4,000 to 5,000 copies
per issue.

Number of pages

Issue pages plus cover. List on
separate sheet.

(Extra prices 8-page colored
inserts.)

Copy details
Type setting
Art
Plate work

Client shall furnish publishing
company camera-ready art with all
type pasted on art boards for one
lineshot per color per page. All
additional lineshots, halftones,
screens, and other camera work are
extra. Publishing company shall
furnish all negatives and plates.
Four color process art to be
furnished by client.

Proofs

A color key proof on four color
process work, and a blue-line
proof on other pages.

Paper

Cover: 80# Book Enamel Cover.

Inside: 60# Enamel Book. *If an
8 pp of other stock included,
extra charges depend on stock.

Presswork

The base bid shall consist of four
color process Cover I & IV. Cover
II & III black only. The inside is
in black only printed front and
back.

Binding

Saddle stitch (2), and trimmed to
bleed 8½ x 11.

Packing
& delivery

Normal delivery time will run from
10 to 16 working days. Bulk pack
in cartons.

Terms

Net, 30 days; 2% discount 10 days
from invoice.

Base prices - 4,000/5,000 copies	4,000	5,000
24 pages plus cover	$1,894.00	$2,189.00
28 pages plus cover	$2,499.00	$2,870.00
32 pages plus cover	$2,558.00	$2,948.00
36 pages plus cover	$2,862.00	$3,302.00
40 pages plus cover	$3,003.00	$3,472.00

One additional color on		
8 page flat	$ 200.00	$ 204.00
Same color both sides	$ 380.00	$ 390.00
Four color process on		
8 page flat	$ 600.00	$ 618.00
Four color process both sides	$1,202.00	$1,235.00

Illustrations:

Halftones - $7.50   Lineshots - $5.20
Cutout halftones - $10.50   Reverses - $13.00
Dropout halftones - $13.00   Screens - $6.00

Four color process strip-in - $25.00

Color separations to be furnished by IMAGE. Branch-
Smith, Inc. guarantees prices for the two fall issues
as presented. Prices for the spring issues will be increased only by the exact amount of any paper price
increases to us.

Printing company   Accepted _____

By: _____   _____
                        Authorized Signature   Date

- The Freedom of Information Act protects trade secrets and information that is confidential, commercial or financial and obtained from outside government.

- Libel laws have three traditional defenses: truth, privilege and fair comment. The necessity to prove "malice" can be considered a protection against libel laws.

- The right of privacy affects the use in publicity and advertising of a person's picture, letter or name. Consent is the best defense.

- Speaking out on issues on behalf of an institution can result in contempt charges if the issue involves a case in litigation.

- Copyright protects a literary form or style from duplication in any manner without the owner's consent. Permission must always be obtained.

- Political activities, including PACs and lobbying, are governed by legislation.

- Contracts PR people are most likely to be making include their role as employers and employees and their role as users of services like photography and printing.

THINGS TO DO

1. Design a self-mailer (a brochure that can be sealed with a sticker or stapled), and be sure it meets all Postal Service requirements.

2. You are planning a promotion for a university charity and want to give away wrapped candy on the downtown streets. What sort of clearances are necessary?

3. A local business has asked you to design a unique promotion piece. Because its business is so competitive, it wants the whole piece copyrighted. What procedures are necessary to accomplish this? What guarantee can you give them it won't be copied?

4. You conducted a successful fund-raising campaign for a local charity and were paid for your work. Now another nonprofit group in the city wants you to "do for us what you did for X." You discover what they want is the same exact campaign design. Is it a legal or ethical issue?

5. The student newspaper's ad manager comes to the paper's photographer and asks for a reprint of a picture taken of a female student after a mud bath during a university social group's Fun Day. The picture is to be used in an ad. What do you do?

SELECTED READINGS

Mark Appleman, *Acquiring Individual Investors* (New York: Corporate Shareholder Press, 1982). Handbook by financial marketing consultant on broadening share-ownership cost-effectively.

Paul P. Ashley, *Say It Safely: Legal Limits in Publishing, Radio and Television*, 5th ed. (Seattle: University of Washington Press, 1976). Dated, but still a good guide. As a supplement, look at Clifton O. Lawhorne's *Defamation and Public Officials: The Evolving Law of Libel* (Carbondale: Southern Illinois University Press, 1971). Unfortunately for scholars, libel law is doing just that—evolving—so the Lawhorne book is also dated; nevertheless, it gives you background for current cases.

John F. Budd, Jr., *How Video Can Vitalize Financial Reporting* (New York: Corporate Shareholder Press, 1983). Advice from experienced professionals on: videotapes for analysts meetings, videocassettes of annual meetings, computer graphics, other ways to use visual media.

Ted Crawford, *The Writer's Legal Aid* (New York: Hawthorne, 1978). This book includes most of the essentials, such as the new copyright law, contracts for authors, censorship, defamation, right of privacy and such.

Marc Franklin, *The First Amendment and the Fourth Estate*, 2d ed. (Mineola, N.Y.: Foundation Press, 1981). Many mass communication law problems center around the First Amendment.

Going Public (New York: Technimetrics, 1983). Investor relations programs of nine companies that recently have gone public, explained by their IR executives.

Joseph J. Graves, Jr., *Managing Investor Relations: Strategies and Techniques* (Homewood, Ill.: Dow Jones–Irwin, 1982). Practical advice on successful communication with security analysts, shareholders, stockbrokers.

Investor Relations: A Practical Guide for NASDAQ Companies (Washington, D.C.: National Association of Securities Dealers, 1982). Basic reference for beginners, but useful to experienced executives; includes information on disclosure policies and press relations, shareholder publications, annual meetings.

Harold Nelson and Dwight Teeter, *Law of Mass Communication*, 4th ed. (Mineola, N.Y.: Foundation Press, 1982). Good resource for all aspects of mass media law.

Don R. Pember, *Mass Media Law*, 2d ed. (Dubuque, Iowa: Wm. C. Brown, 1981). Good reference work.

Kirk Polking and Leonard S. Meranus, eds., *Law and the Writer*, rev. ed. (Cincinnati, Ohio: Writer's Digest, 1981). Particularly good for articles.

Proxy Solicitation; Nominee/Beneficial Owner Identification Program; Tender Offer Defense; Proxy Solicitation in a Fight; Tender Offer Offense (New York: Hill and Knowlton, 1982). Top-ranked public relations firm takes "some of the mystique out of proxy solicitation" by revealing techniques in a series of flow charts.

The SEC: The Stock Exchanges and Your Financial Public Relations (New York: Hill and Knowlton, Financial Relations Unit, 1983). Most useful of all guides through the financial PR labyrinth; also the New York Stock Exchange. The NYSE keeps updates of its three publications on timely disclosure.

Target Cities Reports (New York: Technimetrics, 1982).

CHAPTER **15**

PR and Social Responsibility

What you are stands over you the while, and thunders so that I cannot hear what you say . . .

Ralph Waldo Emerson

Asked what he gained from philosophy, he answered, "To do without being commanded what others do from fear of the laws."

Diogenes Laertius, circa A.D. 200

The "morality" or "ethical" nature—the correctness or rightness—of any action . . . is to be judged in terms of the degree to which it includes and integrates the purposes, and provides for the potential development of those purposes of all other people concerned in the action or possibly affected by it.

Hadley Cantril

Give to every man thine ear but few thy voice.

Shakespeare (Polonius to Laertes in Hamlet)

In Public Relations, Ethical Conflicts Pose Continuing Problems
Lies, Stonewalling, Cover-ups to Protect the Company
Often Are a Way of Life
Indecent Burial of Bad News

The succinct prose of these *Wall Street Journal* headlines poses most of the problems public relations has with its own image, and the story itself covered the activities of some people with the PR title who contributed to that image.[1] PR's image also is tarnished by those who usurp the title.

Chicago police picked up a prostitute in a bar for soliciting. She had been handing out cards with her name, phone number, and address. Below her name were printed two words: Public Relations.

A minor Tammany Hall clubhouse politician in New York, with ties to a former local political leader, acted as the go-between in shady operations. On the door of his office appeared these words: Public Relations.

---

[1] Jim Montgomery, "The Image Makers, in Public Relations, Ethical Conflicts Pose Continuing Problems," *Wall Street Journal*, August 1, 1979, p. 1.

In Washington, a former administrative assistant to a congressman entertained politicians and tried to influence their views on pending legislation without registering as a lobbyist. His letterhead carried the words: Public Relations.

A former newspaperman in Los Angeles was the liaison between the head of a corporation and politicians in the California Legislature, arriving with his little black bag at the right moment before campaigns. He listed himself as a public relations counsel.

There is no restriction on the use of the words "public relations." Anyone can use them. And all sorts of characters do, without performing any of the functions normally associated with the practice of public relations. They are usually the fringe people who, for the lack of another title for their work, are happy to use "public relations."[2]

If a client wants to hire a PR practitioner, what assurances are there that he or she is ethical and responsible? L. L. L. Golden's preceding examples describe the problem well.

Should there be a licensing procedure for PR with education, testing and preliminary practice as prerequisites, as is done for the legal and medical professions? Or should there be something similar to the accounting profession's awarding of a certification (CPA—Certified Public Accountant)? The advantage of licensing is that it would not eliminate those who wished to find employment in public relations, but it would establish a level of competence or professionalism among public relations practitioners.

Just as the CPA has not eliminated the uncertified public accountant and auditor, so there could be licensed and unlicensed PR people, with the qualifications for each being vastly different. Bernays's argument for licensing is that only through controlled entry and exit into the practice of public relations can PR become a profession (see 15.1).

However, many people who come into PR from a news media background feel that if public relations were licensed, a move to license newspeople would not be far behind. Moreover, they argue that an accreditation format already exists in the Public Relations Society of America's program requiring experience, testing and the approval of other professionals. And they point out that even that has resulted in few members being accredited. (About 3,000 current members of PRSA are APPR. Through the years more than 4,000 have been accredited. Currently PRSA membership is over 10,500.) Most significantly in terms of ethics—there have been few cases of censure and suspension although sixty grievances have been filed. Members of PRSA are governed by a Code of Professional Standards. Violations of that code may be called to the attention of the association's Grievance Board with action taken against the offender. (See Appendix A for grievance procedure.) Since the PRSA code was adopted in 1954 (see Appendix A), only three people have been suspended, four censured and one reprimanded. Additionally, the International Association of Business Communicators (IABC), which also includes many PR practitioners, has an accreditation process. The merit of the two accrediting processes has been examined by committees in both organizations and found wanting but, as one executive put it, "It's all we have." Accrediting

---

[2] Reprinted by permission of Hawthorn Books, Inc., from *Only by Public Consent* by L. L. L. Golden, p. 327. Copyright © 1968 by L. L. L. Golden. All rights reserved.

15.1 BERNAYS ON LICENSING

In 1984 Edward L. Bernays wrote a letter to Doug Newsom expounding his views on licensing.

Licensing can be accomplished with ease, without in any way infringing on the rights guaranteed by the first amendment. Lawyers, for instance, are licensed and their freedom of speech is guaranteed by the United States Constitution. So are medical doctors free to speak their minds on any subject. I have taken this question up with lawyers and they assure me that this amendment in the Bill of Rights cannot be infringed upon.

Self licensing is of no use in assuring that standards be maintained. Self licensing carries no legal sanctions with it. In the case of doctors and lawyers, misbehavior brings legal sanction by the state, disbarment or other sanctions.

As for the licensing, the same procedure would be followed as is the case with doctors and lawyers. The state appoints a committee of a Board of Examiners chosen from the profession. The law would stipulate that this group draw up an examination which a practitioner would have to pass. This same board from the profession would, as in the case of doctors and lawyers, serve as the body to inflict punishment as necessary.

As far as the practitioners now practicing they would have the right to continue to practice. Under the circumstances it would take a generation to change the present situation. But all new practitioners would have to go through

the formal procedure. The various educational programs now in existence would, however—in deference to the examinations taking place in each state—obviously have to change their course so that the graduating students would be able to pass the examination.

I have read several good books on the history of the professions. They state that in the early nineteenth century a number of new professions, like civil, electrical, other engineering, needed to protect the public from imposters as well as to ensure standards within their own profession. They asked the state for licensing, registration and legal sanctions. Thus, licensing, registration and legal sanctions became the practice in England and spread to the U.S. Today there are no standards set for public relations practitioners. Any paper hanger can call himself or herself a public relations practitioner. And often does.

Licensing, registration and legal sanctions set up standards and protect the profession and the public alike.

It would be easy for one state to adopt the practice, and it would spread to the satisfaction of profession and public alike.

---

processes serve to identify practitioners recognized by their peers through written and oral examination to be qualified to practice public relations. Policing of members' standards of practice is an internal check against malpractice. However, even if members are denied continued association status, they still can practice public relations.

RESPONSIBILITY TO WHOM?

There will always be some in the business world convinced that all they need is a lawyer to keep them out of jail and a PR practitioner to keep bad news out of the paper. Indeed, one survey found that corporate executives and nonbusinesspeople differed rather markedly on whether particular marketing practices were ethical. In response to statements like "A well-known magazine, very popular with teenagers, obtains a large portion of its revenues from cigarette companies," 62 percent of the corporate executives saw nothing wrong with the practice, compared with 31 percent of nonmanagement workers and 29 percent of the homemakers queried.[3]

And David Finn points out, in a thoughtful article:

> Ethics is, unfortunately, a bad word to use when executives are sitting around a table struggling with practical problems of the day. Any public relations man who has ever had the experience of counseling his client to do something because it is "ethical" knows this to be true. It is considered a *foreign*, if not embarrassingly *naive*, word. Most businessmen react more positively to such phrases as "better from a long-range point of view," "sounder business policy," or even "good public relations" than to the idea of doing something because it is "more ethical."[4]

The result, Finn says, is that public relations, in a frequently disguised form, performs the role of *keeping management in line*: "When functioning well, it acts as the anvil against which management's moral problems can be hammered."[5] In fact, it actually means that when executives are establishing a public relations policy for their company, "they are really concerned with significant ethical questions—without quite realizing it."[6]

Finn's key word is *anvil*. In the same vein, Ed Block, vice president–public relations for AT&T in New York, says:

> Counseling does not mean whining, preaching, hairshirting, pontificating or conducting ceremonial benedictions to the corporate conscience. Counseling means doing. It means action. It means wading into real problems in real time and implementing solutions that are right—and will work. Occasionally it means putting yourself and your reputation at risk in contests of contending viewpoints. I can't imagine myself calling the chairman of the board every morning and saying, "John, it's time for your daily sermon from Ed the tribal wiseman. Please lean back and listen and when I'm through you'll be a wiser and better person." I can't imagine myself calling one of the other vice presidents and saying, "Tim, you and your staff—conscientious and highly motivated though I know you to be—are about to commit a mindless atrocity on our lovable customers and so you must listen to me before it's too late!" Of course not.[7]

The kind of corporate conscience both Finn and Block are talking about creating is the constant awareness by management of the institution's responsibility to all its publics.

Most professional PR practitioners recognize that they have ethical responsibility to nine different publics:

[3] David Finn, "Struggle for Ethics in Public Relations," *Harvard Business Review*, 12 (January–February 1959), p. 9–11.

[4] Ibid.

[5] Ibid.

[6] Ibid.

[7] Ed Block, vice president–public relations, American Telephone and Telegraph Co., New York City, N.Y., in an address to the Texas Public Relations Association, Kerrville, Texas, July 22, 1978. Used by permission.

1. *Clients*: Being responsible to a client means not only being judicious with his or her money, but also not always saying yes, for the customer is *not* always right. When a client is wrong, it is important to say so, to tell truths substantiated by facts discovered through honest research. You may have to spend up to 75 percent of your time convincing a client or management to do what is imperative for sound relations with a public.

2. *The News Media*: These deserve honest and valid use of their channels—that is, you should not involve them in compromising situations, not lie, not feed them insignificant information. PR practitioners are accused by news media more often for sins of omission than commission. A PR person's responsibility is not to call news media attention to bad news but to respond with a straightforward presentation of the facts when the news media have an unfavorable story. Exceptions might be in legal cases where disclosure is required (see SEC rules) or prudent (where events are matters of public record).

3. *Government Agencies*: The PR person should be source and resource for substantive information; this means giving facts, not fantasies.

4. *Educational Institutions*: There should be a good two-way system for sharing research, ideas and resources and for offering opportunities. Both sides can enhance their riches through close, professional cooperation.

5. *Consumers of Information*: An increasingly skeptical and demanding public can be exasperating, especially to those watching the profit and loss sheet, but sincerity and quality go a long way here. They have a right to expect goodwill and integrity in products and services.

6. *Stockholders and Analysts*: Many PR practitioners owe their jobs to the investors in business and those who counsel such investments, since they provide the framework of the economic structure and the overall climate of confidence. Both need adequate information to make good decisions; this demands lucid interpretations of financial status, reliable annual reports and full explanations of company developments.

7. *The Community*: Because it often provides critical elements such as utilities, tax breaks, cooperative zoning plans and chamber of commerce promotion, a community has a right to expect environmental protection, a fair tax return, employment of local people and corporate contributions in both funds and executive time to community projects.

8. *Competitors*: Other businesses have the right to expect from PR-advised firms a fair fight that stays within the limits of the law and does not violate individual rights or their privacy. The obligations of PR practitioners are set forth in the Public Relations Society of America's Code of Professional Standards for the Practice of Public Relations, with Interpretations, which appears in Appendix A, pages 471–482.

9. *Critics*: Public relations practice is likely to generate criticism from all of the preceding, but its very existence stimulates criticism from at least two philosophical points of view. One set of critics complains that public relations practitioners impede instead of facilitate corporate social responsibility by rationalizing corporate actions and manipulating public opinion. They add that for these reasons corporations do not bear the full hostility of their various publics for ignoring the quality of life these critics say the economic indicators do not reflect. These critics are not usually against the capitalistic system, only what they consider its abuses. They think the institutions of our society

should be voluntarily providing improvements in the quality of life as well as economic well-being. They see public relations people as a cushion between management and the public's demand for social responsibility.

Another philosophical set of critics might be categorized as human rights defenders. This group is most likely to speak out against public relations practitioners who represent oppressive countries or go to other countries to work in a professional capacity for the election of leaders who are considered repressive.

PR practitioner Robert W. Smith, Jr., president of his own firm in New Orleans, Louisiana, argues for advocacy as an ethical base.

> Entirely too much has already been written about the public relations practitioner as the super manager who manipulates both his client and the public into some kind of mutuality of interest. . . . We cannot . . . presume to represent both or all sides of an issue, however we-oriented and holistic the world is perceived to be . . . Explain the other side(s), yes. Represent them, no.[8]

The study of ethics falls into two broad categories: comparative ethics, which is the purview of social scientists, and normative ethics, generally the domain of philosophers and theologians. Comparative ethics, sometimes called descriptive ethics, is a study of how different cultures observe ethical standards. Both diversity and similarity are of interest to social scientists. However, the social scientist looks for evidence that can be verified, and in a study of ethics such questions as whether ethical behaviors are a part of human nature spill over into other areas, such as theology and philosophy.

In discussing the viewpoint of philosopher Sissela Bok, author of *Lying* and *Secrecy*, PR educator Hugh Culbertson says she takes a near-absolute position that decisions are either morally right or wrong.[9] But there is another basis for decision making—the technique often referred to as situation ethics, which sees ethical standards not as a constant but as varying or flexible in application to specific occasions or situations. Culbertson's observations of students suggest they lean more toward situation ethics. Bok too recognizes that lies can sometimes serve a good purpose, says Culbertson. (One example is protecting Jewish house guests from discovery by Nazi storm troopers by lying about their presence. A more ordinary example might be telling your friend who asks your opinion that you think her new and expensive outfit is becoming when you think it isn't.) But, says Bok, in choosing between lying and truth telling, the presumption is always against lying, for the following reasons:

1. Dishonesty leads to lack of trust and cynicism—such as when a reporter finds a PR person has told half-truths resulting in an inaccurate story.

2. Lying is an exercise in coercion, forcing someone to act differently from the way he or she would behave given the truth.

---

[8] Letter to *Public Relations Journal*, November 1983, p. 2.

[9] Hugh M. Culbertson, "How Public Relations Textbooks Handle Honesty and Lying," *Public Relations Review*, 9, no. 2 (Summer, 1983), pp. 65–73 (especially pp. 67, 68, 72).

3. Lying is resented by those deceived, even if the deceived are liars themselves.

4. Dishonesty is likely to be discovered and no climate for credibility can be reestablished.

5. Decisions on when to lie are often made without calculating either alternatives or consequences.

6. A lie often demands another lie to cover up, and then others to maintain the prevarications.[10]

Hadley Cantril makes a succinct statement of the basis for ethical conduct:

> The "morality" or "ethical" nature—the correctness or rightness—of any action . . . is to be judged in terms of the degree to which it includes and integrates the purposes, and provides for the potential development of those purposes of all other people concerned in the action or possibly affected by it.[11]

Let us now look at ethics in PR from the standpoint of responsibility in the practice of the profession itself and in the use of advertising and publicity.

RESPONSIBILITY IN PR PRACTICE

There are areas of public relations practice considered legitimate by most practitioners that nonetheless cause public concern and arouse criticism. Among the most obvious are research (and what is done with the information), how to handle the internal battles you lose with management and what to do about international activities in the context of working with foreign governments where different codes of ethics are operating.

Research and Persuasion

Research is critical in all areas of public relations and Chapters 4 and 5 in this book were devoted to the subject. They stressed finding out all you can about the demographics and psychographics of your publics. To what purpose? The first problem is the actual accumulation of information and storage. Probably no PR practitioner is ever going to match any level of government in its accumulation of data on an individual. Most people are in at least a dozen to thirty local and state files as individuals. In addition, the U.S. government has individual citizens classified according to more than 8,000 separate record systems, 6,000 of which are computerized. However, more and more PR people are employing pollsters and market surveyers. If you have a telephone, that's not news. Probably you get at least one call a week from some type of opinion investigator. Further-

---

[10] Sissela Bok, *Lying: Moral Choice in Public and Private Life* (New York: Pantheon Books, 1978).

[11] Hadley Cantril, *Understanding Man's Social Behavior* (Princeton, N.J.: Office of Public Opinion Research, 1947), p. 60. Used by permission.

more, the lists are often sold and compendiums of information are compiled about respondents.

During the 1960s and 1970s there was increasing concern about the use of data banks containing information on individuals. The concern resulted in legislation. The Freedom of Information Act and a consumer credit bill were passed to allow people to see just what information government and business had compiled on them. Nevertheless, both public and private institutions continue to gather substantial data owing to the many different types of public registration (auto and boat licenses, building permits and so on) and mailing lists. The existence of the information is a problem, not only as an invasion of privacy, but also in the enormous potential for misuse. Social scientists' most recent cause for alarm has been the purchase by the Internal Revenue Service of lists drawn from surveys in which people have revealed their level of income. IRS uses the lists to look for tax evaders. Social scientists (and marketing researchers) are afraid such use will discourage participation in surveys.[12]

A second problem is how you use research information. A metropolitan newspaper's managing editor observed how public relations had changed between the 1950s, when its function was largely publicity, and the 1980s, when its function seemed to be to provide information for manipulative use by, say, political figures. He cited a local mayoral race in which attitudinal studies were done before the candidate announced. Then the candidate's strategists couched his position statements in terms consonant with the attitudes the polls had reflected. "That's scary," the editor said.

A lengthy discussion of persuasion appears in Chapter 5, directly connecting information on those you are trying to persuade and the persuasion effort itself. In public relations you become a consenting attitude-change agent. What sort of questions should you ask yourself before you get involved in a persuasive effort?

First, you need to consider if you think the attitude change is one that will benefit the involved publics. Do you believe in what you are doing? Then you need to look at how specific the change needs to be: Will it involve a particular attitude (like how the public feels about the hospital you are working for) or a general set of attitudes (how the public feels about the care of the sick in the United States, in general). You need to examine how long the change will have to last and how many people are involved in the change. What is it you are trying to change? If behavior change is your objective, is it something people have to be aware they are changing (as in stop-smoking campaigns waged by several of the national health agencies) or is it something people will change without being aware (such as automatically turning out lights without thinking consciously of energy conservation)?

Some measure of your effort's effect must be built into the program. The effect might not be what you anticipated. Also, you might have to consider here how your role will be perceived and whether your audience is a captive one. Is it an audience with whom you will be having other dealings? Do you have a prob-

---

[12]John Koten, "IRS Use of Mail-Order Lists Concerns Market Researchers," *Wall Street Journal*, March 8, 1984, p. 29.

lem being identified as a persuader of this particular issue? What is your stake in the effort: personal? professional? both? You may find some roles in conflict. As a volunteer public relations person for the American Cancer Society, for example, you could have difficulty going to the office and effectively representing a tobacco company client.

Internal Battles and Defeat

Public relations people generally try to persuade management to act in ways that will be socially responsible to all publics. Occasionally, though, the interests of two or more publics conflict, or the profits of the company may conflict with one public or another from time to time. Management decisions are not always in line with what the PR person recommends. What happens then? The PR person can first try for a compromise. If that doesn't work, it then becomes a question of how serious the conflict is for the PR person.

Some label themselves "team players" and carry out management's decision as though it were their own. Others may carry out the decision but not as effectively as they would have their own, a subtle sort of sabotage that raises an ethical question in itself. The alternative is to move on to another place where the ethical climate is more compatible. One practitioner said that is difficult to do. "Your ethics may be as good as your credit rating. No one with a big mortgage and lots of bills takes too many risks for a 'cause.'" Not always. Doing something you feel is wrong is often worse for you personally and professionally than job hunting. Crises of confidence, fortunately, rarely occur because most people gravitate to managements with goals compatible with their own.

Foreign Governments

Working with or for foreign governments poses even more complex ethical questions because of different cultural patterns. One CEO from a multinational corporation said, in confidence and with some degree of exasperation, "I wish the federal government would make paying bribes explicitly illegal. We pay bribes abroad—all kinds, to do business. Those crooks just soak us—all the way from border guards to get materials moved among the countries to the heads of state. We have to pass the costs on to our customers. I hate it. It makes me sick. But there is simply no other way to get things done abroad." Anyone who has lived abroad can appreciate his comments, even without agreeing that bribery is necessary.

In response to the surfacing of "questionable payments" by corporations doing business abroad, legislation was passed making bribery illegal. But even with bribes and kickbacks illegal, who is to differentiate these from traditionally acceptable practices like tips, gratuities and gifts? When do these become conditions for doing business? Even in foreign countries where bribes and kickbacks are illegal, such practices exist in custom, which is difficult to work around.

Some companies, like multinational Ingersoll-Rand, try to protect themselves with a committee of outside directors charged with investigating all business practices. Looking at the situation from an outside director's point of view, probably more would prefer to be advisers than police. However, all companies, multinationals in particular, are trying codes of conduct, outside directors and anything else they can to undergird corporate morality. Multinationals have a social responsibility to all of their publics, not just to the nation in which they were originally chartered.

Working for foreign governments poses even more ethical questions. Some questions have been raised about U.S. political strategists, pollsters and political PR campaign managers handling candidates in other countries—even when elections are free and open, not to mention in more coercive political systems. Although attorneys represent clients with public and professional impunity (in fact, their services are supposed to be available to all), public relations firms share the image of their clients. Not only the firms, but also the individuals handling the PR account, find it difficult to defend their working for a country with a reputation for being repressive.

Many countries with records of human rights violations have turned to U.S. public relations firms for help. And looking good in world public opinion is not the only reason for doing so. U.S. aid payments are bigger to nations with better reputations in this area. Tourism may increase as well. Some companies accept only foreign clients with reputations as responsible world citizens, but as one said in discussing the Iranian turnover of 1979, such a judgment gets more and more difficult to make. Burson-Marsteller chairman, Harold Burson, made no apology for his firm's client, Argentina, before the 1983 installation of a civilian regime in that country. The firm told the government it had an image as a dictatorial institution and warned it to halt any campaign that denied civil liberties or human rights. The agency's counsel would, then, seem to be valuable if the client heeds the advice it is paying for.

Foreign governments have begun to rely increasingly on U.S. public relations firms for both government contracts and media relations. An example of media relations use was cited by the *Washington Journalism Review*:

> When a socialist government came to power in Greece in 1981, replacing nearly a decade of right-of-center governments, Prime Minister Andreas Papandreau swiftly hired the New York PR firm Fentom Communications, Inc., at $6,000 a month, to get word to the American press that socialist governments aren't all bad.[13]

Some media people say the PR firms aren't effective and the embassies of the countries could do the same job. Others say the embassies are not skilled at media relations. Apparently the only effective PR people are those whom media people accept as credible sources. When media contacts haven't worked, the foreign countries have often turned to advocacy advertising.

---

[13]James Buie, Maura Casey, Gregory Enns, Vandanna Mathur and Mark Williams with Richard T. Stout, "Foreign Governments Are Playing Our Press," *Washington Journalism Review* (October 1983), p. 23.

RESPONSIBILITY IN ADVERTISING

The first responsibility in advertising is to an agency's clients.

During a casual, informal conversation of the type that sometimes follows a business conference, a young advertising executive was interrupted by a phone call from one of his clients. Answering, the ad executive smiled and responded enthusiastically, "I *am* glad you got over to see the sign. We thought it was handsome, too!" Then he added, somewhat cautiously with a serious expression crossing his face, "Well, it is effective, of course, but we don't know how much more so than some of the other things we are doing, and according to the budget we worked out together, I just don't think we can afford another right now. Let's talk about it and if it really does work out as well as we anticipate, we can plan for others like it in the next year's budget. Okay? Thanks for calling."

The young executive hung up and turned with a big smile to his two associates: "Our client just saw that sign we put up yesterday and wants six more." "Six!" one of the associates gasped. "He can't afford it!" The advertising man nodded in agreement and explained to his other visitors: "We got one of those new multidimensional, lighted, revolving signs for one of our clients, and he's so in love with it he's forgotten how much it cost." Someone asked if he was going to recommend more signs for the client. "I don't think so. He really doesn't have that kind of money, and advertising that causes a business financial problem is sort of defeating its purpose, isn't it?"

Perhaps it's because that young executive makes decisions with his client's best interests in mind that he is in great demand in the metropolitan area where he owns and manages his own advertising agency.

Another advertising executive, vice president of a locally owned agency in another metropolitan area, called one evening to put off a dinner conference for another hour. She is her agency's time buyer and had stayed at her desk all day trying to work out the best broadcast buys for a client. Experienced in all media, she is particularly suited for the latitude her agency's owner and president has given her: "Change the schedules any way you want. What we are after is the best media buys for our customers." She is liked and respected by the media salespeople, who know she will give them a polite hearing and examine their contract suggestions carefully and considerately. She is trusted by the agency's clients, who know there is no competition within the agency to place the ads in a particular medium for personal commission reasons. They also know the bills they get have been carefully checked and the time purchases monitored. That kind of service is worth at least an agency's traditional 15 to 20 percent!

What about so-called kickbacks? This is a source of confusion to many who do not know the difference between the legitimate agency discount and unethical practice. When a client buys time or space directly from the media, it is sold according to the rate for which the client qualifies—local, national, nonprofit and such. The media then prepare the ads or commercials and charge the client not only for the time or space but also usually for any production costs. If the client wants to preserve some kind of uniformity in advertising, the advertising then goes to the media ready for instant use. The agency therefore receives a commission—from the media—which theoretically covers the convenience of their preparing materials (instead of the media) and of bringing the media some business.

To receive such a commission, though, the person placing the ads must really represent a recognized agency. However, unethical practitioners, sometimes working as staff PR, have accepted the commissions from the media—and pocketed the money themselves. Since PR staffers work on a salary, they should not personally benefit from discounts.

The second responsibility in advertising concerns the message itself. Subliminal advertising comes up for discussion from time to time, generally in a classroom setting. Some lecturers manage to draw big crowds with a few examples that purport to reveal sex symbols in the cubes of drinks shown in liquor ads. Books have been written on the subject (see 15.2). However, most social scientists discount the effectiveness of such advertising and mass media gatekeepers (advertising directors in particular) deny that such ads, if submitted, would be published. Nevertheless, subliminal suggestion is possible. You can buy tapes that supposedly help you learn while you sleep, relax or are occupied. The eye can physically detect and relay to the subconscious symbols (words and art) that the conscious mind doesn't react to at the time. But it is unlikely that subliminal advertising exists, much less abounds.

The harshest critics of advertising say it does not need to be subliminal to damage. Stimulating people to buy what they do not need or to buy something instead of spending or saving prudently is also unethical. These kinds of choices, though, are a part of the free marketplace. The view of ethics often depends on the perspective of the beholder.

Protecting the Client

Just as a client's name should be respected, a PR person should protect a client's rights to a trademark, logo or trade name. Sometimes this is difficult. Only the name of the specific design may be protected; there is no law against stealing ideas. This may explain the similarity often found in both symbols and names, and even in advertising ideas.

The only recompense for a copied idea, then, is the realization that imitation is the sincerest form of flattery. If your trademark or logo is copied, you may be able to sue for damages—but only if the *precise* design is used; it does not make any difference legally that the public might not be able to distinguish between your design and the thinly disguised copied one. For instance, the symbol of the famous Texas Boys Choir, a silhouetted choirboy in bow tie holding an open music book, was appropriated by a civic girls' chorus. In the altered design the choir boy's ears were covered with shoulder-length hair and the pants legs were simply filled in to resemble a skirt. A copyright authority said the change was enough to prevent a suit. The alternative was simply for the Boys Choir to stop using the symbol it had created, which it did for several years until the other group's use of it had declined. If you are watchful, you can find examples of close copies, especially with logos or creative advertising concepts and designs.

"Fascinating!
Captivating!
I would
suggest this
informative
and
entertaining
program to
any school."
—Lehigh University

"The lounge
was filled to
capacity and
Key held the
audience
spellbound."
—Bates College

A multi-media presentation
on the secret ways ad men arouse
your sexuality and even your death wish—
to sell and manipulate consumers.

SUBLIMINAL SEDUCTION

In Person
WILSON BRYAN KEY

author of the Signet paperbacks
SUBLIMINAL SEDUCTION and MEDIA SEXPLOITATION

From NEW LINE PRESENTATIONS

© New Line Presentations MCMLXXIX

Reprinted with permission.

Protecting the Consumer

A PR person should also advise a client when his or her product is being erroneously confused with another, thus violating consumer confidence, or when the product itself is creating a consumer problem. For instance, a glue manufacturing firm, Testor's, took direct action when youngsters began sniffing glue for chemically induced elation. It had not run an ad in five years; but when glue-sniffing exploits began to make news, Testor's began putting an ad in hobby trade magazines which read: "You can be sure it's the model—not the kid that's gonna fly. Because . . . you can't sniff Testor's, there's something in it." The ad was the result of a decision made by Charles D. Miller, Testor president, who got a grant for an independent research laboratory to find an additive that would make it impossible for youngsters to sniff glue. Testor's made the new formula available to all its competitors and also made the lab research available to every manufacturer using solvents in retail products.

The ethical behavior of advertising and advertisers is set forth in the advertising profession's own code and an elaborate two-tiered mechanism to deal with truth and accuracy in national advertising (see Appendix A, pp. 471–482), although, of course, there is nothing to prevent those who do not subscribe from plying their trade. But even if advertisers ignore their own code, the media themselves may provide the restraint—at least in matters of taste.

Late in the afternoon of November 21, 1963, a full-page ad headlined "Welcome Mr. Kennedy" was given to the *Dallas Morning News*. It read, in part, "Mr. Kennedy, despite contentions on the part of your administration, the State Department, the Mayor of Dallas, the Dallas Chamber of Commerce, and members of your party, we free thinking and American thinking citizens of Dallas still have through a Constitution largely ignored by you the right to address our grievances to you, to disagree with you and to criticize you." This was followed by a dozen questions regarding government policy, each addressed to the president with a boldface "Why?" The ad was signed by "American Fact Finding Committee, an unaffiliated and nonpartisan group of citizens."[14] In the case of all political advertising, payment with copy is required. A check for more than a thousand dollars was given and the ad accepted.

The advertiser had another thousand dollar-plus check for the city's other daily newspaper. By the time the advertiser reached the fifth-floor offices of the *Dallas Times Herald*, some ten blocks away, most of the advertising staff for that afternoon paper had left for home, since they usually check in about 7 or 8 A.M. A young salesperson read the copy and refused the check saying, in effect, "We don't accept advertising like that at this newspaper." Although it is the prerogative of newspapers as private institutions to accept or reject advertising, the timing of the ad was unfortunate for the *News*. It appeared in the newspaper the morning of November 22, the day President John Kennedy was assassinated in Dallas.

Broadcast stations have less flexibility in rejecting political advertising because of the *equal-time* provision. This provision appeared in the 1934 Broadcast

---

[14]Hearings Before the Presidential Commission on the Assassination of President Kennedy, Vol. 18, Exhibit 1031, U.S. Government Printing Office, 1964, p. 835.

Act because of the incorporation of language from the 1927 Radio Act stating that if a licensee permits any person who is a legally qualified candidate for any public office to use a broadcasting station, the licensee has to give equal opportunity to all other such candidates. Furthermore, the licensee (broadcast station) has no power of censorship over the material broadcast. This distinction was regarded somewhat ruefully by Atlanta, Georgia, broadcasters who in 1974 had taken the advertising of one political candidate and then, under FCC regulations, had to accept the spots of his opponent, Democratic candidate J. B. Stoner. Stoner's taped messages said: "I am the only candidate for the U.S. Senate for white people. The main reason why niggers want integration is that niggers want our white women. I am for law and order. You can't have law and order and niggers." The messages broadcast over radio station WPLO and WSB-TV evoked a deluge of protesting phone calls, but the spots ran for a week anyway.

The equal-time provision was amended in 1959 by the *fairness doctrine*, which stated that legally qualified candidates can appear on bona fide newscasts, news interviews, news documentaries or on-the-spot coverage of news events without the licensee's having to provide equal time to opposing candidates. But, another clause has presented more difficulty in interpretation: Because stations are supposed to be operating in the public interest, they are to afford reasonable opportunity for the discussion of conflicting views on issues of public importance. The fairness doctrine has been interpreted to include advertising as well as program content and was the basis on which two networks, ABC and CBS, refused Mobil's advertising on the energy crisis (see Chapter 13).

Sometimes, the gatekeepers carry out their ethical policies arbitrarily, even to the extent of not telling the advertiser. Such was the case with the promotional logo for the film *The Killing of Sister George*, which had a lesbian theme. The design was like the puzzle drawn for children, where the trick is to find the rabbit or hat hidden in the branches of a tree. The *Sister George* logo seemed to be a woman's picture with the hair curiously draped on one side, but a careful examination of that hair revealed the outline of a nude female. Many newspapers ran the ad, but doctored the hidden nude to suit their own standards (see 15.3).

PR persons have been reminded of their ethics also by the rise of the consumer movement and citizens' complaints about puffery or exaggerated claims in advertising. As a result of this rise, the Federal Trade Commission now requires that advertising claims be substantiated by scientific or otherwise reliable proof. For an offending ad, the FTC can levy a fine, order withdrawal of the offending advertising or sometimes compel the offender to present "corrective" advertising—as Profile Bread had to do to refute its earlier claims that its bread provided substantial help in weight reduction.

Advertising agencies are concerned that they as well as the client are held responsible, but perhaps both should be more worried about their audience than about their legal culpability. A study by Scott Ward, Harvard Business School behavioral scientist, reveals that youngsters start to develop "somewhat cynical attitudes" toward TV ads between the second and fourth grades. That's when children begin to say things like "This commercial is funny, but it isn't true," and what they say is based on their experience with the product. Junior high school students consider ads something to laugh at, not to be believed. By the time they are older, they pay attention only to the program and their attention simply drops or

San Diego Dailies to Refuse Ads for 'X' Rated Movies

SAN DIEGO, Aug. 5—The *San Diego Union* and *Tribune* will no longer "chronicle in its news columns or accept advertising from theaters playing films carrying an 'X' rating or non-rated pictures." An "X" rating by the Motion Picture Assn. of America specifies "persons under 16 not admitted."

Richard W. Tullar, advertising director of the papers, said that this decision includes "X" rated films like "Midnight Cowboy," a new major production acclaimed by critics.

The basis for the decision will not be announced, the company stated. Alex DeBakcsy, general manager, declared: "We have a good reason for not giving our motivation." He said that there has been some reaction, "but we haven't tried to measure it."

■ The *Los Angeles Times,* which altered the logo and requested a change of ad copy for "The Killing of Sister George," was sued by the producer for "capricious and arbitrary censorship of motion picture advertising" (AA, Feb. 17). The case was dismissed May 5 and is now on appeal. #

'L.A. Times' Sued for Insistence on Movie Ad Changes

LOS ANGELES, Feb. 11—Associates & Aldrich (movie producer-director Robert Aldrich) filed suit last week in Los Angeles federal district court against Times Mirror Co., publisher of the *Los Angeles Times,* for "capricious and arbitrary censorship of motion picture advertising" because the paper insisted on changes in an ad for "The Killing of Sister George."

The logo for the film, as published elsewhere, is a girl's face with hair in the form of a nude woman. The *Times* requested that the tagline, "the story of three consenting adults in the privacy of their home" (the picture has a lesbian theme) have the word "consenting" removed.

■ No damages are asked in the case. Well known civil liberties attorney Stanley Flaishman is acting for the plaintiff.

Mr. Aldrich also has filed complaints with the Federal Communications Commission against KMPC and KTLA-TV (Golden West Broadcasters), who refused to run commercials for the picture because it has an X rating. Mr. Aldrich says that the new Motion Picture Assn. of America rating system has not properly been explained, as an X label does not mean a dirty film.

The producer-director further has complained to Jack Valenti, president of MPAA, that by his silence he has created the impression that an "X" film is "a dirty picture not fit for viewing by anyone." #

Before the Times' editing.

Afterward

tunes out when a commercial comes on. Later on, Ward says, they become more and more "jaded to commercial exposure," and if they watch commercials at all, they focus their attention on the commercial itself rather than on the product advertised.

Should there be counteradvertising, that is, ads presenting the opposite point of view? The first counterads to attract significant attention were the antismoking ads, which appeared on TV before cigarette advertising was stopped. Counteradvertising has also been placed by environmental groups. In some cases, broad-

15.4   ADVERTISING SELF-REGULATION PROCEDURES

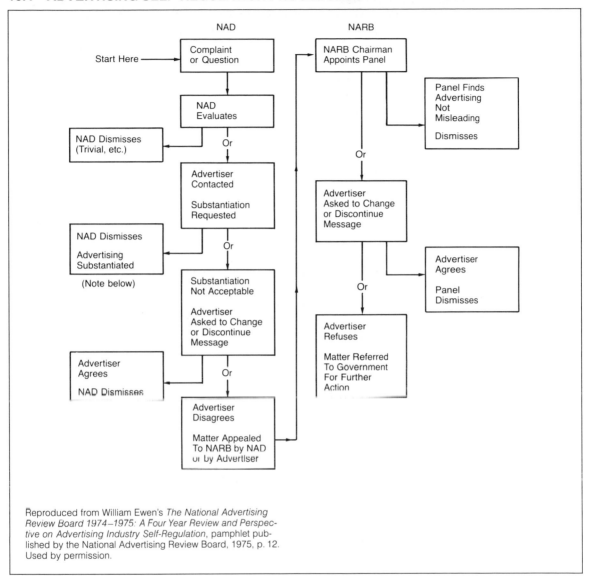

Reproduced from William Ewen's *The National Advertising Review Board 1974–1975: A Four Year Review and Perspective on Advertising Industry Self-Regulation*, pamphlet published by the National Advertising Review Board, 1975, p. 12. Used by permission.

cast stations have been required to run these countercommercials without charge as public service announcements. All stations are alarmed that such rulings requiring "equal time" across the board might mean financial disaster.

An elaborate mechanism was set up in 1971 by the advertising industry to deal specifically with accuracy and truth in advertising (see 15.4). The National Advertising Division (NAD) of the Council of Better Business Bureaus (CBBB) first investigates the case and makes a judgment. NAD's judgment may be appealed to the National Advertising Review Board (NARB), which makes a final judgment.

Complaints from outside the system can go directly to NARB with the permission of the NARB chairman.[15]

The number of commercials in a time segment also has been an element of controversy. Although the time allotment has not changed, the three networks will now allow advertisers to use multiple product ads in a time segment. For example, a 30-second time spot can have two 15-second commercials for different but related products. Only CBS is holding out on its restriction that commercials in the time slot can be unrelated and that no video bridge between the two be used. Until 1967 the networks sold only 60-second spots, and it was Alberto-Culver that led the fight for 30 seconds. The same company has pushed for the split 30s.

Still another question arises when sponsorship is really advertising. Public television is supposed to be devoid of advertising, but programs are openly sponsored. In the early days of public broadcasting, no company could sponsor a program that related to its product or cause. However, sponsored films began to be shown on public television, and then outright sponsorship of programs related to the sponsor were permitted. For example, a computer software company carried in its print ads a line about its upcoming public TV show on computers. The most controversial decision recently has been the changes in underwriting rules for Public Broadcasting Service (PBS), which allow a company that makes or sells liquor to underwrite programming production. Commercial television is prohibited from running liquor or cigarette commercials, and government regulation prohibits cigarette advertising on television. However, the R. J. Reynolds Company, which handles both tobacco and liquor products among others, can sponsor PBS programs.

RESPONSIBILITY IN PUBLICITY

Critics question the ethics of having news appear in the mass media precisely in the form submitted by a PR person. They feel that PR-originated news should carry some identifying label to alert the reader or viewer. Many PR and media people regard this as impractical, even an insult. They believe it is the job of newspeople to know the source of the information they use and to employ discrimination and good editorial judgment about what is disseminated and whether attribution is needed. In the *Columbia Journalism Review*, a critical observer of news media, Jeanne Edwards, made the *Wall Street Journal*'s use of news releases a subject for a 1980 story in which it said some of the press releases were passed off as original material or given *WSJ* bylines. *CJR*'s story reported on seventy companies queried. The accusation and the *WSJ* response are quoted:

---

[15] See Eric J. Zanot, "The National Advertising Review Board, 1971–1976," *Journalism Monographs*, Association for Education in Journalism, no. 59, February 1979.

In 53 cases—72 percent of our responses—news stories were based solely on press releases: in 32 of these examples, the releases were reprinted verbatim or in paraphrase, while in 21 other cases only the most perfunctory additional reporting had been done. Perhaps most troublesome, 20 of these stories (29 percent) carried the slug "By a *Wall Street Journal* Staff Reporter."[16]

In response, Frederick Taylor, executive editor of the *Wall Street Journal*, said, "Ninety percent of our daily coverage is started by a company making an announcement for the record. We're relaying this information to our readers." And those slugs (bylines)? "A staff written piece is a staff written piece—and that's what the slug means."[17]

PR as a Byline

Few newspapers will publish blatantly promotional material from a public relations person, especially if the product is in a highly competitive market. However, the Sunday *New York Times* financial section, March 20, 1977, carried a four-column headline, "Mazda Tries to Get Back in the Race," over a bylined article by Bob Fendell, Mazda account executive at the Al Paul Lefton ad agency. The description of the writer did not so identify him. The author was described as a New York writer on automotive topics. The laudatory quotes from dealers in his piece caused other public relations people concern, but the person who gave out the assignment, which was chosen from among four topics the writer offered to do, said the story was a straight one and he saw no reason to explain the writer's connection to the product.

Others feel publicists should have no access to news columns. A journalism professor and a reporter were discussing a special event of community significance to be handled by a local PR agency. The reporter said he expected the news releases he would receive to be well written because the PR man had newspaper experience and knew what the papers needed and how such releases should be written. "Those are the worst kind for that very reason—they know how to get their stories in with the real news," the professor replied, to the astonishment of the reporter.

Dealing straightforwardly with the news media means adhering to the PRSA code of ethics, and lying to news media representatives or even misleading them is a violation (see Appendix A).

The relationship between PR people and newspeople is rarely the kind of a contest in which the PR practitioner is plotting to see what can be sneaked into print and the reporter is doing his or her best to "get" the PR practitioner's client. Publicity is supposed to *facilitate* the news-gathering process.

This does not mean that there are never any abuses. The U.S. government has a practice of having opinion-making "policy" books printed by a commercial pub-

---

[16]Jeanne Edwards, "Journalists and Public Call for Higher Ethical Standards," *Press Women*, 46, no. 4 (April 1983), pp. 2–4.

[17]Ibid.

lisher (for example, Ralph P. Slater's *The Sword and the Plow* [New York: Praeger, 1965]) so that the reader not only has no idea of the actual source of the book but also pays for it three times: (1) through the subsidy given by the government to the free-lance writer to research and write the book; (2) through the subsidy given the commercial press to print the book; (3) through the retail cost of the book. And at the same time, readers are also paying for a national printing service, the U.S. Government Printing Office, which can produce books inexpensively.[18]

During any election year, look for books about candidates who are already officeholders, and watch out for any heavily promoted books that seem to support a principal plank in a party platform, especially when that party is currently in power. This became an issue in the confirmation of Nelson Rockefeller as vice president in 1974, when it was learned that his brother Laurance had paid for the writing and publication of a book attacking Arthur Goldberg during a New York gubernatorial contest. This sort of subversive publication is, of course, unethical, irresponsible and just one of the many factors that contribute to the overall distrust of publicity.

One deceptive publicity practice that has invaded the magazine field, particularly the specialized magazines, is relatively transparent. A company that buys an elaborate ad—always four-color, usually double-truck (two pages side by side), and sometimes with a foldout—strangely enough almost always has an article with several pictures in the same issue. Sometimes the article carries no byline. Those with bylines are not written by staff writers, and the real identity of the writers is seldom disclosed. In these cases, the writers are probably publicists for the advertisers. In one case, an aviation magazine that carried a prominent four-color advertisement for an airplane manufacturer's new model also published an illustrated four-page article on the plane and gave it the cover.

Xerox got into trouble with something not nearly as devious. As a sponsor of television series such as Alistair Cooke's "America" and Kenneth Clark's "Civilization," the company had been widely applauded. Nothing seemed wrong with doing the same thing in another medium, and Xerox approached *Esquire* about underwriting a special piece. *Esquire* chose the topic and the author with approval from Xerox. The result was a twenty-three-page personal essay by Pulitzer Prize winner Harrison E. Salisbury, "Travels through America." It appeared in the February 1976 issue of *Esquire*, bracketed by modest Xerox ads. The front ad began, "First a word from the sponsor." Xerox paid Salisbury $40,000 as retainer for his six-months' work on the piece, plus $15,000 in expenses, as well as buying $15,000 worth of advertising in *Esquire*. *Esquire* saw nothing wrong with the arrangement because it had final editorial control. Had Xerox not approved of the finished piece, *Esquire* was free to publish it anyway and keep the money too. Criticism of the prestigious piece came from prestigious author E. B. White. White said he felt selling editorial space was a serious erosion of the free press. His criticism was not of the particular piece but of the abuse possibilities such an arrangement offered. The company listened to its critic and canceled two other projects like the *Esquire* essay.

---

[18]William L. Rivers, *The Adversaries* (Boston: Beacon Press, 1969), pp. 157–164.

Matters of Taste

Judgment calls are the name of the game in matters of taste. Even a PR effort that seems to be a public service can be criticized. For example, an effort to dramatize heart disease by having a live telecast of heart surgery resulted in controversy.[19] One hospital PR person compared the event to a circus in the Roman Coliseum. Health care communicators surveyed generally responded favorably to the broadcast but were split almost evenly on whether it should have been live or taped. One hospital PR person noted that a separation of Siamese twins had been telecast live, but without an announcer in the operating room whose voice might have distracted the medical team. She said it would have been just as effective taped, and in any case, nothing should be done to put pressure on the doctors during surgery.

Money Matters

What happens when you, as a publicity writer, have a story accepted by a publication? Does this mean you are entitled to compensation for the story or pictures? No! Publicity is free; magazine editors know it and won't offer payment. Many will give you a byline, and some will identify you as a guest author in that issue. But be sure your identification carries your relationship to the piece you are writing.

What if a magazine staff writer writes a story suggested by a PR firm and allows his or her expenses to be paid by the firm? What if the writer accepts a fee as well as expenses from the firm? The ethical problem is not only with the magazine staffer being "on the take" but also with the PR people offering the temptation. It is permissible for a public relations practitioner to suggest a story to a publication, and if the idea is accepted and a writer assigned, the practitioner may make arrangements for accommodations and see that all expenses involved in getting information for the story are covered. Almost all publications permit such an arrangement on expenses, but many want to pay for transportation and accommodations themselves. Some are flexible about the accommodations.

There is increasing criticism of junkets, trips that are all-expense-paid excursions for movie reviewers to the location of a filming; for travel editors to the opening of a new resort hotel or amusement park; for fashion editors to the site of the introduction of a new line (cosmetics, shoes, sportswear, anything); or for real estate editors to the opening of a new luxury development in a remote area. Some criticize such junkets as the purchasing of editorial talent. Most PR practitioners see nothing wrong with them, particularly since there is no control over what the wined and dined reporters write. Sometimes a strict publication will allow its reporter to go but will insist on paying for the transportation and accommodations. Others permit these to be paid for if the reporter acknowledges such in the copy. Still others permit the reporter to accept the trip package because they believe the gratuities will not affect the reporter's handling of the story.

---

[19] "Was Life/Death Drama Lure of Live TV Operation? Is That Voyeurism?" *pr reporter*, April 11, 1983, p. 1.

15.5 CRUME'S COMMENT ON FREEBIES

You win some and you lose some. That is the only thing that keeps us highly influential newspaper people from becoming entirely corrupt. We get all this free graft from everybody but usually on terms that don't work.

Just this morning, for instance, I received a beautiful beer stein from the new Alpenhof restaurant west of Austin. They forgot to send the beer.

And here we have from Jeanne Eddy a print of the mural in the Sheraton-Dallas' Stampede Room. This is a souvenir from a party which I had to miss. At the time the Stampede Room was opening, I had the genuine Panhandle of Texas variety of the flu and wasn't stampeding much anywhere.

Nevertheless, this is a beautiful print.

The only trouble is that they forgot to send the frame.

And here is a new album by Jim Cullum's boys who do that wonderful job of playing at The Landing in San Antonio. They play jazz the way it ought to be played, highstyle and intellectual instead of crummy the way the kids like it. A man can listen to this music and think he ought to chase some girls again, but I am careful always to remember my bad ankle. The Cullum records are about the best you can get.

However, they forgot to send the phonograph.

It is oversights like this that keep us fortunate people in the media from becoming wholly corrupt.

From Paul Crume's "Big D" column, *Dallas Morning News*, March 8, 1974, p. 1.

The Society of Business Writers was the first to respond to this problem. It adopted a code of ethics that specifically outlaws junkets and "freebies." A member may not accept any special treatment or a gift of more than token value; all out-of-town travel must be paid for by the writer's employer. Other professional journalism organizations followed suit, as did individual newspaper corporations. Most publications already had prohibited outright gifts to their editorial staff members, either directly or through people in their own advertising departments.

Newspapers always seem to watch this practice closest. Some will not allow their reporters to accept any gifts whatsoever; others are aware their reporters often receive small gifts from PR sources and worry only when many stories appear from a single source or when a gift seems large enough to be compromising. One consideration is a ruling by an administrative law judge for the National Labor Relations Board in the case of the Madison (Wisconsin) *Capital Times* that gifts to newspeople were part of a news employee's wages and could not be prohibited by a newspaper. Editorial publisher Miles McMillan appealed the decision to the full NLRB, which upheld the right of the newspaper to establish a code of ethics preventing freebies. One fashion editor is often given free cosmetics, gimmicks and gadgets of all descriptions—but at the risk of the givers. She reports on such gifts and doesn't hesitate to point out bad features. Her editor doesn't worry about news sources compromising *her* integrity. The late columnist and humorist Paul Crume gave the gift situation a light touch (see 15.5).

There is another side to this, though. Public officials are also on PR gift lists. Many companies have certain public officials they want remembered and tell their PR person to "buy something." Many city, county and state governments have strict regulations about what public officials may accept, but just as many don't. Common prudence suggests all gifts be "token" rather than substantial. A rule of thumb is offered by one firm head who shops the catalogs every year for gifts to suggest to his clients: "When I choose something, I always think, how would I feel if I suddenly saw this on the 6 P.M. news? That curbs my buying sprees considerably."

Another kind of remuneration, one that inflates the ego, as well as the pocketbook, is the awarding of prizes, and this affects both press and public officials. Does a reporter embark on a series about arthritis to enlighten the newspaper's readers or to increase the writer's chances for tangible recognition from the Arthritis Foundation? Does a local television station do a documentary on possible fire hazards during the summer to warn its viewers or to receive recognition from the Firefighter's Association? Does a network choose its documentary for overriding public interest or a chance to win an Emmy or Peabody? Does an ambitious lawyer offer to head the local symphony drive for the arts out of love of music or because his eye is on a civic club's annual outstanding citizen award? Commercial as well as nonprofit institutions engage in these incentive programs, which seem to meet with greater editorial acceptance than junkets, although many awards are cash prizes.

There is even a more blatant type of remuneration—the moonlighting that reporters and photographers do at part-time publicity jobs. Although most media executives do not condone the practice, few make serious efforts to stop it. As one newspaper's photo chief said, "Are you kidding? All my good people would quit. They can't live on what this paper pays them." Nevertheless, there are all sorts of ethical ramifications. Certainly it encourages the newsperson so employed to see that the publicity gets in—to keep a paycheck coming.

Keeping the public and private sectors separate caused particular concern in 1978 when attention was focused on the facilities provided for news media in public places (government centers) such as courthouses and state capitols. In many of these places free parking spaces, a paging system and a complete writing facility with desks, typewriters, telephones and even attendants were provided. The taxpayer was picking up the tab, of course. Much of the flurry about such perquisites ("perks") came from the Washington, D.C., news media's criticism and exposure of congressional perks. Wisconsin Democratic Representative David Obey suggested that reporting on perks was the pot calling the kettle black. Suddenly government perks for reporters were under scrutiny everywhere, much to the consternation of some government people hired to handle the news media. When the reporters moved out, the working relationship of these staffs with the news media was complicated. News agencies could preserve their integrity by paying rent for the facilities and furnishings.

Some state governments, whose constitutions bound them to provide the media with free space and prevented reimbursement, were caught in a bind. However, few people working in the public relations role for government saw the facilities issue as a threat to the free press system, and several pointed to an observation made by some newspeople themselves that lack of facilities really inhibited news coverage. The bigger organizations could afford to foot the bill, but some of the smaller media, whose reporters often take a careful look at what their constituents' representatives are doing, were forced to abandon coverage and use wire service copy, which was more general in nature.

Public relations people often have control of more than their budgets. Generally the corporate investments in the community—gifts to civic, social, even national organizations—are within the control of the PR department. Especially national organizations to whom the company gives its support are under the scrutiny of special-interest groups who monitor such gifts to be sure minorities and other disadvantaged groups are not excluded. Also, their reviews are bad if corporate dollars go to groups that do exclude minorities or that practice discrimination or have labor policies that could be criticized as unfair.

A critical review of where an institution's dollars go extends beyond the budget for social and community affairs. Included are investments of all kinds—including the employee pension fund. One company refuses to buy South African rands because of that country's racial policies. A national church group has called for review of investments in its funds because of stock bought in Nestlé, which has been criticized for its marketing practices in some third-world countries.

The Puppet Show

When governments offer space to newspeople, the relationship between the two groups is, at least, a direct one. Less obvious are connections between many organizations that exist in our society and special interests. For example, the false front organization is an old public relations gimmick that hasn't done much for PR credibility and is in violation of the PRSA code of ethics. When a product or a person needs a forum, a club is created. The club appears to be a collection of people with a common interest. Best recognized is a fan club for a star—seldom spontaneous. However, more sophisticated creations have a stated generic rather than specific intent. Not uncommon is the establishment of information centers. Ayerst, which produces the estrogen drug Premarin, was accused by the New York Women's Liberation newspaper of sponsoring such an "Information Center on the Mature Woman," which distributed pamphlets designed to promote the use of the drug. Ayerst denies the center was a "false front," saying the company's tie was always identified. It was so identified on the center's letterhead, which carried at the bottom of the page, although in small type, "Funded by Ayerst Laboratories." However, stories from such centers often find their way into the news media without the explicit tie being shared with the readers or listeners. The question then must be asked, "Who is at fault if the consumer is misled?"

Accusations of misleading a stockbroker public stirred criticism during the late 1970s when PR people developed "brokers' clubs." Trying to reach stock analysts always has been difficult, so some companies began making their pitch directly to the brokers, who are the salespeople anyway and who greatly influence purchases by investors. Clubs for stockbrokers sprang up all over the country, but they were said to meet only when they had a speaker—usually the president of a public corporation. The appearance of the president was arranged by, you guessed it, the corporate PR director.

PACs—Political Action Committees

Another type of organization, political action committees, are identifiable because they are a corporate organization registered in states to raise money for politicians who win their endorsement. These corporate political war chests are sizable. For example, a law firm's PAC funds may be more than $100,000 and one state's professional organization for CPAs has a political fund of more than $200,000. Some PACs are developed by activist groups like antiabortionists and homosexuals. Most states require the registration of PACs and will make public their names, affiliations and assets or the fund and campaign donations. However, in some cases the information is not so easy to get. The public relations ethical questions arise over how the money is raised—through pressure put on employees, for example; how the money is spent—on political candidates who do not behave in the best interests of society; how much information is made public on the institution's PAC and whom it supports. Although big business and big labor dominate PAC activity, many professional and trade associations are also involved. The institutions defend their right to put their dollars behind the candidates they feel will be most supportive of them when in office. The critics of PACs insist there is much room for abuse.

Political PR—
Use of News Media

Politicians and news media are natural adversaries. The cause for conflict, as William Blankenburg identifies it, is that "undefinable thing called news that mixes two combustibles, timely disclosure and objective truth, one of which is chaotic and the other coercive."[20] Caught in the conflict is the political PR person. Although government officials are public servants and should be responsive to the public (represented by news media), the Pentagon's distrust of such responsiveness has gone to the extent of administering lie detector tests even to top-level officials to be sure no "unauthorized information" goes to a reporter. The problem with some of the unauthorized information is that its release would be inconvenient. The PR person is always suspect and is therefore in a high-tension spot. The tension is heightened by the way public officials use the news media and vice versa. *TV Guide* reports on an interview with Henry Kissinger, former secretary of state and a renowned power broker, in which Kissinger made several illuminating comments.

> The news leak is one of Washington's most famous specialties, regardless of the Administration in power. Henry Kissinger told *TV Guide* magazine (April 2 issue) that he discovered how the leak works when President Nixon was considering elevating him from National Security Adviser to Secretary of State.
>
> The President had never discussed the job possibility with Kissinger, so he assumed the news leak reported by Dan Rather of CBS "Evening News" came from an ally trying to secure the Cabinet post for him, or a foe eager to block the appointment.
>
> Kissinger called Rather. "I asked him whether the thing had come from a friend or from a critic, and he very decently told me it was not from a friendly source. He didn't tell me, obviously, who the source was," Kissinger explained.
>
> "There is absolutely no doubt that when an official deals with the press he is trying to 'use' the press," Kissinger said. "And there is no doubt that when a reporter

---

[20]William B. Blankenburg, "The Adversaries and the News Ethic," *Public Relations Quarterly*, 14, no. 4 (Winter 1970) p. 31.

deals with an official, he is trying to 'use' the official. That has to be faced from the beginning.

"An official is very unwise—in addition to being morally wrong—if he deliberately misleads the press. But the press must understand that the official is there not to please them but to achieve his objective," he continued.[21]

RECIPROCAL TRUST

Money, recognition and politics are not at the root of all PR problems with news media and the publics being cultivated. A major area of importance to both is keeping confidences. For example, a reporter on the trail of a story deserves the exclusive he or she is ingenious enough to seek; a PR practitioner should not pull the rug out by offering a general release before the reporter has an opportunity to use the material. Also, a news medium has the right to expect a practitioner to be entirely aboveboard in offering information. Feature ideas or suggestions and pictures should be offered on an "exclusive use" basis. Certainly magazine editors expect stories and pictures submitted to be exclusives. A magazine editor who finds the same or a similar story in another magazine will never trust you again.

A story issued in printed form "for general release" makes it clear to an editor other news media have the story. However, a story marked "Special to the Banner" should be just that. No other news media should receive the story. The quickest way to destroy a welcome in the newsroom is to plant the same story all over the newspapers. Even if the same story is given to the morning and evening editions of the same newspaper, you are in trouble. Each deserves different stories with different approaches. The best way of doing this is to take separate stories to one person at each newspaper. Decide where each story would most appropriately appear or who on the paper would most likely be interested. If it is a column item and more than one newspaper is involved, determine which columnist would be most likely to use the piece and plant it there—only there.

News media should also be able to have enough confidence in publicity sources that they can trust you to have cleared publicity pictures submitted to them by securing a release from those who posed. In addition to protection from invasion of privacy charges, they should also trust you to protect them from copyright complications and libel and lottery laws that can be violated in publicity copy.

When you are supplying news to the media, you are bound, ethically and morally, just as they are, by the codes to which their members subscribe. (See p. 482 for additional codes.)

By the same token, the news media owe public relations practitioners a responsibility to honor release dates and times. Most do. If a story breaks earlier than designated, try to discover why. Often it really is an accident. However, if a publication frequently has "accidents," the solution is simple: Don't give the story to that publication until there is no jeopardy to the client. Do this quietly, without

---

[21]James F. Haughton, *TV Guide* news releases, March 28, 1983. Used by permission.

any warning and certainly without threats. It won't take the publication long to figure out what is happening and why.

Crisis situations are the most trying for relationships because both sides are under pressure and both sides are generally frustrated. Journalists accuse PR people of misrepresentation and covering up information. PR people accuse reporters of bias and inaccuracies. Part of the problem is in how the "truth" appears to each side. PR commentator and practitioner David Finn observed:

> One of the most disturbing discoveries public relations people can make about themselves is that learning "the facts" doesn't always tell them what they should believe. As citizens and readers of newspapers and television viewers they have opinions on as many things as anybody else.
>
> But sometimes their convictions run counter to positions held by a client. Then they study "the facts" and listen to what their client's experts have to say, and those passionate convictions become surprisingly less convincing. They see another point of view and find it more persuasive than they imagined.
>
> The first time this happens, public relations people don't mind admitting they might have been wrong. But when it happens again and again they begin to wonder whether any point of view can be supported by a given set of facts and a particular group of experts. And they fear that a lifetime of listening to all the experts who support their clients' positions weakens their capacity to make independent judgments.[22]

The question of corruption of judgment is a serious one for public relations people. Often what is at question is not facts but interpretation of facts and value systems. The best guide for the public relations person is to return to the formula for socially responsible public relations decision making. Who are the publics? What are the interests of each in the decision or situation? How will an institution's policy, position or action affect each of these publics? What social values are involved? What values are in conflict? What will the effects be? Can the effects be defended? The PR person who loses the public's perspective has forgone public responsibility and become the persuaded instead of the persuader.

POINTS TO REMEMBER

- Lack of formal control of use of public relations as a title leads to abuses and brings up the question of licensing.

- Social responsibility in public relations has to be interpreted in the broadest possible terms since PR practitioners often are in the position to counsel management on policies and programs of great impact.

- PR practitioners have ethical responsibilities to client (management), news media, government agencies, educational institutions, consumers of information, stockholders and analysts, the community, competitors and critics.

- The uses of PR research and the purposes of persuasion must be examined by the practitioner to minimize opportunities for abuse.

---

[22] David Finn, "Medium Isn't Always the Message," in *Dallas Morning News*, May 21, 1981, p. 4D. Used by permission.

- Ethical conflict over policies may arise between PR practitioners and management; the alternatives for the practitioner are to compromise or leave.

- Similar conflict may occur when the PR person works for and in foreign countries with different codes of ethics.

- Advertising and publicity, PR's two message systems, demand protection of the client, the channels of communication and the consumer.

- Responsibility in publicity includes the ethical question of acknowledging the PR source of news.

- PR people must not give or receive compensation from news media for getting information to the public through media channels.

- PR people often control or influence corporate expenditures that have social responsibility implications because of whom the money is going to.

- Political PR people are often caught in the conflict resulting from use of news media by public officials and vice versa.

- Keeping confidences is essential for trust between PR people and the news media.

- At the heart of many conflicts of news media and PR is a subjective view of the "facts."

THINGS TO DO

1. You are handling the campaign of a candidate for governor of your state. Two of his close associates, a major contributor to previous campaigns and an appointee, have just been indicted for a fraudulent land development project. The news media are identifying the two by their relationship to your candidate. What would you do?

2. You take a story to the real estate editor of the daily newspaper. It is a legitimate announcement story on the building by one of your clients of a new office complex. You are told that the story needs some "advertising support" to give it better display, which, translated, means buy an ad or it won't run. What do you do?

3. As public relations director for an annual event promoting the boating industry, a public show produced by a private company with the cooperation of the local marine dealers association, you are suddenly faced with the withdrawal from the show of a core of disgruntled marine dealers. The withdrawal won't hurt you in space sales because you already have more applications than can be accommodated. However, the group sets up a competing show, set for three weeks before your event. Your board of directors wants to initiate advertising that would take a slam at the competing show. Their argument is that not to do so will create confusion in the minds of the public, which will be attracted to the other show and attend it thinking it is your show. What would you do?

4. A newspaper editor whom you have known for a number of years and who has done you a number of favors, calls and says some money he expected to come in from a free-lance job he took is late arriving and he is in financial difficulty. He knows that your firm also represents a bank. Can you "make things happen" to get him a loan. What do you do?

5. You are a partner in a medium-sized public relations firm and you have an exceptionally bright young man working for you. He is twenty-eight, but looks younger. He has been with you for three years, is thoroughly competent and you promote him to account supervisor on a major account involving considerable top management contact. After his first meeting with the client, the client president calls and says, "Bob is a nice young man, but we need someone considerably older to handle our business." What do you do?*

6. You are the public relations director for a major industrial organization and you have a vacancy on your staff. You interview a prospective employee who for the past seven years has been with one of your major competitors. The job applicant is very specific in his criticisms of KMG, the company he has spent the last seven years with. He tells you about their personnel policies, and in fact pulls out of his briefcase a copy of their fringe-benefit booklet and a couple of presentations that the KMG public relations department has made to management in the past several years. He says, "I think you'd be interested in reading these over. Just be sure I get them back. Drop them in the mail tomorrow when you are through with them." What do you do about hiring this man?

7. You are a guest at a dinner party. Over coffee another guest turns to you. "So you're in public relations," she says. "I think it is a very questionable business. To me, public relations is like the pejorative meaning that plastics has: a substitute for the real thing. Nixon nearly ruined the country with public relations and some public relations flack advised Carter to concentrate on form instead of substance. You PR people are in the business of deceit, dishonesty and cover-up. How do you sleep nights?" What is your answer?

8. You are on an international panel of the EAAA (European equivalent of AAAAs) meeting in Stockholm. Besides you, the panel consists of a representative from the Yugoslavia state agency and a representative from Havas, Belgium's leading native agency. The moderator is an editor from one of Italy's more left-wing publications.

    A question from the audience about the impact of television commercials on the young is passed from the Belgium agency representative, who states that his country doesn't condone any commercials at all on TV, to the Yugoslavian. He proceeds to criticize commercials produced in the West that force a false set of values on the young. He uses toy advertising as an example of making children want toys that cost far more than their parents can afford. He cites this as a typical example of capitalistic thinking and mentions that it is in keeping with the fact that your client, ITT, sponsors a program (Big Blue Marble) that attempts to inculcate children around the world with this same sense of tinsel values. The description of the use of children as a tool of industry makes an impact on the audience, and the moderator asks you, as a representative from that part of the world, to comment on its morality. What do you say?

9. Write a definition of PR and compare it with the one you wrote at the end of Chapter 1.

---

*Items 5, 6, 7 and 8 are reprinted with permission from cases prepared for the Sterling Forest Educators' Conference, 1974, by Marsteller, Inc./Burson-Marsteller.

SELECTED READINGS

Samm Baker, *The Permissible Lie* (Boston: Beacon Press, 1968). An advertising man's introspective view of the ethics of his profession.

Charlene J. Brown, Trevor R. Brown and William L. Rivers, *The Media and the People* (New York: Holt, Rinehart and Winston, 1978). For a view that magnifies the warts on PR's growth and development, read the discussion in the chapter on the professional persuaders, which was mostly borrowed from the book's predecessor by the same publisher: *The Mass Media and Modern Society* by William L. Rivers, Theodore Peterson and Jay W. Jensen—long a standard text in media and society courses.

Hugh M. Culbertson, "Three Perspectives on American Journalism," Journalism Monographs no. 83 (Columbia, S.C.: Association for Education in Journalism, June, 1983). An overall view of three different approaches to news: traditional, interpretative and activist.

L. L. L. Golden, *Only By Public Consent* (New York: Hawthorn, 1968). Some case studies of corporate conscience.

John C. Merrill and S. Jack Odell, *Philosophy and Journalism* (New York: Longman, 1983). Takes a critical view of journalistic practices and codes for behavior, as well as looking to the future and asking questions such as "Will journalists be licensed?"

Wilbur Schramm and Clifford Christian, *Responsibility in Mass Communication* (New York: Harper & Row, 1980). Explores ethical pitfalls in all media.

Bruce M. Swain, *Reporters' Ethics* (Ames: Iowa State University Press, 1979). An interesting collection of reporters' personal experiences and opinions on ethical issues.

APPENDIX **A**

Codes

PUBLIC RELATIONS SOCIETY OF AMERICA: CODE OF PROFESSIONAL STANDARDS FOR THE PRACTICE OF PUBLIC RELATIONS *

Declaration of Principles

Members of the Public Relations Society of America base their professional principles on the fundamental value and dignity of the individual, holding that the free exercise of human rights, especially freedom of speech, freedom of assembly and freedom of the press, is essential to the practice of public relations.

In serving the interests of clients and employers, we dedicate ourselves to the goals of better communication, understanding and cooperation among the diverse individuals, groups and institutions of society.

We pledge:

To conduct ourselves professionally, with truth, accuracy, fairness and responsibility to the public;

To improve our individual competence and advance the knowledge and proficiency of the profession through continuing research and education;

And to adhere to the articles of the Code of Professional Standards for the Practice of Public Relations as adopted by the governing Assembly of the Society.

---

* This Code, adopted by the PRSA Assembly, replaces a similar Code of Professional Standards for the Practice of Public Relations previously in force since 1954 and strengthened by revisions in 1959, 1963 and 1977. Used by permission.

The PRSA Research Information Center, 845 Third Ave., New York, NY 10022, will provide help in planning and implementing public relations activities. A bibliography of books and periodicals useful to the public relations practitioner is available on request.

471

Articles of the Code

These articles have been adopted by the Public Relations Society of America to promote and maintain high standards of public service and ethical conduct among its members.

1. A member shall deal fairly with clients or employers, past, present or potential, with fellow practitioners and the general public.

2. A member shall conduct his or her professional life in accord with the public interest.

3. A member shall adhere to truth and accuracy and to generally accepted standards of good taste.

4. A member shall not represent conflicting or competing interests without the express consent of those involved, given after a full disclosure of the facts; nor place himself or herself in a position where the member's interest is or may be in conflict with a duty to a client, or others, without a full disclosure of such interests to all involved.

5. A member shall safeguard the confidences of present and former clients, as well as of those persons or entities who have disclosed confidences to a member in the context of communications relating to an anticipated professional relationship with such member, and shall not accept retainers or employment which may involve the disclosure or use of these confidences to the disadvantage or prejudice of such present, former or potential clients or employers.

6. A member shall not engage in any practice which tends to corrupt the integrity of channels of communication or the processes of government.

7. A member shall not intentionally communicate false or misleading information and is obligated to use care to avoid communication of false or misleading information.

8. A member shall be prepared to identify publicly the name of the client or employer on whose behalf any public communication is made.

9. A member shall not make use of any individual or organization purporting to serve or represent an announced cause, or purporting to be independent or unbiased, but actually serving an undisclosed special or private interest of a member, client or employer.

10. A member shall not intentionally injure the professional reputation or practice of another practitioner. However, if a member has evidence that another member has been guilty of unethical, illegal or unfair practices, including those in violation of this Code, the member shall present the information promptly to the proper authorities of the Society for action in accordance with the procedure set forth in Article XIII of the Bylaws.

11. A member called as a witness in a proceeding for the enforcement of this Code shall be bound to appear, unless excused for sufficient reason by the Judicial Panel.

12. A member, in performing services for a client or employer, shall not accept fees, commissions or any other valuable consideration from anyone other than the client or employer in connection with those services without the express consent of the client or employer, given after a full disclosure of the facts.

13. A member shall not guarantee the achievement of specified results beyond the member's direct control.

14. A member shall, as soon as possible, sever relations with any organization or individual if such relationship requires conduct contrary to the articles of this Code.

Official Interpretations
of the Code

Interpretation of Code Paragraph 2 which reads, "A member shall conduct his or her professional life in accord with the public interest."

> The public interest is here defined primarily as comprising respect for and enforcement of the rights guaranteed by the Constitution of the United States of America.

Interpretation of Code Paragraph 5 which reads, "A member shall safeguard the confidences of both present and former clients or employers and shall not accept retainers or employment which may involve the disclosure or use of these confidences to the disadvantage or prejudice of such clients or employers."

> This article does not prohibit a member who has knowledge of client or employer activities which are illegal from making such disclosures to the proper authorities as he or she believes are legally required.

Interpretation of Code Paragraph 6 which reads, "A member shall not engage in any practice which tends to corrupt the integrity of channels of communication or the processes of government."

1. Practices prohibited by this paragraph are those which tend to place representatives of media or government under an obligation to the member, or the member's employer or client, which is in conflict with their obligations to media or government, such as:

   a. the giving of gifts of more than nominal value;

   b. any form of payment or compensation to a member of the media in order to obtain preferential or guaranteed news or editorial coverage in the medium;

   c. any retainer or fee to a media employee or use of such employee if retained by a client or employer, where the circumstances are not fully disclosed to and accepted by the media employer;

   d. providing trips for media representatives which are unrelated to legitimate news interest;

   e. the use by a member of an investment or loan or advertising commitment made by the member, or the member's client or employer, to obtain preferential or guaranteed coverage in the medium.

2. This Code paragraph does not prohibit hosting media or government representatives at meals, cocktails, or news functions or special events which are occasions for the exchange of news information or views, or the furtherance of understanding which is part of the public relations function. Nor does it prohibit the bona fide press event or tour when media or government representatives are given an opportunity for on-the-spot viewing of a newsworthy product, process or event in which the media or government representatives have a legitimate interest. What is customary or reasonable hospitality has to be a matter of particular judgment in specific situations. In all of these cases, however, it is or should be understood that no preferential treatment or guarantees are expected or implied and that complete independence always is left to the media or government representative.

3. This paragraph does not prohibit the reasonable giving or lending of sample products or services to media representatives who have a legitimate interest in the products or services.

Interpretation of Code Paragraph 13   which reads, "A member shall not guarantee the achievement of specified results beyond the member's direct control."

This Code paragraph, in effect, prohibits misleading a client or employer as to what professional public relations can accomplish. It does not prohibit guarantees of quality or service. But it does prohibit guaranteeing specific results which, by their very nature, cannot be guaranteed because they are not subject to the member's control. As an example, a guarantee that a news release will appear specifically in a particular publication would be prohibited. This paragraph should not be interpreted as prohibiting contingent fees.

An Official Interpretation of the Code as It Applies to Political Public Relations

Preamble   In the practice of political public relations, a PRSA member must have professional capabilities to offer an employer or client quite apart from any political relationships of value, and members may serve their employer or client without necessarily having attributed to them the character, reputation or beliefs of those they serve. It is understood that members may choose to serve only those interests with whose political philosophy they are personally comfortable.

Definition   "Political Public Relations" is defined as those areas of public relations which relate to:

a. the counseling of political organizations, committees, candidates or potential candidates for public office; and groups constituted for the purpose of influencing the vote on any ballot issue;

b. the counseling of holders of public office;

c. the management, or direction, of a political campaign for or against a candidate for political office; or for or against a ballot issue to be determined by voter approval or rejection;

d. the practice of public relations on behalf of a client or an employer in connection with that client's or employer's relationships with any candidates or holders of public office with the purpose of influencing legislation or government regulation or treatment of a client or employer, regardless of whether the PRSA member is a recognized lobbyist;

e. the counseling of government bodies, or segments thereof, either domestic or foreign.

Precepts

1. It is the responsibility of PRSA members practicing political public relations, as defined above, to be conversant with the various statutes, local, state, and federal, governing such activities and to adhere to them strictly. This includes, but is not limited to, the various local, state and federal laws, court decisions and official interpretations governing lobbying, political contributions, disclosure, elections, libel, slander and the like. In carrying out this responsibility, members shall seek appropriate counseling whenever necessary.

2. It is also the responsibility of members to abide by PRSA's Code of Professional Standards.

3. Members shall represent clients or employers in good faith, and while partisan ad-

vocacy on behalf of a candidate or public issue may be expected, members shall act in accord with the public interest and adhere to truth and accuracy and to generally accepted standards of good taste.

4. Members shall not issue descriptive material or any advertising or publicity information or participate in the preparation or use thereof which is not signed by responsible persons or is false, misleading or unlabeled as to its source, and are obligated to use care to avoid dissemination of any such material.

5. Members have an obligation to clients to disclose what remuneration beyond their fees they expect to receive as a result of their relationship, such as commissions for media advertising, printing and the like, and should not accept such extra payment without their clients' consent.

6. Members shall not improperly use their positions to encourage additional future employment or compensation. It is understood that successful campaign directors or managers, because of the performance of their duties and the working relationship that develops, may well continue to assist and counsel, for pay, the successful candidate.

7. Members shall voluntarily disclose to employers or clients the identity of other employers or clients with whom they are currently associated and whose interests might be affected favorably or unfavorably by their political representation.

8. Members shall respect the confidentiality of information pertaining to employers or clients even after the relationships cease, avoiding future associations wherein insider information is sought that would give a desired advantage over a member's previous clients.

9. In avoiding practices which might tend to corrupt the processes of government, members shall not make undisclosed gifts of cash or other valuable considerations which are designed to influence specific decisions of voters, legislators or public officials on public matters. A business lunch or dinner, or other comparable expenditure made in the course of communicating a point of view or public position, would not constitute such a violation. Nor, for example, would a plant visit designed and financed to provide useful background information to an interested legislator or candidate.

10. Nothing herein should be construed as prohibiting members from making legal, properly disclosed contributions to the candidates, party or referenda issues of their choice.

11. Members shall not, through the use of information known to be false or misleading, conveyed directly or through a third party, intentionally injure the public reputation of an opposing interest.

An Official Interpretation of the Code as It Applies to Financial Public Relations

This interpretation of the Society Code as it applies to financial public relations was originally adopted in 1963 and amended in 1972 and 1977 by action of the PRSA Board of Directors. "Financial public relations" is defined as "that area of public relations which relates to the dissemination of information that affects the understanding of stockholders and investors generally concerning the financial position and prospects of a company, and includes among its objectives the improvement of relations between corporations and their stockholders." The interpretation was prepared in 1963 by the Society's Financial Relations Committee working with the Securities and Exchange Commission and with the advice of the Society's Legal Counsel. It is rooted directly in the Code with the full force of the Code behind it and a violation of any of the following paragraphs is subject to the same procedures and penalties as violations of the Code.

1. It is the responsibility of PRSA members who practice financial public relations to be thoroughly familiar with and understand the rules and regulations of the SEC and the laws which it administers, as well as other laws, rules and regulations affecting financial public relations, and to act in accordance with their letter and spirit. In carrying out this responsibility, members shall also seek legal counsel, when appropriate, on matters concerning financial public relations.

2. Members shall adhere to the general policy of making full and timely disclosure of corporate information on behalf of clients or employers. The information disclosed should be accurate, clear and understandable. The purpose of such disclosure is to provide the investing public with all material information affecting security values or influencing investment decisions. In complying with the duty of full and timely disclosure, members shall present all material facts, including those adverse to the company. They shall exercise due care to ascertain the facts and to disseminate only information which they believe to be accurate. They shall not knowingly omit information, the omission of which might make a release false or misleading. Under no circumstances shall members participate in any activity designed to mislead, or manipulate the price of a company's securities.

3. Members shall publicly disclose or release information promptly so as to avoid the possibility of any use of the information by any insider or third party. To that end, members shall make every effort to comply with the spirit and intent of the timely disclosure policies of the stock exchanges, NASD, and the Securities and Exchange Commission. Material information shall be made available to all on an equal basis.

4. Members shall not disclose confidential information the disclosure of which might be adverse to a valid corporate purpose or interest and whose disclosure is not required by the timely disclosure provisions of the law. During any such period of non-disclosure members shall not directly or indirectly (a) communicate the confidential information to any other person or (b) buy or sell or in any other way deal in the company's securities where the confidential information may materially affect the market for the security when disclosed. Material information shall be disclosed publicly as soon as its confidential status has terminated or the requirement of timely disclosure takes effect.

5. During the registration period, members shall not engage in practices designed to precondition the market for such securities. During registration the issuance of forecasts, projections, predictions about sales and earnings, or opinions concerning security values or other aspects of the future performance of the company, shall be in accordance with current SEC regulations and statements of policy. In the case of companies whose securities are publicly held, the normal flow of factual information to shareholders and the investing public shall continue during the registration period.

6. Where members have any reason to doubt that projections have an adequate basis in fact, they shall satisfy themselves as to the adequacy of the projections prior to disseminating them.

7. Acting in concert with clients or employers, members shall act promptly to correct false or misleading information or rumors concerning clients' or employers' securities or business whenever they have reason to believe such information or rumors are materially affecting investor attitudes.

8. Members shall not issue descriptive materials designed or written in such a fashion as to appear to be, contrary to fact, an independent third party endorsement or recommendation of a company or a security. Whenever members issue material for clients or

employers, either in their own names or in the name of someone other than clients or employers, they shall disclose in large type and in a prominent position on the face of the material the source of such material and the existence of the issuer's client or employer relationship.

9. Members shall not use inside information for personal gain. However, this is not intended to prohibit members from making bona fide investments in their company's or client's securities insofar as they can make such investments without the benefit of material inside information.

10. Members shall not accept compensation which would place them in a position of conflict with their duty to a client, employer or the investing public. Members shall not accept stock options from clients or employers nor accept securities as compensation at a price below market price except as part of an overall plan for corporate employees.

11. Members shall act so as to maintain the integrity of channels of public communication. They shall not pay or permit to be paid to any publication or other communications medium any consideration in exchange for publicizing a company, except through clearly recognizable paid advertising.

12. Members shall in general be guided by the PRSA Declaration of Principles and the PRSA Code of Professional Standards for the Practice of Public Relations of which this Code is an official interpretation.

Rules of Procedure for Judicial Panels*

1. Every complaint against a member shall be in writing signed by the complaining party (hereinafter called the complainant) and shall set forth the facts constituting the complaint, plainly and in numbered paragraphs.

2. The complainant shall file nine copies of the complaint with the Chairman of the Panel having jurisdiction (see Section 6 of Article XIII of the Bylaws of the Society, printed in the Society's Register). The Chairman shall send copies of the complaint to members of the Panel, to the Society's counsel, to the Chairman of the Grievance Board and to the Headquarters Office of the Society.

3. In cases where the Grievance Board is not the complainant, the Chairman of the Panel shall acknowledge receipt of the complaint and inform the complainant that if the complaint is found by the Panel to be of sufficient importance and in proper form, the complainant will be expected to prosecute the complaint and a formal hearing will, in due course, be held at which the complainant will be expected to present evidence substantiating the facts set forth in the complaint, in accordance with the obligation imposed by paragraph 10 of the Code. However, the complainant may, on his written application and in the discretion of the Panel, be excused from prosecuting his complaint if the Panel finds that it would be appropriate for the Grievance Board to prosecute the matter. In the latter event, the Chairman of the Panel shall refer the complaint to the Grievance Board and advise the complainant that such action is being taken. The Grievance Board shall then be deemed the complainant and shall then be responsible for investigating the matter and prosecuting the complaint if warranted. Excuse from prosecuting the complaint, however, does not relieve the original complainant of his obligation to appear as a witness.

---

*Adopted by the Board of Directors of the Society, November 18, 1965, and effective as of that date. Used by permission.

4. If the Panel shall deem the complaint to be of sufficient importance and in proper form, the Chairman shall serve a copy of the complaint, together with a copy of these rules, upon the member complained of (hereinafter called the respondent). The foregoing sentence shall not apply to a complaint filed with the Panel by the Grievance Board. In the latter case, such complaint, together with a copy of these rules, shall be automatically served upon the member complained of, as above provided.

5. If the Panel shall determine that the complaint is not of sufficient importance or is not in proper form, the Chairman shall so advise the complainant who shall have the opportunity to file an amended complaint. The rules of procedure regarding complaints shall apply to amended complaints.

6. The respondent shall file with the Chairman of the Panel nine copies and shall serve on the complainant one copy of his written answer, signed by him within twenty days after service of the complaint. The answer shall reply to the complaint by referring to each numbered paragraph of the complaint by number, and each fact alleged by the complaint shall be (a) admitted, or (b) stated to be immaterial, with the reasons why, or (c) denied. The respondent may also include in his answer an affirmative statement of his position. The Chairman shall send copies of the answer to the members of the Panel, to the Society's counsel, to the Chairman of the Grievance Board and the Headquarters Office of the Society.

7. The complainant may within five days of the receipt of the answer, reply thereto by serving on the respondent one copy and filing with the Chairman of the Panel nine copies of a reply specifically replying to any new fact alleged in the answer. The Chairman shall send copies of the reply to members of the Panel, to the Society's counsel, to the Chairman of the Grievance Board and to the Headquarters Office of the Society.

8. If the respondent desires to make a counter-complaint, such counter-complaint shall be made in a separate document and the rules of procedure regarding complaints shall apply to the counter-complaint.

9. The Panel or its Chairman may, at any time in advance of the hearing, require either party to furnish a bill of particulars to the other party, eight copies thereof being filed with the Chairman of the Panel who shall send a copy to members of the Panel, to the Society's counsel and to the Headquarters Office of the Society.

10. After complainant's reply, or after the time to reply has expired, the matter shall be "at issue." When the matter is at issue, the Chairman of the Panel, upon his own motion or upon written request of either party, may direct the holding of pre-hearing depositions in accordance with the following rules:

    a. Depositions may be taken of any party to the proceedings or of any person who appears to be a material witness.

    b. The Chairman of the Panel shall designate a member of the Panel before whom the deposition is to take place.

    c. The designated Panel member shall fix the time and place for the holding of the deposition, giving notice to the parties and to the other Panel members who may attend the deposition.

    d. The taking of the deposition shall not be governed by the rules of evidence pertaining to court procedure. The designated Panel member shall decide all questions of evidence, subject to review at the hearing.

    e. The designated Panel member shall have power to summon any member of the Society to appear at the deposition as a witness and to call for the production of documentary evidence.

f. The designated Panel member and the parties shall have the right to examine and cross-examine the witnesses and be represented by counsel.

g. The designated Panel member shall, at the expense of the Society, provide a public stenographer for the deposition. Copies of the transcript shall be distributed, at the expense of the Society, and prior to the hearing, to all members of the Panel, to the Society's Counsel and to the Headquarters Office of the Society, and if the Grievance Board has been notified of the pendency of the proceedings in accordance with paragraph 26, then the Chairman of the Grievance Board. Copies of the transcript for any other party shall be at the expense of the party.

h. When several depositions are taken in a proceeding, the same or different Panel members may be designated.

11. When the matter is at issue and the Panel or its Chairman have concluded that all appropriate depositions have been taken, the Panel or its Chairman shall set a time and place for a hearing upon the complaint and shall give notice of the hearing to the parties.

12. At the hearing, the transcript of any depositions taken shall be placed in the record of the proceedings.

13. At the hearing the Panel shall not be found by the rules of evidence pertaining to Court procedure, but shall decide all questions of evidence. The Panel may consider the past professional conduct of the respondent.

14. The Panel shall have power to summon any member of the Society to appear at the hearing as a witness and to call for the production of documentary evidence.

15. The Panel, the complainant and respondent shall have the right to call and examine and cross-examine witnesses and be represented by counsel.

16. The Panel Chairman shall, at the expense of the Society, provide a public stenographer for the hearing. Copies of the transcript shall be distributed, at the expense of the Society, to all members of the Panel, to the Society's counsel and to the Headquarters Office of the Society, and if the Grievance Board has been notified of the pendency of the proceedings in accordance with paragraph 26, then the Chairman of the Grievance Board. Copies of the transcript for any other party shall be at the expense of the party.

17. Personal attendance of a quorum of the Panel (four members) throughout the hearing is required. The Panel member or members designated to conduct prehearing depositions under paragraph 10 hereof need not form part of the quorum.

18. The Panel or its Chairman, where circumstances warrant, may accelerate limitations of time herein provided or grant extensions of time to the parties.

19. As promptly as possible after the hearing, the Panel, through its Chairman, shall make a written report to the President of the Society for submission to the Board of Directors of the Society and to the parties, setting forth its findings of fact, conclusions and recommendations with respect to disciplinary action or exoneration.

20. The complainant or respondent, not in default in appearing or answering, may file exceptions to the report within fifteen days from the date of mailing of a copy of such report to them. Such exceptions shall be filed with the President of the Society for submission to the Board of Directors and also with the other party and the Panel Chairman. The other party and the Panel Chairman may reply to such exceptions within ten days thereafter. Such replies shall be filed with the party excepting and with the President of the Society. Thereafter no further statements or exceptions shall be filed.

21. Exceptions shall state plainly and concisely the reasons why the party excepting asserts that the recommendations of the Panel should not be adopted by the Board.

22. Exceptions shall be based solely on the record before the Panel. No evidence not presented to the Panel will be received or considered. Oral argument before the Board of Directors will not be permitted. The matter shall be considered by the Board of Directors solely on the recommendation of the Panel, the record before the Panel, the exceptions if any, and the replies thereto.

23. The Panel may recommend disciplinary action against a member who as a party to a proceeding before the Panel shall, in the judgment of the Panel, be guilty of a violation of the Code (particularly paragraphs 3 and 10 thereof) in his conduct during the proceeding, including the hearing, provided that before the close of the hearing, the Panel shall give the member, if present, notice of the Panel's intention to recommend such disciplinary action and shall at such hearing give such member an opportunity to be heard with respect thereto.

24. The Panel may adopt additional rules of procedure not inconsistent with these rules. In the course of a proceeding, it may determine any points of procedure not covered by these rules.

25. The Society's counsel shall have the following duties and be governed by the following rules:

    a. He shall advise the Panel, the Grievance Board, the parties to the proceedings, and their counsel, and the Board of Directors of the Society as to the application and interpretation of the Rules of Procedure.

    b. At the hearing, he shall act as legal advisor to the Panel to assist it in the discharge of its duties.

    c. He shall, subject to the Panel's control, direct the course of the hearing so that all concerned may have ample opportunity to present the material facts for the decision of the Panel. He shall, subject to the Panel's control, determine the order in which witnesses shall present their testimony and other matters of procedure.

    d. He may participate in the questioning of witnesses for the purpose of clarifying the issues or the testimony of witnesses to assist the Panel in the discharge of its duties.

    e. After the hearing, Counsel may attend the deliberations of the Panel and the Panel may call upon its legal advisor to submit for its consideration proposed findings, conclusions and recommendations as it might indicate.

    f. The foregoing subdivisions of this paragraph 25 shall apply to prehearing depositions where applicable.

26. In a case where the Grievance Board is not a party, the Panel may, in its discretion, at any time in the proceedings notify the Grievance Board of the pendency of the proceedings and of all subsequent steps therein. Thereupon, the Grievance Board may, in its discretion, participate in any subsequent depositions and also at the hearing as if it were a party.

27. When these Rules require or authorize the service of papers they shall be served by certified or registered mail.

28. All documents sent pursuant to these Rules to the Headquarters Office of the Society shall be marked "Personal and Confidential, Attention Staff Assistant for Judicial Matters."

Rules of Procedure for Grievance Board *

1. Copies of source material of complaint, accompanied by an analysis by the Grievance Board Counsel, shall be sent to each member of the Grievance Board by the Grievance Board Chairman with a ballot opinion form to be returned to the Chairman within fifteen (15) days.

2. Investigation of complaints shall be conducted by Grievance Board Counsel as directed by the Grievance Board Chairman after the latter has received ballot opinions from Grievance Board members under Rule 1.

3. The Grievance Board Counsel shall prepare a report on his investigation and findings with a recommendation which shall be sent to all Grievance Board members by the Grievance Board Chairman.

4. Grievance Board members shall take action on the Grievance Board Counsel report filed in accordance with Rule 3, either at a meeting or by ballot, and decide:

    a. to close case as being of insufficient importance to warrant filing charges with a judicial panel,

    b. to ask Grievance Board Counsel for further specific investigation,

    c. to hold case for further development (i.e. court cases), or

    d. to file charges with the proper judicial panel of the Society.

5. If ballot vote is taken under Rule 4, Grievance Board members may have the option of asking that no action be taken until after the complaint has been discussed at a meeting of the Grievance Board, and if any Grievance Board member exercises this option, the Chairman shall call a meeting for this purpose.

6. A majority vote of the Grievance Board members present at a meeting or voting on a mail ballot shall be required under Rule 4d to file charges with a judicial panel of the Society.

7. Six members of the Grievance Board shall constitute a quorum for meetings or ballot voting.

8. In complaints where the Grievance Board votes to file charges, the Grievance Board Counsel shall prepare the complaint which shall then be filed by the Grievance Board Chairman with the proper judicial panel of the Society in accordance with Rules of Procedure for Panels as adopted by the PRSA Board of Directors, November 18, 1965.

9. In cases where the Grievance Board is the complainant in judicial proceedings before a judicial panel, the Grievance Board Chairman and the Grievance Board Counsel shall attend the hearing. The Chairman may designate another Grievance Board member to attend in his stead.

10. In all other procedures involved in a complaint before a judicial panel, including the filing of exceptions, the Grievance Board shall be governed by the Rules of Procedure for Panels adopted by the PRSA Board of Directors, November 18, 1965.

---

*Adopted by the Board of Directors April 7, 1967 and effective as of that date. Used by permission. (There are two main sources of complaints for Grievance Board consideration—(1) complaint from a member when he is not a directly aggrieved party; and (2) information from court proceedings or other events reported in public media.)

11. A quarterly status report of all pending cases before the Grievance Board shall be prepared by the Grievance Board Counsel and circulated by the Grievance Board Chairman to all members of the Grievance Board.

Additional Codes

There are several PR organizations, and PR people also interact with professionals in various communication fields; therefore, codes from the following organizations should be in any PR person's files.

- International Public Relations Association
  Attn: Secretary General, IPRA
  49 Wellington St.
  Covent Garden
  London WC2E 8BN
  England

- International Association of Business Communicators
  Attn: Executive Director
  870 Market St.
  San Francisco, CA 94102

- Better Business Bureau (for Code of Advertising)
  Attn: Executive Director
  Industry Division, Council of Better Business Bureaus
  1515 Wilson Blvd. N
  Arlington, VA 22209

- Society of Professional Journalists, Sigma Delta Chi
  Attn: Executive Director
  Suite 801W
  840 N. Lakeshore Dr.
  Chicago, IL 60611

- American Society of Journalists and Authors, Inc.
  (formerly Society of Magazine Writers)
  Attn: Executive Director
  1505 Broadway, Suite 1907
  New York, NY 10036

- The American Society of Newspaper Editors
  Attn: Executive Director
  Box 551, Easton, PA 18042

- Associated Press Managing Editors Association
  Attn: Executive Director
  c/o Milwaukee Journal
  Milwaukee, WI 53201

(Additionally, many newspaper chains, individual newspapers and broadcast stations, as well as regional associations such as county medical associations, have codes of conduct of interest to PR practitioners.)

APPENDIX B

Careers in Public Relations *

The Public Relations Society of America, founded in 1948, is the major force in developing the increased professionalism required of today's practitioners of public relations.

PRSA, headquartered in New York City, has more than 80 chapters located throughout the United States. Its members, totaling more than 10,000, come from business corporations, public relations counseling firms, government agencies, educational institutions, trade and professional groups, and other nonprofit organizations.

The Society enforces a code of professional standards and conducts an Accreditation program which offers members an opportunity to take written and oral examinations to demonstrate their competence in the practice of public relations, PRSA carries on a program of continuing education for its members. And it publishes the monthly *Public Relations Journal* and the annual *Public Relations Register*.

In 1968, PRSA established the Public Relations Student Society of America (PRSSA) to cultivate a favorable and mutually useful relationship between students and professional public relations practitioners. Chapters of PRSSA are located on the campuses of more than 100 colleges and universities, with membership exceeding 4,000.

Public Relations Today

Public relations is difficult to grasp at first. For one thing, the term is used to describe both a way of looking at an organization's performance and a program of activities.

Another difficulty is that the public relations function takes many forms in different organizations. And the function goes under many other names, too. Among them: public

* 1983 edition, Public Relations Society of America, Inc., 845 Third Avenue, New York, NY 10022.

information, investor relations, public affairs, corporate communications, employee relations or communications, marketing or product publicity, consumer service or customer relations.

Basic to *all* public relations, however, is communicating. Well-thought-out, effectively handled communications are increasingly seen as essential to the success and even existence of organizations and causes in today's complex, fast-changing world. Every organization—governmental, business, labor, professional and membership, health, cultural, educational and public service—depends on people. Their attitudes, attention, understanding and motivation can be critical factors in whether an organization or an idea succeeds or fails.

Public relations, at its best, does not only tell an organization's "story" to its publics. The public relations practitioner also helps shape the organization and the way it performs. Through research, feedback communications and evaluation, the practitioner should find out the concerns and expectations of the organization's various publics and explain them to its management. A responsible—and effective—public relations program should be based on the understanding and support of its publics.

The number of people in public relations work has been estimated to be as many as 120,000. The rate of growth of public relations jobs at all levels is thought to have been higher than that of any other management function. A high growth rate reflects increased recognition of the importance of communications and of professional competence in its planning and implementation. For example, it is rare today for medium- or large-sized corporations not to have public relations staffs, consultants or both. Thirty years ago, a major number of such companies had not formalized their public relations functions. Increasingly, the person responsible for the public relations department of major companies is a corporate officer.

Salaries

Because they have been in a growth field, public relations practitioners tend to be well paid, although the range of compensation is quite broad. Earnings depend on such factors as the individual's qualifications and experience, responsibilities of the position, financial strength of the organization and the general state of the economy.

A trainee in public relations for business may begin at $10,000 or more.* An account executive of a consulting firm can earn upwards of $35,000 as will a person with comparable responsibility in a company's public relations department. A director of public relations for a small to medium-sized company may earn $35,000 to $40,000, while the range for the larger corporation more likely would be $40,000 to $60,000. Salaries from $75,000 to $150,000 are earned by a number of seasoned public relations executives, who more often than not carry the title of vice president and enjoy commensurate fringe benefits.

Depending upon the profitability of public relations consulting firms (or agencies), the incomes of their senior members may exceed those of public relations officials on the payrolls of corporations.

Various industries and companies tend to pay their employees higher or lower than others, and these characteristic compensation patterns generally apply to their public relations workers. Variations according to geographic location may also be found, with New York and Chicago personnel tending to be higher paid.

---

*Salaries based on 1981 data.

Kind of Work Done

Most public relations positions involve one or more of these functions:

1. *Programming*. This involves analyzing problems and opportunities, defining goals and the publics (or groups of people whose support or understanding is needed), and recommending and planning activities. It may include budgeting and assignment of responsibilities to the appropriate people, including non-public relations personnel. For example, an organization's president or executive director is often a key figure in public relations activities.

2. *Relationships*. Successful public relations people develop skill in personally gathering information from management, from colleagues in their organizations and from external sources. Continually evaluating what they learn, they formulate recommendations and gain approval for them from their managements.

   Many public relations activities require working with, and sometimes through, other functions, including personnel, legal and marketing staffs. The practitioner who learns to be persuasive with others will be most effective.

   Public relations people also represent their organizations. Sometimes this is formal, in that they are official representatives to a trade or professional association. But in all their relationships with others—including people in industry groups, regulatory agencies and government, educational institutions and the general public—public relations personnel are at work in behalf of their organizations.

3. *Writing and Editing*. Since the public relations worker is often trying to reach large groups of people, the tool most often used is the printed word. Examples of its use are found in reports, news releases, booklets, speeches, film scripts, trade magazine articles, product information and technical material, employee publications, newsletters, shareholder reports and other management communications, directed to both organization personnel and external groups. A sound, clear style of writing, which effectively communicates, is virtually a must for public relations work.

4. *Information*. Setting up channels of dissemination of material to appropriate newspaper, broadcast, general and trade publication editors, and contact with them with a view toward enlisting their interest in publishing an organization's news and features are normal public relation activities. This requires a knowledge of how newspapers and other media operate, the areas of specialization of publications and the interests of individual editors. Competition is keen for the attention of editors and broadcasters who have a limited amount of space and time at their disposal. As one public relations practitioner puts it, "You have to get to the right editor of the right publication with the right story at the right time." Although ideas are accepted on the basis of news and other readership value, an ability to develop relationships of mutual respect and cooperation with the press can be useful to both the practitioner and the newsman.

5. *Production*. Brochures, special reports, films and multi-media programs are important ways of communicating. The public relations practitioner need not be an expert in art, layout, typography and photography, but background knowledge of the techniques of preparation is needed for intelligent planning and supervision of their use.

6. *Special Events*. News conferences, convention exhibits and special showings, new facility and anniversary celebrations, contest and award programs, tours and special meetings make up a partial list of special events used to gain attention and acceptance of groups of people. They involve careful planning and coordination, attention to detail, preparation of special booklets, publicity and reports.

7. *Speaking*. Public relations work often requires skill in face-to-face communication—

finding appropriate platforms, the preparation of speeches for others and the delivery of speeches. The person who can effectively address individuals and groups will enjoy an advantage over those whose facility of expression is limited to writing.

8. *Research and Evaluation.* The first activity undertaken by a public relations practitioner is always fact gathering. As previously indicated, this can be highly personal, through interviews, review of library materials and informal conversations. It can also involve the use of survey techniques and firms specializing in designing and conducting opinion research.

After a program is completed, the public relations practitioner should study its results and make an evaluation about the program's implementation and effectiveness. More and more managements expect research and evaluation from their public relations advisers.

The Day

Public relations offices are busy places; work schedules are choppy and frequently interrupted. The junior employee will answer calls for information from the press and the public, work on invitation lists and details for a press conference, escort visitors and clients, help with research, write brochures, deliver releases to editorial offices, work up contact and distribution lists, scan newspapers and journals, paste scrapbooks of clippings.

The employee will brief his or her superior on forthcoming meetings, help write reports, speeches, presentations and letters, research case histories, help produce displays and other audiovisual materials, proofread, select photographs for publication, arrange for meetings, perform liaison jobs with advertising and other departments, arrange for holiday and other remembrances, conduct surveys and tabulate questionnaires, work with letter shops and printers.

The telephone, typewriter, photocopier, postage meter, telecopier, postal system and messenger services are communications tools. All are familiar in the public relations work environment.

Not infrequently, public relations programs operate against deadlines. Under such high-pressure conditions, nine-to-five schedules go out the window. While the public relations executive will not be tied to his desk for long periods, meetings, community functions, business lunches, travel assignments, special speaking and writing commitments, and unscheduled work on "crisis" situations often mean long hours—sometimes creating envy of those engaged in occupations with more settled routines.

Personal Qualifications and Preparation

Because public relations covers many kinds of tasks, there is no single set of "ideal" qualifications. Most people think of the public relations executive as a highly articulate and imaginative individual with more than a little salesmanship in his or her makeup. Yet public relations executives themselves stress *judgment* as the most important single qualification needed in their field. The public relations practitioner is a "counselor" whose advice and services are often sought out when an organization faces the prospect of trouble. Therefore, it is important to develop the capacity to think analytically under pressure, to draw out necessary information and to express persuasive practical solutions. Other qualities needed by the public relations worker include:

- imagination, for coping with new problems and commanding the attention of others
- verbalizing skills, with demonstrable competence in writing

- personal confidence, for successful frequent face-to-face contacts with individuals and groups

- sensitivity to other people; to profess a liking for people will not help a candidate get a job—however, both diplomacy and a more than ordinary ability to place oneself in the shoes of another are important in public relations work

- organizing and planning ability, applied both to oneself and others—as with many other occupations, managerial skills are invaluable assets for successfully climbing the public relations career ladder

Academic Preparation

A college degree is almost a necessity for work at the professional level. Though public relations is a relatively new field, more than 300 colleges and universities offer at least one course in the subject and some fifty institutions offer sequences of Public Relations courses.

Students may major in Public Relations at a number of educational institutions, several of which also offer the opportunity for graduate study in Public Relations. The courses are generally administered by Journalism or Communications departments.

Although an increasing number of students of Public Relations, including those with master's degrees, are entering the field, many employers emphasize the value of a broad liberal arts program of study. Courses in English, Creative Writing, Economics, Journalism, Psychology, Sociology, and Marketing are considered most helpful as preparation.

Work Experience

Most of today's senior public relations practitioners started in journalism. For the majority with this background, public relations work represented a change of career objectives. A number of young people still seek out journalism jobs but as a specific stepping stone to public relations. With the growth of college training for public relations, it is possible that the importance of a journalism apprenticeship will diminish.

There remains something to be said about a journalism background. The experience gained in writing, personal contact and other aspects of publications work for metropolitan or smaller newspapers, general or trade magazines and broadcast media is still deemed important by a majority of public relations employers. To a far lesser extent, experience in general business, marketing, advertising and selling are considered useful for public relations work in business and industry.

Sometimes experience in specialized fields—such as finance, engineering, medicine and public or educational administration—can be valuable qualifications for a particular public relations position.

Outside activities—such as free-lance writing, community organization work, election and fund campaigning, public speaking—are often looked upon favorably as supporting experience.

Fields of Public Relations

Business Corporations.   The greatest amount of public relations activity will be found in business and industry. Public relations had its origins in this sector of our life at the beginning of this century and now represents expenditures of billions of dollars annually.

The extent of organized public relations programs and the size of staffs will generally vary according to the size of companies. Some very large companies have staffs exceeding one hundred persons. The average public relations staff is not large—a half-dozen or fewer—while many small companies consolidate public relations responsibility with advertising or sales or place it with the president or another official or top management.

The nature of the public relations job will vary with the type of industry. A service company—for example, a public utility dependent upon good customer and government relations—may give high priority to the public relations function. A consumer products company will call for different approaches (based on the interests of its various publics) from those of an industrial goods company, selling chiefly to other companies.

Associations.   There are more than 14,000 active national associations, the majority of which are headquartered in New York City, Washington or Chicago. Associations are not engaged directly in the marketing of products, but rather in creating a favorable climate for an industry or a cause.

Similar activities are maintained by information bureaus, institutions, councils, and foundations, which frequently derive support from business and industry and are devoted to matters of public concern, such as conservation, safety and nutrition.

Professional societies, both national and regional, also have their public relations activities organized on lines similar to trade membership groups. Legal and medical groups are examples.

Labor Unions.   Trade unions, like the businesses which employ their members, recognize the importance of building public support for their positions and programs. The AFL-CIO, many of its affiliated unions and major independent unions at the international or national, state and local levels operate news bureaus, sponsor radio and television programs, offer films and educational programs to schools and civic groups, organize speakers' bureaus and publish a variety of newspapers, brochures and other materials. Public relations people who start in the labor movement tend to remain in this field throughout their careers.

Schools and Colleges.   Few institutions of higher learning are without organized public relations activities, which are frequently combined with "development" or fund raising for the institution. While fund raising itself is a specialized field, a number of the tools used, including brochures, letters, and special events, are similar to those used in other public relations work. Large colleges and universities may have offices of public relations for information separate from the development department. These offices will handle press relations, community relations, special observances, speakers' bureaus and speech writing and other typical public relations activities. Publications, including the school catalog, descriptive brochures, bulletins and news publications are frequently an important part of the communications function.

More and more secondary schools and school systems are also undertaking organized public relations programs. Cultural institutions, such as museums, historical societies, musical organizations, art councils, theaters and libraries also employ public relations personnel to further their ends.

Volunteer Agencies.   Sometimes called the nonprofit, public service, or social sector, voluntary agencies include those in the health and welfare field involved with rehabilitation, recreation and family service. Another segment is the hospital field which provides work opportunity in press, community and patron relations, as well as in fund raising. Other service organizations, including the Red Cross, Girl Scouts, Young Men's Christian Association, along with religious, community and special fund organizations and fraternal groups also use public relations for acceptance and support.

Government. Government units, including those of the Armed Forces, designate their public relations activity as "public information." In addition to the numerous federal agencies, commissions and other bodies which have press and information officers, state, regional, county and municipal units are also staffed with persons responsible for good relations with the public and for reporting on their organizations' activities. On the international level, the United States Information Agency (USIA) is charged with informing people outside our country about its ideals and the operation of the American system.

Public Relations Firms. Most public relations firms or counselors are located in large metropolitan centers, with heavy concentration in New York City and Chicago. (Together, these two cities account for nearly half of the approximately 4,000 firms.) Public relations firms range in staff size from several employing more than one hundred people to the great majority with fewer than a dozen workers. There is hardly any kind of public relations job that is not handled by consulting firms. Some specialize in financial or investor relations, government relations, employee communications, education and social programs, or industrial products or consumer marketing programs. The great majority have varied accounts. In some instances, they offer advertising as well as public relations services.

Some public relations workers are well suited for either a company staff or a consulting firm, but the conditions of employment and qualifications called for are somewhat different. Job tenure and benefits may sometimes be less advantageous for those working for the consulting firm. But those who chafe at the routines of the larger organization, and enjoy the creative ferment that often characterizes the consulting firm, may find themselves happier in that environment. Candidates for positions with firms are usually selected on the basis of experience and public relations proficiency.

Finding the First Job

No job is harder than finding a job, particularly your first. This is true of any field and certainly so of public relations. Success requires planning, preparation, energy and enthusiasm—all in large quantities.

Research the field in which you have the greatest interest. Not only should you use library resources, but also find people who work in these fields and particularly those engaged in public relations activities. Sometimes a journalist can also provide useful insights. The knowledge you acquire from all these sources will confirm your interest in the field and will be evidence of your alertness and maturity.

You will need a written résumé of your background. This should contain a convincing, but not lengthy, account of yourself, particularly as it might bear on your potential usefulness in a job. It should include name, address, telephone number, age, possibly a statement of job objectives, your education and work experience including part-time work while at college, reported chronologically or in terms of the types of skills demonstrated or the work accomplished.

You should be attentive to the impression your résumé makes by its layout and the way you express yourself. Check and recheck your résumé, particularly for typographical errors. Duplicated processing is acceptable and you probably will find it useful to have your résumé run off in quantity.

You may learn about possible job openings in advance of contacting employers, or you may conduct a personal mail campaign, sending your résumé with a covering letter to organizations where there is some possibility of staff needs. Personal contacts are perhaps the best source for job leads, and personal referrals are most advantageous. Placement agencies, associations, firms which service other organizations and "help wanted" advertisements are also sources of information about specific openings.

Business directories may be consulted when making direct canvass by letter and résumé. Especially useful for this purpose are two directories published by J. R. O'Dwyer Co., Inc., New York: *O'Dwyer's Directory of Public Relations Firms* and *O'Dwyer's Directory of Corporate Communications*.

When possible, you should address by name the person immediately responsible for the department in which you might be employed. It is often effective to follow up your letter by telephone to attempt to arrange an interview, even if a position is not immediately available.

It is important to prepare for interviews by attempting to learn as much as possible about the organization beforehand. For major business corporations, financial information may be available from their shareholder relations or corporate secretary office.

Showing samples of your work can prove helpful, but bear in mind that they should represent your best efforts. Quality is more impressive than quantity.

Be ready to take the initiative in describing your qualifications and what you believe you can accomplish on the job, if the interviewer does not choose to lead the discussion. Also be aware of the fact that the quality of your questions about the company and the position can be as impressive and revealing of your potential as your background, particularly if your experience is limited.

Every candidate for a public relations position must keep in mind that the number of persons hired for any particular opening is small compared with the number interviewed. Rejection is no cause to suppose you will not qualify elsewhere. Consider your job hunt as a learning experience. Through perseverance you can win the opportunity to begin your public relations career.

Good luck—and may you find your career rewarding in every way.

GLOSSARY

ABC Audit Bureau of Circulations, an organization giving accurate circulation data on U.S. print media.

A-B rolling (1) Preparation of film for printing. All odd-numbered shots are put on one reel (A-roll), with black leader replacing the even shots. The even-numbered shots, with black leader replacing the odd shots, make up the B-roll. Both rolls are then printed together onto one film, thus eliminating splices. (2) Electronic A-B rolling means that on one film chain an SOF (sound on film) film is projected, while on the second film chain a silent film is projected. The films can be intermixed (A-B rolled) through the television switcher.

academy leader A specifically marked film with numbers one second apart used for cueing film in the projector.

account Contract agreement with client.

acetate Transparent plastic sheet used in layouts, called "cell" for cellulose acetate; also is base for photographic film, used for magnetic tape too important to risk stretching.

Acetate does not stretch and breaks cleanly.

across the board A show aired at the same time daily at least five days a week. Also called a strip show.

adjacencies Broadcast term referring to programs or time period; usually means commercials placed next to specific programming.

advance News story about an event to occur in the future.

aerial shot Photo taken from helicopter or plane. (Has different meaning for movie film production and printing—refers to a particular effect.)

affidavit Proof that commercials were aired at specific time periods, a sworn statement.

affiliate A radio or TV station that is part of a network but not owned and operated by the network.

AFM American Federation of Musicians, a union.

AFTRA A union whose membership consists of anyone who performs live on videotape. Filmed TV shows require membership in SAG—Screen Actors Guild.

agate Typographic term for 5½-point type, standard unit of measurement for advertising lineage; fourteen agate lines to the inch.

air brush Brush used by artists which operates with compressed air; is used to retouch photos or create special effects in illustrations.

air check Tape made of radio or TV program or a commercial when it is aired.

air time Time when a radio or TV program starts.

alignment (1) Straightness or crookedness of letters in a line of type. Also refers to positioning of the elements in an ad for a desirable effect. (2) "Setup" of head on audio or video tape machine.

alphanumeric A set of characters used in computer programming that includes letters, digits and other special punctuation marks.

AM May mean either a morning newspaper or standard radio broadcasting (amplitude modulation of 535 to 1605 KHZ, soon to change to 1705).

angle Particular emphasis of a

media presentation; sometimes called a slant.

animation   Process of filming a number of slightly different cartoon drawings to create the illusion of movement.

annual report   Financial statement by management, used as a communication to all stockholders, security analysts and other interested publics, required by Securities and Exchange Commission for publicly held companies.

answer print   In 35mm film, the first print off a negative or, in 16mm, off a reversal after work print is completed; used to check quality.

AOR   Designation for a type of radio station format, album-oriented rock music.

AP   Associated Press, a cooperative or membership news-gathering service, dating from 1848, serving both print and broadcast media with stories and pictures. AP is international in scope and has its own correspondents, in addition to receiving material from member media.

Arbitron   Ratings company sales research organization for broadcasting (also known as ARB).

arc   To move the camera in an arcing motion about a subject.

art   General term for all illustrations in any medium.

art-type   Adhesive-backed, paste-on type used for special effects.

ASCAP   American Society of Composers, Authors and Publishers; licensing clearing house. Sets fees and controls artistic performance activity. *See* BMI.

ascender   The element of a lower-case letter extending above the body of the letter such as in b, d, h. *See* descender.

aspect ratio   TV picture measurement—three units high and four wide. Also used for film measurement—varying with the format.

assemble mode   The adding of

shots on videotape in a consecutive order.

audience   Group or groups receptive to a particular medium.

audio   Sound.

audio mixer   (1) Control room technician who mixes sound from different sources. (2) Equipment for mixing sound.

author's alterations   (AA) Typesetter's term for changes made on proofs by the author after type has been set. *See* printer's error.

availabilities   Unsold time slots for commercials.

back light   (1) Diffused illumination from behind the subject and opposite the camera. (2) In three-point lighting, a light opposite the camera to separate subject from the background.

back of the book   In magazines, the materials appearing after the main editorial section.

backroom or backshop   Mechanical section of a newspaper plant.

backtiming   (1) In broadcasting, a method of determining the time at which various program segments must begin to bring a program out on time. (2) In PR campaign, a scheduling to determine completion dates for various component parts to climax.

backup   (1) In newspaper assignments, a second reporter or photographer used as a backup in case the first does not or cannot complete the job. (2) In printing, when one side of a sheet has been printed and the reverse side is being printed.

backup lead-in   A silent lead-in to sound film or video tape recording when original recording preceding the sound is uncut; lead-in sound may be blooped or faded out by audio mixer.

bad break   In typesetting, an incorrect word division at end of line of type.

bank   (1) Composing-room table for galleys. (2) A strip of lights.

banner   Also called a streamer; a long line of type.

banner head   Headlines set in large type and usually stretching across a page.

barter   Paying for goods through advertising rather than money, or airing programs with commercials or time availabilities without paying directly for the program.

BASIC   (Beginners All-Purpose Symbolic Instruction Code)—a common time-sharing and business computer language for terminal-oriented programming.

beat   A reporter's regular run, such as "city hall beat."

beeper   (1) Recorded telephone conversation or interview. (2) Device frequently attached to the telephone that "beeps" every 14 seconds as required by FCC to indicate that a recording is being made.

beep-tape   Magnetic tape reproducing a continuous beep.

Ben Day   Process carrying its originator's name which makes possible a variety of shadings in line plates through photoengraving rather than the more expensive halftone.

bicycling   Transporting of film or audio or video recording from one station to another instead of making a duplicate.

bit   (Binary Digit)—either a "0" (zero) or "1" (one).

black leader   Also called opaque leader. (1) Black film used in editing. (2) Film used in 16mm "A" and "B" or checkerboard editing. The black film, without images, makes putting sequences together easier.

blanking out   Printing in two or more colors means forms must be broken or separated and spacing material placed where lines or illustrations have been lifted to print in different colors. Also called breaking for color.

bleed   Running a picture off the edge of a page. Allow at least one-eighth of an inch additional on all bleed sides of an illustration to be sure it "bleeds" after trimming.

block programming   Scheduling the same type of shows back to back; the opposite of magazine format, which is varied.

bloop   To erase sound track—by degaussing (wiping out) if magnetic; or by opaquing (blocking out) if optical.

blow up   Photographically enlarging the visual size of any item.

blurb   Short promotional description of story or article.

BMI   Broadcast Music, Inc. Copyright-holding organization from whom permission for usage of musical selections may be received without asking individual copyright holders. Permission from BMI (or ASCAP) is through a license fee. Copyright covers anything broadcast which exceeds four bars. Non-commercial stations get special consideration.

board   Audio control board that sends programming to the transmitter for broadcast or to the tape machine for recording.

body type   Type used for text matter, as distinguished from display (headlines or headings) type.

boldface type or BF   Blacker, heavier type than the rest of the type face, so it stands out from surrounding copy.

booklet   Compilation of six-plus pages, printed with paper cover and bound.

boomerang effect   When person affected by public opinion reacts in opposite from expected way.

border   Frame around piece of type matter.

box or boxed   Type enclosed with printed borders.

break   (1) Story available for publication. (2) Stopping point—may designate commercial break.

breaking for color   *See* blanking out.

break up   To kill or break up a type form so it cannot be used to print from again.

bridge   (1) Phrase or sentence connecting two stories. (2) In broadcasting, transitional program music.

bright   Light, humorous news story.

broadside   Message printed on one side of a single sheet no smaller than 18 × 25 inches. Designed for quick reading and prompt response.

brochure   Printed piece of usually six or more pages. More elaborate than a booklet, but without a backbone. Differs from a pamphlet by its use of illustrations and color.

brownlines   Lithographer's proofs.

BTA   Best Time Available—commercial at the best time available for the station.

bulletin   (1) Important news brief. (2) Wire service message to kill or release a story.

burnish/burnishing   Spreading dots in a halftone to deepen certain areas; also rubbing down to make paste-ups stick.

business publications   Periodicals published by and/or directed toward business.

bust shot   Photographic framing of a person from the upper torso to the top of the head.

busy   Too cluttered, as in a print illustration, still photograph or TV scene.

butted slug   Type matter that is too wide to set in one line on composing machine; it is set on two slugs and butted together to make one continuous line.

B & W   Black and white (monochrome) photograph (as opposed to color photo).

byline   reporter's name preceding a newspaper or broadcast story.

byte   A set of adjacent bits considered as a unit.

cable television   *See* CATV.

cameo lighting   Foreground figures are lighted with highly directional light, with the background remaining dark.

camera chain   TV camera and associated equipment, including power supply and sync generator.

camera copy   Copy ready for reproduction. Also called repros.

camera negative   Original negative film shot by film camera.

campaign   Organized effort to affect opinion of a group or groups on particular issue.

caps   Capital letters.

caption or cutline   Editorial material or legend accompanying illustration.

card image   Computer language for image of punched card as represented by some other medium, such as a tape or disc.

casting off   Estimating space required for copy set in given type size.

cathode ray tube (CRT)   Electronic vacuum tube with screen, on which information, news stories, etc., can be displayed.

CATV   Community Antenna Television. Also called Cable TV, a system in which home receivers get amplified signals from a coaxial cable connected to a master antenna. The CATV companies charge a monthly fee for this service.

CCTV   Closed-circuit TV. Program telecast not to public but only to a wired network of specific TV receivers.

cell or photocell   Optical reader.

center spread   Two facing center pages of publication; printed on single, continuous sheet.

chain   *See* film chain, double chain.

channel   (1) In broadcasting, a radio spectrum frequency assigned to a radio or TV station or stations. (2) In computer science, a path for electrical communication or transfer of information; imaginary line parallel to edge of tape along which lines are punched.

character Any single unit of type—letter, number, punctuation mark.

character generation Projection on the face of a CRT of typographic images, usually in high-speed computerized photocomposition system. The series of letters and numbers appears directly on the television screen or is keyed into a background picture.

chase Metal frame around a type form.

cheesecake Photographs depending for their appeal upon display of sexual images.

chroma key Electronic process for matting (imposing) one picture into another. Called "shooting the blue," because it generally uses the blue camera signal of color TV cameras, but may use any color.

circular Flyer, mailing piece, free distribution item, usually one sheet and inexpensive.

circulation (1) In broadcasting, refers to number of regular listeners or viewers or area in which they regularly attend to a station. (2) In print media, refers to subscribers, but may include street or newsstand sales.

class publications Periodicals designed for well-defined audiences, with focus limited to certain subjects.

CLC "Capital and lower case" letters, to designate typesetting.

client Institution, person or business hiring PR services.

clip (1) Newspaper clipping. (2) In broadcasting, a short piece of film or tape used as program insert. (3) Also may mean to cut off high and low frequencies of audio of a program. (4) To compress the white

and/or black picture information or to prevent the video signal from interfering with the sync signals.

clipping returns Clippings, mentioning a specific subject, from newspapers, magazines, trade journals, specialized publications and internal publications. Commercial services supply clippings from numerous publications for monthly charge and per-clipping charge or flat rate per clipping.

clipsheet Stories and illustrations printed on one page and sent to publications. Offers a number of releases in one mailing, works best with small publications that cannot afford syndicated matter.

close-up (CU) Object or any part of it seen at close range and framed tightly. The close-up can be extreme (XCU or ECU) or rather loose (MCU) (medium close-up).

coated paper Paper with enameled coating to give smooth, hard finish suitable for best halftone reproduction.

coincidental interview Method of public opinion surveying in which a phone interview is conducted to gain information.

cold comp Type composition by various "cold methods"—from typewriter to high-speed computerized photocomposition systems.

cold light Fluorescent .

cold reading Broadcasting copy read by announcer without prior rehearsal.

colophon (1) Credit line at end of book for designer and printer; tells what type faces and paper stock used. (2) Publisher's logo. *See* logo.

color (1) "Mood" piece to go with a straight news story. (2) Lively writing. (3) Exaggerate, falsify. (4) Colored ink or art.

column rule Vertical line separating columns of type.

combination plate Halftone and line plate combined in one engraving.

commercial protection Specific time between competitive commercials granted by a station.

community Immediate area affected by company policy and production.

composition (1) Typesetting and makeup. (2) Arrangement of words into stylistic format.

compositive or composite (1) In broadcasting, sound track with desired mix of sounds. (2) In photography, mixing of elements from different negatives to create false image.

computer network Two or more computers interconnected.

computer program Set of instructions that, converted to machine format, causes computer to carry out specified operations to solve a problem.

condensed Type that is narrower than regular face.

conservation Support of an existing opinion held by a public to keep it from changing.

console Part of computer through which operator or repair person communicates with machine and vice versa. Normally has display device such as typewriter.

continuity Radio and television copy.

continuity strip Ad in comic strip format.

control group Group comprised of members chosen for particular characteristics or opinions. Used as a comparison to a *test group*.

control track The area of the videotape that is used for recording the synchronization information (sync spikes), which is essential for videotape editing.

control unit In a digital computer, the parts that effect retrieval of instruction in correct sequence. The unit interprets each instruction and applies proper signals to arithmetic unit in compliance with instructions.

conversion To influence opinion away from one side of an issue to another.

co-op advertising Sharing of costs of advertising by two advertisers. In broadcasting nearly always refers to a national/local share.

coppering Revising old news to give it feeling of currency.

copy (1) Any broadcast writing, including commercials. (2) Any written material intended for publication, including advertising.

copy desk News desk at newspaper, magazine, radio or TV station where copy is edited and headlines written.

copyreader Newsroom employee who reads and corrects (edits) copy and writes headlines.

core (1) "Memory" of computer. (2) Small hub on which film is wound for storage or shipping.

correspondent Out-of-town reporter.

cost per thousand CPM cost to advertiser to reach 1,000 listeners or viewers with given message; figured by dividing time cost by size of audience (in thousands).

cover (1) To reporter, getting all available facts about an event. (2) Outer pages of a magazine—specifically, outside front (first cover), inside front (second cover), inside back (third cover), outside back (fourth cover).

cover shot Shot of the scene used as a reserve if you miss the action with the first shot.

cover stock (1) Sturdy paper for magazine covers. (2) Also used for pamphlets, booklets, tent cards, posters and other printed matter where weight and durability are important.

CPI (1) In typesetting, characters per inch. (2) In computer science, density of magnetic tape or drum.

CPM Cost per thousand (*M* means "thousand")—the ratio of the cost of a given TV segment to audience reached in thousands.

CPS Characters per second—relates to paper tapes or typewriter speeds.

CPU Central processing unit—the main frame of a computer with circuits that control operations.

crawl graphics Usually credit copy that moves slowly up the TV or cinema screen; often mounted on a drum, or crawl. More exactly, an up-and-down movement of credits is called a roll, and a horizontal movement a crawl. Both the roll and the crawl can be produced by the character generator.

credits List of people who participated in a TV or film production.

cropping Changing the shape or size of an illustration to make it fit a designated space or to cut out distracting or undesirable elements.

cross-fade (1) In audio, a transition method in which the preceding sound is faded out and the following sound faded in simultaneously. The sounds overlap temporarily. (2) In video, a transition method whereby the preceding picture is faded to black and the following picture is faded in from black.

CRT *See* cathode ray tube.

crystallization Creating an awareness of previously vague or subconscious attitudes held by a public.

CTC or CTK Copy to come.

CTG Copy to go.

CTR Computer tape reader—attached when needed to photo-typesetting device.

CU *See* close-up; usually head and just below shoulders of person, in TV, film or still photograph.

cue (1) In TV, film or radio, a signal to initiate action. (2) Mark in a TV script for technical and production staffs. (3) White or black dots on film indicating end. (4) To find the proper place of a transcription.

cumulative audience ("cume") Audience reached by a broadcast station in two or more time periods or more than one station in a specific time period (such as a week).

custom-built network Linking of stations temporarily for special broadcast.

cut (1) To delete part of some copy or to end a program suddenly. (2) Track or groove in a transcription. (3) Engraving, metal plate bearing an illustration, either lined or screened, to be used in letterpress printing (with a raised printing surface made from a matrix). (4) Instantaneous transition from one film or video source to another. *See* engraving.

cutaway shot A shot of an object or event peripherally connected with the overall event and neutral as to screen direction (usually a straight-on shot). Used to intercut between two shots in which the screen direction is reversed. Also used to cut between two takes with the same shot, avoiding a jump cut.

cutline Caption or legend accompanying illustration.

data base/data bank A collection of data used by an organization, capable of being processed and retrieved.

dateline Line preceding story giving date and place of origin; usually only location is printed.

deadline The time a completed assignment is due and *must* be delivered.

dealer imprint Name and address of dealer printed on leaflet, pamphlet, poster or similar matter, usually in space set aside for this purpose.

deck (1) Part of a headline. (2) A recording machine only (audio or video).

deck head Headline having two or more groups of type.

deckled edge Ragged edge of a sheet or paper.

demographics Refers to certain characteristics in the audience for any medium—sex, age, family, education, economics.

department Regular section on a particular subject in a newspaper or magazine.

depth of field The measure in which all objects, located at different distances from the camera, appear in focus. Depth of field depends on focal length of the lens, f-stop, and distance between object and camera.

descender Bottom part of a lowercase letter which extends below the body of the letter, as in p, q and y. *See* ascender.

dirty copy Written material with considerable errors or corrections.

disc Record or transcription.

display type Type or hand lettering for headlines; usually larger than 14 points.

dissolve In TV or film, a gradual transition from shot to shot whereby the two images temporarily overlap. Also called lap-dissolve, or lap.

documentaries Informational film presentation with specific message.

dolly To move the camera toward (dolly in) or away from (dolly out or back) the object.

donut A commercial in which live copy runs between the opening and close of a produced commercial, usually a singing jingle.

dope News information or background material.

double chain Film story using two film chains simultaneously. *See* film chain.

double-page spread Two facing pages; may be editorial material or advertising, with or without illustrations.

double projection Shooting and recording sound and pictures separately for later simultaneous projections. Gives higher quality reproduction.

double-spot Two TV commercials run back to back.

double system sound In film and TV, picture and sound portion are recorded separately and later may be combined on one film through printing; married printing.

double truck Center spread, or two full facing pages.

download A news release will be in the organization's computer; a newspaper or other medium can call by phone and have the information fed directly into the medium's computer for typesetting, etc.

dress (1) The appearance of a magazine. (2) In broadcasting, a final "dress" rehearsal, or what people will wear on camera. (3) Set dressing, properties.

drive out In typesetting, to space words widely to fill the line.

drop folio In books and publications, page number at bottom of page.

drop-in ads Small advertising messages added to or "dropped in" regular advertisements of a different character; e.g., a one-column-inch community-fund-drive ad in a department store's regular half-page ad.

dry A "slow" or "dry" news day when not much is going on.

dry brush drawing A drawing usually on coarse board made with a thick ink or paint.

dry run A rehearsal, usually for TV, before the taping or airing, if live.

dub The duplication of an electronic recording or an insertion into a transcription. Dubs can be made from tape to tape or from record to tape. The dub is always one generation down (away) from the recording used for the dubbing and is therefore of lower quality.

dubbing Transcribing a sound track from one recording medium to another, such as film sound to audio tape.

dummy Suggested layout for a publication showing positions of all elements. A hand dummy is rough and general. A paste-up dummy is proofs carefully pasted in position.

duotones Two-color art. Two halftone plates are made from a one-color illustration and etched to produce a two-tone effect.

dupe Duplicate proof.

ears Boxes or type appearing at the upper left- and right-hand corners of publications alongside the flag (newspaper nameplate).

easel shots or "limbos" Still pictures or models photographed by a TV camera.

edge key A keyed (electronically cut-in) title whose letters have distinctive edges, such as dark outlines or a drop shadow.

edit To modify, correct, rearrange or otherwise change data in the computer.

editing Emphasizing important matter or deleting the less significant. (1) In live TV, selecting from preview monitors pictures that will be aired, the selection and assembly of shots. (2) In print media, the collection, preparation, layout and design of materials for publication.

edition All identical copies, printed in one run of the press.

editorialize Injection of opinion into a news story.

editorial matter Entertainment or educational part of a broadcast program or publication, exclusive of commercial messages.

EDP Electronic data processing.

electronic editing Inserting or assembling a program on videotape without physically cutting the tape.

electronic film transfer Kinescoping a program from videotape to film by filming the images that appear on a very sharp television monitor.

electronic newspaper Videotex or Teletext system in which the individual becomes his or her own gatekeeper, selecting a tailored mix of news and other information.

electros or electrotype Printing plates made by electrolysis from original composition or plates. Made from wax or lead molds, they are much cheaper than original and duplicate photoengravings. Used when long runs or several copies of plates or forms are required. If the expense of shipping would be an additional cost factor, mats or flongs should be used instead of electros.

em The square of any given type body. Usually refers to the pica em, which is 12 points square. Common method of measuring type composition: number of ems in a line is multiplied by the number of lines.

embossing An impression made by pressing a piece of paper between two metal dies so that it stands above the surface of the sheet.

en Half an em, unit of measure in typesetting. Equal to width of a capital "N" in the particular size of type face being used.

enameled stock *See* coated paper.

end rate Lowest rate for commercial time offered by a station.

engraving ("cut") Zinc or copper plate that has been etched, generally with acid, to get a raised surface that, when inked, will print on paper. Engravings are reproductions of either line illustrations or halftones (screened); also called photoengravings, because they are made by being brought into contact with film negatives of illustrations. In commercial usage, the term engravings refers almost solely to letterpress printing, although in the past the term "engraving" referred to the intaglio processes.

essential area The section of the television picture, centered within the scanning area, that is seen by the home viewer, regardless of masking of the set or slight misalignment of the receiver. Sometimes called critical area.

establishing shot Orientation shot, usually a long shot; a wide angle giving relationship of place and action; sometimes called a *cover* shot.

ET Electrical transcription. Like a record but produced only for broadcast stations.

etching proofs Sharp, clean proofs from which zinc etchings can be made.

ETV Educational TV.

exclusive Correspondent's report or story limited to a single station, network or periodical.

extended or expanded Extra wide face of type.

external publication Publication issued by an organization to people outside its own employee or membership groups, such as to customers, the local community, the financial world, etc.

extra condensed Type compressed, very thin.

face The printing surface of type. Also used to identify one style of type from another, such as plain face, heavy face.

fact sheet Page of significant information prepared by PR people to help news media in covering a special event.

fade (1) In audio, the physical or mechanical decrease of volume, either voice or music, to smooth a transition between sounds. (2) In video, the gradual appearance of a picture from black (fade-in) or disappearance to black (fade-out).

family Complete series of one type face, with all variations (bold, italic, small caps, etc.).

fax Slang for "facsimile." Exact reproduction of printed matter (words and photos) by radio transmission; also used to refer to TV facilities.

FCC Federal Communications Commission, the government regulatory body for broadcasting.

feature (1) To play up or emphasize. (2) A story, not necessarily news; usually more of human interest.

feed Electronic signal. Generally a source like a network from which a station can record or what one station sends to another station or stations.

file Send story by wire, Telex or other form of transmission. In computer language, information on a related record, treated as a unit.

fill (1) In broadcasting, additional program material kept ready in case a program runs short. (2) To fill out for timing or space.

fill copy Pad copy. Material not significant used to "fill out."

fill light Additional direction light, usually opposite the key light, to illuminate shadow areas.

filler A short, minor story to fill space where needed in making up the page of a publication. Copy set in type for use in emergencies.

film chain A motion picture film projector, slide projector and TV camera, all housed in single unit called a "multiplexor," used to convert film pictures and sound or still pictures mounted on slides into electronic signals.

film clip Short piece of film.

film counter Device used in measuring film length while editing.

film lineup List of films in broadcast order.

film rundown List of cues for film story.

fixed position Spot delivered at a guaranteed time.

fixed service Short-range TV transmission on 2,500-megacycle band; generally used for closed-circuit TV.

flack Slang for press agent or publicist, primarily those in the entertainment fields, and apparently coined by writer Pete Martin, since the first recorded use was by him in the April 1, 1950, issue of *Saturday Evening Post*. Martin defined the term in a May 5, 1956, issue of the

Post with these words, "And since 'flack' is Hollywood slang for publicity man . . ." This word has a few meanings from obsolete provincial English usage: As a verb: to palpitate, to hang loosely, to beat by flapping. Also as a noun: a stroke or touch, a blow, a gadding woman. The word flak came into use during World War II and is an acronym for the German Flieger AbwehrKanone, an aircraft defense cannon, literally translated to mean "the gun that drives off raiders." The Old English word and the military word may or may not have anything to do with the inspiration of its application to PR.

flag   (1) Front page title or nameplate of a newspaper. (2) Device to block light in film lighting.

flagship station   The major network-owned station or the major station in a community-owned group of stations.

flighting   Broadcast advertising technique for periods of concentrated advertising with period of inactivity—usually six-week patterns help a small advertiser get impact.

flong   *See* electros, matrix.

flyer   *See* circular.

FM   Frequency Modulation. Radio broadcasting (88 to 108 megacycles) with several advantages over standard (AM) broadcasting such as elimination of static, no fading, generally more consistent quality reception.

fold   Where the front page of a newspaper is folded in half.

folder   A printed piece of four pages or a four-page, heavy-paper container for other printed materials.

folio   Page number.

follow-up   A story presenting new developments of one previously printed; also known as a second-day story.

follow copy   Instruction to typesetter to set type exactly like copy in every detail.

font   An assortment of type face in one size and style.

form   Pages of type and illustrations locked in a rectangular iron frame called a chase.

format   (1) The size, shape and appearance of a magazine or any publication. (2) The skeletal structure or outline of a program, or even the kind of programming a station does.

foundry proofs   (1) Etching proofs. (2) Heavy borders of black foundry rules.

four-color process   Reproduction of full-colored illustrations by the combination of plates for yellow, blue, red and black ink. All colored illustrations are separated photographically into these four primary colors. Four-color process is available to the letterpress, offset and gravure process.

frame   (1) A single picture on a storyboard. (2) A single picture in film footage. (3) 1/30 second TV; 1/24 second in film. (4) A command to a camera operator to compose the picture.

free lance   An unaffiliated writer or artist, available for hire on a per-story basis or retainer.

freeze frame   Arrested motion, which is perceived as a still shot.

frequency discount   Lower rate available to volume advertisers.

fringe time   Broadcast time generally considered to be 5:30–7:00 P.M. and 10:30 P.M.–1:00 A.M., early and late fringe bracketing prime time.

front of the book   Main editorial section of a magazine.

front timing   The process of figuring out clock times by adding given running times to the clock time at which the program starts.

f-stop   The calibration on the lens indicating the ratio of the aperture diameter or diaphragm opening to the focal length of the lens (apertures control the amount of light transmitted through the lens). The larger the f-stop number, the smaller the aperture or diaphragm opening; the smaller the f-stop number, the larger the aperture or diaphragm opening.

fully scripted   A TV script indicating all words to be spoken and all major video information.

gain   Amplification of sound.

galley   Shallow metal tray for holding type after lines have been set.

galley proofs   Proofs reproduced from the type as it stands in galley trays before being placed in page forms or, with cold type, as photocopied from the master print or repro.

gel or cell   Sheet of transparent colored plastic used to change the color of a still photo, key light or graphic, or clear material used in film animation. (Inserted in front of key lights, on top of art.)

ghost writer   Writer whose work appears under the byline of another.

glossy print   A smooth, shiny surfaced photograph; most suitable form for black and white reproduction in print media. Also called glossy.

grain   (1) Direction in which paper fibers lie and the way paper folds best. Folded against the grain, it is likely to crack or fold irregularly. (2) Unwanted silver globs in a photograph.

graphics   (1) All visual displays in broadcasting. (2) Art and display lettering as well as design in print media.

gravure   A form of intaglio printing. *See* intaglio printing.

gross rating points   Broadcast time periods have rating points. The gross rating points is simple addition of quarter hour ratings for time period when each scheduled commercial for a single, specific advertiser was aired.

guideline   Slugline. Title given

news stories as a guide for editors and printers.

gutter   The space between left- and right-hand pages of a printed publication.

halftone   A screened reproduction (composed of a series of light and heavy dots) of a photograph, painting or drawing.

hand composition   Type set by hand.

handout   Publicity release.

hardware   Physical equipment of the computer.

head   Headline. Name, headline, title of a story.

headnote   Short text accompanying the head and carrying information on the story, the author or both.

headroom   The space left between the top of the head and the upper screen edge in television display.

highlight halftone   A halftone in which whites are intensified by dropping out dots, usually by hand tooling.

hold   Not to be published without release or clearance.

hold for release (HFR)   News not to be printed until a specified time or under specified circumstances.

holdover audience   Listeners or viewers inherited from a preceding program.

Home Box Office   A company that supplies pay TV programs to cable systems.

Home Information System (H.I.S.)   A computer-based, electronic information system that links the home to a variety of data bases; individual consumer controls information mix delivered.

hometown stories   Stories for the local newspapers of individuals participating in an event or activity, usually written so the name and perhaps address can be filled into a general story.

horsing   Reading a proof without the copy.

house ad   An ad either for the publication in which it appears or for another medium held by the same owner.

house magazine   House organ, company magazine. Internal house publications are for employees. External house publications may go only to company-related persons (customers, stockholders and dealers) or to the public.

HTK   Head to come. Information telling the typesetter that the headline is not with the copy but will be provided later.

human interest   Feature material appealing to the emotions—drama, humor, pathos.

HUTS   Households using television—number with sets in use at one time.

ID   Identification. In broadcasting, includes call letters and location in a 10-second announcement that identifies the station, usually in a promotional way.

impose   To arrange pages in a chase so they will be in sequence when the printed pages are folded.

independent station   A broadcast station not affiliated with a network.

indicia   Mailing information data required by the Postal Service.

initial letter   First letter in a block of copy, usually two or three copy lines deep; used for emphasis; frequently in another color.

inline   Letter with a white line cut in it.

insert   (1) New material inserted in the body of a story already written. (2) Printed matter prepared for enclosure with letters. (3) In film, a matted portion of a picture or an additional shot added to a scene.

institutional ads, commercials and programs   All planned for long-term effects rather than immediate response.

intaglio printing   A process in which the design is scratched or etched below the general level of the metal and filled with ink so the transfer in printing will show only the design. Rotogravure is intaglio printing.

integrated commercial   May be either a "cast" delivered commercial incorporated into a show or a multiple-brand announcement for a number of products by the same manufacturers.

intercut   TV film technique of cutting back and forth between two or more lines of action.

internal communications   Communications within a company or organization to personnel or membership.

internal publication   A publication directed to personnel or membership of a company or organization.

interviewee   Person being interviewed.

interviewer   (1) A person who seeks information by asking questions either formally or informally. (2) One who asks respondents the questions specified on a questionnaire in an opinion or market survey.

investigative reporting   Searching below the surface for facts generally concealed.

island   An ad surrounded by editorial material.

italic   Type in which letters and characters slant.

item   News story, usually short.

jingle   Musical signature or logo used as broadcast identification and as vehicle for message.

job press   Press taking small sheet size, normally under 25 × 38 inches.

jump   (1) To continue a story from one page of a publication to another. (2) In film, to break continuity in time or space. *See* jump cut.

jump cut   Cutting between shots that are identical in subject yet slightly different in screen location. Through the cut, the subject seems to jump from one screen location to another for no apparent reason.

jump the gutter   Titles or illustrations that continue from a left- to a right-hand page over the center of the publication.

jump head   The title or headline over the continued portion of a story on another page.

jump lines   Short text matter explaining the destination of continued text.

justification   Arranging type and spacing in a line so the type completely fills the line and makes it the same length as adjoining lines.

key   (1) An electronic effect. Keying means the cutting in of an image (usually lettering) into a background image. (2) Key light means the principal source of illumination.

kicker   A short line over the source of directional illumination, headline and a type of television light.

kill   (1) To strike out or discard part or all of a story. (2) In films or TV, to stop production.

kinescope   Film of a TV program film taken directly from a receiving tube. Also called a "transfer."

lapel   Small microphone worn as a lapel button.

lavaliere mike   Also called "lav." Small microphone suspended around neck, worn on tie, collar, etc.

layout   Dummy.

LC   Lowercase (uncapitalized) letters.

lead ("led")   Spacing metal, usually lead alloy, placed horizontally between lines of type to give more space between lines. Leads can be 1, 2 or 3 points thick. Ten-point type lines separated by 2-point leads are said to be "10 point leaded 2 points." *See* slug.

lead ("leed")   (1) Introductory sentence or paragraph of a news story. (2) A tip that may develop into a story. (3) Also the news story of greatest interest, usually placed at the beginning of a newscast and generally in the upper right-hand corner of a newspaper, although some papers favor the upper left-hand position.

leaders   (1) In print, dots used to direct the eye from one part of the copy to another. (2) In broadcasting, timed visual used at the beginning of sequences for cues. *See* academy leader, black leader.

lead-in line   Section of film, videotape or copy such as first sentence used by newscaster to cue the technical staff or news anchorperson.

leaflet   Printed piece of about four pages, usually from a single sheet, folded.

leg   Part of any network; usually a principal branch off the main trunk.

legend   Cutline. *See* caption.

leg man   Reporter who calls in information to a rewrite person.

letterpress   Printing process in which raised type and plates are inked and then applied to paper through direct pressure.

letterspacing   Putting narrow spaces between letters.

level   (1) In audio, it means volume. (2) In video, it means number of volts.

light level   Measured in footcandles or in lumens.

light pen   A penlike tube containing a photocell, which when directed at a cathode-ray tube display, reacts to light from the display. The response goes to the computer and text in the data store can be deleted or inserted.

lighting ratio   The relative intensities of key, back and fill light.

limbo   Any set area used for shooting small commercial displays, card easels and the like, having a plain, light background. It appears as if the floor and the background go on forever.

lineprinter   Drum, chain or cathode-ray tube printer, which is usually capable of printing a complete line of characters in one cycle of operation. The whole line is composed in the computer.

linotype   Typesetting machine that casts lines instead of single characters.

lithographic printing   Chemically transferring an inked image from a smooth surface to paper, as in offset lithography, offset printing, photo-offset.

lithography   Printing from a flat surface.

live   Performed at broadcast time.

live copy   Copy read by station announcer, in contrast to electronic transcriptions or tapes.

live tag   Message added to recorded commercial by announcer, usually to localize spot.

localize   To stress the local angle.

log   Second-by-second daily account of what was broadcast.

logo   Logotype or ligature: (1) Combination of two or more letters on the same body—e.g., *fl*. (2) Company trade name or product identification. (3) In broadcasting, a musical or sound signature used for identification.

long shot   Object seen from far away or framed very loosely. The extreme long shot shows the object from a great distance.

loop   (1) In audio, a technical way to keep up special sound effects or a background noise like rain by constant transmission from one spot of tape. (2) In video, loops used with videotape may replace kinescope pictures and sound recordings for national dissemination of TV programs. Loop feeds make it possible for the affiliated local station's programs and news reports to be picked up by the network. Film loops permit continuous repetition of picture.

LS Long shot, as with a TV or film camera.

machine format Broadcast format in which elements are not prefixed by time or relative position, but are varied. Opposite of segmented.

magazine format *See* block programming.

make good When an ad or commercial is not run because of media error or when there is a misprint or malfunction, the offender must publish or broadcast it free at a later date.

make ready Preparing a form on the press for printing.

makeup (1) Getting type and engravings in printing form correctly. (2) Placement of information and pictures on a publication's page. (3) Planning a group of pages. (4) In film, putting several films on one big reel.

markup Proof with changes indicated.

mass publications Periodicals with a wide appeal and large, general circulation.

master Original of a film or videotape. Master positive—positive film made from edited camera negative and composite sound track with optical effects.

masthead Name of publication and staff that appears in each issue of magazine or paper, usually on the editorial page in a box also giving information about the paper such as company officers, subscription rates and address.

matrix or mats A papier-maché impression of a printing plate which may be used as a mold for a lead casting to reproduce the copy or art. Used for publicity primarily because of economy of mailing and used by small publications without engraving facilities.

matte (1) Imposition of a scene

or title over another scene, excluding background. Not a blend or a super. (2) Name for a box placed in front of lens to shade and hold filters and effects. (3) Dull finish needed for still photos used by TV so lights will not be reflected.

mediastat A broadcast rating service.

medium shot *See* MS.

memory Same as storage.

MICR Magnetic Ink Character Recognition. Automatic reading by machine of graphic characters printed in magnetic ink.

microwave relay Use of ultra high-frequency radio relay stations to transmit television signals from one point to another in line of sight, usually about twenty-five miles.

milline Unit of space and circulation used in advertising to measure the cost of reaching an audience. Milline rate means cost per million for a one-column line of agate type.

minicam A highly portable TV camera and videotape unit that can be easily carried and operated by one person.

mixer (1) Audio control console. (2) Person working this console.

mixing (1) In audio, the combining of two or more sounds in specific proportions (volume variations) as determined by the event (show) context. (2) In video, the combining of various shots via the switcher.

mock-up Scale model used for study, testing or instruction.

model release Document signed by a model allowing use of photographs or art in which he or she appears.

monitor (1) To review a station's programming and commercials. (2) TV set that handles video signals.

montage In TV and film, a rapid succession of images to give idea association. *Also see* composite.

MOR Type of radio station pro-

gramming that is "middle of the road."

more Written at the bottom of a page of copy indicating a story is not complete, that there is more to come.

morgue Newspaper library for clippings, photos and reference material.

MOS "Mitout sound." Film recorded without sound.

movieola Device used to view film during editing.

MS Medium shot of TV or film camera.

mult box Portable electronic box (usually like a large travel case) that allows dozens of tape recorders to be plugged in at once to record off the public address (PA) system so the speakers' remarks will be captured and transmitted to all simultaneously. *See* multiplexes.

multigraphing Trademarked process for making numerous copies of typewritten or hand-drawn material. More closely resembles hand typing than does mimeographing.

multiplexer (1) System of movable mirrors or prisms that takes images from several projection sources and directs them into one stationary television film camera. (2) Instrument for mixing signals.

must Written on copy or art to designate that it must appear.

NABET National Association of Broadcast Employees and Technicians. Union for studio and master control engineers; may include floor personnel.

nameplate The name of the publication appearing on page one of a newspaper. *See* flag.

national rate Rate offered to advertisers in more than one market.

Neilsen The A.C. Neilsen Company is the biggest name in broadcast ratings. Reputations and shows literally live or die on their Neilsen ratings.

NET   National Educational Television.

network   Any link, by any technology, of two or more stations so they can each separately broadcast the same program.

network option time   Broadcast hours a network preempts on its affiliates and the stations it owns.

Nexis   Data base.

new lead   Replacement for a lead already prepared, usually offering new developments or information. *See* lead.

newsprint   A rough, relatively inexpensive paper, usually made from wood pulp, used for many newspapers and also for other inexpensive printed material.

news wheel   News show in which content is repeated with some updating.

NPR   National Public Radio.

obituary   News biography of a dead person.

OCR   Optical Character Recognition. Electronically reading printed or handwritten documents.

offset   Lithographic process.

on the nose   (1) On time. (2) Correct.

online   To be in direct communication with the computer CPU.

open-end   Recorded commercial with time at close for "tag."

open spacing   Widely leaded spacing.

optical center   A point equidistant from the left and right sides of a sheet of paper and five-eighths of the way from the bottom. In the optics so important to film is the optical center point of a lens, a point which may have no relationship to equal distances from perimeters.

optical reader   Electronic reader of copy.

opticals   In film, any variations to the picture achieved after or during filming, such as mattes or dissolves. May be done during filming or by control board when multiple cameras are used.

optical scanner   Visual scanner. Scans printed or written data and generates their digital representation.

outline   The gist of a written article or program.

outtake   Filmed or taped scenes or sequences not used in final production.

overdubbing   Recording of separate channels on a multichannel tape separately, then adding and synchronizing so that the original sound track is added to. Makes it possible for a few voices to become a chorus and a few instruments an orchestra.

overline   Kicker.

overrun   Legitimate printing trade practice that permits delivery and charge for up to 10 percent more than the quantity of printed matter ordered.

overset   More type set than there is space to use.

pace   Overall speed of show or performance.

pad   Fill.

page proof   Proof of type and engravings as they will appear.

pamphlet   A printed piece of more than four pages with a soft cover. Differs from brochure in its size and simplicity, lack of illustrations.

pan   Horizontal turning of the camera.

panel   (1) An area of type sometimes boxed but always different in size, weight or design from the text and partially or entirely surrounded by text. (2) In broadcasting and communication research, a group brought together to discuss one subject or related subjects.

paper tape   Strip of paper on which data may be recorded, usually in the form of punched holes. Punched paper tape capable of being sensed by a reading head to transfer the data. Each charge is represented by a pattern of holes, called a row or frame.

participation spot   Shared time in a program for spot commercials or announcements.

paste-up   *See* dummy.

patch   Temporary equipment connection. Patch panels or patch board: an assembly of jacks into which various circuits are permanently tied and into which patch cords may be inserted. They are essential at "on site" special events.

PBS   Public Broadcasting System.

perforator   Keyboard unit used to produce punched paper tape.

personal   A brief news item about one or more persons.

photo composition   A photographic method of setting type to produce proofs on paper.

photoprint   Reproduction of art or a printed or written piece by any one of many different photographic copying processes.

photostat   A trademarked device for making photographic copies of art or text.

pica   Standard printing measure of 12 points. There are six picas to the inch.

pied type   Type that is all mixed up.

PIQ   Program Idea Quotient. Annual study by Home Testing Institute to get reactions to new program ideas. Ratings are on a 6-point scale from "favorite" to "wouldn't watch."

pix   Pictures.

place   Refers to all types of printing surfaces, as well as the engravings and electrotypes.

play up   To emphasize, give prominence.

plug   A free and favorable mention.

PM Afternoon paper.

point Printers' standard unit of measure equal to 0.01384 inch. Roughly 72 points equal one inch. Sizes of type and amount of leading are specified in points.

poll Survey of the attitudes and beliefs of a selected group of people.

position Where elements in any publication appear; usually indicates relative significance.

postdubbing The adding of a sound track to an already recorded (and usually fully edited) picture portion.

poster type Large, garish letters.

pot Potentiometer. A volume-control device on audio consoles.

power structure The socially, politically and economically advantaged.

PR Public relations.

precinct principle Organization of a campaign through delegation of local responsibilities to chosen leaders in each community. These may be opinion leaders and not necessarily political leaders.

preempt In broadcasting, to replace a regular program with a commercial or a news event of greater importance.

preemptible spot Commercial time sold at a lower rate by a station, which has the option of taking it back if it has a buyer at full rate, unless the first purchaser wants it still at full rate.

presentational TV performance where camera is addressed as audience.

presidential patch Portable sound system with outlets for amplifiers to be connected. Unity gain amplifier with numerous mike-level outputs used in pool remotes to cut down on the number of mikes needed.

pretesting Testing a research plan, any of its elements or any elements in a campaign before launching the entire program.

printer's error (PE) Typographical errors made by typesetter.

privilege Constitutional privilege granted the press to print with immunity news that might otherwise be libelous—e.g., remarks made in open court.

process plates and progressive proofs Each of the color plates in a set printed singly. These may be laid over each other for effect. In progressive prints, in addition to the single prints of each color, the colors are shown in proper color combination and rotation to suggest the final printed result.

program Set of instructions that make the computer perform the desired operations.

promo Broadcast promotional statement, film, videotape/recording, slide or combination.

promotion Creating interest in a person, product, institution or cause through special activities.

proof Trial impression of type and engraved matter taken on paper to make corrections.

propaganda devices Specific devices—spoken, written, pictorial or even musical— to influence human action or reaction.

PR wires Commercial wire services received by print and electronic media.

psychographics Refers to media audience attitudes and images held.

public, publics Any group of people tied together by some common bond of interest or concern. *See* audience.

publicity Information about a client (person, company or institution), about a product or about services that appears as news in any medium, print or electronic.

public relations All activities and attitudes intended to judge, adjust to, influence and direct the opinion of any group or groups of persons in the interest of any individual, group or institution.

public television Noncommercial broadcasting. Stations are financed by federal grants, private donations and public subscriptions.

puffery Unsubstantiated and exaggerated claims with no factual basis that appear in either advertising or publicity.

pulp Magazines printed on rough, wood-pulp paper in contrast to "slicks," magazines printed on coated or calendared stock.

punch To give vigor to the writing or editing process.

quads (1) Blank pieces of metal used to fill large spaces in a line of type. (2) A type of videotape recorder.

query Letter addressed to an editor that summarizes an article idea and asks if the piece might be considered for publication.

questionnaire The body of questions asked of subjects in a research effort.

quoins ("coins") Metal wedges of triangular-shaped steel used in locking up a type form.

quote Quotations, estimate of costs.

RADAR Radio's All Dimension Audience Research, a survey conducted by Statistical Research Inc., for NBC, CBS, ABC and Mutual networks.

radio-TV wire (1) Broadcast wire. (2) The news service's wire copy written in broadcast style.

RAM (Random Access Memory). A storage device in which the time needed to find data is not affected significantly by where the data are physically located.

raster The scanned area of the CRT tube. Line scans traced across the face of a CRT tube by a flying spot.

rating service Company that surveys broadcast audience for total homes or individuals listening or gives percentages of total listening for specific stations and also for specific shows.

raw stock Unexposed film. Called camera stock when it is unexposed film for use in a motion picture camera. Called print stock when it is unexposed film for making duplicate copies of still photographs.

reach Number of people or households a station, commercial or program is heard by in a given time period. Used with frequency to measure station's audience for evaluation of worth, generally for advertising dollar.

real time Online processing, with data received and processed quickly enough to produce output; interactive.

rear screen projection Projection of positive transparencies onto translucent screen.

rebate Extra discount on ads earned from using more time or space than contract specifies.

recap Recapitulation of news.

reduce Decreasing the size of anything visual when reproducing it.

register (1) The correct position in which a form is to print so that the pages when printed back to back will be in the proper places. (2) In color printing, the precise position for superimposition of each color for the colors to blend properly.

rejection slip Letter or printed form from a publication's editor accompanying a manuscript returned to its author.

release print In TV, film print made from negative and given to stations to use.

relief printing Letterpress. Letters on the block or plate are raised above the general level so that when an inked roller is passed over the surface the ink can touch only the raised portions.

remote A broadcast live videotape recording originating outside the regular studios.

reprint A second or new impression of a printed work, either text or art.

repro *See* camera copy.

respondent Those to whom questions are directed in a survey.

retail rate Local rate or lower for advertising.

retouch To improve photographs before reproduction by artwork.

reversal print A copy made on reversal print stock.

reverse To print text or art in white on a dark background, or, in making a cut from a picture, to turn over or "flop" the negative so that everything goes in an opposite direction.

review Critique or commentary on any aspect of human events—politics, society or the arts.

rewrite person Newspaper staff member who rewrites stories and takes phoned-in reports but does not leave the office to cover news.

rim On newspapers, outer edge of a copy desk where copy readers work under the direction of a "slot" person or copy chief.

roots of attitudes Attitudes are grounded in our institutions, observations, responses of others to us, socialization, education and media.

ROP Run of Paper. Means ad may be placed on any page of the publication.

ROS Run of Station or Run of Schedule. Costs less; usually preemptible.

rotary press Press that prints from curved stereotypes bolted to a cylinder.

rotogravure Printing by means of a sensitized copper cylinder on which is etched the image to be reproduced.

rough Preliminary visualization of art.

rough cut First editing of film, without effects.

roundup Comprehensive story

written with information gathered from several sources.

routing Cutting out a part of plate or engraving to keep it from printing.

rule Thin strip of type-high metal that prints as a slender line.

run-in To combine one or more sentences to avoid making an additional paragraph.

running foot Identification information printed in the bottom margin in some magazines.

running head Identification information printed in the top margins.

running story or breaking story Fast-breaking story usually written in sections.

saddle stitching Binding pages by stitching with wire through fold.

SAG Screen Actors Guild.

sample The portion of the total population queried in a survey, intended to be representative of the total population.

sandwich Donut. In broadcasting, a commercial with live copy between musical open and close.

sans serif Type face without serifs.

scaling Measuring and marking illustrations for engraving to be sure illustration appears in appropriate, designated size and in proper proportion.

scanner Optical scanner.

scanning The movement of the electron beam from left to right and from top to bottom on a screen.

scanning area Picture area that is scanned by a television camera's pickup tube; more generally, the picture area actually reproduced by the camera and relayed to the studio monitors.

segue An audio transition method whereby the preceding sound goes out and the following sound comes in immediately after.

set close   To thin space and omit leads.

set open   To open spaces with leads as slugs.

set solid   To set without extra space between horizontal type lines.

sets in use   Rating service team for percentage of total homes in coverage area in which at least one radio set is on at any given time; radio equivalent of HUT (Households Using Television).

setwise   Differentiates width of a type from its body size.

share of audience or share   Percentage of audience tuned into each station at any given time.

shared ID   When an organization or institution appears on the TV station's channel identification.

shelter books   Magazines that focus on housing or related subjects.

short rate   Charge back to advertiser for not fulfilling contract.

show   Program

side stitching   Method of stitching thick booklets by pressing wire staples from the front side of the booklet and clinching in back, making it impossible to open the pages flat.

silhouette or outline halftone   Halftone with all background removed.

silk screen   Stencil process using fine cloths painted so that the surface is impenetrable except where color is supposed to come through.

silver print or Van Dyck   Proof of negative for offset plate taken on sensitized paper and used as a final proof before plates are made.

simulcast   Simultaneous transmission over radio and television.

sizing   Scaling.

skip frame   Printing of alternate frames to speed up action on film.

slant   Angle. (1) Particular emphasis of a media presentation. (2) To emphasize an aspect of a policy story.

slanting   (1) Emphasizing a particular point or points of interest in the news. (2) Disguised editorializing.

slick   A publication, usually magazine, published on coated, smooth paper.

slicks   Glossy prints used instead of mats in sending releases or art to offset publications.

slidefilm   Filmstrip. A continuous strip of film with frames in a fixed sequence, but not to simulate motion. A recorded sound track usually is synchronized with the succession of the film frames.

slides   Individual film frames, usually positive but can be negative transparencies, projected either in the room where an oral presentation is being given or from a TV control room.

slip sheet   Paper placed between sheets of paper to prevent smudging.

slot   On newspapers, the inside of a copy desk where the copy chief or copy editor sits.

slow motion   A scene in which the objects appear to be moving more slowly than normal. In film, slow motion is achieved through high-speed photography (exposing many frames that differ only minutely from one another) and normal (24 frames per second, for example) playback. In television, slow motion is achieved by multiple scanning of each television frame.

slug   Lead thicker than 4 points used between lines of type.

slug lines   Notation placed at the upper left of a story to identify the story during typesetting and makeup of a publication.

slushpile   Collection of unsolicited manuscripts received by magazines.

SOF   Sound on film.

soft news   Feature news or news that does not depend upon timeliness.

software   The programs and routines associated with the operation of a computer; as opposed to "hardware."

SOT   Sound on videotape.

sources of motivation   Motivations are founded in socially based or personal need and avoidance or elimination of stress often caused by the power of others.

splice   The spot where two shots are actually joined or the act of joining two shots. Generally used only when the material (such as film or audiotape) is physically cut and glued (spliced) together again.

split run   The regional division of a national magazine before printing to accommodate advertisers desiring a specific regional market and often with regional editorial emphasis.

split screen   Divided screen to show two or more pictures; often used in TV titles and commercials.

sponsor   (1) The underwriter of broadcast programming whose messages are presented with the program. Most advertisers buy spot time and are not sponsors. (2) Underwriter of an event or activity who gets publicity for participation.

spot announcement or spot   Broadcast commercial that lasts usually less than one minute.

spread   (1) Long story, generally illustrated. (2) Ad group of related photographs. (3) Copy that covers two facing pages in a publication, generally without gutter separation and usually printed from a single plate.

SPSS   Social science statistical package used in research.

stand-by   Signal given in broadcast studio before on-air signal given.

standing head   A regularly used title.

standing matter   Type kept set

from one printing to another, such as staff names on a newspaper.

station break   Break to a station for a contracted local spot. May include on-the-hour legal identification required of broadcasters by the FCC.

stereotype   Plate cast by pouring molten metal into a matrix or flong. Inexpensive form of duplicating plates generally used by newspapers.

stet   Proofreader's designation to say that the copy should stand as originally written, that the change marked was an error.

stop-motion   A slow motion effect in which one frame jumps to the next, showing the object in a different position.

storyboard   (1) Art work that shows the sequence of a TV commercial. (2) In film work, drawings and text showing major visual changes in proposed show. Grew out of animated film, pioneered by Walt Disney.

straight matter   Plain typesetting set in conventional paragraph form, as opposed to some kind of display.

straight news   Hard news. A plain recital of news facts written in standard style and form.

stuffer   Printed piece intended for insertion into bills and receipts, pay envelopes, packages delivered to customers or any other medium of delivery.

style book   Manual setting up standards for handling copy, detailing rules for spelling, capitalization, abbreviations, word usages and such.

subhead   Small head inserted in the body of a news story to break up long blocks of type.

summary lead   Beginning paragraphs in a news story usually including the H and five W's (who, what, when, where, why and how).

super   In film or TV, superimposition of one scene or characters over

another scene, called a take-out or add videotape.

supercard   A studio card with white lettering on a dark background, used for superimposition of a title or for keying of a title over a background scene. For chromakeying, the white letters are on a chromakey blue background.

surprint   In printing, superimposing type or lettering upon an illustration so the type remains solid, unbroken by a screen.

survey   An analysis of a market or opinions held by a specified group.

suspended interest   News story with climax at the close.

sync   Synchronization. Keeping one operation in step with another (1) between sound and picture or (2) between a scanning beam and a blinking pulse.

synchronization rights   Rights granted by a mechanical rights agency to use music licensed by them.

system cue   Network identification.

tabloid   Newspaper format—usually five columns wide, with each page slightly more than half the size of a standard paper. Tabloid format often is the use of just a picture and headlines on page one.

tag   Final section of a broadcast story, usually stand-up (personally given rather than taped) following film or VTR. Announcement at the end of a recorded commercial or music at the end of live copy.

tailpiece   A small drawing at the end of a story.

take   (1) In print, a portion of copy in a running story. (2) In broadcasting, a complete scene. (3) Also means to cut.

talent   Any major personality or models for ads or publicity photos. In TV or radio, anyone in front of the camera or on the air.

tally light   Red light on video

camera that indicates which camera is on air or being recorded.

teaser   (1) In print, ads or statements that pique interest or stimulate curiosity without giving away facts; used to build anticipation. (2) Technique in which the beginning of a film has scenes and sounds related to the theme of the program rather than a title.

telecommunications   Long-distance transmission of signals by any means.

tele line   Equipment room where film and slide projectors are located.

teleprocessing   Information handling in which a data-processing system uses communication facilities.

Teletext   A one-way electronic information system; noninteractive. *See* H.I.S.

teletypesetter (TTS)   Trademark applied to a machine that transmits to a linotype and causes news to be set into type automatically.

terminal   Point in a communication system or network where data can either enter or leave.

test group   Selection of a group used to measure reactions to or use of a product or an idea.

testing   Sampling of opinions, attitudes or beliefs of a scientifically selected group on any particular set of questions.

text   Written material, generally used in referring to editorial rather than commercial matter; excludes titles, heads, notes, references and such.

TF   Till Forbid. Means to run until advertiser terminates or contract expires.

thirty (30)   In newspaper, means "that's all." Reporter writing story places at the last of the written material to signify end.

tie-back   Previously printed information included in a story to give background or frame of reference and to refresh the reader's memory.

tie-in Promotional term used to describe the joint or combined activities of two or more organizations on a single project or to describe a promotional activity designed to coincide with an already scheduled event.

tight In broadcast and print media, means little time or space left for additional material.

time base corrector An electronic accessory to a videotape recorder that helps to make playbacks or transfers electronically stable. A time base corrector helps to maintain picture quality even in dubbing.

time classifications Broadcast time rated by audience level and priced accordingly as Class AA, Class A, Class BB, Class B, etc.

timesharing Use of computer hardware by several persons simultaneously.

tint block Solid color area on a printed piece, usually screened.

tip Information offered that could lead to a story.

Tipping-in Hand insertion or attachment of extra pages in a publication, usually of a different stock than other items.

title slide Graphic giving name of TV show.

total audience plan Spot package designed to reach all of a station's audiences.

track Physical location on magnetic tape in which the signal is recorded for a specific source—the channel 1, 2, etc. of audio, the video signal, the control signal, etc.

trade publications Periodicals carrying information of interest to a particular trade or industry.

traffic Department in ad agencies that handles production schedules; in broadcasting, traffic handles everything that goes on the air.

trim (1) In newspapers, means shorten copy. (2) In printing, the final process that cuts all pages to the same size.

turnover In advertising refers to ratio of *net unduplicated* cumulative audience over several time periods to average audience per time period.

TWX "TWIX," a teletype machine.

type face Particular type design; sometimes carries the name of the designer or a descriptive name.

type family Name given to two or more type series that are variations of the same basic design.

type page Printed area on a page bordered by margins.

type series Collective name for all sizes of one design of type faces.

typo Typographical error.

UC and LC Upper and lower case; capitals and small letters.

UHF Ultra High Frequency—TV channels broadcasting at frequencies higher than channel 13.

under and over In broadcasting scripts, use of sound to be dominated by (under) or to dominate (over) another sound.

underrun Printing practices permit an allowance of 10 percent less than the total printing order as completion of an order when excessive spoilage in printing or in binding causes a slight shortage. *See* overrun.

upcut In TV or film, unintentionally to overlap sound picture with another sound.

update To alter a story to include the most recent developments.

UPI United Press International—international wire service to which any media may subscribe for news copy and photos. Unlike AP, which is a membership corporation, UPI is a stock company with clients.

upper case Capital letters.

Van Dyck *See* silver print.

varitype Typewriter with alternate type fonts.

VDT Visual or Video Display Terminal. Electronic device for use in typesetting and word processing, with a television-type screen to display data.

vertical saturation Scheduling commercials heavily on one or two days before a major event.

VHF Very high frequency—TV channels broadcasting at channels 2 through 13.

video All television visual projection.

Videotex Electronic data transmission system; interactive; establishes two-way link from individual's television set or home computer to a data base. *See* H.I.S.

vidicon Special camera tube often used in closed-circuit operations and TV film cameras.

vignette Story or sketch, often a "slice of life" drama.

vignetted halftones A halftone with edges that soften gradually until completely faded out.

visual scanner Optical scanner.

VO Voice Over—broadcasting or film script designation.

VTR (1) In TV, videotape recording. Cheaper and more flexible than film but not so permanent. (2) In radio, voice transmitter and receiver—small device attached to the phone, which makes it possible to call in a story and preserve broadcast quality.

wash drawing Water color or diluted India ink brush drawing requiring halftone reproduction.

watermark Identification mark left in texture of quality paper stock. Revealed when paper is held up to the light.

when room Designation on copy or art that means usable any time.

wide open Publication or news script with ample room for additional material.

widow Short line (one word to two) at the end of a paragraph of type. To be avoided, especially in the first line of a column and in captions.

wild track Related footage with sound track not intended to be in sync with picture.

wipe A transitional television technique in which one scene gradually replaces another.

wood cuts Wooden printing blocks with impression carved by hand. Now an art form, was forerunner to zinc engravings.

woodshedding In broadcasting, reading and rehearsing news script.

working drawings Final drawings, usually black and white, prepared for use by engraver. Shows how final art will appear.

work print Film print used in first editing. Usually one "light print," not printed for full quality reproduction.

WOW Pitch distortion or variation caused by changes in speed of film or tape; also used to describe sound distortions in records.

wrap-up Summary or closing.

wrong font Letter from one font of type mixed with others of a different font.

XCU, ECU In TV or film, extreme close-up. For a person, might be eyes and nose only.

yak Narration.

Z-axis The imaginary line that extends in the direction the lens points from the camera to the horizon. Z-axis motion is the movement toward or away from the camera. (Not standardized term in the industry.)

zinc etching Line engraving etched in zinc.

INDEX

Uncontrolled advertising, 224
United Automotive Workers (UAW), 48
United Nations, 184 (**7.4**)
United Press International, 271
Unwin, Stephen, 89
Urban II, Pope, 30
U.S. Census, 91 (**4.4**)
U.S. Chamber of Commerce, 45
U.S. Government Printing Office, 86
U.S. News & World Report, 91

Vail, Theodore N., 38
Validity, 112
VALS, 153
Vanderbilt, William Henry, 38, 40
Variance, 134
Veloro boards, 240 (**9.7A**)
Videotape, 241 (**9.7A**), 242–43 (**9.7B**), 310–15
Vietnam war, 51–52
Virgil, 30

Virginia Company, 31
Vocal activists, 182

Wall Street Journal, 62, 64, 92, 96–97, 113, 355, 458–59
Wallace, Mike, 363
Walsh, Frank, 422 (**14.5**), 428
Ward, Scott, 455
Warfel, Barry, 169–70
Warner, Charles Dudley, 171
Washington, George, 33, 176
Washington Public Power Supply (WPPSS), 319
Watkins, Frederick D., 58–59
Weiner, Richard, 213
Westinghouse Corporation, 25–26, 39
Wheaton, Anne Williams, 49
Whitaker and Baxter, 49
White, E. B., 460
Wilson, Sloan, 48
Wilson, Woodrow, 43, 177
Wire services, 277–81

Wirtz, John R., 122 (**5.2**)
Women, salaries of, 72
Women's Christian Temperance Union, 35
World Future Society, 91
World War I, 42–43
World War II, 46–48
Writers, free-lance, 258–59
Writer's Market, 86
Wycliffe, John, 31
Wylie, Frank, 17, 70 (**3.3**), 83, 325

Yale University, 37
YMCA, 41
Young and Rubicam, 69

Ziegler, Ronald, 177
Zimbardo, Philip, 183, 202